HMH | into Algebra 1™

Dear Students and Families,

Welcome to *Into Algebra 1*! In this program, you will develop skills and make sense of mathematics by solving real-world problems, using tools and strategies, and collaborating with your classmates.

Every lesson includes Spark Your Learning, Build Understanding, and Step It Out tasks. A Spark Your Learning task provides an opportunity to make sense of the mathematics using concepts and procedures you know to try and solve it. The Build Understanding tasks guided by your teacher focus on understanding new concepts, and Step It Out tasks guided by your teacher focus on building efficient procedures and applying those procedures.

With the support of your teacher and by engaging with meaningful practice, you will learn to persevere when solving problems. *Into Algebra 1* will not only help you deepen your understanding of mathematics, but also build your confidence as a learner of mathematics.

We want you to be successful in learning math because it opens up a world of possibilities to you. By engaging and persevering in the learning tasks in *Into Algebra 1*, you will be well on the path to becoming college, career, and civic ready in mathematics. Enjoy your time with *Into Algebra 1*!

Sincerely,
The Authors

Authors

Edward B. Burger, PhD
President, Southwestern University
Georgetown, Texas

Robert Kaplinsky, MEd
Mathematics Educator
Long Beach, California

Juli K. Dixon, PhD
Professor, Mathematics Education
University of Central Florida
Orlando, Florida

Matthew R. Larson, PhD
Past-President, National Council
of Teachers of Mathematics
Lincoln Public Schools
Lincoln, Nebraska

Timothy D. Kanold, PhD
Mathematics Educator
Chicago, Illinois

Steven J. Leinwand
Principal Research Analyst
American Institutes for Research
Washington, DC

Consultants

English Language Development Consultant

Harold Asturias
Director, Center for Mathematics
Excellence and Equity
Lawrence Hall of Science, University of California
Berkeley, California

Program Consultant

David Dockterman, EdD
Lecturer, Harvard Graduate School of Education
Cambridge, Massachusetts

Blended Learning Consultant

Weston Kiercshneck
Senior Fellow
International Center for Leadership in Education
Littleton, Colorado

Open Middle™ Consultant

Nanette Johnson, MEd
Secondary Mathematics Educator
Downey, California

STEM Consultants

Michael A. DiSpezio
Global Educator
North Falmouth, Massachusetts

Marjorie Frank
Science Writer and
Content-Area Reading Specialist
Brooklyn, New York

Bernadine Okoro
Access and Equity and
STEM Learning Advocate and Consultant
Washington, DC

Cary I. Sneider, PhD
Associate Research Professor
Portland State University
Portland, Oregon

Real Numbers and Connections to Algebra

MODULE 1 Real Numbers and Real-World Quantities

Build Conceptual Understanding   Connect Concepts and Skills   Apply and Practice

MODULE 2 Linear Equations and Inequalities in One Variable

Unit 2
Linear Functions and Equations

MODULE 3 Linear Equations in Two Variables

MODULE 4 Linear Functions and Models

©Houghton Mifflin Harcourt

○ Build Conceptual Understanding   ○ Connect Concepts and Skills   ○ Apply and Practice

MODULE 5 Relationships Among Linear Functions

(Bottom Left) ©Peepo/iStock/Getty Images; (Bottom Right) ©Houghton Mifflin Harcourt

Build Linear Functions and Models

MODULE 6 Fit Linear Functions to Data

(Top) ©AleksandarNakic/E+/Getty Images; (Bottom) ©kali9/E+/Getty Images

Build Conceptual Understanding   Connect Concepts and Skills   Apply and Practice

Linear Systems

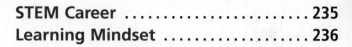

MODULE 9 Systems of Linear Equations

MODULE 10 Linear Inequalities

Build Conceptual Understanding   Connect Concepts and Skills   Apply and Practice

Unit 5

Exponential Functions and Equations

MODULE 11 Exponential Functions and Models

MODULE 12 Relationships Among Exponential Functions

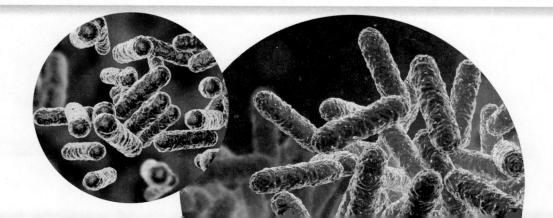

Unit 6

Build Exponential Functions and Models

MODULE 13 Fit Exponential Functions to Data

MODULE 14 Discrete Exponential Functions

● Build Conceptual Understanding   ● Connect Concepts and Skills   ● Apply and Practice

Build Conceptual Understanding   Connect Concepts and Skills   Apply and Practice

©PeopleImages/E+/Getty Images

xv

MODULE 18 Use Square Roots to Solve Quadratic Equations

©Steve Debenport/E+/Getty Images

9 Functions and Models

MODULE 19 Build Quadratic Functions and Models

● Build Conceptual Understanding   ● Connect Concepts and Skills   ● Apply and Practice

MODULE 20 Function Analysis

(Left) ©Hero Images/Getty Images; (Right) ©Tomwang112/iStock/Getty Images Plus/Getty Images

Unit 10 Data Analysis

Build Conceptual Understanding   Connect Concepts and Skills   Apply and Practice

STUDENT RESOURCES

Unit 1

Real Numbers and Connections to Algebra

Chemist

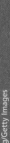

©YinYang/Getty Images

Chemists work in labs or in the field investigating how different substances interact with one another. In their work, chemists sometimes mix substances together. The substances, called reactants, may react to form new substances, called products. Chemists use a chemical equation to describe the reaction.

STEM Task

A *balanced* chemical equation has the same number of atoms for each element before and after the reaction.

Suppose you are combining molecules of the elements nitrogen (N_2) and hydrogen (H_2) to form ammonia (NH_3). The subscripts indicate the number of atoms of an element in each molecule.

$$\underline{\quad?\quad} N_2 + \underline{\quad?\quad} H_2 \rightarrow \underline{\quad?\quad} NH_3$$

1 nitrogen atom and 3 hydrogen atoms

Find the missing numbers of nitrogen, hydrogen, and ammonia molecules to balance the equation.

Learning Mindset

Resilience Monitors Knowledge and Skills

How do you know that you are learning? Whenever you approach a new topic, it is important that you monitor your understanding of it. Checking in with yourself before, during, and after learning can help you see that you're making progress and keep you focused on your learning goal. Here are some questions you can ask yourself to monitor your learning:

- What am I trying to learn? What is the goal or objective?

- How is the new topic connected to something I already know? What is the new information?

- What skills should I be able to perform in order to demonstrate my understanding of the topic?

- What additional knowledge about the topic did I gain today?

- What am I *not* understanding yet? What do I need to do to understand better?

- Can I explain or demonstrate to someone else what I have learned?

Reflect

Q How do you know that you are improving your understanding of a mathematical concept or skill?

Q What did you need to understand in order to balance the chemical equation in the STEM Task?

Module Performance Task: Spies and Analysts™

Stack
Soda Cans
to the Ceiling

To make a soda tower that will reach to the ceiling, how many soda cans do you need to stack?

Are You Ready?

Complete these problems to review prior concepts and skills you will need for this module.

Evaluate Algebraic Expressions

Evaluate each expression.

1. $2x + 6$ for $x = 12$

2. $-3x - 5$ for $x = 18$

3. $\frac{1}{5}x + 14$ for $x = 20$

4. $\frac{x}{2} \cdot 16$ for $x = 5$

5. $\frac{2}{x-1} + 4$ for $x = 0$

6. $x^2 - 4x$ for $x = -1$

Square Roots and Cube Roots

Evaluate each expression.

7. $\sqrt[3]{216}$

8. $\sqrt{169}$

9. $\sqrt{225}$

10. $\sqrt{\frac{49}{144}}$

11. $\sqrt[3]{27}$

12. $\sqrt[3]{125}$

Properties of Exponents

Simplify each expression.

13. $3^4 \cdot 3^5$

14. $(2 \cdot 3)^2$

15. $5^5 \div 5^2$

16. $\left(4^2\right)^3$

17. $\frac{6^7}{6^5}$

18. $8\left(\frac{1}{2}\right)^4$

Connecting Past and Present

In middle school, you learned:

- to identify rational and irrational numbers,
- to operate with rational numbers, and
- to round decimals to any place.

In Algebra 1, you will learn:

- to use properties of rational and irrational numbers,
- to simplify expressions involving radicals and rational exponents, and
- to report unit measurements with accuracy and appropriate levels of precision.

Real Numbers

(I Can) operate with real numbers and understand closure properties in the real number system.

Spark Your Learning

In a cable-stayed bridge, cables run in straight lines from the tower to the bridge deck providing support.

The distance, along the bridge deck, from the tower to the end of the longest cable is 130 m.

Complete Part A as a whole class. Then complete Parts B–D in small groups.

- **A.** What is a mathematical question you can ask about this situation? What information would you need to know to answer your question?

- **B.** What formula can you use to answer this question? What assumption(s) would you need to make? Are they reasonable?

- **C.** To answer your question, what strategy and tool would you use along with all the information you have? What answer do you get?

- **D.** Does your answer make sense? How do you know?

  Turn and Talk Examine your answer closely.
- Is it possible to state your answer as a whole number?
- Is it possible to state your answer without losing any information?
- How would an engineer most likely state the answer? Explain your reasoning.

Build Understanding

Investigate the Set of Real Numbers

Every point on the number line represents a **real number,** including both rational and irrational numbers. A **rational number** is a number that can be written in the form $\frac{a}{b}$, where a and b are integers and $b \neq 0$. An **irrational number** cannot be expressed as the ratio of two integers, and its decimal form is non-repeating and non-terminating. For example, the decimal form of π, 3.14159265..., neither repeats nor terminates.

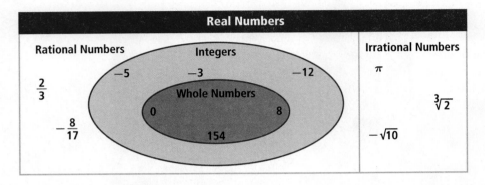

Every real number can be classified as a rational or irrational number.

1 Use the definitions of rational and irrational numbers to justify each statement.

    A. $\sqrt{5}$ is an irrational number.

    B. -5 is a rational number.

    C. 5.26262626... is a rational number.

 Turn and Talk John says that the number π is a rational number because it is equivalent to 3.14 and $\frac{22}{7}$. Is John correct? Explain.

Prove Closure

Examine the following *closure* statements.

Integers are *closed* under addition, subtraction, and multiplication.

$$-120 + 50 = -70$$

$$-2 - (-5) = 3$$

$$4(-6) = -24$$

Integers are *not closed* under division.

$$-24 \div 14 = -1\frac{5}{7}$$

$$15 \div -6 = -2.5$$

> **Connect to Vocabulary**
>
> A set of numbers is said to be closed, or to have **closure**, under a given operation if the result of the operation on any two numbers in the set is also in the set.

2 In this activity, you will explore the closure property with rational and irrational numbers under addition.

A. Copy and complete the table by finding the indicated sums of the given rational and irrational numbers.

+	$\frac{1}{4}$	0	$\sqrt{3}$	$-\sqrt{3}$
$\frac{1}{4}$	$\frac{1}{2}$	?	?	$\frac{1}{4} - \sqrt{3}$
0	?	?	?	?
$\sqrt{3}$	?	?	?	?
$-\sqrt{3}$	?	?	?	?

B. Describe the patterns you see for (1) the sum of two rational numbers, (2) the sum of a rational number and an irrational number, and (3) the sum of two irrational numbers. Is each of the three types of sums always, sometimes, or never a rational number?

C. Copy and complete the proof that the sum of two rational numbers is rational.

Let a, b, c, and d be integers such that $b \neq 0$ and $d \neq 0$.
Then by definition, $\frac{a}{b}$ and $\frac{c}{d}$ are ___?___ numbers.

$\frac{a}{b} + \frac{c}{d} = \frac{ad}{bd} + \frac{?}{bd}$ Rewrite each fraction with a denominator of bd.

$= \frac{?}{bd}$ Add the fractions.

$ad + bc$ and bd are integers because integers are closed under ___?___ and ___?___.

Therefore, $\frac{ad + bc}{bd}$ is a ___?___ number by the definition of rational numbers.

D. Copy and complete the proof, called a *proof by contradiction,* that the sum of a rational number and an irrational number is irrational.

Assume that the sum of a rational number a and an irrational number b is a rational number. In other words, $a + b = c$ for some ___?___ number c.

Solving for b, you get $b = c - a = c + (?)$.

Therefore b is the sum of two rational numbers, c and $-a$, and must itself be a ___?___ number as proved in Part C.

But this contradicts the given fact that b was an irrational number, so the assumption must be wrong. So, the sum of a rational number and an irrational number must be ___?___.

Turn and Talk When is the sum of two irrational numbers rational?

Step It Out

Apply Closure Properties

The table shows the types of numbers that are closed under each operation.

		Set of Numbers		
		Rational numbers	**Irrational numbers**	**Real numbers**
Operation	**Addition**	closed	not closed	closed
	Subtraction	closed	not closed	closed
	Multiplication	closed	not closed	closed
	Division	closed	not closed	closed

3 Given that 2 is a rational number and $\sqrt{2}$ is an irrational number, classify each number described as either rational or irrational. Justify your answer.

A. $2 + \sqrt{2}$

B. $2 - \sqrt{2}$

C. $2 \cdot \sqrt{2} + \sqrt{2}$

D. $\dfrac{2 \cdot \sqrt{2}}{2}$

To prove that a statement is false, you only need to find one counterexample. Determine whether each statement is true or false. If false, give a counterexample.

E. Irrational numbers are closed under addition.

F. The sum of a rational and irrational number is a rational number.

G. Irrational numbers are closed under division.

H. The sum of a rational and irrational number is a real number.

 Turn and Talk What are some closure statements that you can disprove by giving a counterexample?

Check Understanding

Use the definitions of rational and irrational numbers to justify each statement.

1. $\sqrt{14}$ is an irrational number.

2. -4 is a rational number.

Identify each statement as true or false. Justify your answer.

3. The difference of two rational numbers is an irrational number.

4. The sum of two irrational numbers is always an irrational number.

Determine whether each statement is true or false. If false, give a counterexample.

5. Irrational numbers are closed under subtraction.

6. Irrational numbers are closed under multiplication.

On Your Own

Identify each real number as either rational or irrational. Justify your answer.

7. $5 + \pi$

8. $2 + \dfrac{1}{7}$

9. $0 \times \pi$

10. $1.030030003\ldots$

11. 2×0.5

12. $\dfrac{\pi}{2}$

13. $2.222\ldots + 4$

14. $2\pi - 2\pi$

15. $\sqrt{16}$

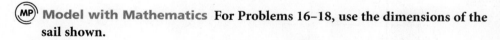 **Model with Mathematics** For Problems 16–18, use the dimensions of the sail shown.

16. Is the height of the sail a rational or irrational number? Explain.

17. Is the width of the sail a rational or irrational number? Explain.

18. Is the length of the diagonal a rational or irrational number? Explain.

5 m

2 m

MP **Model with Mathematics** Sal's Pizza baked the largest pizza in town. The size of the record-breaking pizza is shown. Use this information for Problems 19–21.

19. Is the diameter of the pizza a rational or irrational number? Explain.

20. Is the circumference of the pizza a rational or irrational number? Explain.

21. Is the area of the pizza a rational or irrational number? Explain.

3 m

22. **MP** **Use Structure** Look back at the table in Task 2.

   A. Create a similar table showing all the possible products of the numbers -5, 10, $\sqrt{2}$, and π.

   B. Will the product of two rational numbers sometimes, always, or never be a rational number?

   C. Will the product of two irrational numbers sometimes, always, or never be a rational number?

   D. Will the product of a nonzero rational number and an irrational number sometimes, always, or never be a rational number?

23. **MP** **Construct Arguments** Prove that the product of two rational numbers is rational.

24. **MP** **Construct Arguments** Prove that the product of a nonzero rational number and an irrational number is irrational.

25. **(Open Middle™)** Using the digits 1 to 9 at most one time each, fill in the boxes to make a true statement.

$$\sqrt{\boxed{}\boxed{}} + \sqrt{\boxed{}\boxed{}} = \boxed{}\boxed{}$$

Spiral Review • Assessment Readiness

26. Which expressions can represent the area of a circle? Select all that apply.

   Ⓐ 16π ft^2 Ⓑ 4π m^2

   Ⓒ 18π yd   Ⓓ 2π cm^3

27. At the end of the first year, a zoo has 10 monkeys. If the number of monkeys doubles each year, how many will there be at the end of the fifth year?

   Ⓐ 50   Ⓑ 60   Ⓒ 160   Ⓓ 320

28. Simplify the following expression.
$$2x + 3x^2 + 5x^3 + 7x + 17$$

   Ⓐ $5x^3 + 5x^2 + 7x + 17$

   Ⓑ $5x^3 + 3x^2 + 9x + 17$

   Ⓒ $5x^3 + 2x + 3x^2 + 24x$

   Ⓓ $7x^3 + 3x^2 + 7x + 17$

I'm in a Learning Mindset!

What math skills do I need to classify numbers as rational or irrational?

Radicals and Rational Exponents

(I Can) simplify expressions involving radicals and rational exponents.

Spark Your Learning

Police Officers are trained to analyze pieces of trace evidence left behind. They can determine if a car was speeding by measuring the length of a skid mark.

A car skidded a long distance after applying the brakes before it was able to stop completely.

Complete Part A as a whole class. Then complete Parts B–D in small groups.

A. What is a mathematical question you can ask about this situation? What information would you need to know to answer your question?

B. What variable(s) are involved in this situation? What unit of measurement would you use for each variable?

C. To answer your question, what strategy and tool would you use along with all the information you have? What answer do you get?

D. Does your answer make sense in the context of the situation? How do you know? Is there anything that could change the answer?

Turn and Talk Predict how your answer would change for each of the following changes in the situation:
- The asphalt was slightly wet.
- The roadway was made of dirt instead of asphalt.
- The skid marks were longer or shorter.

Build Understanding

Convert Between Radical Form and Rational Exponent Form

A **radical expression** is an expression that contains the radical symbol $\sqrt{}$. In the radical expression $\sqrt[n]{a}$, a is called the **radicand**, and n is called the **index**, which must be an integer value greater than 1. For example, the radical expression $\sqrt[5]{8}$ has an index of 5 and a radicand of 8 and is read as "the fifth root of 8". When $n = 2$, the radical is called a square root, and the index 2 is usually not shown.

Recall that a *power* is a quantity that can be expressed as a *base* with an *exponent*.

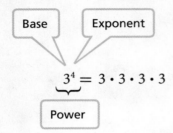

Base   Exponent

$$3^4 = 3 \cdot 3 \cdot 3 \cdot 3$$

Power

Recall the properties of exponents.

Properties of Exponents		
Property	**Symbols**	**Examples**
Product of Powers	For all real numbers a, and all integers m and n, $a^m \cdot a^n = a^{m+n}$.	$3^4 \cdot 3^2 = 3^{4+2} = 3^6$
Quotient of Powers	For all real numbers $a \neq 0$, and all m and n, $\frac{a^m}{a^n} = a^{m-n}$.	$\frac{3^4}{3^2} = 3^{4-2} = 3^2$
Power of a Product	For all real numbers a and b, and all n, $(a \cdot b)^n = a^n \cdot b^n$.	$(3 \cdot 4)^2 = 3^2 \cdot 4^2 = 144$
Power of a Quotient	For all real numbers a and $b \neq 0$, and all integers n, $\left(\frac{a}{b}\right)^n = \left(\frac{a^n}{b^n}\right)$.	$\left(\frac{3}{2}\right)^2 = \left(\frac{3^2}{2^2}\right) = 2.25$
Power of a Power	For all real numbers a, and all integers m and n, $(a^m)^n = a^{m \cdot n}$.	$(3^4)^2 = 3^{4 \cdot 2} = 3^8$
Zero Exponent	For all real numbers $a \neq 0$, $a^0 = 1$.	$5^0 = 1$
Negative Exponent	For all real numbers $a \neq 0$ and all integers n, $a^{-n} = \frac{1}{a^n}$.	$4^{-3} = \frac{1}{4^3}$

You can define exponential expressions with rational exponents in terms of radicals by making sure the properties of integer exponents still hold true.

1 Determine what real number $3^{\frac{1}{2}}$ represents.

A. Suppose you square $3^{\frac{1}{2}}$ to get $\left(3^{\frac{1}{2}}\right)^2$. What property of exponents could you use to simplify this expression?

B. Use that property to simplify the result of squaring $3^{\frac{1}{2}}$.

$$\left(3^{\frac{1}{2}}\right)^2 = \underline{\quad ? \quad}.$$

C. The definition of a square root says that a is a square root of b whenever $a^2 = b$. You have squared $3^{\frac{1}{2}}$ and gotten 3. What does this tell you about $3^{\frac{1}{2}}$?

D. Generalize your result:

If $a > 0$, then $a^{\frac{1}{2}} = \underline{\quad ? \quad}.$

 Turn and Talk How would you define $a^{\frac{1}{3}}$ and, in general, $a^{\frac{1}{n}}$, where n is an integer greater than 1? Explain your reasoning.

2 Examine the methods below to see how the Power of a Power Property can be used to define $a^{\frac{m}{n}}$ for any positive real number a and any integers m and n, where $n > 1$.

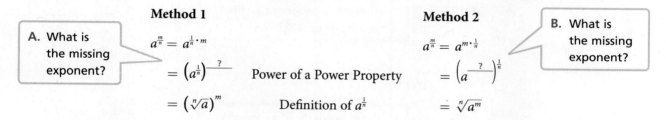

Method 1

A. What is the missing exponent?

$a^{\frac{m}{n}} = a^{\frac{1}{n} \cdot m}$

$= \left(a^{\frac{1}{n}}\right)^{\underline{?}}$ Power of a Power Property

$= \left(\sqrt[n]{a}\right)^m$ Definition of $a^{\frac{1}{n}}$

Method 2

B. What is the missing exponent?

$a^{\frac{m}{n}} = a^{m \cdot \frac{1}{n}}$

$= \left(a^{\underline{?}}\right)^{\frac{1}{n}}$

$= \sqrt[n]{a^m}$

Methods 1 and 2 show that when you are simplifying a rational exponent, raising to the *m*th power and taking the *n*th root can be considered in either order.

C. Give your own example of evaluating $a^{\frac{m}{n}}$ by choosing values of m, n, and a, where $n > 1$, $a > 0$, and a is an *n*th power.

D. Did you use Method 1 or Method 2 in Part C? Explain why you chose that method.

 Turn and Talk Which method do you prefer for evaluating $8^{\frac{5}{3}}$? Explain why.

Step It Out

Evaluate Numerical Expressions Involving Rational Exponents

You can use the rules that you derived from the properties of exponents for rewriting expressions involving radicals and rational exponents to evaluate expressions with rational exponents.

Definition of Rational Exponent
For any real number a and any integers m and n, where $n > 1$:
$\sqrt[n]{a} = a^{\frac{1}{n}}$ $\qquad$ $a^{\frac{m}{n}} = \sqrt[n]{a^m}$ $\qquad$ $a^{\frac{m}{n}} = \left(\sqrt[n]{a}\right)^m$

The properties of integer exponents can be extended to rational exponents because rational exponents were defined to be consistent with the properties of exponents.

3 Evaluate each expression.

$9^{\frac{3}{2}} = \left(\sqrt{9}\right)^3$

$\qquad = (3)^3$

$\qquad = 27$

A. Which form of the definition of rational exponent justifies writing $9^{\frac{3}{2}}$ as $\left(\sqrt{9}\right)^3$?

$8^{\frac{2}{3}} = \sqrt[3]{8^2}$

$\qquad = \sqrt[3]{64}$

$\qquad = 4$

B. Which form of the definition of rational exponent justifies writing $8^{\frac{2}{3}}$ as $\sqrt[3]{8^2}$?

$4^{-\frac{3}{2}} = \left(\sqrt{4}\right)^{-3}$

$\qquad = 2^{-3}$

$\qquad = \dfrac{1}{2^3}$

$\qquad = \dfrac{1}{8}$

C. What property of exponents justifies writing 2^{-3} as $\frac{1}{2^3}$?

$64^{\frac{2}{3}} - 125^{\frac{1}{3}} = \left(\sqrt[3]{64}\right)^2 - \sqrt[3]{125}$

$\qquad = (4)^2 - 5$

$\qquad = 11$

D. Which form of the definition of rational exponent justifies writing $125^{\frac{1}{3}}$ as $\sqrt[3]{125}$?

 Turn and Talk What is another way to evaluate each expression shown above? For each expression, tell which method you prefer and why.

Simplify Algebraic Expressions Involving Rational Exponents

The rules for converting between forms with radicals and rational exponents can be used along with all of the properties of exponents to simplify algebraic expressions involving variables and rational exponents.

4 Select from the list of properties of exponents stated earlier to justify the steps taken to simplify each expression. Assume all variables are positive.

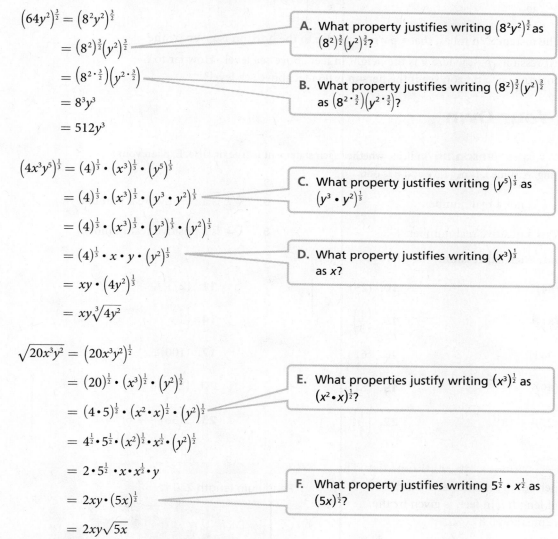

$$\left(64y^2\right)^{\frac{3}{2}} = \left(8^2y^2\right)^{\frac{3}{2}}$$
$$= \left(8^2\right)^{\frac{3}{2}}\left(y^2\right)^{\frac{3}{2}}$$
$$= \left(8^{2\cdot\frac{3}{2}}\right)\left(y^{2\cdot\frac{3}{2}}\right)$$
$$= 8^3y^3$$
$$= 512y^3$$

A. What property justifies writing $\left(8^2y^2\right)^{\frac{3}{2}}$ as $\left(8^2\right)^{\frac{3}{2}}\left(y^2\right)^{\frac{3}{2}}$?

B. What property justifies writing $\left(8^2\right)^{\frac{3}{2}}\left(y^2\right)^{\frac{3}{2}}$ as $\left(8^{2\cdot\frac{3}{2}}\right)\left(y^{2\cdot\frac{3}{2}}\right)$?

$$\left(4x^3y^5\right)^{\frac{1}{3}} = (4)^{\frac{1}{3}} \cdot \left(x^3\right)^{\frac{1}{3}} \cdot \left(y^5\right)^{\frac{1}{3}}$$
$$= (4)^{\frac{1}{3}} \cdot \left(x^3\right)^{\frac{1}{3}} \cdot \left(y^3 \cdot y^2\right)^{\frac{1}{3}}$$
$$= (4)^{\frac{1}{3}} \cdot \left(x^3\right)^{\frac{1}{3}} \cdot \left(y^3\right)^{\frac{1}{3}} \cdot \left(y^2\right)^{\frac{1}{3}}$$
$$= (4)^{\frac{1}{3}} \cdot x \cdot y \cdot \left(y^2\right)^{\frac{1}{3}}$$
$$= xy \cdot \left(4y^2\right)^{\frac{1}{3}}$$
$$= xy\sqrt[3]{4y^2}$$

C. What property justifies writing $\left(y^5\right)^{\frac{1}{3}}$ as $\left(y^3 \cdot y^2\right)^{\frac{1}{3}}$

D. What property justifies writing $\left(x^3\right)^{\frac{1}{3}}$ as x?

$$\sqrt{20x^3y^2} = \left(20x^3y^2\right)^{\frac{1}{2}}$$
$$= (20)^{\frac{1}{2}} \cdot \left(x^3\right)^{\frac{1}{2}} \cdot \left(y^2\right)^{\frac{1}{2}}$$
$$= (4 \cdot 5)^{\frac{1}{2}} \cdot \left(x^2 \cdot x\right)^{\frac{1}{2}} \cdot \left(y^2\right)^{\frac{1}{2}}$$
$$= 4^{\frac{1}{2}} \cdot 5^{\frac{1}{2}} \cdot \left(x^2\right)^{\frac{1}{2}} \cdot x^{\frac{1}{2}} \cdot \left(y^2\right)^{\frac{1}{2}}$$
$$= 2 \cdot 5^{\frac{1}{2}} \cdot x \cdot x^{\frac{1}{2}} \cdot y$$
$$= 2xy \cdot (5x)^{\frac{1}{2}}$$
$$= 2xy\sqrt{5x}$$

E. What properties justify writing $\left(x^3\right)^{\frac{1}{2}}$ as $\left(x^2 \cdot x\right)^{\frac{1}{2}}$?

F. What property justifies writing $5^{\frac{1}{2}} \cdot x^{\frac{1}{2}}$ as $(5x)^{\frac{1}{2}}$?

Turn and Talk Discuss how to evaluate $\sqrt{36x^{16}y^{36}}$. Compare your method with that of other students, using the properties of exponents to justify each step.

Check Understanding

1. Which two of the expressions shown below are equivalent? Explain.

$$4^{\frac{5}{2}} \qquad\qquad 8^{\frac{4}{3}} \qquad\qquad 16^{\frac{5}{4}}$$

Simplify each expression. Assume all variables are positive.

2. $\sqrt[5]{-32y^{10}}$

3. $\left(\dfrac{64y^6}{9x^2}\right)^{-\frac{1}{2}}$

4. The distance, in miles, that a person can see to the horizon is given by the expression $\sqrt{\dfrac{3h}{2}}$, where h is the height in feet above sea level. How far to the horizon can a person see if the person is 96 feet above sea level?

On Your Own

(MP) **Critique Reasoning** Indicate whether each statement is true or false. Explain your reasoning. Assume k is negative and n is odd.

5. $\sqrt[n]{k}$ is not a real number.

6. $\sqrt[n]{k}$ is a negative real number.

7. k^n is a positive real number.

8. $\sqrt[n]{k}$ is a positive real number.

Evaluate each expression.

9. $(64)^{\frac{1}{3}}$

10. $(25)^{-\frac{1}{2}}$

11. $(27)^{-\frac{1}{3}}$

12. $(81)^{\frac{1}{2}}$

13. $\left(\dfrac{1}{3}\right)^{-2}$

14. $\left(\dfrac{1}{2}\right)^{-4}$

15. $(343)^{\frac{2}{3}}$

16. $(625)^{\frac{3}{4}}$

17. $(100)^{\frac{3}{2}}$

18. $(49)^{\frac{3}{2}}$

19. $(8)^{\frac{5}{3}}$

20. $(25)^{\frac{3}{2}} + (16)^{\frac{3}{2}}$

21. $(27)^{\frac{4}{3}} + (8)^{\frac{4}{3}}$

22. $\left(\dfrac{1}{4}\right)^{-\frac{3}{2}}$

23. $2(36)^{-\frac{1}{2}} + 6^{-1}$

24. (MP) **Model with Mathematics** The period, in seconds, of a pendulum of length l, in feet, is given by the expression $0.81\sqrt{2l}$.

The Foucault pendulum, named after the French physicist Leon Foucault and shown here, was created to demonstrate the Earth's rotation. Find the approximate period of the Foucault pendulum.

Pendulum length 220 ft

Simplify each expression. Assume all variables are positive.

25. $\left(10{,}000x^4y^8\right)^{\frac{3}{4}}$

26. $\left(4x^2\right)^{\frac{5}{2}}$

27. $\left(9x^2y^8\right)^{\frac{3}{2}}$

28. $\sqrt{50x^3y^2}$

29. $\left(8x^5y\right)^{\frac{1}{3}}$

30. $\sqrt[4]{27x^7y^5}$

31. $\sqrt{12x^7y^2}$

32. $\left(125x^9y^5\right)^{\frac{2}{3}}$

33. 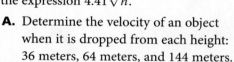 **Use Structure** Alicia noticed that the expression she was asked to simplify, $\sqrt[3]{3} \cdot \sqrt[3]{9}$, has the form $a^{\frac{1}{3}} \cdot b^{\frac{1}{3}}$, which she knows can be written as $(ab)^{\frac{1}{3}}$. Explain how this helps Alicia simplify the original expression, then use this to simplify the expression.

34. **Open Ended** Andre simplified the expression $(16)^{\frac{1}{4}}$ by thinking of $\frac{1}{4}$ as $\frac{1}{2} \cdot \frac{1}{2}$. The steps of his process to simplify the expression are shown.

$$16^{\frac{1}{4}} = \left(16^{\frac{1}{2}}\right)^{\frac{1}{2}}$$
$$= 4^{\frac{1}{2}}$$
$$= 2$$

A. Is Andre correct? Explain.

B. Is there another way to simplify the expression? Explain.

35. **STEM** When an object is dropped from a height of h, in meters, above the ground, the object will hit the ground with a velocity, in meters per second, given by the expression $4.41\sqrt{h}$.

A. Determine the velocity of an object when it is dropped from each height: 36 meters, 64 meters, and 144 meters.

B. What happens if the initial height is quadrupled? Justify your answer.

C. What if the initial height increases from 9 meters to 144 meters (an increase by a factor of 16)? Draw a conclusion based on your answers.

D. Predict how the factor of the increase in height h affects the increase in velocity.

36. STEM A formula that gives the resting heart rate h, in beats per minute, of a mammal based on its mass m, in kilograms, is $h = a \cdot m^{-\frac{1}{4}}$ where a is a constant.

A. Use the information in the photo to determine the value of a.

B. Find the resting heart rate of an elephant that has a mass of 4500 kilograms.

C. As the mass of mammals increases, does the resting heart rate increase or decrease? Explain how you know from the formula alone (without knowing any masses or resting heart rates of specific mammals).

37. (MP) **Use Structure** When simplifying the expression $\sqrt[3]{8x^8y^8}$, Adrian reported the answer as $2x^2y^2$, stating that he simply applied the cube root to all numerical values in the expression. Is his solution correct? Explain why or why not.

Mass: 24 g
Resting heart rate: 610 bpm

38. Demonstrate how you can use the Product of Powers Property instead of the Power of a Power Property to show that $2^{\frac{1}{2}} = \sqrt{2}$.

39. (Open Middle™) Using the digits 1 to 9, at most one time each, fill in the boxes to create a true statement.

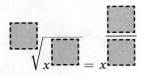

Spiral Review • Assessment Readiness

40. Which expressions simplify to $\frac{1}{27}$? Select all that apply.

(A) $3^2 \times 3^{-5}$ (D) $\dfrac{3^3}{3^{-6}}$

(B) $\dfrac{3}{3^4}$ (E) 3×3^{-2}

(C) $3^2 \times 3$ (F) 3×3^{-4}

41. Which of the expressions are irrational numbers? Select all that apply.

(A) $\sqrt{2}$ (C) $\sqrt{3}$

(B) $\sqrt{4}$ (D) π

42. Write 0.00112 in scientific notation.

(A) 1.12×10^{-3} (C) 112×10^{-5}

(B) 11.2×10^{-4} (D) 0.112×10^{-2}

43. Which equations have graphs that are lines? Select all that apply.

(A) $y = 3x + 4$ (D) $y = 6x$

(B) $y = 2^x$ (E) $y = x^2 + 3x - 1$

(C) $y = x^2 + 1$ (F) $y = 4$

 I'm in a Learning Mindset!

What skills do I need to evaluate expressions with rational exponents?

Precision and Accuracy in Calculations

(I Can) report quantities with accuracy and appropriate levels of precision.

Spark Your Learning

Mickey and Danni are mounting a shelf on the wall and need to determine where the mounting brackets should be placed. To ensure that the shelf is level, they need to make measurements that are as precise as possible.

They use a tape measure that has markings for both inches and centimeters.

Complete Part A as a whole class. Then complete Parts B–D in small groups.

A. What is a mathematical question you can ask about this situation? What information would you need to know to answer your question?

B. What measurement unit subdivisions are involved in this situation? Which subdivisions would you compare to answer your question? Explain your reasoning.

C. To answer your question, what strategy and tool would you use along with all the information you have? What answer do you get?

D. How would your answer change if they used a tape measure where the smallest measurement unit subdivisions marked are $\frac{1}{8}$ inch and $\frac{1}{2}$ centimeter?

 Turn and Talk Using the tape measure shown, they measure three different lengths to all be 91.4 centimeters. Is this possible? Explain why or why not.

Build Understanding

Compare Accuracy and Precision in Measurements

Accuracy is the closeness of a measured value to the actual value.

Precision is the level of detail of a measurement, determined by the smallest unit or fraction of a unit that can be reasonably measured.

Accuracy involves comparing a measurement to the actual value, while precision involves comparing repeated measurements to each other. In general, a measurement that is closer to the actual value than another measurement is more accurate than the other measurement, and repeated measurements that are close together are more precise than repeated measurements that are far apart.

1 Examine the targets below to understand how accuracy and precision compare. The *bull's eye* represents the actual correct value.

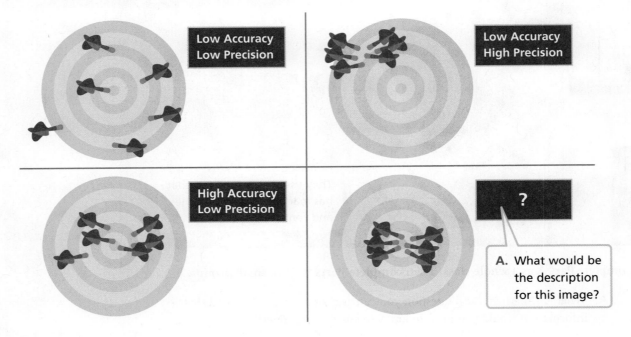

B. Explain why the target in the upper left of the image above shows low accuracy and low precision.

C. Explain why the target in the upper right of the image above shows low accuracy and high precision.

D. Explain why the target in the lower left of the image above shows high accuracy and low precision.

 Turn and Talk Compare and contrast the target showing low accuracy and high precision with the target showing high accuracy and low precision.

Step It Out

Determine Precision of Measurements

Measurements are obtained using a measuring tool, and the precision of the tool determines the precision of the measurements. For instance, the smallest unit on the ruler shown is a millimeter. So, while the actual length of the insect is between 1.2 cm and 1.3 cm, you would report the length as either 1.2 cm or 1.3 cm depending on whether the actual length appears to be closer to 1.2 cm or closer to 1.3 cm. Since in this case the insect's length appears to fall exactly halfway between 1.2 cm and 1.3 cm, you would round 1.25 up and report the length as 1.3 cm.

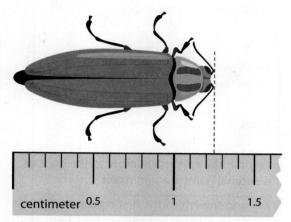

A reported measurement and the actual value of what was measured can differ by as much as half the unit of measurement. For the ruler shown above, the unit of measurement is 0.1 cm (that is, 1 millimeter), so half the unit of measurement is 0.05 cm. For example, if you are told that the insect's length is 1.3 cm, you know that the actual length could be anything from 1.25 cm up to (but not including) 1.35 cm.

2 ▶ The ribbon shown is between Ruler A with centimeter markings and Ruler B with millimeter markings. For each ruler, state what the length of the ribbon would be reported as, and give a range of values for the actual length of the ribbon.

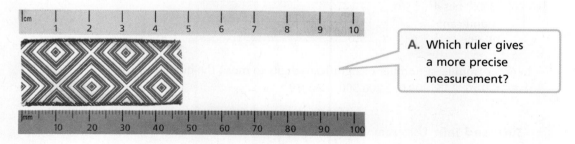

> **A.** Which ruler gives a more precise measurement?

Using Ruler A, the ribbon's length would be reported as 5 cm. The range of actual values for the length is between $(5 - 0.5)$ cm and $(5 + 0.5)$ cm.

So, 4.5 cm $\leq$ actual length < 5.5 cm using Ruler A.

Using Ruler B, the ribbon's length would be reported as 4.8 cm. The range of actual values for the length is between $(4.8 - 0.05)$ cm and $(4.8 + 0.05)$ cm.

So, 4.75 cm $\leq$ actual length < 4.85 cm using Ruler B.

Turn and Talk A tape measure has markings to a sixteenth of an inch. For a reported measurement m, what is the range of values for the actual measurement?

Identify Significant Digits

A **significant digit** is a digit in a measurement that carries a meaning in terms of the precision of the measurement

Rules for Significant Digits	
Words	**Examples**
All nonzero digits are significant.	4.316 has 4 significant digits. 295 has 3 significant digits.
Zeros between two other significant digits are significant.	305 has 3 significant digits. 0.600008 has 6 significant digits.
Zeros at the end of a number to the right of a decimal point are significant.	4.1000 has 5 significant digits. 0.9450 has 4 significant digits.
Zeros to the left of the first nonzero digit in a decimal number between −1 and 1 are *not* significant.	0.00015 has 2 significant digits. 0.09108 has 4 significant digits.
Zeros at the end of a number without a decimal point are assumed to be *not* significant.	50,700 has 3 significant digits. 94,000,000 has 2 significant digits.

3 Order the quantities by the number of significant digits.

Quantity	Number of significant digits
2.15	3
0.16	2
2,200,300	5
0.0004	1
300.0	4
4.30010	6

A. Explain why 300.0 has 4 significant digits.

B. Explain why 2,200,300 has 5 significant digits.

In order from least number of significant digits to most, the quantities are 0.0004, 0.16, 2.15, 300.0, 2,200,300, 4.30010.

 Turn and Talk Use examples to explain when zeros are not significant.

Calculate with Significant Digits

The rules for calculations involving significant digits are given in the table.

Rules for Calculations Involving Significant Digits	
Operation	**Rule**
Multiplication or division	The result should be given with the same number of significant digits as the value with the fewest significant digits.
Addition or subtraction	The result should be given with the same precision as the least precise value in the calculation.

4 ▶ Lisa is measuring a poster that she wants to frame. She finds that the poster's width is 32 cm and its length is 45.6 cm. What length of frame and what area of glass are needed to frame the poster?

A. The calculation of the length of the frame is shown below. Using the rules of significant digits, how should Lisa round the result?

Length of frame = 32 + 45.6 + 32 + 45.6

= 155.2 cm

B. The calculation of the area of the glass is shown below. Using the rules of significant digits, how should Lisa round the result?

Area of glass = 32 × 45.6

= 1459.2 cm²

Turn and Talk Suppose you use the perimeter formula $P = 2\ell + 2w$ to calculate the length of the frame. Does the presence of the two 2s in the formula have an effect on how the length of the frame should be rounded? Explain.

When a calculation involves multiple operations, round the result of the calculation so that it has the same number of significant digits as the value(s) with the least number of significant digits. However, rounding should always occur at the end of a calculation to avoid round-off error.

5 ▶ Average speed is the distance traveled divided by the time taken to travel that distance. Two methods of finding the average speed of the dog walker are shown below,

A. Contrast the two methods.

B. Identify which method produces a round-off error. Explain why.

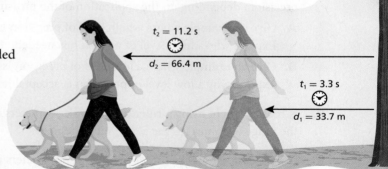

Preferred Method	Flawed Method
Average speed = $\dfrac{d_2 - d_1}{t_2 - t_1}$	Change in distance = $d_2 - d_1 = 66.4 - 33.7 = 32.7$
$= \dfrac{66.4 - 33.7}{11.2 - 3.3}$	The change in distance is 33 m rounded to 2 significant digits.
$= \dfrac{32.7}{7.9}$	Change in time = $t_2 - t_1 = 11.2 - 3.3 = 7.9$
$= 4.139\ldots$	Average speed = $\dfrac{d_2 - d_1}{t_2 - t_1} = \dfrac{33}{7.9} = 4.177\ldots$
The average speed is 4.1 m/s rounded to 2 significant digits.	The average speed is 4.2 m/s rounded to 2 significant digits.

Check Understanding

1. Would the manufacturing of components for the International Space Station require high precision, high accuracy, or both? Explain your reasoning.

2. A measurement using a ruler marked to an eighth of an inch is reported as $3\frac{1}{2}$ inches. What is the range of values for the actual measurement?

Identify the number of significant digits in each number. Justify your answer.

3. 3.0020

4. 0.00100100310

5. Over a 1.35-hour period of time, a family walks 0.75 km, stops to talk to the neighbor, then walks another 1.15 km before reaching the destination. What is the average speed of the family during this walk?

On Your Own

6. **(MP) Critique Reasoning** An old adage used when cutting during construction is shown. Does this practice increase precision, accuracy, or both? Explain.

Measure **twice** and **cut** once.

7. **(MP) Attend to Precision** Measurements can be reported at a variety of levels of precision, depending on the application of the measurement.

   A. Give an example where a high level of precision is needed in a measurement. Explain why a high level of precision is needed.

   B. Give an example where a low level of precision is acceptable in a measurement. Explain why a low level of precision is acceptable.

8. A measurement using a ruler marked in centimeters is reported as 6 cm. What is the range of values for the actual measurement?

9. A measurement using a ruler marked in millimeters is reported as 9.2 cm. What is the range of values for the actual measurement?

10. A measurement using a ruler marked to a sixteenth of an inch is reported as $4\frac{3}{16}$ inches. What is the range of values for the actual measurement?

Identify the number of significant digits in each measurement.

11. 0.000501 in. | 12. 32.0202 s | 13. 4.5 in.

14. 0.50 h | 15. 10 m | 16. 100 ft

17. 403 km | 18. 9.120 ft | 19. 0.005 cm

Calculate. State your answer using the rules for calculations with significant digits.

20. 4.5 cm + 3.77 cm

21. 3 ft × 2.7 ft

22. 7.46 h + 8.25 h − 2.5 h

23. $\dfrac{22.6 \text{ m}}{3.5 \text{ s}}$

24. $\dfrac{(8.75 + 3.45 + 7.71 + 8.65 + 5.42) \text{ lb}}{5 \text{ days}}$

25. $\dfrac{(4.54 - 1.31) \text{ cm}}{(5.0 - 2.25) \text{ h}}$

26. Monique is having her living room carpeted. The dimensions of her living room are 4.9 meters by 6 meters.

A. The length of tack strips needed to hold the carpet in place is determined by the perimeter of the carpet. Using the rules for significant digits, what is the perimeter of the carpet?

B. The amount of carpet needed to cover the living room floor is determined by the area of the carpet. Using the rules for significant digits, what is the area of the carpet?

27. STEM A scientist wants to know the density of some metal fragments. First he measures the mass of the metal using a balance and a beaker to hold the metal. Then he measures the volume using a graduated cylinder filled with water and reading the displacement. His measurements are recorded in the table shown.

Description	Measurement
Mass of empty beaker	48.886 grams
Mass of beaker and metal	143.37 grams
Volume of water	75.5 mL
Volume of water and metal	87.5 mL

A. Using the rules for significant digits, what is the mass of the metal?

B. Using the rules for significant digits, what is the volume of the metal?

C. The formula $d = \dfrac{m}{V}$ gives the density d in grams per milliliter, where m is the mass in grams, and V is the volume in milliliters. Using the rules for significant digits, what is the density of the metal?

28. Debi is riding down the zipline shown. It takes her 9 seconds to complete the zipline.

1.8 m

27.4 m

A. How can you find the length of the zipline?

B. What is Debi's average speed going down the zipline?

29. Open Ended A person gets three caricatures made from the same artist. Will the likeness of the caricatures more likely be precise or accurate in the three drawings? Explain your reasoning.

30. **(MP) Critique Reasoning** Jamie is taking a trip where he will be driving on a highway for 104 miles and then driving in a city for 28 miles. He knows that his car gets 30 miles per gallon of gas for highway driving and 24 miles per gallon of gas in city driving. He calculates his average fuel efficiency for the entire trip (rounding to 2 significant digits when necessary) as shown. Is this the most accurate method? Explain.

Total miles: $104 + 28 = 132$ miles

Total gas: $\dfrac{104}{30} + \dfrac{28}{24} \approx 4.6$ gallons

Average fuel efficiency: $\dfrac{132}{4.6} \approx 29$ mpg

31. **Financial Literacy** A family is assembling a budget for their finances. Their expenses include rent, food, transportation, clothing, and entertainment. What level of precision will be acceptable as they assemble this budget? Explain your reasoning.

Spiral Review • Assessment Readiness

32. John collects postcards. He buys them in packages of 8. He currently has 96 postcards. Write an equation to model the size of his collection after buying x packages.

Ⓐ $8x = 96$ Ⓒ $y = 96 + 8$

Ⓑ $y = 96x + 8$ Ⓓ $y = 8x + 96$

33. Which real numbers are rational? Select all that apply.

Ⓐ $\sqrt[3]{64}$ Ⓓ $\dfrac{\pi}{\pi}$

Ⓑ 4π Ⓔ $\sqrt{15}$

Ⓒ $0.999\ldots$ Ⓕ $\pi + 4$

34. Match the expression on the left with the equivalent value on the right.

Expression	Value
A. $4^3 \times 4^2$	**1.** 16
B. $3^3 \times 3^7 \div 3^8$	**2.** 2401
C. $2^3 \times \sqrt{4}$	**3.** 1024
D. $\dfrac{5^3 \times 5^2}{\sqrt{25}}$	**4.** 625
E. $7^5 \div 7$	**5.** 9

I'm in a Learning Mindset!

What skills do I need in order to attend to precision in my calculations with measurements?

Review

Real Numbers

Reviewing the real number system can help you understand operations with rational and irrational numbers.

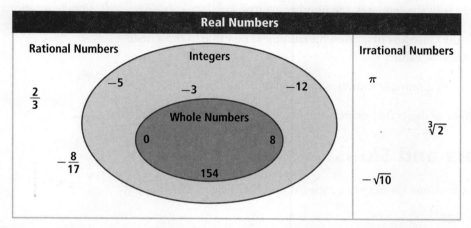

Radicals and Rational Exponents

You can write radical expressions as equivalent expressions with rational exponents.

     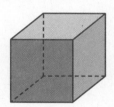

Area:
2 square units

Volume:
2 cubic units

Side length:
$\sqrt{2} = 2^{\frac{1}{2}}$ units

Side length:
$\sqrt[3]{2} = 2^{\frac{1}{3}}$ units

The properties of exponents can be extended to rational exponents.

$A = \sqrt{2} \cdot \sqrt[3]{2}$
$\quad = 2^{\frac{1}{2}} \cdot 2^{\frac{1}{3}}$
$\quad = 2^{\left(\frac{1}{2} + \frac{1}{3}\right)}$
$\quad = 2^{\frac{5}{6}}$ sq units

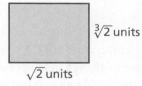

Note that $2^{\frac{5}{6}} = \sqrt[6]{2^5}$ or $\left(\sqrt[6]{2}\right)^5$.

Precision and Accuracy in Calculations

You use the rules for significant digits to report calculated measurements based on the significant figures of the measurements used in the calculation.

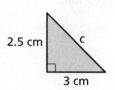

$c^2 = 2.5^2 + 3^2$
$c^2 = 6.25 + 9$
$c^2 = 15.25$
$c = \sqrt{15.25}$
$c \approx 4$ cm

The length of the hypotenuse should be reported based on the leg length with the fewer number of significant digits. So, the length of the hypotenuse is reported as 4 cm.

Vocabulary

Complete the following to review your vocabulary for this module.

1. $\sqrt[3]{8}$ is a ___?___ expression, and the number under the radical symbol is the ___?___.

2. For the radical expression $\sqrt[4]{9}$, the 4 is the ___?___, also known as a root.

3. When you add, subtract, multiply or divide with a set of numbers and the answer is in the same set, the number set has ___?___.

4. ___?___ is the closeness of a given measurement or value to the actual measurement or value.

5. The ___?___ of a number indicates the level of detail.

6. The number of digits that express the precision of a measurement are the ___?___.

Concepts and Skills

7. Which expressions simplify to a rational number? Select all that apply.

   (A) $24 - 4.25$

   (B) $\sqrt{16} + \sqrt[3]{8}$

   (C) 3π

   (D) $-\dfrac{7}{8} \cdot \dfrac{2}{5}$

   (E) $\dfrac{\sqrt{2}}{2}$

   (F) $-3(4 + 5)$

8. Which operation is not closed for integers?

   (A) addition

   (B) multiplication

   (C) subtraction

   (D) division

Simplify each expression.

9. $\sqrt[3]{8}$

10. $\sqrt[4]{81}$

11. $\sqrt{10{,}000}$

12. $\sqrt[3]{1000}$

13. $\sqrt[4]{25^2}$

14. $\sqrt[3]{125}$

15. $\sqrt[4]{16}$

16. $\sqrt[3]{16^3}$

Identify the number of significant digits in each value.

17. 2000

18. 200.00

19. 0.0020

20. (MP) **Use Tools** A digital thermometer shows that the temperature is 12.7 °F at 7:12 p.m. and 9.3 °F at 8:45 p.m. What is the average rate of change in temperature with respect to time measured in hours? State what strategy and tool you will use to answer the question, explain your choice, and then find the answer.

Linear Equations and Inequalities in One Variable

Module Performance Task: *Spies and Analysts™*

Clothing Coupon Choices

How can you decide which digital coupon to use?

©Digital Vision/Getty Images

Are You Ready?

Complete these problems to review prior concepts and skills you will need for this module.

Simplify Algebraic Expressions

Simplify each expression.

1. $(4x - 1) + (2x + 3)$

2. $(1 + 3y) - (2 - 5y)$

3. $2(6n + 4) - 5n$

4. $-8x - 3(2x - 1)$

Solve Two-Step Equations

Solve each equation.

5. $3b + 4 = -8$

6. $106 = 43 + 7x$

7. $-\frac{1}{4}s - \frac{3}{2} = \frac{3}{4}$

8. $2m + 1.5 = -11.7$

Write Two-Step Inequalities

Write an inequality to model each situation.

9. Bob has two 8-foot sections of prebuilt fencing left over from a previous fencing project. He plans to buy s 6-foot sections of the fencing so that he will have more than 40 feet of fencing.

10. Vijay has loaded 35 pounds of soil onto a cart. He will add b bricks that each weigh 4 pounds, but he does not want to exceed a total weight of 100 pounds in the cart.

11. Ana is baking cookies for a cookie exchange. She has already baked 20 cookies, and she will bake 1 dozen cookies at a time in each of the next b batches. She wants to take at least 50 cookies to the exchange.

Connecting Past and Present Learning

Previously, you learned:

- to write and simplify simple algebraic expressions,
- to write and solve linear equations and inequalities in one variable, and
- to use expressions, equations, and inequalities to model real-world situations.

In this module, you will learn:

- to justify the steps you take when solving equations and inequalities in one variable,
- to rewrite formulas and solve literal equations, and
- to use expressions, equations, and inequalities to model more complicated real-world situations.

Write, Interpret, and Simplify Expressions

(I Can) write an algebraic expression, interpret the parts of the expression, and use the **Distributive Property** to simplify the expression.

Spark Your Learning

Carlos dropped the phone he had received for his birthday and broke the screen. He knows he has to pay for the replacement himself and does some research to find the least cost. He is trying to decide between two stores offering different deals on the same-priced phone.

Store A
Buy the phone and get a rebate later.

Store B
Buy the phone with a discount now.

Complete Part A as a whole class. Then complete Parts B–D in small groups.

A. What is a mathematical question you can ask about this situation? What information would you need to know to answer your question?

B. What is the difference between a rebate and a discount? How does that affect how the tax rate (if there is one) is used in a calculation of final cost?

C. To answer your question, what strategy and tool would you use along with all the information you have? What answer do you get?

D. Compare the final costs at each store. Which is the better deal? Explain how you know.

 Turn and Talk Suppose your teacher gave you the original full price of the phone. How could you use that information to verify your answer about where Carlos should buy the phone?

Image Credit: ©Piyawan/Adobe Stock

Build Understanding

Interpret Expressions

An **expression** is a mathematical phrase that combines numbers and/or variables using mathematical operations. The parts of an expression that are added are called **terms**. Numerical expressions contain only numbers (constant terms) and operations. Algebraic expressions, also called variable expressions, include one or more variables. The numerical factor in a variable term (including 1 if a term does not have a numerical factor) is called a **coefficient**. You can understand what an expression modeling a real-world situation means by looking at its different parts. Each term and coefficient means something in the context of the situation.

 Look back at the situation on page 31. An algebraic expression that represents Carlos buying his replacement phone at Store A is $1.05p - 50$.

   A. What do you think p represents in this situation? What about $1.05p$?

   B. What do you think the term -50 represents in this situation?

   C. What do you think the whole expression represents in this situation?

 Turn and Talk Why might it be important to interpret the meaning of each part of an expression?

Analyze Units of Measurement

Consider the situation below. Here, the cost involves one unit but the weight involves another. You will need to use a conversion factor to make the units the same.

 At the store, Keeley buys a total of 44 ounces of apples and grapes. Let a represent the weight in ounces of the apples Keeley buys.

APPLES
$2.00 per pound

GRAPES
$1.50 per pound

   A. Explain why $44 - a$ is an expression for the weight of the grapes in ounces.

   B. Show how to use the conversion factor $\frac{1 \text{ pound}}{16 \text{ ounces}} = 0.0625$ pound per ounce to write expressions for the weights of the fruits so that the units are compatible with the costs.

Weight in ounces	Weight in pounds
Apples: a	Apples: ___?___ · a
Grapes: $44 - a$	Grapes: $0.0625(\underline{\quad?\quad} - a)$

 Turn and Talk You changed the weights to pounds to be compatible with the prices, which were in dollars per pound. How could you instead change the prices to dollars per ounce so that they are compatible with the given weights in ounces?

Step It Out

Write and Simplify Expressions

Expressions may contain grouping symbols such as parentheses or brackets. To eliminate grouping symbols, you can use the Distributive Property to multiply the number outside the parentheses by each term inside the parentheses.

> **Distributive Property**
>
> For all real numbers a, b, and c, $a(b + c) = ab + ac$.
> **Example:** $3(4 + 2) = 3 \cdot 4 + 3 \cdot 2 = 12 + 6 = 18$.

Variable terms whose variables and their exponents are the same are **like terms**. You can combine like terms by adding their coefficients. You simplify an expression by eliminating any grouping symbols and combining like terms so that the expression is easier to read and use. Two expressions are **equivalent expressions** if they have the same value for all values of the variable(s).

3 Consider your work on compatible units from Task 2. Write and simplify an expression to represent the amount Keeley spent on fruit at the store.

Use the compatible units found in Task 2 to write a verbal model.

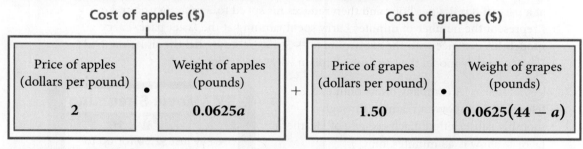

Cost of apples ($)

Price of apples (dollars per pound)	Weight of apples (pounds)
2	$0.0625a$

Cost of grapes ($)

Price of grapes (dollars per pound)	Weight of grapes (pounds)
1.50	$0.0625(44 - a)$

Write the expression.

$2(0.0625a) + 1.50\left[0.0625(44 - a)\right]$

> **A.** Which part of this expression represents the total cost of the apples? the total cost of the grapes?

Simplify the expression.

$2(0.0625a) + 1.50\left[0.0625(44 - a)\right] = 0.125a + 1.50\left[0.0625(44 - a)\right]$ Multiply by 2.

> **B.** Why is 0.09375, and not 0.0625, the coefficent of a?

$= 0.125a + 1.50(2.75 - 0.0625a)$ Distribute 0.0625.

$= 0.125a + 4.125 - 0.09375a$ Distribute 1.50.

$= 0.03125a + 4.125$ Combine like terms.

 Turn and Talk Suppose Keeley bought each of these different numbers of ounces of apples. How can you verify that the original expression and the simplified expression for the cost of the fruit are equivalent expressions? Explain your reasoning.

- $a = 12$ ounces
- $a = 20$ ounces
- $a = 36$ ounces

Check Understanding

1. At the movies, children's tickets are $6 each and adult's tickets are $10 each. Shandra buys 14 tickets. Let a be the number of adults going to the movies. Write an algebraic expression to represent the total price Shandra pays.

2. How many feet are in y yards?

Simplify each expression. Then substitute the given value for the variable in each given expression and each simplified expression to determine if the given expression and the simplified expression are equivalent expressions.

3. $2m + 6\left(\dfrac{2}{3} - m\right)$; $m = 4$

4. $3(0.5 - p) + 4(p + 0.75)$; $p = 2$

5. Michael spends a half hour adding water to his pool, part of the time at a rate of 15 gallons per minute and the rest of the time at a rate of 9 gallons per minute. Let t be the time in minutes that he adds water at the faster rate. Write an algebraic expression to represent the total amount of water added to the pool.

On Your Own

6. (MP) **Critique Reasoning** Larry spends a total of 45 minutes running. He begins at a pace of 8 miles per hour and then reduces his speed to 5 miles per hour. Let t represent the number of minutes Larry spent running at the faster pace. Larry models his distance with the expression $8t + 5(45 - t)$ to model the situation. Did Larry correctly model the situation? Explain why or why not.

7. (MP) **Reason** A company offers online television and movie streaming through a monthly subscription. Each episode of Heather's favorite show is 48 minutes long.

   TV / Movie Streaming
   PLAN
   - Pay just **$2.50** for up to 10 hours of streaming.
   - Then pay **$0.50** per hour for time over 10 hours.

   A. Is the unit of time used in the advertisement compatible with the unit of time for an episode of Heather's show? Explain.

   B. How many hours long is an episode of Heather's favorite show?

   C. Write an expression to determine how much Heather will pay if she watches s episodes per month for a total of more than 10 hours.

8. Jackson buys tickets for two concerts. The tickets for the concert featuring the local artist are $25 each. The tickets for the concert featuring the international artist are $75. Jackson buys a total of 20 tickets.

   A. Let x be the number of tickets Jackson buys for the concert featuring the local artist. How many tickets does Jackson buy for the concert featuring the international artist?

   B. Write an algebraic expression to represent the total cost of both concerts for Jackson.

   C. Interpret the parts of the expression by identifying how much Jackson pays for tickets for each of the two concerts.

9. As a speed skater, Kyle cycles between sprinting and recovering on the 111.12-meter short track during practice every day for 50 minutes. Let t be the time in hours that Kyle sprints during a practice.

Sprint: 48 km/h
Recovery: 18 km/h

   A. Write the unsimplified expression to represent the total distance Kyle skates. It may help you to make a verbal model to represent the total distance Kyle skates. Be sure to use compatible units.

   B. Interpret the parts of the expression.

   C. Simplify the algebraic expression.

   D. If Kyle spent 40 minutes sprinting yesterday, how far did he skate in all?

Simplify each expression.

10. $8(3x + 4) - 20$

11. $4(5x + 1) - 3x$

12. $4(2x + 3) + 6x + 9$

13. $3(4x + 2) + 2(x - 1)$

14. $\frac{1}{3}(6x - 15) - 3x$

15. $-7(x - 5) - 3(4 - 5x)$

16. $0.6(3 - 2x) - 0.4(1.5x + 2)$

17. $\frac{2}{3}(3x + 9) - \frac{4}{7}(21x - 14)$

18. $\frac{3}{5}(10x + 20) + \frac{4}{9}(9x - 27)$

19. $0.2(4.9x + 6) + 0.8(2 - 3x)$

20. A work crew is building a new biking path that will be 28 miles long. Each day, the crew builds 0.5 mile of the path. Write an expression for the length of the bike path left to build at any point during the construction. Explain what your variable represents.

21. **(MP) Use Structure** Matthew makes bracelets and necklaces using beads. He uses 34 beads for each bracelet and 72 beads for each necklace. He makes two more necklaces than bracelets. Let b represent the number of bracelets he makes.

   A. Copy and complete the table. What pattern do you see in the table?

   B. Write an expression that represents the total number of beads he uses to make bracelets and necklaces.

Bracelets	Beads used in bracelets	Necklaces	Beads used in necklaces
1	34	3	3 • 72, or 216
2	68	4	4 • 72, or 288
3	102	5	5 • 72, or 360
⋮	⋮	⋮	⋮
b	?	?	?

   C. Simplify the expression from Part B. What does each part of the simplified expression mean in the context of the situation?

   D. Is the simplified expression equivalent to the original expression? Justify your answer.

22. (MP) **Model with Mathematics** Rather than charging an entrance fee, a museum suggests that visitors donate d dollars per person. The log shows the number of people who entered the museum in a 15-minute period and how much each person paid.

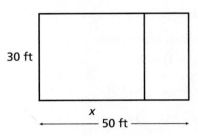

Visitor Donations

Suggested amount	ⅢⅠ ⅢⅠ
$2 more	ⅢⅠ ⅢⅠ ⅢⅠ
$3 less	ⅠⅠ

A. Write an algebraic expression to represent how much the visitors paid.

B. Identify what each part of the expression represents.

23. Open Ended Write an expression that can only be simplified by using the Distributive Property twice. Simplify the expression. How do you know that the unsimplified and simplified expressions are equivalent?

24. Trevor has a rectangular patch of dirt that has a length of 50 feet and a width of 30 feet. He wants to divide this area into two rectangular gardens as shown.

A. Write an expression to represent the area of the garden on the left.

B. Write an expression to represent the area of the garden on the right.

C. If the area of the garden on the left is greater, what is the difference of the areas of the two gardens? Simplify your answer.

30 ft

x

50 ft

Spiral Review • Assessment Readiness

25. Which radical has a value of 2?

Ⓐ $\sqrt[3]{125}$ Ⓒ $\sqrt{64}$

Ⓑ $\sqrt[5]{32}$ Ⓓ $\sqrt[4]{81}$

26. Which is equivalent to $\dfrac{15a^{-2}b^7}{3a^4b^{-3}}$?

Ⓐ $\dfrac{5b^{10}}{a^6}$ Ⓒ $5a^6b^{10}$

Ⓑ $\dfrac{a^6}{5b^{10}}$ Ⓓ $\dfrac{5b^4}{a^2}$

27. For each value, identify the number of significant digits in the value.

Value	1 significant digit	2 significant digits	3 significant digits
A. 0.0302	?	?	?
B. 0.003	?	?	?
C. 0.032	?	?	?

 I'm in a Learning Mindset!

What skills do I need to use to simplify algebraic expressions?

Write and Solve Equations

(I Can) use the properties of equality and the Distributive Property to solve an equation with the variable on both sides.

Spark Your Learning

Lynn and Anna are joggers who use the same running trail.

Lynn starts jogging before Anna does.

Anna jogs at a faster rate than Lynn does.

Complete Part A as a whole class. Then complete Parts B–D in small groups.

A. What is a mathematical question you can ask about this situation? What information would you need to know to answer your question?

B. What variable(s) are involved in this situation? What unit of measurement would you use for each variable?

C. To answer your question, what strategy and tool would you use along with all the information you have? What answer do you get?

D. Does your answer make sense in the context of the situation? How do you know?

Turn and Talk Predict how your answer would change for each of the following changes in the situation:

- Anna starts jogging 3 minutes earlier.
- Lynn's average jogging speed is 0.2 mile per hour faster.
- Lynn and Anna jog at the same average speed.

Build Understanding

Investigate Properties of Equality

An **equation** is a mathematical statement comparing two expressions using the symbol $=$. When you solve an equation, the **solution** produces a true statement when substituted for the variable in the equation. Solving an equation involves using properties of equality to write simpler **equivalent equations**, which all have the same solution as the original equation. In the Symbols column of the table below, a, b, and c are real numbers.

Properties of Equality		
Property	**Words**	**Symbols**
Addition Property of Equality	Adding the same number to both sides of an equation produces an equivalent equation.	If $a = b$, then $a + c = b + c$. **Example:** If $x - 2 = 3$, then $x - 2 + 2 = 3 + 2$.
Subtraction Property of Equality	Subtracting the same number from both sides of an equation produces an equivalent equation.	If $a = b$, then $a - c = b - c$. **Example:** If $x + 4 = -1$, then $x + 4 - 4 = -1 - 4$.
Multiplication Property of Equality	Multiplying both sides of an equation by the same nonzero number produces an equivalent equation.	If $a = b$ and $c \neq 0$, then $ac = bc$. **Example:** If $\frac{x}{3} = 2$, then $\frac{x}{3} \cdot 3 = 2 \cdot 3$.
Division Property of Equality	Dividing both sides of an equation by the same nonzero number produces an equivalent equation.	If $a = b$ and $c \neq 0$, then $\frac{a}{c} = \frac{b}{c}$. **Example:** If $-2.5x = 10$, then $\frac{-2.5x}{-2.5} = \frac{10}{-2.5}$.

1 **A.** Using a spreadsheet, create a table like the one shown for the equation $x = -1$. The formula in cell B2 is an if-then-else statement that checks the value in cell A2. Fill down the formula from cell B2 to cell B8. What do you observe?

B2	⬍	✕ ✓	fx	$=$ IF(A2 $= -1$,"YES", "NO")		
	A	**B**		**C**	**D**	**E**
1	x	Is x a solution?				
2	-3	NO				
3	-2					
4	-1					
5	0					
6	1					
7	2					
8	3					

If the number in cell A2 equals -1, then the word YES is shown in cell B2. Otherwise, the word NO is shown in cell B2.

B. Suppose you use the Multiplication Property of Equality to rewrite the equation $x = -1$ as $2x = -2$. Use the new equation in if-then-else statements you enter in cells C2 through C8. What do you observe?

C. Suppose you use the Addition Property of Equality to rewrite the equation $2x = -2$ as $2x + 3 = 1$. Use the new equation in if-then-else statements you enter in cells D2 through D8. What do you observe?

 Turn and Talk You used properties of equality to build the equation $2x + 3 = 1$ from $x = -1$. How can you use properties of equality to solve the equation $2x + 3 = 1$?

Step It Out

Solve Equations Using the Distributive Property

Previously, you solved one-step and two-step equations. Now you will solve multistep equations. Such equations may contain grouping symbols. In order to free the terms in an equation that contains grouping symbols, you can use the Distributive Property.

 The steps for solving the equation $5(2x - 3) + 4 = -6$ and checking the solution are shown below, but the steps have been scrambled.

A. Write the solution steps in the correct order.

$$10x - 11 = -6$$

$$x = 0.5$$

$$10x - 15 + 4 = -6$$

$$5(2x - 3) + 4 = -6$$

$$10x = 5$$

B. Write the check steps in the correct order.

$$-6 = -6 \checkmark$$

$$5(2(0.5) - 3) + 4 \stackrel{?}{=} -6$$

$$5(-2) + 4 \stackrel{?}{=} -6$$

$$5(1 - 3) + 4 \stackrel{?}{=} -6$$

$$-10 + 4 \stackrel{?}{=} -6$$

 Turn and Talk Can you solve the equation $5(2x - 3) + 4 = -6$ *without* using the Distributive Property as one of the steps? Show how or explain why not.

Recall that the Distributive Property also allows you to combine like terms.

3 The steps for solving the equation $-2x + \frac{1}{2}(6x - 5) = \frac{3}{2}$ are shown, but some justifications are missing.

$$-2x + \frac{1}{2}(6x - 5) = \frac{3}{2} \qquad \text{Given equation}$$

$$-2x + 3x - \frac{5}{2} = \frac{3}{2} \qquad \underline{\quad ? \quad}$$

$$(-2 + 3)x - \frac{5}{2} = \frac{3}{2} \qquad \underline{\quad ? \quad}$$

$$x - \frac{5}{2} = \frac{3}{2} \qquad \text{Simplify the coefficient of } x.$$

$$x = 4 \qquad \underline{\quad ? \quad}$$

A. What property justifies rewriting $\frac{1}{2}(6x - 5)$ as $3x - \frac{5}{2}$?

B. What property justifies rewriting $-2x + 3x$ as $(-2 + 3)x$?

C. What property justifies adding $\frac{5}{2}$ to each side of the equation?

 Turn and Talk Is it possible to eliminate the fractions as a first step in solving the equation $-2x + \frac{1}{2}(6x - 5) = \frac{3}{2}$? Show how or explain why not.

Solve Equations with the Variable on Both Sides

When a variable appears on both sides of an equation, you can use the Addition Property of Equality or the Subtraction Property of Equality to move the variable from one side to the other. Doing so allows you to isolate the variable on one side.

4 ▶ The steps for solving the equation $4(x + 1) + 1 = -3(x + 3)$ are shown, but some justifications are missing.

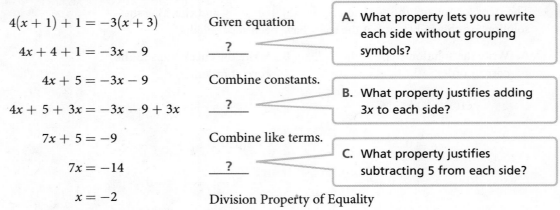

$$4(x + 1) + 1 = -3(x + 3)$$ Given equation

$$4x + 4 + 1 = -3x - 9$$ ___?___

A. What property lets you rewrite each side without grouping symbols?

$$4x + 5 = -3x - 9$$ Combine constants.

$$4x + 5 + 3x = -3x - 9 + 3x$$ ___?___

B. What property justifies adding $3x$ to each side?

$$7x + 5 = -9$$ Combine like terms.

$$7x = -14$$ ___?___

C. What property justifies subtracting 5 from each side?

$$x = -2$$ Division Property of Equality

 Turn and Talk How is solving $4(x + 1) + 1 = 4(x + 3)$ different from solving $4(x + 1) + 1 = -3(x + 3)$? What is different about solving $4(x + 1) + 8 = 4(x + 3)$?

Use an Equation to Solve a Real-World Problem

When solving a real-world problem, you may have to use a formula, such as the formula $P = 2\ell + 2w$ for the perimeter of a rectangle or the formula $d = rt$ for the distance traveled at a constant rate. When using a formula, you should pay attention to the units of measurement associated with the variables to ensure that the units are consistent.

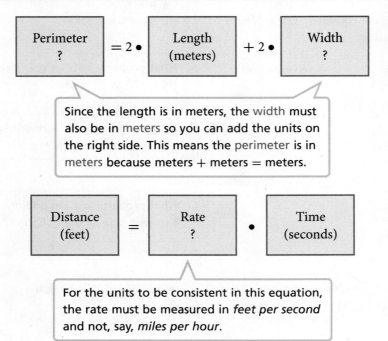

| Perimeter ? | $= 2 \bullet$ | Length (meters) | $+ 2 \bullet$ | Width ? |

Since the length is in meters, the width must also be in meters so you can add the units on the right side. This means the perimeter is in meters because meters + meters = meters.

| Distance (feet) | $=$ | Rate ? | $\bullet$ | Time (seconds) |

For the units to be consistent in this equation, the rate must be measured in *feet per second* and not, say, *miles per hour*.

5 Two friends, Jon and Josh, live at opposite ends of a trail. They bike toward each other at the speeds shown. At what distance along the trail, measured from Jon's starting point, do the two friends meet?

Jon

Josh starts biking 20 minutes before Jon does.

Josh

15 mi/h

12 mi/h

22 mi

Use a verbal model.

Although you are asked to find distance, you will do so by expressing distance in terms of time. Note that the units *miles per hour* and *minutes* are incompatible. So, let t represent the time in *hours* that Jon spends biking.

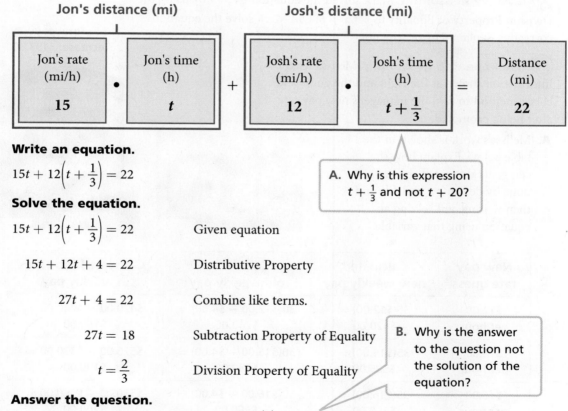

Jon's distance (mi)

Jon's rate (mi/h)	Jon's time (h)
15	t

Josh's distance (mi)

Josh's rate (mi/h)	Josh's time (h)
12	$t + \frac{1}{3}$

Distance (mi)
22

Write an equation.

$15t + 12\left(t + \frac{1}{3}\right) = 22$

Solve the equation.

$15t + 12\left(t + \frac{1}{3}\right) = 22$ Given equation

$15t + 12t + 4 = 22$ Distributive Property

$27t + 4 = 22$ Combine like terms.

$27t = 18$ Subtraction Property of Equality

$t = \frac{2}{3}$ Division Property of Equality

A. Why is this expression $t + \frac{1}{3}$ and not $t + 20$?

B. Why is the answer to the question not the solution of the equation?

Answer the question.

The two friends will meet at a distance of $15\left(\frac{2}{3}\right) = 10$ miles from Jon's starting point on the trail.

 Turn and Talk Suppose the trail in Task 5 is only 3 miles long. Write and solve a new equation to find the time Jon spends biking. Does your solution make sense? Explain.

Check Understanding

1. Which two of the equations shown below are equivalent? Explain your reasoning.

$$2x + 7 = 1 \qquad -3x + 4 = 12 \qquad x = -3$$

Solve each equation. Justify your solution steps, and check each solution.

2. $6(2x - 5) - 8 = 4$

3. $\frac{1}{2}(4x - 3) = \frac{3}{4}(4x - 5)$

4. The local art center sells two types of memberships each year. The premium membership is $90, and the regular membership is $60. The center wants to sell a total of 100 memberships. How many premium memberships must the center sell in order to earn $7260 in membership sales?

On Your Own

5. (MP) **Critique Reasoning** Mark solved the equation $\frac{2}{3}x = 9$ by using the Division Property of Equality to get $x = 6$. Did Mark solve the equation correctly? Explain why or why not.

6. (MP) **Use Repeated Reasoning** Melissa used the information shown at the right and the guess and check method to find the manager's new pay rate after being promoted.

   A. Melissa's work is shown in the table below. Explain how she can generalize what she has done by defining a variable and then writing and solving an equation using that variable.

Total pay increase: $197.50

Increase in time worked: 5 hours per week

Pay increase: $4 per hour

30 hours worked per week

Before Promotion

After Promotion

New pay rate guess	Calculated new weekly pay	Calculated old weekly pay	Calculated increase in weekly pay
$12.00 per hour	35($12.00) = $420.00	30($12.00 − $4.00) = $240.00	$420.00 − $240.00 = $180.00 ✗
$15.00 per hour	35($15.00) = $525.00	30($15.00 − $4.00) = $330.00	$525.00 − $330.00 = $195.00 ✗
$16.00 per hour	35($16.00) = $560.00	30($16.00 − $4.00) = $360.00	$560.00 − $360.00 = $200.00 ✗
$15.50 per hour	35($15.50) = $542.50	30($15.50 − $4.00) = $345.00	$542.50 − $345.00 = $197.50 ✓

   B. Suppose the question had been, "What was the manager's old pay rate?" Define the variable in a way that will answer this question. Then write and solve a new equation to show that you get a solution that is consistent with the one from Part A.

Solve each equation. Justify your solution steps, and check each solution.

7. $4(3x - 10) + 7 = 15$

8. $6 - 5(2x + 1) = 21$

9. $2 - \dfrac{3}{4}(8x - 6) = 11$

10. $0.2(4 - 5x) + 1 = 2.4$

11. $5(x + 1) - 2(3x - 4) = 14$

12. $2(5 - x) + 3(4x - 1) = -6$

13. $4x - 3 = 7x + 6$

14. $-2x + 5 = 3x + 1$

15. $5(2x + 3) - 7 = -2(x + 2)$

16. $8 - 3(2x - 5) = 4(x + 2)$

17. $0.4(2x + 3) = 0.3x + 0.8$

18. $\dfrac{1}{2}(6x - 5) = x - \dfrac{3}{2}$

19. **Financial Literacy** Kiera recently bought a used car from a relative, who agreed to let her pay for the car over time. She also borrowed money from her parents for a summer internship in Washington, D.C. She is paying off both loans in equal weekly payments. Use the information in the photos to determine how many weeks it takes for the balances of the loans to be the same.

$6500 loan, $200 weekly payments

$1600 loan, $25 weekly payments

20. (MP) **Use Structure** Jan noticed that the equation $3(4x - 7) + 2(4x - 7) = 5$ has the form $3\square + 2\square = 5$ where $\square = 4x - 7$. Explain how Jan can use this observation to solve the equation. Then use the same method to solve the equation $2(3x + 4) - 5(3x + 4) = 33$.

21. **Open Ended** Write an equation that can be solved using the Subtraction Property of Equality and the Division Property of Equality. Show another way to solve the same equation using the Addition Property of Equality and the Multiplication Property of Equality. Explain your reasoning.

22. Two subscription services offer deliveries of boxes of nutritious, organic snack foods each month. For how many months of deliveries will the two plans cost the same?

SNACKS 4 U
Pay just $4 per month for the first 3 months of deliveries.
Then pay $14 per month for deliveries after the third month.

HEALTHY TIMES
Get 1 free month of deliveries.
Then pay $10 per month for deliveries after the first month.

23. Luke wants to mix dry roasted peanuts and dried cranberries to make a trail mix. He wants to make 20 ounces of trail mix and spend $11. What weight of peanuts does he need to buy?

ORGANIC
DRY ROASTED
PEANUTS
$8 per pound

ORGANIC
DRIED
CRANBERRIES
$10 per pound

24. (MP) **Reason** Consider the equation $3(2x - 5) = ax + b$ where a and b represent constants.

  A. For what values of a and b would any value of x be a solution of the equation? Explain your reasoning.

  B. For what values of a and b would the equation not have any solutions? Explain your reasoning.

  C. For what values of a and b would the equation have exactly one solution?

25. (Open Middle™) Using the integers from -9 to 9 at most one time each, replace the boxes to create an equation that has a positive solution. Then repeat this activity to create a second equation that has a negative solution.

$$\frac{\square}{\square}\left(\square x - \square\right) + \square x = \square x - \square$$

Spiral Review • Assessment Readiness

26. Which expressions are equivalent to $4x^2y^6$? Select all that apply.

  (A) $\left(2xy^3\right)^2$

  (B) $\left(2x^2y^6\right)^2$

  (C) $2xy^2 + 2xy^4$

  (D) $2x^2y^6 + 2x^2y^6$

  (E) $\left(16x^8y^{24}\right)^{\frac{1}{4}}$

  (F) $\left(16x^4y^{12}\right)^{\frac{1}{2}}$

27. A circular mulch bed has a radius of 1.6 feet. A bag of mulch contains 2 cubic feet of mulch. If all of the mulch is spread evenly on the bed, what is the mulch's depth to an appropriate number of significant digits?

  (A) 0.2 foot

  (B) 0.25 foot

  (C) 0.249 foot

  (D) 0.2487 foot

28. To make salsa, you buy 8 tomatoes that weigh t pounds each and that cost $2.20 per pound. You also buy 2 peppers that weigh p pounds each and that cost $3.40 per pound. Which expression gives the total cost (in dollars) of the items?

  (A) $2.2t$

  (B) $3.4p$

  (C) $2.2t + 3.4p$

  (D) $17.6t + 6.8p$

29. Which formulas can be used to find the perimeter P of a rectangle with length ℓ and width w? Select all that apply.

  (A) $P = \ell + w$

  (B) $P = \ell w$

  (C) $P = 2\ell + 2w$

  (D) $P = (2\ell)(2w)$

  (E) $P = 2(\ell + w)$

  (F) $P = 4\ell w$

 I'm in a Learning Mindset!

What properties did I learn to use to justify the steps in solving an equation?

Rewrite Formulas and Solve Literal Equations

(I Can) solve both simple and more complicated literal equations for a given variable.

Spark Your Learning

Cheetahs are built for speed, which they need to catch their prey, such as fast-moving gazelles. Although cheetahs can run faster than their prey, they cannot sustain a high speed for very long. About half of the time, their prey escapes.

The gazelle starts running before the cheetah can reach the gazelle.

The cheetah runs faster than the gazelle.

Complete Part A as a whole class. Then complete Parts B–D in small groups.

A. What is a mathematical question you can ask about this situation? What information would you need to know to answer your question?

B. Your teacher will define the constants d, r_g, and r_c for this situation. What is the variable in this situation, and what should be true about the units of measurement for the constants and the variable?

C. What equation can you write to model the situation?

D. To solve the equation for the variable identified in Part B, what strategy and tool would you use along with all the information you have? What answer do you get?

 Turn and Talk If you successfully solved the equation, you expressed the variable in terms of d, r_g, and r_c. Now examine the expression involving those constants.

- Why does it make sense mathematically for r_c to be greater than r_g?
- For $r_c > r_g$, you can think of r_c as equal to r_g plus the excess speed $r_c - r_g$. How can you use this information to make sense of the expression involving the constants d, r_g, and r_c?

Build Understanding

Solve a Formula for a Variable of Interest

You have seen many formulas from your study of math, such as the formula $A = \ell w$
that gives the area A of a rectangle in terms of the rectangle's length ℓ and width w.
A formula usually shows just one variable on the left side so that you can easily calculate
the value of that variable using known values of the variables on the right side.

1 ▶ The table below shows perimeter formulas for some *regular polygons*. A *polygon* is
a closed figure made up of line segments, called *sides*, that intersect only at their
endpoints and that lie on distinct lines. A *regular* polygon is a polygon whose sides
all have the same length and whose angles all have the same measure.

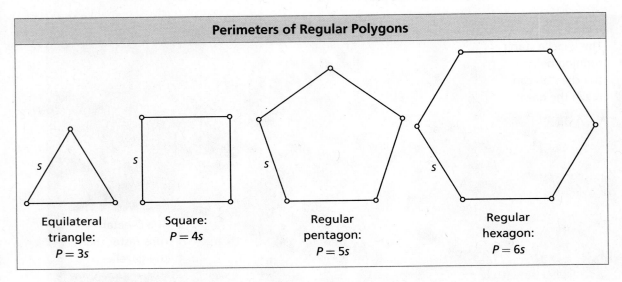

Perimeters of Regular Polygons

Equilateral
triangle:
$P = 3s$

Square:
$P = 4s$

Regular
pentagon:
$P = 5s$

Regular
hexagon:
$P = 6s$

A. Suppose you want to write a formula that allows you to calculate the side length
s of a regular polygon if you know the perimeter P. What would be the formula
for each of the four regular polygons shown above? Explain your reasoning.

B. A polygon with n sides is sometimes called an n-gon. What would be a
formula for finding the perimeter P of a regular n-gon? What would be a
formula for finding the side length s of a regular n-gon?

C. Can you write a formula for finding the number n of sides of a regular n-gon
if you know the perimeter P and side length s? If so, write the formula. If not,
explain why not.

D. The formula for the sum S of the angle measures in a polygon with n sides is
$S = 180(n - 2)$, where the angles are measured in degrees. What is a formula
for the number of sides of a polygon if you know the sum of its angle measures?

Turn and Talk What is the mathematical relationship between the perimeter
formula for a regular n-gon and the perimeter formulas for the four regular
polygons shown above?

Step It Out

Rewrite Formulas

Formulas are equations that express one variable in terms of one or more other variables and constants. Consider the formula for the perimeter of a rectangle: $P = 2\ell + 2w$. If you know the values of the length ℓ and width w, you can easily calculate the value of the perimeter P. But what if you know the values of P and w and want to calculate the value of ℓ?

2 ▶ Trisha has enough wire fencing to build 30 feet of fencing around her rectangular vegetable garden. She wants to use all of the fencing but hasn't decided on the dimensions of the garden. Complete the calculations below.

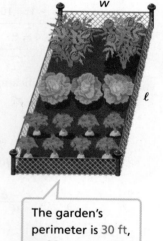

Let the width be 5 feet.	**A.** Let the width be 6 feet.	**B.** Let the width be 7 feet.
$P = 2\ell + 2w$	$P = 2\ell + 2w$	$P = 2\ell + 2w$
$30 = 2\ell + 2(5)$	$30 = 2\ell + 2(6)$	$30 = 2\ell + 2(7)$
$30 = 2\ell + 10$	$30 = 2\ell + \underline{\quad?\quad}$	$30 = 2\ell + \underline{\quad?\quad}$
$20 = 2\ell$	$\underline{\quad?\quad} = 2\ell$	$\underline{\quad?\quad} = 2\ell$
$10 = \ell$	$\underline{\quad?\quad} = \ell$	$\underline{\quad?\quad} = \ell$

The garden's perimeter is 30 ft, so $30 = 2\ell + 2w$.

> **Turn and Talk** What is the area of each of the three rectangles whose lengths were calculated above? Which area is greatest? Do you think there is some other width and length that would maximize the area? Explain.

You can rewrite a formula to express any of the variables in the formula in terms of the others.

3 ▶ The steps for solving $P = 2\ell + 2w$ for ℓ are shown, but some justifications are missing.

$P = 2\ell + 2w$ Given formula

$P - 2w = 2\ell$ $\underline{\quad?\quad}$

A. What property justifies subtracting $2w$ from each side of the equation?

$\dfrac{P - 2w}{2} = \ell$ $\underline{\quad?\quad}$

B. What property justifies dividing each side of the equation by 2?

> **Turn and Talk** Suppose you start with the equivalent perimeter formula $P = 2(\ell + w)$. What result do you get if you solve this formula for ℓ? Is your result equivalent to the rewritten formula above? Explain.

Solve Literal Equations

You can often use a literal equation to express the general form of a class of equations. When a literal equation contains variables from the end of the alphabet, letters from the beginning of the alphabet are commonly used for the constants.

Specific Equations
$2x + 5 = 9$
$-3x + 1 = 10$
$x - 4 = 2$

Literal Equation
$ax + b = c$ where $a \neq 0$

4 ▶ Give the justifications for the solution steps when solving the literal equation $ax + b = c$ for x.

$ax + b = c$ Given equation

$ax = c - b$ ___?___

A. What property justifies subtracting b from each side of the equation?

$x = \dfrac{c - b}{a}$ ___?___

B. What property justifies dividing each side of the equation by a?

The literal equation's solution is used below to solve $2x + 5 = 9$.

$a = 2$

$b = 5$

$c = 9$

$x = \dfrac{c - b}{a}$

$= \dfrac{9 - 5}{2}$ Substitute.

$= 2$ Simplify.

C. Use the literal equation's solution to solve $-3x + 1 = 10$.

$a = $ ___?___

$b = $ ___?___

$c = $ ___?___

$x = \dfrac{c - b}{a}$

$= \dfrac{? - ?}{?}$ Substitute.

$= $ ___?___   Simplify.

D. Use the literal equation's solution to solve $x - 4 = 2$.

$a = $ ___?___

$b = $ ___?___

$c = $ ___?___

$x = \dfrac{c - b}{a}$

$= \dfrac{? - ?}{?}$ Substitute.

$= $ ___?___   Simplify.

Turn and Talk

- For the literal equation $ax + b = c$, why is the restriction "where $a \neq 0$" necessary? Does it matter whether $c - b = 0$? Explain.
- How do you think solving a literal equation would be helpful to a software developer creating an app for giving students practice in solving equations?

Check Understanding

1. Your friend claims to have drawn a regular polygon with sides of length 8 centimeters and a perimeter of 52 centimeters. Use the formula $n = \frac{P}{s}$ that you wrote in Task 1 to explain why your friend must have made a mistake.

2. The formula for the volume of a right circular cone is shown. Rewrite the formula so that it expresses the height h in terms of the volume V and base radius r.

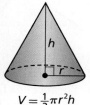

$V = \frac{1}{3}\pi r^2 h$

3. Solve the literal equation $a(bx + c) = d$ for x. State any necessary restrictions on the letters representing constants in the equation. Then use the solution of the literal equation to solve $-3(2x + 1) = 4$.

4. Alma is choosing a new smartphone and cellular service plan. Let p be the phone's price in dollars, m be the cost of the selected plan in dollars per month, and C be Alma's total cost in dollars after time t, measured in months of service. Write an equation that expresses C in terms of p, m, and t. Then solve your equation for t.

On Your Own

5. **(MP) Model with Mathematics** Two cars are traveling in the same lane along a stretch of highway. The second car is catching up to the first car.

The blue car's average speed is r_b.

The blue car has a head start of time t_1.

The yellow car's average speed is r_y, which is greater than r_b.

   A. Write an equation that you could use to find the time t it takes the yellow car to catch up to the blue car. Then solve your equation for t.

   B. **(MP) Use Structure** In Part A, you obtained a fractional expression involving the constants t_1, r_b, and r_y. Interpret the numerator and denominator of the fraction in the context of the situation. Then explain why it makes sense to divide the numerator by the denominator.

6. **STEM** The table shows formulas for the speed of a falling object on three planets. In the formulas, s is the object's speed in feet per second and t is the time in seconds that the object has been falling. The formulas differ because the force of gravity on each planet differs.

   A. Solve each formula in the table for t.

   B. The coefficient of t in each formula is the acceleration due to gravity, measured in feet per second squared. For example, the acceleration due to gravity on Earth is 32 ft/s². Let a be the acceleration due to gravity on *any* planet. Write a formula for s in terms of a and t. Then solve your formula for t.

Speed of a Falling Object	
Planet	Speed formula
Earth	$s = 32t$
Jupiter	$s = 75t$
Mercury	$s = 12t$

In Problems 7–10, solve the geometric formula for the indicated variable.

7. The formula for the area A of a triangle is $A = \frac{1}{2}bh$. Solve for h.

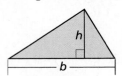

8. The formula for the area A of a trapezoid is $A = \frac{1}{2}(b_1 + b_2)h$. Solve for b_1.

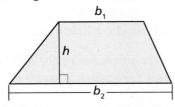

9. The formula for the surface area S of a right circular cylinder is $S = 2\pi r^2 + 2\pi rh$. Solve for h.

10. The formula for the surface area S of a right rectangular prism is $S = 2\ell w + 2\ell h + 2wh$. Solve for h.

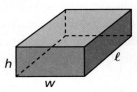

11. STEM The *density* of an object tells you how much mass the object has per unit of volume. An object's average density D is given by $D = \frac{m}{V}$ where m and V are the mass and volume of the object, respectively.

A. Express V in terms of the other variables in the formula.

B. Osmium is the densest metal known. Use the information shown to find the volume of a sample of osmium that has a mass of 200 grams.

C. Suppose the sample of osmium in Part B is shaped like a cube. What is the length of each edge of the cube?

Density of osmium: 22.6 g/cm³

12. Each figure below involves a rectangle and two semicircles. (Dashed lines are not part of a figure.) Write formulas for the perimeter P and area A of each figure, and then rewrite the formulas to express ℓ in terms of the other variables and constants in the formulas.

A.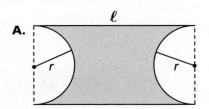

B.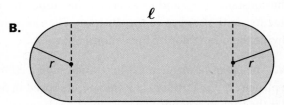

Solve the literal equation for x. State any necessary restrictions on the letters representing constants in the equation.

13. $ax = b$

14. $x + a = b$

15. $a(x + b) = c$

16. $ax = bx + c$

17. $ax + b = cx + d$

18. $a(x + b) = c(x + d)$

19. **Model with Mathematics** A local arts council is organizing a dinner to thank supporters. Guests will have three choices for their dinner: chicken, seafood, or vegetarian. The caterer's prices and the council's estimates for the percent of guests who will choose each dinner option are shown.

Chicken	Seafood	Vegetarian
$15 per guest	$20 per guest	$12 per guest
50% of guests	30% of guests	20% of guests

A. Choose letters to represent the number of guests who attend the dinner and the council's estimated total cost for the food. Then write an equation that gives the estimated total cost in terms of the number of guests.

B. Solve your equation from Part A for the number of guests.

C. If the council has budgeted $2500 for the food, what is the maximum number of guests who can attend the dinner?

20. Financial Literacy Tony is planning to start a small business selling fresh-squeezed lemonade. The variables and constants he must consider are listed in the table.

Fixed costs	He must buy equipment, such as a stand from which to sell the lemonade, a trailer to haul the stand, and a juicer.
Variable costs	Each serving of lemonade that he sells involves the cost of the cup, the lemons, and the added sugar. There may be other ongoing costs as well, such as the cost of hauling his stand.
Income	He must set a selling price for a serving of lemonade so that each sale will eventually generate income.

Initially, Tony's costs will exceed his income, and he will operate at a loss. But once he sells enough servings of lemonade, he will reach a *break-even point* where costs equal income. After that, he will operate at a profit.

A. Choose letters for all of the variables and constants in this situation. Write an equation relating the variables and constants and then solve the equation to obtain a formula for calculating the break-even point.

B. Interpret the formula in the context of the situation.

C. Tony has $3600 in fixed costs and $0.75 per serving of lemonade in variable costs. He sells the lemonade for $3 per serving. What is his break-even point?

21. **Critique Reasoning** Jen solved the formula $x = \frac{x_1 + x_2}{2}$ for x_1 and obtained $x_1 = x - \frac{x_2}{2}$. Is Jen correct? Explain why or why not.

22. A basketball player's free-throw percentage is the ratio (expressed as a percent) of successful free throws to attempted free throws. For example, if a player makes 30 free throws in 40 attempts, the free-throw percentage is $\frac{30}{40} = 75\%$. If the player then makes a string of consecutive free throws, the free-throw percentage rises as shown in the table.

Consecutive free throws made	5	10	15
Free-throw percentage	$\frac{30+5}{40+5} = \frac{35}{45} \approx 78\%$	$\frac{30+10}{40+10} = \frac{40}{50} = 80\%$	$\frac{30+15}{40+15} = \frac{45}{55} \approx 82\%$

Develop a formula for calculating the number of consecutive free throws a player must make to raise the player's current free-throw percentage to a desired target.

23. (MP) **Reason** Three well-known formulas for a circle are $d = 2r$, $C = 2\pi r$, and $A = \pi r^2$ where d, r, C, and A are a circle's diameter, radius, circumference, and area, respectively. Use these formulas to write two new formulas for a circle's area. One formula should give the area in terms of the diameter. The other formula should give the area in terms of the circumference. Explain your reasoning.

Spiral Review • Assessment Readiness

24. Which inequality is represented by the graph?

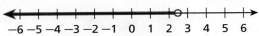

Ⓐ $x < 2.5$ Ⓒ $x \le 2.5$

Ⓑ $x > 2.5$ Ⓓ $x \ge 2.5$

25. Ella wants to buy gasoline and get a car wash at a local gas station. She can spend at most $20. Gasoline costs $2.75 per gallon, and a car wash costs $9. Which inequality represents the possible amounts g of gasoline (in gallons) that Ella can buy?

Ⓐ $9g + 2.75 \ge 20$ Ⓒ $2.75g + 9 \ge 20$

Ⓑ $9g + 2.75 \le 20$ Ⓓ $2.75g + 9 \le 20$

26. A family drove for 2 hours to visit relatives. Part of the time was spent driving on a highway at an average speed of 55 mi/h, and the rest of the time was spent driving in a city at an average speed of 25 mi/h. If t is the time, in hours, spent driving in the city, match the expression on the left with its real-world interpretation on the right.

Expression

A. $25t$

B. $55(2 - t)$

C. $25t + 55(2 - t)$

D. $\dfrac{25t + 55(2 - t)}{2}$

Real-world interpretation

1. The total distance traveled

2. The average speed for the entire trip

3. The distance traveled in the city

4. The distance traveled on the highway

I'm in a Learning Mindset!

What did I learn about solving equations in one variable that I could apply to solving a literal equation for a variable?

Write and Solve Inequalities

(I Can) write inequalities to model real-world problems and use properties of inequality to solve the inequalities.

Spark Your Learning

An airline company must plan the amount of fuel needed for a flight.

Jets burn gallons of fuel every mile they travel.

Jets also burn gallons of fuel to reach cruising altitude.

Complete Part A as a whole class. Then complete Parts B–D in small groups.

  A. What is a mathematical question you can ask about this situation? What information would you need to know to answer your question?

  B. What variable(s) are involved in this situation? What are the units of measurement for the variable(s)?

  C. To answer your question, what strategy and tool would you use along with all the information you have? What answer do you get?

  D. Does your answer make sense in the context of the situation? How do you know?

 Turn and Talk How would your answer be different for each of the following changes in the situation?
  - The airplane's fuel capacity is greater.
  - The airplane uses more fuel per mile flown.
  - The airplane uses less fuel to reach cruising altitudes.

Build Understanding

Investigate Properties of Inequality

An **inequality** is a mathematical statement comparing two expressions using one of the following inequality symbols: $<, >, \leq, \geq,$ or $\neq$.

Meanings of Inequality Symbols	
Symbol	**Words**
$>$	greater than
$<$	less than
$\geq$	greater than or equal to
$\leq$	less than or equal to

When solving inequalities, you will use the following properties of inequality. These properties are similar to the properties of equality, with one important difference. When you multiply or divide both sides of an inequality by a negative number, you must reverse the inequality symbol. In the Symbols column in the table below, a, b, and c are real numbers. Similar properties exist for each of the other inequality symbols.

Properties of Inequality	
Property	**Symbols**
Addition Property of Inequality	If $a < b$, then $a + c < b + c$.
Subtraction Property of Inequality	If $a < b$, then $a - c < b - c$.
Multiplication Property of Inequality	If $a < b$ and $c > 0$, then $ac < bc$. If $a < b$ and $c < 0$, then $ac > bc$.
Division Property of Inequality	If $a < b$ and $c > 0$, then $\frac{a}{c} < \frac{b}{c}$. If $a < b$ and $c < 0$, then $\frac{a}{c} > \frac{b}{c}$.

1 **A.** Using a spreadsheet, create a table like the one shown for the inequality $x < 1$. The formula in cell B2 is an if-then-else statement that checks the value in cell A2. Copy the formula from cell B2 to cells B3 through B8. What do you observe?

B2	X ✓	fx = IF(A2 < 1,"YES", "NO")			
	A	B	C	D	E
1	x	Is x a solution?			
2	-3	YES			
3	-2				
4	-1				
5	0				
6	1				
7	2				
8	3				

If the number in cell A2 is less than 1, then the word YES is shown in cell B2. Otherwise, the word NO is shown in cell B2.

B. Suppose you use the Multiplication Property of Inequality to restate the inequality $x < 1$ as $2x < 2$. Use the new inequality in the if-then-else statements you enter in cells C2 through C8. What do you observe?

C. Suppose you restate $x < 1$ as $-x < -1$. Use the new inequality in the if-then-else statements in cells D2 through D8. What do you observe?

D. How are the spreadsheet and the results here different from the spreadsheet and results from Task 1 in Lesson 2.2?

 Turn and Talk You can use properties of inequality to build the inequality $2x < 2$ from $x < 1$. How can you use properties of inequality to solve the inequality $2x < 2$?

Step It Out

Solve Inequalities

Previously, you solved multistep equations, including equations that contained grouping symbols. Now you will solve multistep inequalities using the properties of inequality. Any number that produces a true statement when substituted for the variable in the inequality is a **solution** of the inequality.

2 ▶ The steps for solving the inequality $3x + 2 \geq \frac{1}{2}(x + 5)$ are shown, but one of the justifications is missing.

$3x + 2 \geq \frac{1}{2}(x + 5)$ Given inequality

$3x + 2 \geq \frac{1}{2}x + \frac{5}{2}$ _____?_____

> **A.** What property justifies writing
> $3x + 2 \geq \frac{1}{2}(x + 5)$ as
> $3x + 2 \geq \frac{1}{2}x + \frac{5}{2}$?

$\frac{5}{2}x + 2 \geq \frac{5}{2}$ Subtraction Property of Inequality

$\frac{5}{2}x \geq \frac{1}{2}$ Subtraction Property of Inequality

$x \geq \frac{1}{5}$ Division Property of Inequality

> **B.** What is true about the solutions of $x \geq \frac{1}{5}$ and the given inequality?

 Turn and Talk You can graph the solutions of an inequality on a number line. How can you show the solutions of the inequality $3x + 2 \geq \frac{1}{2}(x + 5)$ on a graph?

Recall that when you multiply or divide both sides of an inequality by a negative number, you must reverse the direction of the inequality symbol.

3 ▶ The steps for solving $-4x + \frac{3}{4}(4x - 12) \geq 3$ and the justifications are shown below, but both have been scrambled.

A. Write the solution steps in the correct order.

$x \leq -12$
$-x - 9 \geq 3$
$-4x + \frac{3}{4}(4x - 12) \geq 3$
$-x \geq 12$
$-4x + 3x - 9 \geq 3$

B. Write the justifications in the correct order.

Distributive Property
Simplify.
Division Property of Inequality
Addition Property of Inequality
Given inequality

 Turn and Talk Is it possible to eliminate the fraction as a first step in solving the inequality $-4x + \frac{3}{4}(4x - 12) \geq 3$? Show how or explain why not.

Use Inequalities to Solve a Real-World Problem

Real-world situations are sometimes modeled using inequalities. Look for relationships such as "no more than" or "at least" to determine which inequality symbol to use in your model.

 Two newspapers charge different rates for an ad in the paper. For how many weeks must an ad be placed in order for the total cost of the ad in the *Daily Info* to be less expensive than the total cost of placing an ad in *Citywide Times*?

Daily Info:
Set up fee $650
$80 per week

Citywide Times:
$145 per week

Write a verbal model with units for this situation.

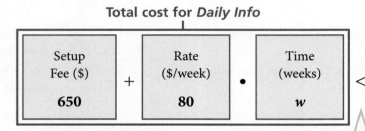

Total cost for *Daily Info*

Setup Fee ($)		Rate ($/week)		Time (weeks)
650	+	80	•	w

Total cost for *Citywide Times*

Rate ($/week)		Time (weeks)
145	•	w

$<$

Write an inequality for this situation.

$650 + 80w < 145w$

> **A.** Explain why this is the correct symbol to use in the verbal model.

Solve the inequality.

$650 + 80w < 145w$	Given inequality
$650 < 65w$	Subtraction Property of Inequality
$10 < w$	Division Property of Inequality
$w > 10$	Write an equivalent inequality.

Graph the solution.

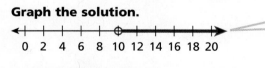

0 2 4 6 8 10 12 14 16 18 20

> **B.** Why is there an open circle at 10? Why does the arrow point to the right?

Answer the question.

An ad must be placed for more than 10 weeks for the total cost of the ad at the *Daily Info* to be less expensive than the cost at *Citywide Times*.

 Turn and Talk Suppose the problem had asked for how many weeks it would take in order for the total cost of the ad in the *Daily Info* to be no greater than the total cost of the ad in *Citywide Times*. How would that change the inequality? How would that change the answer?

Check Understanding

1. Mark claims that the Multiplication Property of Inequality is exactly like the Multiplication Property of Equality, except that it involves an inequality symbol instead of an equals sign. Explain why Mark is not correct.

Solve each inequality. Justify your solution steps and graph the solution.

2. $4x - 5 \geq \frac{1}{4}(x + 40)$

3. $2(x + 3) < \frac{1}{2}(6x + 14)$

4. Micah is shopping for work shirts. The short-sleeve shirts cost $18 each and the long-sleeve shirts cost $24 each. He wants to buy 2 more short-sleeve shirts than long-sleeve shirts, and he is willing to spend no more than $120 total. How many long-sleeve shirts can he buy?

5. Kiaya has to have at least $100 in her checking account to avoid a fee from the bank. She has $376 in her account now. Each week, she makes a $25 withdrawal. For how many weeks can she make this withdrawal and avoid a fee?

On Your Own

6. **(MP) Critique Reasoning** Paige solved the inequality $-\frac{1}{2}x > -6$ by using the Division Property of Inequality to get $x > 12$. Did Paige solve the inequality correctly? Explain why or why not.

7. Orange Taxi charges a pickup fee of $4 plus $0.75 per mile. Blue Taxi charges $1.25 per mile.

   A. Complete a verbal model with units for Orange Taxi and one for Blue Taxi. Each model should give the cost for a ride of m miles.

   B. Write and solve an inequality to model when using Blue Taxi is a better deal.

   C. When is using Blue Taxi a better deal? Explain your answer.

8. Kevin is choosing which of two new video games to download and play while his friends are over. Both games offer a 60-minute free trial.

   Game A:
   5 min setup
   7 min/level

   Game B:
   10 min setup
   6 min/level

   A. Let l = the number of levels completed. Write expressions for the time spent on each game.

   B. Write and solve inequalities to model how many levels they can complete during the 60-minute free trial.

   C. Which video game would allow them to play more levels for free?

   D. Suppose the free trial for both games shortens to 15 minutes. Which video game allows them to play more levels for free now? Explain your answer.

9. (MP) **Use Repeated Reasoning**
The manager at Apex Gym wants to know
when the new pricing model (higher per-
class fee but lower membership fee) will
be better than the old pricing model used
last year. He uses a table to calculate the
members' costs for different numbers of
classes.

Pricing Last Year

$15 per class
and
$140 membership
fee

New Pricing

$30 per class
and
$50 membership
fee

A. Copy and complete the table.

Number of classes	Cost under old model ($)	Cost under new model ($)
2	$2(15) + 140 = 170$	$2(30) + 50 = 110$
4	?	?
5	?	?
6	?	?
7	?	?

B. Let c be the number of classes. What expression models the cost under the old
pricing? What expression represents the cost under the new pricing?

C. For gym members, the new pricing is better than the old pricing when they
pay less than they did before. The inequality that models this situation is
$30c + 50 < 15c + 140$. Use the results of the table to solve the inequality.
Explain your answer.

D. Explain why the manager might use a different inequality for Part C.

10. (MP) **Reason** The solutions of an inequality are often written as another inequality.
For example, the solutions of $-\frac{3}{4}x + 5 > 11$ can be written as $x < -8$. What is
true about both inequalities? Explain your answer.

Solve each inequality. Justify your solution steps and graph the solutions.

11. $165 \geq -7(4n - 4) - 3$

12. $276 < 7n + 8(6n + 7)$

13. $2r - \frac{11}{3}r > -\frac{5}{6}$

14. $-1.3 + 4.9(1 - 3.6x) \leq 81.216$

15. $19 > 2(1 + 3x) - (1 - 3x)$

16. $2(1 - 3r) + 3(r + 2) > 5$

17. $n + 3 - 2n \geq 5 + n - 1 + 3$

18. $3 - 4x \geq -9 - 2x$

19. $5 + 2(n - 3) \leq 3(n + 2)$

20. $-3(1 - 5p) \leq 3(1 + 4p)$

21. $-2.3(3.5x + 3) \leq 28.1 - 1.8x$

22. $\frac{1}{2}(4x - 5) \leq x - \frac{9}{2}$

23. A band wants to rent a rehearsal space. They will be charged a cleaning fee and an hourly rate for use of the room.

Cleaning fee: $50
Rate: $24 per hour

Room A

Cleaning fee: $80
Rate: $18 per hour

Room B

The band has $250 to spend. Let t be the time (in hours) the band rents the room.

A. Write and solve an inequality to represent the time (in hours) the band could rent Room A.

B. Write and solve an inequality to represent the time (in hours) the band could rent Room B.

C. Which room should the band rent? Explain your answer.

24. Financial Literacy Kelly receives a loan from her parents to buy a bike. She pays $100 of the initial cost and her parents pay the rest. She makes weekly payments of $20.

Kevin receives a loan from his parents to buy a laptop. He pays $230 of the initial cost and his parents pay the rest. He makes weekly payments of $50.

Use the information in the photos to determine how many weeks it takes for Kevin to owe less than Kelly.

Cost: $400

Cost: $800

25. (MP) **Use Structure** Use the properties of inequality to solve each inequality for x. Assume $a < b < c < d$, and $a > 0$.

A. $-\dfrac{a}{b}x - c < d$

B. $a(x - c) \geq b$

C. $ax - b > cx + d$

D. $a(x + c) \leq d - bx$

26. Kaya works a total of 15 hours each week. She babysits for $10 per hour and tutors for $12 per hour. She wants to earn at least $160.

    A. Write an inequality to model this situation. Solve the inequality.

    B. What does the solution mean?

    C. (MP) **Reason** Suppose Kaya wants to earn more than $160 per week. How does the solution change?

27. **Open Ended** Write an inequality that can be solved using the Subtraction Property of Inequality and the Multiplication Property of Inequality. Show another way to solve the same inequality using the Addition Property of Inequality and the Division Property of Inequality. Explain your reasoning.

28. (MP) **Reason** Callie's company has a fixed monthly expense of $3200. In addition, each of the company's pillows costs $2.40 to make.

    A. If each pillow sells for $18, how many pillows must the company sell each month to have a profit? (Profit is the amount of money left after paying all of the expenses.) Explain your reasoning.

    B. The company tracks how much profit it makes each quarter, which is a period of 3 months. For the first 2 months of a quarter, the company sold 375 pillows. How many pillows must the company sell during the third month to have a profit for the quarter?

29. (**Open Middle**™) Using the digits 1–9 at most one time each, replace the boxes to write an inequality whose solution is $x \geq -\frac{3}{4}$.

$$\square x + \square \leq \square x + \square$$

Spiral Review • Assessment Readiness

30. Which expressions are equivalent to $4(2x + 1) - 3(x - 2)$? Select all that apply.

    (A) $8x + 4 - 3x + 6$ (D) $11x + 10$

    (B) $8x + 4 - 3x - 6$ (E) $5x + 10$

    (C) $4 + 5x + 6$ (F) $5x - 2$

31. Solve $4(2x + 3) = 6x - 12$.

    (A) $x = -24$ (C) $x = 0$

    (B) $x = -12$ (D) $x = 12$

32. Solve $w = \frac{x - y}{2}$ for y.

    (A) $y = \frac{x}{2w}$ (C) $y = 2w - x$

    (B) $y = \frac{2w}{x}$ (D) $y = x - 2w$

33. A ticket to an evening performance of a play costs $3 more than a ticket to an afternoon performance. You can buy 8 evening tickets for the same price as 10 afternoon tickets. What is the cost of an afternoon ticket?

    (A) $9   (C) $15

    (B) $12   (D) $24

 I'm in a Learning Mindset!

What steps do I need to follow when I solve inequalities?

Write and Solve Compound Inequalities

(I Can) write, solve, and graph compound inequalities, and use compound inequalities to model real-world problems.

Spark Your Learning

David wants to provide the proper environment for his pet iguana.

An iguana regulates its body temperature by moving back and forth between cooler and warmer areas.

Complete Part A as a whole class. Then complete Parts B–D in small groups.

A. What is a mathematical question you can ask about this situation? What information would you need to know to answer your question?

B. Your teacher will give you some information about the iguana's preferred environment. What is the unit of measurement for that information?

C. To answer your question, what strategy and tool would you use along with all the information you have? What answer do you get?

D. Does your answer make sense in the context of the situation? How do you know?

Turn and Talk Denise says that 100 °F is an acceptable temperature in the enclosure because it is greater than the minimum temperature. Is she correct? Explain why or why not.

Build Understanding

Compound Statements

A compound statement is made of two statements connected by an *and* or an *or*.

> *Mary is a ninth grader and she plays softball.*
>
> *Francis walked to school today or he rode the bus to school today.*

Any given statement might be True or False. This is called its *truth value*. A compound statement will be True or False depending on the truth values of its two statements together with the connecting conjunction.

1 For Parts A–D, consider how the truth values for each pair of given statements help determine whether a given compound statement is true or false.

A.

Mary is a ninth grader.	Mary plays softball.

Assume that the two given statements are both true. Is the compound statement, *Mary is a ninth grader and she plays softball,* true? Explain why or why not.

Is the compound statement, *Mary is a ninth grader or she plays softball,* true? Explain why or why not.

B.

Francis walked to school today.	Francis rode the bus to school today.

Assume that the two given statements are not both true. Is the compound statement, *Francis walked to school today and he rode the bus to school today,* true? Explain why or why not.

Assume that the two given statements are not both false. Is the compound statement, *Francis walked to school today or he rode the bus to school today,* true? Explain why or why not.

C.

Animal X is a cat.	Animal X is a bird.

Can one of the given statements be true? Can both statements be true? Is there an animal such that *Animal X is a cat and a bird*? So, can that compound statement ever be true? Explain your reasoning.

Is there an animal such that *Animal X is a cat or it is a bird*? So, can that compound statement ever be true? Explain your reasoning.

D.

5.2 is an integer.	2.5 is a whole number.

Is either of the statements true? Is the compound statement, *5.2 is an integer and 2.5 is a whole number,* ever true? Explain your reasoning.

Is the compound statement, *5.2 is an integer or 2.5 is a whole number,* ever true? Explain your reasoning.

 Turn and Talk Use your own words to describe how you know when a compound statement with AND is true and when it is false. Then describe how you know when a compound statement with OR is true and when it is false. Use your own examples to support your descriptions.

Step It Out

Solve Compound Inequalities Involving AND

Previously, you solved inequalities involving one inequality symbol. Now you will solve inequalities with two symbols.

The graph of a compound inequality involving AND consists of points that appear on *both* graphs of the simple inequalities.

The compound inequality $-2 \leq x \leq 3$ means that $x \geq -2$ AND $x \leq 3$. The solutions are all numbers between -2 and 3. Here, the endpoints -2 and 3 are included.

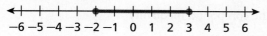

The compound inequality $-1 < x < 2$ means $x > -1$ AND $x < 2$. The solutions are all numbers between -1 and 2. Here, the endpoints -1 and 2 are not included.

2 ▸ Solve $-6 \leq 4x - 2 < 10$. Then graph the solutions.

$-6 \leq 4x - 2 < 10$			Given inequality
$-6 \leq 4x - 2$	AND	$4x - 2 < 10$	Separate into two inequalities.
$-4 \leq 4x$	AND	$4x < 12$	Addition Property of Inequality
$-1 \leq x$	AND	$x < 3$	Division Property of Inequality

A. Explain how to separate the original inequality into two inequalities.

Now, graph the solutions of the simple and compound inequalities.

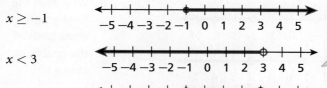

$x \geq -1$

$x < 3$

$-1 \leq x < 3$

B. Why does the final graph show only the overlapping part of the graphs above it?

3 ▸ Solve $x - 2 > -1$ AND $4x \leq -8$. Then graph the solutions.

$x - 2 > -1$	AND	$4x \leq -8$
$x > 1$	AND	$x \leq -2$

There are no solutions.

A. Are there any values of x that are both greater than 1 AND less than or equal to -2? What does this mean?

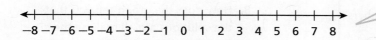

B. How would the graph change if you replaced AND with OR in the compound inequality?

 Turn and Talk Explain why two inequalities connected with AND can be written as a compound inequality with the variable expression in between two inequality symbols.

Solve Compound Inequalities Involving OR

The graph of a compound inequality involving OR consists of points that appear on *either* graph of the simple inequalities.

Consider the graph of the compound inequality
$x < -2.5$ OR $x \geq 0$. In order for a compound
inequality involving OR to be true,
at least one of the inequalities must be true.

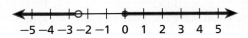

Using the graph above, you can see that -4 is a solution and 3 is a solution, but that -1 is not a solution. You can check using the inequalities:

$-4 < -2.5$, so it makes the compound inequality true.

$3 \geq 0$, so it makes the compound inequality true.

Neither $-1 < -2.5$ nor $-1 \geq 0$, so it does not make the compound inequality true and that coordinate is not on the graph.

4 ▶ **Solve $3x - 8 \leq -14$ OR $5x + 7 > 17$. Then graph the solutions.**

$3x - 8 \leq -14$	OR	$5x + 7 > 17$
$3x \leq -6$	OR	$5x > 10$
$x \leq -2$	OR	$x > 2$

> **A.** What properties did you use to obtain the inequality $x > 2$ from the original inequality $5x + 7 > 17$?

Now, graph the solutions of the simple and compound inequalities.

$x \leq -2$

$x > 2$

$x \leq -2$ OR $x > 2$

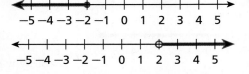

> **B.** Why does the final graph show both of the graphs above it?

5 ▶ **Solve $3x + 6 > 3$ OR $-2x + 5 > 5$. Then graph the solutions.**

$3x + 6 > 3$	OR	$-2x + 5 > 5$
$3x > -3$	OR	$-2x > 0$
$x > -1$	OR	$x < 0$

> **A.** How do you know that the entire number line should be shaded?

The solutions are all real numbers.

> **B.** How does the graph tell you that the solutions are all real numbers?

Turn and Talk Explain why two inequalities connected with OR cannot be written as a single compound inequality with the variable expression in between two inequality symbols.

64

Use a Compound Inequality to Solve a Real-World Problem

6 ▸ A manufacturer makes single-serving packages of oatmeal to sell for breakfast use. For quality control, there is an acceptable range of weight for each package. The acceptable weight range for each package should be within 0.025 ounce of the ideal weight. Write and graph a compound inequality to represent the situation. What is the weight range the manufacturer will accept for a package?

The ideal weight of an oatmeal package is 1.58 ounces.

Use a verbal model.

Let w represent the actual weight of an oatmeal package. The difference between the actual and ideal weights is a value within the *tolerance* bounds of -0.025 to 0.025 ounces.

Difference in weights

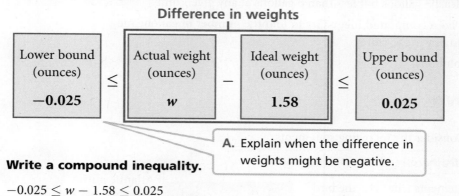

Lower bound (ounces)		Actual weight (ounces)	Ideal weight (ounces)		Upper bound (ounces)
-0.025	$\leq$	w	1.58	$\leq$	0.025

A. Explain when the difference in weights might be negative.

Write a compound inequality.

$-0.025 \leq w - 1.58 \leq 0.025$

Write the compound inequality as two inequalities and solve the inequalities.

$-0.025 \leq w - 1.58 \leq 0.025$ Given inequality

$-0.025 \leq w - 1.58$ AND $w - 1.58 \leq 0.025$ Separate into two inequalities.

$1.555 \leq w$ AND $w \leq 1.605$ Addition Property of Inequality

$1.555 \leq w \leq 1.605$ Rewrite as a compound inequality.

Graph the compound inequality.

B. Would a 1.63-ounce package be rejected? Explain.

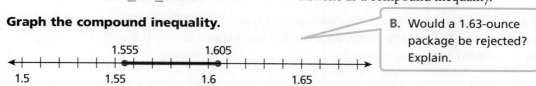

Answer the question.

The manufacturer will sell oatmeal packages with weights between 1.555 ounces and 1.605 ounces, inclusive. Packages with weights outside those bounds will be rejected.

Turn and Talk Is it possible to have a real-world scenario involving a range of measurements within which some measure must lie that can be described with a compound inequality involving OR?

Check Understanding

1. Consider the following statements.

| Your dog is a mammal. | Your dog is a lion. |

    A. Is the compound statement, *Your dog is a mammal and it is a lion,* true? Explain why or why not.

    B. Is the compound statement, *Your dog is a mammal or it is a lion,* true? Explain why or why not.

Solve each inequality. Graph the solutions.

2. $-8 < 6a + 10 < 58$

3. $p - 8 > -6$ OR $1 + 4p \leq -39$

4. The Smith family has 2 gallons of cold water in the cooler at the moment. They want to have at least 3 gallons but less than 6 gallons at any given time.

    A. Write and solve a compound inequality to find the number of gallons the family should buy at the store.

    B. Graph the solutions.

On Your Own

5. (MP) **Reason** Consider the following statements.

| All birds have feathers. | All birds swim. |

    A. Are both statements true? Use the bird shown in the photo and other examples to explain your reasoning.

    B. Is the compound statement, *All birds have feathers and all birds swim,* true? Explain your reasoning.

    C. Is the compound statement, *All birds have feathers or all birds swim,* true? Explain your reasoning.

Atlantic puffin

For the groups of numbers or words in Problems 6–11, give the AND and OR compound statements. For each group, what are the numbers or names, if any, that make each compound statement true?

6. even numbers less than 15
multiples of 3 that are less than 16

7. months whose names have 7 letters
months whose names begin with a "J"

8. the set of all real numbers
the irrational numbers $\sqrt{5}, \pi, 2\sqrt{7}$

9. prime numbers less than 30
perfect cubes less than 30

10. days of the week whose names have fewer than 8 letters
days of the week whose names have no "s" in them

11. states that border on bodies of salt water
states whose names begin with an "M"

12. (MP) **Critique Reasoning** Susan graphed the solutions of the compound inequality $x < -1$ OR $x > 2$.

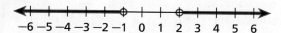

Susan says that there are no solutions. Is she correct? Explain why or why not.

Solve each inequality. Graph the solutions.

13. $-6 + 2a \geq 22$ OR $10 + 3a \leq 22$

14. $4n - 5 \geq 23$ OR $n - 2 \leq 1$

15. $7x - 6 \geq 43$ OR $10x + 4 < -76$

16. $-18 < 9m \leq -54$

17. $p + 10 > 7$ OR $-9p > -45$

18. $5m - 10 \leq -45$ AND $-1 - m \geq -4$

19. $52 < 4 + 6x \leq 64$

20. $-5x - 4 > 36$ OR $3 - 7x \leq 24$

21. $3 + 2n \leq -3$ AND $1 - 3n < 19$

22. $5 - 10x \leq 45$ OR $x + 4 < -1$

Does each graph show an AND situation or an OR situation? Write the compound inequality represented by each graph.

23.
```
<-+--+--O--+--+--+--+--+--+--O--+--+--+->
 -8 -7 -6 -5 -4 -3 -2 -1  0  1  2  3  4  5  6
```

24.
```
<-+--+--+--+--+--+--+--+--+--+--●--+--+--+->
 -8 -7 -6 -5 -4 -3 -2 -1  0  1  2  3  4  5  6
```

25.
```
<-+--+--+--+--+--O--+--+--●--+--+--+--+--+->
 -3 -2 -1  0  1  2  3  4  5  6  7  8  9  10 11
```

26.
```
<-+--+--+--+--+--●--+--+--+--+--O--+--+--+->
 -1  0  1  2  3  4  5  6  7  8  9  10 11 12 13
```

27. STEM Robert wants to put a koi pond in his back yard. What are the possible temperatures of the koi pond in degrees Fahrenheit?

Use the formula $T_C = \frac{5}{9}(T_F - 32)$, where T_C is the temperature in degrees Celsius and T_F is the temperature in degrees Fahrenheit. Write and interpret the solutions. Round to the nearest degree Fahrenheit. Then graph the solutions.

The temperature should be between 15 °C and 25 °C, including the endpoints.

28. (MP) **Use Structure** George solves the compound inequality $9 - 4x \leq 29$ AND $5x + 6 \geq 26$ and records the solutions to be $x \geq 4$. Explain why the result is a simple inequality. Use a graph to justify your answer.

29. To get an A on a test, Mario must get between 90 and 100 points, including the endpoints. If each question is worth 2.5 points, how many questions must he answer correctly to make an A? Graph the solutions.

30. (MP) **Reason** Can more than one inequality be represented by the same graph? Explain your answer.

31. Health and Fitness In a weightlifting class, athletes may perform squats with barbells to strengthen their legs and improve stability. Let p be the number of pounds an athlete of a certain weight is expected to squat in the weight room. If an athlete weighs 120 pounds, explain the compound inequality below in terms of this situation. Then solve and interpret the solutions.

$$0.70 \leq \frac{p}{120} \leq 0.80$$

32. A grocery delivery service charges $8 per mile traveled and a flat fee of $10 for each delivery. The minimum charge is $18, and the maximum charge is $100.

   A. Write an inequality to represent the cost of delivery. What does your variable represent?

   B. Solve your inequality. What does the solution mean in this context?

33. (Open Middle™) Using the digits 1 to 9 at most one time each, make a compound inequality whose least and greatest solutions are as far apart as possible.

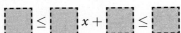

Spiral Review • Assessment Readiness

34. A school purchases a lab book and a $30 textbook for each student for $1134. There are 27 students in the class. Let b be the cost of the lab book. Which equation could you use to find the cost of the lab book?

   (A) $b(30 + 27) = 1134$

   (B) $27(30 + b) = 1134$

   (C) $30(27 + b) = 1134$

   (D) $27b + 30b + b = 1134$

35. Solve $4(x + 1) - 3(x - 6) > 7x - 10$.

   (A) $x > \frac{16}{3}$ (C) $x < \frac{16}{3}$

   (B) $x > -\frac{16}{3}$ (D) $x < -\frac{16}{3}$

36. The formula for the area A of a trapezoid with bases b_1 and b_2 and height h is $A = h \cdot \frac{b_1 + b_2}{2}$. Which shows the formula solved for b_2?

   (A) $b_2 = \frac{2A}{h} - b_1$ (C) $b_2 = \frac{2h}{A} - b_1$

   (B) $b_2 = \frac{2A}{h} + b_1$ (D) $b_2 = b_1 - \frac{2A}{h}$

37. Which expressions are equivalent to $\frac{1}{2}(10x - 4) - (x + 1)$? Select all that apply.

   (A) $5x - 1 - x$ (D) $5x - 2 - x - 1$

   (B) $6x - 1 + x$ (E) $6x - 3 - x$

   (C) 2 (F) $4x - 3$

I'm in a Learning Mindset!

What skills do I use when I write compound inequalities?

Review

Expressions

Youth Center Classes	
Swim classes	$8 each
Dance classes	$12 each

Ben chooses 10 classes.

Let $x =$ his number of swim classes.

So, $10 - x =$ his number of dance classes.

Expression for Ben's total cost:

$$8x + 12(10 - x)$$

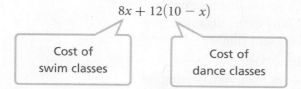

Cost of swim classes

Cost of dance classes

Equations

Ben spends $108 on his classes at the youth center. To find how many swim classes and how many dance classes he takes, solve an equation.

$$8x + 12(10 - x) = 108$$
$$8x + 120 - 12x = 108$$
$$-4x + 120 = 108$$
$$-4x = -12$$
$$x = 3$$

Ben takes 3 swim classes.

He takes $10 - 3 = 7$ dance classes.

Literal Equations

The equation used to find how many swim classes and dance classes Ben takes,

$$8x + 12(10 - x) = 108,$$

is a specific instance of this literal equation:

$$ax + b(c - x) = d.$$

You can solve the literal equation for x.

$$ax + b(c - x) = d$$
$$ax + bc - bx = d$$
$$ax - bx = d - bc$$
$$(a - b)x = d - bc$$
$$x = \frac{d - bc}{a - b}$$

To avoid division by 0, $a \neq b$.

You can use the literal equation's solution to confirm the solution of $8x + 12(10 - x) = 108$.

$a = 8$, $b = 12$, $c = 10$, and $d = 108$.

$$x = \frac{d - bc}{a - b} = \frac{108 - 12(10)}{8 - 12} = \frac{-12}{-4} = 3$$

Inequalities

Ben's friend Jude also wants to take 10 classes at the youth center but can spend at most $88. To find how many swim classes Jude can take, solve an inequality.

$$8x + 12(10 - x) \leq 88$$
$$8x + 120 - 12x \leq 88$$
$$-4x + 120 \leq 88$$
$$-4x \leq -32$$
$$x \geq 8$$

When multiplying or dividing both sides of an inequality by a negative number, reverse the inequality symbol.

Jude can take at least 8 swim classes.

You can graph the solutions of the inequality on a number line. For this situation, the solutions that make sense are 8, 9, and 10.

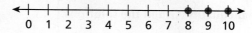

Vocabulary

Choose the correct term from the box to complete each sentence.

1. $3x + 4x - 2(x - 1)$ is a(n) __?__, and $3x$ and $4x$ are __?__.

2. Two equations are __?__ if they have the same solution(s).

3. A(n) __?__ is an equation in which constants have been replaced by letters.

4. A(n) __?__ is made up of two inequalities joined by *and* or *or*.

Concepts and Skills

Simplify the expression.

5. $4(2 - x) - 3(6x - 5)$

6. $\frac{1}{3}(7x + 9) + \frac{2}{3}(4x)$

7. Rosa works out 1 hour each day at the gym. She spends part of that time on the treadmill and the rest of the time on the stair climber. Rosa burns 10 calories per minute on the treadmill and 7 calories per minute on the stair climber.

A. Let t be Rosa's time spent on the treadmill in minutes. Write, but do not simplify, an expression for the total number of calories Rosa burns during her workout. Interpret each part of the expression in the context of the situation.

B. Simplify your expression from Part A.

Solve the equation. Justify your solution steps, and check the solution.

8. $3(2x - 1) + 4 = -17$

9. $5.2(x + 4) = -2.3(x - 1) + 21.5$

10. (MP) **Use Tools** Declan is moving into a college dormitory and needs to rent a moving truck. For the type of truck he wants, Company A charges a $30 rental fee plus $0.95 per mile driven, while Company B charges a $45 rental fee plus $0.65 per mile driven. For how many miles is the cost of renting the truck the same at both companies? State what strategy and tool you will use to answer the question, explain your choice, and then find the answer.

11. The surface area S of a right circular cone is given by $S = \pi r^2 + \pi r \ell$ where r is the radius of the base and ℓ is the slant height. Solve this formula for ℓ.

Solve the literal equation for x. State any necessary restrictions on the letters representing constants in the equation.

12. $ax + b = 0$

13. $a(x + b) + cx = d$

14. A bank offers two credit cards. Card A gives 1.5% cash back on every purchase. Card B gives 2% cash back on every purchase but has a $95 annual fee. When is Card B a better deal than Card A? (Assume no interest is paid on purchases.)

Solve the inequality. Graph the solutions.

15. $7x - 4 \geq 5x + 2$

16. $-3.5(x + 4) < 2(1 - x) - 13$

17. $-3x + 1 > -2$ or $2x - 3 > 1$

18. $-12 \leq 5x + 3 \leq 23$

Linear Functions and Equations

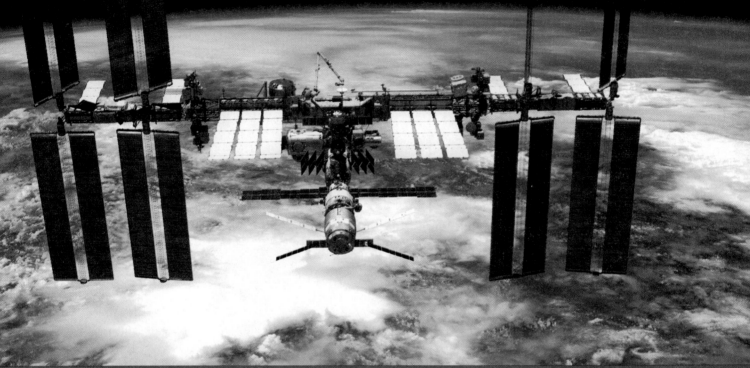

Aerospace Engineer

STEM
POWERING INGENUITY

©Stocktrek Images/Getty Images

Aerospace engineers are responsible for designing spacecraft and equipment that must endure long missions to distant places while operating extraordinarily sensitive detectors. They are deeply involved throughout each stage of the project, from development to implementation and ongoing modification. The International Space Station (ISS), in orbit around Earth, was designed and developed by a team of aerospace engineers.

STEM Task

Solar activity can alter the atmospheric density, increasing drag on the ISS and lowering its altitude. Higher altitudes reduce the need to counteract the effect of drag. Determine how the orbit time would change if the altitude increased to 600 km and the speed stayed at 27,600 km/h.

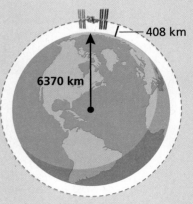

408 km

6370 km

Learning Mindset
Perseverance Sustains Focus

How do you stay focused on what you're learning? Sometimes it is difficult to stay focused on a task, especially if you feel you aren't learning as much or as quickly as you think you should be. In these situations, staying focused can help you continue to progress and reach your learning goals. Keep these tips in mind to help you sustain focus on a task.

- Remember that learning this concept will benefit you now and in the future. Think of a few of these benefits.

- Look ahead to your learning goal. Focus on how your current task will help you reach your goal.

- Sometimes, a task can feel so big that you do not feel you are making any measurable progress. Identify specific parts of the task to serve as checkpoints. Keep track of when you complete checkpoints and celebrate each success.

- Your mindset affects your ability to focus and engage with a task. Try to reset your mindset and approach the task from a fresh perspective.

Reflection

Q When were you unable to remain focused on a task? When were you able to successfully sustain your focus? How did your focus affect the outcome? How can you use your experiences to improve your future?

Q If you are an aerospace engineer working on an ISS project that will last many years, how can you keep your focus on the project?

Linear Equations in Two Variables

Module Performance Task: *Spies and Analysts*™

Sandwich
Cookie
Tower

How many cream-filled sandwich cookies would you need to reach your own height if you used only one bottom cookie, the stuffing, and one top cookie?

©Houghton Mifflin Harcourt

Are You Ready?

Complete these problems to review prior concepts and skills you will need for this module.

Find Unit Rates

1. Lisa takes 27 minutes to run 3 miles.

    A. Write Lisa's unit rate in minutes per mile.

    B. Write Lisa's unit rate in miles per minute.

    C. At this rate, how many miles will Lisa have run after 45 minutes?

    D. At this rate, how long would it take Lisa to run 7 miles?

2. A 5-pound bag of carrots costs $2.69, and a 2-pound bag costs $1.89.

    A. Which bag provides a greater weight per dollar spent?

    B. How much does 10 pounds of carrots cost when purchasing 5-pound bags?

    C. How much does 10 pounds of carrots cost when purchasing 2-pound bags?

    D. What is the difference in price between each option when purchasing 10 pounds of carrots?

Solve Two-Step Equations

Solve each equation.

3. $5x + 2 = 9$

4. $\frac{2}{3}x - 3 = -7$

5. $2(x + 1) = 10$

6. $\frac{4}{5}(15x - 1) = -8$

Graph $y = mx$

Graph each equation.

7. $y = 3x$

8. $y = \frac{4}{5}x$

9. $y = -2x$

10. $y = -1.5x$

Connecting Past and Present Learning

Previously, you learned:

• to write and interpret algebraic expressions,

• to use equations and inequalities to model real-world problems, and

• to find and use unit rates to solve real-world problems.

In this Module, you will learn:

• to write linear equations in standard form,

• to calculate, use, and interpret slope, and

• to create linear equations to model real-world problems.

Linear Equations in Standard Form

(I Can) connect solutions of equations to points on their graphs.

Spark Your Learning

Dina isn't tall enough to go on carnival rides with a height requirement, but Donald is.

Donald and Dina have 24 tickets, and they want to use all of them.

Complete Part A as a whole class. Then complete Parts B–D in small groups.

   A. What is a mathematical question you can ask about this situation? What information would you need to know to answer your question?

   B. What variable(s) are needed in this situation? What must be true of the values for these variables in this question?

   C. To answer your question, what strategy and tool would you use along with all the information you have? What answer do you get?

   D. Does your answer make sense in the context of the situation? How do you know?

Turn and Talk Predict how your answer would change for each of the following changes in the situation:

- All rides require 5 tickets.
- Dina uses all of the tickets.
- They have 28 tickets.

©Corbis

Build Understanding

Graph Linear Equations

A **linear equation in two variables** is an equation that can be written in the form $Ax + By = C$, where A, B, and C are real numbers and A and B are not both zero. There are many equivalent ways to express the linear relationship between two variables x and y, but the form $Ax + By = C$ is called the **standard form of a linear equation**.

 The table shows examples and non-examples of linear equations in two variables.

A. Rewrite each equation from the left column in standard form.

B. Examine the equations in the right column. Explain why each one cannot be written in standard form.

Linear equations	NOT linear equations
$2x - 5y = 8$	$2x - y^3 = 4$
$y = -3x - 2$	$x^2 + y^2 = 9$
$4y = -\frac{1}{2}x + 5$	$\frac{x^2}{9} - \frac{y^2}{16} = 1$
$2.5x = \pi - y$	$x^3 + 2y^2 = 4$

 Turn and Talk Would you classify $-2x + y = 0$ as a linear equation? Why or why not? How would you classify $y = 3x^2 - 1$? Explain.

The graph of a linear equation is the set of all pairs of x- and y-values that satisfy the equation.

2 Examine the table of values for $2x + y = 4$ and its corresponding graph.

x	$2x + y = 4$	y	Point on graph
-1	$2(-1) + y = 4$	6	$(-1, 6)$
0	$2(0) + y = 4$	4	$(0, 4)$
$\frac{1}{2}$	$2\left(\frac{1}{2}\right) + y = 4$	3	$\left(\frac{1}{2}, 3\right)$
1	$2(1) + y = 4$	2	$(1, 2)$
2	$2(2) + y = 4$	0	$(2, 0)$
$\sqrt{13}$	$2\left(\sqrt{13}\right) + y = 4$	$4 - 2\sqrt{13}$	$\left(\sqrt{13}, 4 - 2\sqrt{13}\right)$

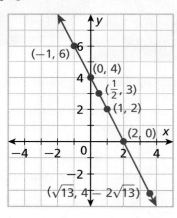

A. How are the first and third columns related to the corresponding equation in the second column?

B. How are the first and third columns related to the corresponding point on the graph in the fourth column?

C. Would the points $(5, -6)$ and $(-4, 10)$ be points on the graph of the linear equation? Explain.

 Turn and Talk Using words such as *coordinates*, *coordinate plane*, *x-coordinate*, and *y-coordinate*, describe how a linear equation and its graph are related.

Identify Intercepts

The **x-intercept** is the x-coordinate of the point where the graph of a relation intersects the x-axis. The **y-intercept** is the y-coordinate of the point where the graph of a relation intersects the y-axis. In general, an intercept is indicated by a point on a graph where the curve or line crosses an axis on a coordinate plane. It also refers to the number read from the axis to identify the point.

 3 Consider the linear equation $2x - 3y = 6$. When one of the variables is zero, the other variable can be found as shown.

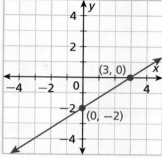

For $y = 0$:

$2x - 3(0) = 6$

$2x = 6$

$x = \dfrac{6}{2}$

$x = 3$

For $x = 0$:

$2(0) - 3y = 6$

$-3y = 6$

$y = \dfrac{6}{-3}$

$y = -2$

A. How does the calculation for $y = 0$ correspond to a point on the graph?

B. How does the calculation for $x = 0$ correspond to a point on the graph?

C. Can the intercepts for a linear equation be used to create its graph? Explain.

 Turn and Talk Since two points determine a line, just one mistake with any of the four x- and y-coordinates may lead to graphing an equation incorrectly. Beyond double-checking your work, how else can you confirm that you've graphed the line correctly?

Use Slope and Intercepts to Categorize Lines

 4 You have seen linear equations of the form $Ax + By = C$, where A, B, and C are nonzero real numbers. The table shows special cases of linear equations in standard form.

Condition	Equation	Type of line	Example
$A = 0$	$By = C$	Horizontal line	$4y = 12$
$B = 0$	$Ax = C$	Vertical line	$x = 5$
$C = 0$	$Ax + By = 0$	A line through the origin	$2x + 3y = 0$

A. Show how you know that when $A = 0$, there is no x-intercept.

B. Show how you know that when $B = 0$, there is no y-intercept.

C. Show how you know that when $C = 0$, the x-intercept and the y-intercept both occur at the origin.

 Turn and Talk What would be the characteristics of the line that has $A = 0$ and $C = 0$? What would be the characteristics of the line that has $B = 0$ and $C = 0$? Explain your answers.

Step It Out

Use Linear Equations to Model Real-World Situations

When you use a linear equation in standard form to model a real-world situation, you should pay close attention to what the variables represent. In many situations, the variables can represent only nonnegative numbers. In some cases, the numbers can be real, but in other cases the numbers must be integers.

 5 Gary is making punch to serve at his party. The recipe calls for mixing lemon-lime soda and cranberry-apple juice in no particular ratio. Gary can buy lemon-lime soda for $1 per liter and cranberry-apple juice for $1.50 per liter. He wants to spend $9 on the ingredients used in the punch. What are some possible amounts of the ingredients?

Use a verbal model.

Let x represent the amount, in liters, of lemon-lime soda, and let y represent the amount, in liters, of cranberry-apple juice.

> **A.** Can x and y be any real numbers? Explain.

Total cost of lemon-lime soda ($)

Total cost of cranberry-apple juice ($)

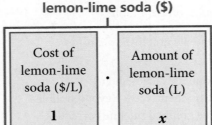
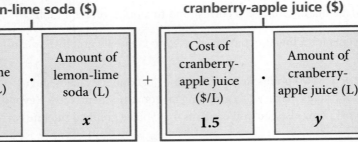
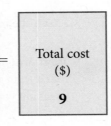

Cost of lemon-lime soda ($/L)	·	Amount of lemon-lime soda (L)	+	Cost of cranberry-apple juice ($/L)	·	Amount of cranberry-apple juice (L)	=	Total cost ($)
1		x		1.5		y		9

Write an equation.
$x + 1.5y = 9$

Identify the possible solutions.
Draw the graph of the equation in Quadrant I because only nonnegative values of x and y make sense in this situation.

The graph shows five possible solutions. For instance, the point (4.5, 3) represents using 4.5 liters of lemon-lime soda (at a cost of $4.50) and 3 liters of cranberry-apple juice (also at a cost of $4.50) to make the punch.

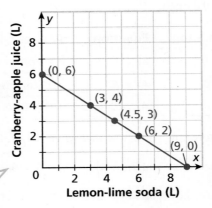

> **B.** What is another possible solution besides the five shown here?

 Turn and Talk Suppose Gary buys the ingredients in 1-liter bottles and wants to empty the bottles when making the punch. How does this change the possible solutions?

6 Jeanine is shopping for T-shirts and sweatshirts. She plans to spend $100. How many T-shirts and how many sweatshirts can she buy?

T-shirts: $10 each

Sweatshirts: $20 each

Use a verbal model.

Let x represent the number of T-shirts, and let y represent the number of sweatshirts.

> **A.** Can x and y be any real numbers? Explain.

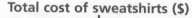

Total cost of T-shirts ($)   Total cost of sweatshirts ($)

Cost of a T-shirt ($)		Number of T-shirts		Cost of a sweatshirt ($)		Number of sweatshirts		Total spent ($)
10	·	**x**	+	**20**	·	**y**	=	**100**

Write an equation.

$10x + 20y = 100$

> **B.** Why can't the value of x be an odd positive integer?

Identify the possible solutions.

Method 1 Make a table of possible values of x and y. Decide whether the ordered pair (x, y) is a solution of the problem.

Value of x	Value of y	Solution?
0	5	Yes
1	4.5	No
2	4	Yes
3	3.5	No
4	3	Yes
5	2.5	No
6	2	Yes
7	1.5	No
8	1	Yes
9	0.5	No
10	0	Yes

Method 2 Using a scale of 1 on both axes and letting x and y be real numbers, graph the equation in Quadrant I. Since horizontal and vertical grid lines intersect at points with integer coordinates, observe where the line includes those points.

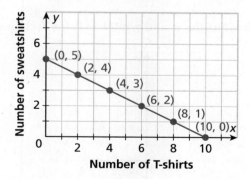

Turn and Talk If Jeanine wants to spend $95 on T-shirts and sweatshirts, how many of each could she buy? How do you know?

Check Understanding

1. Which of the equations are linear equations? Explain your reasoning.

$$5x - 4y = 3 \qquad 3x + 3y = 2 \qquad 2x^2 - 4y^2 = 11$$

Determine if $(4, 7)$ is on the graph of each linear equation. Justify your answers.

2. $4x + 7y = 28$

3. $4x - 3y = -5$

4. Mimi wants to spend a $25 gift card on two kinds of in-app purchases for her favorite game: premium skins that cost $2.99, and tools that cost $4.99. Write an equation that models the skins and tools that Mimi can afford with the gift card.

On Your Own

5. Write two examples of linear equations and two examples of equations that are not linear. Explain your choices.

6. Without calculating, determine if the linear equation $3x + 5y = 45$ has integer solutions for intercepts. Verify by finding each intercept.

Determine whether each equation is linear.

7. $x + 3y^2 = -6$

8. $3x - 2y = 12$

9. $2x - 3y = -3$

Determine whether the point $(2, -3)$ is on the graph of each equation.

10. $x + y = 1$

11. $2x - y = 7$

12. $3x + 5y = -9$

13. $4x + y = 11$

14. $10x - 4y = 23$

15. $8x + 7y = -5$

Determine the x- and y-intercepts for each indicated line.

16. $2x - 5y = 10$

17. $2x - y = 4$

18. $7x + 2y = -14$

19. $x + 4y = 8$

20. $2x + y = 7$

21. $3x - 4y = 48$

Determine the x- and y-intercepts for each line.

22.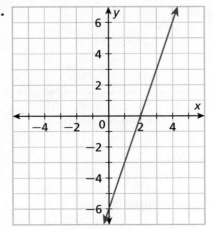

23.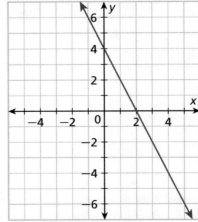

Determine the *x*- and *y*-intercepts for each line.

24.
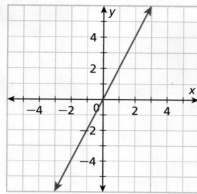

25.
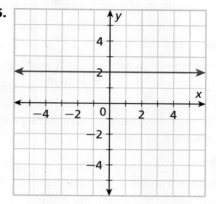

26. **Open Ended** Describe how you would graph the equation $x + 4y = -4$.

27. **STEM** The relationship between a temperature in degrees Fahrenheit and its equivalent in degrees Celsius is given by the linear equation $5F - 9C = 160$, where *F* is the temperature in degrees Fahrenheit and *C* is the temperature in degrees Celsius.

   A. Write the intercepts as points for this linear equation.

   B. Create the graph of this equation using these intercepts.

Give three examples of equations for each situation.

28. linear equations that represent horizontal lines

29. linear equations that represent vertical lines

30. linear equations that pass through the origin

31. A cake recipe calls for 9 large eggs. A large egg weighs 2 ounces, and a medium egg weighs 1.75 ounces.

   A. Write an equation to model the possible combinations of large and medium eggs that result in 18 ounces of eggs.

   B. Find all possible whole-number solutions of the equation.

32. A reception hall has two kinds of tables.

   A. Write an equation that represents the number of round and rectangular tables that could seat 80 people.

   B. Use the equation that you wrote in Part A to determine all three possible solutions if every table must be full.

Round tables seat 6.
Rectangular ones seat 10.

33. Dennis is selling soap sets and candle sets for a school fundraiser. He needs to raise a total of $300.

   A. What are all the possible numbers of each item he can sell to raise $300?

   B. How does your answer to Part A relate to the linear equation $30x + 20y = 300$?

   C. Give an example of a solution of the linear equation that is not a reasonable answer to the problem in this situation.

34. (Open Middle™) Using the digits 1 through 9 at most one time each, fill in the boxes to create two linear equations: one where the x- and y-intercepts both have integer values and one where the x- and y-intercepts both have non-integer values.

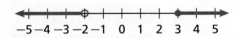

35. Tim is mixing his own birdseed by combining black oil sunflower seeds and dried cranberries. The price of the sunflower seeds is $1 per pound. The price of the cranberries is $6 per pound.

   A. Tim wants to spend $50 total on the seeds and cranberries. Write a linear equation to model the possible amounts of these two ingredients.

   B. Use the equation that you wrote in Part A to determine the weight of the seeds if Tim's mix contains $30 of the cranberries.

   C. Use the equation that you wrote in Part A to determine the weight of the cranberries if Tim's mix contains $30 of the sunflower seeds.

Spiral Review • Assessment Readiness

36. Which compound inequality is represented by the graph?

$$\xleftarrow{\quad} \begin{array}{ccccccccccc} & & & & & & & & & & \\ -5 & -4 & -3 & -2 & -1 & 0 & 1 & 2 & 3 & 4 & 5 \end{array} \xrightarrow{\quad}$$

   Ⓐ $x < -2$ OR $x > 3$

   Ⓑ $x < -2$ OR $x \geq 3$

   Ⓒ $x < -2$ AND $x > 3$

   Ⓓ $x < -2$ AND $x \geq 3$

37. Solve $P = 2(x + y)$ for x. Select all that apply.

   Ⓐ $x = \dfrac{P}{2} - y$ Ⓒ $x = \dfrac{P - 2y}{2}$

   Ⓑ $x = 2P - y$ Ⓓ $x = 2P + y$

38. Which of the following is the solution of $2x - 1 > 5$?

   Ⓐ $x > 2$

   Ⓑ $x < 3$

   Ⓒ $x < 2$

   Ⓓ $x > 3$

39. Which of the following is equivalent to $\dfrac{-3 - (-2)}{3 - 2}$?

   Ⓐ -5 Ⓒ 1

   Ⓑ -1 Ⓓ 2

 I'm in a Learning Mindset!

What strategies do I use to persevere through problems involving writing linear equations that model real-world situations? How do I know when I have succeeded?

Slopes of Lines and Rates of Change

(I Can) numerically describe and interpret the slope of a line.

Spark Your Learning

Howard is taking a trip in his car.

Howard is driving on a highway at a constant speed.

Complete Part A as a whole class. Then complete Parts B–D in small groups.

A. What is a mathematical question you can ask about this situation? What information would you need to know to answer your question?

B. What variable(s) are involved in this situation? What unit of measurement would you use for each variable?

C. To answer your question, what strategy and tool would you use along with all the information you have? What answer do you get?

D. Does your answer make sense in the context of the situation? How do you know?

Turn and Talk Predict how your answer would change for each of the following changes in the situation:
- The amount of time traveled is greater than 3 hours.
- The distance traveled is greater.
- Howard stopped during the travel time.

Build Understanding

Investigate Slope

The **slope** of a line is a measure of its steepness and direction. A line that rises from left to right has positive slope. A line that falls from left to right has negative slope.

1 ▶ A. Which lines shown have positive slope? Which have negative slope?

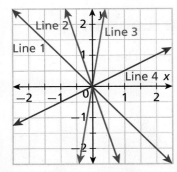

B. Of the two lines with positive slope, which one rises more steeply? That is, which line is more vertical?

C. Of the two lines with negative slope, which one falls more steeply? That is, which line is more vertical?

You can compare the steepness of two nonvertical lines by comparing their slopes. The line whose slope has the greater absolute value is steeper.

D. Line 4 has a slope of $\frac{1}{2}$. Line 1 has a slope of -1. Of these two lines, which is steeper? How can you tell from the given slopes?

Slope is a ratio of vertical change over a given horizontal change. It is calculated by taking the *rise* of the line and dividing it by the *run* of the line.

$$\text{slope} = \frac{\text{rise}}{\text{run}}$$

The rise is determined by counting along the vertical grid lines. The run is determined by counting along the horizontal grid lines. When counting rise and run, be sure to account for the scales of their respective axes.

Slope is most often represented by the letter m.

For the line with positive slope:

$$m = \frac{\text{rise}}{\text{run}}$$
$$= \frac{16 - 10}{10 - 4}$$
$$= \frac{6}{6}$$
$$= 1$$

For the line with negative slope:

$$m = \frac{\text{rise}}{\text{run}}$$
$$= \frac{3 - 6}{10 - 4}$$
$$= -\frac{3}{6}$$
$$= -\frac{1}{2}$$

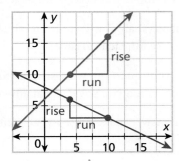

 Turn and Talk How would you characterize the slope of a horizontal line, such as $y = -2$? How would you characterize the slope of a vertical line, such as $x = 1$?

Interpret Slope as a Rate of Change

A **rate of change** is a ratio of the amount of change in the dependent variable to the amount of change in the independent variable. It can be determined by calculating the slope of the line that represents the linear relation between the variables.

In a purely mathematical graph, the slope is just a ratio of the change in y (the rise) to the change in x (the run). There are no physical measurements involved. In a real-world graph, however, the variables do have associated units of measurement. This means that the unit of measurement for the rate of change is a ratio of the unit of measurement in the dependent variable to the unit of measurement in the independent variable.

2 ▶ Consider a car traveling at a constant speed.

The graph shows the relationship between the gasoline left in the tank and the distance traveled.

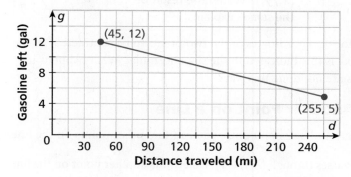

A. Determine the rise between the two points. What does the rise represent? What units are associated with this rise?

B. Determine the run between the two points. What does the run represent? What units are associated with this run?

C. Find the slope. What does the slope represent? What units are associated with the slope?

 Turn and Talk How would the graph and slope change if the horizontal axis represented gasoline used and the vertical axis represented distance traveled?

Step It Out

Calculate Slope

The slope of a line can be calculated if the coordinates of two points on the line are known or if the coordinates of two points can be identified from a graph of the line.

Slope Formula

For any two points (x_1, y_1) and (x_2, y_2) on the graph of a line, the slope m of the line can be calculated using the formula:

$$\text{slope} = \frac{\text{rise}}{\text{run}}$$

$$m = \frac{y_2 - y_1}{x_2 - x_1}$$

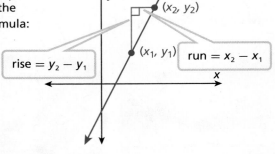

rise $= y_2 - y_1$

run $= x_2 - x_1$

---

3 ▸ Use the labeled points on the line shown to find the slope of the line.

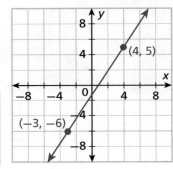

Use the slope formula with $(x_1, y_1) = (-3, -6)$ and $(x_2, y_2) = (4, 5)$:

$$m = \frac{5 - (-6)}{4 - (-3)}$$

$$= \frac{11}{7}$$

> **A.** Could the ordered pair $(4, 5)$ have been selected as the point (x_1, y_1)? Would the result be the same? Explain.

B. It is important for the coordinates of the two points to be subtracted "in the same order." How is this indicated in the slope formula? What happens if the subtractions are not done this way?

Use Slope to Find Another Point on a Line

If you know the slope of a line and one point on it, you can find other points on the line.

4 ▸ A line with slope $\frac{3}{5}$ passes through $(-1, -1)$. Determine another point on the line.

Begin by plotting the given point. Then use the given slope to find another point on the line.

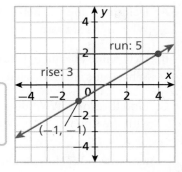

The slope indicates that the rise is 3 and the run is 5.

Moving 3 units up from $(-1, -1)$ takes you to the point $(-1, 2)$. Moving 5 units to the right from $(-1, 2)$ takes you to the point $(4, 2)$.

> **A.** Why are the movements up and to the right?

The point $(4, 2)$ is another point on the line.

B. How can the slope formula be used to verify that $(4, 2)$ is on the line?

Find Average Rate of Change

Linear relationships involve a constant rate of change. That rate of change is the slope of the line that models the relationship. Some real-world situations involve more than one rate of change. In these situations, an average rate of change can be determined.

5 Tracy runs every Saturday to stay healthy. After stretching, he always begins by jogging at a steady pace. He uses a fitness watch to monitor both his time running and his pace. At the end of his jog, he immediately increases his pace to his regular running speed for the remainder of his workout. Find the average rate of change (average speed) for his entire workout.

The graph models his time and distance run during his workout.

Jogging: 10 minutes
Running: 40 minutes

Determine the rate of change for the 10 minutes while he is jogging.

$$m = \frac{0.5 - 0}{10 - 0} = \frac{0.5}{10}$$
$$= \frac{1}{20}$$

A. What are the units for this rate of change?

Determine the rate of change for the 40 minutes while he is running.

$$m = \frac{5.5 - 0.5}{50 - 10}$$
$$= \frac{5}{40}$$
$$= \frac{1}{8}$$

B. How were the values used in this calculation determined?

C. How does this rate compare to his rate of change while jogging?

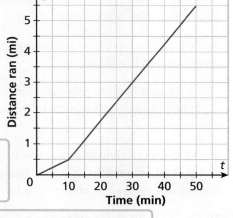

Now determine the average rate of change for his entire workout.

$$m = \frac{5.5 - 0}{50 - 0} = \frac{5.5}{50} = \frac{11}{100}$$

So his average rate of change for his entire workout is $\frac{11}{100}$, or 0.11 mile per minute.

D. How does Tracy's average rate of change compare to his jogging and running rates? Explain why this makes sense for this real-world situation.

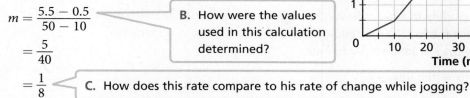

Turn and Talk Discuss why the average rate of change for the entire workout is not simply the average of the jogging and running rates of change.

Check Understanding

1. Which rates of change could be used to measure the pattern of the growth of a tree? Select all that apply.

   centimeters/month   liters/day   miles per gallon   feet/year

Determine the slope of the line passing through the given points.

2. $(4, 2)$ and $(-2, 1)$

3. $(5, 3)$ and $(7, 9)$

4. Preet wants to determine the rate of change in gas prices. In week one of his study, he found the price to be $2.86 per gallon. In week five of his study, he found the price to be $3.14 per gallon. What is the average rate of change in gas prices, based on the data collected by Preet?

On Your Own

5. (MP) **Critique Reasoning** Louise and Martha are debating the slopes of two lines, one with a slope of 2 and the other with a slope of -2. Louise states that the slope of 2 is greater than the slope of -2 since 2 is greater than -2. Martha argues that the two are basically the same, with the only difference being that the line with a slope of 2 moves up and to the right while the line with a slope of -2 moves down and to the right. Who is correct? Explain.

6. A slope is found to be -1. Give two ratios of rise and run values that would correspond to this slope.

7. (MP) **Critique Reasoning** Julia was asked to find the slope between the points $(3, 1)$ and $(4, -2)$. She reported the slope to be $-\frac{1}{3}$. Is she correct? Explain why or why not.

8. **STEM** Lucy is sailing in a race. She reaches the quarter mile buoy at 1:30 p.m. At 1:36 p.m., she reaches the mile buoy. Use this information to determine her average rate of change, in miles per minute.

Determine the slope of the line.

9.

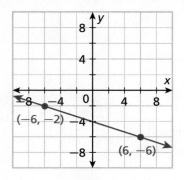

10.

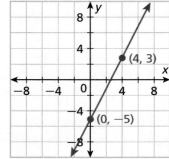

11.

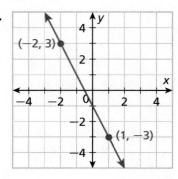

Calculate the slope of the line determined by the ordered pairs in the table.

12.

x	y
1	11
2	9
3	7
4	5

13.

x	y
−4	5
−2	8
0	11
2	14

Determine the slope of a line containing the two points.

14. $(0, 3)$ and $(4, 2)$

15. $(0, 0)$ and $(5, 4)$

16. $(5, 3)$ and $(12, 11)$

17. $(6, -3)$ and $(-3, 6)$

Use the slope and the given point to determine a second point that is on the line.

18. $m = 4$ through $(1, 3)$

19. $m = \frac{3}{2}$ through $(0, 0)$

20. $m = -\frac{1}{5}$ through $(7, -2)$

21. $m = \frac{5}{4}$ through $(5, 4)$

22. Given a slope $m = \frac{b}{a}$ of a line and a point (x, y) on that line, how can you determine the coordinates of another point on the line?

For each situation, first determine the rate of change for each part of the graph. Then find the average rate of change over the entire time period shown.

23.

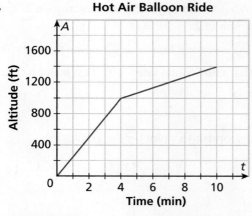

Hot Air Balloon Ride

24.

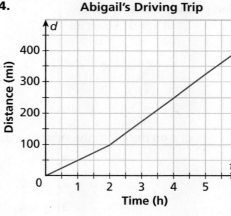

Abigail's Driving Trip

25. Open Ended You are given the point $Q(-2, -5)$,

A. Identify a point (x_1, y_1) that along with point Q defines a line with a positive slope.

B. Identify a point (x_2, y_2) that along with point Q defines a line with a negative slope.

26. Andre ran a 100-meter race in 12 seconds. What was his average speed as he ran the race?

27. Use the information about the bamboo plant to determine and interpret the average rate of change, in inches per day.

28. Suzanne completed a 1500-piece jigsaw puzzle in 4 hours 10 minutes. What was her average speed, in pieces per minute?

200 in.

25 in.

Monday
noon

Saturday
noon

29. During a storm a rain gauge collects rain. The rain gauge is shown at two different times during the storm.

   A. By how much did the water level increase?

   B. How many hours passed between the two photos?

   C. Use this information to determine the average rate of change in rainfall.

4.0 inches at 3:30 p.m.

1.5 inches at 2:00 p.m.

30. (Open Middle™) Using the integers −9 to 9 at most one time each, fill in the boxes to create a slope that matches the corresponding table of values.

$m = \dfrac{\boxed{}}{\boxed{}}$

x			
y			

Spiral Review • Assessment Readiness

31. Which value(s) satisfy the compound inequality $x \le -2$ OR $x > 3$? Select all that apply.

   Ⓐ $x = -2$ Ⓓ $x = 0$

   Ⓑ $x = 3$ Ⓔ $x = 2$

   Ⓒ $x = 6$ Ⓕ $x = -4$

32. What would be the correct description of the graph of $2x + 3y = 0$?

   Ⓐ a vertical line   Ⓒ a line through $(0, 0)$

   Ⓑ a horizontal line   Ⓓ This is not a line.

33. Match the value of x on the left to the value of y that corresponds to a point on the graph.

   A. $x = -3$ **1.** $y = -2$

   B. $x = -2$ **2.** $y = 2$

   C. $x = 0$ **3.** $y = 4$

   D. $x = 1$ **4.** $y = -4$

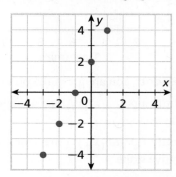

I'm in a Learning Mindset!

What strategies do I use to persevere through understanding the calculations of rates of change? How do I know when I have succeeded?

Review

Standard Form

David needs to measure out 30 cups for a recipe. He can measure out 1 cup at a time, *x*, or 4 cups using a quart, *y*.

To determine the number of each type of measurement, he writes a linear equation.

$$x + 4y = 30$$

The coefficients represent the number of cups for each type of measurement.

The standard form of a linear equation is $Ax + By = C$.

Intercepts

David graphed the equation to visualize the relationship between the number of cups and the number of quarts he would measure out.

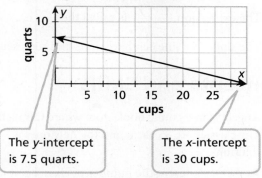

The *y*-intercept is 7.5 quarts.

The *x*-intercept is 30 cups.

When David uses 0 cups, he would have to measure out 7.5 quarts.

When David uses 0 quarts, he would have to measure out 30 cups.

Slope Between Two Points

The slope of a line, *m*, can be determined by comparing the coordinates of two points.

The change in *y*-coordinates represents the "rise" of the line.

$$m = \frac{y_2 - y_1}{x_2 - x_1}$$

The change in *x*-coordinates represents the "run" of the line.

Another way of saying this is "rise over run".

The slope is equivalent for any two points chosen on the line.

Slope as a Rate of Change

David uses the points $(0, 7.5)$ and $(30, 0)$ to determine the slope of the line.

The variable *y* is measured in quarts.

$$m = \frac{y_2 - y_1}{x_2 - x_1} = \frac{0 - 7.5}{30 - 0} = -\frac{7.5}{30} = -\frac{1}{4}$$

The variable *x* is measured in cups.

He interprets the slope as a rate of change by analyzing the units of each variable. For every quart he measures for the recipe, he needs to measure 4 fewer cups.

Vocabulary

Choose the correct term from the box to complete each sentence.

1. The ___?___ of a line is calculated by taking the ___?___ of the line and dividing it by the ___?___ of the line.

2. $Ax + By = C$ is called the ___?___ of a linear equation.

3. With $Ax + By = C$, when you substitute $x = 0$, you are solving for the ___?___, and when you substitute $y = 0$, you are solving for the ___?___.

4. The expression $\frac{y_2 - y_1}{x_2 - x_1}$ is called the ___?___.

5. The slope of a line can have units and represent a ___?___ of the variables.

Concepts and Skills

6. Angela is in a comic book store where they sell classic and new comic books. The classics are $5 each, and the new ones are $2. Where necessary, use integer solutions.

   A. Let x represent the number of classic comic books she can purchase, and let y represent the number of new comics she can purchase. Write an equation in standard form to represent her purchases if she has $15 to spend in the store.

   B. Use your equation to determine how many comic books she can purchase if she only buys new comic books.

   C. Use your equation to determine how many comic books she can purchase if she only buys classics.

Find the x- and y-intercepts of the line represented by each equation.

7. $2x - 7y = 28$

8. $5x + 3y = 30$

9. $4x + 5y = 60$

10. $-3x + 8y = 24$

11. When driving on a highway, Ian passed the 23 mile marker with 15 gallons of gas in the tank. When he passed the 73 mile marker, he had 12.5 gallons of gas left.

    A. If the number of gallons is the dependent variable, find the slope of a graphed line that passes through these two points. What would the slope represent in terms of the context?

    B. (MP) **Use Tools** How much gas would Ian have left when passing the 100 mile marker? Round to the nearest gallon. State what strategy and tool you will use to answer the question, explain your choice, and then find the answer.

    C. How would the graph and rate of change be different if the gasoline used were the independent variable and the distance traveled were the dependent variable?

12. A line with a slope of $\frac{3}{4}$ passes through $(2, 3)$. Find a second point on the line.

Find the slope of the line that passes through the two points given.

13. $(4, 3)$ and $(5, -3)$

14. $(-2, -5)$ and $(0, 13)$

15. $(1, 4)$ and $(6, -1)$

16. $(-5, -4)$ and $(-2, -3)$

Module Performance Task: *Spies and Analysts™*

Veggie Burger Fundraiser

BBQ Veggie Burger
Sell-a-Thon

How many veggie burgers will
have to be sold to reach the goal?

BBQ Goal

$400

$300

$200

$100

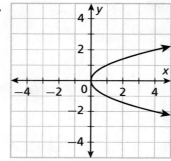

Are You Ready?

Complete these problems to review prior concepts and skills you will need for this module.

Write Equations for Proportional Relationships

Write an equation that describes each relationship.

1. The number of students whom Ian tutors is proportional to the amount that he earns as shown in the table.

2. Kim drives 144 miles every 3 hours.

Number of students, x	5	7	9
Amount earned ($), y	150	210	270

Slopes of Lines

Determine the slope of a line passing through each pair of points.

3. $(0, 0)$ and $(6, 3)$

4. $(2, 1)$ and $(-8, 5)$

5. $(-2, -3)$ and $(-3, 1)$

6. $(-5, 2)$ and $(3, 2)$

Understand Functions

Determine if each relation is a function

7.

Hour	Temperature, °C
10	5
16	8
20	5

8.

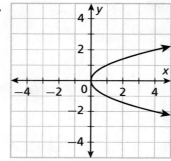

Connecting Past and Present Learning

Previously, you learned:

• to determine if a relation is a function,

• to write equations in standard form, and

• to determine and interpret the slope of a linear equation.

In this module, you will learn:

• to write linear equations in point-slope form,

• to describe characteristics of linear functions, and

• to build linear functions that model real-world problems.

Relations and Functions

(I Can) **identify how functions and relations are related.**

Spark Your Learning

Mr. Fry and some volunteers take a science class to a museum.

The group purchased 20 tickets before they visited the museum.

Complete Part A as a whole class. Then complete Parts B–D in small groups.

A. What is a mathematical question you can ask about this situation? What information would you need to know to answer your question?

B. What variable(s) are needed in this situation? What must be true of the values for these variables in this question?

C. To answer your question, what strategy and tool would you use along with all the information you have? What answer do you get?

D. Does your answer make sense in the context of the situation? How do you know?

Turn and Talk Predict how your answer would change for each of the following changes in the situation:

- There are 25 people in the group.
- Tickets are $15 each.
- The group discount is 15% for groups of 15 or more.

Build Understanding

Describe Relations

A **relation** is a set of ordered pairs (x, y) where x is the input value and y is the output value. The **domain** is the set of all possible inputs for the relation. The **range** is the set of all possible outputs for the relation.

 Consider the relation $\left\{(5, 2), (4, 1), (3, 0), (2, 5), (7, 4), (4, 3)\right\}$.

A. What are the elements of the domain for these ordered pairs?

B. What are the elements of the range for these ordered pairs?

C. A *mapping diagram* shows how the elements in the domain and range correspond to one another. How is the element 4 in the domain different from all other domain elements?

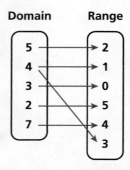

> **Turn and Talk** Why are there only 5 elements in the domain even though there are 6 ordered pairs in the relation?

Identify Functions

A **function** is a relation in which every domain value corresponds to exactly one range value.

 You can use a mapping diagram to determine whether a relation is a function.

A. Describe how the mapping diagrams of the two relations shown are different.

B. Which mapping diagram represents a function? Explain why.

C. Which mapping diagram does not represent a function? Explain why.

> **Turn and Talk** Would a relation in which every domain value corresponds to the same range value be a function? Explain.

When a relation is graphed, you can use the *vertical line test* to determine if the relation is a function. According to the **vertical line test**, a relation is a function if and only if no vertical line passes through two or more points on the graph.

3 You can also use a table of values to determine whether a relation is a function.

x	y
0	7
2	2
4	−3
3	5
1	1

x	y
2	4
0	2
3	1
2	5
1	7

A. What *y*-value(s) are associated with the *x*-value of 2 in the first table? What *y*-value(s) are associated with the *x*-value of 2 in the second table?

B. Explain how you can determine whether a relation is a function by considering a table of values.

 Turn and Talk What change would you make in the second table so that the relation becomes a function?

4 The graphs of two relations are shown.

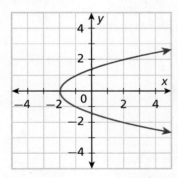 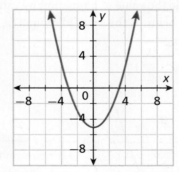

A. Is there at least one vertical line that crosses the first graph more than once? Would any vertical line cross the second graph more than once?

B. A vertical line crosses the *x*-axis. How does this test help you determine whether every domain value is paired with exactly one range value?

 Turn and Talk Would it make sense to have a horizontal line test for functions as well? Explain.

Use Function Notation

If the ordered pairs (x, y) for a function have a pattern that can be expressed algebraically, you can write an equation that shows how to calculate the value of y from the value of x. For instance, if the value of y is always 1 more than the value of x, you can write $y = x + 1$. Because the value of y depends on the value of x, y is called the **dependent variable**, and x is called the **independent variable**.

You can name a function by using a letter, typically f, but g and h are often used as well. You can then use the *function notation* $f(x)$, which is read "the value of f at x" or simply "f of x," in place of the dependent variable y. For instance, you can write the ordered pair (x, y) as $(x, f(x))$, and you can write the function represented by the equation $y = x + 1$ as $f(x) = x + 1$. The expression $x + 1$ is called the *function rule*. A **function rule** is an algebraic expression that defines a function.

5 You can determine the value of a function by substituting a given value for the independent variable.

A ball is dropped from a platform 30 feet above the ground. The ball's height h, in feet, above the ground can be modeled by the function $h(t) = -16t^2 + 30$, where t is the time, in seconds, since the ball was dropped.

A. What is the independent variable? the dependent variable?

B. What does $h(1)$ represent?

C. Describe how to find $h(1)$.

6 You can also determine the value of a function by using a graph. The graph of a function g shown below is the set of all points $(x, g(x))$, where x is in the domain of the function.

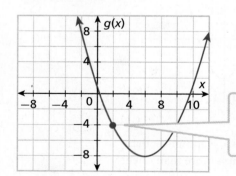

This point on the graph is located at $x = 2$. The associated y-coordinate is -4, so $g(2) = -4$.

A. What is the domain of the function?

B. For the given graph, determine $g(-2)$ and $g(6)$.

C. Describe how to use a graph to locate a function value for a given value of x.

 Turn and Talk Write an ordered pair representing a point on the graph of a function f for each of the following x-values: 0, -2, and a.

Step It Out

Analyze Real-World Functions

7 An artist spends an afternoon making bracelets using beads she already has. She uses 15 beads for each bracelet. The remaining number R of beads in her supply can be modeled by the function shown, where b represents the number of bracelets she makes. Find and interpret $R(0)$ and $R(3)$. Then graph $R(b)$.

Find and interpret $R(0)$.

$$R(b) = 90 - 15b$$

$R(0) = 90 - 15(0) = 90$

$R(0)$ represents the remaining number of beads when $b = 0$.

So, before she makes any bracelets, she has 90 beads left.

Find and interpret $R(3)$.

$R(3) = 90 - 15(3) = 45$ ◁———— **A.** Why wouldn't you find $R(3.5)$?

$R(3)$ represents the remaining number of beads when $b = 3$.

So, after making 3 bracelets, she has 45 beads left.

Graph $R(b)$.

The domain is restricted to the input values that make sense in the context of this real-world function. Use the function rule to identify all points on the graph of the function. Then graph the function by plotting the points.

B. Why is the graph of the function R limited to the first quadrant? Explain your reasoning.

C. What is the domain of the function?

D. What is the range of the function?

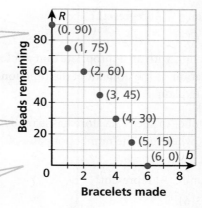

Turn and Talk How would the graph of the function change if the artist started with only 60 beads?

Check Understanding

1. Consider the relation $\{(1, 6), (8, 4), (2, 6), (5, 4), (3, 9), (2, 7)\}$.

   A. Create a mapping diagram for the ordered pairs. What are the domain and range?

   B. Is this relation a function? Explain why or why not.

2. Does the y-axis represent a function? Explain.

3. For any function f, what does the value of $f(0)$ represent graphically?

4. The function $A(t) = 500 + 5t$ represents the amount A, in dollars, of an investment, where t is the time in months.

   A. What does $A(2)$ represent?

   B. Find $A(2)$.

On Your Own

5. Explain how the vertical line test is used to determine if the graph of a relation is a function.

6. Create a graph of a relation that is a function and a graph of a relation that is not a function. Be sure to include the reasoning you used to generate each graph.

Determine whether each relation is a function.

7. $(3, 2), (1, 2), (4, 3), (6, -2)$ 8. $(-1, -1), (-2, -2), (-3, 2), (-2, 3)$

For each function, find $f(-1), f(1)$, and $f(3)$.

9. $f(x) = 3x - 4$ 10. $f(x) = 4$

11. The cost C, in dollars, of a large pizza with t toppings is modeled by the function $C(t) = 10.95 + t$.

    A. What do $C(0)$ and $C(2)$ represent?

    B. Find $C(0)$ and $C(2)$.

    C. Graph the function with an appropriate domain for this real-world situation. Is the domain of the function all real numbers? Explain.

12. The remaining number of socks S a store has is modeled by $S(p) = 14 - 2p$, where p is the number of pairs of socks sold.

    A. What do $S(0)$ and $S(6)$ represent?

    B. Find $S(0)$ and $S(6)$.

    C. Graph the function with an appropriate domain for this real-world situation. Is the domain of the function all real numbers? Explain.

Pizza Italiano

Large cheese pizza
$10.95

Toppings
$1.00 each

For each relation, create a mapping diagram and give the domain and range.

13. $\{(2, 0), (5, -2), (6, -5), (7, 3), (3, 1)\}$

14. $\{(8, 4), (6, 4), (-1, -2), (8, 5), (6, 5)\}$

15. Determine if the relations in Problems 13 and 14 are functions. Explain your reasoning.

Use the vertical line test to determine whether each graph represents a function.

16.

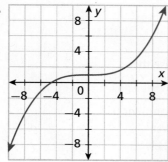

17.

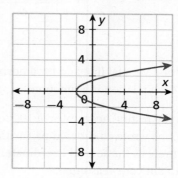

18.

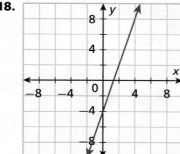

19.

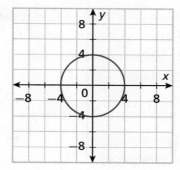

Use the graph of f to determine each indicated function value.

20. $f(-6)$

21. $f(-4)$

22. $f(0)$

23. $f(4)$

24. $f(6)$

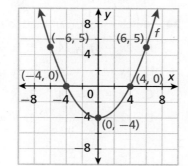

25. **(MP)** **Reason** A new movie is released and shown in a local theater. Let $p(t)$ be the number of people, in thousands, who see the movie t days after the movie is released.

   A. Is p a function? Explain your reasoning.

   B. What does $p(0) = 12$ mean?

   C. What does $p(10) < p(5)$ mean?

   D. What does $p(3) + p(4) = 19$ mean?

   E. If $p(t) = 0$ for some value of t, what does that mean?

Use each table of values to determine if the relation represented is a function.

26.

x	y
−2	4
−1	1
0	0
1	1
2	4
3	9

27.

x	y
1	8
2	11
3	14
1	17
4	20
5	23

28. Create a table of values for a vertical line and for a horizontal line, and use these tables to demonstrate if each relation is a function. Explain your reasoning.

29. Deena collected data on the resting heart rates of 100 individuals based on their age. For each individual, she wrote an ordered pair with the age as the first coordinate and the heart rate as the second coordinate. Is this relation likely to represent a function? Explain your reasoning.

30. (MP) **Model with Mathematics** The cost C, in dollars, of buying t T-shirts and s sweatshirts is modeled by the *multivariate function* $C(t, s) = 13.75t + 35s$.

A. What are the independent variables? What is the dependent variable?

B. Find and interpret $C(3, 1)$.

Spiral Review • Assessment Readiness

31. The formula for the perimeter P of a rectangle is $P = 2l + 2w$. How can you rewrite this formula so that it is solved for w?

Ⓐ $w = \dfrac{P - 2l}{2}$ Ⓒ $w = \dfrac{P + 2l}{2}$

Ⓑ $w = 2(P - 2l)$ Ⓓ $w = 2(P + 2l)$

32. A compound inequality is created by joining two inequalities with the word AND. Under which circumstances does x satisfy the compound inequality?

Ⓐ x satisfies the first inequality.

Ⓑ x satisfies the second inequality.

Ⓒ x satisfies both inequalities.

Ⓓ x satisfies neither inequality.

33. Maureen drives 120 miles in 120 minutes. What is her rate of change in mi/h?

Ⓐ 1 mi/h   Ⓒ 60 mi/h

Ⓑ 50 mi/h   Ⓓ 120 mi/h

34. Match each linear relation to its intercepts.

A. $2x - 3y = 24$ **1.** $x = 8, y = -12$

B. $3x - 2y = 24$ **2.** $x = 8, y = 12$

C. $2x + 3y = 24$ **3.** $x = 12, y = -8$

D. $3x + 2y = 24$ **4.** $x = 12, y = 8$

I'm in a Learning Mindset!

What strategies do I use to identify functions and relations? How do I know when I have succeeded?

Linear Functions

(I Can) describe the graphs of linear functions.

Spark Your Learning

A truck is being loaded with 19 pallets.

There are weight restrictions for roadways, highways, and bridges. This truck will need to use a bridge but will only travel on highways.

Complete Part A as a whole class. Then complete Parts B–D in small groups.

A. What is a mathematical question you can ask about this situation? What information would you need to know to answer your question?

B. What variable(s) are needed in this situation? What must be true of the values for these variables in this question?

C. To answer your question, what strategy and tool would you use along with all the information you have? What answer do you get?

D. Does your answer make sense in the context of the situation? How do you know?

 Turn and Talk Predict how your answer would change for each of the following changes in the situation:

- The empty truck weight is 25,000 pounds.
- A loaded pallet weighs 5000 pounds.
- The lowest load restriction is 58,000 pounds.

Build Understanding

Analyze Linear Functions

A **linear function** is a relation that can be written in the form $f(x) = mx + b$, where x is the independent variable and m and b are real numbers.

A. In the general form of a linear function, replace $f(x)$ with y and then rewrite the equation so that both variables are on one side of the equation.

B. Describe how your rewritten equation from Part A fits the definition of the standard form of a linear equation.

C. Use what you know about the graph of a linear equation in standard from to describe the graph of a linear function.

D. Write the general linear function $f(x) = mx + b$ when $m = 0$.

E. Write the equation for a linear function with $m = 0$ and $b = 4$. What is the corresponding y-value for any x-value?

F. Describe the graph of the function you wrote in Step E.

A linear function with $m = 0$ can be written as $f(x) = b$ and pairs every x-value with the constant b. This type of linear function is called a *constant function,* and its graph is a horizontal line.

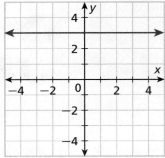

G. Write the constant linear function whose graph is shown.

For any function of the form $f(x) = mx + b$, you can see that $f(0) = b$ and $f(1) = m + b$. It follows that the points $(0, b)$ and $(1, m + b)$ are on the graph of a linear function as shown.

H. How is the value of b related to the graph of $f(x) = mx + b$?

I. You already know that the slope of a line is the ratio of the change in y to the change in x. Find the slope of the line $y = mx + b$ using the points shown on the graph.

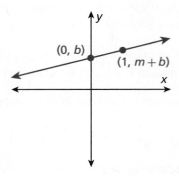

Therefore, the form $f(x) = mx + b$ is known as **slope-intercept form** where m is the slope and b is the y-intercept.

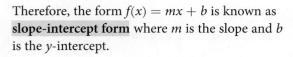

Turn and Talk Can a vertical line be written in slope-intercept form? Can a horizontal line? Explain.

Graph Linear Functions

You can represent an equation like $y = \frac{3}{4}x + 2$ graphically by choosing x-values, finding the corresponding y-values, plotting the pairs (x, y), and drawing a line through the points.

x	y
−1	$1\frac{1}{4}$
0	2
1	$2\frac{3}{4}$
2	$3\frac{1}{2}$

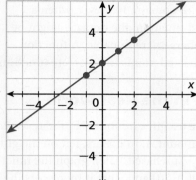

2 ▶ You can use the y-intercept and slope to obtain a graph of the equation as well.

$$y = \frac{3}{4}x + 2$$

A. In the drawing, how are the y-intercept of 2 and the slope of $\frac{3}{4}$ being used to obtain the graph of the line?

B. Can you use a different, but equivalent, slope to graph the line? If so, show how. If not, explain why not.

C. Match each equation to its graph by plotting points or using the slope and y-intercept.

1. $y = -\frac{3}{4}x - 2$ **2.** $y = -\frac{3}{4}x + 2$ **3.** $y = \frac{3}{4}x - 2$

A.

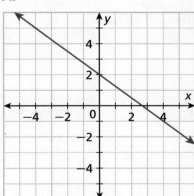

B.

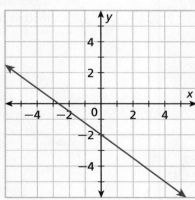

C.

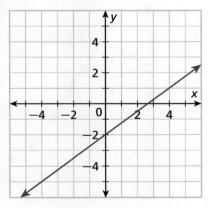

 Turn and Talk Describe the graph of $y = 2$ by first identifying the slope and y-intercept and then explaining how those facts allow you to visualize the graph.

Step It Out

A function whose graph on an interval of the x-axis is connected with no gaps or breaks is a **continuous function**. A linear function is a continuous function on its entire domain. However, when a linear function models a real-world situation, the domain might be restricted because not all real numbers are reasonable. A function whose graph is made up of unconnected points is a **discrete function**.

BUBBLE TEA
$4

GIFT CARD
$80

Apply Linear Functions in the Real World

3 ▶ Cameron received a bubble tea gift card for his birthday. Write a linear function for the amount A, in dollars, left on the gift card after x bubble teas are purchased. Then graph the function and determine the value of $A(20)$ and what it represents in this situation.

Write a verbal model.

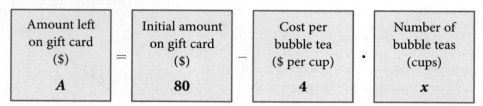

Amount left on gift card ($)		Initial amount on gift card ($)		Cost per bubble tea ($ per cup)		Number of bubble teas (cups)
A	=	80	−	4	·	x

Write the function.

$A(x) = 80 - 4x$

> **A.** What would be the domain and range for the general function $f(x) = 80 - 4x$?

Graph the function.

Only non-negative integer values of x make sense in this real-world situation, so A is a discrete function.

> **B.** Why is it reasonable to show only the first quadrant when graphing the function that models this real-world situation?

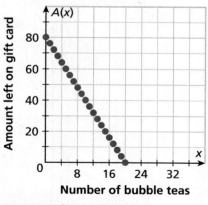

> **C.** What are the domain and range?

Answer the question.

$A(20)$ is the x-intercept of the graph and is equal to 0. It represents the amount on the gift card after Cameron buys 20 bubble teas.

 Turn and Talk How would the graph change with each of the following changes in the situation?

- The cost per bubble tea is doubled while the initial amount on the gift card stays the same.
- The initial amount on the gift card is doubled while the cost per bubble tea stays the same.

Check Understanding

1. Which of the functions are linear? Explain your reasoning.

$$f(x) = x^2 + 2x - 3 \qquad g(x) = 3x + 8 \qquad h(x) = 4$$

Explain how to graph each linear function using the slope and y-intercept.

2. $f(x) = 2x - 7$

3. $f(x) = -\frac{2}{5}x + 1$

4. Suppose you are in a building at 28 feet above ground level and you take an escalator down to ground level. On the escalator, your distance above ground level changes by -2 feet per second. Write a linear function to describe the distance d that you are from ground level over time t in seconds.

On Your Own

5. (MP) **Construct Arguments** If you are told that the points $(3, p)$ and $(4, q)$ are on a line, what does the value $q - p$ represent? Explain your reasoning.

6. **Open Ended** Vladimir is looking to retire in 10 years. He has a plan to put $25,000 into an investment today that earns interest at a fixed amount per year. What would be a reasonable domain and range for a function modeling the total amount of the investment, including interest? Explain your answer.

Graph each linear function.

7. $f(x) = 5x - 2$

8. $f(x) = \frac{2}{3}x + 1$

9. $f(x) = 6$

10. $f(x) = -\frac{1}{4}x - 4$

11. $f(x) = \frac{3}{4}x - 2$

12. $f(x) = -\frac{1}{2}x + 1$

13. Until a Labrador puppy is 30 weeks old, it gains about the same amount of weight each week. A newborn Labrador puppy weighs 2 lb.

50 lb at 28 weeks old

   A. Use the information shown to write a linear function describing the weight of the Labrador puppy over time. Be sure to define your variables.

   B. What is the domain of this function?

State the domain and range for each function graphed.

14.

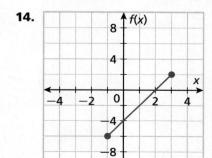

15.

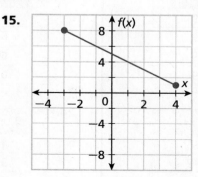

State the domain and range for each function graphed.

16.

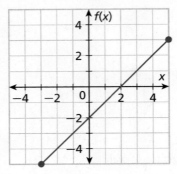

17.

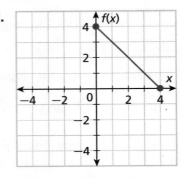

18. You make an investment in a plan that will pay simple interest. The table indicates the value of this investment as time goes on. Year zero is the year that you made the investment.

A. What does the value at year 0 represent, if this linear function is graphed?

B. What would the difference between any two consecutive values of investment determine for this linear function?

C. Write a linear function $V(t)$ for this information.

D. What is $V(10)$? What does this value represent?

E. Graph the function.

Year	Value of investment
0	$2000
1	$2100
2	$2200
3	$2300
4	$2400
5	$2500

Determine the slope of the linear function from the given table of values. If possible, write the linear function in slope-intercept form.

19.

x	f(x)
−3	14
−2	11
−1	8
0	5

20.

x	f(x)
4	6
5	8
6	10
7	12

21.

x	f(x)
3	9
2	9
1	9
0	9

22.

x	f(x)
6	5
6	2
6	−2
6	−5

23.

x	f(x)
0	−3
2	−2
4	−1
6	0

24.

x	f(x)
1	17
3	14
5	11
7	8

25. (MP) **Critique Reasoning** Wendy is given the equation of a function as $f(x) = \frac{1}{2x} + 5$, and she suggests that this is a linear function with a slope of 2 and a y-intercept of 5. Is Wendy correct? Explain your answer.

26. **STEM** Etienne is studying the movement of a plastic puck on an air table. He records his data in the table shown.

    A. What does the value at 0 seconds represent if this linear function were to be graphed?

    B. What is the rate of change of this linear function?

    C. Write a rule $d(t)$ to model the data. What do d and t represent?

    D. What is $d(8)$? What does this value represent?

Time (s)	Distance traveled (cm)
0	1.0
1	2.5
2	4
3	5.5
4	7
5	8.5

27. Julio is graphing a linear function. He starts at the x-intercept and then uses the slope to locate additional points. His friend Estella tells him that he made a mistake, as he needed to start at the y-intercept to graph this function. Who is correct? Explain your reasoning.

28. Give an example of a real-world discrete linear function.

29. Give an example of a real-world continuous linear function.

30. The cost of providing water bottles at a high school football game is $35 for the rental of the coolers and $0.50 per bottle of water.

    A. What does $35 represent in the function for this situation?

    B. What does $0.50 represent in the function for this situation?

    C. Write a function for the amount C, in dollars, of providing b water bottles.

    D. What is an appropriate domain for the function?

    E. Graph the function over the appropriate domain.

31. The normal water level of a river is 12 feet above the base of a dam. Engineers are controlling the water level by letting more water through for a period of 24 hours. The water level drops at a rate of 1 inch every two hours.

    A. How would you use the quantities *12 feet* and *1 inch per 2 hours* when writing a rule for the function that gives the river's water level over the period of time that the water level is dropping?

    B. Write a linear function to model the height of the water. Define the variables you use.

    C. What is the domain of the function?

    D. What is the range of the function? Explain how you found it.

32. Aaron gets two quotes for the cost to add a cedar deck to his home. The two quotes are shown here. Aaron estimates that the job will take 18 hours to complete.

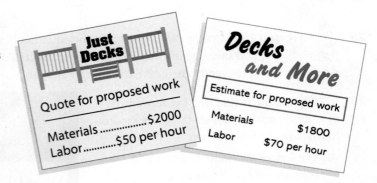

A. Write a function to represent the cost of each quote.

B. Based on these quotes, which company should Aaron use?

33. Daniel is cutting 800 feet of wood trim for a client. He begins the day with 200 feet of trim completed and completes an additional 250 feet of trim every three hours. Let $f(t)$ represent the amount of trim completed t hours after Daniel begins the day.

A. What is the initial value of the function f?

B. What is the rate of change of the function f?

C. Write the rule for $f(t)$.

34. (Open Middle™) Using the integers −9 to 9, at most one time each, create two linear functions f and g as well as an ordered pair that the functions have in common.

$$f(x) = \dfrac{\Box}{\Box}\, x + \Box \qquad g(x) = \dfrac{\Box}{\Box}\, x + \Box \qquad \text{Ordered pair shared by } f \text{ and } g: \left(\Box, \Box\right)$$

Spiral Review • Assessment Readiness

35. Which relations are functions? Select all that apply.

Ⓐ $x - y^2 = 39$ Ⓓ $2x - 3y = 4$

Ⓑ $y = 2x + 5$ Ⓔ $y = 5$

Ⓒ $y = x^2 - 5$ Ⓕ $x = 2$

36. What is the slope between the points $(3, 4)$ and $(8, 14)$?

Ⓐ $m = 2$ Ⓒ $m = \dfrac{1}{2}$

Ⓑ $m = \dfrac{4}{3}$ Ⓓ $m = 0$

37. Let $f(x) = 4x - 4$. Match each x-value in the domain of f to its corresponding y-value in the range.

A. $x = 0$ **1.** $y = 396$

B. $x = 1$ **2.** $y = -4$

C. $x = 100$ **3.** $y = 0$

D. $x = -100$ **4.** $y = -404$

I'm in a Learning Mindset!

What strategies do I use to find the slope and y-intercept of the graph of a linear function? How do I know when I have succeeded?

Characteristics of Linear Functions

(I Can) **identify the characteristics of linear functions.**

Spark Your Learning

A high-speed train offers service with limited stops between Boston, MA, and Washington, D.C. One of the stops along the way is Penn Station in New York City.

A passenger arrives at Penn Station at 10:00 a.m. worried that they missed the train.

Complete Part A as a whole class. Then complete Parts B–D in small groups.

- **A.** What is a mathematical question you can ask about this situation? What information would you need to know to answer your question?

- **B.** What variable(s) are needed in this situation?

- **C.** To answer your question, what strategy and tool would you use along with all the information you have? What answer do you get?

- **D.** Does your answer make sense in the context of the situation? How do you know?

Turn and Talk Predict how your answer would change for each of the following changes in the situation:

- The number of stops between Boston and New York City decreases.
- The train leaves Boston at 6:45 a.m.

©Robert Quinlan/Alamy

Build Understanding

Identify Increasing and Decreasing Functions

A function is **increasing** on an interval if the output of the function increases (or stays the same) as the input increases. For an increasing function, $f(b) \geq f(a)$ for any a and b in the interval such that $b > a$.

A function is **decreasing** on an interval if the output of the function decreases (or stays the same) as the input increases. For a decreasing function, $f(b) \leq f(a)$ for any a and b in the interval such that $b > a$.

Increasing Function

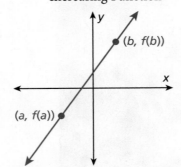

Decreasing Function

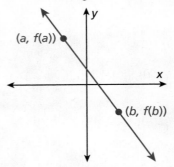

1 You can determine if a function is increasing or decreasing by analyzing the input and output values.

Consider what happens when you increase the input x of a linear function by 1 unit.

$f(x) = mx + b$	Given equation
$f(x + 1) = m(x + 1) + b$	Substitute x with $x + 1$ in the function rule.
$f(x + 1) = mx + m + b$	Apply the Distributive Property.
$f(x + 1) = mx + b + m$	Apply the Commutative Property of Addition.
$f(x + 1) = f(x) + m$	Substitute $f(x)$ for $mx + b$.

A. What does the parameter m represent?

B. What must be true for the value of m if the function is to increase as you move from $f(x)$ to $f(x + 1)$?

C. What must be true for the value of m if the function is to decrease as you move from $f(x)$ to $f(x + 1)$?

D. Give an example of an increasing function and an example of a decreasing function. Explain your reasoning.

Turn and Talk If a linear function is increasing over one interval, is it increasing over its entire domain? Explain your reasoning.

Determine End Behavior

The **end behavior** of a function f describes the trend in the output values $f(x)$ as the input values x either increase without bound (approach positive infinity) or decrease without bound (approach negative infinity). The notation $x \to +\infty$ is read "x approaches positive infinity," and the notation $x \to -\infty$ is read "x approaches negative infinity." As x approaches positive or negative infinity, $f(x)$ can approach positive infinity (written $f(x) \to +\infty$), $f(x)$ can approach negative infinity (written $f(x) \to -\infty$), or $f(x)$ can approach a constant value c (written $f(x) \to c$).

 2 Consider the function $f(x) = \frac{1}{2}x - 3$.

A. Identify the domain of f. Is there a largest value in the domain? Explain your reasoning.

B. If the graph were extended to the left, what would the graph look like? How would the outputs be changing?

C. What is the end behavior as $x \to -\infty$?

D. If the graph were extended to the right, what would the graph look like? How would the outputs be changing?

E. What is the end behavior as $x \to +\infty$?

F. How would the end behavior change if the function were defined as $f(x) = -\frac{1}{2}x - 3$ instead? Explain your reasoning.

 Turn and Talk What are the possible end behaviors of $f(x) = mx + b$? Explain your reasoning.

Identify Zeros

A **zero** of a function f is any value of x such that $f(x) = 0$.

 3 The graph and table represent the linear functions f and g, respectively.

A. How can you find the zero of f? What is the zero?

B. How can you find the zero of g? What is the zero?

C. Which function has the greater zero?

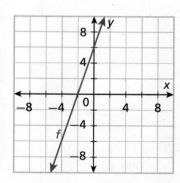

x	−2	2	6	10	14
g(x)	9	6	3	0	−3

 Turn and Talk Does a linear function always have a zero? Explain your reasoning.

Step It Out

Determine Extreme Values

The **minimum** of a function is the *y*-value of the lowest point on the graph of the function. Similarly, the **maximum** of a function is the *y*-value of the highest point on the graph of the function.

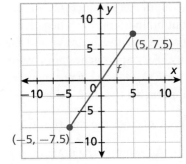

4 Consider the functions *f* and *g*. For each function, find the domain, range, maximum, and minimum.

The domain of *f* is $-5 \leq x \leq 5$.

A. What are the endpoints of the graph of *f*?

The range of *f* is $-7.5 \leq y \leq 7.5$.

The maximum of *f* is 7.5.

The minimum of *f* is -7.5.

B. Does the graph of *g* have endpoints?

The domain of *g* is all real numbers.

The range of *g* is all real numbers.

g has no maximum or minimum.

C. Why doesn't *g* have a maximum or minimum?

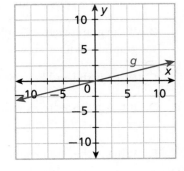

 Turn and Talk Is it possible for a linear function to not have a maximum nor a minimum on a finite interval? Explain your reasoning.

5 Tasha is filling a car with gasoline. The volume of gas in the tank increases steadily until the pump stops when the tank is full, as shown in the graph. Identify the minimum and maximum of the function given by the graph, and tell what the minimum and maximum represent.

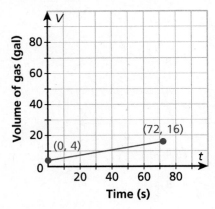

The minimum is 4, which is the number of gallons of gas in the tank before Tasha begins filling it. The maximum is 16, which is the number of gallons of gas the tank can hold.

A. What does the *t*-coordinate 72 of the graph's right endpoint represent?

B. What would happen in this context if the domain were extended beyond 72 seconds?

Identify Characteristics of Linear Functions

6 Match the given linear functions to the corresponding characteristics so that each function is paired with only one characteristic.

Function	Characteristic
A. $f(x) = -2x + 4$	**1.** y-intercept of 5; $f(x) \to -\infty$ as $x \to +\infty$
B. $f(x) = x - 2$	**2.** y-intercept of 5; $f(x) \to +\infty$ as $x \to +\infty$
C. $f(x) = 3x + 5$	**3.** Decreasing; 2 is a zero
D. $f(x) = -3x - 12$	**4.** Increasing; 2 is a zero
E. $f(x) = -x + 5$	**5.** Decreasing; −4 is a zero

Turn and Talk Describe the characteristics of the function $f(x) = ax - 2$ in each of the following cases.

- $a = 0$
- $a < 0$
- $a > 0$

7 A hybrid poplar tree was planted at a tree farm. The tree grew for 10 weeks at the farm and then was sold and transplanted to a customer's lawn. The graph shows the tree's height $h(t)$ as a function of time t while it was at the farm. Tell whether the function is increasing or decreasing. Then identify the function's domain, range, minimum, and maximum.

The function is increasing.

The domain is $0 \le t \le 10$. The range is $40 \le h(t) \le 55$.

The function's minimum is 40, and its maximum is 55.

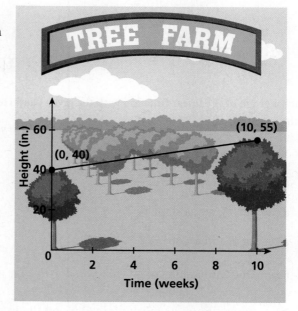

A. What do the minimum and maximum values represent in this situation?

B. Does the function have any zeros? Explain.

Turn and Talk How much did the tree grow while it was on the farm? Explain.

Check Understanding

1. For which two functions does $f(x) \to +\infty$ as $x \to +\infty$? Explain your reasoning.

$$f(x) = \frac{1}{4}x + 3 \qquad g(x) = -\frac{3}{5}x - 8 \qquad h(x) = 2x - 1$$

Determine whether each function is increasing or decreasing on the interval of $2 \le x \le 5$. Justify your answer.

2. $f(x) = x + 4$

3. $g(x) = -\frac{2}{3}x - 2$

4. Give an example of a linear function that has a minimum value but no maximum value. Specify the domain and whether the function is increasing or decreasing.

5. How can you find a zero of a linear function from an equation, graph, or table?

On Your Own

Graph each function and describe the end behavior.

6. $f(x) = -5x + 1$

7. $g(x) = 3x + 4$

Determine whether each linear function is increasing or decreasing. Explain your reasoning.

8.

x	0	$\frac{1}{3}$	$\frac{2}{3}$	1
f(x)	4	3	2	1

9.

x	5	6	8	12
g(x)	80	96	128	192

Sketch a graph of the linear function with the given characteristics. Then write an equation for the function.

10. a zero at 2, and a slope of -2

11. a zero at 5, and a slope of -1

12. a zero at -3, and a slope of 3

13. a zero at 1, and a slope of 1

14. a zero at 0, and a slope of $\frac{5}{4}$

Identify any maximum or minimum values on the interval $-2 \le x \le 3$.

15. $f(x) = 5x - 2$

16. $f(x) = -2x - 4$

17. $f(x) = -5$

18. $f(x) = \frac{3}{2}x + 1$

19. $f(x) = \frac{2}{3}x - 6$

20. $f(x) = \frac{1}{2}$

21. $f(x) = -x + 3$

22. $f(x) = 20 - 3x$

Determine the zeros of each linear function.

23. $f(x) = 5x - 1$

24. $g(x) = 4x - 2$

25.

x	h(x)
−4	12
−2	8
0	4
2	0

26.

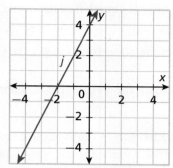

27. Why would a linear function describing an investment made at a bank have a minimum value but no maximum value? Explain.

Identify the zero, y-intercept, maximum, and minimum of each function from its graph.

28.

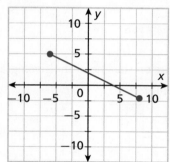

29.

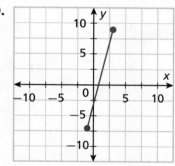

When a toy car is allowed to move along a lab table, it moves according to the linear function given by the following graph. Use the graph for problems 30–33.

30. State the domain and range of this linear function.

31. What is the y-intercept? What does it represent in this context?

32. What is the slope? What are its units, and what does the slope represent in this context?

33. Identify the maximum and minimum values. What do they represent in this context?

34. Open Ended Elizabeth stated that the function $f(x) = 0$ has no x-intercept, because it does not change in y-values from positive to negative or from negative to positive. Lucy argues that this linear function has an infinite number of x-intercepts because the function $f(x) = 0$ is the equation of the x-axis.

   A. Who is correct? Explain.

   B. What characteristics does the linear function $g(x) = 4$ share with the linear function $f(x) = 0$?

   C. What can you conclude about the zeros of the function $f(x) = c$, where c is a constant?

35. (Open Middle™) Using the integers -9 to 9, at most one time each, fill in the boxes to make two separate true statements: one where the line has a positive slope and one where the line has a negative slope.

$$\boxed{}\,x + \boxed{}\,y = \boxed{}$$

$$x\text{-int.} = \boxed{}, \; y\text{-int.} = \boxed{}, \; \text{point on the line} = \left(\boxed{}, \boxed{}\right)$$

Spiral Review • Assessment Readiness

36. Which of the following is an example of a function?

   Ⓐ $(3, 1), (1, 3), (2, 2), (2, 6)$

   Ⓑ $(1, 7), (2, 7), (3, 7), (5, 7)$

   Ⓒ $(6, 1), (6, 2), (6, 4), (6, 6)$

   Ⓓ $(1, 5), (2, 3), (4, 8), (2, 4)$

37. Which points are on the line of the given graph? Select all that apply.

   Ⓐ $(0, -2)$

   Ⓑ $(0, 2)$

   Ⓒ $(2, 0)$

   Ⓓ $(3, 1)$

   Ⓔ $(4, 1)$

   Ⓕ $(5, 3)$

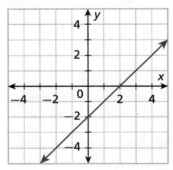

38. Match the form of an equation to an example of that form.

Form	Example
A. Point-slope form	**1.** $(y - 2) = \frac{1}{2}(x - 4)$
B. Standard form	**2.** $y = 3x - 1$
C. Slope-intercept form	**3.** $2x + 5y = 10$

 I'm in a Learning Mindset!

What strategies do I use to identify characteristics of linear functions? How do I know when I have succeeded?

Linear Models and Point-Slope Form

(I Can) use linear functions to model real-world scenarios.

Spark Your Learning

Ernie is using a pump to empty a pool for repair.

The pool had 20,000 gallons before the pump began to drain the pool.

Complete Part A as a whole class. Then complete Parts B–D in small groups.

A. What is a mathematical question you can ask about this situation? What information would you need to know to answer your question?

B. What variable(s) are needed in this situation? What must be true of the values for these variables in this question?

C. To answer your question, what strategy and tool would you use along with all the information you have? What answer do you get?

D. Does your answer make sense in the context of the situation? How do you know?

Turn and Talk Predict how your answer would change for each of the following changes in the situation:
- Two pumps are used instead of one.
- There are only 9000 gallons of water left to empty.
- The pump has been running for 2 hours instead of 1 hour.

©Tom Dowd/Dreamstime

Build Understanding

Interpret Linear Functions

 1 Mitchell uses an older digital camera that he got at a thrift store. Each picture takes 3 megabytes (MB) of space on a memory card. If S represents the amount of space left on the memory card and p represents the number of pictures taken, then the amount of space remaining on the card can be modeled by the function $S(p) = -3p + 498$.

Mitchell takes a few pictures and keeps track of the available space in a table. He then draws a line through the points to model the relationship.

Pictures taken	Available storage space (MB)
0	498
10	468
20	438
30	408

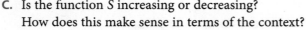

A. What does $S(0)$ represent in this context? How does this value appear in the table and on the graph?

B. What does the slope of -3 represent in this context? How does this appear in the table and on the graph?

C. Is the function S increasing or decreasing? How does this make sense in terms of the context?

D. What does a zero of the function represent in this context?

After clearing the memory, Mitchell changes the settings on the camera to obtain a higher resolution. Each high-resolution picture takes 8 MB of space. Consider a function S_h that models the relationship between the amount of storage space in megabytes and the number of high-resolution pictures taken.

E. What does the input and output of S_h represent? How does this compare to S?

F. How would the slope of the graph of S_h compare to the slope of the graph of S?

G. How would the intercepts of the graph of function S_h compare to the intercepts of the graph of function S?

H. Sketch a graph of function S_h, and write a rule for $S_h(p)$.

 Turn and Talk Is it possible to write an increasing linear function that describes the number of pictures taken in terms of the available storage space?

Step It Out

Model with Linear Functions

2 ▸ Jim has a long drive home from a conference. He notes that his odometer reads 1500 miles at the beginning of his journey. Jim reaches home after 4 hours of driving. How can you model the mileage on his odometer as a function of driving time? Graph the function, and identify any minimum or maximum values.

> Jim drives at an average speed of 50 mi/h.

Use a verbal model to write a function rule.

Mileage on odometer (mi)		Average speed (mi/h)		Driving time (h)		Starting mileage (mi)
$O(t)$	=	50	·	t	+	1500

$O(t) = 50t + 1500$

> **A.** Why does it make sense for $O(t)$ to be a linear function?

Graph the function.

Identify a point on the graph of the function O.

$O(0) = 50(0) + 1500 = 1500$

So, $(0, 1500)$ is on the graph of the function O.

> **B.** What does $O(0)$ represent?

Identify the slope of the function O.
The slope is 50.

> **C.** How does the slope help you sketch a graph?

> **D.** Is the function increasing or decreasing? How does that make sense in this context?

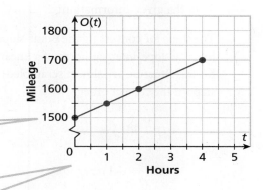

The domain of the function is limited to the hours of Jim's drive home. The minimum number of miles on his odometer occurs at the beginning of his trip, so the minimum value of the function O is 1500 miles. Since Jim reached home after 4 hours of driving, then $O(4) = 1700$ miles is a maximum value of $O(t)$.

> **E.** What do the domain and range of $O(t)$ represent in this context? How many miles did Jim drive for?

🐢 **Turn and Talk** If Jim drives at a slower average speed, how does that affect the function and its domain and range? Explain.

Module 4 • Lesson 4.4

121

You can use the *point-slope form* of a linear function when you know the rate of change and some function value.

Consider a line with slope m that contains the point (x_1, y_1) for some linear function f. The **point-slope form** of a linear equation is a direct consequence of the slope formula.

$$\frac{y - y_1}{x - x_1} = m \qquad \text{Slope formula.}$$

$$y - y_1 = m(x - x_1) \qquad \text{Multiply both sides by } (x - x_1).$$

$$f(x) - f(x_1) = m(x - x_1) \qquad \text{Substitute function notation.}$$

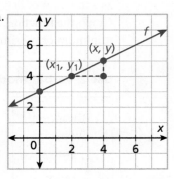

When the known point (x_1, y_1) is the y-intercept, $(0, b)$, point-slope form can be rewritten to obtain the slope-intercept form.

$y - y_1 = m(x - x_1)$ Point-slope form

$y - b = m(x - 0)$ Substitute.

$y - b = mx$ Simplify.

$y = mx + b$ Addition Property of Equality

3   A bald eagle is shown diving toward its prey. Its distance from the ground is decreasing at an average rate of 140 feet per second during the dive.

A. What is the rate of change in this context?

B. What point $\left(t_1, h(t_1)\right)$ can you determine from the given information?

C. The steps for converting the point-slope form into the slope-intercept form of a linear equation for this situation are shown scrambled. Write the steps in the correct order.

$$h(t) - h(t_1) = m\left(t - t_1\right)$$

$$h(t) = -140t + 160$$

$$h(t) - 62 = -140t + 98$$

$$h(t) - 62 = -140(t - 0.7)$$

D. What is the bald eagle's initial height?

Turn and Talk How would the function h change for each scenario?

- The bald eagle had a slower rate of change.
- The bald eagle was at a height of 80 ft after 0.7 s.
- The bald eagle was at 62 ft after 0.5 s.

4 Lakshmi adds the same amount of money to a savings account each week. After 8 weeks, a total of $576 had been saved. After 20 weeks, a total of $1140 had been saved. Use the information in the table to find the initial amount in the savings account.

Time t (weeks)	Savings S ($)
8	$576
20	$1140

A. Why draw a line through the two data points?

B. Estimate the initial amount from the sketch.

Identify the slope:

$$m = \frac{S(t_2) - S(t_1)}{t_2 - t_1} = \frac{S(20) - S(8)}{20 - 8} = \frac{1140 - 576}{20 - 8} = 47$$

C. What are the units of the slope? How does this relate to the rate of change?

Substitute into point-slope form and rewrite in slope-intercept form:

$S(t) - S(t_1) = m(t - t_1)$ Point-slope form

$S(t) - 576 = 47(t - 8)$ Substitute.

$S(t) - 576 = 47t - 376$

D. What justifies this step?

$S(t) = 47t + 200$ Addition Property of Equality

E. The initial amount occurs for what value of t?

So, the initial amount in the savings account was $200.

 Turn and Talk How would your answer change if you substituted $\left(t_2, S(t_2)\right)$ into the equation for point-slope form instead? Explain your reasoning.

Check Understanding

1. Racetracks often charge an annual membership fee and an entry fee per race. One racer paid a total of $76 after 3 races. Another racer paid a total of $124 after 7 races.

   A. Sketch a graph that models the situation. Explain why it is okay to draw a line and what it represents even though this is a discrete function.

   B. What are the domain and the range of the function? Explain your reasoning.

   C. Determine the slope of the function. What does this represent in the situation?

   D. Determine the initial value. What does this represent in this situation?

   E. Write a linear function that models the situation.

On Your Own

2. A rental car company has a special deal on one of the available rentals. Let C be the cost, in dollars, of the rental car as a function of the distance d, in miles, it is driven in one day.

   A. What would the value $C(75)$ represent in this context?

   B. Is function C increasing or decreasing? What are the units of the slope in this situation?

   C. Identify any maximum or minimum values of the function. What do they represent in this situation? State any assumptions that you make.

   D. Would the graph of C have any intercepts? What would they represent in this situation?

   E. Write a rule for $C(d)$, and sketch a graph of the function.

3. A chef needs 5 tablespoons of paprika for a recipe but has only a teaspoon available for measuring. It is known that 3 teaspoons can fill exactly 1 tablespoon.

   A. Create a table that shows the relationship between the number of tablespoons still needed, T, and the number of teaspoons already used, t.

   B. Sketch a graph of T as a function of t from your table.

   C. Identify any intercepts of your graph. What do they represent in this situation?

   D. Is the function T increasing or decreasing? How does that make sense in this situation?

   E. Write a rule for $T(t)$. What does the value $T(10)$ represent in this situation?

4. A container has a mass of 200 grams when it is empty. Each item that is placed in the container has a mass of 5 grams.

   A. Write the mass m of the container as a function of the number n of items added to it.

   B. Sketch a graph of the function.

   C. Determine any intercepts of the graph. What do they represent in this situation?

   D. Determine the value of the slope of the graph. What are the units in this situation?

5. The cost C, in dollars, to construct a concrete sidewalk is based on the length ℓ, in meters.

A. Write a linear function to represent the cost to construct a concrete sidewalk given that the cost of a 300 m sidewalk was found to be a total of $4500.

B. Identify and interpret the C-intercept of the cost function.

C. Does the function have any maximum or minimum values? Explain your reasoning.

D. What is the end behavior of the function? Explain your reasoning.

6. The cost of a taxi ride is determined by the distance traveled as shown in the graph.

A. Find and interpret the C-intercept.

B. Find and interpret the slope.

C. Write a linear function $C(d)$ that models this situation.

D. Define a reasonable domain for the function. Explain your reasoning.

E. What does the value $C(15)$ represent in this situation?

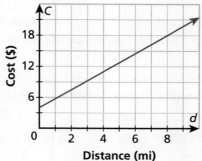

7. The graph shows the altitude of an airplane as it descends to land at an airport.

A. Write a function that models this situation.

B. Is the function increasing or decreasing?

C. What are the domain and range?

D. Find and interpret the A-intercept.

E. Find and interpret the slope.

F. What does the value $A(30)$ represent in this situation?

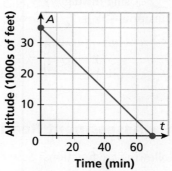

Use the point-slope form of a linear equation to write an equation of the line.

8. $m = 4$ through $(3, -2)$

9. $m = \frac{1}{3}$ through $(0, 2)$

10. $m = -5$ through $(-3, -4)$

11. $m = 2$ through $(-5, 2)$

12. $m = -\frac{3}{4}$ through $(5, 0)$

13. $m = 0$ through $(-1, 6)$

14. through $(4, -2)$ and $(5, -3)$

15. through $(6, 4)$ and $(9, 11)$

16. through $(-2, 0)$ and $(-1, 4)$

17. through $(3, 2)$ and $(4, 2)$

18. Open Ended Think about a real-world situation where the rate of change of one variable with respect to another is constant or almost constant. You may want to do some research online. Identify the variables in the situation and their units of measure. Create a linear function to model the situation, graph the function, and describe its characteristics.

19. **STEM** The temperature T, in degrees Celsius, of a layer of water in the ocean is measured between a depth, d, of 15 meters and 45 meters. The water has a temperature of 13 °C at the top of the layer and decreases at an average rate of 1 °C for every 10 meters of additional depth.

   A. Create a table that gives two input-output pairs of the function $T(d)$.

   B. Identify the slope, and explain how the units make sense in this situation.

   C. Write the rule for $T(d)$.

   D. What does the value $T(45)$ represent in this situation?

13 °C	-----	15 m
−1 °C		+10 m
12 °C	-----	25 m
−1 °C		+10 m
11 °C	-----	35 m
−1 °C		+10 m
10 °C	-----	45 m

20. A grain cart filled with corn is unloaded at a rate of 15 bushels per second. After one minute, 300 bushels of corn still remain in the grain cart.

   A. Write a linear function to model the amount of corn in the grain cart while it is being unloaded. Define each variable.

   B. Sketch a graph of the function.

   C. Identify and interpret the intercepts of the graph in this context.

21. **(Open Middle™)** Using the digits −9 to 9, at most one time each, fill in the boxes to rewrite the equation $-3x + 2y = 5$ from standard form to point-slope form.

   $$\left(y - \boxed{}\right) = \frac{\boxed{}}{\boxed{}}\left(x - \boxed{}\right)$$

Spiral Review • Assessment Readiness

22. Which of the following are functions? Select all that apply.

   Ⓐ $y = 2x - 4$ Ⓓ $f(x) = 3x^4 + 5x$

   Ⓑ $x = y^2$ Ⓔ $y = 4 \pm x$

   Ⓒ $2x - 6y = 11$ Ⓕ $x = 4$

23. The graph of a linear function f has a y-intercept of 3 and an x-intercept of 2. Which is a rule for $f(x)$?

   Ⓐ $f(x) = -\frac{2}{3}x + 3$ Ⓒ $f(x) = -\frac{3}{2}x + 3$

   Ⓑ $f(x) = -\frac{3}{2}x + 2$ Ⓓ $f(x) = -\frac{2}{3}x + 2$

24. What is the maximum value for the linear function $f(x) = 2x + 1$ in the domain $0 \leq x \leq 3$.

   Ⓐ 1   Ⓒ 6

   Ⓑ 3   Ⓓ 7

25. Which formula can be used to find slope? Select all that apply.

   Ⓐ $m = \frac{y_2 - y_1}{x_2 - x_1}$ Ⓓ $m = \frac{x_2 - x_1}{y_2 - y_1}$

   Ⓑ $m = \frac{\text{rise}}{\text{run}}$ Ⓔ $m = \frac{x}{y}$

   Ⓒ $m = \frac{y}{x}$ Ⓕ $m = \frac{\text{run}}{\text{rise}}$

 I'm in a Learning Mindset!

What strategies do I use to persevere through modeling with linear functions?
How do I know when I have succeeded?

Review

Relations and Functions

A relation is a function if there is exactly 1 output for every input of the domain. One way to test this is by graphing the relation and using the vertical line test.

Function

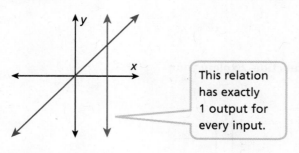

This relation has exactly 1 output for every input.

Not a Function

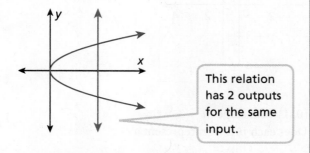

This relation has 2 outputs for the same input.

Characteristics of Linear Functions

Vanessa is a captain, and she models the distance her ship travels away from port with a graph.

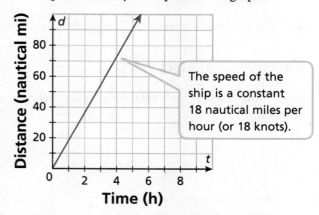

The speed of the ship is a constant 18 nautical miles per hour (or 18 knots).

She begins her graph at the point $(0, 0)$ because she knows that at the start of her trip, when $t = 0$, the ship has traveled $d = 0$ nautical miles.

Her graph is a straight line because the ship is traveling at a constant speed.

Slope-Intercept Form

Vanessa wants to write an equation to model her journey so that she can predict how far she is from port at any given point in time.

She starts with a y-intercept of 0, and she keeps a steady speed of 18 knots away from port.

The slope represents her rate of change.

The y-intercept represents her starting distance.

$$y = mx + b$$
$$d = 18t + 0$$
$$d = 18t$$

Vanessa uses the slope-intercept form because she knows these two pieces of information.

Point-Slope Form

At 2:00, Vanessa changes her course and speed to return to port. She must rewrite her equation to reflect the new situation.

She notes that at 2:15 she is 50 nautical miles from port with a speed of 30 knots.

$$y - y_1 = m(x - x_1)$$
$$d - 50 = -30\left(t - \frac{1}{4}\right)$$

She measures her time from 2:00 as $\frac{1}{4}$ of an hour.

Her rate of change is -30 because she is returning to port.

Vocabulary

Choose the correct term from the box to complete each sentence.

1. A ___?___ is a relation that has exactly one element in its ___?___ for every value in its ___?___.

2. Another name for the x-intercept of the graph of a function is a ___?___ of the function.

3. The equation $y - y_1 = m(x - x_1)$ is called the ___?___ of a linear function.

4. The equation $y = mx + b$ is called the ___?___ of a linear function.

Concepts and Skills

Determine whether each relation graphed below is a function. Explain your reasoning.

5.
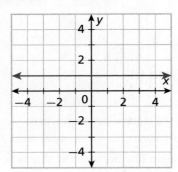

6.
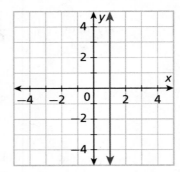

7. Given that the graph of f passes through the point $(0, 1)$ with slope $m = 3$, write $f(x)$ in slope-intercept form and point-slope form. Does each function represent a different line? Explain your reasoning.

8. How many zeros does a linear function have? Explain your reasoning.

9. The slope of the graph of a linear function is -2, and it has a zero at $x = 3$. Write the slope-intercept form of the function.

Write a linear function in point-slope form for each slope and point given.

10. slope of 0.5 through point $(5, 4)$

11. slope of $-\frac{4}{3}$ through point $(0, 3)$

12. **(MP) Use Tools** After opening an account with $20, Enrico puts in an additional $25 per week so that he can save up to visit a friend.

   A. Write a function to model the savings in the account for a given time. Be sure to define your variables.

   B. How much will be saved after eight weeks? State what strategy and tool you will use to answer the question, explain your choice, and then find the answer.

Relationships Among Linear Functions

Module Performance Task: *Spies and Analysts*™

Hot Dog Competition

How can you figure out how many hot dogs each person would eat in the *n*th round? At what round would Lucy eat 13 hot dogs?

SCORE

ROUND	LUCY	DAN
1	1	2
2	3	4
3	5	6

Are You Ready?

Complete these problems to review prior concepts and skills you will need for this module.

Represent Equations with Tables and Graphs

For each equation, create a table with 3 points and then graph the equation.

1. $y = x - 2$

2. $y = -\dfrac{5}{2}x$

Compare Proportional Relationships

For each pair of models, state which model represents the lesser unit rate.

3. $y = 3x$

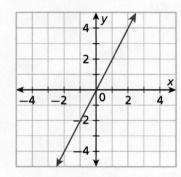

4. $y = 1.5x$

x	y
3	5
6	10
9	15
12	20

Translate Figures in the Coordinate Plane

Identify the coordinates of $\triangle ABC$ under each translation.

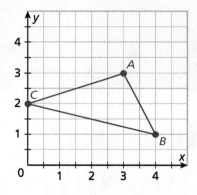

5. 2 units down

6. 3 units to the right and 4 units down

7. 2 units to the left and 1 unit up

Connecting Past and Present Learning

Previously, you learned:

- to transform figures on the coordinate plane,
- to build linear functions to model real-world problems, and
- to write and compare unit rates in context.

In this module, you will learn:

- to transform graphs of linear functions,
- to compare linear functions represented in different representations, and
- to write and confirm linear inverse functions.

Transform Graphs of Functions

(I Can) determine how transformations to functions affect their graphs.

Spark Your Learning

Parker is designing wallpaper borders.

This design uses transformations of various shapes.

Complete Part A as a whole class. Then complete Parts B–D in small groups.

A. What is a mathematical question you can ask about this situation? What information would you need to know to answer your question?

B. Describe the shapes that you see in the design.

C. To answer your question, what strategy and tool would you use along with all the information you have? What answer do you get?

D. Does your answer make sense? How do you know?

Turn and Talk What is the smallest portion of the design that Parker could draw to form the border pattern using only translation? to form the pattern using only reflection? Explain.

Build Understanding

Transformations That Affect the Range of a Function

Given the graph of a function f and a nonzero constant k, you can create a new function g by adding k to $f(x)$ or by multiplying $f(x)$ by k. In both cases, g and f pair the same domain values to different range values. The graph of g is a transformation of the graph of f.

1 ▶ The graph of f is the semicircle shown in blue. Note that the semicircle is centered at the origin, has endpoints at $(-2, 0)$ and $(2, 0)$, and passes through the point $(0, 2)$. The mapping diagram shows $g(x) = f(x) + 2$, and the graph of g is red.

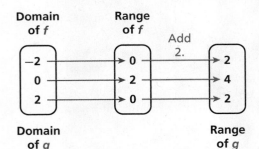

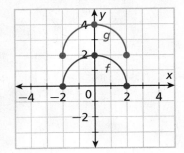

A. Describe how the graph of f is transformed to obtain the graph of g.

B. Now let $g(x) = f(x) - 2$. How is the graph of f transformed to obtain the graph of g?

2 ▶ The graph of f is the same semicircle shown in Task 1. The mapping diagram shows $g(x) = 2f(x)$, and the graph of g is red.

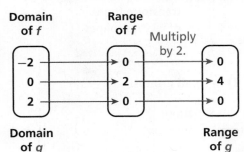

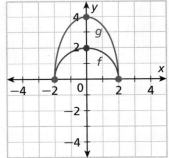

A. Describe how the graph of f is transformed to obtain the graph of g.

B. Now let $g(x) = -2f(x)$. How is the graph of f transformed to obtain the graph of g?

C. Finally, let $g(x) = \frac{1}{2}f(x)$. How is the graph of f transformed to obtain the graph of g?

Turn and Talk For any function f, describe how the graph of f is transformed to obtain the graphs of $g(x) = f(x) + k$ and $g(x) = k \cdot f(x)$ for a nonzero constant k.

Transformations That Affect the Domain of a Function

When you create a new function g by adding a nonzero constant k to x in $f(x)$ or by multiplying x in $f(x)$ by k, g pairs different domain values than f does to the same range values. The graph of g is a transformation of the graph of f.

3 The graph of f is the same semicircle shown in Task 1. The mapping diagram shows $g(x) = f(x + 2)$, and the graph of g is red. Note that in the mapping diagram, you have to work backwards from the domain of f to obtain the domain of g.

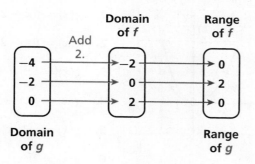 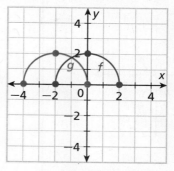

A. Describe how the graph of f is transformed to obtain the graph of g.

B. Now let $g(x) = f(x - 2)$. How is the graph of f transformed to obtain the graph of g?

> **Turn and Talk** For any function f, describe how the graph of f is transformed to obtain the graph of $g(x) = f(x + k)$ for a nonzero constant k.

4 The graph of f is the same semicircle shown in Task 1. The mapping diagram shows $g(x) = f(2x)$, and the graph of g is red. Note that in the mapping diagram, you have to work backwards from the domain of f to obtain the domain of g.

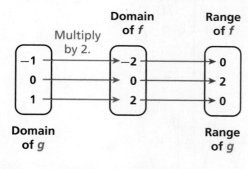 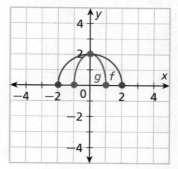

A. Describe how the graph of f is transformed to obtain the graph of g.

B. Now let $g(x) = f(-2x)$. How is the graph of f transformed to obtain the graph of g?

C. Finally, let $g(x) = f\left(\frac{1}{2}x\right)$. How is the graph of f transformed to obtain the graph of g?

> **Turn and Talk** For any function f, describe how the graph of f is transformed to obtain the graph of $g(x) = f(kx)$ for a nonzero constant k.

Step It Out

Identify Transformations

5 Compare the graphs in each coordinate plane. The original function *f* is graphed in blue. The red graph of *g* is the result of a transformation of the original function. Match each equation relating *g* to *f* with the corresponding pair of graphs.

A.
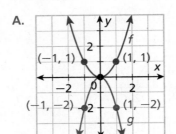

B.
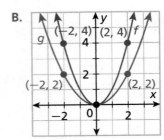

1. $g(x) = f(x + 2)$

2. $g(x) = f(x - 2)$

3. $g(x) = f(x) + 2$

4. $g(x) = f(x) - 2$

5. $g(x) = -2f(x)$

6. $g(x) = 2f(x)$

7. $g(x) = -\frac{1}{2}f(x)$

8. $g(x) = \frac{1}{2}f(x).$

C.
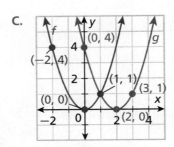

D.
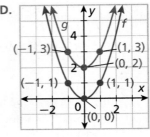

E.
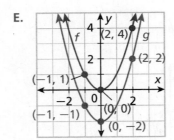

F.
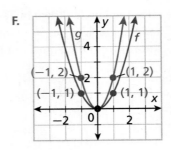

G.
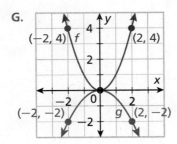

H.
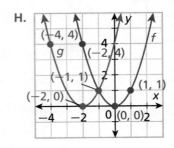

 Turn and Talk Which transformations change the shape of the graph? Which transformations change the location but not the shape of the graph?

Check Understanding

Describe how the graph of *f* is transformed to obtain the graph of *g*.

1.

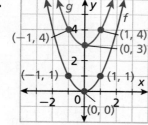

2.

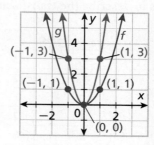

3. How is the graph of $g(x) = f(x + 5)$ related to the graph of *f*?

4. How is the graph of $g(x) = \frac{1}{3}f(x)$ related to the graph of *f*?

On Your Own

Describe how the graph of *f* is transformed to obtain the graph of *g*.

5.

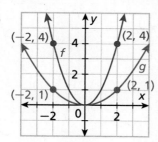

6.

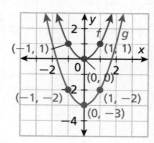

7. How is the graph of $g(x) = f(x - 5)$ related to the graph of *f*?

8. How is the graph of $g(x) = -\frac{1}{4}f(x)$ related to the graph of *f*?

9. How is the graph of $g(x) = f(x) + 7$ related to the graph of *f*?

10. How is the graph of $g(x) = f(x + 8)$ related to the graph of *f*?

11. How is the graph of $g(x) = 5f(x)$ related to the graph of *f*?

12. How is the graph of $g(x) = f(x) - 6$ related to the graph of *f*?

Tell whether *g* pairs different domain values than *f* does to the same range values, or whether *g* and *f* pair the same domain values to different range values.

13. $g(x) = 4 \cdot f(x)$

14. $g(x) = f(x + 9)$

15. $g(x) = f(3x)$

16. $g(x) = f(x) - 7$

17. (MP) **Use Structure** Describe how you can change the shape of a function's graph by altering the function's rule.

18. (MP) **Use Structure** Describe how you can change the location but not the shape of a function's graph by altering the function's rule.

19. How can you alter a function's rule to reflect its graph across the x-axis without changing the shape of the graph?

Use the tables of values to describe the transformation of the graph of f to obtain the graph of g.

20.

$f(x)$	
−2	16
−1	4
0	0
1	4
2	16

$g(x)$	
−2	48
−1	12
0	0
1	12
2	48

21.

$f(x)$	
−2	16
−1	4
0	0
1	4
2	16

$g(x)$	
−2	20
−1	8
0	0
1	8
2	20

22.

$f(x)$	
−2	16
−1	4
0	0
1	4
2	16

$g(x)$	
−5	16
−4	4
−3	0
−2	4
−1	16

23.

$f(x)$	
−2	16
−1	4
0	0
1	4
2	16

$g(x)$	
−2	−4
−1	−1
0	0
1	−1
2	−4

Describe the indicated transformation of the graph of f to obtain the graph of g.

24. $g(x) = 2f(x)$

25. $g(x) = f(x - 3)$

26. $g(x) = f(x) + 1$

27. $g(x) = -3f(x)$

28. $g(x) = f(x + 5)$

29. $g(x) = f(x) - 5$

30. The graph of g is a transformation of the graph of f such that $g(x) = 2.5f(x)$. Give the coordinates of the point where the graph of g crosses the y-axis.

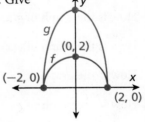

31. (MP) **Use Repeated Reasoning** Free-standing towers often require cables to help stabilize them. These tensioned cables are called *guy wires*. A meteorological (MET) tower is used to collect wind data for an area that is being considered for a wind farm. Identify transformations that you see in the diagram of a MET tower shown.

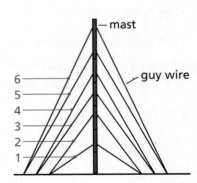

32. (MP) **Use Structure** Roger designs a pattern of V-shapes to make a logo for his new business. What transformations of a V-shape can he use to create the logo shown?

33. (MP) **Attend to Precision** Karen says she can draw a quarter circle and then alter the rule for the function to make a half-circle when combined with the original shape. Is she correct? Explain.

34. Explain why the graph of $g(x) = f(x + 1)$ is a translation of the graph of f to the left 1 unit rather than to the right 1 unit.

35. Copy and complete the table of values for $f(x) = x^2$ and the functions $g(x) = -f(x)$ and $h(x) = f(-x)$. Describe the graphs of g and h.

f(x)	
x	**y**
−2	4
−1	1
0	0
1	1
2	4

g(x) = −f(x)	
x	**y**
−2	?
−1	?
0	?
1	?
2	?

h(x) = f(−x)	
x	**y**
−2	?
−1	?
0	?
1	?
2	?

36. The graph of a function f is shown. The graph is called a *triangle wave*.

A. Make a table of values for f using the points labeled.

B. Make a table of values for a function g such that $g(x) = f(x - 1.5)$.

C. Graph f and g on the same coordinate plane.

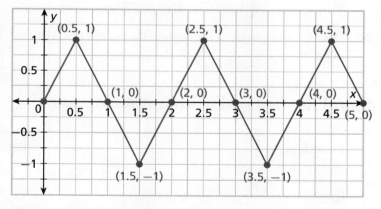

A function f is transformed as indicated to produce a new function g. Write g in terms of f.

37. The graph of f is translated down 2 units.

38. The graph of f is stretched vertically by a factor of 3.

39. The graph of f is translated left 3 units.

40. The graph of f is compressed horizontally by a factor of $\frac{1}{2}$ and translated up 3 units.

41. The graph of f is translated right 2 units and up 4 units.

42. The graph of f is compressed vertically by a factor of $\frac{1}{3}$ and translated up 1 unit.

43. The graph of f is stretched vertically by a factor of 8 and translated left 1 unit.

44. The graph of f is translated 3 units to the right and vertically stretched by a factor of 2 to obtain the graph of g. Use the table of values for f to determine the corresponding points on the graph of g. Copy and complete the table for g.

f		g	
x	**f(x)**	**x**	**g(x)**
2	1	?	?
4	4	?	?
6	3	?	?
8	−6	?	?

45. The graph of f is horizontally compressed by a factor of $\frac{1}{2}$, reflected about the x-axis, and translated down 1 unit to obtain the graph of g. Use the table of values for f to determine the corresponding points on the graph of g. Copy and complete the table for g.

f		g	
x	**f(x)**	**x**	**g(x)**
−4	−3	?	?
−2	1	?	?
0	−2	?	?
2	8	?	?

46. (MP) **Critique Reasoning** Keara and Tiana are applying transformations to the graph of $f(x) = x^2$ to obtain the graph of $g(x) = 2x^2 + 1$. Keara translates the graph of f up 1 unit first and then vertically stretches the graph by a factor of 2 to obtain the graph of g. Tiana vertically stretches the graph of f by a factor of 2 first and then translates the graph up 1 unit to obtain the graph of g. Do both Keara and Tiana obtain the correct graph of g? Explain your reasoning.

47. Describe a sequence of transformations of the graph of f that would map the point $(2, 6)$ on the graph of f to the point $(-1, -12)$ on the graph of g.

Spiral Review • Assessment Readiness

48. What is the y-intercept of the graph of the linear function?
$$y = 3x + 2$$

   (A) 3   (C) $\frac{1}{3}$

   (B) 2   (D) −2

49. What is the x-intercept of the graph of the linear function?
$$y = -3x + 6$$

   (A) 6   (C) −2

   (B) 2   (D) −6

50. Match the equation of the line with two points that lie on the line.

   A. $y = -3x + 1$ **1.** $(0, 5)\ (10, 5)$

   B. $y = 2x - 3$ **2.** $(2, 1)\ (3, 3)$

   C. $y = 5$ **3.** $(0, 1)\ (3, -8)$

I'm in a Learning Mindset!

What did I learn about transformations to the graphs of functions that I can use in my future learning?

Transform Linear Functions

(I Can) relate all linear functions to the linear parent function $f(x) = x$.

Spark Your Learning

The Get-Up-and-Go Company produces recreational vehicles (RVs).

This year, the company increased its monthly rate of production of RVs.

Complete Part A as a whole class. Then complete Parts B–D in small groups.

- **A.** What is a mathematical question you can ask about this situation? What information would you need to know to answer your question?

- **B.** What is unknown in this situation?

- **C.** To answer your question, what strategy and tool would you use along with all the information you have? What answer do you get?

- **D.** What should be true about the total production of last year and this year for any given month?

 Turn and Talk How might the graph of the production function for this year change if the company bought 10 RVs from another manufacturer that went out of business at the beginning of the year?

Build Understanding

Transform the Graph of a Parent Function

A **family of functions** is a group of functions that have basic characteristics in common. Graphs of functions in the same family are transformations of the graph of the *parent function*. The **parent function** is the most basic function with the defining characteristics of the family of functions.

The parent function of all linear functions is $f(x) = x$. Notice that $f(x) = x$ has the form $f(x) = mx + b$ when $m = 1$ and $b = 0$. So, the graph of the parent linear function has a slope of 1 and a y-intercept of 0.

1 Consider families of linear functions whose graphs are transformations of the graph of the parent linear function. When comparing transformed graphs to the graph of $f(x) = x$, observe the following three characteristics:

- **Direction** – Determine whether the graph is still rising, falling, or neither rising nor falling from left to right.
- **Steepness** – Determine whether the graph is more vertical, less vertical, or horizontal compared to the graph of $f(x) = x$.
- **y-intercept** – Determine whether the y-intercept has changed.

A. You can translate the graph of the parent linear function by adding to or subtracting from the range values. The graphs of g_1 and g_2 are translations of the graph of $f(x) = x$.

$$g_1(x) = f(x) + 2$$
$$g_2(x) = f(x) - 2$$

In general, how do the characteristics of the graph of $g(x) = f(x) + k$ compare with the characteristics of the graph of $f(x) = x$?

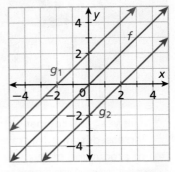

B. You can reflect the graph of the parent linear function across the x-axis by multiplying the range values by -1.

$$g(x) = -f(x)$$

How do the characteristics of the graph of $g(x) = -f(x)$ compare with the characteristics of the graph of $f(x) = x$?

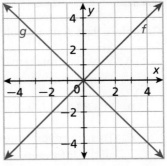

C. You can stretch or compress the graph of the parent linear function by multiplying the range values by a number.

$$g_1(x) = 2f(x)$$
$$g_2(x) = \frac{1}{2}f(x)$$

In general, how do the characteristics of the graph of $g(x) = kf(x)$ compare with the characteristics of the graph of $f(x) = x$?

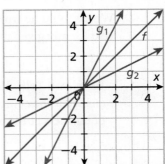

Combine Transformations

You can combine a vertical stretch or compression (which may or may not include a reflection across the *x*-axis) with a vertical translation. For instance, consider the graph of *g* shown.

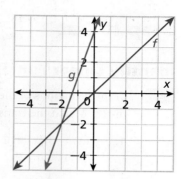

D. What vertical stretch or compression must be applied to the graph of *f* to obtain the correct slope for the graph of *g*? What vertical translation must be applied to the graph of *f* to obtain the correct *y*-intercept for the graph of *g*?

E. What is the rule for *g(x)* in terms of *f(x)*?

> **Turn and Talk** Consider the graph of the general linear function $g(x) = mx + b$. Interpret the graph as a sequence of transformations applied to the graph of $f(x) = x$.

Translate the Graph of the Parent Linear Function Horizontally

2 The graphs below show translations of the graph of the parent linear function.

Horizontal Translations

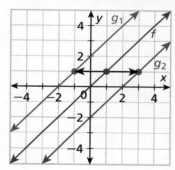

Vertical Translations

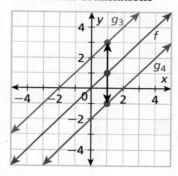

A. Do horizontal translations of the graph of *f* affect the domain of the function, the range of the function, or both? Explain.

B. The graph of $g(x) = f(x + k)$ is a horizontal translation of *k* units of the graph of $f(x) = x$. If $k > 0$, then the graph translates *k* units to the left. If $k < 0$, then the graph translates *k* units to the right. Use this information to write rules for $g_1(x)$ and $g_2(x)$ in terms of $f(x)$.

C. Write rules for $g_3(x)$ and $g_4(x)$ in terms of $f(x)$.

D. Given that $f(x) = x$, write the rules for $g_1(x)$, $g_2(x)$, $g_3(x)$, and $g_4(x)$ in terms of *x* instead of $f(x)$.

E. Why are the graphs of g_1 and g_3 identical? Why are the graphs of of g_2 and g_4 identical?

> **Turn and Talk** When the graph of $f(x) = x$ is translated 2 units to the left, what are the new *x*-intercept and *y*-intercept? What will be the new *x*-intercept of the graph that results after *f* is translated 5 units up?

Step It Out

Identify Linear Function Transformations

3 Transformations of the graph of the parent linear function $f(x) = x$ are shown in red. Match the transformation of the graph with its function.

1. $g_1(x) = 3f(x) + 2$

2. $g_2(x) = 2f(x) + 3$

3. $g_3(x) = \frac{1}{2}f(x) - 3$

4. $g_4(x) = f(x - 3)$

5. $g_5(x) = f(x) + 3$

6. $g_6(x) = -\frac{1}{2}f(x) + 3$

A.
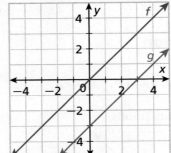

B.
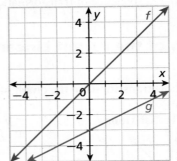

C.
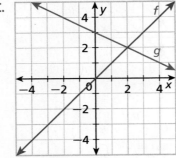

D.
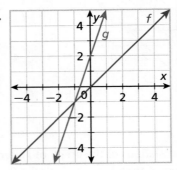

E.
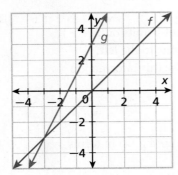

F.
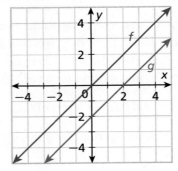

 Turn and Talk What strategies do you use to identify transformations of the graph of a linear function?

Transformations with Real-World Functions

4 ▶ Write and graph a function that models Marcie's cell phone cost plan.

Suppose Marcie's cell phone service provider decides to double the per-gigabyte charge for using data. Write a function that gives the new monthly cost in terms of the original function. Then describe how the graph of the new function is related to the graph of the original function.

Marcie pays $40 per month plus $10 per GB of data for her cell phone.

Write and graph a function for the original plan.

The total monthly cost $C(d)$ is a function of Marcie's monthly data usage d (in gigabytes).

Total monthly cost (dollars) $C(d)$		Data usage cost (dollars/GB) 10		Monthly data usage (GB) d		Monthly fee (dollars) 40
	$=$		$\cdot$		$+$	

The graph of $C(d) = 10d + 40$ is shown.

> **A.** What is the y-intercept of the graph? How do you know?

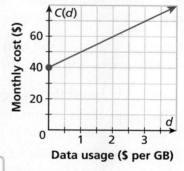

Monthly cost ($) vs. Data usage ($ per GB)

Write and graph a function for the new plan.

To write a function $C_1(d)$ for the new total monthly cost as a function of the original total monthly cost $C(d)$, first double the original function.

$$C_1(d) = 2C(d)$$

> **B.** How is the graph of C transformed?

However, multiplying $C(d)$ by 2 doubles both the per-gigabyte charge and the monthly fee.

To get the monthly fee back to $40, subtract 40 from $C_1(d)$:

$$C_1(d) = 2C(d) - 40$$

The graph of C_1 is the graph of C vertically stretch by a factor of 2 and translated down 40 units.

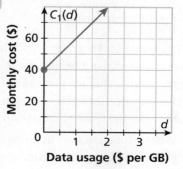

Monthly cost ($) vs. Data usage ($ per GB)

Turn and Talk Suppose the original plan changes so $C_2(d) = \frac{1}{2}C(d) + 20$ represents the new monthly cost as a function of the original plan. How did the plan change?

Check Understanding

1. What function is a vertical compression of $f(x) = x$? Explain.

   $g(x) = 2f(x) + 1$ $h(x) = -f(x) - \dfrac{4}{5}$ $j(x) = -\dfrac{1}{2}f(x)$

2. What function is a shift of $f(x) = x$? Explain.

   $g(x) = f(x) - 5$ $h(x) = -4f(x)$ $j(x) = 3f(x)$

3. In the function $g(x) = f(x) + k$, $f(x)$ is the parent linear function, and k is a constant added to the range values of the function. How is the graph of g related to the graph of f?

4. Tracy has plans to save $40 per week from the money she earns washing cars.

   A. Write a rule $S(w)$ for the total amount of money she saves after w weeks.

   B. Suppose Tracy decides to change her weekly savings to $\dfrac{3}{4}$ of her original weekly savings. Also, Tracy adds $50 from birthday gifts to her savings. Write a rule $S_1(w)$ for the new total amount of money she saves after w weeks in terms of $S(w)$.

   C. Explain how to transform the graph of S to create the graph of S_1.

On Your Own

5. Suppose a family of linear functions can be described by $p(x) = mx$. What is true about all of the graphs of the functions in the family?

6. Suppose $b_1(x) = a(x) - 5$ and $b_2(x) = a(x - 5)$ for $a(x) = x$. How are the graphs of b_1 and b_2 related? Explain.

7. Use the graph to answer the questions.

   A. Which graph shows a vertical translation of the graph of the parent linear function?

   B. Which graph shows a compression of the graph of the parent linear function?

   C. Which graph shows a stretch of the graph of the parent linear function?

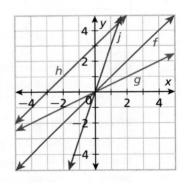

8. **(MP)** **Attend to Precision** Bubbly Car Wash offers three price plans as shown. Let f be the cost of x car washes per month with the no membership fee plan. Let g be the cost of x car washes per month with the Silver Membership, and let h be the cost of x car washes with the Gold Membership.

   A. Write a function for f in terms of x. Then write functions for g and h in terms of the function f.

   B. How can you transform the graph of f to create the graph of g?

   C. How can you transform the graph of f to create the graph of h?

   D. Zachary gets his car washed 4 times a month. Which plan should he choose? Why?

9. What transformation of the graph of the parent linear function gives the graph of g shown? What is a rule for $g(x)$ in terms of $f(x)$?

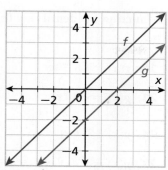

10. How is the graph of $f(x) = x$ transformed to obtain the graph of $g(x) = \frac{1}{4}f(x)$?

11. How is the graph of $f(x) = x$ transformed to obtain the graph of $g(x) = -f(x) + 7$?

12. How is the graph of $f(x) = x + 1$ transformed to obtain the graph of $g(x) = 3f(x)$?

In Problems 13–15, write a rule for $g(x)$ in terms of $f(x)$.

13. The graph $f(x) = 2x$ is translated up by 50 units to obtain the graph of g.

14. The graph $f(x) = x - 4$ is stretched by a factor of 2 and then translated down by 9 units to obtain the graph of g.

15. The graph $f(x) = 3x + 8$ is reflected in the y-axis and then compressed by a factor of $\frac{1}{2}$ to obtain the graph of g.

16. (MP) **Use Structure** Carlos builds a ramp for access to the community center. The graph of $g(x) = \frac{1}{16}x$ represents the slope of the ramp. The graph of a function f represents a ramp with the maximum possible slope allowed by the ADA. Is the graph of g a stretch or a compression of the graph of f? Is the ramp Carlos built ADA compliant?

The *Americans with Disabilities Act* (ADA) requires the slope of ramps to be no more than 1 foot in height for each 12 feet in distance.

Describe the graph of each linear function by identifying the transformation(s) of the parent linear functions $f(x) = x$.

17. $g(x) = f(x) + 5$

18. $g(x) = f(8 + x)$

19. $g(x) = 6f(x)$

20. $g(x) = \frac{1}{6}f(x)$

21. $g(x) = -3f(x)$

22. $g(x) = -\frac{1}{2}f(x)$

23. $g(x) = \frac{f(x)}{2}$

24. $g(x) = \frac{4}{3}f(x)$

25. $g(x) = 5 - 3f(x)$

26. $g(x) = 1 - f(x)$

27. $g(x) = 9 + f(x)$

28. $g(x) = f(x - 7)$

29. Jerry walks to the bus stop each morning from his home at a constant rate of 120 meters per minute. The bus stop is 1800 meters from his home.

  A. Write a function $f(t)$ that models Jerry's walk to the bus stop, where t is the time in minutes since Jerry left his home and $f(t)$ is the distance remaining to the bus stop.

  B. Suppose Jerry walks to a closer bus stop only 1000 meters from his home. Write a function $g(t)$ for the new distance remaining to the bus stop in terms of $f(t)$. How is graph of g related to the graph of f?

  C. Suppose Jerry walks at a constant rate of 80 meters per minute to the bus stop 1800 meters from his home. Write a function $h(t)$ for the new distance remaining to the bus stop in terms of $f(t)$. How is graph of h related to the graph of f?

30. The graph of the linear function $g(x)$ passes through $(-1, -3)$ and $(2, 0)$. How is the graph of g related to the graph of $f(x) = x$? Write a rule for $g(x)$ in terms of $f(x)$.

Spiral Review • Assessment Readiness

31. What is the y-intercept of the line $2y + 4x = 8$?

  (A) 2

  (C) 6

  (B) 4

  (D) 8

32. What is the equation of the line containing $(3, 4)$ and $(5, 14)$?

  (A) $y = -5x + 11$

  (C) $y = 3x - 11$

  (B) $y = 5x - 11$

  (D) $y = 5x - 14$

33. Which transformation of the graph of a linear function changes the direction of the graph?

  (A) shift

  (C) stretch

  (B) reflection

  (D) compression

34. What is the linear function given by the ordered pairs?

$$\left\{ (0, -1), (1, 3), (2, 7), (3, 11), (4, 15) \right\}$$

  (A) $y = 4x + 1$

  (C) $y = -x - 4$

  (B) $y = 4x - 1$

  (D) $y = x - 4$

 I'm in a Learning Mindset!

What strategies do I use to persevere to transform linear equations? How do I know when I have succeeded?

Keep Going to ► Journal and Practice Workbook

Compare Linear Functions

(I Can) compare functions given in different forms.

Spark Your Learning

Kyle and Emma watch the same movie, but on different devices.

As each device is used to watch the same movie, the battery charge is depleted at different rates for the two devices.

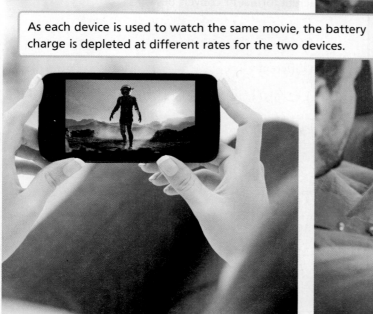

Complete Part A as a whole class. Then complete Parts B–D in small groups.

A. What is a mathematical question you can ask about this situation? What information would you need to know to answer your question?

B. What information do you have? Is the information you have presented in the same form?

C. To answer your question, what strategy and tool would you use along with all the information you have? What answer do you get?

D. Without recharging their devices, will Kyle and Emma finish the movie? Who will need to plug in first?

Turn and Talk The information about Emma's battery is a function rule. The information about Kyle's battery is a table. Would representing both functions as graphs be helpful? Explain.

Build Understanding

Examine Linear Functions in Different Forms

You can represent functions in various ways, including graphs, equations, tables, or sets of ordered pairs. As you solve problems in this lesson, think about what representation is most efficient for you to use to find the information you need.

When you compare multiple functions, to obtain the information you need, you may need to represent one or more of the functions in a different format or convert between representations.

1 Below are four linear functions, represented in different ways.

$$f(x) = 4x + 3$$

$$h = \left\{(0, -1), (2, 6), (4, 14), (6, 22), (8, 30), \ldots\right\}$$

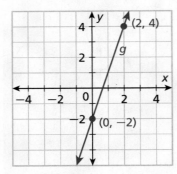

x	j(x)
0	1
1	6
2	11
3	16
4	21
⋮	⋮

Identify the rate of change of each function. Explain how you calculated the slope for each form.

A. Function represented by a rule: function f.

B. Function represented by a graph: function g.

C. Function represented by a set of ordered pairs: function h.

D. Function represented by a table: function j.

Identify each function value when $x = 0$. Explain how you calculated the function value for each form.

E. Function represented by a rule: function f.

F. Function represented by a graph: function g.

G. Function represented by a set of ordered pairs: function h.

H. Function represented by a table: function j.

 Turn and Talk A function can also be represented by a verbal description. Create a verbal description to represent function f.

Step It Out

Compare Linear Functions

2 Below are four linear functions represented in different ways. Identify the function that has the greatest value when $x = 15$.

Equation

$f(x) = 2x + 4$

$$f(15) = 2(15) + 4 = 34$$

> **A.** How is the verbal description used to write a rule for $h(x)$?

Verbal Description

As x increases by 1, $h(x)$ increases by 2. When $x = 4$, $h(x) = 5$.

$$h(x) - 5 = 2(x - 4)$$
$$h(x) = 2x - 8 + 5$$
$$h(x) = 2x - 3$$

So, $h(x) = 2x - 3$.

$$h(15) = 2(15) - 3 = 27$$

Graph

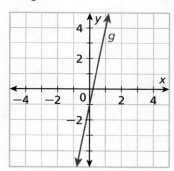

y-intercept: -1

$$m = \frac{4 - (-1)}{1 - 0} = 5$$

So, $g(x) = 5x - 1$.

$$g(15) = 5(15) - 1 = 74$$

> **B.** How is the graph used to write a rule for $g(x)$?

Table of Values

x	$j(x)$
0	4
1	7
2	10
3	13
4	16
⋮	⋮

$j(0) = 4$.

$$m = \frac{7 - 4}{1 - 0} = 3$$

So, $j(x) = 3x + 4$.

$$j(15) = 3(15) + 4 = 49$$

> **C.** How is the table used to write a rule for $j(x)$?

So, the function g has the greatest value when $x = 15$.

Identify the function that has the least x-intercept.

> **D.** Why are the function values set equal to 0?

$f(x) = 2x + 4$	$g(x) = 5x - 1$	$h(x) = 2x - 3$	$j(x) = 4x + 4$
$0 = 2x + 4$	$0 = 5x - 1$	$0 = 2x - 3$	$0 = 4x + 4$
$-2 = x$	$0.2 = x$	$1.5 = x$	$-1 = x$

The graph of function f has the least x-intercept.

Module 5 • Lesson 5.3

Check Understanding

Use the functions for Problems 1–3.

$f(x) = 2x + 10$

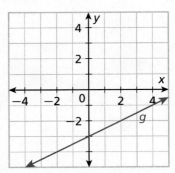

$h = \left\{(0, 3), (1, 6), (2, 9), (3, 12), (4, 15), \ldots\right\}$

x	0	1	2	3	4	...
j(x)	−4	6	16	26	36	...

1. What function graph has the greatest slope?

2. What function graph has the greatest y-intercept?

3. Compare and contrast representing a function with an equation, a graph, an ordered set of pairs, and a table.

On Your Own

Use the functions for Problems 4–10.

$f(x) = \frac{1}{2}x + 2$

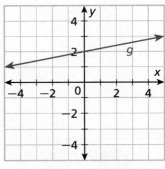

$h = \left\{(0, 5), (2, 15), (4, 25), (6, 35), (8, 45), \ldots\right\}$

x	0	1	2	3	4	...
j(x)	7	7.1	7.2	7.3	7.4	...

4. Which function graph has the least steep slope?

5. Which function has the greatest value when $x = 20$?

6. Which function has the least value when $x = 2$?

7. Which two function graphs have the same y-intercept?

8. Which function graph has the greatest x-intercept?

9. Which function graphs have the same end behavior?

10. Which function has the greatest maximum value and which function has the least minimum value on the interval $-10 \leq x \leq -5$?

Use the functions for Problems 11–14.

$f(x) = -2x + 2$

$h = \left\{ (0, -7), (1, -9), (2, -11), (3, -13), (4, -15), \ldots \right\}$

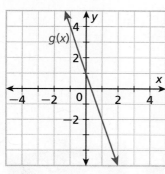

x	j(x)
0	2
2	−8
4	−18
6	−28
8	−38
⋮	⋮

11. Identify the rate of change for each function, and order them from least to greatest.

12. Identify each function value when $x = 0$, and order them from least to greatest.

13. Compare and contrast how to find each function value when $x = 20$ across the four representations.

14. Write a verbal description to represent each function.

15. Mark and Tamara begin walking along a hiking and biking trail at noon. Tamara's distance in miles from the start of the trail at t hours after noon is represented by $g(t) = 3.75t + 0.5$. Mark begins at the start of the trail at noon. His pace is shown.

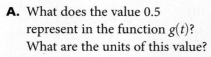

Mark's pace is 4 mi/h.

   A. What does the value 0.5 represent in the function $g(t)$? What are the units of this value?

   B. Write the function, $f(t)$, that gives Mark's distance from the start.

   C. Which person walked the farthest before a storm hits at 1:30 pm?

16. The cost of large boxes of Cruncho breakfast cereal at a Save Rite grocery store is represented by the function f, shown in the graph. At Members Save shopping club, the cost of a lifetime membership is $20, and each large box of Cruncho breakfast cereal costs $3. The function g represents the cost of large boxes of Cruncho breakfast cereal at Members Save.

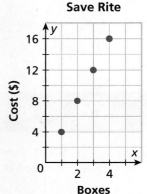

Save Rite

   A. Which function has the greater value for $x = 0$? What does this value represent?

   B. Which function has the lesser value for $x = 10$? What does the answer mean in terms of buying Cruncho cereal at the two stores?

   C. Which function has the lesser value for $x = 25$? What does the answer mean in terms of buying Cruncho cereal at the two stores?

17. (MP) **Use Structure** Susan's In-Home Tutoring Service fees are shown in the table. Best Online Tutors charges a rate of $75 per hour.

Susan's In-Home Tutoring Service					
h	0	1	2	3	4
$S(h)$	25	85	145	205	265

   A. Which service charges more for 2 hours of tutoring?

   B. Which service charges more for 3 hours of tutoring?

   C. Which tutoring service has the greater hourly rate?

18. (MP) **Attend to Precision** The charges for two different student-managed lawn services are shown.

   A. Write a function g for the cost of using Grassy Blades Lawn Service for t hours.

   B. Write a function h for the cost of using Mow No More Lawn Service for t hours.

   C. Which lawn service charges less for 40 minutes? What assumption(s) did you make?

   D. Which plan has a greater hourly rate?

Spiral Review • Assessment Readiness

19. Which of the following is the point-slope form of a linear equation?

   (A) $y - y_1 = m(x - x_1)$ (C) $y = mx + b$

   (B) $m = \dfrac{y_2 - y_1}{x_2 - x_1}$ (D) $Ax + By = C$

20. Which describes a reflection of the graph of f across the x-axis?

   (A) $g(x) = -f(x)$ (C) $g(x) = f(x) - 1$

   (B) $g(x) = 1 - f(x)$ (D) $g(x) = f(-x)$

21. Which describes a vertical shift of the graph of f down 5 units?

   (A) $g(x) = \dfrac{1}{5} - f(x)$ (C) $g(x) = \dfrac{1}{5} f(x)$

   (B) $g(x) = f(x) - 5$ (D) $g(x) = f(x) - \dfrac{1}{5}$

22. Which point is on the graph of $f(x) = 2x + 5$?

   (A) $(3, 10)$ (C) $(1, 5)$

   (B) $(2, 9)$ (D) $(8, 20)$

I'm in a Learning Mindset!

What strategies do I use to persevere through learning which form of a linear function is best to find the information I need?

Inverses of Linear Functions

(I Can) write an equation for the inverse of a linear function and use inverses of linear functions to solve problems.

Spark Your Learning

Sandra and Roger have the same cell phone service plan. The plan has a fixed monthly cost for unlimited phone calls and texting, plus an additional cost for each gigabyte of data used.

Sandra wants to know her monthly cost if she uses a certain amount of data.

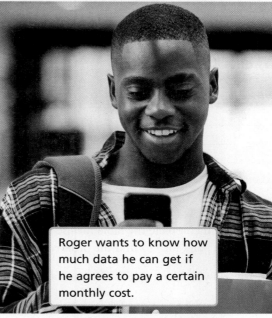

Roger wants to know how much data he can get if he agrees to pay a certain monthly cost.

Complete Part A as a whole class. Then complete Parts B–E in small groups.

A. What is a mathematical question you can ask about each person in this situation? What information would you need to know to answer your questions?

B. What variables are involved in this situation?

C. To answer your question, what strategy and tool would you use along with all the information you have? What answer do you get?

D. What is Sandra's monthly cost for cell phone service if she uses 3 gigabytes of data?

E. How much data can Roger use if he agrees to spend $60 per month on cell phone service?

 Turn and Talk How can you use an equation that gives monthly cost as a function of data used to write an equation that gives data used as a function of monthly cost?

Build Understanding

Investigate the Inverse of a Function

A function f maps each input value in its domain to exactly one output value in its range. The **inverse** of a function f maps the output values back to their original input values. If the inverse of f is itself a function, then it is denoted by f^{-1} (read as "f inverse") and is called an **inverse function**.

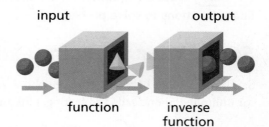

input output

function inverse function

1 ▶ The first table shows a set of ordered pairs for a function f. The second table, which is partially completed, is for the inverse of f.

Function f	
x	**y**
−2	0
−1	2
0	4
1	6
2	8

Inverse of f	
x	**y**
0	?
2	?
4	?
6	?
8	?

A. Copy and complete the table for the inverse of f. How did you use the ordered pairs for f to find the ordered pairs for the inverse?

B. How do you know that the inverse of f is a function?

C. What are the equations for $f(x)$ and $f^{-1}(x)$?

D. The steps for finding $f\left(f^{-1}(x)\right)$ are shown below. Find $f^{-1}\left(f(x)\right)$. What do you notice about $f\left(f^{-1}(x)\right)$ and $f^{-1}\left(f(x)\right)$? Why does this make sense?

$$f\left(f^{-1}(x)\right) = f\left(\frac{1}{2}x - 2\right)$$
$$= 2\left(\frac{1}{2}x - 2\right) + 4$$
$$= x - 4 + 4$$
$$= x$$

E. Graph $y = f(x)$, $y = f^{-1}(x)$, and $y = x$ in the same coordinate plane. How are the three graphs related?

Turn and Talk In the table for the function f, suppose the ordered pair $(-2, 0)$ is replaced with $(-2, 6)$. Is the inverse of f still a function? Explain.

Step It Out

Write Equations for Inverse Functions

2 The steps for finding an equation of the inverse of $f(x) = -3x + 5$ are shown below, but some justifications are missing.

$$f(x) = -3x + 5 \qquad \text{Given function}$$

$$y = -3x + 5 \qquad \text{Replace } f(x) \text{ with } y.$$

$$y - 5 = -3x \qquad \underline{\quad ? \quad}$$

$$-\frac{1}{3}y + \frac{5}{3} = x \qquad \underline{\quad ? \quad}$$

$$-\frac{1}{3}x + \frac{5}{3} = y \qquad \text{Switch } x \text{ and } y.$$

> **A.** What property justifies subtracting 5 from each side?

> **B.** What property justifies multiplying each side by $-\frac{1}{3}$?

Replace y with $f^{-1}(x)$. An equation for the inverse function is $f^{-1}(x) = -\frac{1}{3}x + \frac{5}{3}$.

3 Karen wants to buy a karaoke machine from an online store, which quotes prices that do not include sales tax or the cost of shipping. Write an equation that gives Karen's total cost c as a function of the quoted price p. Then write an equation for the inverse function.

> The online store charges 6% sales tax plus $12 for shipping.

Use a verbal model to write an equation for the total cost as a function of the quoted price.

Total cost	=	Quoted price	+	Sales tax	+	Shipping cost

$$c = p + 0.06p + 12$$

$$c = 1.06p + 12$$

Solve the equation for p to find the inverse function.

$$c = 1.06p + 12$$

$$c - 12 = 1.06p$$

$$\frac{c - 12}{1.06} = p$$

The inverse function is $p = \dfrac{c - 12}{1.06}$.

> **A.** Why don't you switch the variables as you did in Task 2?

> **B.** If Karen can pay a total of at most $90, what is the greatest price her karaoke machine can have before tax and shipping?

> **Turn and Talk** What are the domain and range of the function $c = 1.06p + 12$ and the inverse function? How are the domain and range of the function and its inverse related?

Check Understanding

1. How can you determine whether a function g is the inverse of a function f by examining the graphs of the two functions?

Verify that g is the inverse of f by showing that $f(g(x)) = x$ and $g(f(x)) = x$.

2. $f(x) = x + 4$, $g(x) = x - 4$

3. $f(x) = 2x + 1$, $g(x) = \frac{1}{2}x - \frac{1}{2}$

Find an equation for the inverse function.

4. $f(x) = -4x - 7$

5. $f(x) = \frac{1}{2}x + \frac{5}{2}$

6. Janet drives at an average speed of 50 miles per hour to visit her grandparents, who live 200 miles away from Janet's house.

   A. Write an equation that gives Janet's distance d from her grandparents' home (in miles) as a function of her driving time t (in hours).

   B. Write an equation for the inverse of the function from Part A.

   C. Janet stops at a gas station located 75 miles from her grandparents' home. Use the inverse function to find how much time it took Janet to reach the gas station.

On Your Own

Each table represents a function. Make a table that represents the inverse of the function. Then tell whether the inverse is itself a function. Explain your reasoning.

7.

x	y
−2	5
−1	2
0	−1
1	−4
2	−7

8.

x	y
−2	4
−1	1
0	0
1	1
2	4

Verify that g is the inverse of f by showing that $f(g(x)) = x$ and $g(f(x)) = x$.

9. $f(x) = \frac{7}{2}x$, $g(x) = \frac{2}{7}x$

10. $f(x) = 3x + 3$, $g(x) = \frac{1}{3}x - 1$

11. $f(x) = 5x - 10$, $g(x) = \frac{1}{5}x + 2$

12. $f(x) = -\frac{3}{4}x + 2$, $g(x) = -\frac{4}{3}x + \frac{8}{3}$

13. **(MP) Construct Arguments** Is the inverse of a constant function $f(x) = c$ also a function? Explain why or why not.

14. **Open Ended** Write equations for two functions f and g such that g is the inverse of f and the graphs of f and g are parallel lines.

Tell whether the function *g* is the inverse of the function *f*. Explain your reasoning.

15.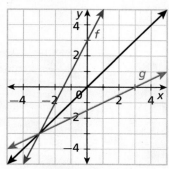

16.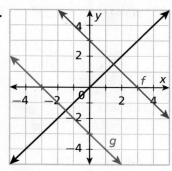

Find an equation for the inverse function.

17. $f(x) = x - 7$

18. $f(x) = -6x$

19. $f(x) = 3x + 4$

20. $f(x) = -x + 9$

21. $f(x) = -0.25x - 8$

22. $f(x) = \frac{4}{5}x - \frac{1}{5}$

23. (MP) **Model with Mathematics** Use the information in the photo about the number of students enrolled at a university.

  A. Write an equation that gives the university's expected enrollment *E* at time *t* (measured in years from now).

  B. Write an equation for the inverse of the function from Part A.

  C. Predict the number of years it will take for enrollment to reach 10,000 students.

A university has 5500 students. Enrollment is expected to increase by 250 students each year.

24. **STEM** At sea level, the total pressure on a diver is 1 atmosphere (atm) due to the weight of the air above the diver. As the diver descends below the surface of the water, the total pressure increases by 1 atm for each 33 feet of depth due to the additional weight of the water above the diver.

  A. Copy and complete the table.

  B. Write an equation that gives the total pressure *p* on a diver as a function of the diver's depth *d*. What are the domain and range of the function?

  C. Write an equation for the inverse of the function from Part B. What are the domain and range of the inverse function?

  D. The diver who set the world record for the deepest scuba dive experienced a total pressure of about 34 atm. Find the approximate depth of the record dive.

Depth, *d* (ft)	Pressure, *p* (atm)
0	?
33	?
66	?
99	?

25. (MP) **Use Structure** Write an equation for the inverse of the general linear function $f(x) = ax + b$ where $a \neq 0$. Then use your equation to find the inverse of $f(x) = 7x - 2$.

26. **Financial Literacy** Theo, who lives in the United States, is planning a trip to Berlin, Germany. Before the trip, he goes to his bank to exchange dollars for euros. The bank offers the exchange rate shown. (The symbol for euros is €.)

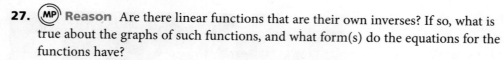

$1 = €0.86

A. Write an equation that gives the number E of euros Theo receives as a function of the number D of dollars he exchanges.

B. Write an equation for the inverse of the function from Part A.

C. When Theo returns from his trip, he still has €300. If he exchanges his euros for dollars at the exchange rate shown, how many dollars will he receive?

27. (MP) **Reason** Are there linear functions that are their own inverses? If so, what is true about the graphs of such functions, and what form(s) do the equations for the functions have?

28. Consider the equation $2x - 5 = 3$. Let f be the function defined by the left side of the equation so that $f(x) = 2x - 5$ and the equation can be written as $f(x) = 3$.

A. Explain why the solution of $2x - 5 = 3$ is $f^{-1}(3)$.

B. Write an equation for $f^{-1}(x)$. Then use the equation to solve $2x - 5 = 3$.

Spiral Review • Assessment Readiness

29. The graph of which function is the graph of f shifted 3 units to the left?

Ⓐ $g(x) = f(x) + 3$ Ⓒ $g(x) = f(x + 3)$

Ⓑ $g(x) = f(x) - 3$ Ⓓ $g(x) = f(x - 3)$

30. The graph of which function is a vertical stretch of the graph of $f(x) = x$?

Ⓐ $g(x) = 2x$ Ⓒ $g(x) = x + 2$

Ⓑ $g(x) = 0.5x$ Ⓓ $g(x) = x + 0.5$

31. Let $f(x) = 3x + 5$, $g(x) = 5x + 3$, and $h(x) = -6x + 1$. The graph of which linear function has the greatest slope?

Ⓐ the function f Ⓒ the function h

Ⓑ the function g Ⓓ cannot be determined

32. What is an equation of the line passing through the points $(-2, -8)$ and $(3, 22)$?

Ⓐ $y = 14x + 20$ Ⓒ $y = 6x - 4$

Ⓑ $y = 14x - 20$ Ⓓ $y = 6x + 4$

 I'm in a Learning Mindset!

What strategies did I use to persevere when learning how to find inverses of linear functions?

Transform Graphs

The graph of g is a transformation of the graph of f such that $g(x) = -\frac{1}{2} f(x)$. The range values of f are multiplied by $-\frac{1}{2}$, which reflects the graph across the x-axis and compresses the graph vertically by a factor of $\frac{1}{2}$.

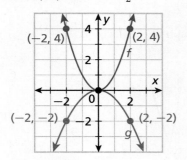

Transform Linear Functions

You can transform the graphs of linear functions by translating, stretching, compressing, or reflecting the graph of the parent function.

Edwin is shipping a package. One option is to pay $1 for the shipping box and $0.50 per pound of weight added to it. He graphs the relationship by vertically compressing the graph of the parent function by a factor of 0.5 or $\frac{1}{2}$ and then translating the graph up 1 unit.

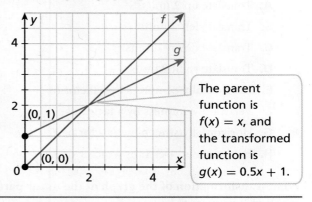

The parent function is $f(x) = x$, and the transformed function is $g(x) = 0.5x + 1$.

Compare Linear Functions

Another shipping option is represented by the function shown in the table.

Weight (x)	Price (y)
1 pound	$1.00
2 pounds	$1.60
3 pounds	$2.20

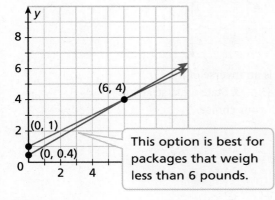

This option is best for packages that weigh less than 6 pounds.

Inverses of Linear Functions

Edwin uses the first option where $g(x) = 0.5x + 1$. The inverse function can tell Edwin the weight x when he knows the fee y. To find the inverse, substitute y for $g(x)$, solve for x, then switch the variables.

$$y = 0.5x + 1$$
$$0.5x = y - 1$$
$$x = 2y - 2$$
$$y = 2x - 2$$

Suppose Edwin wants to spend $8. Since $2(8) - 2 = 14$, the package will weigh 14 lb.

Price (x)	$y = 2x - 2$	Weight (y)
$2	$y = 2(2) - 2 = 2$	2 pounds
$3	$y = 2(3) - 2 = 4$	4 pounds
$4	$y = 2(4) - 2 = 6$	6 pounds
$5	$y = 2(5) - 2 = 8$	8 pounds

Vocabulary

Choose the correct term from the box to complete each sentence.

1. The ___?___ of all linear functions is $f(x) = x$.

2. The ___?___ of a function exchanges the ___?___ and ___?___.

3. A(n) ___?___ is a change in the position, size, or shape of a figure or graph.

Concepts and Skills

4. How is the function $g(x) = mx + b$ related to the parent function $f(x) = x$?

5. Determine the transformations to the graph of f that result in the graph of g. Select all that apply from the list.

A. Translate up 2 units.

B. Translate left 2 units.

C. Translate down 2 units.

D. Translate right 2 units.

E. Horizontally compress by a factor of $\frac{1}{3}$.

F. Vertically compress by a factor of $\frac{1}{3}$.

G. Horizontally stretch by a factor of 3.

H. Horizontally stretch by a factor of 3.

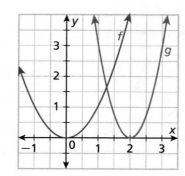

What transformation of the graph of the linear parent function $f(x) = x$ does the graph of g represent?

6. $g(x) = 4f(x)$

7. $g(x) = f(x) + 5$

8. $g(x) = 3f(x) - 4$

9. $g(x) = f(x - 2)$

The table and the graph represent linear functions presented in different formats.

h(x)				
x	0	1	2	3	4
y	4	5	6	7	8

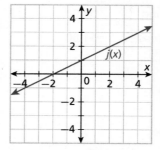

10. What function has the greater slope?

11. What function has the greater y-intercept?

12. What function has the lesser value when $x = 10$?

13. **(MP)** **Use Tools** How do you verify that a function $g(x)$ is an inverse of $f(x)$? Explain your reasoning using $g(x) = \frac{2}{3}x + 2$ and $f(x) = \frac{3}{2}x - 3$. State what strategy and tool you will use to answer the question and explain your choice.

Determine the inverse of each function.

14. $f(x) = 5x$

15. $f(x) = 2x + 2$

16. $f(x) = -2x$

17. $f(x) = 3x + 4$

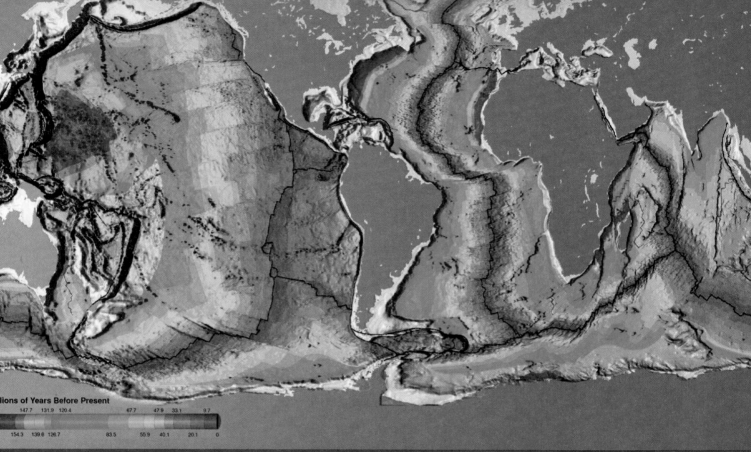

Unit 3
Build Linear Functions and Models

Millions of Years Before Present

147.7 131.9 120.4   67.7   47.9 33.1   9.7

154.3 139.6 126.7   83.5   55.9 40.1   20.1   0

©Dr. Peter Sloss, formerly of NGDC/NOAA/NCEI

Geologist

STEM
POWERING INGENUITY

A geologist analyzes the current condition of Earth to make inferences about its past and future. Rocks, minerals, and fossils reflect the different conditions at the time of their formation. Analyzing these artifacts along with their geographic distribution allows geologists to infer how the conditions on Earth have changed over long periods of time.

STEM Task

Volcanic activity at mid-ocean ridges creates new rock that aligns with the polarity of Earth's magnetic field. The sea floor slowly spreads, creating a record of Earth's magnetic history.

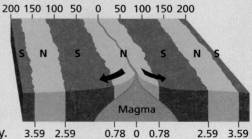

Distance from ridge (km)

200 150 100 50 0 50 100 150 200

S   N   S   N   S   N   S   N   S

Magma

3.59 2.59   0.78 0 0.78   2.59 3.59

Time (millions of years)

Approximately how many years does it take for the Atlantic Ocean sea floor, which is shown in the diagram, to spread by one kilometer? Explain.

Learning Mindset
Challenge-Seeking Makes Decisions

How do you make thoughtful decisions? Thoughtful decision-making comes from good communication and strategic planning. Communication must be clear, concise, and frequent. Strategic planning involves listing and prioritizing your needs at the onset of the task, and then adjusting this prioritization as the work progresses. It is imperative that your communication and strategic planning are thorough enough to help you stay focused on your learning goal. Here are some questions you can ask yourself when making decisions:

- Am I allowing myself the proper amount of time to go through each part of the task?

- How do I decide which resources offer me the most reliable information? Which resources have I used successfully in the past?

- What is the best way to convey the information I have gathered? With a graph, an essay, a video, or some other type of presentation?

- What do I do if it turns out the decision I made doesn't work out?

Reflect

Q Think about a time when you made a thoughtful decision and about a time when you did not. How did those decisions affect you and those around you?

Q What would you need to do if you think that the information you have gathered or analyzed is unreliable? What would happen if you based your research on unreliable information? Explain your reasoning.

Module Performance Task: *Spies and Analysts*™

Rubber Band Bungee

How many rubber bands are needed so that when the doll jumps, it will just miss the floor?

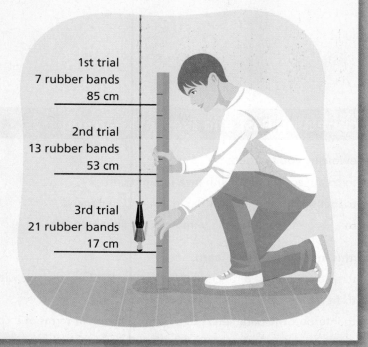

1st trial
7 rubber bands
85 cm

2nd trial
13 rubber bands
53 cm

3rd trial
21 rubber bands
17 cm

Are You Ready?

Complete these problems to review prior concepts and skills you will need for this module.

Evaluate Algebraic Expressions

Evaluate each expression for the given information.

1. $x = 5, y = -5$

$6x + 4y = \underline{\quad?\quad}$

2. $x = \frac{1}{2}, y = 4$

$3x + 6y = \underline{\quad?\quad}$

Slopes of Lines

Find the slope of the line passing through the two points on the line.

3. $(1, 2)$ and $(5, 1)$

4. $(-1, -3)$ and $(2, 6)$

5. $(4, 3)$ and $(6, -2)$

6. $(-2, -2)$ and $(-8, -14)$

Point-Slope Form

Write the equation of a line in point-slope form using the given information.

7. slope, $m = 3$, passing through the point $(6, 8)$

8. slope, $m = -2$, passing through the point $(2, 3)$

9. passing through the points $(1, 2)$ and $(0, 8)$

10. passing through the points $(1, -1)$ and $(3, 4)$

Connecting Past and Present Learning

Previously, you learned:

- to create scatter plots with bivariate data,
- to identify a linear association in bivariate data, and
- to interpret the slope and y-intercept of linear models.

In this module, you will learn:

- to assess the fit of a function using residuals informally and with technology,
- to fit a function to data to solve problems, and
- to interpret the parameters of a linear function in terms of a context.

Scatter Plots, Correlation, and Fitted Lines

(I Can) create a line fitted to data that shows a linear correlation and use it to make predictions.

Spark Your Learning

A high school basketball league has 16 teams.

The team that was champion of the league had the most wins. This was NOT the team that scored, on average, the most points per game.

Complete Part A as a whole class. Then complete Parts B–D in small groups.

A. What is a mathematical question you can ask about this situation? What information would you need to know to answer your question?

B. How can you visualize the relationship between average number of points scored per game and number of games won?

C. To answer your question, what strategy and tool would you use along with all the information you have? What answer do you get?

D. Explain why it makes sense that the average number of points scored per game and total number of wins would be related.

> **Turn and Talk** How can you use the average number of points scored per game to predict the total number of wins a team has in this league?

Build Understanding

Determine Correlation

In this lesson, you will study **bivariate data**, which are paired values of two variables. **Scatter plots**, which are graphs of bivariate data, can reveal a linear relationship between the two variables. The measure of the direction and strength of the linear relationship is called **correlation**.

1 In a scatter plot, you can observe whether there appears to be a correlation between two variables and what type of correlation there is. Data can have positive, negative, or no correlation.

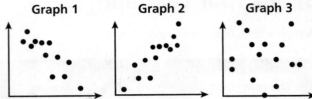

Graph 1   **Graph 2**   **Graph 3**

A. A *positive correlation* is when both values increase together. Which graph shows this?

B. A *negative correlation* is when one value decreases as the other increases. Which graph shows this?

C. *No correlation* is when the data follow no pattern. Which graph shows this?

2 Hattie sells hot cocoa at a farmers' market. She believes that people tend to buy more hot cocoa as the weather gets colder. The table shows data for the average daily air temperature and corresponding number of cups of hot cocoa sold.

Temperature (°F)	Cups sold
30	300
42	265
45	250
46	225
58	192
62	150
70	75
77	45
85	40
95	30
98	25

A. The air temperatures are shown in increasing order. What do you notice about the number of cups of hot cocoa sold as the air temperature increases?

B. Make a scatter plot of the data. Does your scatter plot support your answer to Part D? What type of correlation do these data have?

Turn and Talk What type of correlation would you expect to see between cold lemonade sales and air temperatures? Explain.

Estimate the Correlation Coefficient of a Linear Fit

Characterizing a correlation as positive or negative indicates the direction of the linear relationship between the variables. To indicate the strength of the linear relationship, you can use words like *strong* and *weak*.

3 Examine the lines of fit graphed with the data in each scatter plot.

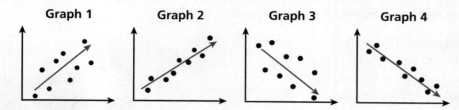

Graph 1   Graph 2   Graph 3   Graph 4

A. Which two scatter plots display bivariate data that are clustered tightly around the line of fit? These scatter plots display bivariate data that have a *strong correlation*.

B. Of the graphs with a strong correlation, which has a *strong positive correlation* and which has a *strong negative correlation*?

C. Which two scatter plots display bivariate data that are clustered more loosely around the line of fit? These scatter plots display bivariate data that have a *weak correlation*.

D. Of the graphs with a weak correlation, which has a *weak positive correlation* and which has a *weak negative correlation*?

A **correlation coefficient**, denoted by r, where $-1 \leq r \leq 1$, is a statistic that describes how closely the points in a scatter plot cluster about a line. A strong positive correlation has a correlation coefficient close to 1, and a strong negative correlation has a correlation coefficient close to -1. If there is no apparent correlation, then $r \approx 0$.

4 Use the information in Tasks 2 and 3 to answer the questions.

A. Which of the graphs display data that would have a correlation coefficient described here?

- r is close to -1.
- r is close to 1.
- r is between 0 and -1.
- r is between 0 and 1.

B. Estimate the correlation coefficient that describes the hot cocoa data in Task 2. Based on your answer, what advice would you give someone selling hot cocoa?

Turn and Talk What variables can you think of that might have a correlation coefficient of about -1? Explain.

Distinguish Between Correlation and Causation

A common error when interpreting bivariate data is to observe a correlation and conclude that a *causation* has been demonstrated. Causation is when a change in one variable causes a change in the other variable. If there is causation, it is reasonable to expect correlation between the variables. However, a strong correlation does not imply causation. Both variables may instead be influenced by a variable not included in the data set, or the causation may be the reverse of what was assumed.

5 Below are descriptions of three studies. Use the given information to complete Parts A–G. The results of a study about the age of children and their respective heights are given.

The height of a child and the age of that child have a strong positive correlation.

A. Based on the correlation noted, what happens to the height of a child as his or her age increases?

B. Do you think that the correlation is due to causation? Explain.

The results of a study about student absences and student grades are given.

The number of absences a student has and that student's grade point average have a strong negative correlation.

C. Based on the correlation noted, what happens to grade point averages as the number of absences increases?

D. Do you think that the correlation is due to causation? Explain.

The results of a study about the number of people jogging and the number of people biking outdoors are given.

E. Based on the correlation noted, what happens to the number of joggers as the number of people biking increases?

The number of people jogging and the number of people biking outdoors have a strong positive correlation.

F. Do you think that the correlation is due to causation? Explain.

G. Explain how another variable could have a causal relationship with each of the original two variables.

Turn and Talk Even though correlation does not necessarily imply causation, do you think causation necessarily implies correlation? Justify your response using examples.

Step It Out

Fit a Linear Function to Data

When there is a strong correlation between two variables, you can use a **line of fit** to construct a linear model for the data. To estimate a line of fit, position a straightedge through the middle of the plotted data points so that the data points are evenly dispersed above and below the line. Use the straightedge to draw a line. Then select two points on the line to write the equation.

6 ▶ The scatter plot for the data of hot cocoa sales from Task 2 is shown. Draw a line of fit, and write an equation for the line of fit.

Draw the line of fit.
Use a straightedge to draw a line of fit, such as the blue dashed line that is shown. The data points should appear to be clustered around the line.

Write an equation for the line of fit.
Select two points (not necessarily data points) on the line: $(30, 300)$ and $(60, 160)$.
Find the slope of the line.

$$m = \frac{y_2 - y_1}{x_2 - x_1} = \frac{160 - 300}{60 - 30} = -\frac{140}{30} = -\frac{14}{3}$$

> **A.** How do you know what points to select?

Use point-slope form to write an equation of the line.

$$y - y_1 = m(x - x_1)$$
$$y - 300 = -\frac{14}{3}(x - 30)$$
$$y - 300 = -\frac{14}{3}x + 140$$
$$y = -\frac{14}{3}x + 440$$

> **B.** What do the slope and y-intercept represent in this line of fit?

Turn and Talk What does the sign of the slope of a line fitted to bivariate data tell you about the correlation between the variables?

Use a Line of Fit to Solve Problems

You can use a line of fit to solve real-world problems by *interpolation* and *extrapolation* of the data. **Interpolation** is making a prediction using a value of the independent variable from *within* the model's domain. **Extrapolation** is making a prediction using a value of the independent variable *outside* the model's domain.

7 The scatter plot and line of fit for hot cocoa sales is shown. A shaded rectangle indicates the values that are within the model's domain.

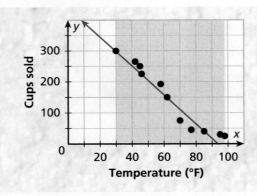

Interpolation: Predict the number of cups of hot cocoa that would sell on a day with an average air temperature of 80 °F.

> **A.** Explain why this is interpolation.

Use the equation of the line of fit from Task 6.

$$y = -\frac{14}{3}x + 440$$

$$y = -\frac{14}{3}(80) + 440$$

$$y \approx 67$$

About 67 cups of hot cocoa would be sold.

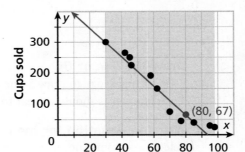

Extrapolation: Predict the number of cups of hot cocoa that would sell on a day with an average air temperature of 20 °F.

> **B.** Explain why this is extrapolation.

Use the equation of the line of fit from Task 6.

$$y = -\frac{14}{3}x + 440$$

$$y = -\frac{14}{3}(20) + 440$$

$$y \approx 347$$

About 347 cups of hot cocoa would be sold.

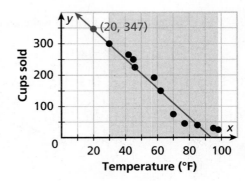

 Turn and Talk Which of the two predictions is more reliable? Explain.

Check Understanding

1. Describe the three linear correlation types: positive correlation, negative correlation, and no correlation.

2. What is an example of bivariate data that would have a correlation coefficient $r = 1$? What about an example of data that might have a correlation coefficient of $r = 0$?

3. If bivariate data are found to have a strong correlation, does that mean there must be causation? Explain.

4. The table shows the measured height of a tree sapling for several years.

Time after planting (years)	0	1	2	3	4	5
Height (in.)	25	52	60	87	97	122

   A. Make a scatter plot of the data. Draw a line of fit and write an equation of the line of fit.

   B. Use extrapolation to predict the height of the tree 8 years after it is planted.

On Your Own

Tell whether each data set shows *positive correlation*, *negative correlation*, or *no correlation*. Justify your answer.

5.

x	1	1	2	3	3	4	5	5	6
y	2	3	4	4	5	5	5	7	8

6.

x	2	2	3	6	8	8	11	15	20
y	−5	−6	−6	−4	−9	−8	−12	−11	−19

7.

x	−3	−1	1	0	3	5	7	6	8
y	6	2	7	−4	−1	0	9	4	−1

8. The table shows the average winter temperature for 8 winters and the number of gallons of maple syrup produced that winter by one farm. Describe the type of correlation and estimate the correlation coefficient.

Average winter temperature (° F)	Maple syrup produced (gal)
24	154
26	128
25	141
22	168
28	104
21	170
24	144
22	160

For each scatter plot, estimate the value of the correlation coefficient, *r*. Tell whether it would be *close to −1, close to −0.5, close to 0, close to 0.5,* or *close to 1*.

9.

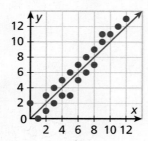

10.

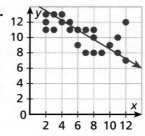

(MP) **Model with Mathematics** Describe the type of correlation you would expect to see between each pair of variables. If there is a correlation between the variables, determine whether it is *strong* or *weak*. Explain your reasoning.

11. the volume of water poured into a container and the amount of empty space left in the container

12. a person's shoe size and the length of the person's hair

13. the outside temperature and the number of people at the beach

14. the speed of a runner and the distance she can cover in 10 minutes

Read each description. Describe how the variables change in relation to one another. Explain whether the correlation is a result of causation.

15. A study about the age of children and the hours they sleep shows they have a strong negative correlation.

16. A study about the number of musical instruments a student plays and the student's grade in math shows they have a strong positive correlation.

17. A study about the number of movie tickets sold at two different theaters shows they have a strong positive correlation.

18. Which line shown is a better line of fit for the scatter plot? Explain your reasoning.

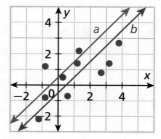

Make a scatter plot of the data. Describe the correlation of the data. If possible, fit a line to the data and write an equation of the line.

19.

x	10	12	15	20	30	45	60	99
y	−2	4	9	16	32	55	87	128

20.

x	−5	−3	−3	0	1	2	5	6
y	−4	12	10	−6	8	0	3	−9

21. The table contains data for the total amount of money, in dollars, collected at a movie theater concession stand and the total number of movie tickets sold each day for 5 days.

Movie tickets sold	23	42	60	85	124
Concession stand sales ($)	155	189	341	420	565

   A. Make a scatter plot and describe any correlation.

   B. Do you think there is any causation? Explain.

   C. Fit a line to the data in your scatter plot and write an equation for it.

   D. What do the slope and y-intercept of the line of fit represent in this situation?

   E. Use your line of fit to predict the concession stand sales when 75 movie tickets are sold. Is this an interpolation or extrapolation?

   F. Use your line of fit to predict the concession stand sales when 200 movie tickets are sold. Is this an interpolation or extrapolation?

22. Reina opens a car wash and logs the weekly earnings in thousands of dollars, as shown in the table.

Weeks after opening	Earnings ($1000s)
0	1.05
1	1.7
2	2.4
3	2.0
4	3.5
5	3.6

   A. Make a scatter plot and describe any correlation.

   B. Do you think there is any causation? Explain.

   C. Fit a line to the data in your scatter plot and write an equation for it.

   D. If you use a line of fit to estimate the earnings for 8 weeks after opening, would that be an interpolation or an extrapolation? Explain.

   E. Do you think it is reasonable to use this data for estimating the earnings of the car wash for 5 years after opening? Explain your answer.

23. The table shows the weights, in pounds, of two alligators during a feeding trial.

Weeks	0	9	18	27	34	43	49
Alligator 1 weight (lb)	6	8.6	10	13.6	15	17.2	19.8
Alligator 2 weight (lb)	6	9.2	12.8	13.6	20.2	21.4	24.3

   A. Make two scatter plots, one for each alligator, where x is the number of weeks and y is the weight of the alligator.

   B. Draw lines of fit for both scatter plots. Compare the approximate growth rates.

24. STEM The mesosphere is a layer of atmosphere that extends from about 50 kilometers above Earth's surface to about 90 kilometers above Earth's surface. The diagram shows the temperature at certain altitudes in the mesosphere.

A. Make a scatter plot of the altitude and temperature data in the mesosphere.

B. Write an equation for a line of fit for the data. Explain what your line models.

C. At about what rate does the temperature change with increasing altitude in the mesosphere?

25. (MP) **Critique Reasoning** The table shows the time, in hours, it takes a landscaping work crew with different numbers of people to complete a job. Stanley claims the variables should have a strong negative correlation because the time to complete a landscaping job decreases as the number of people working increases. What is the error in Stanley's reasoning? Explain.

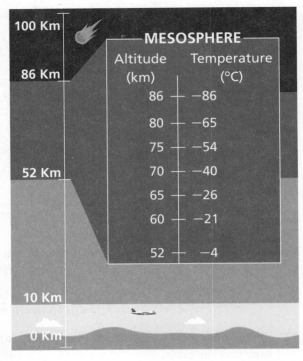

MESOSPHERE

Altitude (km)	Temperature (°C)
86	−86
80	−65
75	−54
70	−40
65	−26
60	−21
52	−4

Number of people working	8	4	7	5	1	3	2
Time to complete job (h)	5	10	7	8	40	13	20

Spiral Review • Assessment Readiness

26. Which function includes a vertical reflection of the graph of $f(x) = x$?

Ⓐ $f(x) = x + 2$ Ⓒ $f(x) = 0.5x$

Ⓑ $f(x) = 2x$ Ⓓ $f(x) = -(x - 4)$

27. Which equation has a graph with a negative slope?

Ⓐ $2x + 2y = 8$ Ⓒ $y = -12 + 3x$

Ⓑ $y = 2x + 3$ Ⓓ $-2x + 3y = 10$

28. Which is the inverse of the function $f(x) = 2x + 5$?

Ⓐ $g(x) = \dfrac{x - 5}{2}$ Ⓒ $g(x) = 2x - 5$

Ⓑ $g(x) = x - 5$ Ⓓ $g(x) = 5x + 2$

29. Which line contains the points $(6, 3)$ and $(2, 2)$?

Ⓐ $-\dfrac{1}{4}x + y = 1.5$ Ⓒ $y = -4x + 3$

Ⓑ $y = -\dfrac{1}{4}x + 1.5$ Ⓓ $\dfrac{1}{4}x + 3y = 1.5$

I'm in a Learning Mindset!

How do my time management skills impact decision-making?

Residuals and Best-Fit Lines

(I Can) use the linear regression function on a graphing calculator to find a line of best fit for a bivariate data set.

Spark Your Learning

Sandra wants to study abroad in the northern hemisphere where the average temperature is about 70 °F.

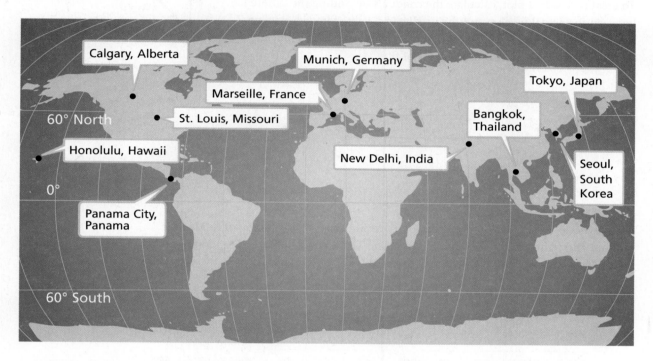

Complete Part A as a whole class. Then complete Parts B–D in small groups.

A. What is a mathematical question you can ask about this situation? What information would you need to know to answer your question?

B. What variable(s) are involved in this situation? Does there appear to be causation between the variables?

C. To answer your question, what strategy and tool would you use along with all the information you have? What answer do you get?

D. Does your answer make sense in the context of the situation? Explain.

 Turn and Talk Why may your prediction differ from another student's prediction?

Build Understanding

Plot Residuals

You can use the location of data points with respect to a line of fit to determine how well the line fits the data. The signed vertical distance between a data point and a line of fit is a **residual**. A **residual plot** is a scatter plot of the data points generated by the values of the independent variable and the corresponding residuals.

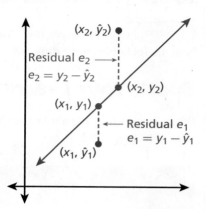

To create a residual plot, calculate the residuals by finding the difference between the actual y-value and the predicted y-value for each x-value. Then plot the residuals. The plots below show how residuals may be distributed for three data sets and lines of fit.

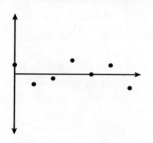 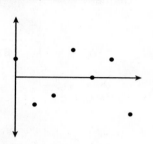 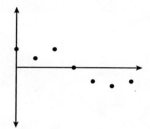

Distribution of residuals is random and tight. The line fits the data very well.

Distribution of residuals is random but loose. The line fits the data weakly.

Distribution of residuals is tight but not random. The line does not fit the data well.

 1 The table shows the mean height and girth (circumference) measurements for Douglas fir trees in a mountain range. A line of fit for the data is $y = 0.04x + 2.32$, where x is the height and y is the girth, both in meters.

Height (m)	60	61	62	63	64	65	66	67	68
Girth (m)	4.83	5.10	4.93	5.15	4.77	4.93	4.89	4.57	5.04

A. Using a spreadsheet, create a table like the one shown. What is the formula for the predicted y-value in cell C2? Fill down the formula for cells C2–C10 to find the predicted values.

B. To determine the residual in cell D2, what formula do you use? Fill down the formula for cells D2–D9 to find the residual values.

C. Use a graphing calculator to graph a residual plot of x-values and residuals.

	A	B	C	D
1	x	y (Actual)	y (Predicted)	Residual
2	60	4.83		
3	61	5.1		
4	62	4.93		
5	63	5.15		
6	64	4.77		
7	65	4.93		
8	66	4.89		
9	67	4.57		
10	68	5.04		

D. Evaluate the quality of fit to the data for the line $y = 0.04x + 2.32$.

 Turn and Talk If you were to compare two lines of fit for a single data set, how would the residual plot show which line is the better model?

Analyze Squared Residuals

Different people may find different lines of fit for the same data set. You can use the sum of squared residuals to compare different lines of fit. The closer the sum of the squared residuals is to zero, the better the line of fit.

2 The table below gives data about the tolls on the Massachusetts Turnpike. In the table, the variable d represents the distance, in miles, that you travel from the western end of the turnpike, heading toward Boston. The variable T, in dollars, is the toll that you pay when you leave the turnpike at one of the turnpike's exits. Adam and Helen each modeled the bivariate data with a line of fit.

Adam's line of fit: $T = 0.03d$
Helen's line of fit: $T = 0.035d$

d	0	7.7	37.5	42.8	46.1	48.4	52	59.9	75.6	87.3
T	0	0.25	1.25	1.55	1.55	1.55	1.55	2.00	2.55	3.05

A. To analyze Adam's model, use a spreadsheet to create a table like the one shown. What are the formulas to find the predicted T-value in cell C2 and residual for cell D2? Fill down the formulas to find all the values for columns C and D.

	A	B	C	D	E
1	d	T (Actual)	T (Predicted)	Residual	Residual squared
2	0	0			
3	7.7	0.25			
4	37.5	1.25			
5	42.8	1.55			
6	46.1	1.55			
7	48.4	1.55			
8	52	1.55			
9	59.9	2			
10	75.6	2.55			
11	87.3	3.05			

B. To determine the values in column E, square each residual. What is the formula you would use in cell E2? Fill down the formula for cells E2–E11 to find the square of each residual. What is the sum of the squared residuals?

C. Analyze Helen's model using the same methods you used in Parts A and B.

D. Which model is the better fit? Explain.

 Turn and Talk What do you know about a line of fit for which the sum of the squared residuals is 0?

Step It Out

Perform Linear Regression

A **line of best fit** is a line that comes closest to all of the points in a data set. The line of best fit for which the sum of the squares of the residuals is as small as possible is called the **least-squares line**. You can use a graphing calculator to perform **linear regression**, which is a statistical method used to find the least-squares line for a given data set.

3 Suppose a study is conducted of adolescents who are asked to log the amount of time (hours per day) spent with different screen-based media (TV/video, game console, PC/internet, mobile phone) and the number of times they engage in fitness activities (sessions per week). The adolescents track their screen time and fitness for several months. The table shows the average values of screen time and fitness recorded by several adolescents.

Screen time (hours per day)	0.5	1.4	3.6	4.0	5.3	5.8	7.0
Fitness (sessions per week)	6.5	5.2	4.9	4.8	3.9	2.3	1.6

Use a graphing calculator and linear regression to find the equation of the line of best fit for the data.

The correlation coefficient is -0.9348.

A. What does the correlation coefficient tell you?

An equation of the line of best fit is $y = -0.681783x + 6.8596$.

B. What do the slope and y-intercept represent in this situation?

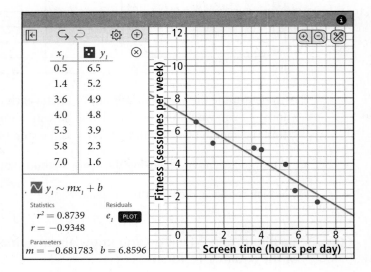

Use Linear Regression

Linear regression models can be used to solve real-world problems, such as how to estimate the relationship between the height and weight of infants.

4 The data show the average height and weight for male babies for the first few months after birth.

Weight (lb), x	7.4	9.8	12.3	14.1	15.4	16.6	17.5
Length (in.), y	19.6	21.6	23.0	24.2	25.2	26.0	26.6

Use a graphing calculator to find the equation of the line of best fit for the data. Then use the equation of the line of best fit to estimate the length of a baby boy when he weighs 20 pounds.

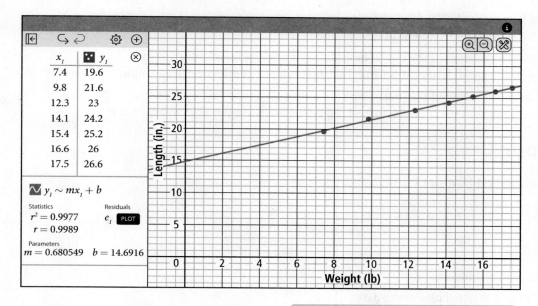

The correlation coefficient is 0.9989. An equation of the line of best fit is $y = 0.680549x + 14.6916$.

A. What does the correlation coefficient tell you?

B. Is the line of best fit a good model for the data? Use residuals to explain how you know.

To estimate the length of the baby boy when he weighs 20 pounds, substitute 20 for x in the model of the line of best fit.

$$y = 0.680549(20) + 14.6916$$
$$y = 13.61098 + 14.6916$$
$$y \approx 28.3$$

When a baby boy weighs 20 pounds, he is approximately 28.3 inches long.

 Turn and Talk Is the y-intercept a meaningful value in this situation? Why or why not?

Check Understanding

1. The temperature T, in degrees Fahrenheit, is displayed on an oven while it is heating. The table shows the displayed temperature for the time t, in seconds, since the oven was turned on. A line of fit for the data is $y = 0.6x + 160$.

Time, t (sec)	Temperature, T (°F)
31	175
104	225
202	275
285	325
380	375

   A. Find the residuals. Then create a residual plot.

   B. Based on the residual plot, is the model a good fit for the data? Explain your reasoning.

   C. If another line of fit for the data is determined to be $y = 0.55x + 161$, how could you use squared residuals to determine which line fits the data better?

   D. Use a graphing calculator and linear regression to find an equation of the line of best fit for the data. Interpret the correlation coefficient. What do the slope and y-intercept represent in this situation?

   E. Use the equation of the line of best fit to estimate the temperature of the oven 420 seconds after it is turned on. Is this interpolation or extrapolation?

   F. Use the equation of the line of best fit to estimate the temperature of the oven 250 seconds after it is turned on. Is this interpolation or extrapolation?

On Your Own

2. Use the data shown and the line of fit $y = 3.5x + 20$.

x	1	2	3	4	5	6	7	8	9
y	20	27	30	32	39	41	42	45	56.0

   A. Find the residuals.

   B. Create a residual plot of the data.

   C. Based on the residual plot, does the line $y = 3.5x + 20$ fit the data well? Explain your reasoning.

   D. Compare the sum of squared residuals for the line $y = 3.5x + 20$ from Part C and the line $y = 3.5x + 15.5$. Which line fits the data better? Explain your reasoning.

3. Explain how to find the line of best fit for a set of bivariate data with a strong correlation.

4. (MP) **Reason** Do you think it is easier to compare the residuals or the sum of squared residuals when comparing two linear models for a data set? Explain your reasoning.

5. (MP) **Use Structure** The residual plot for a line of fit has x-values that are close to the x-axis from $x = 0$ to $x = 16$ but has values that are far from the x-axis from $x = 16$ to $x = 36$. Is this a strong or weak relationship? Explain your reasoning.

6. **Health and Fitness** In an attempt to encourage healthy sleeping habits, a school surveys students to determine if there is a relationship between the average number of hours they sleep per day and their grade point averages. The data from the survey are shown.

Average sleep (hours per day)	4.75	5.25	6.00	7.75	8.50	9.00
Grade point average	2.6	2.5	2.75	3.0	4.0	3.75

07:15

A. Use a graphing calculator and linear regression to find an equation of the line of best fit for the data.

B. Interpret the correlation coefficient. What do the slope and y-intercept represent in this situation?

C. Based on your equation from Part A, what grade point average would you expect from students who averaged about 8 hours of sleep per day?

D. Use residuals to determine how well the line from Part A fits the data.

(MP) **Use Tools** For each table of data, compare the two given lines of fit. Calculate the residuals and the sum of the squared residuals. Identify which line is a better fit.

7.

x	1	2	3	4
y	3	21	9	15

$y = 2x + 6$

$y = 2.2x + 6$

8.

x	2	4	6	8
y	5	15	7	11

$y = 0.5x + 6$

$y = 0.5x + 6.2$

9.

x	1	2	3	4
y	15	7	8	3

$y = -3.5x + 16$

$y = -3x + 17$

10.

x	2	4	6	8
y	100	85	92	83

$y = -2x + 99$

$y = -2x + 100.5$

11.

x	1	2	3	4
y	4	8	10	17

$y = 4x - 1$

$y = 4.5x - 2$

12.

x	2	4	6	8
y	21	18	25	27

$y = x + 16$

$y = 1.5x + 16.5$

13. Suppose you have found a line of fit for a set of bivariate data. You examine a residual plot to examine the goodness of fit.

A. You observe that there are far more positive residuals than negative residuals. What does this tell you about the line of fit?

B. You observe that the residuals are positive, then they are negative, and then they are positive again. What does this tell you about the line of fit?

14. The data shows the population, in millions, of Australia in the years since 1980.

   A. Use the given data and a graphing calculator to find an equation for the line of best fit.

   B. Interpret the slope and y-intercept of the line of best fit.

   C. Use the line of best fit to estimate the population of Australia in 2012.

   D. Use the line of best fit to determine in what year you would expect the population of Australia to be about 20 million.

Time (years since 1980)	Population (millions)
0	14.649
5	15.730
10	17.041
15	18.077
20	19.066
25	20.239
30	22.120
35	23.800

15. (MP) **Use Structure** Explain why you use the sum of the squared residuals and not the sum of the residuals to analyze the goodness of fit of a line modeling a data set.

16. (Open Middle™) Using the integers -9 to 9, at most one time each, fill in the boxes twice to create two linear functions with corresponding x- and y-coordinates, one with a positive slope and one with a negative slope.

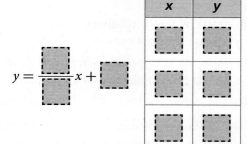

©Taras Vyshnya/Alamy

Spiral Review • Assessment Readiness

17. Which equation has a graph with a positive slope?

  Ⓐ $3x + 2y = 8$ Ⓒ $y = -12 - 5x$

  Ⓑ $y = -5x + 3$ Ⓓ $-2x + 3y = 10$

18. Which is the inverse of $f(x) = 0.5x + 2$?

  Ⓐ $g(x) = \dfrac{x-2}{0.5}$ Ⓒ $g(x) = 2(x-2)$

  Ⓑ $g(x) = x + 0.5$ Ⓓ $g(x) = 0.5x - 2$

19. What type of correlation does $r = -0.5$ describe?

  Ⓐ strong negative   Ⓒ weak positive

  Ⓑ strong positive   Ⓓ weak negative

20. For the given pattern, what operation can you perform to find the next number?

$$10, 5, 2.5, \ldots$$

  Ⓐ multiply by 2   Ⓒ divide by 2

  Ⓑ add 2   Ⓓ subtract 2

 I'm in a Learning Mindset!

Did I learn anything new about lines of fit that was outside my comfort zone?

Correlation

Isaiyah is investigating the relationship between altitude and the boiling point of water.

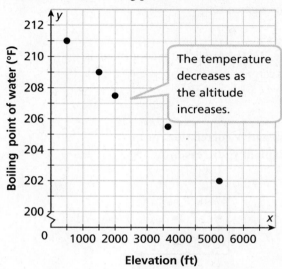

After creating a scatter plot, Isaiyah notices that there is a strong negative correlation between altitude and the boiling point of water.

Linear Regression

Isaiyah wants to predict the boiling point of water at other elevations. He uses graphing software to perform linear regression and obtains the least-squares line.

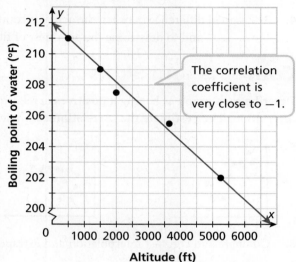

Least-squares line: $T(h) = -0.0018h + 211.706$

Interpolation and Extrapolation

Isaiyah predicts the boiling point of water in San Salvador using the least-squares line.

$$T(2160) \approx 208 \text{ °F}$$

This is interpolation because the input came from within the model's domain.

Isaiyah predicts the boiling point of water in La Paz using the least-squares line.

$$T(11,900) \approx 190 \text{ °F}$$

This is extrapolation because the input came from outside the model's domain.

Residuals

Isaiyah wants to know how good the model is and creates a table to analyze some residuals, the difference between the predicted and actual values.

Altitude (ft)	500	2000
Actual boiling point (°F)	211.0	207.5
Predicted boiling point (°F)	210.8	208.1
Residual	0.2	−0.6
Squared residual	0.04	0.36

A smaller sum of squared residuals indicates a better fit. Linear regression minimizes the sum of squared residuals to determine the least-squares line.

Vocabulary

Choose the correct term from the box to complete each sentence.

Vocabulary
bivariate data
correlation coefficient
correlation
linear regression
residual
residual plot

1. The ___?___ for a set of bivariate data can be categorized as positive, negative, or none.

2. The ___?___ is a number r that describes how closely data clusters around a line.

3. ___?___ is a method that finds the least-squares line for a given set of ___?___.

4. The signed difference between the actual y-coordinate and the predicted y-coordinate is the ___?___, and to determine the goodness of fit, you can use a ___?___

Concepts and Skills

Describe each graph as having a positive correlation, a negative correlation, or no correlation. Then estimate the correlation coefficient. Explain your reasoning.

5.   6.    7.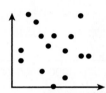

8. Compare and contrast interpolation and extrapolation.

9. Mona is reading a long novel. The table shows the cumulative number of pages p read for various times t (days of the year).

t	10	12	15	20	30	45	60	80
p	0	30	75	142	287	500	730	1050

A. Create a line of fit.   B. Create a residual plot.

C. Assess your line of fit. Use your residual plot in your explanation.

D. Would your model give a more reliable prediction for the cumulative number of pages read on day 50 or day 100? Explain.

E. Use your model to approximate $p(50)$. Explain what it would represent in this context.

10. To determine which of two lines of fit is better, which analysis is more useful: looking at residual plots or comparing sums of squared residuals?

11. **(MP) Use Tools** State what strategy and tool you will use to answer the question, explain your choice, and then find the answer. Matt is letting his hair grow out. The length ℓ, in inches, of Matt's hair is measured at time t, in months (where a time ending in .5 represents half of a month).

t	0	0.50	1.00	1.50	2.00	2.50	3.00	3.50	4.00
ℓ	1.00	1.50	1.75	2.00	2.50	2.75	3.15	3.60	3.90

A. Use linear regression to determine the line of best fit.

B. What is the correlation coefficient, r? What is the strength of the correlation?

C. What is the length of Matt's hair after letting it grow for 1.25 months? Explain.

Module Performance Task: *Spies and Analysts*™

Address the Address

If your friend lives 15 buildings away on the same side of the street, what is your friend's address?

4672

U.S. MAIL

©zodebala/iStock/Getty Images Plus/Getty Images

Are You Ready?

Complete these problems to review prior concepts and skills you will need for this module.

Add and Subtract Rational Numbers

Simplify each expression.

1. $-\dfrac{1}{2}+\dfrac{5}{6}$

2. $-1.24-2.54$

3. $1.24+6.52$

4. $\dfrac{3}{4}-\dfrac{7}{8}$

5. $\dfrac{2}{9}+\dfrac{1}{5}$

6. $5.81-9.1$

Multiply and Divide Rational Numbers

Simplify each expression.

7. $\left(\dfrac{1}{2}\right)\left(\dfrac{7}{8}\right)$

8. $1.11(0.5)$

9. $378\div5$

10. $\dfrac{3}{5}\div\dfrac{7}{8}$

11. $\left(-\dfrac{2}{3}\right)\left(\dfrac{9}{13}\right)$

12. $0.0768\div0.024$

Evaluate Algebraic Expressions

Evaluate the expression for the given information.

13. $-3+5(n-1)$ for $n=6$

14. $2-6(n+2)$ for $n=3$

15. $-5-7(n-1)$ for $n=10$

16. $2+3(n-8)$ for $n=20$

17. $2(n+1)-12$ for $n=5$

18. $-3(n-3)+3$ for $n=-3$

Connecting Past and Present Learning

Previously, you learned:

• to generate sequences given a rule or identify a rule from a pattern,

• to use function notation,

• to work with linear functions.

In this module, you will learn:

• to write recursive and explicit formulas for arithmetic sequences,

• to construct functions and sequences that model graphs and descriptions, and

• to evaluate functions for inputs to solve real-world problems.

Arithmetic Sequences Defined Recursively

(I Can) use arithmetic sequences defined recursively to solve real-world problems.

Spark Your Learning

A pass for the food festival includes entry admission and tickets for tastings. Different passes include different numbers of tastings.

One admission with 5 tastings costs $22.

Complete Part A as a whole class. Then complete Parts B–D in small groups.

A. What is a mathematical question you can ask about this situation? What information would you need to know to answer your question?

B. How would you find the cost per tasting for each type of pass?

C. To answer your question, what strategy and tool would you use along with all the information you have? What answer do you get?

D. In the relationship between the total cost and the number of tastings, how would you classify the numbers in the domain? In the range?

 Turn and Talk Predict how your answer would change for each of the following:

- The cost of three tastings is cut in half.
- The cost of 8 tastings is $32.
- A ticket for 9 tastings is introduced.

Build Understanding

Examine Sequences and Function Notation

A **sequence** is a list of numbers in a specific order. Each number in a sequence is a **term (of the sequence).**

1 ▶ The table displays part of a sequence that models the total cost of piano lessons based on the number of hours of piano lessons.

Piano Lessons:
$50 first hour
$75 for each additional hour

The positions in the sequence give the hours of piano lessons, and the terms of the sequence give the corresponding total costs.

Position, n	1	2	3
Term, $f(n)$	50	125	200

A. Copy and complete the table for integer values of n from 1 through 10.

B. Using the table, find the total cost for 5, 8, and 10 hours of piano lessons. Write your answers using function notation.

C. What is the domain, and what does it represent?

D. What is the range, and what does it represent?

E. What does the ordered pair $(7, 500)$ represent?

F. How many hours of piano lessons can you get for $350?

 Turn and Talk For a sequence, every domain value is paired with how many range values? How does this relate to the definition of a function?

Use Recursive Rules for Arithmetic Sequences

An **arithmetic sequence** is a sequence in which consecutive terms differ by the same number d, called the **common difference**. The sequence of piano-lesson costs in Task 1 is an example of an arithmetic sequence with a common difference of 75.

$$50, \quad 125, \quad 200, \quad 275, \quad 350, \quad 425, \ldots, f(n-1), f(n), \ldots$$

$$+75 \quad +75 \quad +75 \quad +75 \quad +75 \qquad +75$$

You can write a rule for an arithmetic sequence that describes how to find the nth term. A **recursive rule** for a sequence gives the beginning term or terms and then a *recursive equation* that defines the nth term by relating it to one or more previous terms. For example, the following is a recursive rule for the sequence of piano-lesson costs:

$$f(1) = 50, f(n) = f(n-1) + 75$$

2 The first several figures in a pattern are shown below.

Figure 1: □

Figure 2: □□□

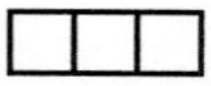

Figure 3: □□□□□

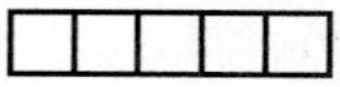

⋮

Figure $n - 1$: □□□□□ ··· □

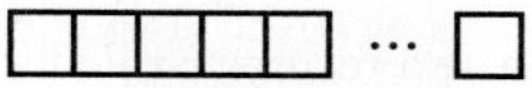

Figure n: □□□□□ ··· □□□

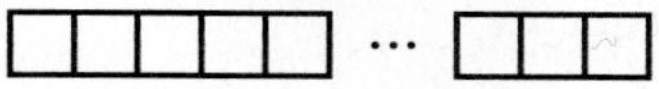

A. Draw Figure 4 and Figure 5.

B. Let $s(n)$ = the number of squares in the nth figure. Write the first 5 terms of the sequence defined by $s(n)$.

C. Is the sequence defined by $s(n)$ an arithmetic sequence? If so, what is the common difference?

D. Write a recursive rule for $s(n)$. Use the recursive rule to find $s(6)$ and $s(7)$.

> **General Recursive Rule for an Arithmetic Sequence**
>
> A recursive rule for an arithmetic sequence with common difference d is given by:
> $$f(1) = \text{value of 1st term}, \quad f(n) = f(n - 1) + d \text{ for } n \geq 2$$

3 The photo shows the cost of admission to an art museum. Let $f(n)$ = the total cost in dollars of n visits to the museum during the same month.

A. Write the first 5 terms of the sequence defined by $f(n)$.

B. Is the sequence defined by $f(n)$ an arithmetic sequence? If so, what is the common difference, and what does it represent in this situation?

C. What is a recursive rule for the sequence?

D. What is the value of $f(8)$, and what does it represent?

Monthly Admission:
$25 first admission
$5 for each additional
visit in the month

 Turn and Talk Why must the first term of an arithmetic sequence be given as part of the recursive rule?

Step It Out

Graph Arithmetic Sequences

You can graph a sequence on a coordinate plane by plotting the points $(n, f(n))$. Since the domain is generally the set of natural numbers or whole numbers, the function is a discrete function. Recall that a discrete function has a graph made up of unconnected points.

4 Given the table representing an arithmetic sequence, write a recursive rule for the sequence, graph it, and find the 9th term of the sequence.

Position, n	1	2	3	4	5
Term, $f(n)$	20	16	12	8	4

Graph the arithmetic sequence given in the table.

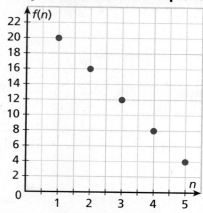

A. How is the common difference, d, represented in the graph?

B. Why is the graph a set of disconnected points instead of a continuous line?

Write a recursive rule.

Write the first term: $f(1) = 20$.

C. What point represents the first term?

Find the difference between successive terms to find the common difference, d.
The difference between the second and first terms is $16 - 20 = -4$, so $d = -4$.

$f(n) = f(n - 1) + d$, for $n \geq 2$
$f(n) = f(n - 1) - 4$, for $n \geq 2$

Find $f(9)$ for this sequence.

The last term known is the 5th term, 4, or $f(5) = 4$.

$f(5) = 4$
$f(6) = 4 - 4 = 0$
$f(7) = 0 - 4 = -4$
$f(8) = -4 - 4 = -8$
$f(9) = -8 - 4 = -12$

D. Why do the steps for finding the 9th term of this sequence begin with the 5th term?

 Turn and Talk Can you think of a way involving multiples of the common difference, -4, that you could find the 9th term of this sequence?

Model with Arithmetic Sequences

5 The photo shows the transporter rental charges for a guided tour for a group of 25 or less.

Make a table and a graph for the arithmetic sequence that models this situation. Then write a recursive rule for the sequence, and use the rule to find the cost for transporter rentals for a group of 8 people.

Create a table for the first five terms.

n	1	2	3	4	5
$f(n)$	40	60	80	100	120

A. What do n and $f(n)$ represent?

Transporter Rental:
$40 for first rental
$20 for each additional rental

Graph the sequence for $1 \leq n \leq 5$.

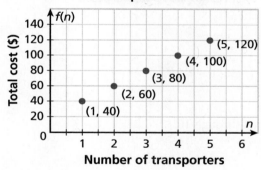

Transporter Rental

(5, 120)
(4, 100)
(3, 80)
(2, 60)
(1, 40)

Total cost ($)
Number of transporters

Write a recursive rule for the sequence.

$f(1) = 40$
$f(n) = f(n - 1) + 20$, for $2 \leq n \leq 25$

B. Explain how and why the domain is limited in this situation.

Find the cost for a group of 8 to go on this guided tour.

$f(5) = 120$
$f(6) = 120 + 20 = 140$
$f(7) = 140 + 20 = 160$
$f(8) = 160 + 20 = 180$

 Turn and Talk What is the cost for 25 tourists to rent transporters? Explain.

Check Understanding

1. Do the terms of an arithmetic sequence correspond to the domain or to the range of the related function? Explain.

2. Does a recursive rule for an arithmetic sequence always need to include at least one term of the sequence? Explain.

3. Explain how to determine whether a sequence is arithmetic.

4. Consider the sequence 6, 9, 12, 15, 18, . . .
   A. What is the domain?
   B. What is $f(7)$?

5. A mini-golf course charges $9 for the first game and $4 for each additional game for up to 5 games. Write a recursive rule that models this situation. How much does it cost to play 4 games?

On Your Own

6. Why is a sequence a function?

7. The table shows part of a sequence that models the total cost of movie tickets based on the number of tickets purchased using a special offer.

Tickets, t	1	2	3	4	5	6
Cost, $c(t)$	10	18	26	34	42	50

   A. What does the ordered pair $(5, 42)$ represent?
   B. Copy and complete the table for values of t from 1 through 10.
   C. How many movie tickets can you purchase for $74?

8. The first three figures in a pattern are shown below.

   Figure 1: Figure 2:   Figure 3:

   A. Draw the next figure in the pattern.
   B. Let $d(n)$ = the total number of dots in the nth figure. Is the sequence defined by $d(n)$ an arithmetic sequence? If so, what is the common difference?
   C. Write a recursive rule for $d(n)$. Use the recursive rule to find $d(8)$.

9. Do all infinite arithmetic sequences have the same domain? Do all infinite arithmetic sequences have the same range? Explain.

10. (MP) **Reason** In an arithmetic sequence given by the rule $f(n) = f(n-1) + d$, for $n \geq 2$, why is n always a natural number?

11. (MP) **Construct Arguments** Is the sequence 2, 4, 8, 16, ... an arithmetic sequence? Explain why or why not.

Write a recursive rule for each of the sequences shown in a table. Then graph the sequence.

12.

Position, n	1	2	3	4	5
Term, $g(n)$	7	13	19	25	31

13.

Position, n	1	2	3	4	5	6
Term, $g(n)$	8	−2	−12	−22	−32	−42

14. Part of an arithmetic sequence is shown in the graph. Write a recursive rule for the sequence.

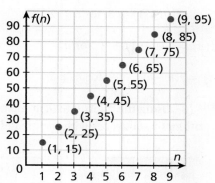

15. For an arithmetic sequence, if $f(1) = 250$ and $d = 15$, what is $f(4)$?

16. For an arithmetic sequence, if $f(18) = 176$ and $d = 11$, what is $f(15)$?

17. For an arithmetic sequence, if $f(1) = 100$ and $f(5) = 160$, what is d?

18. (MP) **Reason** Wylie knows the fourth term in a sequence is 1 and the ninth term in the same sequence is −9. Explain how Wylie can find the common difference for the sequence. Then use the common difference to find the second term of the sequence.

19. **Open Ended** Write and solve a real-world problem involving a situation that can be represented by the sequence $f(n) = 15 + 2(n - 1)$.

Write a recursive rule for each arithmetic sequence. Then find the 15th term.

20. −12, −5, 2, 9, 16, ...

21. 4, −3, −10, −17, −24, ...

22. 135, 114, 93, 72, 51, ...

23. 3, 17, 31, 45, 59, ...

24. $\frac{1}{4}, \frac{3}{8}, \frac{1}{2}, \frac{5}{8}, \frac{3}{4}, \ldots$

25. $2\frac{1}{3}, 2, 1\frac{2}{3}, 1\frac{1}{3}, 1, \ldots$

26. $2, 3\frac{1}{2}, 5, 6\frac{1}{2}, 8, 9\frac{1}{2}, \ldots$

27. 0.25, −0.75, −1.75, −2.75, ...

28. (MP) **Use Structure** Slade works as a caregiver in the home health industry. His charges are shown.

A. Write a recursive rule to model the amount Slade earns based on hours worked.

B. How much does Slade earn for 4 hours of caregiving?

Home Health Charges
$25 first hour
$12 each additional hour

29. The graph models the balance (in dollars) of Roberto's savings account.

A. What was Roberto's first deposit?

B. Is the sequence defined by $f(n)$ an arithmetic sequence? If so, write a recursive rule for the sequence.

C. If he continues to make the same deposit each time, how much money will he have after the 10th deposit?

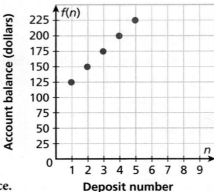

Graph the first five terms of each arithmetic sequence.

30. $f(1) = 2, f(n) = f(n - 1) - 3$, for $n \geq 2$

31. $f(1) = 15, f(n) = f(n - 1) + 3$, for $n \geq 2$

32. $f(1) = -\frac{1}{4}, f(n) = f(n - 1) + \frac{3}{4}$, for $n \geq 2$

33. $f(1) = \frac{1}{4}, f(n) = f(n - 1) - \frac{3}{4}$, for $n \geq 2$

34. (Open Middle™) Using the digits 0 to 9, at most one time each, fill in the boxes to make two arithmetic sequences with the greatest common differences.

Spiral Review • Assessment Readiness

35. What function is the inverse of $f(x) = 3x - 3$?

Ⓐ $g(x) = \dfrac{x + 3}{3}$ Ⓒ $g(x) = \dfrac{x - 3}{3}$

Ⓑ $g(x) = \dfrac{3x + 1}{3}$ Ⓓ $g(x) = \dfrac{x}{3} + 3$

36. In a scatter plot, the values of two variables increase together. What type of correlation exists?

Ⓐ positive   Ⓒ none

Ⓑ negative   Ⓓ weak

37. What point lies on the same line as $(4, 5)$ and $(8, 7)$?

Ⓐ $(2, 6)$ Ⓒ $(0, 6)$

Ⓑ $(2, 4)$ Ⓓ $(6, 2)$

38. Which description of the distribution of residuals in a residual plot shows a line that fits the data very well?

Ⓐ random but loose

Ⓑ random and tight

Ⓒ not random but tight

Ⓓ not random and loose

 I'm in a Learning Mindset!

How do I know I used appropriate sources of information when I made decisions for writing recursive rules?

Arithmetic Sequences Defined Explicitly

(I Can) use arithmetic sequences defined explicitly to solve real-world problems.

Spark Your Learning

At a wholesale gift-wrap outlet, the price of the first roll purchased is a set amount. Each additional roll purchased is the same price, which is less than the price of the first roll.

Mr. Phillips wants to buy 20 rolls of gift-wrap from the wholesale gift-wrap outlet.

Complete Part A as a whole class. Then complete Parts B–D in small groups.

A. What is a mathematical question you can ask about this situation? What information would you need to know to answer your question?

B. To answer your question, what strategy and tool would you use along with all the information you have? What answer do you get?

C. What is the price of the first roll purchased?

D. Does your answer make sense in the context of the situation? How do you know?

Turn and Talk An arithmetic sequence can be used to model the situation.
- What is a recursive rule for the sequence?
- What is the disadvantage of using a recursive rule when finding $f(n)$ for large values of n?

Build Understanding

Write and Use Explicit Rules for Arithmetic Sequences

In the previous lesson, you wrote recursive rules for arithmetic sequences. In this lesson, you will write *explicit* rules that describe how to find the nth term of a sequence. An **explicit rule** for a sequence defines the nth term of the sequence as a function of n. For instance, an explicit rule for the arithmetic sequence 5, 15, 25, 35, . . . is $f(n) = 5 + (n - 1)10$.

1 ▷ The first several figures in a pattern are shown below.

Figure 1: ☐

Figure 2: ☐☐☐

Figure 3: ☐☐☐☐☐

⋮

Figure $n - 1$: ☐☐☐☐☐ ⋯ ☐

Figure n: ☐☐☐☐☐ ⋯ ☐☐☐

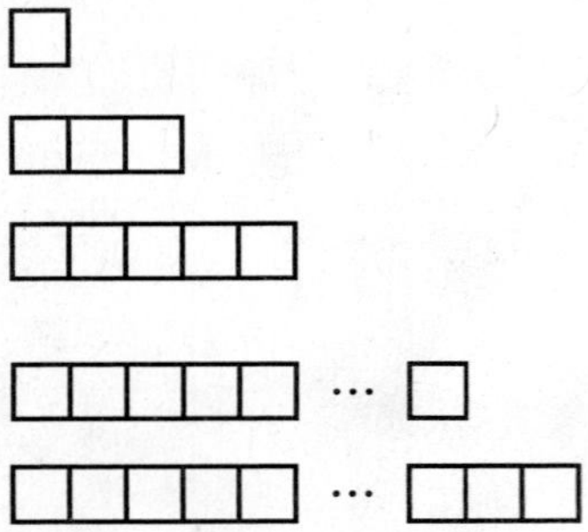

A. Let $s(n) =$ the number of squares in the nth figure. Is the sequence defined by $s(n)$ an arithmetic sequence? If so, what is the common difference?

B. The table shows $s(n)$ expressed as the sum of the first term and a multiple of the common difference. Copy and complete the table for values of n from 1 through 6.

C. Generalize the results from the table to write an explicit rule for $s(n)$. Use the rule to find $s(13)$.

n	$s(n)$
1	$1 + 2(0) = 1$
2	$1 + 2(1) = 3$
3	$1 + 2(2) = 5$

General Explicit Rule for an Arithmetic Sequence

An explicit rule for the nth term of an arithmetic sequence with common difference d is given by:

$$f(n) = f(1) + (n - 1)d$$

2 ▷ An arithmetic sequence is defined by the explicit rule $f(n) = 12 + (n - 1)(9)$ for $1 \le n \le 10$.

A. What is the first term of the sequence?

B. What are the domain and range values of the function?

C. An arithmetic sequence is equivalent to a linear function with a restricted domain. Show that the explicit rule for the sequence can be written as a linear function of the form $f(n) = mn + b$.

Turn and Talk Suppose the points $(n, f(n))$ for the sequence in Task 2 are plotted on the coordinate plane. Do the points lie on a line? If so, how is the slope of the line related to the sequence?

Convert Between Forms of Arithmetic Sequences

Every arithmetic sequence can be described using both recursive and explicit rules.

3 ▶ The photo shows the cost of admission to an aquarium for a group. Let $f(n)$ = the total cost in dollars of n admission tickets.

Group Admission:
$30 for first person
$11 for each additional person

A. What are the first 3 terms of the sequence defined by $f(n)$?

B. What is an explicit rule for this sequence?

C. What is a recursive rule for this sequence?

D. What is the cost for 20 tickets? Which rule did you use to find the answer? Explain your choice.

Turn and Talk How many tickets can be purchased for $294? Which rule did you use to find the answer? Explain your choice.

Given a recursive rule for an arithmetic sequence, you can write an explicit rule. Similarly, given an explicit rule, you can write a recursive rule.

4 ▶ Consider the sequence defined by the recursive rule shown.

$$g(1) = 120, g(n) = g(n - 1) + 18, \text{ for } n \geq 2$$

A. Suppose you want to write an explicit rule for the sequence. What information do you need to write the explicit rule?

B. Can you use the recursive rule to find the values that you need to write the explicit rule? If so, what are the values?

C. What is an explicit rule $g(n)$ for the sequence?

D. Check your explicit rule by verifying that it gives the same value as the recursive rule for $g(3)$ and $g(5)$.

E. Kati says that an explicit rule for the sequence is $g(n) = 120 + 18n - 1$. Is her rule correct? Explain why or why not.

Turn and Talk Why does the explicit rule involve multiplying the common difference by $(n - 1)$ instead of by n?

Step It Out

Graph Arithmetic Sequences

5 The table shows the terms of an arithmetic sequence and the position of each term in the sequence. Graph the sequence, and then write an explicit rule for the sequence.

Position, n	1	2	3	4	5
Term, $f(n)$	35	53	71	89	107

Graph the sequence.

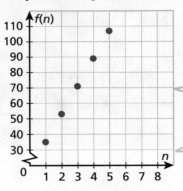

A. What is the sequence represented by the graph?

B. How is the 5th term in the sequence represented in the graph?

Write an explicit rule.

$f(1) = 35$ and $d = 18$

$f(n) = f(1) + (n - 1)d$

$f(n) = 35 + (n - 1)18$

$\quad = 17 + 18n$ for $1 \le n \le 5$

C. Explain why 35 is substituted for $f(1)$ and 18 is substituted for d.

D. Why are the domain values limited to $1 \le n \le 5$?

6 The graph shows an arithmetic sequence. Write an explicit rule for the sequence. Then use the rule to find $f(8)$.

Write an explicit rule.

The first term is 60, so $f(1) = 60$.

The common difference is $d = 90 - 60 = 30$.

$f(n) = f(1) + (n - 1)d$

$f(n) = 60 + 30(n - 1)$

$\quad = 30 + 30n$ for $1 \le n \le 8$

A. Why are the domain values $1 \le n \le 8$?

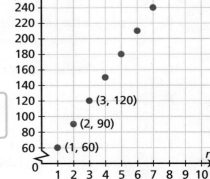

Use the rule to find $f(18)$.

$f(18) = 30 + 30(8) = 270$

B. What point represents $f(18)$?

Turn and Talk How can you tell whether the graph of a sequence is the graph of an arithmetic sequence?

Model with Arithmetic Sequences

7 ▶ A plumbing company creates a fee chart for their labor charges. What is the total charge for 9 hours of labor?

Number of hours, n	1	2	3	4	5	...
Total charge in dollars, $f(n)$	75	125	175	225	275	...

An arithmetic sequence can model this situation since consecutive terms have a common difference. A recursive or explicit rule can be used to find $f(9)$.

Recursive Rule

$f(1) = 75 \quad d = 50$

$f(n) = f(n - 1) + 50$

$f(2) = 75 + 50 = 125$

$f(3) = 125 + 50 = 175$

$f(4) = 175 + 50 = 225$

$\vdots \qquad \vdots$

$f(9) = 425 + 50 = 475$

Explicit Rule

$f(1) = 75 \quad d = 50$

$f(n) = 75 + (n - 1)(50)$ or $f(n) = 25 + 50n$

$f(9) = 25 + 50(9) = 475$

A. How are the two methods alike, and how are they different?

B. What are the terms of the sequence that are not shown here?

The total charge for 9 hours of labor is $475.

8 ▶ Julio is visiting a college. What is the total cost for 8 hours of parking?

Arrange the solution steps in the correct order.

$f(8) = 3.5 + 28$

$f(n) = 3.5 + 3.5n$

$f(n) = 7 + (n - 1)(3.5)$

$f(8) = 31.5$

$f(8) = 3.5 + 3.5(8)$

Parking Costs:
$7.00 for the first hour
$3.50 for each additional hour

The total cost for parking 8 hours is $31.50.

Turn and Talk What is a reasonable domain for this sequence?

Check Understanding

1. Part of an arithmetic sequence is shown in the table.

Position, n	1	2	3
Term, $f(n)$	10	17	24

   A. What is $f(1)$?

   B. What is the common difference d?

   C. What is an explicit rule for the sequence?

2. A sequence is defined by the explicit rule $f(n) = 8 + (n - 1)(3)$ for $1 \leq n \leq 15$.

   A. What is the first term?

   B. What is the 15th term?

   C. What is a recursive rule for the sequence?

3. What is an explicit rule for the graph?

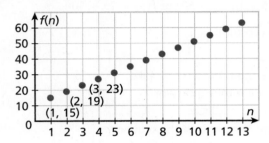

4. Ainsley is a private chef who charges \$50 for the first hour of work and \$30 for each additional hour. Write the explicit rule for the arithmetic sequence that models the chef's total charges, and find the amount charged for 8 hours.

On Your Own

5. Grayson uses toothpicks to create figures like the ones below.

   Figure 1　**Figure 2**　**Figure 3**

   A. Let $t(n)$ be the number of toothpicks in the nth figure. Does $t(n)$ define an arithmetic sequence? If so, what is the common difference?

   B. How many times is the common difference added to the first term of the sequence to find the 4th term? the 5th term?

6. An arithmetic sequence is defined by $f(n) = 52 + (n - 1)(-7)$ for $1 \leq n \leq 6$. What are the domain and range values of $f(n)$?

7. **Personal Finance** To save money for a school trip, Monika does light yardwork.

   A. Write an explicit rule and a recursive rule that model this situation.

   B. Monika spends 4 hours working for the Ziegler family. How much does she earn? Explain how you found the answer.

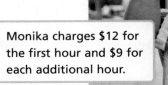

Monika charges \$12 for the first hour and \$9 for each additional hour.

Write an explicit rule for each arithmetic sequence defined by the given recursive rule.

8. $g(1) = 100, g(n) = g(n - 1) + 10$ for $n \geq 2$

9. $g(1) = 88, g(n) = g(n - 1) - 6$ for $n \geq 2$

10. $g(1) = 15, g(n) = g(n - 1) + 20$ for $2 \leq n \leq 5$

11. An arithmetic sequence is defined by the rule $h(n)$.

$h(n) = 16 + 6n$ for $1 \leq n \leq 5$

A. Graph the sequence.

B. How many data points are shown on the graph?

C. Write a recursive rule for the sequence.

12. A grocery cart is 38 inches long. When the grocery carts are put away in a nested row, the length of the row depends on how many carts are nested together. Part of the sequence that models the row length is shown in the graph.

A. Write a recursive rule for the sequence.

B. Write an explicit rule for the sequence.

C. Find the length of a row with 15 nested carts.

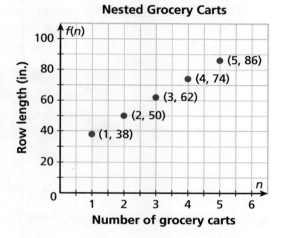

Nested Grocery Carts

13. Nadya's parents loan her $52. A week later, she starts paying back the debt by making weekly payments. Part of the sequence that models the remaining debt is shown in the graph.

A. Write a recursive rule for the sequence. Do not specify a domain.

B. Write an explicit rule for the sequence. Do not specify a domain.

C. Find the amount remaining to be paid after 7 weeks.

D. In what week will the loan be paid off?

Paying Off Debt

14. The wolf population in a local wildlife area is currently 12. Due to a new conservation effort, conservationists hope the wolf population will increase by 2 each year for the next 50 years. Assume that the plan will be successful.

A. Write an explicit rule for the sequence that models this situation.

B. Use the rule to predict the number of wolves in the wildlife area in the 50th year.

15. The graph shows part of an infinite arithmetic sequence. Write an explicit rule for the sequence.

16. (MP) **Attend to Precision** Karen keeps track of the total amount of money she has saved so far during the year by writing the sequence that gives her total amount saved (in dollars) at the end of each week.

28, 40, 52, 64, …

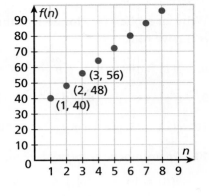

A. What is an explicit rule for this sequence? Use a reasonable domain.

B. What is $f(12)$?

17. (MP) **Reason** Carlos has some money saved for a scooter and would like to have more. Let $f(0)$ represent his initial savings, and let $f(n)$ represent his savings after n months. The diagram shows the total amount Carlos plans to have saved after 2 different months. Write an explicit rule for $f(n)$ assuming Carlos saves the same amount of money each month.

Savings Plan
Month 4: $500
Month 5: $550

Spiral Review • Assessment Readiness

18. Perform linear regression on the data set $\{(1, 3), (2, 6), (3, 7), (4, 10)\}$. What is the correlation coefficient, r?

(A) 0.8909

(C) 0.9768

(B) 0.968

(D) 0.9839

19. Liam earns an hourly wage for babysitting and earned $105 babysitting for 5 hours. What function gives the amount of money (in dollars) that Liam earns in x hours?

(A) $f(x) = 105$

(C) $f(x) = 5x$

(B) $f(x) = 21x$

(D) $f(x) = 105x$

20. Match the description with the equation.

A. A phone plan costs $40 per month plus $5 per gigabyte of data.

1. $y = 1.25x + 8$

B. A pizza costs $12 plus $2 per topping.

2. $-2x + y = 12$

C. A restaurant charges $8 for a plate of wings and $1.25 for each dipping sauce.

3. $y = 5x + 40$

 I'm in a Learning Mindset!

How do I make thoughtful decisions about my academic needs?

Review

Recursive Rules for Arithmetic Sequences

Esther is saving money. She saves $100 the first month and then saves $25 each month that follows. The table shows part of a sequence that models the total amount of money Esther has saved after m months.

Position, m	1	2	3
Term, $f(m)$	100	125	150

$+25$ $+25$

> This is an arithmetic sequence since consecutive terms have a common difference.

Use the first term $f(1) = 100$ and the common difference $d = 25$ to write a recursive rule for the sequence. You can use the rule to find how much Esther has saved after 5 months.

$$f(n) = f(n - 1) + 25 \text{ for } n \geq 2$$

$$f(1) = 100$$

$$f(2) = f(1) + 25 = 125$$

$$f(3) = f(2) + 25 = 150$$

$$f(4) = f(3) + 25 = 175$$

$$f(5) = f(4) + 25 = 200$$

Esther has saved $200 after 5 months.

Explicit Rules for Arithmetic Sequences

The graph shows how much money Esther has saved after m months.

The information in the graph can be used to write a recursive rule for the arithmetic sequence that models the total amount of money Esther has saved.

$$f(n) = f(1) + (n - 1)d$$

$$f(n) = 100 + (n - 1)25$$

$$= 100 + 25n - 25$$

$$= 75 + 25n$$

> The sequence shown in the graph is arithmetic since the points lie on a line.

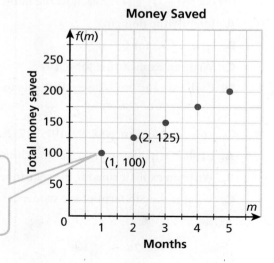

Money Saved

You can use the explicit rule to find how much Esther has saved after 48 months.

$$f(48) = 75 + 25(48) = 1275$$

Esther has saved $1275 after 48 months.

Vocabulary

Choose the correct term from the box to complete each sentence.

1. The ___?___ of the sequence 14, 16, 18, … is 2.

2. A sequence with successive numbers having the same difference is a(n) ___?___ .

3. A(n) ___?___ defines the nth term of an arithmetic sequence by relating it to previous terms.

4. A(n) ___?___ defines the nth term of an arithmetic sequence by adding the common difference $n - 1$ times to the first term.

5. A(n) ___?___ is a list of numbers in a specific order.

Concepts and Skills

6. **(MP) Use Tools** State what strategy and tool you will use to answer the question, explain your choice, and then find the answer. The table shows part of an arithmetic sequence that models the height $h(n)$ of a building based on the floor of the building.

Position number, n	1	2	3	4
Term of the sequence, $h(n)$	15	25	35	45

   A. What is the common difference d of the sequence?

   B. What is $h(1)$? What does it represent in this situation?

   C. Write a recursive rule for the sequence.

   D. Write an explicit rule for the sequence.

   E. Find $h(7)$.

7. The recursive rule for a particular arithmetic sequence $f(n)$ is $f(1) = 16$ and $f(n) = f(n - 1) + 4$ for each whole number greater than 1.

   A. Identify the domain.

   B. Graph $f(n)$ for $1 \leq n \leq 10$.

   C. Write an explicit rule for $f(n)$.

   D. Carli says she used the explicit rule to find $f(5.5) = 34$. Is her answer correct? Explain your reasoning.

8. Consider the sequence 82, 92, 102, 112, …

   A. Explain why the sequence is an arithmetic sequence.

   B. Write an explicit rule for the sequence.

   C. What is the 8th term of the sequence?

Piecewise-Defined Functions

Module Performance Task: *Spies and Analysts*™

TAKING THE PRESSURE OFF

What is an acceptable range for a football's air pressure?

Are You Ready?

Complete these problems to review prior concepts and skills you will need for this module.

Find and Interpret Absolute Values of Numbers

Determine the absolute value of the following numbers.

1. -5

2. 0

3. 11

4. $-\pi$

5. The state of California requires that hot food being served at any facility over a period of time be held at a temperature of 135 °F or higher before food is removed from the temperature control to be served. If the holding oven used has a tolerance of 2 °F and shows a temperature of 138 °F, is the holding temperature within the state requirement?

6. The length of a bolt should be 18.0 cm. The allowable range of bolt length is from 17.5 cm to 18.5 cm. What is the tolerance of the bolt length?

Solve Two-Step Inequalities

Find the solution for each two-step inequality.

7. $2x - 1 \geq 9$

8. $\dfrac{x - 4}{5} > 8$

9. $3x + 6 < -15$

10. $\dfrac{x + 3}{4} \leq -2$

Graph Linear Equations in Slope-Intercept Form

Create a graph for each given function.

11. $y = -2x - 3$

12. $y = 3x + 1$

13. $y = \dfrac{1}{3}x + 2$

14. $y = -\dfrac{2}{5}x + 10$

Connecting Past and Present Learning

Previously, you learned:

- to write an equation in point-slope form when given information graphically,
- to write two-step inequalities to model real-world scenarios, and
- to use function notation to characterize relationships among linear functions.

In this module, you will learn:

- to write and solve absolute value equations and inequalities algebraically,
- to graph and model with piecewise functions, and
- to graph and construct absolute value functions.

Graph Piecewise-Defined Functions

(**I Can**) write, graph, and use piecewise-defined functions
to solve real-world problems.

Spark Your Learning

A digital rain gauge keeps track of how much rain has fallen over the
course of the day.

At day's end, the
gauge has provided
24 hourly readings.

Complete Part A as a whole class. Then complete Parts B–D in small groups.

> **A.** What is a mathematical question you can ask about this situation? What
> information would you need to know to answer your question?
>
> **B.** Would a graph modeling this situation be continuous or discrete? Explain.
>
> **C.** To answer your question, what strategy and tool would you use along with all the
> information you have? What answer do you get?
>
> **D.** Does your answer make sense in the context of the situation? How do you know?

Turn and Talk Predict how your answer would change for each of the following
changes in the situation:

- The rate of the rainfall was constant over the 24-hour period.
- There was no rain for the day.

Build Understanding

Describe Piecewise-Defined Functions

A **piecewise-defined function** is a function that has different rules for different intervals of its domain. These intervals must be distinct, because a function cannot produce two different $f(x)$-values for the same x-value.

1 ▷ A deep farmhouse sink is slowly being filled with water at a rate of 2 gallons per minute. After 4 minutes, the stopper accidently comes loose, and over the next 2 minutes, the volume decreases by 15 quarts. Once the stopper is properly put back in, water fills the sink at a rate of 3 gallons per minute to fill the sink to a capacity of 22 gallons.

> After 8 minutes of washing dishes, the stopper is pulled on purpose, and water is completely drained from the sink at an average rate of 8 gallons per minute.

   A. Explain why this situation can be modeled using a piecewise-defined function.

A graph modeling the volume of water in the sink is shown.

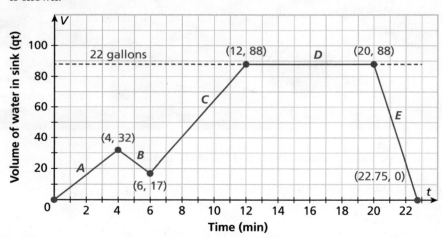

B. What is the domain of the function? What is the range?

C. Where is the graph increasing? What do these intervals correspond to in this situation?

D. Where is the graph decreasing? What do these intervals correspond to in this situation?

E. Where is the graph constant? What does this interval correspond to in this situation?

 Turn and Talk What would the graph of the function look like if the stopper had not come loose after the first 4 minutes?

Evaluate Piecewise-Defined Functions

You can evaluate a piecewise-defined function by substituting values of the domain for the variable in the function rule. When evaluating a piecewise-defined function, you need to first determine which piece of the function to use.

2 **A.** Consider a relation in which one value in the domain is associated with two different values of the range. For example:

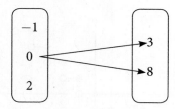

Is this relation a function? Explain.

B. A piecewise-defined function is shown below. The three intervals for the domain do not overlap. Explain why this relation is a function.

$$f(x) = \begin{cases} -2x & \text{if } x < -3 \\ 3x + 1 & \text{if } -3 \leq x < 2 \\ x - 1 & \text{if } x \geq 2 \end{cases}$$

C. The graph of f is shown. Which piece of the graph is related to each equation?

- $y = -2x$
- $y = 3x + 1$
- $y = x - 1$

D. Which piece(s) of the graph are the following:

- line segments
- rays

E. Explain how each piece of the graph relates to the domain intervals.

F. To evaluate $f(x)$ for values in the function's domain, first identify which piece of the function to use. Explain how you know which piece of the function to use to evaluate each of the following. Then find the value.

$f(-3)$ $f(0)$ $f(2)$

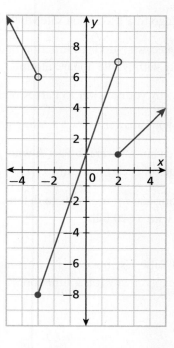

 Turn and Talk Why couldn't the domain for the third piece of the function be $x \geq 1$ instead of $x \geq 2$?

Graph Piecewise-Defined Functions

A **step function** is a piecewise-defined function that is constant over each interval of its domain. An example of a step function is the **greatest integer function**, denoted by $f(x) = \lfloor x \rfloor$, which rounds the number x down to the greatest integer that is less than or equal to x.

3 The greatest integer function is written here as a piecewise-defined function, and the graph is shown.

$$f(x) = \begin{cases} \vdots \\ -2 & \text{if } -2 \leq x < -1 \\ -1 & \text{if } -1 \leq x < 0 \\ 0 & \text{if } 0 \leq x < 1 \\ 1 & \text{if } 1 \leq x < 2 \\ 2 & \text{if } 2 \leq x < 3 \\ \vdots \end{cases}$$

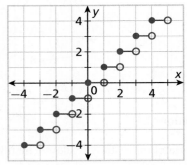

A. Describe the domain intervals. Do they overlap? Explain.

B. How is the function rule related to the corresponding domain interval for each piece of the greatest integer function?

4 Suppose you go to a used book sale where all the books are being sold for $3.

A. Write a piecewise-defined function that models the number of books you could buy with whole dollar amounts.

B. Explain why your answer to Part A represents a step function.

C. Rewrite your answer to Part A using greatest integer function notation.

D. Compare your answers to Part A with your answer to Part C. What are the advantages of each notation?

E. Apply your answer to Part C to determine the greatest number of books you can buy with a $20 bill.

 Turn and Talk Use the domain intervals of the step function that you wrote in Part A to explain why it is a function.

Step It Out

Write Piecewise-Defined Functions

5 The graph of a piecewise-defined function f is shown. Write a rule for $f(x)$.

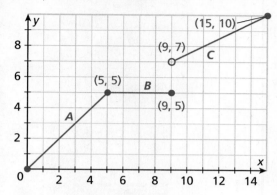

First find the equation for segment A.

$m = \dfrac{5 - 0}{5 - 0} = 1$

$y = mx + b$ ———————— **A.** Why is slope-intercept form used?

$y = 1x + 0$

$y = x$

Then find the equation for segment B.

$y = 5$ ———————— **B.** What is the general form of the equation for a horizontal line?

Finally, find the equation for segment C.

$m = \dfrac{10 - 7}{15 - 9} = \dfrac{1}{2}$ or 0.5

$y - y_1 = m(x - x_1)$ ———————— **C.** Why is point-slope form used?

$y - 7 = 0.5(x - 9)$ ———————— **D.** What point on segment C is used to write the equation?

$y = 0.5x + 2.5$

Use the equations for each segment to write the piecewise-defined function with the appropriate domain intervals.

$$f(x) = \begin{cases} x & \text{if } 0 \leq x \leq 5 \\ 5 & \text{if } 5 < x \leq 9 \\ 0.5x + 2.5 & \text{if } 9 < x \leq 15 \end{cases}$$

E. How are the domain intervals determined?

 Turn and Talk Does it matter whether $x = 5$ is part of the first domain interval or the second? Does it matter whether $x = 9$ is part of the second domain interval or the third? Explain.

Model with Piecewise-Defined Functions

Some real-world situations can be modeled by piecewise-defined functions.

6 A shipping service's charges are based on the weight of the envelope or package being sent. Write a function that models this situation, and then graph the function. How much would it cost to mail an envelope that weighs 3.5 oz?

Envelopes up to 1 ounce: **$1.00**

Each additional ounce: **$0.21**

Use a piecewise-defined function. Let w be the weight (in ounces) of the envelope, and let C be the shipping cost (in dollars).

$$C(w) = \begin{cases} 1.00 & \text{if } 0 < w \le 1 \\ 1.21 & \text{if } 1 < w \le 2 \\ 1.42 & \text{if } 2 < w \le 3 \\ 1.63 & \text{if } 3 < w \le 4 \\ \vdots \end{cases}$$

A. Why is 0 not included in the domain?

B. What is the rule for the next domain interval?

The graph of the function is shown.

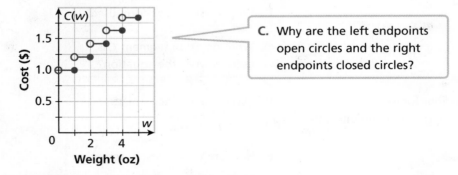

C. Why are the left endpoints open circles and the right endpoints closed circles?

To find the cost of shipping a 3.5-ounce envelope, find the domain interval that includes 3.5.

3.5 is in the interval $3 < w \le 4$, so $C(3.5) = 1.63$.

The cost of shipping a 3.5-ounce envelope is $1.63.

Turn and Talk Explain how the model would change if the additional amount per ounce were to increase to $0.25 per ounce.

Check Understanding

1. A large barrel is filled at a rate of 3 gallons per hour. After 2 hours, the water level reaches a hole in the side of the barrel, and water pours out at the same rate that it flows in for another 2 hours. Describe the graph of this situation.

2. Evaluate $f(-2), f(2), f(3),$ and $f(6)$ for $f(x) = \begin{cases} -x & \text{if } x < 2 \\ 2x + 3 & \text{if } 2 \leq x < 4 \\ x + 6 & \text{if } x \geq 4 \end{cases}$.

3. Graph g.
$$g(x) = \begin{cases} x & \text{if } x < 2 \\ 2x + 3 & \text{if } 2 \leq x < 4 \\ -2x & \text{if } x \geq 4 \end{cases}$$

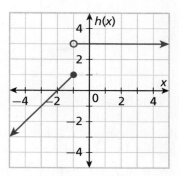

4. Write the function h, whose graph is shown.

On Your Own

5. The cost C for photocopying at a local copy shop is based on the number of pages p.

   A. Write a rule for $C(p)$.

   B. How much would it cost to make 50 copies?

   C. How much would it cost to make 65 copies?

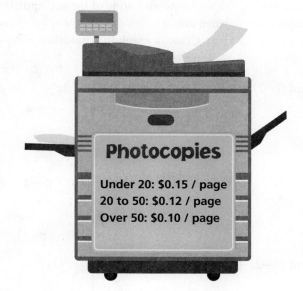

6. **(MP) Critique Reasoning** Clint was given the following information and told to write a rule for $C(t)$ to give the total calories burned C at time t, in minutes, during the workout.

   While exercising, a person's workout consists of using a rowing machine and an elliptical trainer for 30 minutes each. The person burns calories at the following rates:

   • 7 calories per minute on the rowing machine
   • 9 calories per minute on the elliptical trainer

   Clint produced the result shown. What did Clint do wrong and what is a correct answer?

   $$C(t) = \begin{cases} 7t & \text{if } 0 \leq t \leq 30 \\ 210 + 9t & \text{if } 30 < t \leq 60 \end{cases}$$
   ✗

7. **STEM** The velocity of a professional parachuter after the initial jump was approximated at 10 times. Write a piecewise-defined function for the resulting graph.

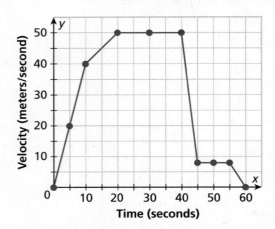

8. (MP) **Model with Mathematics** A late fall day began with the temperature below 32 °F. At 6:00 a.m., the first snow of the season began to fall at a rate of 2 inches per hour. After two hours of steady snowfall, it slowed to 1 inch per hour. From 9:00 a.m. until noon, it did not snow, and none of the accumulated snow melted. Then the temperature warmed enough that the snow started to melt at a rate of 0.5 inch per hour until 2:00 p.m. Create a graph that models the depth of the snow over time.

9. Find $f(-2), f(2), f(5)$, and $f(7)$ for $f(x) = \begin{cases} 2x + 2 & \text{if } x < 2 \\ 3x + 3 & \text{if } 2 \le x < 7. \\ -x + 6 & \text{if } x \ge 7 \end{cases}$

10. Find $h(-3), h(-1)$, and $h(1)$ for $h(x) = \begin{cases} \dfrac{2}{x} & \text{if } x \le -2 \\ x & \text{if } -2 < x < 0. \\ 1 & \text{if } x \ge 0 \end{cases}$

11. Find $k(-2), k(-1), k(0), k(4)$, and $k(9)$ for $k(x) = \begin{cases} -x & \text{if } x \le -2 \\ 2x & \text{if } -2 < x < 2. \\ x + 6 & \text{if } 2 \le x \le 4 \\ 3x + 8 & \text{if } x > 4 \end{cases}$

12. Find $g(-6), g(-2.2), g(1.4)$, and $g(3.6)$ for $g(x) = -2\lfloor x \rfloor$.

Graph each function.

13. $f(x) = \begin{cases} -x & \text{if } x < 0 \\ x + 1 & \text{if } x \ge 0 \end{cases}$

14. $f(x) = \begin{cases} 3 & \text{if } x < 2 \\ 4 & \text{if } 2 \le x < 4 \\ 5 & \text{if } x \ge 4 \end{cases}$

15. $f(x) = \begin{cases} x - 3 & \text{if } x < 4 \\ 2x - 7 & \text{if } x \ge 4 \end{cases}$

16. $f(x) = \begin{cases} -3 & \text{if } x < -1 \\ 2x - 3 & \text{if } x \ge -1 \end{cases}$

17. The *least integer function* or *ceiling function*, denoted by $f(x) = \lceil x \rceil$, rounds the number x up to the least integer that is greater than or equal to x. Write the domain intervals that correspond to $f(x) = -2, -1, 0, 1,$ and 2, and then graph this step function.

18. Open Ended Give an example of a piecewise-defined function that is not continuous. Include an explanation of why this function is not continuous.

19. Personal Finance An initial investment of $8000 paid interest of $500 annually. After 20 years, the original investment plus all the earnings are drawn down at a rate of $800 per year until they are gone. Assume that money accumulated and is later drawn down on a continuous basis even though the annual changes in the total amount of money actually happen all at once when interest is paid or withdrawals are made. Write a piecewise-defined function that models this situation.

Write a piecewise-defined function for each graph.

20.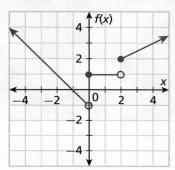

21.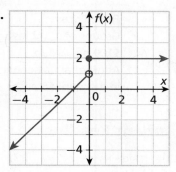

22.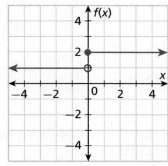

23.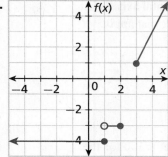

24. The cost of a taxi ride is a function of d, the number of miles driven.

   A. Write a piecewise-defined function $C(d)$ that models this situation.

   B. What would be the cost of a taxi ride that is 8.3 miles long?

   C. Graph this function.

   D. Use your graph to identify whether or not this piecewise-defined function is a step function.

TAXI

$3.50 base fee

Additional $2.75 for each full mile

25. Sophia is planning a pizza party. Her budget allows her to buy 10 pizzas. She uses the spreadsheet shown to determine how many friends she can invite without not having enough pizza for everyone.

	A	B
1	Number of pizzas =	10
2	Number of slices per pizza =	8
3	Number of slices per person =	3
4	Number of people to invite =	26

 A. Describe the steps performed on the numbers in cells B1, B2, and B3 to produce the output in cell B4.

 B. The spreadsheet function [INT] is equivalent to the greatest integer function. Use [INT] and your answer from Part A to give the formula used in cell B4 of the spreadsheet.

26. The cost for a ferry ride is a function of the size of the group taking the ride, as shown.

 A. What is the piecewise-defined function that models this situation?

 B. What would be the cost for a group of 18 people?

> **Ferry Prices:**
> Groups of 15 or less:
> $100 per group
> Additional passengers in a group: $5 each

Spiral Review • Assessment Readiness

27. A residual plot shows that the residuals are large, but they are randomly distributed above and below the horizontal axis. What does this indicate? Select all that apply.

 Ⓐ The line is a good fit.

 Ⓑ The line is not a good fit.

 Ⓒ Correlation is strong.

 Ⓓ Correlation is not strong.

28. The cost of a charm bracelet is $30 for the plain bracelet and $10 for each charm added to it. What recursive formula models this situation?

 Ⓐ $f(0) = 10, f(n) = f(n-1) + 30$

 Ⓑ $f(0) = 40, f(n) = f(n-1) + 10$

 Ⓒ $f(0) = 30, f(n) = f(n-1) + 10$

 Ⓓ $f(0) = 30, f(n) = 10f(n-1)$

29. Which is the correct explicit definition of an arithmetic sequence to get from the first to the nth term?

 Ⓐ $f(n) = f(1) + nd$

 Ⓑ $f(d) = f(n) + 1$

 Ⓒ $f(n) = f(n-1) + d$

 Ⓓ $f(n) = f(1) + (n-1)d$

30. Which correlation coefficients show a strong correlation? Select all that apply.

 Ⓐ $r = 0.51$ Ⓓ $r = 0.98$

 Ⓑ $r = -0.74$ Ⓔ $r = 1.55$

 Ⓒ $r = -0.96$ Ⓕ $r = -0.37$

I'm in a Learning Mindset!

How do I know I used appropriate sources of information when I made decisions for analyzing graphs of piecewise-defined functions?

Graph Absolute Value Functions

(I Can) evaluate and graph absolute value functions.

Spark Your Learning

Ernie sees several geese flying together in a V formation.

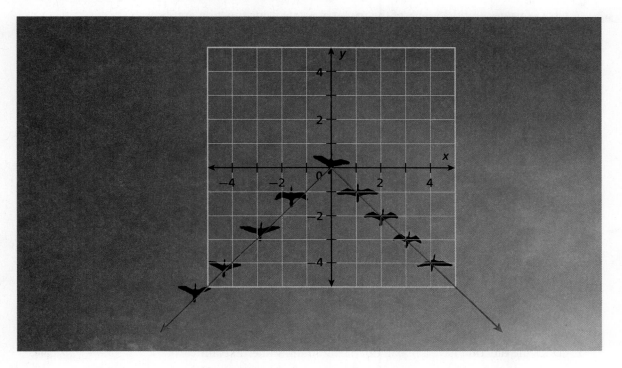

Complete Part A as a whole class. Then complete Parts B–D in small groups.

A. What is a mathematical question you can ask about this situation? What information would you need to know to answer your question?

B. What type of function could be used in this situation?

C. To answer your question, what strategy and tool would you use along with all the information you have? What answer do you get?

D. Compare the two pieces of the function.

Turn and Talk Predict how your answer would change for each of the following changes in the situation:

- The geese spread out so that the horizontal distance between the geese is doubled.
- The geese change their path so that they fly 5 units to the right of their current position.
- The geese fly south instead of flying north.

Build Understanding

Understand the Parent Absolute Value Function

The parent **absolute value function**, denoted $f(x) = |x|$, is a piecewise function given by the following rule:

$$f(x) = \begin{cases} -x & \text{if } x < 0 \\ x & \text{if } x \geq 0 \end{cases}$$

1 ▶ A table of values and the graph of the parent absolute value function are shown.

x	f(x) = |x|
−3	3
−2	2
−1	1
0	0
1	1
2	2
3	3

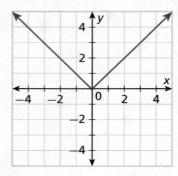

A. Describe the shape of the graph of the parent absolute value function.

B. Identify the domain and range of the parent absolute value function.

C. What are the *x*- and *y*-intercepts of the graph?

D. At what point does the graph of the parent absolute value function change direction? This point is called the *vertex of an absolute value graph*.

E. Does the function have a maximum or minimum value? Explain.

F. For what values of the domain is the function increasing, and for what values of the domain is the function decreasing? Identify the slope of the graph for each part of the domain.

G. What line divides the graph of the parent absolute value function into two congruent reflected halves? This line is called the *axis of symmetry*.

H. Describe how the function rule works for values of *x* that are less than 0, greater than 0, and equal to 0.

I. Explain why the piecewise definition of the parent absolute value function has two parts.

J. What is the minimum number of points you would need to plot in order to draw the graph of the parent absolute value function?

Turn and Talk Susie says that the parent absolute value function can be defined as $f(x) = \begin{cases} -x & \text{if } x \leq 0 \\ x & \text{if } x > 0 \end{cases}$ instead. Is she correct or incorrect? Explain.

Graph Transformations of the Absolute Value Function

You can *translate* the graph of the parent absolute value function $f(x) = |x|$ by changing the values of h and k in $g(x) = |x - h| + k$, where h and k are real numbers.

2 ▶ Compare a translated graph of the parent absolute value function with the graph of the parent absolute value function.

x	g(x) = |x − 3| + 2
2	3
3	2
4	3

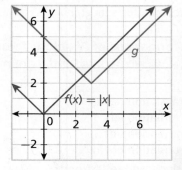

A. How is the graph of g translated from the graph of the parent function? How do the values of h and k affect the vertex, axis of symmetry, intercepts, and minimum value of g?

B. What is the domain of g? What is the range of g? Does a horizontal or vertical translation affect these values? Explain.

You can vertically *stretch or compress* the graph of the parent absolute value function $f(x) = |x|$ by changing the value of a in $g(x) = a|x|$, where a is a nonzero real number.

3 ▶ Compare a stretched or compressed graph of the parent absolute value function with the graph of the parent absolute value function.

x	g(x) = 3|x|
−1	3
0	0
1	3

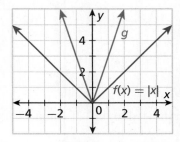

A. How is the graph of g stretched or compressed from the graph of the parent function? How does the value of a affect the slope of each piece of the graph of g?

B. What is the domain of g? What is the range of g? Can changing the value of a ever affect the domain and range? Explain.

 Turn and Talk In a graph of an absolute value function in the form $y = a|x - h| + k$, how is the graph transformed if $h = -3$, $k = -2$, and $a = -3$?

Step It Out

Construct Functions for Transformations of the Absolute Value Function

You can use what you know about transformations to write an absolute value function given its graph. The graphic organizer summarizes how each parameter in an equation for an absolute value function affects its graph.

Transformations of Absolute Value Functions $g(x) = a\lvert x - h \rvert + k$, where a, h, and k are real numbers and $a \neq 0$	
Translations	
$h > 0$	Translation right
$h < 0$	Translation left
$k > 0$	Translation up
$k < 0$	Translation down
Stretches, compressions, and reflections	
$a > 1$	Vertical stretch
$0 < a < 1$	Vertical compression
$-1 < a < 0$	Vertical compression and reflection across x-axis
$a = -1$	Reflection across x-axis
$a < -1$	Vertical stretch and reflection across x-axis

4 ▶ Construct the function of the form $g(x) = a\lvert x - h \rvert + k$ for the given graph.

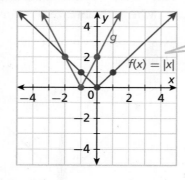

A. How does the vertex indicate what the values of h and k are?

- The graph is translated to the left 1 unit, so $h = -1$.

- The graph is not translated vertically, so $k = 0$.

- The graph is stretched vertically by a factor of 2, so $a = -2$ or $a = 2$.

- Since the graph is not reflected across the x-axis, a is not negative. So, $a = 2$.

The function is $g(x) = 2\lvert x - 1 \rvert + 0$ or $g(x) = 2\lvert x - 1 \rvert$.

B. How can you use the reference points on the transformed graph to draw this conclusion?

C. How does the end behavior tell you whether the graph has been reflected or not?

 Turn and Talk How can you use the vertex to determine the range of the function? What additional information would you need to make a final conclusion?

5 ▶ Jen is making a bank shot in a game of pool on a regulation size table that has a playing field of 46 inches by 92 inches. Using a coordinate plane to describe the location, the cue ball is at $(-30, 3)$ before she hits the ball as described. Write an absolute value function whose graph models the path of this cue ball.

First graph the path described.

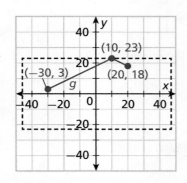

Jen hits the ball to bank off a side at point $(10, 23)$ and hit another ball located at $(20, 18)$.

The vertex of the graph is located at $(10, 23)$. So, $h = 10$ and $k = 23$.

> **A.** The values of h and k relate the vertex to what part of the table?

The slope between the initial point $(-30, 3)$ and the vertex $(10, 23)$ is given by

$$m = \frac{y_2 - y_1}{x_2 - x_1} = \frac{23 - 3}{10 - (-30)} = \frac{20}{40} = \frac{1}{2}$$

> **B.** How would the slope change if you used the vertex and the final point? Would this affect the value of a? Explain.

The graph is a vertical compression and reflection across the x-axis of the graph of the parent absolute value function.

So, $a = -\frac{1}{2}$.

> **C.** How can you tell that the graph is a reflection?

An absolute value function that models the path of the cue ball is given by $g(x) = -\frac{1}{2}|x - 10| + 23$, but the domain must be restricted to match the situation.

The domain is restricted to $-30 \le x \le 20$.

> **D.** What points determine the domain? What do they represent in this context?

So, the range is restricted to $3 \le g(x) \le 23$.

> **E.** What points determine the range? What do they represent in this context?

Turn and Talk Predict how the vertex of g would change in each situation:
- The cue ball was translated to the left.
- The cue ball was translated down.
- The target ball was translated down.

Check Understanding

1. Describe the graph of the parent absolute value function. What is the domain? What is the range?

2. Write a function in the form $f(x) = a|x - h| + k$ for the function whose graph is shown.

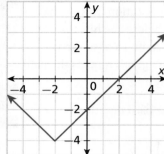

State the effect of the constants in each function when compared to the parent absolute value function.

3. $f(x) = -4|x + 5| - 2$

4. $g(x) = \frac{2}{3}|x - 3| + 1$

5. In general, how is the graph of $f(x) = a|x - h| + k$ related to the graph of the parent absolute value function?

6. Explain how you know from the equation of an absolute value function whether it has a maximum or a minimum value? How can you identify the coordinates where this value occurs?

On Your Own

7. Is the following piecewise function a valid definition for the parent absolute value function? Explain.

$$f(x) = \begin{cases} x & \text{if } x > 0 \\ 0 & \text{if } x = 0 \\ -x & \text{if } x < 0 \end{cases}$$

8. **(MP) Critique Reasoning** Asha suggests that if k is negative and h is positive in $f(x) = |x - h| + k$, then the graph of the parent absolute value function is translated to the right and down. Is her reasoning correct? Explain why or why not.

Create a table of values for each indicated function. Then, graph the function using your table.

9. $f(x) = |x + 3| - 3$

10. $f(x) = |x - 1| + 2$

11. $f(x) = 2|x + 1| - 2$

12. $f(x) = -|x - 3| + 2$

13. $f(x) = -\frac{1}{2}|x - 3| + 6$

14. $f(x) = \frac{1}{4}|x - 6| + 4$

15. A function of the form $f(x) = a|x|$ includes the ordered pair $(-1, -4)$. What is the value of a for this function? How is the graph of f a transformation of the graph of the parent absolute value function?

Determine the values of *a*, *h*, and *k* for each function. Then, describe the effect of each constant on the graph of the function.

16. $f(x) = -3|x + 2| - 4$

17. $f(x) = -|x - 1| - 3$

18. $f(x) = |x - 3| + 1$

19. $f(x) = \frac{2}{5}|x| + 6$

Determine the vertex of the graph of each function.

20. $f(x) = |x + 3| - 1$

21. $f(x) = 2|x + 2| + 2$

22. $f(x) = -4|x| + 1$

23. $f(x) = \frac{3}{7}|x - 9|$

24. Wendy sees the roof of a building reflected in a puddle. She is 6 ft tall and is standing 3 ft away from the puddle.

    A. What assumptions would you need to make a drawing of this situation on a coordinate plane?

    B. Write a function, *p*, that models the path of light as it travels from the roof of the building to Wendy's eye.

    C. Determine the height of the building if its base is 12 ft away from where Wendy is standing.

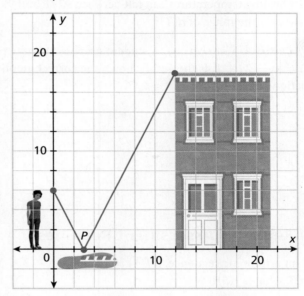

Write an equation of the form $f(x) = a|x - h| + k$ for each graph.

25.

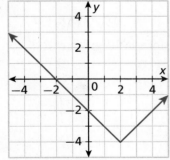

26.

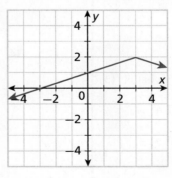

27.

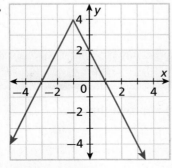

28.

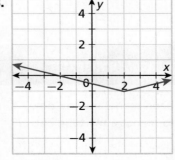

29. STEM A significant difference in a person's body temperature from the average is dangerous.

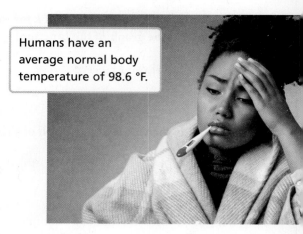

Humans have an average normal body temperature of 98.6 °F.

  A. Complete the absolute value function below that is used to describe the absolute difference $d(T)$, in degrees Fahrenheit, of the body temperature T of a person and the average body temperature.

  $$d(T) = \left| T - \boxed{?} \right|$$

  B. How is the graph of $d(T)$ related to the graph of the parent absolute value function?

  C. If healthy temperatures can fall between 97 °F and 99 °F, what is the range of $d(T)$?

30. (MP) **Critique Reasoning** A student graphed the function $f(x) = |x - 2| + 1$. Is the graph shown the correct graph for this function? Explain.

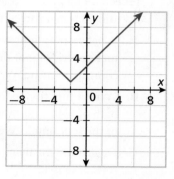

Spiral Review • Assessment Readiness

31. For an arithmetic sequence, if $f(1) = 10$ and $d = 3$, what is $f(5)$?

  (A) 15

  (B) 22

  (C) 25

  (D) 30

32. For $f(x) = \begin{cases} x + 2, & x \le 3 \\ 2x - 2, & x > 3 \end{cases}$, what is $f(3)$?

  (A) 7   (C) 4

  (B) 5   (D) $\frac{1}{5}$

33. Which fills in the blank correctly? If the first term in an arithmetic sequence with common difference d is $f(1)$, then $f(n) = \boxed{?}$.

  (A) $f(1) + nd$ (C) $f(1) + (n - 1)d$

  (B) nd (D) $f(1) \cdot n + d$

34. For what values of x is the graph of $f(x) = x - 4$ above the x-axis?

  (A) $x > -4$

  (B) $x > 4$

  (C) $x < -4$

  (D) $x < 4$

 I'm in a Learning Mindset!

How well have I been managing my time? What skill could I improve that would allow me to manage my time better?

Solve Absolute Value Equations and Inequalities

(I Can) solve absolute value equations and inequalities both graphically and algebraically.

Spark Your Learning

An ice cream stand lists a scoop of ice cream as weighing 6 ounces on their menu. The actual weight of a scoop of ice cream varies a little each time an ice cream cone is prepared.

A customer receives a 5.6-ounce scoop of ice cream.

Complete Part A as a whole class. Then complete Parts B–D in small groups.

A. What is a mathematical question you can ask about this situation? What information would you need to know to answer your question?

B. What type of equation or inequality could be written to help determine if the size of the ice cream scoop the customer received was fair?

C. To answer your question, what strategy and tool would you use along with all the information you have? What answer do you get?

D. What is the acceptable range for the amount of ice cream that can be served as one scoop? What could cause the variation in weight?

Turn and Talk Predict how your answer would change for each of the following changes in the situation:
- The listed weight was 6.5 ounces.
- You were given 7.3 ounces of ice cream.

©Daniel Madrigal Madrigal/Shutterstock

Build Understanding

Solve Absolute Value Equations Graphically

To solve a one-variable equation of the form $f(x) = g(x)$ by graphing, you can find the point(s) of intersection of the graphs of the functions $y = f(x)$ and $y = g(x)$. The x-coordinate of each point of intersection is a value of x for which $f(x) = g(x)$ and is therefore a solution of the original equation.

  The graphs of $f(x) = |x - 5|$ and $g(x) = 3$ are shown in the same coordinate plane. You can use these graphs to solve a related equation $|x - 5| = 3$.

A. Explain how the equation $|x - 5| = 3$ is related to the functions $f(x) = |x - 5|$ and $g(x) = 3$.

B. For what x-coordinates do the graphs of $f(x) = |x - 5|$ and $g(x) = 3$ have the same y-coordinate? In other words, for what x-values is $|x - 5| = 3$ true? Explain.

C. How can you verify that the intersection points of the graphs correspond to solutions of the equation $f(x) = g(x)$?

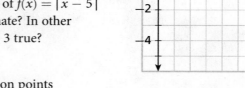

The graphs of $f(x) = |x - 5| - 2$ and $g(x) = 1$ are shown in the same coordinate plane. You can use these graphs to solve a related equation $|x - 5| - 2 = 1$.

D. Explain how the equation $|x - 5| - 2 = 1$ is related to the functions $f(x) = |x - 5| - 2$ and $g(x) = 1$.

E. For what x-coordinates do the graphs of $f(x) = |x - 5| - 2$ and $g(x) = 1$ have the same y-coordinate? In other words, for what x-values is $|x - 5| - 2 = 1$ true? Explain.

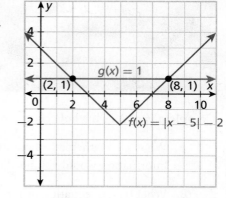

F. How are the two equations you solved, shown again here, alike? How are they different?

$$|x - 5| - 2 = 1 \qquad |x - 5| = 3$$

 Turn and Talk Explain why a solution of an equation in one variable found by graphing should be considered approximate until verified by substitution.

Solve Absolute Value Inequalities Graphically

You can solve an absolute value inequality by graphing in a way that is similar to how you have graphically solved absolute value equations. However, with an inequality, the points of intersection indicate endpoints of a possible range of solutions.

2 Examine the graphs of $f(x) = |x - 5|$ and $g(x) = 3$ together again.

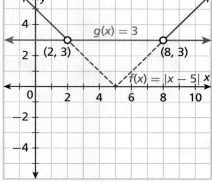

A. How can you use the graphs to determine for what x-values the function values of $f(x) = |x - 5|$ are greater than those of $g(x) = 3$? In other words, for what x-values is $|x - 5| > 3$ true? Explain.

B. Are the x-coordinates of the points of intersection included in the solutions of $|x - 5| > 3$? How is this represented in the graphs?

C. What does the portion of the graph of f that is dashed on the graph represent? What does the portion that is solid represent?

Examine the graphs of $f(x) = |x - 3| + 1$ and $g(x) = 5$ shown here.

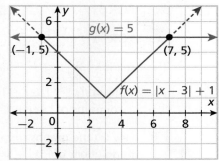

D. Use the graphs to find the solutions of $|x - 3| + 1 \leq 5$.

E. Are the x-coordinates of the points of intersection included in the solutions of $|x - 3| + 1 \leq 5$? How is this represented in the graphs?

F. How can you use the graphs to determine for what x-values the function values of $f(x) = |x - 3| + 1$ are greater than those of $g(x) = 5$? In other words, for what x-values is $|x - 3| + 1 > 5$ true? Explain.

G. The graph of $f(x) = |x + 3| - 2$ is shown. Use the graph to write a related absolute value equation that has no solution and a related absolute value inequality that has no solution.

H. Let $g(x) = c$ for some real number c. How many solutions can $f(x) = g(x)$, $f(x) > g(x)$, and $f(x) \geq g(x)$ have? Explain.

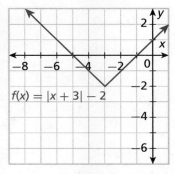

 Turn and Talk How is solving an absolute value inequality by graphing similar to solving an absolute value equation by graphing? How is it different?

Step It Out

Solve Absolute Value Equations Algebraically

Recall that the parent absolute value function $f(x) = |x|$ can be expressed as the piecewise-defined function $f(x) = \begin{cases} x & \text{if } x \geq 0 \\ -x & \text{if } x < 0 \end{cases}$. When solving an absolute value equation, both cases must be considered.

> ### Solving an Absolute Value Equation
>
> The equation $|ax + b| = c$ where $c \geq 0$ is equivalent to the statement $ax + b = c$ OR $ax + b = -c$.

3 ▶ **Solve $|3x| + 1 = 7$.**

$$|3x| + 1 = 7$$

$$|3x| = 6 \qquad \text{Subtraction Property of Equality}$$

$$3x = 6 \text{ OR } 3x = -6 \qquad \boxed{\textbf{A. Why are there two cases to consider?}}$$

$$x = 2 \text{ OR } x = -2 \qquad \text{Division Property of Equality}$$

The equation $|3x| + 1 = 7$ has two solutions, 2 and -2.

The graphs of $f(x) = |3x| + 1$ and $g(x) = 7$ support the conclusion that the solutions of $|3x| + 1 = 7$ are -2 and 2.

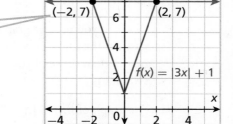

> **B. How do the graphs support the conclusion that the solutions of $|3x| + 1 = 7$ are -2 and 2?**

Solve $|3x| + 1 = 1$.

$$|3x| + 1 = 1$$

$$|3x| = 0 \qquad \text{Subtraction Property of Equality}$$

$$3x = 0 \qquad \boxed{\textbf{C. Why is there only one case to consider?}}$$

$$x = 0 \qquad \text{Division Property of Equality}$$

> **D. If an absolute value equation $f(x) = c$ has exactly one solution, how is the solution related to the graph of f?**

The equation $|3x| + 1 = 1$ has exactly one solution, 0.

Solve $|3x| + 1 = 0$.

> **E. Use the definition of absolute value to explain why no value of x makes this equation true.**

$$|3x| + 1 = 0$$

$$|3x| = -1$$

> **F. How can you use a graph to support this conclusion?**

The equation $|3x| + 1 = 0$ has no solution.

 Turn and Talk How can you show that the equation $|2x| + 5 = 3$ has no solution algebraically? How can you show this using graphs?

Solve Absolute Value Inequalities Algebraically

Solving an absolute value inequality algebraically is much like solving absolute value equations.

Solving Absolute Value Inequalities

The inequality $|ax + b| < c$ where $c > 0$ is equivalent to this compound inequality:
$$-c < ax + b < c$$

The inequality $|ax + b| > c$ where $c > 0$ is equivalent to this compound inequality:
$$ax + b < -c \text{ OR } ax + b > c$$

In the absolute value and compound inequalities above, the symbols, $<$ and $>$ can be replaced with $\leq$ and $\geq$, respectively.

Tolerance is the amount by which a measurement is permitted to vary from a prescribed measure. It is the allowable amount of variation in a quantity. For example, a bolt needed in a machine cannot be too long or too short. If the tolerance for a 2.5-centimeter bolt is 0.1 centimeter, then the bolt must be between 2.4 and 2.6 centimeters long, inclusive.

4 ▸ A bolt is supposed to be to be 2.75 centimeters in length with a tolerance of 0.04 centimeter. Find the acceptable lengths for the bolt.

Solve $|x - 2.75| \leq 0.04$.

$$|x - 2.75| \leq 0.04$$

> **A.** How could you write this inequality as two simple inequalities joined by AND?

$$-0.04 \leq x - 2.75 \leq 0.04$$

$$2.71 \leq \quad x \quad \leq 2.79$$

> **B.** What property justifies this step?

An acceptable length of a bolt must be between 2.71 and 2.79 centimeters, inclusive.

The graphs of $f(x) = |x - 2.75|$ and $g(x) = 0.04$ support the conclusion that the solutions of $|x - 2.75| \leq 0.04$ are $2.71 \leq x \leq 2.79$.

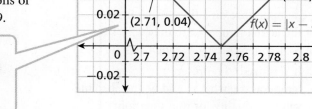

> **C.** How do the graphs support the conclusion that the solutions of $|x - 2.75| \leq 0.04$ are $2.71 \leq x \leq 2.79$?

 Turn and Talk Predict how the graphs would change if you prescribed a more precise tolerance.

Check Understanding

1. Explain how you would solve the equation $|x - 2| + 3 = 12$.

Solve each equation by graphing.

2. $|x - 3| + 2 = 5$

3. $2|x + 1| + 3 = 7$

4. Explain why the solution of $|x| > a$ is all real numbers if a is a negative number.

5. Solve $4|3x - 1| + 3 > 11$.

On Your Own

Solve each equation algebraically.

6. $2|x + 1| + 3 = 7$

7. $-5|-3x + 2| - 2 = -2$

8. $-2|x + 5| + 4 = 2$

9. $3|x + 1| + 3 = 9$

10. $|x - 3| + 2 = 5$

11. $|3x - 4| + 2 = 1$

Solve each inequality algebraically.

12. $|x| + 2 \geq 5$

13. $|4 - x| + 15 > 21$

14. $|x + 4| - 11 \leq -3$

15. $\frac{1}{2}|x| + 2 < 3$

16. $2|x - 1| < 3$

17. $8|x + 4| + 10 < 2$

Use the graph of $f(x) = |2x - 5| - 1$ and $g(x) = 8$ to solve each equation or inequality. Explain how the x-coordinates of the intersection points relate to the solutions of the equation or inequality.

18. $|2x - 5| - 1 = 8$

19. $|2x - 5| - 1 \leq 8$

20. $|2x - 5| - 1 \geq 8$

21. $|2x - 5| - 1 < 8$

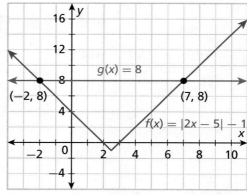

22. The temperature on a thermostat is set to 68 °F, but the actual temperature may vary from the set temperature by as much as 2 °F.

  A. If T is used to represent the actual temperature, what would be the absolute value inequality for this situation?

  B. What is the range of possible actual temperatures?

230

23. **(MP) Model with Mathematics** The bottom of a river makes a shape that can be modeled by $d(h) = \frac{1}{5}|h - 240| - 48$, where d represents the depth of the river bottom, in feet, and h represents the horizontal distance, in feet, to the left-hand shore.

A ship risks running aground if the bottom of its keel (its lowest point under the water) reaches down to the river bottom.

A. Suppose you are the harbormaster and you want to place buoys where the river bottom is 30 feet below the surface. How far from the left-hand shore should you place the buoys?

B. How would your solution change if the surface of the river dropped by 2 feet?

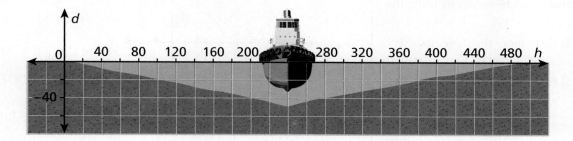

24. Write two absolute value inequalities that can be solved using the given graphs.

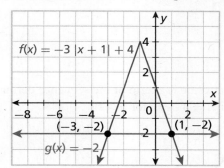

25. **Open Ended** What are examples of real-world quantities for which a negative solution of an absolute value equation would not make sense?

26. Identify the error:

$$-3|x - 4| - 4 = 3$$
$$-3|x - 4| = 7$$
$$|x - 4| = -\frac{7}{3}$$
$$x = \frac{5}{3} \quad \text{OR} \quad x = \frac{19}{3}$$

27. **(MP) Model with Mathematics** Swimmers in a men's 200-meter butterfly event finished with times from 1 minute 54.04 seconds to 1 minute 57.48 seconds. Let t represent a possible finishing time (in seconds). Write an absolute value inequality that describes the situation.

28. **(MP)** **Use Structure** Let f be a non-constant linear function, g be an absolute value function, and c be a real number. How do the ranges of f and g differ? Use this fact to explain why the equation $f(x) = c$ always has a solution but the equation $g(x) = c$ may not have a solution.

29. Use the given graph.

   A. Write an absolute value equation that could be solved by using the graph.

   B. Write an absolute value inequality that could be solved by using the graph.

   C. Is there more than one possible answer to Part A? Explain your answer.

   D. Is there more than one possible answer to Part B? Explain your answer.

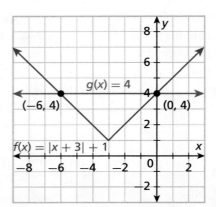

30. **(Open Middle™)** Using the digits 1 to 9, at most one time each, fill in the boxes to create a true statement.

$$\left| \boxed{} x - \boxed{} \right| \geq \boxed{}, \quad x \geq \boxed{}, \quad x \leq \boxed{}$$

Spiral Review • Assessment Readiness

31. Which of the functions represents an absolute value function with a vertex of $(3, 4)$?

   (A) $f(x) = |x + 3| + 4$ (C) $f(x) = |x - 3| + 4$

   (B) $f(x) = |x - 3| - 4$ (D) $f(x) = |x + 3| - 4$

32. Which statements are true of the piecewise-defined function

$$f(x) = \begin{cases} 2x - 2 \text{ if } x > 3 \\ x + 5 \text{ if } x \leq 3 \end{cases}?$$

Select all that apply.

   (A) $f(2) = 2$ (D) $f(3) = 4$

   (B) $f(5) = 10$ (E) $f(1) = 6$

   (C) $f(3) = 8$ (F) $f(0) = -2$

33. What value is a term of the sequence defined by $f(n) = 4 + 3n$ for $n \geq 0$?

   (A) 3   (C) 10

   (B) 5   (D) 17

34. Which point lies on both lines given by the equations $f(x) = 2x - 1$ and $g(x) = -x + 2$?

   (A) $(1, 1)$

   (B) $(3, 5)$

   (C) $(3, 1)$

   (D) $(4, 2)$

I'm in a Learning Mindset!

What are the potential long-term effects of my academic decisions?

Piecewise-Defined Functions

Tareek drove his car through the city at an average speed of 20 miles per hour for 30 minutes before getting on the highway and driving at an average speed of 50 miles per hour for 1.5 hours.

$$d(t) = \begin{cases} 20t & \text{for } 0 \le t \le 0.5 \\ 50t - 15 & \text{for } 0.5 < t \le 2 \end{cases}$$

Let t represent the time Tareek drove, in hours, and let $d(t)$ represent the distance he traveled, in miles.

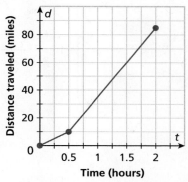

Absolute Value Functions

The graph of an absolute value function can be used to determine its equation.

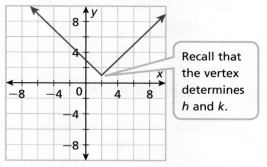

Recall that the vertex determines h and k.

The vertex is $(2, 1)$, so $h = 2$ and $k = 1$ in $f(x) = a|x - h| + k$.

$$f(x) = a|x - 2| + 1$$

Substitute the y-intercept $(0, 3)$ to find a.

$$3 = a|0 - 2| + 1$$
$$3 = a(2) + 1$$
$$2 = 2a$$
$$a = 1$$

So, the function is $f(x) = |x - 2| + 1$.

Absolute Value Equations

The U.S. Mint requires that dimes be manufactured with a mass of 2.268 g. There can be deviations from this target mass, but the maximum absolute deviation allowed is 0.091 g.

You can express this manufacturing requirement by writing the equation

$$|m_d - 2.268| = 0.091$$

where m_d is the mass of a dime.

Solving this equation for m_d gives you the minimum mass and the maximum mass that the U.S. Mint allows.

$$m_d - 2.268 = -0.091 \quad \text{or} \quad m_d - 2.268 = 0.091$$
$$m_d = 2.177 \quad \text{or} \quad m_d = 2.359$$

So, the minimum mass allowed is 2.177 g, and the maximum mass allowed is 2.359 g.

Absolute Value Inequalities

The U.S. Mint requires that quarters be manufactured with a mass of 5.67 g. The maximum absolute deviation from 5.67 g allowed is 0.227 g.

You can express the range of acceptable masses of quarters by writing the inequality

$$|m_q - 5.67| \le 0.227$$

where m_q is the mass of a quarter.

The solution of this inequality is shown below.

$$-0.227 \le m_q - 5.67 \le 0.227$$
$$5.443 \le \quad m_q \quad \le 5.897$$

So, any mass between and including 5.443 g and 5.897 g is acceptable.

Unacceptable masses are given by the inequality $|m_q - 5.67| > 0.227$. The solutions of this inequality are $m_q < 5.443$ or $m_q > 5.897$.

Vocabulary

Choose the correct term from the box to complete each sentence.

1. A __?__ is composed of different rules for different intervals in its domain.

2. The amount by which a measurement is permitted to vary from a specified value is called the __?__ of the measurement.

3. A piecewise-defined function where the rule for each domain interval is a constant is called a __?__ .

4. The vertex of the graph of an __?__ lies on the __?__ of the graph.

> **Vocabulary**
>
> absolute value function
> axis of symmetry
> piecewise-defined function
> step function
> tolerance

Concepts and Skills

5. Which piecewise-defined function has the graph shown?

Ⓐ $f(x) = \begin{cases} x + 1 & \text{if } x < 4 \\ 2x - 6 & \text{if } x \geq 4 \end{cases}$ Ⓒ $f(x) = \begin{cases} 2x - 6 & \text{if } x < 4 \\ x + 1 & \text{if } x \geq 4 \end{cases}$

Ⓑ $f(x) = \begin{cases} x + 1 & \text{if } x \leq 4 \\ 2x - 6 & \text{if } x > 4 \end{cases}$ Ⓓ $f(x) = \begin{cases} 2x - 6 & \text{if } x \leq 4 \\ x + 1 & \text{if } x > 4 \end{cases}$

6. Graph the piecewise-defined function

$$f(x) = \begin{cases} -5x & \text{if } -2 < x < -\frac{1}{2} \\ 4 & \text{if } -\frac{1}{2} \leq x \leq 1 \\ -2x + 6 & \text{if } x > 1 \end{cases}$$

Identify the vertex and y-intercept of each function's graph.

7. $f(x) = -2|x + 4| - 3$

8. $f(x) = |x + 7| + 2$

9. Graph the absolute value function $f(x) = \frac{3|x + 1|}{2}$.

10. Solve the absolute value equation $\frac{1}{2}|x + 3| = 1$ by graphing.

11. Solve the absolute value equation $4|x - 2| + 1 = 9$ algebraically. Show each step of your solution.

12. Solve the absolute value inequality $|x - 4| - 3 > 2$ by graphing.

13. Solve $|x + 2| - 4 \geq -2$ algebraically. Show each step of your solution.

14. A box of cereal is supposed to weigh 13.8 ounces, with a tolerance of 0.3 ounces. Write and solve an absolute value inequality to find the range of acceptable weights for the cereal.

15. (MP) **Use Tools** State what strategy and tool you will use to answer the question, explain your choice, and then find the answer. A bridge is rated for vehicles weighing a maximum of 30,000 pounds. A shipping company loads each of its 15,000-pound trucks with 13,000 pounds of cargo. The scale the company uses to measure the weight of the loaded truck has a tolerance of 500 pounds. Are the trucks able to cross the bridge safely? Explain.

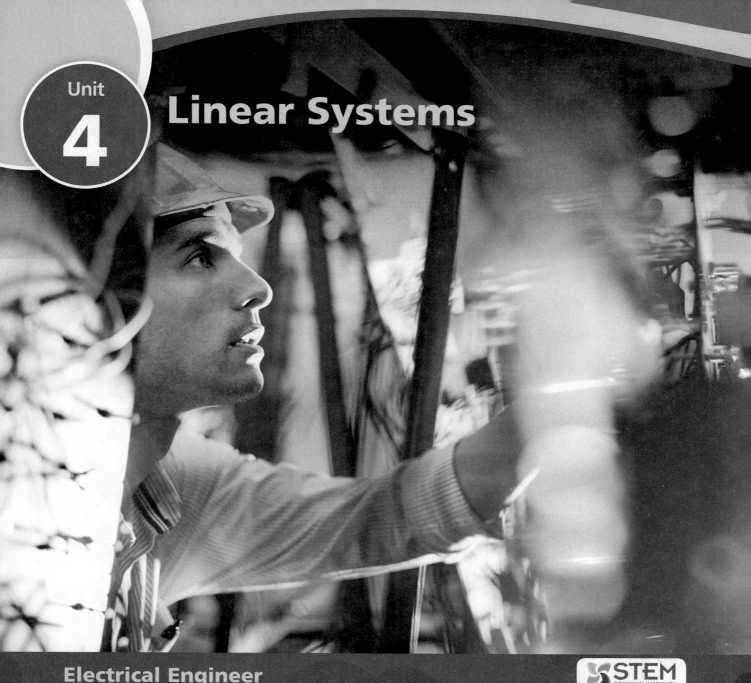

Linear Systems

Electrical Engineer

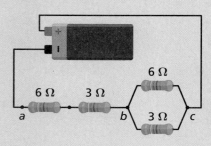
STEM
POWERING INGENUITY

Any product that uses an electrical source was designed by and is maintained by an electrical engineer. When designing an electrical circuit for a new product, electrical engineers have to calculate electrical resistance, measured in ohms (Ω), at different points. Resistors are placed in a circuit to control the flow of energy. For example, more resistance in a battery-powered lighting circuit means the light will be dimmer but the battery will last longer.

©Westend61/Getty Images

STEM Task

Equivalent resistance is determined by the equation $R_{eq} = R_1 + R_2 + \ldots$ when set in series, as shown between points a and b, and the equation $\frac{1}{R_{eq}} = \frac{1}{R_1} + \frac{1}{R_2} + \ldots$ when set in parallel, as shown between points b and c.

Determine the equivalent resistance for the electrical circuit shown.

Learning Mindset

Strategic Help-Seeking Identifies Need for Help

©Monika Sakowska/Eye Em/Getty Images

How can you be sure that you are asking for assistance at the right time? Whenever you approach a new topic, it is important that you give your best attempt before asking for help. You will be able to better focus on your learning goal if you periodically converse with your peers to see if it is time to seek help or to continue on your own. Here are some things to keep in mind as you identify if you need help:

- Struggle helps us grow, but only if it is productive. Try to complete the task on your own, recognizing that you may need assistance.

- Make a list of ways to attack the problem. If you reach the end of the list, ask someone if they can add to the list.

- We grow through discourse. Engaging our peers in problem solving allows us to reflect, evaluate, and grow together.

- If you recognize that you do not have enough time to complete a task on your own, ask someone if they can help speed things up.

- If you are unsure of how to proceed, let your teacher know. It is better to be proactive, and your teacher will be understanding.

Reflect

Q Think of a time you needed to ask for help but did not. How did this affect the outcome of the project?

Q When an electrical engineer is tasked with researching and testing a new product, how and when do you think they will determine if they need help?

Systems of Linear Equations

Module Performance Task: *Spies and Analysts™*

Down the Drain

When will both toilets use the same amount of water?

Single flush mechanism

1.28
gallons per flush

Double flush mechanism

1.6 gpf
for solids

1.0 gpf
for liquids

Are You Ready?

Complete these problems to review prior concepts and skills you will need for this module.

Simplify Algebraic Expressions

Simplify each expression.

1. $-2x + 5x + 3$

2. $-x + 6 + (-2x)$

3. $1.5x + 7 + 2.5x$

4. $2(x + 3) + 3$

5. $4(x - 1) - 8$

6. $-2(2x + 1) + 7x$

7. $3(x + 4) + 4(x + 3)$

8. $-5(x - 2) + 2(x + 6)$

Graph Linear Equations in Slope-Intercept Form

Graph each equation.

9. $y = -2x - 1$

10. $y = \frac{1}{2}x + 5$

11. $y = -2x - 10$

12. $y = \frac{4}{3}x + 3$

Graph Linear Equations in Standard Form

Graph each equation.

13. $-2x + y = -1$

14. $-x + 6y = -26$

15. $3x + 2y = 10$

16. $5x - 5y = -5$

Connecting Past and Present Learning

Previously, you learned:

- to use operations to simplify expressions,
- to write and solve linear equations in two variables, and
- to graph linear functions.

In this module, you will learn:

- to solve systems of linear equations by graphing, substitution, and elimination, and
- to create linear equations that represent relationships and constraints in real-world contexts.

Solve Linear Systems by Graphing

(**I Can**) write linear systems to model real-world problems and solve them by graphing.

Spark Your Learning

Raul wonders whether he should take a taxi or use a ridesharing service.

Taxi: Cost = base fare + charge per mile + tip

Ridesharing: Cost = base fare + charge per mile (minimum fare applies)

Complete Part A as a whole class. Then complete Parts B–D in small groups.

  A. What is a mathematical question that you can ask about this situation? What information would you need to know to answer your question?

  B. What variables are involved in this situation? How can you create a model for the situation?

  C. To answer your question, what strategy and tool would you use along with all the information you have? What answer do you get?

  D. Does your answer make sense in the context of the situation? How do you know?

 Turn and Talk How can mathematical equations help you solve real-world problems? For this situation, what information is not conveyed in a mathematical equation?

Build Understanding

Understand Systems of Linear Equations

A **system of equations** is made up of two or more equations having the same variables. You know that every point on the graph of an equation in two variables represents an ordered pair that is a solution of the equation. A **solution of a system of equations** is any ordered pair that satisfies all the equations in the system.

1 The graph of the following system of linear equations is shown.

$$\begin{cases} y = x + 3 \\ y = 2x + 2 \end{cases}$$

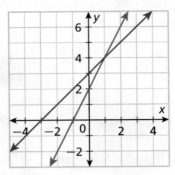

A. Which points represent solutions of $y = x + 3$?

B. Which points represent solutions of $y = 2x + 2$?

C. What ordered pair appears to be the solution to the system? Explain.

D. How can you check that the solution you identified in Part C is correct?

> **Turn and Talk** Suppose the first equation was $y = -x + 3$ instead of $y = x + 3$. Would you be able to identify the exact solution of the new system just by looking at the graph of the system? Explain.

Classify Systems of Linear Equations

You can classify systems by the number of their solutions. An **independent system** has exactly one solution. A **dependent system** has an infinite number of solutions. A **consistent system** has at least one solution. A system with no solutions is an **inconsistent system**.

2

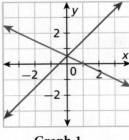
Graph 1

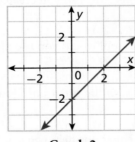
Graph 2

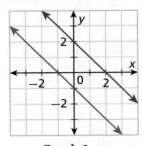
Graph 3

A. Which graph shows one solution?

B. Which graph shows infinitely many solutions?

C. Which graph shows no solutions?

D. Classify the system represented by each graph based on the number of solutions.

> **Turn and Talk** What do you observe about the slopes of the lines in an independent system? in an inconsistent system?

Step It Out

Apply Systems of Linear Equations

 Circular and rectangular tables are set up for a banquet. There are 9 tables set up with 80 chairs. Each circular table has 8 chairs and each rectangular table has 10 chairs. How many tables of each type have been set up?

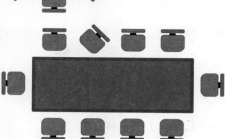

You can model the situation algebraically and with a graph.

To model the situation algebraically, first define the variables. Let c represent the number of circular tables, and let r represent the number of rectangular tables.

Write one equation in standard form to model the number of tables and a second equation to model the number of chairs.

There are 9 tables altogether.

$c + r = 9$

$c = 9$ when $r = 0$, so the c-intercept is at $(9, 0)$.

$r = 9$ when $c = 0$, so the r-intercept is at $(0, 9)$.

> **A.** How do the intercepts help you graph the equations?

There are 80 chairs altogether, 8 at each circular table and 10 at each rectangular table.

$8c + 10r = 80$

$c = 10$ when $r = 0$, so the c-intercept is at $(10, 0)$.

$r = 8$ when $c = 0$, so the r-intercept is at $(0, 8)$.

> **B.** Why are the lines restricted to the first quadrant of the graph?

Graph the system $\begin{cases} c + r = 9 \\ 8c + 10r = 80 \end{cases}$.

Identify the point where the lines intersect.

The intersection point appears to be $(5, 4)$.

C. How can you confirm that $(5, 4)$ is a solution of the system?

This means that 5 circular tables and 4 rectangular tables have been set up.

D. Why is using 6 circular tables and 3 rectangular tables not a viable option even though there would be a total of 9 tables?

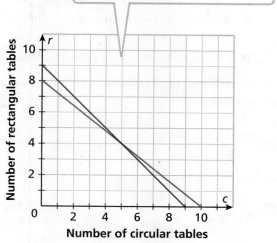

Number of circular tables

 Turn and Talk Suppose 100 chairs are needed for the banquet. Is there a viable solution to the problem in Task 3 if 9 tables must still be used? Explain.

Check Understanding

1. How many solutions does an independent system have?

2. How can you identify the graph of an inconsistent system?

3. How do you identify the solution of a system using a graph?

4. What is the solution for the system shown in the graph at the right?

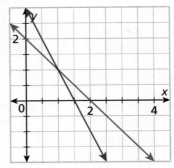

5. Solve the system by graphing. What is the solution?

$$\begin{cases} 3x + 3y = 6 \\ -x + y = 4 \end{cases}$$

On Your Own

Solve the system of linear equations by graphing.

6. $\begin{cases} y = x + 4 \\ x + y = 6 \end{cases}$

7. $\begin{cases} y = x + 4 \\ -x + y = 4 \end{cases}$

8. $\begin{cases} y = 2x + 8 \\ -2x + y = 3 \end{cases}$

9. $\begin{cases} x + 2y = 10 \\ -2x + y = 5 \end{cases}$

10. $\begin{cases} -7 = 2y + x \\ y = -3x - 16 \end{cases}$

11. $\begin{cases} y + x = 0 \\ -7y - 3x = 6 \end{cases}$

12. Graph the system: $\begin{cases} y = 5x + 5 \\ 2x - y = 6 \end{cases}$

   A. Estimate the coordinates of the solution to the nearest integer solution of the system.

   B. Do you think that your estimated solution is reasonable? Explain your answer.

Graph each system of equations. Estimate the coordinates of the solution to the nearest integer.

13. $\begin{cases} x + 3y = 10 \\ -x + y = 5 \end{cases}$

14. $\begin{cases} 2x + y = 10 \\ -2x + 2y = 7 \end{cases}$

15. $\begin{cases} -3x + 2y = 15 \\ 12 = 2x + y \end{cases}$

16. $\begin{cases} 3x - 5y = 25 \\ 10 = x + y \end{cases}$

17. $\begin{cases} 2x + 3y = 18 \\ 5x - 2y = -10 \end{cases}$

18. $\begin{cases} x + 6y = 6 \\ -3x + 4y = 12 \end{cases}$

19. Two friends are playing the same game on their phones. One is already on level 6, and levels up every two hours. Her friend is on level 3, but levels up every 60 minutes. After how many hours will they have reached the same level? What level will that be?

20. (MP) **Model with Mathematics**
The owner of a frozen yogurt stand considers different pricing options for a serving of yogurt plus toppings. For what number of toppings do the two options give the same price?

$3 plus $0.75 per topping

$4 plus $0.50 per topping

   A. Define the variables.
   B. Write a system of equations that models this situation.
   C. Graph the system. What is the intersection point?
   D. What is the solution of the problem?
   E. Is the solution reasonable for this situation? Explain.

21. Describe the graph of an independent system.

22. (MP) **Reason** The equations in a system of linear equations have different slopes. What does that mean about the number of solutions that the system could have?

23. (MP) **Reason** The equations in a system of linear equations have the same slope and the same y-intercept. What does that mean about the number of solutions that the system could have?

24. (MP) **Reason** The equations in a system of linear equations have the same slope and different y-intercepts. What does that mean about the number of solutions that the system could have?

25. (MP) **Construct Arguments**
Without graphing, how can you identify the solution of the system? Explain.
$$\begin{cases} y = 3x + 4 \\ -6x + 2y = 8 \end{cases}$$

26. (MP) **Critique Reasoning** Karen says that the graph of the system below consists of two lines with the same slope, so the system has infinitely many solutions. What is her mistake?
$$\begin{cases} y = 2x + 2 \\ -4x + 2y = 8 \end{cases}$$

27. **Music** A seamstress is creating costumes for a show choir. High school students will each wear a 5-piece costume, and middle school students will each wear a simpler 3-piece costume. There are 10 students in the show choir and enough fabric to make 41 costume pieces. How many high school students and how many middle school students should be chosen for the choir?

   A. Define the variables.
   B. Write a system of linear equations that models this situation.
   C. Graph the system and estimate the intersection point.
   D. What is the solution of the problem?
   E. Is the solution reasonable for this situation? Explain.

©Victoria Kurylo/Shutterstock

28. (MP) **Use Tools** Two printing companies have different pricing for photo books. Company A charges $5.00 plus $0.60 per page. Company B charges $10.00 plus $0.25 per page. For what number of pages is the cost of a photo book at the two companies the same?

A. Define the variables and write a system of equations that models the two photo book pricing structures.

B. Choose a tool to graph the system. What is the intersection point?

C. Interpret the intersection point in the context of the situation. Does the intersection point represent a reasonable solution to the problem? Explain.

29. (Open Middle™) Using the digits 1 to 9, at most one time each, fill in the boxes to create three separate sets of equations: one where there is no solution, one where there is one solution, and one where there are infinitely many solutions. You can reuse all the digits for each set of equations.

$$\begin{cases} \square x + \square y = \square \\ \square x + \square y = \square \end{cases}$$

Spiral Review • Assessment Readiness

30. Which type of function has a graph composed of two or more pieces?

(A) absolute value

(B) quadratic

(C) linear

(D) exponential

31. What is the shape of the graph of an absolute value function?

(A) V-shaped

(B) V- or U-shaped

(C) U-shaped

(D) neither V- nor U-shaped

32. Solve algebraically: $|4x - 4| + 4 \leq 5$.

(A) $1 \leq x \leq 2$

(B) $x \leq -1$ or $x \geq 1$

(C) $\frac{3}{4} \leq x \leq \frac{5}{4}$

(D) no solution

33. Given the system $\begin{cases} 4x + y = 12 \\ y = x + 2 \end{cases}$, which statements are equivalent? Select all that apply.

(A) $4x + y = 6(y - x)$

(B) $12 - 4x = x + 2$

(C) $4(y - 2) + y = 12$

(D) $4x + (x + 2) = 12$

 I'm in a Learning Mindset!

What skills do I have that benefit collaboration? Which collaboration skills still need improvement?

Solve Linear Systems by Substitution

(I Can) write systems of linear equations to model real-world situations and solve them by substitution.

Spark Your Learning

A bowling alley usually requires that bowlers wear a special type of shoe to protect the lanes. Shoes from outside that are worn on the bowling lanes may have dirt or grit on them that can scratch the bowling lanes. When you pay for bowling, there is often a shoe rental fee included to rent the bowling shoes from the bowling alley.

Pins Down Bowling Club and Flying Pin Bowling Center charge different rates per game, but Pins Down Bowling Club loans their bowling shoes for FREE!

Complete Part A as a whole class. Then complete Parts B–D in small groups.

A. What is a mathematical question you can ask about this situation? What information would you need to know to answer your question?

B. What variables are involved in this situation?

C. To answer your question, what strategy and tool would you use along with all the information you have? What answer do you get?

D. Does your answer make sense in the context of the situation? How do you know?

Turn and Talk For how many games is Pins Down Bowling Club a better deal? For how many games is Flying Pin Bowling Center better? Explain.

©Digital Vision/Getty Images

Build Understanding

Understand the Substitution Method

You can solve systems of two linear equations using the **substitution method**. The first step in this method is to solve either equation for either variable. In some systems, one or even both equations may already be solved for one of the variables.

 The system of two linear equations at the right involves two equations given in slope-intercept form. That is, both equations are already solved for y.

$$\begin{cases} y = x + 2 \\ y = \dfrac{3}{4}x + 3 \end{cases}$$

A. The first equation shows that y is equivalent to the expression $x + 2$. So $x + 2$ can be substituted for y in the second equation. What does the second equation show is equivalent to y? Into which equation could this expression be substituted for y in order to solve for x?

B. What equation results by substituting $x + 2$ for y in the second equation? After the substitution, only the variable x remains. Perform the steps needed to find the value of x using this equation. Justify each step.

C. Do you think the value of x will be the same if you used the second equation to make a substitution for y in the first equation? Do the work to verify your answer. Were you correct?

D. Now that you know the value of x, you can use this value to find the value of y by substituting into either equation. Is there an advantage to selecting one equation over the other? Explain your answer.

E. How might you verify that the solution is $(4, 6)$?

 In the system of linear equations at the right, both equations are in standard form. That is, both equations have x and y on the same side of the equation.

$$\begin{cases} x + 2y = 3 \\ 2x - y = -1 \end{cases}$$

A. For this system, one of the equations needs to be solved for either variable before making a substitution in the other equation. Which equation would you use if you choose to solve for y? Since either equation could be used, justify your choice. Which equation would you use if you choose to solve for x? Again, justify your choice.

B. The process from this point onward is the same as discussed in Task 1. If your process led to finding the value of y, which equation would you use to find the value of x? If you find the value of x first, which equation would you use to find the value of y? Explain your choices.

C. The solution of this system is the ordered pair $(0.2, 1.4)$. How could you use a graphing calculator to verify this result?

 Turn and Talk Compare the graphing and substitution methods for solving a system of linear equations. Which method always gives exact results? Which method often gives approximate results? Explain.

Solve Systems with Different Types of Solutions

When solving systems by graphing, you learned to recognize each of the types of linear systems from their graphs. Independent systems intersect in a single point, dependent systems graph as the same line, and inconsistent systems graph as parallel lines. When using the substitution method to solve systems of these three types, three different outcomes will occur during the process. In Tasks 1 and 2, you encountered two independent systems. The substitution method resulted in an ordered pair solution for those systems. The tasks below discuss what happens when using the substitution method to solve a dependent system of equations and an inconsistent system of equations.

 Solve this system of equations by substitution. $\begin{cases} -2x + 2y = 6 \\ y = x + 3 \end{cases}$

Since the second equation is $y = x + 3$, substitute $x + 3$ for y in the first equation and solve for x.

$$-2x + 2(x + 3) = 6$$
$$-2x + 2x + 6 = 6$$
$$6 = 6$$

The final step of the solution process yields a true numerical fact. Notice that the middle step, $-2x + 2x + 6 = 6$, is true for all values of x. When a true numerical fact is the result, the system is a dependent system of equations.

A. What does the graph of a dependent system look like? What does this indicate for the number of solutions of the system?

B. Look at the two equations in the system. What is the result if you divide each term of the first equation by 2 and then add x to both sides? What do you notice about this equivalent form of the equation?

C. When the equations in a system are equivalent, what does this indicate about the number of solutions of the system?

 Solve this system by substitution. $\begin{cases} 3y = 2x \\ 3y = 2x + 3 \end{cases}$

Notice that the left side of both equations is $3y$. Since $3y = 2x$ in the first equation, you can substitute $2x$ for $3y$ in the second equation. Then solve for x.

$$2x = 2x + 3$$
$$0 = 3$$

The result is a false numerical statement. Notice that the substitution into the second equation results in an equation, $2x = 2x + 3$, that is never true for any value of x. When a false numerical result occurs, the system is an inconsistent system of equations.

A. What does the graph of an inconsistent system look like? What does this indicate for the number of solutions of the system?

B. When the equations in a system differ only by their constant term, what does this indicate about the number of solutions of the system?

 Turn and Talk What are you able to conclude about the system $2x + 3y = 5$ and $2x + 3y = 8$ just by looking at the equations? Explain.

Step It Out

Solve Systems Using Substitution

The steps for solving systems using the substitution method are:

1) Solve one of the equations for one of its variables.

2) Substitute the expression from Step 1 into the other equation and solve for the other variable.

3) Substitute the value from Step 2 into either original equation and solve to find the value of the other variable.

5 Use the substitution method to solve the system of equations shown below.

$$\begin{cases} y = 2x + 4 \\ 2x + 3y = 9 \end{cases}$$

Choose the equation that is already solved for y: $y = 2x + 4$.

> **A.** Must $y = 2x + 4$ be chosen? Can you start with the other equation instead? Explain.

Substitute $2x + 4$ for y in the second equation and solve for x.

$$2x + 3(2x + 4) = 9$$

$$2x + 6x + 12 = 9$$

> **B.** What property justifies this step in the solution?

$$8x = -3$$

$$x = -\frac{3}{8}$$

Now substitute $-\frac{3}{8}$ for x in either of the original equations.

$$y = 2\left(-\frac{3}{8}\right) + 4$$

> **C.** Is there an advantage to selecting one equation over the other here also? Explain your answer.

$$= -\frac{3}{4} + 4$$

$$= 3\frac{1}{4}$$

> **D.** How would you verify that this ordered pair is indeed correct?

The solution of the system is the ordered pair $\left(-\frac{3}{8}, 3\frac{1}{4}\right)$.

E. Graphing a system of linear equations can help you check a solution of the system that you found algebraically. Would graphing the system above by hand be a reasonable means for verifying the solution? Would graphing the system using a graphing calculator be reasonable? Explain both of your answers.

 Turn and Talk What will result from using the substitution method to solve a system that is dependent? a system that is inconsistent?

Solve Real-World Problems Using Substitution

6 ▶ On opening night for a new play, a theater sold 639 tickets for the main floor and the balcony. They sold $5,824 more in main floor tickets than balcony tickets. How many of each type of ticket were sold?

Balcony ticket: $17

Main floor ticket: $24

Write a system of equations to model the situation using the given information.

Use a verbal model to write each equation. Let x represent the number of main floor tickets sold and y represent the number of balcony tickets sold.

Main floor tickets sold	+	Balcony tickets sold	=	Total tickets sold		Value of main floor tickets	−	5824	=	Value of balcony tickets
x	+	y	=	639		24x	−	5824	=	17y

So the system of equations is $\begin{cases} x + y = 639 \\ 24x - 5824 = 17y \end{cases}$.

Use the substitution method to solve the system.

$x + y = 639$

A. Does it matter which variable, x or y, you solve for?

$x = 639 - y$

Next, substitute this expression into the other equation.

$24(639 - y) - 5824 = 17y$

$15{,}336 - 24y - 5824 = 17y$

$9512 = 41y$

$y = 232$

B. Is this the number of main floor or balcony tickets sold?

Now use the value of y to solve for x.

$x + 232 = 639$

$x = 407$

C. Is this the number of main floor or balcony tickets sold?

The solution of the system is the ordered pair $(407, 232)$.

The theater sold 407 main floor tickets and 232 balcony tickets.

 Turn and Talk Is the solution to this real-world problem reasonable? Explain.

Check Understanding

1. Solve this system by substitution. $\begin{cases} y = x + 2 \\ 2x + 2y = 16 \end{cases}$

   A. Into which equation will you make the substitution? Explain.

   B. What is the solution of this system?

   C. Describe the graph of this system.

2. Solve this system by substitution. $\begin{cases} x + y = 10 \\ 2y = x + 6 \end{cases}$

   A. Which variable will you select to solve for first? Explain.

   B. What is the solution of this system?

   C. Describe the slopes and y-intercepts of this system.

3. What result of substitution tells you a system has infinite solutions?

4. What result of substitution tells you a system has no solution?

5. Justin goes to a store to buy jeans and T-shirts. The jeans cost $40 each and the T-shirts cost $20 each. If Justin spends $100 on 4 items, how many pairs of jeans and how many T-shirts did he buy?

On Your Own

For Problems 6–17, solve the system by substitution.

6. $\begin{cases} y = 3 \\ y = 11 - 2x \end{cases}$

7. $\begin{cases} y = x + 3 \\ y = -x + 7 \end{cases}$

8. $\begin{cases} x = y + 3 \\ x = -2y + 12 \end{cases}$

9. $\begin{cases} x = 3y + 9 \\ x = -4y + 2 \end{cases}$

10. $\begin{cases} y = -3x + 14 \\ x = 3y - 12 \end{cases}$

11. $\begin{cases} x = y + 5 \\ y = -3x + 15 \end{cases}$

12. $\begin{cases} y - 4x = 0 \\ x + y = 5 \end{cases}$

13. $\begin{cases} 3x + y = -3 \\ -2x + y = 7 \end{cases}$

14. $\begin{cases} 6x - y = 2 \\ x + 2y = -17 \end{cases}$

15. $\begin{cases} -x + 2y = -6 \\ 2x + y = 2 \end{cases}$

16. $\begin{cases} 3x + y = 14 \\ x - 3y = -2 \end{cases}$

17. $\begin{cases} -x + y = 2 \\ x - 2y = 4 \end{cases}$

18. Kayla and Clarice ride scooters starting from the same spot. After Kayla has gone 2 miles, Clarice starts riding her scooter in the same direction. The system of equations below represents this situation.

    $\begin{cases} d = 5t + 2 \quad d \text{ is distance in miles.} \\ d = 6t \qquad\quad t \text{ is time in hours.} \end{cases}$

    A. Which equation models Kayla's distance from the starting point using the time since Clarice began riding?

    B. What is the time and distance when Clarice catches up to Kayla?

    C. Is your answer to Part B reasonable?

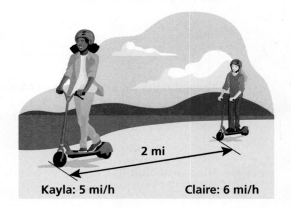

Kayla: 5 mi/h   Claire: 6 mi/h

For Problems 19–33, solve the system by substitution.

19. $\begin{cases} 5x + y = 8 \\ 2x + y = 5 \end{cases}$

20. $\begin{cases} 4y = 1 \\ 8x - 4y = 3 \end{cases}$

21. $\begin{cases} -y = 2x - 6 \\ x - y = 3.9 \end{cases}$

22. $\begin{cases} x + y = 4 \\ -x - y = 6 \end{cases}$

23. $\begin{cases} x - 3y = 6 \\ 4x - 12y = 24 \end{cases}$

24. $\begin{cases} x - y = -2.75 \\ x - 2y = -5.5 \end{cases}$

25. $\begin{cases} 7x + 2y = 24 \\ \dfrac{7}{2}x + y = 12 \end{cases}$

26. $\begin{cases} -3x + y = 12 \\ 6x - 2y = 18 \end{cases}$

27. $\begin{cases} x + y = 1 \\ 10x - 5y = 1 \end{cases}$

28. $\begin{cases} -x + 7y = -14 \\ \dfrac{1}{7}x - y = 2 \end{cases}$

29. $\begin{cases} y = x + 0.5 \\ -2x + 2y = 4 \end{cases}$

30. $\begin{cases} x - 3y = 10 \\ x + 5y = -22 \end{cases}$

31. $\begin{cases} y = \dfrac{3}{10} \\ 2x - y = \dfrac{1}{5} \end{cases}$

32. $\begin{cases} x + y = \dfrac{5}{8} \\ 2y = -2x + \dfrac{5}{4} \end{cases}$

33. $\begin{cases} x + y = -0.05 \\ -3x + y = 1.15 \end{cases}$

34. **(MP) Use Structure** A community center is hosting presentations of a puppet show. For the Saturday matinee show, 480 tickets have been sold for total proceeds of $3050.

Adult tickets: $10

Children tickets: $5

A. If x represents the number of adult tickets sold for the matinee, what might y represent in this situation?

B. Write a system of equations to model the situation.

C. How many adult tickets were sold? How many children tickets?

D. For which variable did you substitute? How did you decide?

E. Describe what the graph of this system would look like.

35. Other than graphing both equations on the same coordinate grid, how can you verify the solution for a system of equations?

36. **Open Ended** Write a system that has no solution. How do you know what equations to write?

37. **Financial Literacy** For her catering business, Mrs. Smith orders jars of items from an online site. She placed two orders for pickles and olives. The first order was for 10 jars of pickles and 12 jars of olives. The second order was for 12 jars of pickles and 15 jars of olives.

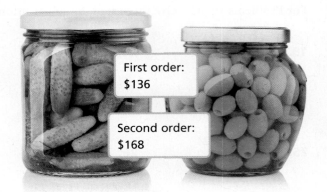

First order: $136

Second order: $168

    A. Write the system of equations to model this situation.

    B. What is the price of one jar of pickles? one jar of olives?

    C. Describe what the graph of this system would look like.

38. Without using substitution or graphing, how can you know that a system of equations has an infinite number of solutions?

Spiral Review • Assessment Readiness

39. What does the graph of the function $f(x) = -|-x|$ look like?

    Ⓐ V-shaped opening upwards

    Ⓑ U-shaped opening upwards

    Ⓒ V-shaped opening downwards

    Ⓓ U-shaped opening downwards

40. If the graph of a system of linear equations displays only one line, how can you describe the equations that comprise the system?

    Ⓐ same slope with different y-intercept

    Ⓑ different slope and different y-intercept

    Ⓒ different slope with same y-intercept

    Ⓓ same slope and same y-intercept

41. Sally has $200 in a personal safe at her home and plans to add $50 per month. Match the expression with the real-world interpretation.

Expression	Real-World Interpretation
A. 200	**1.** the initial amount in the safe
B. 50	**2.** the total amount Sally will have in the safe in 18 months
C. $50x$	**3.** the total amount added to the safe in x months
D. $50(18) + 200$	**4.** the amount added to the safe each month

 I'm in a Learning Mindset!

How did helping my peers solve systems of linear equations by substitution benefit me? What impact did it have on my learning outcome?

Solve Linear Systems by Adding or Subtracting

(I Can) write linear systems to model real-world situations and solve the systems by adding or subtracting.

Spark Your Learning

Lea is training for a triathlon, which is an event that involves first swimming, then bicycling, and finally running. This week, Lea trains for the swimming and running portions of the triathlon.

On Monday, Lea swims and runs a total of 14 miles in 3 hours.

On Thursday, Lea swims and runs a total of 20 miles in 4 hours.

Complete Part A as a whole class. Then complete Parts B–D in small groups.

A. What is a mathematical question you can ask about this situation? What information would you need to know to answer your question?

B. What variables are involved in this situation? What unit of measurement would you use for each variable?

C. To answer your question, what strategy and tool would you use along with all the information you have? What answer do you get?

D. Does your answer make sense in the context of the situation? How do you know?

 Turn and Talk Why was it necessary to assume that Lea's swimming speed and her running speed were the same on each day in order to answer the question? Why might this assumption not be true?

Build Understanding

Understand the Elimination Method

To *eliminate* something means to get rid of it. The **elimination method** for solving a system of two equations eliminates one variable in the system by adding or subtracting the equations.

Steps in the Elimination Method
1. Add or subtract the equations in the system to eliminate one variable, and then solve for the variable that was not eliminated.
2. Substitute the value of the variable you found into either original equation and solve for the other variable.
3. Write the solution as an ordered pair.

1 ▶ Consider the following system of equations.

$$\begin{cases} x + y = 4 \\ x - y = 2 \end{cases}$$

A. Without actually graphing, how do you know that the graphs of the two equations in the system intersect at a single point?

B. The graph of the system is shown. What does the graph tell you about the solution of the system?

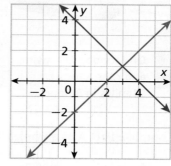

C. Find the sum of the left sides of the two equations and the sum of the right sides. Why are these sums equal?

D. Equate the two sums from Part C and solve for x. Then substitute the value of x into either original equation and solve for y. What do you notice about the values of x and y you obtained?

E. Now use a similar process to once again solve for x and y, but this time subtract each side of the second equation from the corresponding side of the first equation. Do you get the same values of x and y?

F. Can you solve the system below by adding or subtracting the equations? Explain. What must be true about a system for adding or subtracting to work?

$$\begin{cases} 2x + 3y = 1 \\ 4x - y = 9 \end{cases}$$

 Turn and Talk What method(s) could you use to solve the system of equations in Part F of Task 1? What is the solution?

Step It Out

Solve Linear Systems Using Elimination

You can solve a linear system by subtracting or adding to eliminate a variable, provided that the coefficients of the variable you want to eliminate are the same or are opposites.

2 Use elimination to solve the system.

$$\begin{cases} 7x + 2y = 4 \\ 3x + 2y = 12 \end{cases}$$

Subtract the equations to eliminate y. Then solve for x.

$$\begin{array}{r} 7x + 2y = 4 \\ -(3x + 2y = 12) \\ \hline 4x \qquad = -8 \\ x = -2 \end{array}$$

A. Why do you subtract the equations instead of adding them?

Substitute -2 for x in either original equation and solve for y.

$$3x + 2y = 12$$

$$3(-2) + 2y = 12$$

$$-6 + 2y = 12$$

$$2y = 18$$

$$y = 9$$

B. Would you get the same value of y if you substituted -2 for x in the first equation instead of the second equation? Explain.

The solution is $(-2, 9)$.

 Turn and Talk Suppose the second equation in the system in Task 2 is replaced with $3x - 2y = 12$. How would your strategy for solving the system change?

3 **A.** Matias tries to solve the linear system below by adding the equations. Why does his result show that the system has infinitely many solutions?

$$\begin{cases} 5x + 4y = 8 \\ -5x - 4y = -8 \end{cases} \Rightarrow \begin{array}{r} 5x + 4y = 8 \\ +(-5x - 4y = -8) \\ \hline 0 = 0 \end{array}$$

B. Matias then tries to solve the following linear system by subtracting the equations. Why does his result show that the system has no solution?

$$\begin{cases} 2x + 3y = 8 \\ 2x + 3y = 1 \end{cases} \Rightarrow \begin{array}{r} 2x + 3y = 8 \\ -(2x + 3y = 1) \\ \hline 0 = 7 \end{array}$$

 Turn and Talk How can you tell that the linear system in Part B of Task 3 has no solution *without* subtracting the equations?

Apply Systems of Linear Equations

4 ▸ Jamie is paddling her kayak on a river. She first paddles downstream (with the current) from her campsite to a picnic area, where she eats lunch. She then paddles upstream back to her campsite. What are Jamie's paddling speed in still water and the speed of the river's current?

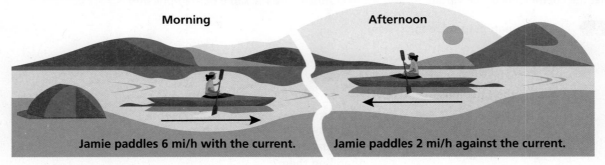

Morning   **Afternoon**

Jamie paddles 6 mi/h with the current.   Jamie paddles 2 mi/h against the current.

Write a verbal model.

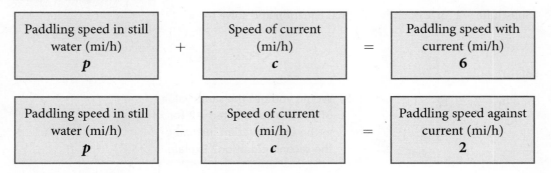

| Paddling speed in still water (mi/h) p | $+$ | Speed of current (mi/h) c | $=$ | Paddling speed with current (mi/h) 6 |

| Paddling speed in still water (mi/h) p | $-$ | Speed of current (mi/h) c | $=$ | Paddling speed against current (mi/h) 2 |

Write a system of equations.

$$\begin{cases} p + c = 6 \\ p - c = 2 \end{cases}$$

A. How do you know that you can add the equations to solve the system?

Add the equations to eliminate c. Then solve for p.

$$\begin{array}{r} p + c = 6 \\ +(p - c = 2) \\ \hline 2p \quad\;\; = 8 \\ p = 4 \end{array}$$

Substitute 4 for p in either original equation and solve for c.

$$p + c = 6$$
$$4 + c = 6$$
$$c = 2$$

B. Why does it make sense in this situation that the value of c is less than the value of p?

Answer the question.
Jamie's paddling speed in still water is 4 mi/h. The speed of the current is 2 mi/h.

Turn and Talk How would your answer for Task 4 change if Jamie is able to paddle 5 mi/h with the current and 4 mi/h against the current?

256

Check Understanding

1. Using your own words, describe the elimination method for solving a system of two linear equations in two variables.

Tell whether you would add the equations or subtract the equations to eliminate one of the variables.

2. $\begin{cases} 2x - y = 5 \\ x + y = 1 \end{cases}$

3. $\begin{cases} 6x + 2y = 8 \\ 6x + y = 7 \end{cases}$

4. $\begin{cases} 4x - 5y = 7 \\ -2x - 5y = 19 \end{cases}$

Use the elimination method to solve the system.

5. $\begin{cases} 3x + 2y = 10 \\ 3x - y = 22 \end{cases}$

6. $\begin{cases} -2x + y = 3 \\ 3x - y = -2 \end{cases}$

7. $\begin{cases} 7x - 9y = 4 \\ -7x + 9y = -5 \end{cases}$

8. An aquarium charges one price for adults and a different price for students under 18. Two classes visit the aquarium. The first class has 4 adult chaperones and 20 students, and pays a total of $320 for admission. The second class has 4 adult chaperones and 23 students, and pays a total of $356 for admission. Find the price of an adult ticket and the price of a student ticket.

On Your Own

9. **(MP) Use Structure** What must be true in order for you to be able to solve a system of linear equations using the elimination method?

Use the elimination method to solve the system.

10. $\begin{cases} x + y = 1 \\ -2x + y = 4 \end{cases}$

11. $\begin{cases} 4x - 9y = -21 \\ 4x + 3y = -9 \end{cases}$

12. $\begin{cases} -2x + 5y = 7 \\ 2x - 5y = -7 \end{cases}$

13. $\begin{cases} x + 2y = 13 \\ -x + y = 5 \end{cases}$

14. $\begin{cases} x + 4y = 47 \\ 3x - 4y = -19 \end{cases}$

15. $\begin{cases} -10x + 2y = -7 \\ -10x + 2y = 0 \end{cases}$

16. **(MP) Reason** Consider the system shown, where both a and c are nonzero. Under what conditions will the system have exactly one solution? no solution? infinitely many solutions? $\begin{cases} x + ay = b \\ x + cy = d \end{cases}$

17. **(MP) Model with Mathematics** Katie and her friend Alma went to their county's annual fair. Use the information in the photo to write a system of equations. Then solve the system to find the cost of admission and the cost of a ride at the fair.

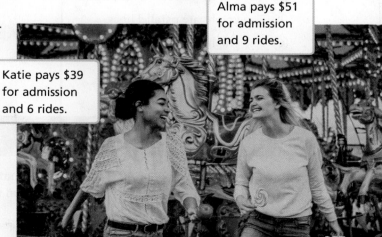

Alma pays $51 for admission and 9 rides.

Katie pays $39 for admission and 6 rides.

18. **Open Ended** Write a system of two linear equations in two variables that you can solve by adding the equations, and whose solution is $(-2, 4)$.

©Solstock/E+/Getty Images

19. Geography Airplanes can travel faster from west to east than from east to west because an airplane flying east travels with the wind, while an airplane flying west travels against the wind. Suppose a commercial airliner takes 5 hours to complete the 2440-mile flight from San Francisco, California, to Washington, D.C., but takes 6 hours to complete the return trip.

2440 mi

San Francisco   Washington, D.C.

A. Find the airliner's average speed for the trip from San Francisco to Washington, D.C., and for the return trip.

B. Write and solve a system of equations to find the airliner's speed with no wind and the speed of the wind.

C. Is the answer to Part B reasonable? Explain.

20. Juan is buying flowers for his mother. He has $18 to spend and sees that roses are $3 each and carnations are $1.50 each. He wants to buy 3 times as many carnations as roses and spend all of his money on flowers. Write a system of equations that models this situation. Is there a viable solution that meets Juan's conditions? Explain.

Spiral Review • Assessment Readiness

21. What are the solutions of the equation $|x - 3| = 5$?

Ⓐ only 8
Ⓒ 8 and 2
Ⓑ 5 and −5
Ⓓ 8 and −2

22. For a system of two linear equations in two variables, what is true about the graphs of the equations if the system has no solution?

Ⓐ The graphs intersect at exactly one point.
Ⓑ The graphs are parallel lines.
Ⓒ The graphs are the same line.
Ⓓ none of the above

23. Lydia has 10 dimes and quarters in her pocket. The value of her coins is $1.45. How many dimes and how many quarters does Lydia have?

Ⓐ 5 dimes and 5 quarters
Ⓑ 6 dimes and 4 quarters
Ⓒ 7 dimes and 3 quarters
Ⓓ 8 dimes and 2 quarters

24. Which expression is equivalent to $-2(3x - 7y)$?

Ⓐ $-6x + 14y$
Ⓒ $-6x + 7y$
Ⓑ $-6x - 14y$
Ⓓ $-6x - 7y$

 I'm in a Learning Mindset!

How did receiving help with the elimination method for solving linear systems benefit me? What impact did it have on my learning outcome?

Solve Linear Systems by Multiplying First

(I Can) write linear systems to model real-world problems and solve them by multiplying first.

Spark Your Learning

Karen and Leona are purchasing art supplies for art class.

Each canvas has the same price.
Each tube of paint has the same price.

Complete Part A as a whole class. Then complete Parts B–D in small groups.

A. What is a mathematical question you can ask about this situation? What information would you need to know to answer your question?

B. What must be true for you to use a system of linear equations in order to solve this problem?

C. To answer your question, what strategy and tool would you use along with all the information you have? What answer do you get?

D. Does your answer make sense in the context of this situation? How do you know?

  Turn and Talk How might your strategy to solve the problem change if Karen buys 4 canvases and 3 tubes of paint, spending $19.20, and Leona buys 4 canvases and 2 tubes of paint, spending $16?

Build Understanding

Understand the Elimination Method

In the previous lesson, elimination worked when at least one pair of like terms had the same or opposite coefficient. You can also use elimination to solve systems that have like terms that do not have the same or opposite coefficient.

1 Consider the system defined by the equations $Ax + By = C$ and $Dx + Ey = F$, where A, B, C, D, E, and F are constants. Multiply the second equation by a nonzero constant k to get the new equation $kDx + kEy = kF$.

$$Ax \quad + \quad By \quad = \quad C$$
$$+(kDx \quad + \quad kEy \quad = \quad kF)$$
$$\overline{(A + kD)x + (B + kE)y = C + kF}$$

Add the new equation to the first equation.

The proof that follows shows that if (x_1, y_1) is a solution of the original system, then it is also a solution of the new system written below.

$$\begin{cases} Ax + By = C \\ (A + kD)x + (B + kE)y = C + kF \end{cases}$$

$Ax_1 + By_1 = C$	(x_1, y_1) is a solution of $Ax + By = C$.
$Dx_1 + Ey_1 = F$	(x_1, y_1) is a solution of $Dx + Ey = F$.
$k(Dx_1 + Ey_1) = kF$	Multiplication Property of Equality
$kDx_1 + kEy_1 = kF$	Distributive Property
$C + kDx_1 + kEy_1 = C + kF$	Addition Property of Equality
$Ax_1 + By_1 + kDx_1 + kEy_1 = C + kF$	Substitute $Ax_1 + By_1$ for C on the left side.
$Ax_1 + kDx_1 + By_1 + kEy_1 = C + kF$	Commutative Property of Addition
$(A + kD)x_1 + (B + kE)y_1 = C + kF$	Distributive Property

Since $(A + kD)x_1 + (B + kE)y_1 = C + kF$, (x_1, y_1) is a solution of the new system.

A. Use graphing to identify the solution of the system of equations $\begin{cases} 4x + 5y = 12 \\ 2x + 3y = 8 \end{cases}$.

B. Write a new system whose first equation is obtained by multiplying the second equation in Part A by -2 and adding the result to the first equation in Part A, and whose second equation is the second equation in Part A. Compare the solutions of the new and original systems.

C. Why do you think the value chosen for k in Part B is -2?

 Turn and Talk For the system in Part A, multiply the first equation by 3 and the second equation by 5. Does this new system have the same solution? Explain.

Step It Out

Solve Linear Systems by Multiplying

2 Solve the linear system using the elimination method.
$$\begin{cases} -2x + 3y = 7 \\ 5x + 4y = 17 \end{cases}$$

Rewrite both equations in this system by multiplying.

$$\begin{cases} 5(-2x + 3y = 7) \\ 2(5x + 4y = 17) \end{cases} \Rightarrow \begin{cases} -10x + 15y = 35 \\ 10x + 8y = 34 \end{cases}$$

A. How do you choose what numbers to multiply by for each equation?

Use addition to eliminate one of the variables.

$$\begin{cases} -10x + 15y = 35 \\ 10x + 8y = 34 \end{cases}$$

B. Why do you use addition and not subtraction to eliminate a variable in this system?

$$-10x + 15y = 35$$
$$\underline{+(10x + 8y = 34)}$$
$$23y = 69$$

$$y = 3$$

Solve for the other unknown variable by substituting into one of the original equations.

$$5x + 4(3) = 17$$

$$5x + 12 = 17$$

$$5x = 5$$

$$x = 1$$

The solution of the system is $(1, 3)$.

C. Why is the solution written as an ordered pair?

Check the solution by substituting into both equations in the system.

$$-2x + 3y = 7 \qquad\qquad 5x + 4y = 17$$

$$-2(1) + 3(3) \overset{?}{=} 7 \qquad\qquad 5(1) + 4(3) \overset{?}{=} 17$$

$$7 = 7 \checkmark \qquad\qquad 17 = 17 \checkmark$$

D. What is another way you could check your solution?

 Turn and Talk Consider the system in Task 2. Are you able to solve the system by any of the following methods? Explain your answers.

- Multiply the equations in the original system by different constants than the ones shown to solve the system another way.
- Graph to solve the system.
- Add the original equations in the system.

Apply Systems of Linear Equations

3 Carl drives a delivery truck. Each month, he drives the same two routes, but not the same number of times each month. What is the length of each route?

	Times Route A driven	Times Route B driven	Total miles
Jan.	7	13	636
Feb.	11	5	552

Write a verbal model for the situation for each month.

January:

| Times Carl drove Route A **7** | · | Length of Route A (mi) **x** | + | Times Carl drove Route B **13** | · | Length of Route B (mi) **y** | = | Total miles **636** |

February:

| Times Carl drove Route A **11** | · | Length of Route A (mi) **x** | + | Times Carl drove Route B **5** | · | Length of Route B (mi) **y** | = | Total miles **552** |

Write the system of linear equations. $\begin{cases} 7x + 13y = 636 \\ 11x + 5y = 552 \end{cases}$

A. Why do you use the same variables in both equations?

Multiply each equation in the system.

$$\begin{cases} 11(7x + 13y = 636) \\ 7(11x + 5y = 552) \end{cases} \Rightarrow \begin{cases} 77x + 143y = 6996 \\ 77x + 35y = 3864 \end{cases}$$

Use subtraction to eliminate one of the variables.

$$77x + 143y = 6996$$
$$-(77x + 35y = 3864)$$
$$\overline{108y = 3132}$$
$$y = 29$$

Solve for the other unknown variable.

$$7x + 13(29) = 636$$
$$7x + 377 = 636$$
$$7x = 259$$
$$x = 37$$

B. Could you have used the other equation to solve for x? Explain.

The solution is $(37, 29)$. Route A is 37 miles long and Route B is 29 miles long.

 Turn and Talk How would the solution for Task 3 change if the number of times Carl drove Route A and the number of times he drove Route B were switched for January and also switched for February?

Check Understanding

1. How does the solution of a linear system change if you multiply one or both of the equations by a nonzero constant?

Explain how you would use multiplication to solve each of these linear systems by elimination.

2. $\begin{cases} 2x + 3y = 54 \\ 4x + 7y = 85 \end{cases}$

3. $\begin{cases} 3x + 2y = 54 \\ 4x + 5y = 85 \end{cases}$

4. $\begin{cases} 2x + 3y = 54 \\ -4x + 7y = 85 \end{cases}$

5. Use the elimination method to solve the system.
$\begin{cases} 2x - y = 10 \\ 10x + 4y = 5 \end{cases}$

   A. Which equation(s) would you rewrite? Explain.

   B. What is the solution of the system?

6. A florist sells two types of bouquets. The first bouquet has 4 roses and 5 sunflowers and costs $13. The second bouquet has 6 roses and 3 sunflowers and costs $15. How much does each rose cost? How much does each sunflower cost?

On Your Own

7. **(MP) Attend to Precision** When would you need to multiply one of the equations in a system before you can add or subtract to eliminate a variable?

8. **A.** The graph of a system of equations is shown. Write the equations of the lines that form this system in standard form.

   B. What happens when you use the elimination method to solve this system? Explain your answer.

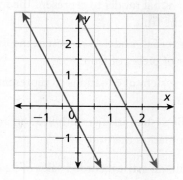

Use the elimination method to solve the system.

9. $\begin{cases} x + 4y = 20 \\ -3x + 7y = 35 \end{cases}$

10. $\begin{cases} 2x + 3y = 12 \\ 6x + 4y = 26 \end{cases}$

11. $\begin{cases} -x + 3y = 11 \\ 7x + y = -11 \end{cases}$

12. $\begin{cases} x + 3y = 10 \\ -2x + 2y = 18 \end{cases}$

13. $\begin{cases} -x + 6y = 7 \\ 6x + 2y = -4 \end{cases}$

14. $\begin{cases} -2x + 3y = 16 \\ 3x + 4y = -7 \end{cases}$

15. $\begin{cases} -5x + 5y = 35 \\ 12x + 4y = -20 \end{cases}$

16. $\begin{cases} 5x - y = 13 \\ 7x + 2y = 25 \end{cases}$

17. $\begin{cases} 3x - 4y = -9 \\ 2x - 3y = -8 \end{cases}$

18. $\begin{cases} -5x + 5y = 20 \\ 2x + 2y = 8 \end{cases}$

19. $\begin{cases} -5x - 3y = -32 \\ 4x + 2y = 23 \end{cases}$

20. $\begin{cases} -2x + 3y = 4 \\ 3x + 3y = 9 \end{cases}$

21. (MP) **Critique Reasoning** For the system of equations shown below, Eloise says she needs to multiply the first equation by 7 and then add to eliminate the variable x. What error did she make?

$$\begin{cases} -2x + 5y = 35 \\ 7x + 4y = -7 \end{cases}$$

22. (MP) **Critique Reasoning** Manny says he should multiply the first equation in the system of equations below by 3 and the second equation by 2. Is there a more efficient way to solve this system? Explain your answer.

$$\begin{cases} -2x + y = 15 \\ 3x + 4y = -12 \end{cases}$$

Use the elimination method to solve each system.

23. $\begin{cases} 1.5x - 0.75y = 5.25 \\ -3x + 4.5y = -7.5 \end{cases}$ **24.** $\begin{cases} 1.75x + 2.5y = 22 \\ 1.5x + 0.5y = 9 \end{cases}$ **25.** $\begin{cases} 0.8x + 2y = 3.2 \\ 1.2x + 3.5y = 5.8 \end{cases}$

26. $\begin{cases} 1.8x - 3y = 0.6 \\ 1.2x + 0.4y = -2.6 \end{cases}$ **27.** $\begin{cases} 2.5x + 3.5y = 9 \\ -2x + 3y = -13 \end{cases}$ **28.** $\begin{cases} 1.5x + 2.5y = 8.5 \\ 2.5x + 1.5y = 7.5 \end{cases}$

29. (MP) **Use Structure** Miguel spends $11 to buy 16 apples and oranges. How many of each type of fruit did he buy?

 A. Identify the variables in this situation.

 B. Write a verbal model to represent the total cost of the fruit.

 C. Write a verbal model to represent the total number of pieces of fruit.

 D. Write a system of equations to represent the situation.

 E. Solve the system using multiplication and the elimination method.

apple: $0.75

orange: $0.65

30. At an art fair, an artist recorded sales of 52 candles of two different sizes and a total of $269 collected. The smaller candle sells for $4 and the larger candle sells for $7.

 A. Based on the artist's records, how many of each size of candle were sold?

 B. Is your answer reasonable? What might this imply about the artist's records?

31. (MP) **Reason** How is solving a system of linear equations using multiplication and the elimination method related to finding the least common multiple of two numbers?

32. The sum of the measures of two angles is 90°. The difference of the measure of the larger angle and twice the measure of the smaller angle is 30°. What is the measure of each angle? Solve the problem by writing a system of equations and solving the system using the elimination method.

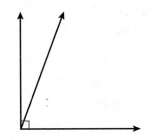

33. The Lynn and Cohen families go to see the new baby panda at the zoo. The Lynn family spends $84 on tickets. The Cohen family spends $76 on tickets. What is the price of each type of ticket? Solve the problem by writing a system of equations and solving the system using the elimination method.

Lynn family:
3 adults, 3 children

Cohen family:
2 adults, 4 children

34. (MP) **Reason** Write a system of linear equations in two variables that has an infinite number of solutions. Then use the elimination method to solve the system. What is the solution that you get? Explain how this solution relates to the fact that the system has an infinite number of solutions.

35. Each month Hannah uses the bus and subway to travel around her city. The table shows the number of times she rides the bus, the number of times she rides the subway, and the total amount she spends on the rides in May and in June.

A. Write a system of equations to model this situation.

B. How much does it cost for one bus ride?

C. How much does it cost for one subway ride?

D. Hannah can travel to her friend's house either by subway or by bus. Which mode of transportation do you think she should use? Explain your answer.

	Bus rides	Subway rides	Total amount spent
May	8	6	$27.10
June	10	7	$32.75

36. A store sells bags that contain tubes of lip balm and travel-size lotions. A bag that has 2 tubes of lip balm and 3 lotions costs $21. A bag that has 3 tubes of lip balm and 4 lotions costs $29. How much would a bag that has 5 tubes of lip balm and 5 lotions cost?

37. (MP) **Critique Reasoning** Nina says you can solve the system shown by multiplying the first equation by 5 and then adding the result to the second equation. Kara says you can solve the system by multiplying the first equation by 4 and the second equation by 3, and then adding the resulting equations. Who is correct? Explain.

$$\begin{cases} -x + 3y = 8 \\ 5x - 4y = -18 \end{cases}$$

38. Jordan listens to two different playlists while he runs. On Monday, he ran for 42 minutes and listened to all of playlist A and half of playlist B. On Wednesday, he ran for 48 minutes and listened to all of playlist B and half of playlist A.

A. How many minutes long is each playlist?

B. How long can he run if he listens to each playlist exactly one time?

C. Assume that each song on the playlists is about 3 minutes long. How many songs are on each playlist?

39. **(MP) Reason** A system of linear equations is given. $\begin{cases} x + 2y = -4 \\ 3x + y = -32 \end{cases}$

    A. Solve the system using the substitution method.

    B. Solve the system again using the elimination method by multiplying the second equation by -2 and adding the resulting equation to the first equation.

    C. Does your result from Part B support the idea that replacing one equation in a system with a multiple of it produces a system with the same solution? Explain.

40. Rebecca creates a painting that has the dimensions shown.

    A. Write a system of equations that can be used to find the length and width of the painting.

    B. What method would you use to solve this system of equations? Explain.

    C. What are the length and width of the painting?

perimeter = 24 feet
length = 2 times the width

41. **(Open Middle™)** Using the digits 0 to 9, at most one time each, fill in the boxes to create a system of equations and its solution.

$\begin{cases} \square\, x + \square\, y = \square \\ y = \square\, x - \square \end{cases}$ $(\square, \square)$

Spiral Review • Assessment Readiness

42. The number of times Susan sings a solo in the school chorus is less than 5 and at least 2. Which inequality represents this situation?

    (A) $2 < x < 5$ (C) $2 \leq x < 5$

    (B) $2 > x > 5$ (D) $2 \geq x < 5$

43. Which system consists of equations whose graphs are the same line?

    (A) $\begin{cases} y = -x + 3 \\ 2x - 2y = 8 \end{cases}$ (C) $\begin{cases} -x + 3 = y \\ 2x + 2y = 6 \end{cases}$

    (B) $\begin{cases} x = 3 + y \\ 2x - 2y = 10 \end{cases}$ (D) $\begin{cases} x + y = 3 \\ 2x + 2y = 8 \end{cases}$

44. Solve the system by substitution.

$\begin{cases} \dfrac{1}{2}y = -2x + 10 \\ 8x + 2y = 20 \end{cases}$

    (A) $(-1.25, 15)$ (C) $(1.25, 15)$

    (B) $(-2.5, 10)$ (D) no solution

45. If applying the elimination method to a system of equations results in a false statement, what do you know about the system? Select all that apply.

    (A) infinite number of solutions   (D) independent system

    (B) one solution   (E) consistent system

    (C) no solution   (F) inconsistent system

I'm in a Learning Mindset!

How did helping my peers solve systems of linear equations using the elimination method with multiplication benefit me? What impact did it have on my learning outcome?

Solve Linear Systems by Graphing

The cost of a hot dog and a drink is $5. The cost of two hot dogs and a drink is $8. You can use a graph to solve the system of two linear equations that models this situation.

$$\begin{cases} h + d = 5 \\ 2h + d = 8 \end{cases}$$

The point of intersection is $(3, 2)$. So, $(3, 2)$ is the solution of the system. This means that the cost of a hot dog is $3 and the cost of a drink is $2.

Solve Linear Systems by Substitution

You can use the substitution method to solve the system of equations.

$$\begin{cases} h + d = 5 \\ 2h + d = 8 \end{cases}$$

Solve either equation for one of the variables.

$$h + d = 5$$
$$d = 5 - h$$

Substitute for d in the other equation.

$$2h + 5 - h = 8$$
$$h + 5 = 8$$
$$h = 3$$

Find the value of d using either original equation.

$$3 + d = 5$$
$$d = 2$$

The solution is $(h, d) = (3, 2)$.

Solve Linear Systems by Adding and Subtracting

Subtract to solve by the elimination method.

Subtract the first equation from the second equation to eliminate d.

$$\begin{array}{r} 2h + d = 8 \\ -(h + d = 5) \\ \hline h \quad\;\; = 3 \end{array}$$

Find the value of d using either original equation.

$$3 + d = 5$$
$$d = 2$$

The solution is $(h, d) = (3, 2)$.

Solve Linear Systems by Multiplying First

Use the elimination method with multiplication.

Multiply the first equation by 2. Then subtract the second equation from the result to eliminate h.

$$2(h + d = 5) \quad \rightarrow \quad 2h + 2d = 10$$
$$2h + 2d = 10$$
$$\begin{array}{r} -(2h + \;\; d = 8) \\ \hline d = 2 \end{array}$$

Find the value of h using either original equation.

$$h + 2 = 5$$
$$h = 3$$

The solution is $(h, d) = (3, 2)$.

Vocabulary

Choose the correct term from the box to complete each sentence.

1. A system of equations that has exactly one solution is a(n) ___?___, and a system of equations that has no solution is a(n) ___?___.

2. Two or more equations having the same variables form a(n) ___?___.

3. When you add or subtract to solve a system of equations, you are using the ___?___ method.

4. Solving one equation in a system of equations for one of its variables is the first step of the ___?___ method.

Concepts and Skills

Write a system of linear equations for each type.

5. independent

6. dependent

7. inconsistent

Identify each system of equations as independent, dependent, or inconsistent. Then solve the system.

8. $\begin{cases} y = -3x + 3 \\ y = 3x + 6 \end{cases}$

9. $\begin{cases} y = x + 2 \\ y = x + 5 \end{cases}$

10. $\begin{cases} y = x + 1 \\ -2x + 2y = 2 \end{cases}$

11. $\begin{cases} y = 2x + 3 \\ y = 4x + 6 \end{cases}$

12. (MP) **Use Tools** State what strategy and tool you will use to answer the question, explain your choice, and then find the answer. Two companies charge different amounts for the use of their dance halls. Party Time charges a $100 flat fee plus $50 per hour. Let's Dance Company charges a $175 flat fee plus $25 per hour. For what number of hours do the two companies charge the same amount?

   A. Write a system of linear equations to model the situation.

   B. Solve the system graphically. Then answer the question.

   C. Show that the solution results in the same charge for both companies.

13. Isabella begins riding a bike on a trail at mile 6 at a rate of 8 mi/h. Tanaysha beings riding a bike from the beginning of the trail at a rate of 9 mi/h.

   A. Write a system of linear equations to model the situation.

   B. Identify the system as independent, dependent, or inconsistent. Justify your reasoning.

Linear Inequalities

Calorie Count Cafe

How much bacon and eggs can you eat while staying under 300 calories?

Are You Ready?

Complete these problems to review prior concepts and skills you will need for this module.

Solve Two-Step Inequalities

Solve each inequality and graph the solution on a number line.

1. $6 + \dfrac{x}{2} > 10$

2. $-2 + \dfrac{x}{3} \le 6$

Write Linear Equations in Slope-Intercept Form

Write an equation for each line in slope-intercept form.

3.

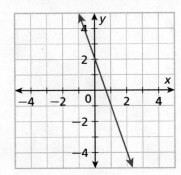

4.

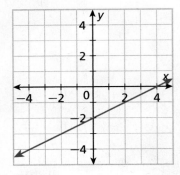

Solve Systems of Linear Equations by Graphing

Solve each system by graphing.

5. $\begin{cases} y = -x + 3 \\ y = \dfrac{1}{2}x - 6 \end{cases}$

6. $\begin{cases} -4x + 12y = 12 \\ -2x + 4y = 6 \end{cases}$

Connecting Past and Present Learning

Previously, you learned:

- to solve systems of linear equations,
- to write and solve inequalities, and
- to use compound inequalities to model real-world problems.

In this module, you will learn:

- to write and graph linear inequalities in two variables,
- to write and graph systems of linear inequalities, and
- to use systems of inequalities to model real-world problems.

Linear Inequalities in Two Variables

(I Can) write and graph linear inequalities in two variables to model and solve real-world problems.

Spark Your Learning

Students are having a fundraiser by selling popcorn. Their goal is to raise at least $3000.

They buy flavored popcorn in bulk and then put them in small and large bags to sell for the fundraiser.

Complete Part A as a whole class. Then complete Parts B–D in small groups.

A. What is a mathematical question you can ask about this situation? What information would you need to know to answer your question?

B. What are the variables of this problem? How can you use them in an expression to to answer your question?

C. To answer your question, what strategy and tool would you use along with all the information you have? What answer do you get?

D. Do all of the possible solutions make sense in the context of this real-world situation? Explain.

 Turn and Talk How would your answer change for each of the following changes in the situation?

- The bulk popcorn costs 10% more for the students to buy.
- The students sell the popcorn for 15% more.

Build Understanding

Graph Linear Inequalities in Standard Form

Inequalities that can be written in one of the following five forms are called **linear inequalities in two variables**:

$$Ax + By < C \qquad Ax + By > C$$
$$Ax + By \leq C \qquad Ax + By \geq C \qquad Ax + By \neq C$$

Here A, B, and C are real numbers, and A and B are not both 0.

A **solution of an inequality in two variables** is any ordered pair that makes the inequality true.

You can represent solutions of an inequality with a graph and manipulate inequalities much like you manipulate equations.

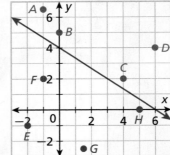

 Consider an inequality in standard form, such as $2x + 3y \leq 12$.

A. Are the points on the line $2x + 3y = 12$, graphed here, solutions to the inequality $2x + 3y \leq 12$? Explain.

B. Copy and complete the table.

Point	Inequality	True or false?
$A(-1, 6.5)$	$2(-1) + 3(6.5) \leq 12$	?
$B(0, 5)$	$2(0) + 3(5) \leq 12$	?
$C(4, 2)$	$2(4) + 3(2) \leq 12$	?
$D(6, 4)$	$2(6) + 3(4) \leq 12$	?
$E(-2, -1)$	$2(-2) + 3(-1) \leq 12$	?
$F(-1, 2)$	$2(-1) + 3(2) \leq 12$	?
$G(1.5, -2.5)$	$2(1.5) + 3(-2.5) \leq 12$	?
$H(5, 0)$	$2(5) + 3(0) < 12$	?

C. In the table, you identified four solutions of the inequality. How could you use shading on the graph to show ALL solutions of the inequality?

 Turn and Talk Describe a general process for graphing a linear inequality of the form $Ax + By \leq C$ or $Ax + By \geq C$.

272

Graph Linear Inequalities in Slope-Intercept Form

A **half-plane** is a part of the coordinate plane on one side of a line. This line, which divides the coordinate plane into two half-planes, is called the **boundary line**.

The graph of a strict "greater than" inequality or a strict "less than" inequality does not include the points on its boundary line. To represent the exclusion of those points, draw the boundary line with dashes.

2 ▶ Consider an inequality in slope-intercept form, such as $y > 2x + 3$.

A. Point $P(-2, -1)$ lies on the boundary line of $y > 2x + 3$. Choose three other points with the same x-coordinate as P and y-coordinates greater than that of P. Where do your points fall relative to the boundary line?

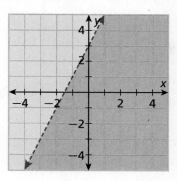

B. Choose a new point Q on the boundary line. Repeat what you did in Part A, selecting three points with the same x-coordinates as Q and y-coordinates greater than that of Q. Where do these points fall relative to the boundary line?

C. Based on your answers to Parts A and B, what can you conclude about all such points that lie vertically above the boundary line?

D. Based on your answer to Part C, which half-plane would you shade to show ALL solutions of the inequality $y > 2x + 3$?

E. What would the other half-plane represent?

F. Pick a point in that unshaded half-plane and use it to confirm your answer to Part E.

G. The graph at right shows a dashed boundary line and both half-planes shaded. What inequality does it represent?

 Turn and Talk Describe a general process for graphing a linear inequality in slope-intercept form, and compare it to the general process that you came up with for graphing a linear inequality in standard form.

Step It Out

Write Linear Inequalities

You can write a linear inequality from its graph.

3 Write a linear inequality to represent the graph.

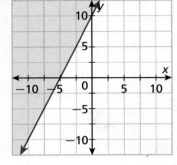

1) Write an equation for the boundary line.

   - y-intercept: 10
   - slope: 2

   $y = 2x + 10$

2) Determine the inequality symbol.

   - Shading is *above* the boundary line.
   - The boundary line is *solid*.

   The inequality is $y \geq 2x + 10$.

   A. The inequality symbol $\geq$ is a combination of a greater than symbol, $>$, and an equality symbol, $=$. Which of these two symbols is affected by the location of the shading in the graph? By the appearance of the boundary in the graph?

3) Check using substitution.

   - A point in the solution region is $(-10, 0)$.
     $y \geq 2x + 10$
     $0 \geq 2(-10) + 10$
     $0 \geq -10$ true

   - A point on the boundary line is $(-5, 0)$.
     $y \geq 2x + 10$
     $0 \geq 2(-5) + 10$
     $0 \geq 0$ true

   B. How do you know whether a point on the boundary line should be included in the solution?

   - A point NOT in the solution region is $(0, 0)$.
     $y \geq 2x + 10$
     $0 \geq 2(0) + 10$
     $0 \geq 10$ false

Note that for the same boundary line there are the following related inequalities.

 Turn and Talk Shown below are three graphs related to the graph in Task 3. What inequality represents each of these graphs? Explain your reasoning.

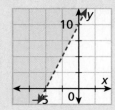 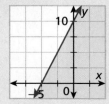 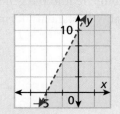

Model with Linear Inequalities

4 ▶ A realtor has a budget of $200 for cheese and crackers for an open house.

Write a linear inequality to describe this situation, graph it, and then use the graph to identify three possible combinations of cheese wheels and boxes of crackers that stay within the realtor's budget.

Crackers:
$4 per package

Cheese:
$8 per wheel

Use a verbal model.

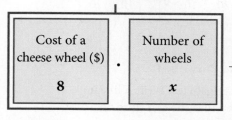
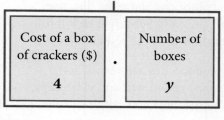

Total cost of cheese ($)

| Cost of a cheese wheel ($) **8** | · | Number of wheels ***x*** |

+

Total cost of crackers ($)

| Cost of a box of crackers ($) **4** | · | Number of boxes ***y*** |

≤

| Budget ($) **200** |

Write an inequality in standard form.

$8x + 4y \leq 200$

A. Why is the symbol $\leq$ being used?

Identify the *x*- and *y*-intercepts of the boundary line.

x-intercept: Let $y = 0$.

$8x + 4(0) = 200$

$8x = 200$

$x = 25$

y-intercept: Let $x = 0$.

$8(0) + 4y = 200$

$4y = 200$

$y = 50$

Graph the inequality.

Graph the boundary line and then shade the appropriate half-plane.

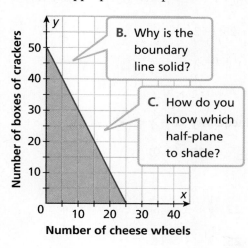

B. Why is the boundary line solid?

C. How do you know which half-plane to shade?

Identify two points in the solution region, confirm that they make the inequality true, and interpret them in the context of the situation.

One point in the solution region is $(10, 15)$.

$$8(10) + 4(15) = 140$$

$$140 \leq 200? \text{ True}$$

The realtor can buy 10 wheels of cheese and 15 boxes of crackers.

Another point in the solution region is $(15, 20)$.

$$8(15) + 4(20) = 200$$

$$200 \leq 200? \text{ True}$$

D. Why isn't $(5, 45)$ a solution?

The realtor can buy 15 wheels of cheese and 20 boxes of crackers.

Turn and Talk Is every point within the solution region an acceptable solution in the context of this problem? Explain.

Check Understanding

1. What inequality symbols are associated with a dashed line in the graph of a linear inequality in two variables?

2. What does shading indicate on a graph of a linear inequality in two variables?

3. Use the graph shown.

   A. What inequality symbol is indicated by the graph?

   B. Write the inequality.

   C. Select three points: one above the line, one below it, and one on it. Substitute each into the inequality and show the results.

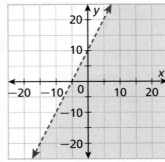

4. A music video producer has a library of audio samples, each 2 gigabytes in size, and video clips, each 10 gigabytes. Write a linear inequality that models how many of these audio and video files she can store on a thumb drive that has a maximum capacity of 32 gigabytes.

On Your Own

Determine whether each relation is a linear inequality in two variables.

5. $5x - 10y < 170$

6. $0.5x - 3y \le 6$

7. $2x + 3y^2 > 25$

8. $x > y$

9. Consider an inequality of the form $Ax + By > C$ where A, B, and C are real numbers and $B > 0$. If a point P makes this inequality false, where does it fall relative to the boundary line?

Tell whether the ordered pair is a solution of the inequality.

10. $2x + 3y \ge 14; \ (5, 2)$

11. $4x - 7y > 28; \ (-2, 4)$

12. $x - y \le 5; \ (8, 3)$

13. $x \ge -3; \ (-4, 0)$

14. $y < 8; \ (-9, -7)$

15. $-3y - 2x \ne 12; \ (5, -6)$

Determine whether the ordered pair is a solution of the inequality $3x - y < -5$.

16. $(0, -5)$

17. $(2, 3)$

18. $(-5, -5)$

19. $(5, 0)$

Graph the linear inequality.

20. $y > x + 3$

21. $y \le x - 2$

22. $y < 3x + 5$

23. $y \ge -2x + 8$

24. $x + y < -8$

25. $x - y > 11$

26. $x + 8y > 16$

27. $5x - y \ge 1$

28. $y - 4 \ne x - 6$

29. $-4y \le 16x$

30. $y \le -4$

31. $x > -5$

Write the inequality shown.

32.
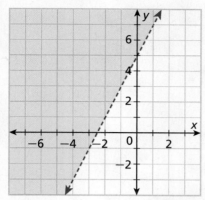

33.
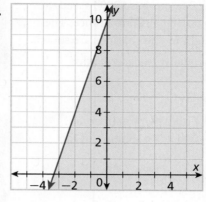

34. **Open Ended** How can you verify if a point in the solution region of the graph of a linear inequality in two variables is a reasonable solution in the context of a problem? Explain.

35. **Open Ended** How can you represent the algebraic form of a linear inequality in two variables given its graph? Explain.

36. **(MP) Use Structure** The president of the high school Pep Club buys bottles of tempera paint and poster boards to make signs for the upcoming pep rally. The budget for supplies is $25.

   A. Write a linear inequality to describe this situation. Let x represent the number of bottles of paint and y the number of poster boards.

   B. Graph your inequality from Part A.

   C. Why is $(10, 0)$ the only point with an x-coordinate of 10 that is a solution of the inequality?

37. The combined weight of the athletes and bobsled in a two-person bobsled competition must not exceed 860 pounds. Write and graph an inequality that describes this situation. Identify and interpret one of the solutions.

38. The number y of passengers riding in an elevator can be no greater than the elevator's maximum weight capacity divided by 150. Write and graph an inequality that describes this situation. Identify and interpret one of the solutions.

39. The authors of a nutritional study conclude that the fat calories consumed per day should be at most 30% of the total calories consumed per day. Write and graph an inequality that describes this conclusion. Identify and interpret one of the solutions.

40. **(MP)** **Use Structure** Marcus has $2000 saved to spend on lodging during a trip to France. The average prices per night for two options are shown.

A. Write a linear inequality to describe this situation.

B. Graph the inequality.

C. Why is $(40, 0)$ the only point with an x-coordinate of 40 that is a solution of the inequality?

41. **(Open Middle™)** Using the digits 1 to 9, at most one time each, fill in the boxes to create a linear inequality, the coordinates of a point that is a solution, and the coordinates of a point that is not a solution.

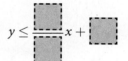

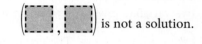

Youth Hostel:
$50 per night

Hotel:
$120 per night

Spiral Review • Assessment Readiness

42. Solve the system for x: $\begin{cases} x + 2y = 3 \\ 3x - 2y = 1 \end{cases}$

Ⓐ 1   Ⓒ 0

Ⓑ −1   Ⓓ 3

43. To solve $\begin{cases} 3x + 4y = 18 \\ 4x + 5y = 23 \end{cases}$ by elimination, what is the first step?

Ⓐ Determine the LCM of the coefficients of one of the variables.

Ⓑ Substitute to eliminate a variable.

Ⓒ Write the equations in slope-intercept form.

Ⓓ Solve one equation for one variable.

44. Sally wants to spend at least $10 on a combination of $1 energy drinks and $3 protein bars. Select the answer that describes the shading of the graph of the inequality corresponding to this situation.

Ⓐ above the dashed line

Ⓑ above the solid line

Ⓒ below the dashed line

Ⓓ below the solid line

45. Which points are solutions of both $y > -x - 2$ and $y \leq 3x + 6$? Select all that apply.

Ⓐ $(0, 0)$ Ⓒ $(0, -2)$

Ⓑ $(-3, 0)$ Ⓓ $(0, 1)$

⊹⊙⊹ **I'm in a** Learning Mindset!

Was collaboration an effective tool for graphing linear inequalities in two variables? Explain.

Graph Systems of Linear Inequalities

(I Can) write and graph systems of linear inequalities to model and solve real-world problems.

Spark Your Learning

In a bowling-style arcade game, you roll a ball up an alley over a ball-hop to launch the ball into a ring worth points. A grand prize is awarded for scoring at least 450 points in the game.

When aiming for a 100-point ring, you risk getting only 10 points if you miss.

Complete Part A as a whole class. Then complete Parts B–D in small groups.

A. What is a mathematical question you can ask about this situation? What information would you need to know to answer your question?

B. What is the constraint on the number of 10-point and 100-point rolls that can be made? What is the constraint on the total score needed to win the grand prize?

C. To answer your question, what strategy and tool would you use along with all the information you have? What answer do you get?

D. What must be true about the answers in your solution set for them to make sense in the context of this situation? Explain.

Turn and Talk How would your chance to win the grand prize change for each of the following changes to the situation?

- The minimum score is 0 points.
- There is a 200-point ring.
- There are 10 balls in each game.

Build Understanding

Graph Systems of Linear Inequalities

In a previous lesson, you learned to solve systems of linear equations. Now you will investigate a **system of inequalities** that consists of two or more inequalities having the same variables. A **solution of a system of inequalities** is any ordered pair that satisfies all inequalities in the system.

1 ▶ The graph of the following system of linear inequalities is shown.

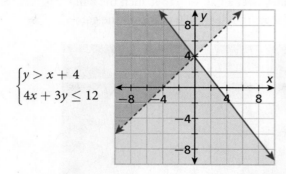

$$\begin{cases} y > x + 4 \\ 4x + 3y \leq 12 \end{cases}$$

A. You can verify the solution region by checking points from each region and on each ray algebraically. A point must satisfy both inequalities upon substitution to be a part of the solution for the system. Copy and complete the table.

Point	$y > x + 4$	$4x + 3y \leq 12$	$\begin{cases} y > x + 4 \\ 4x + 3y \leq 12 \end{cases}$
$(-6, 0)$	true	true	true
$(0, 6)$	?	?	?
$(6, 0)$	?	?	?
$(0, -6)$	?	?	?
$(-4, 0)$	false	true	false
$(-3, 8)$	?	?	?
$(2, 6)$	?	?	?
$(3, 0)$	?	?	?

B. Which of the shaded regions are part of the solution?

C. Which of the rays are part of the solution?

D. Is the ordered pair $(0, 4)$ part of the solution? Explain.

Turn and Talk Explain how the solution of the system of linear inequalities relates to the solutions of the individual inequalities.

Previously, you learned that systems of linear equations whose graphs are parallel lines have no solutions. Now you will learn that systems of linear inequalities whose graphs include parallel boundary lines will sometimes have no solution.

 The graph of the following system of linear inequalities is shown.

$$\begin{cases} y < 2x - 5 \\ y > 2x + 2 \end{cases}$$

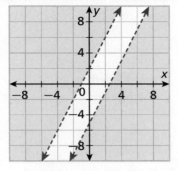

A. First consider $y < 2x - 5$. Which shaded region represents the solution to this inequality?

B. Then consider $y > 2x + 2$. Which shaded region represents the solution to this inequality?

C. Does the system have a solution? Explain.

D. You can verify the solution region by checking points from each region algebraically. A point must satisfy both inequalities upon substitution to be a part of the solution for the system. Copy and complete the table.

Point	$y < 2x - 5$	$y > 2x + 2$	$\begin{cases} y < 2x - 5 \\ y > 2x + 2 \end{cases}$
$(-4, 0)$	false	true	false
$(0, 0)$	?	?	?
$(4, 0)$	?	?	?

E. How would the solution of the system change if the inequalities were changed to $y > 2x - 5$ and $y < 2x + 2$?

F. How would the solution of the system change if the inequalities were changed to $y < 2x - 5$ and $y < 2x + 2$?

G. How would the system change if the inequalities were changed to $y > 2x - 5$ and $y > 2x + 2$?

 Turn and Talk What determines if a system of linear inequalities having parallel boundary lines has a solution?

Step It Out

Write a System of Linear Inequalities

3 Use the graph to write the system of linear inequalities and identify the solution region.

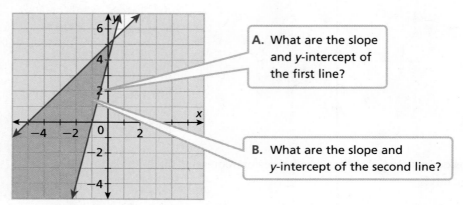

A. What are the slope and y-intercept of the first line?

B. What are the slope and y-intercept of the second line?

First write the equation for each boundary line in slope-intercept form.

$y = 4x + 4$

$y = x + 5$

C. How can you justify that the inequality symbol is $\geq$ for the first inequality?

Then write the system.

$$\begin{cases} y \geq 4x + 4 \\ y \leq x + 5 \end{cases}$$

D. How can you justify that the inequality symbol is $\leq$ for the second inequality?

You can verify the solution region by checking points from each region algebraically. A point must satisfy both inequalities upon substitution to be a part of the solution for the system.

Point	$y \geq 4x + 4$	$y \leq x + 5$	$\begin{cases} y \geq 4x + 4 \\ y \leq x + 5 \end{cases}$
$(-5, 5)$	true	false	false
$(-3, 0)$	true	true	true
$(1, 7)$	false	false	false
$(0, 0)$	false	true	false

The solution region is the darker part of the graph, which represents the overlap of the graphs of the individual inequalities. The solution region includes the solid rays along its boundaries.

 Turn and Talk Is the point of intersection of the boundary lines part of the solution? Explain.

Model with Systems of Linear Inequalities

4 Jessica goes to a garden center to buy potted plants for her garden. Her favorites are pansies and mums. She wants to spend no more than $30, and she wants to buy at least 8 potted plants. Write a system and create a graph to model all the combinations of pansies and mums she can buy.

Pansies $5

Mums $2

To write the system, let x represent the number of pots of pansies and y represent the number of pots of mums.

$x + y \geq 8$

$5x + 2y \leq 30$ **A.** What does this inequality represent?

Graph the system.

$\begin{cases} x + y \geq 8 \\ 5x + 2y \leq 30 \end{cases}$ **B.** What do $5x$ and $2y$ represent?

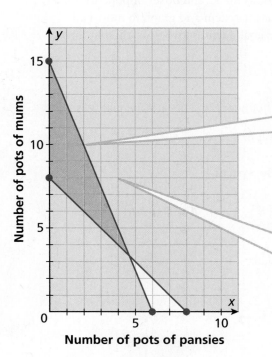

Number of pots of mums

Number of pots of pansies

C. What combination of pots of pansies and pots of mums does this point represent? Does it meet Jessica's requirements?

D. What combination of pots of pansies and pots of mums does this point represent? Does it meet Jessica's requirements?

Turn and Talk What combinations of pots of pansies and pots of mums are solutions of the system? Are there points in the solution that are not reasonable for this real-world situation? Explain.

Check Understanding

1. Graph the system $\begin{cases} 3x - y \leq -3 \\ y < 2x + 4 \end{cases}$. Explain why the boundary line of each inequality is solid or dashed, and justify the shading in your graph.

Indicate whether each ordered pair is a solution of the system $\begin{cases} x - y \leq -2 \\ 2x - y > -3 \end{cases}$.

2. $(0, 0)$ 3. $(4, 8)$ 4. $(-2, 4)$ 5. $(-6, -6)$

6. Does the system $\begin{cases} y < x - 3 \\ y > x + 3 \end{cases}$ have a solution? Explain.

Write the system of inequalities that is graphed.

7.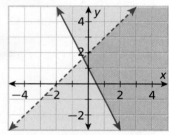

8.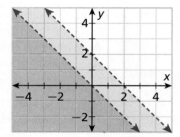

9. A club needs to raise at least $200 selling baked goods for $2 and boxes of popcorn for $1. The display table can hold at most 250 items. Create a system and graph to model all combinations of items the club can sell to meet its goal. Identify two possible solutions.

On Your Own

10. Graph the system $\begin{cases} y \geq 5x + 3 \\ x - y \leq -4 \end{cases}$. Explain why the boundary line of each inequality is solid or dashed, and justify the shading in your graph.

Indicate whether each ordered pair is a solution of the system $\begin{cases} x - y \leq -5 \\ 2x - y > 0 \end{cases}$.

11. $(0, 0)$ 12. $(2, 5)$ 13. $(-2, 4)$ 14. $(10, 16)$

15. Does the system $\begin{cases} y < x - 1 \\ y > x + 5 \end{cases}$ have a solution? Explain.

Write the system of inequalities that is graphed.

16.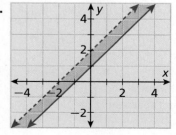

17.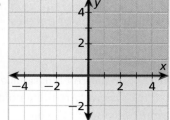

18. **(MP) Construct Arguments** Can the solutions of a system of linear inequalities be the points on a line? Explain.

Graph the system of inequalities.

19. $\begin{cases} x > -5 \\ x < 2 \end{cases}$

20. $\begin{cases} y \le 10 \\ y \ge 6 \end{cases}$

21. $\begin{cases} x > 3 \\ y > x \end{cases}$

22. $\begin{cases} y < -2x + 3 \\ y \ge 4 \end{cases}$

23. $\begin{cases} y \ge 0 \\ y < 2.5x - 1 \end{cases}$

24. $\begin{cases} y \ge 2x + 1 \\ y < -x + 4 \end{cases}$

25. $\begin{cases} x < 8 \\ x - 4y \le -8 \end{cases}$

26. $\begin{cases} y \ge -2 \\ 2x + 3y > -6 \end{cases}$

27. $\begin{cases} y - 2x < 7 \\ y + 2x > -1 \end{cases}$

28. $\begin{cases} x < 4 \\ y > 1 \\ y \ge -x + 1 \end{cases}$

29. $\begin{cases} x \ge 0 \\ y \ge 0 \\ 6x - y < 12 \end{cases}$

30. $\begin{cases} x + y \le 10 \\ x - y \ge 2 \\ y \ge 2 \end{cases}$

31. **(MP) Use Structure** Carlos buys chicken sandwiches and salmon burgers for his family. He has only $50, and he wants to buy at least 9 items. Let x represent the number of chicken sandwiches and y represent the number of salmon burgers.

$5.00 Salmon Burger

$6.00 Chicken Sandwich

   A. Create a system and graph to model all combinations of items Carlos can buy.

   B. Does Carlos have enough money to buy 5 chicken sandwiches and 4 salmon burgers? Determine the answer algebraically.

   C. Does Carlos have enough money to buy 8 chicken sandwiches and 4 salmon burgers? Use the graph to determine your answer.

   D. Suppose Carlos has only $40 to spend. How would this change the graph? How would this change the solution?

32. **(MP) Use Tools** Mr. Jones has $24, and he wants to buy at least 8 containers of yogurt. Yogurt is packaged in both large and small containers. Large containers cost $4, and small containers cost $2.

   A. Create a system and graph to model all the combinations of yogurt containers he can buy. Define the variables you use.

   B. Does he have enough money to buy 5 large and 5 small containers? Determine the answer algebraically.

   C. Does he have enough money to buy 3 large and 5 small containers? Use the graph to determine your answer.

   D. Give an example of an ordered pair that is part of the solution region but is not reasonable for this real-world situation. Explain.

33. Financial Literacy Roger received $200 for his birthday. He wants to use the money to buy new clothes for work. He can buy pants for $30 and shirts for $20. He wants at least 6 new items.

A. Create a system and graph to model all combinations of items Roger can buy. Define the variables you use.

B. Is $(4, 4)$ a solution for the system? Is this a reasonable solution in the context of this situation?

C. Is $(3.5, 3.5)$ a solution for the system? Is this a reasonable solution in the context of this situation? Explain.

34. Open Ended Write a system of linear inequalities that does not have a solution.

35. (Open Middle™) Using the digits 0 to 9, at most one time each, fill in the boxes to create a system of three linear inequalities whose solutions are all in the first quadrant.

$$\begin{cases} y > \boxed{}x + \boxed{} \\ y < -\dfrac{\boxed{}}{\boxed{}}x + \boxed{} \\ y < \boxed{}x + \boxed{} \end{cases}$$

Spiral Review • Assessment Readiness

36. Solve the linear system by adding or subtracting. What is the solution?
$$\begin{cases} x - y = -1 \\ 2x - y = -5 \end{cases}$$
Ⓐ $(4, 3)$ Ⓒ $(-4, 3)$
Ⓑ $(-4, -3)$ Ⓓ $(4, -3)$

37. Solve the linear system by multiplying first. What is the solution?
$$\begin{cases} 2x - 3y = 5 \\ x - 2y = 6 \end{cases}$$
Ⓐ $(8, 7)$ Ⓒ $(-8, 7)$
Ⓑ $(8, -7)$ Ⓓ $(-8, -7)$

38. Which ordered pair is a solution of the inequality?
$$y < 2x + 6$$
Ⓐ $(0, 5)$ Ⓒ $(-3, 0)$
Ⓑ $(-5, 5)$ Ⓓ $(-10, -10)$

39. Carlos invests $1000 in an account that earns 10% interest each year. What is the value of his investment after 1 year?
Ⓐ $100.00   Ⓒ $1000.10
Ⓑ $1010.00   Ⓓ $1100.00

I'm in a Learning Mindset!

How did I benefit from receiving help with graphing systems of linear inequalities? What impact did it have on my learning outcome?

Linear Inequalities in Two Variables

The 122-member marching band is performing at an away game. The band will take a combination of vans that can hold 15 passengers and buses that can hold 48 passengers to the game. Let x represent the number of vans and y represent the number of buses. This situation can be modeled by the inequality $15x + 48y \geq 122$. The graph of the inequality is shown.

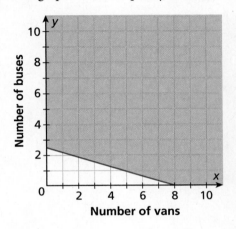

Points located in the shaded region guarantee that there are enough vans and buses for all of the members.

The number of vans and buses cannot be negative or a fraction, so only ordered pairs with nonnegative integers are solutions to the problem.

The line is solid because having seats for exactly 122 passengers would be sufficient. Anything above the line means that there are extra seats.

Systems of Linear Inequalities

The marching band has a travel budget of $2500. The cost of renting a van is $250, and the cost of renting a bus is $700. Adding this constraint, this situation can be modeled by the system $\begin{cases} 15x + 48y \geq 122 \\ 250x + 700y \leq 2500 \end{cases}$. The graph of the system is shown.

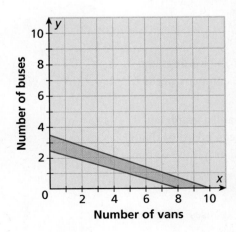

The solution region is where the graphs of the individual inequalities overlap.

If 0 vans are rented, the band must rent 3 buses. If 0 buses are rented, the band can rent 9 or 10 vans.

Can the band rent 2 vans and 2 buses?

$15(2) + 48(2) = 126 \geq 122$

$250(2) + 700(2) = 1900 \leq 2500$

Since $(2, 2)$ satisfies both inequalities, the band can rent 2 vans and 2 buses.

Vocabulary

Choose the correct term from the box to complete each sentence.

1. A ___?___ can be written in various linear forms, including $Ax + By > C$.

2. A ___?___ divides a coordinate plane into two ___?___.

3. A ___?___ is any point that makes the inequality true.

4. Two or more inequalities having the same variables makes a ___?___.

5. The overlap of shaded regions identifies the ___?___.

Concepts and Skills

Graph the inequality or the system of inequalities.

6. $3x + 2y < 6$

7. $y \geq -x + 4$

8. $\begin{cases} x + y < 7 \\ 4x - 3y > 12 \end{cases}$

9. $\begin{cases} y > -5x - 1 \\ y \leq 2x + 8 \end{cases}$

Write the inequality or the system of inequalities graphed.

10.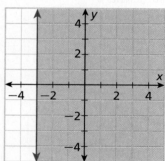

11.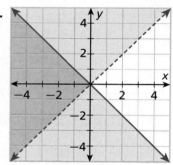

12. The Spanish class is attending an international film festival. Each film ticket costs $5, and items for lunch can be purchased for $2. Every student is given a budget of $20.

    A. Write a linear inequality to describe this situation. Define the variables that you use.

    B. Graph the inequality. Describe the boundary line.

    C. Identify and interpret one possible solution.

13. (MP) **Use Tools** A company that boards small animals charges $32 for dogs and $22 for cats. There are enough spaces to board 50 animals. The company needs to make at least $1000 to cover its expenses.

    A. State what strategy and tool you will use to create a system and a graph to model all combinations of cats and dogs that the company can board so that it covers its expenses. Explain your choice, and then solve and graph the system.

    B. Can the company board 10 dogs and 30 cats and cover its expenses? Determine the answer algebraically.

    C. Can the company board 30 dogs and 10 cats and cover its expenses? Use your graph to determine the answer.

    D. Give an example of an ordered pair that is part of the solution region but is not reasonable for this real-world situation.

Exponential Functions and Equations

Industrial Engineer

An industrial engineer is tasked with designing and building systems that adhere to very precise standards that are unique to each project. Mathematical modeling allows industrial engineers to construct and modify automated procedures that meet the requirements of the project.

STEM Task

Industrial engineers are tasked with designing control systems that regulate temperature with extreme precision. The Law of Cooling helps them construct their designs: The rate of heat loss is proportional to the difference between the object's temperature and the ambient temperature.

$$T_{n+1} = T_n - k(T_n - T_a)h$$

Given that $k = 0.0267 \frac{1}{min}$, when will the water reach the required temperature of 205 °F?

Initial temperature T_0: 212 °F
Ambient temperature T_a: 74 °F
Time step h: ?

Learning Mindset

Perseverance Checks for Understanding

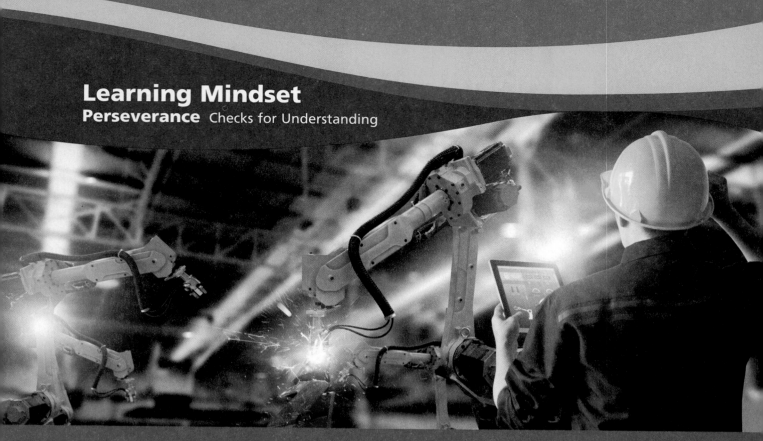

How do you know that you are understanding the task at hand? Whenever you are working on a task, it is important that you monitor how well you are grasping each part of the problem. You should periodically stop and reflect on your own, and with a peer, to think about how each part fits into the overarching learning goal. Here are some questions you can ask yourself to check how well you are understanding the task:

- How do I make sure that I understand the Law of Cooling?

- How will I make sure I understand how the Law of Cooling is being applied to the rate of heat loss of a body?

- Am I using the proper amount of time to complete the task?

- With whom should I check that my understanding is on the right path?

- Is my understanding of functions progressing as I anticipated? What adjustments do I need to make for my learning to improve?

Reflect

Q When have you paused to check your understanding? How did it help you? How was the outcome or experience different from a project where you did not stop to check on your understanding?

Q How many times might an industrial engineer check in to make sure they understand the specifications of the system they are designing? Would one time be enough? Explain your reasoning.

Exponential Functions and Models

Module Performance Task: *Spies and Analysts*™

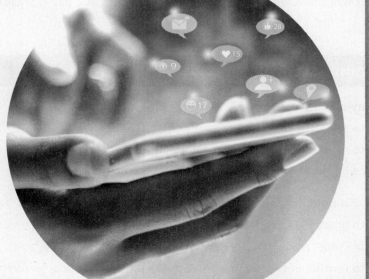

Going Viral

How can you tell if a post is going viral?

Are You Ready?

Complete these problems to review prior concepts and skills you will need for this module.

Percent Increase and Decrease

Solve each problem.

1. Determine the percent increase if the price of an item changes from $70 to $84.

2. An item is initially priced at $38. It is currently on sale for 20% off. What is the sale price?

3. The items on a rack of clothing at a store have already been marked down by 50%. A new sign states that 50% of the previously reduced price will be taken off at checkout. If the original price of an item was $100, how much must be paid at checkout?

4. A baseball card is purchased for $40 and increases in value by 5% each year over the next two years. How much is the card worth at the end of the two-year period?

Evaluate Expressions with Exponents

Evaluate each expression.

5. $3^2 \times 2^3$

6. $\dfrac{8^2}{2^3}$

7. $2^2 \times 4^3 \times 2^{-3}$

8. $5^2 - 3^2 \times 2^0$

Construct Linear Models

Write a linear function to model each relationship.

9. There are 16 cups in a gallon.

10. A phone plan charges a fixed $20 monthly fee plus $0.25 per text message.

11. A car travels at a constant rate, traversing 80 km in 2 hours.

12. A water tank with 24 gallons in it is being filled at a rate of 5 gal/min.

Connecting Past and Present Learning

Previously, you learned:
- to rewrite exponential expressions,
- to model situations with linear functions, and
- to interpret rates of changes in real-world scenarios.

In this module, you will learn:
- to graph exponential growth and decay functions,
- to model real-world problems with exponential functions, and
- to rewrite an exponential model if the units for the independent variable change.

Exponential Growth Functions

(I Can) write, graph, and analyze exponential growth functions.

Spark Your Learning

Colin and Sofia want to invest some money.

The bank pays 2.5% interest on the account balance at the end of each year and deposits the interest back into the account.

Complete Part A as a whole class. Then complete Parts B–D in small groups.

A. What is a mathematical question you can ask about this situation? What information would you need to know to answer your question?

B. What is the interest rate expressed as a decimal? What can you multiply the initial investment by to find the total amount in the account after the first year? What can you multiply by to find the total after two years?

C. To answer your question, what strategy and tool would you use along with all the information you have? What answer do you get?

D. Does your answer make sense in the context of the situation? How do you know?

Turn and Talk Predict how your answer would change for each of the following changes in the situation:
- The annual interest rate is increased to 3.5%.
- The annual interest rate is decreased to 2%.
- The investment is $50,000.

Build Understanding

Explore Exponential Growth Functions

An **exponential function** can be expressed in the form $f(x) = ab^x$, where a and b are real numbers with $a \neq 0$, $b > 0$, and $b \neq 1$. The parameter a is the value of $f(x)$ when $x = 0$ and also the y-intercept of the graph of f. The parameter b is the base of the exponential function. If $a > 0$ and $b > 1$, then the function is referred to as an **exponential growth function**.

 Consider the exponential function $f(x) = 2^x$.

    A. Copy and complete the table of values. Examine how the points are used to generate the graph.

x	$f(x) = 2^x$	(x, y)
-3	$2^{-3} = \dfrac{1}{2^3}$	$\left(-3, \dfrac{1}{8}\right)$
-2	$2^{-2} = \dfrac{1}{2^2}$	?
-1	$2^{-1} = \dfrac{1}{2^1}$	?
0	$2^0 = 1$	$(0, 1)$
1	$2^1 = 1$	$(1, 2)$
2	2^2	?
3	2^3	?
4	2^4	?

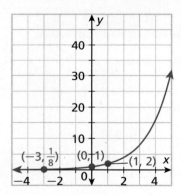

The x-values chosen in the table are integers. However, based on your work in Lesson 1.2, exponential functions are defined for all rational-number inputs. Exponential functions are also defined for inputs that are irrational.

    B. Suppose $x = 4\frac{1}{2}$. What is the value of $f\!\left(4\frac{1}{2}\right)$?

    C. If the domain of f is restricted to only integer values, describe the graph of f.

    D. Explain why the domain of f must include all rational and irrational values of x to obtain the smooth curve shown in the graph.

Use Graphs to Analyze Characteristics of $y = b^x$ When $b > 1$

2 ▶ The graphs of three exponential growth functions are shown.

$$f(x) = 2^x$$

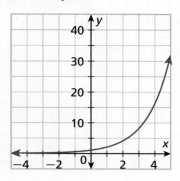

$$g(x) = 3^x$$

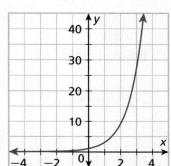

$$h(x) = 4^x$$

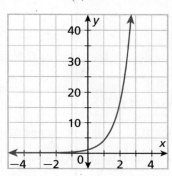

A. What is the y-intercept for each of the graphs? Do any of the graphs have an x-intercept? Explain.

B. Examine the graphs of the exponential growth functions $f(x)$, $g(x)$, and $h(x)$. What appears to be true about the domain and range values of these three exponential growth functions?

C. For each function, what happens to the value of the function as the value of x increases without bound?

D. What happens to the value of each function as the value of x decreases without bound?

E. What is the value of the base b for each of the functions f, g, and h? For which value of b does the function increase most rapidly?

F. An **asymptote** is a line that a graph gets closer to as the value of x increases or decreases without bound. Does a horizontal asymptote exist for each of these functions? Explain.

 Turn and Talk What is a real-world situation that could be modeled by an exponential growth function? Explain.

Use Graphs to Analyze Characteristics of $y = ab^x$ When $a > 0$, $b > 1$

In Lesson 5.1, the graph of $y = af(x)$ was described as a vertical stretch or vertical compression of the graph of $y = f(x)$. You can use what you know about transformations of functions to graph exponential growth functions of the form $g(x) = ab^x$.

3 The graph of $f(x) = 2^x$ is shown. Consider the function $g(x) = 3(2)^x$.

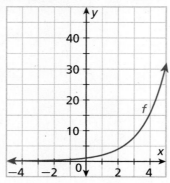

A. What is the y-intercept of the graph of f? What will be the y-intercept of the graph of g?

B. What is the domain of f? What is the domain of g?

C. What is the range of f? What is the range of g?

D. As x increases without bound, what happens to the graph of f? What happens to the graph of g as x increases without bound?

E. As x decreases without bound, what happens to the graph of f? What happens to the graph of g as x decreases without bound?

F. Of the key characteristics discussed in Parts A–E, what is the only characteristic of the graph of $f(x) = 2^x$ that is different for the graph of $g(x) = 3(2)^x$? Use the graph of $g(x) = 3(2)^x$ below to justify your answer.

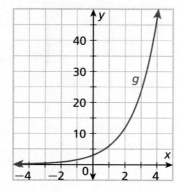

 Turn and Talk How do you know the graphs of $f(x) = 2^x$ and $g(x) = 3(2)^x$ never cross the x-axis as x decreases without bound?

Step It Out

Model Exponential Growth

Exponential growth functions can be used to model situations represented by an initial amount a and a growth rate r. In these situations, the base b is replaced by the growth factor $(1 + r)$, and the exponential growth model becomes $f(x) = a(1 + r)^x$.

4 A new investment account is opened with $4000 at the interest rate shown. If no additional money is invested, what will be the value of the investment after 5 years?

Write the exponential growth function that models this situation.

$$f(x) = a(1 + r)^x$$
$$= 4000(1 + 0.045)^x$$

> **A.** How was the value of a determined?

$$= 4000(1.045)^x$$

> **B.** How was the value of r determined?

Find the value in 5 years.

$$f(x) = 4000(1.045)^x$$
$$f(5) = 4000(1.045)^5$$

> **C.** What does the variable x represent in this situation?

$$\approx 4984.73$$

After 5 years, the investment will be worth $4984.73.

Invest Now!

4.50%
ANNUAL INTEREST

NO FEES
NO MINIMUM

 Turn and Talk Suppose the interest rate in Task 4 doubles. Does the value of the investment after 5 years double as well? Explain.

If you know at least two ordered pairs that satisfy an exponential growth function, you can use them to write an equation for the function.

Time (days)	Number of bacterial cells
0	36
1	108
2	324
3	972

5 The number of bacterial cells in a lab culture is growing exponentially. How many cells will there be in 10 days?

Use the data in the table to write an exponential growth function of the form $P = ab^t$, where P is the population (number of cells) and t is the time (in days).

Using the points $(t, P) = (0, 36)$ and $(t, P) = (1, 108)$:

$$P = ab^t \qquad\qquad P = ab^t$$
$$36 = ab^0 \qquad\qquad 108 = 36b^1$$
$$36 = a \qquad\qquad 3 = b$$

> **A.** Why has a been replaced by 36 in this calculation?

So the exponential growth function is $P = 36(3)^t$. Evaluate the function when $t = 10$.

$$P = 36(3)^{10}$$
$$= 2{,}125{,}764$$

> **B.** Which operation is performed first according to the order of operations?

There will be 2,125,764 bacterial cells in the culture in 10 days.

Check Understanding

1. Are irrational numbers such as π included in the domain of the function $f(x) = 7^x$? Explain.

Determine which function has the greater rate of growth.

2. $f(x) = 2(3)^x$ or $g(x) = 3(2)^x$

3. $f(x) = 7(1.05)^x$ or $g(x) = 2(1.08)^x$

4. Which key characteristic of the graph of $g(x) = 3^x$ is different from the graph of $f(x) = 4(3)^x$?

5. The function $f(x) = 3000(1.005)^x$ models the value of an investment where $f(x)$ is in dollars and x is in months. What is the growth rate, expressed as a percent?

6. The ordered pairs $(0, 5)$ and $(1, 15)$ satisfy an exponential growth function. Write an equation of the form $f(x) = ab^x$ for the function.

On Your Own

For each function of the form $y = ab^x$, identify the values of a and b.

7. $f(x) = 3(2)^x$

8. $g(x) = 2(3)^x$

Create a table of values for each exponential growth function using integer values of x from -3 to 3. Then graph the function.

9. $f(x) = 5^x$

10. $g(x) = 2(3)^x$

11. $h(x) = 3(4)^x$

12. **(MP)** **Reason** Describe in words what happens to the value of $f(x) = b^x$ when the value of x increases by 1.

$$f(x + 1) = b^{x+1}$$

$$f(x + 1) = b^x \cdot b^1$$

$$f(x + 1) = f(x) \cdot b$$

Identify the y-intercept, domain, range, and end behavior of each graphed function.

13.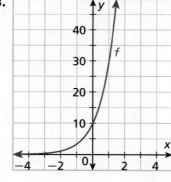

14.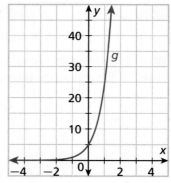

15. Identify a key characteristic that all exponential growth functions of the form $f(x) = b^x$ share.

16. Which key characteristic is different for the exponential growth functions $f(x) = b^x$ and $g(x) = ab^x$ where $a \neq 1$? Explain.

Determine which function has the greater growth rate.

17. $f(x) = 5^x$ or $g(x) = 5(2)^x$

18. $f(x) = 0.5(3)^x$ or $g(x) = 2(1.5)^x$

Write a function of the form $f(x) = a(2)^x$ that is represented by the graph.

19.

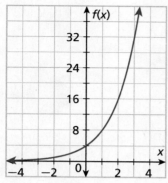

20.

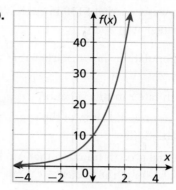

Graph each function.

21. $f(x) = 6^x$

22. $g(x) = 5(2)^x$

23. $g(x) = 4(3)^x$

24. (MP) **Reason** Explain how a part of the graph of an exponential function may appear to be the graph of a linear function.

25. Financial Literacy An investment of $25,000 is made in a savings plan that offers 4% annual interest.

    A. Identify the growth rate r in this situation.

    B. What is the base, or growth factor, of the exponential function for the situation?

    C. Write the exponential growth function that can be used to model this investment.

    D. If no additional money is invested, how much will the investment be worth in 15 years?

For each investment amount and time period, determine which plans are available. Then determine which plan pays the most interest. Explain.

26. An investment of $25,000 for 5 years

27. An investment of $50,000 for 2 years

28. An investment of $40,000 for 1 year

29. An investment of $20,000 for 2 years

Investment Options!

Plan 1:
3.5% per year, minimum $40,000

Plan 2:
3.8% per year, minimum 3 years

Plan 3:
3.1% per year, no conditions

30. Edwin purchased a rare baseball card 3 years ago. The value of the card each year since his purchase is shown in the table below.

Years since purchase	0	1	2	3
Value ($)	450	540	648	777.60

The value of the card has been increasing exponentially since he bought it. If the value continues to increase at the same rate, what will the card be worth 7 years from now?

31. The ordered pairs $(0, 0.5)$ and $(1, 2)$ satisfy an exponential growth function. Write an equation of the form $f(x) = ab^x$ for the function.

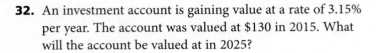
A bacteria population increases by 50% every week.

32. An investment account is gaining value at a rate of 3.15% per year. The account was valued at $130 in 2015. What will the account be valued at in 2025?

33. STEM The bacteria population shown starts with 200 bacterial cells.

   A. Identify the growth rate r in this situation.

   B. What is the base, or growth factor, of the exponential function for the situation?

   C. Write the exponential growth function that can be used to model the population of the bacteria.

   D. How many cells will be in the population after 12 weeks?

34. Open Ended Which factor or factors most affect the value of an investment that can be modeled using an exponential growth function? Explain.

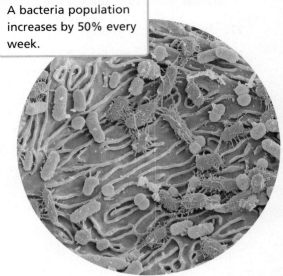

Spiral Review • Assessment Readiness

35. Which best describes the graph of the system? $\begin{cases} y < x - 2 \\ y > -3x + 5 \end{cases}$

   (A) The solution region is above both boundary lines.

   (B) The solution region is below both boundary lines.

   (C) The solution region is between the boundary lines.

   (D) There is no solution region.

36. Which describes the graph of $y \leq x - 6$?

   (A) the region of the coordinate plane below $y = x - 6$, not including the line

   (B) the region of the coordinate plane below $y = x - 6$, including the line

   (C) the region of the coordinate plane above $y = x - 6$, not including the line

   (D) the region of the coordinate plane above $y = x - 6$, including the line

37. Which transformations are applied to the graph of f to produce the graph of $g(x) = 3f(x) - 2$? Select all that apply.

   (A) a vertical stretch by a factor of 3

   (B) a horizontal stretch by a factor of 3

   (C) a translation 2 units down

   (D) a translation 2 units up

   (E) a translation 2 units to the left

   (F) a translation 2 units to the right

 I'm in a Learning Mindset!

Is my understanding of exponential functions progressing as I anticipated? What, if any, adjustments do I need to make to enhance my learning?

Exponential Decay Functions

(**I Can**) analyze the characteristics of exponential decay functions.

Spark Your Learning

A new computer at a business depreciates as it ages. Eventually, the business will need to buy a new computer.

Purchase price: $3200

Complete Part A as a whole class. Then complete Parts B–D in small groups.

A. What is a mathematical question you can ask about this situation? What information would you need to know to answer your question?

B. What variable(s) are needed in this situation?

C. To answer your question, what strategy and tool would you use along with all the information you have? What answer do you get?

D. Does your answer make sense in the context of the situation? How do you know?

 Turn and Talk Will the value of this computer ever reach $0?

Build Understanding

Explore Exponential Decay Functions

An exponential function of the form $f(x) = ab^x$, where a and b are real numbers with $a > 0$ and $0 < b < 1$, is called an **exponential decay function**. The parameter a is the value of $f(x)$ when $x = 0$ and also the y-intercept of the graph of f. The parameter b is the base of the exponential function.

1 Consider the exponential function $f(x) = \left(\frac{1}{2}\right)^x$. You can create a table of values and use the points generated to create a graph.

x	f(x)
−3	$\left(\frac{1}{2}\right)^{-3} = 2^3 = 8$
−2	$\left(\frac{1}{2}\right)^{-2} = 2^2 = 4$
−1	$\left(\frac{1}{2}\right)^{-1} = 2^1 = 2$
0	$\left(\frac{1}{2}\right)^{0} = 1$
1	$\left(\frac{1}{2}\right)^{1} = \frac{1}{2}$
2	$\left(\frac{1}{2}\right)^{2} = \frac{1}{4}$
3	$\left(\frac{1}{2}\right)^{3} = \frac{1}{8}$

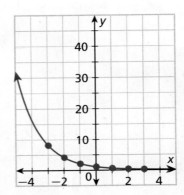

As in the previous lesson, the x-values chosen in the table are integers. Like exponential growth functions, exponential decay functions are defined for all real numbers.

A. Based on the table, how is $f(x)$ related to $f(x − 1)$ and $f(x + 1)$? Does this make sense based on what you know about the laws of exponents?

B. Evaluate the function at another integer value of x, at a rational value of x that is not an integer, and at an irrational value of x.

C. Evaluate the function for $x = 10$, $x = 100$, and $x = 1000$. Will the value of the function ever reach 0? Explain your reasoning.

D. How is the graph of an exponential decay function similar to the graph of an exponential growth function?

E. How is the graph of an exponential decay function different from the graph of an exponential growth function?

 Turn and Talk What is a real-world situation that could be modeled by an exponential decay function? Explain.

Use Graphs to Analyze Characteristics of $y = b^x$ When $0 < b < 1$

2 ▶ The graphs of three exponential decay functions are shown below.

$$f(x) = \left(\frac{1}{2}\right)^x$$

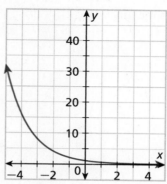

$$g(x) = \left(\frac{1}{3}\right)^x$$

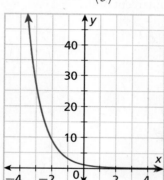

$$h(x) = \left(\frac{1}{4}\right)^x$$

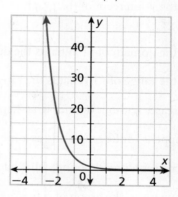

A. What is the *y*-intercept for each of these graphs? Do any of the graphs have an *x*-intercept? Explain.

B. In each of these graphs, notice that the curve is continuous and is above the *x*-axis for all values of *x*. What does this imply about the domain and range for an exponential decay function?

C. For each of these functions, what happens to the value of the function as the value of *x* decreases without bound? What happens as *x* increases without bound?

D. Does the graph of each decay function have a horizontal asymptote? Explain.

E. What is the value of the base *b* for each of the functions *f*, *g*, and *h*? For which value of *b* does the function decrease most slowly?

 Turn and Talk How are the characteristics of exponential decay functions similar to and different from the characteristics of exponential growth functions?

Use Graphs to Analyze Characteristics of $y = ab^x$ When $a > 0$, $0 < b < 1$

You can use what you know about transformations of the graph of $f(x) = b^x$ to graph exponential decay functions of the form $g(x) = ab^x$.

3 ▸ A graph of $f(x) = \left(\frac{1}{2}\right)^x$ is shown. Graph the function $g(x) = 3\left(\frac{1}{2}\right)^x$.

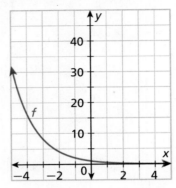

A. What is the y-intercept of the graph of f? What will be the y-intercept of the graph of g?

B. What is the domain of f? What is the domain of g?

C. What is the range of f? What is the range of g?

D. As x increases without bound, what happens to the graph of f?

What happens to the graph of g as x increases without bound?

E. As x decreases without bound, what happens to the graph of f?

What happens to the graph of g as x decreases without bound?

F. Of the key characteristics discussed in Parts A–E, what is the only characteristic of the graph of $f(x) = \left(\frac{1}{2}\right)^x$ that is different for the graph of $g(x) = 3\left(\frac{1}{2}\right)^x$? Use the graph of $g(x) = 3\left(\frac{1}{2}\right)^x$ below to justify your answer.

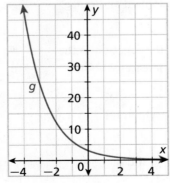

 Turn and Talk Which transformation could you apply to an exponential decay function to create the graph of an exponential growth function? How can you explain this algebraically?

Step It Out

Model Exponential Decay

Exponential decay functions can be used to model situations that have an initial amount a and a decay rate r, where $0 < r < 1$. In these situations, the base b is replaced by the decay factor $(1 - r)$, and the exponential decay model becomes $f(x) = a(1 - r)^x$.

4 ▶ The value of a new vehicle purchased at the price shown depreciates at a rate of 20% each year. What is the value of the vehicle after 8 years?

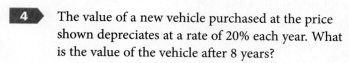

Write the function that models this situation.

$$f(x) = a(1 - r)^x$$
$$= 18{,}000(1 - 0.20)^x$$
$$= 18{,}000(0.8)^x$$

A. How was the value of a determined?

B. How was the value of r determined?

Find the value after 8 years.

$$f(x) = 18{,}000(0.8)^x$$
$$f(8) = 18{,}000(0.8)^8 \approx 3019.90$$

C. What does the variable x represent in this situation?

After 8 years, the car will be worth about $3020.

Turn and Talk Will the exponential decay function in this situation model the actual value of the vehicle indefinitely? Explain.

5 ▶ A scientist has 360 grams of a radioactive material that has a half-life of 2 years. Half-life is the length of time needed for half of the radioactive material to decay. How many grams of the radioactive material will remain in 7 years?

Write a function of the form $A(t) = ab^t$ for this situation, where A is the amount of radioactive material remaining, in grams, and t is the time, in years.

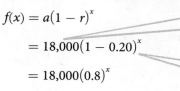

Use the points $(t, A(t)) = (0, 360)$ and $(t, A(t)) = (2, 180)$.

$$A(t) = ab^t \qquad A(t) = ab^t$$
$$360 = ab^0 \qquad 180 = 360b^2$$
$$360 = a \qquad 0.5 = b^2$$
$$0.71 \approx b$$

A. Why has a been replaced by 360?

So the function is $A(t) = 360(0.71)^t$. Evaluate the function when $t = 7$.

$$A(7) = 360(0.71)^7 \approx 32.74$$

B. How can you use the graph to check this result?

There will be about 33 grams of the radioactive material remaining in 7 years.

Check Understanding

1. How are the graphs of $f(x) = \left(\frac{1}{3}\right)^x$ and $g(x) = 3^x$ alike and how are they different?

For each pair of functions, determine the decay rate of each function and identify which function has the lesser decay rate.

2. $f(x) = 2\left(\frac{1}{3}\right)^x$ and $g(x) = 3\left(\frac{1}{2}\right)^x$

3. $f(x) = 7(0.85)^x$ and $g(x) = 2(0.90)^x$

4. Which of the following are key characteristics for the function $f(x) = 5\left(\frac{2}{3}\right)^x$?
   - The domain is all real numbers.
   - The y-intercept is 1.
   - The horizontal asymptote is the x-axis.

5. A piece of construction equipment depreciates by 25% each year. What is the base, or decay factor, of the exponential decay function describing its value?

6. The ordered pairs $(0, 2)$ and $\left(1, \frac{3}{2}\right)$ satisfy an exponential decay function. Write an equation of the form $f(x) = ab^x$ for the function.

On Your Own

For each function of the form $y = ab^x$, identify the values of a and b.

7. $g(x) = \frac{5}{3}\left(\frac{1}{4}\right)^x$

8. $h(x) = 0.5(0.47)^x$

Create a table of values for each exponential decay function using integer values of x from -3 to 3. Then graph the function.

9. $f(x) = (0.4)^x$

10. $g(x) = 2\left(\frac{1}{3}\right)^x$

11. $h(x) = 3\left(\frac{1}{4}\right)^x$

12. Describe the domain and range of the exponential decay function of the form $g(x) = ab^x$ using inequalities.

13. Recall from Lesson 4.3 that *end behavior* describes a key characteristic of the graph of a function as the x-values approach positive and negative infinity. Describe the end behavior of an exponential decay function.

Identify the y-intercept, domain, range, and end behavior of each graphed function.

14.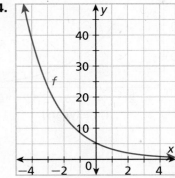

15.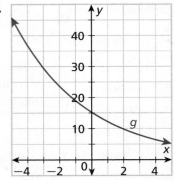

16. Identify a key characteristic that all exponential decay functions of the form $f(x) = b^x$ share.

17. Identify a key characteristic of the function $f(x) = b^x$ that changes when the function rule is multiplied by a positive constant a.

Determine which function has the lesser rate of decay.

18. $f(x) = \left(\frac{3}{7}\right)^x$ and $g(x) = \left(\frac{3}{8}\right)^x$

19. $f(x) = 10(0.31)^x$ and $g(x) = 8(0.42)^x$

Write a function in the form $f(x) = a\left(\frac{1}{2}\right)^x$ that is represented by the graph.

20.
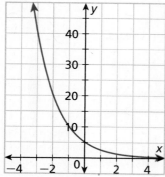

21.
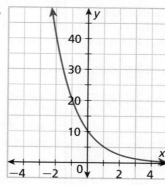

Graph each function.

22. $f(x) = \left(\frac{2}{3}\right)^x$

23. $g(x) = 7\left(\frac{1}{7}\right)^x$

24. $g(x) = 20(0.6)^x$

25. (MP) **Reason** A student was asked to find the value of a \$2000 item after 5 years. The student was told that the item was depreciating at a rate of 30% per year. What is the error in the student's work shown below?
$$2000(0.3)^5 = 4.86$$

26. A vehicle depreciates at a rate of 22% each year after it is purchased.

   A. What is the base of the exponential decay function that models this situation?

   B. Write the exponential decay function that can be used to model the value of the vehicle.

   C. How much will the vehicle be worth 8 years after it was purchased?

27. **Open Ended** Give an example of a real-world exponential decay function in which the domain would be all real numbers greater than or equal to zero.

28. **Open Ended** What is an exponential decay function whose graph passes through the point $(3, 10)$?

For Sale
Used Luxury Car
Purchase price: \$30,000

29. STEM A radioactive material with a half-life of 3 days is being used in an experiment. At the beginning of the experiment there are 250 mg of the material.

A. Write an exponential decay function that can be used to model the amount A (in milligrams) of the radioactive material remaining after time t (in days). Round the value of b, the decay factor, to the nearest hundredth.

B. How much of the radioactive material will still be left after 10 days?

Write an exponential decay function to model each situation. Then find the value of the function after the given amount of time.

30. The value of a textbook is $53 and depreciates at a rate of 15% per year for 4 years.

31. The value of a couch is $1000 and depreciates at a rate of 6% per year for 10 years.

32. The population of a town is 154,927 and is decreasing at a rate of 2.5% per year for 7 years.

33. Andrew just purchased a new laptop for $1800. The value of the laptop will decrease exponentially over the time that he owns it. The graph shows the value of the laptop over time. Write an exponential function that models the value v (in dollars) of the laptop over time t (in years). To the nearest dollar, what will be the value of the laptop if Andrew still owns it 5 years after he purchased it?

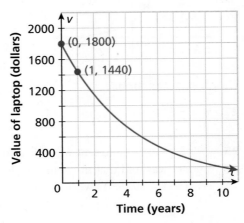

Spiral Review • Assessment Readiness

34. A system of inequalities is given by $y < 0$ and $x \leq 0$. Which portion of an axis is included in the solution?

Ⓐ positive x-axis   Ⓒ negative x-axis

Ⓑ positive y-axis   Ⓓ negative y-axis

35. Which of these ordered pairs are solutions of the system of inequalities $y \leq 1$ and $x < 2$? Select all that apply.

Ⓐ (2, 1)   Ⓓ (0, 1)

Ⓑ (−2, 4)   Ⓔ (5, −5)

Ⓒ (−2, −2)   Ⓕ (1, 2)

36. Which function represents an exponential growth function?

Ⓐ $f(x) = 2x - 2$ Ⓒ $f(x) = 4\left(\frac{1}{3}\right)^x$

Ⓑ $f(x) = x^2$ Ⓓ $f(x) = \frac{1}{2}(2)^x$

37. Which statement is *not* always true about an exponential function $f(x) = ab^x$?

Ⓐ The domain consists of all real numbers.

Ⓑ The x-axis is an asymptote of the graph.

Ⓒ $f(x)$ increases as x increases.

Ⓓ The y-intercept of the graph is a.

 I'm in a Learning Mindset!

Does my work meet the expectations for understanding exponential decay functions? What evidence supports this claim?

Rewrite Exponential Models

(I Can) use the properties of exponents to write exponential models.

Spark Your Learning

Biologists conducted an experiment to determine how quickly two types of bacteria increase in population.

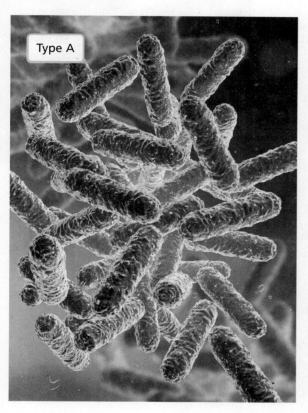

Type A

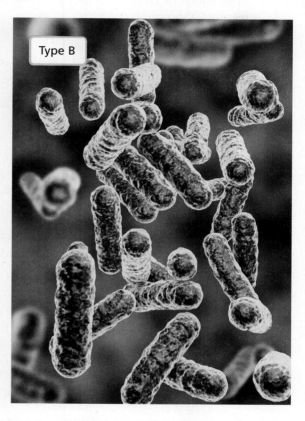

Type B

Complete Part A as a whole class. Then complete Parts B–D in small groups.

A. What is a mathematical question you can ask about this situation? What information would you need to know to answer your question?

B. What are the variables in this situation?

C. To answer your question, what strategy and tool would you use along with all the information you have? What answer do you get?

D. Suppose a colony of Type A bacteria and a colony of Type B bacteria initially have the same population. Compare the populations of the two colonies after 90 hours.

Turn and Talk Could you determine which bacteria population is greater at any given time? Explain.

Build Understanding

Explore Equations of Exponential Models

Exponential models can be rewritten in equivalent forms to reveal new information. You can use this technique to determine the rate of growth or decay for a different time scale.

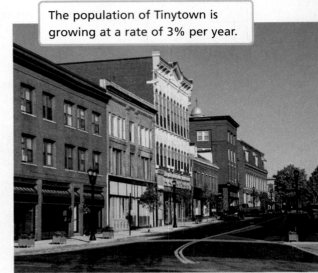

The population of Tinytown is growing at a rate of 3% per year.

1 ▶ The population of Tinytown is currently 4000 and increasing, as shown.

 A. Use the exponential growth model $f(t) = ab^t$, where a is the initial amount, b is the growth factor, and t is the time in years, to write a function that models the annual growth of Tinytown.

What is the decadal growth rate?

 B. Find the decadal growth factor d by raising the annual growth factor to the 10th power. What is the decadal growth rate expressed as a decimal?

 C. Use your result from Part B to write a function that models Tinytown's population $g(t)$ where t is the time in decades.

What is the monthly growth rate?

 D. Find the monthly growth factor by finding the value of m that, when raised to the 12th power, equals the annual growth factor. What is the monthly growth rate expressed as a decimal?

 E. Use your result from Part D to write a function that models Tinytown's population $g(t)$ where t is the time in months.

 F. As the units of measure for time increase from months to years to decades, does the corresponding growth rate increase or decrease? Explain.

 G. Suppose the population of Tinytown was decreasing at a rate of 2% per year. What function would model the population if the time t is measured in years? in decades? in months?

 H. Use your results from Part G to determine how the decay rate changes as the units of measure for time increase from months to years to decades.

Turn and Talk Suppose the function $f(t) = ab^t$ models the amount of a quantity over time where t is measured in years. Write functions $g(t)$ and $h(t)$ that model the amount of the quantity if t is measured in decades or months, respectively.

Step It Out

Analyze Exponential Models

You can rewrite an exponential growth model to reveal information about the rate of growth for a particular time interval.

2 The value of a collectible is $25, and its value increases by 8% per year after it is sold.

Show the model where t is measured in years:

$$f(t) = 25(1.08)^t$$

Show the model where t is measured in decades:

$$g(t) = 25(1.08)^{10t} = 25[(1.08)^{10}]^t \approx 25(2.16)^t$$

A. What is the decadal growth rate expressed as a percent?

Show the model where t is measured in months:

$$h(t) = 25(1.08)^{\frac{t}{12}} = 25[(1.08)^{\frac{1}{12}}]^t \approx 25(1.006)^t$$

B. What is the monthly growth rate expressed as a percent?

Turn and Talk Without doing any calculations, what can you say about the values of $f(10)$, $g(1)$, and $h(120)$? Explain.

One form of an exponential decay function that is used by scientists is the half-life form, where the base of the function is $\frac{1}{2}$. Recall that half-life is the length of time required for half of a sample of radioactive material to no longer be radioactive. You can write an exponential decay function in half-life form if it is not given in this form.

3 A scientist has a sample of radioactive material for which the rate of decay is known. What is the half-life form of the exponential decay function for this material?

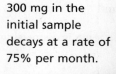
300 mg in the initial sample decays at a rate of 75% per month.

The rate of decay is 75% per month, so the decay factor is $1 - 0.75 = 0.25$.

A model for this situation is $A(t) = 300(0.25)^t$, where A represents the amount of radioactive material (in milligrams) and t represents the time (in months).

Rewrite the exponential decay function with base $\frac{1}{2}$.

$$A(t) = 300\left(\frac{1}{4}\right)^t$$

A. Why has 0.25 been replaced by $\frac{1}{4}$?

$$= 300\left(\left(\frac{1}{2}\right)^2\right)^t$$

B. Why was $\frac{1}{4}$ rewritten as $\left(\frac{1}{2}\right)^2$?

$$= 300\left(\frac{1}{2}\right)^{2t}$$

C. Which property of exponents justifies this step?

The half-life form of the exponential decay function is $A(t) = 300\left(\frac{1}{2}\right)^{2t}$.

Check Understanding

For Problems 1–3, use the following information: The population of a colony of bacteria was 200 at the beginning of an experiment. It was observed that the number of bacteria doubled every hour.

1. Write an exponential growth model for this situation.

2. Rewrite the function so that time is measured in minutes.

3. Rewrite the function so that time is measured in days.

4. Given the function $f(x) = 800(16)^x$, write an equivalent function with a base of 2.

5. Which function, where t is time in years, models slower exponential decay? Explain.
$$f(t) = 800\left(\frac{1}{4}\right)^t \text{ or } g(t) = 400\left(\frac{1}{8}\right)^t$$

On Your Own

Determine the monthly interest rate for the given annual interest rate.

6. 6% annually

7. 3% annually

For Problems 8 and 9, use the following information: The value of a $25,000 investment is modeled by the function $A(t) = 25{,}000(1.06)^t$, where t is the time in years.

8. Rewrite the function so that time is measured in months.

9. Rewrite the function so that time is measured in decades.

10. A model for the growth in the number of bacteria in a lab culture is $P(t) = 8^t$, where t is time in hours. Find the time it takes for the number of bacteria to double.

11. The population of a town is decreasing at a rate of 5% each year. In 2018, there were 1200 people.
   A. Write a function that models the population over time t in years.
   B. Write a function that models the population over time t in months.
   C. Find the time in years it would take for the population to decrease to 1000.

12. (MP) **Model with Mathematics** A colony of termites has been discovered in the wood in Norman's garage. The population of this termite species is known to increase by a factor of 8 every month.
   A. Let t represent time in months. Write a population function $P(t)$ for these termites.
   B. Rewrite this function using a base of 2.
   C. When will the population double?
   D. When will the population reach 1000?

The initial population of termites was found to be 100.

13.  **Model with Mathematics** A piece of farm equipment depreciates exponentially over time.

   A. Write a function that models the value v in dollars of the equipment over time t in years.

   B. Write a function that models the value v in dollars of the equipment over time t in months.

14. Annual sales for a company are $155,000 and increase at a rate of 8% per year.

   A. Write a function that models the annual sales A in dollars over time t in years.

   B. Find the annual sales after 5 years.

   C. Rewrite the function from Part A so that time is measured in decades.

> Originally purchased for $45,000, the equipment decreases in value at a rate of 25% annually.

15. A savings account is opened with $300 and gains 3% annually.

   A. Write a function for the account balance A over time t in years.

   B. Find the account balance after 5 years.

   C. Write a function for the account balance A over time t in months.

   D. Find the account balance after 32 months.

16. The value of a resource book is $249 and decreases at a rate of 15% per year.

   A. Write a function for the value v in dollars of the book over time t in years.

   B. Find the value of the book after 4 years.

   C. Write a function for the value v in dollars of the book over time t in months.

   D. Find the value of the book after 18 months.

17. The value of a new office building is $3.4 million and decreases at a rate of 2.39% annually due to poor economic conditions.

   A. Write a function for the value v in dollars of the building over time t in years.

   B. Find the value of the building after 8 years.

   C. Write a function for the value v in dollars of the building over time t in months.

   D. Find the value of the building after 42 months.

18. A new home has a value of $258,000 and appreciates at a rate of 2.5% annually.

   A. Write a function for the value v in dollars of the home over time t in years.

   B. Find the value of the home after 10 years.

   C. Write a function for the value v in dollars of the home over time t in decades.

   D. Find the value of the home after three decades.

   E. Find the time in years and decades when the home will be valued at $500,000.

19. **Critique Reasoning** Alan says that a growth rate of 12% per year is equivalent to a growth rate of 1% per month because there are 12 months in a year and $12\% \div 12 = 1\%$. Explain why Alan is mistaken, and approximate the correct monthly growth rate that is equivalent to an annual growth rate of 12%.

20. The population of a colony of bacteria doubles every 8 hours. The exponential growth function $P(t) = P_0(2)^{\frac{t}{8}}$ models the bacteria population after t hours, where P_0 is the initial population. How long does it take for the population to triple?

21. The function $f(t) = 20(16)^t$ models exponential growth, where t is time in years. How long does it take for the initial value to double?

22. STEM Carbon-14 has a half-life of 5730 years.

A. Write the half-life form of the exponential decay function that gives the amount A of carbon-14 remaining after t years, where A_0 is the initial amount of carbon-14.

B. How much of a 255-milligram sample of carbon-14 would still remain after 7500 years?

23. (Open Middle™) Using the digits 1 through 9 at most two times each, fill in the boxes to create an exponential function, with its graph's asymptote and greatest possible y-intercept.

$$y = \boxed{} \cdot \boxed{}^{\left(x + \boxed{}\right)} + \boxed{}, \quad \text{asymptote: } y = \boxed{} \quad y\text{–intercept: } \boxed{}$$

Spiral Review • Assessment Readiness

24. Which of the following are characteristics of the function $f(x) = 3 \cdot 2^x$? Select all that apply.

(A) no x-intercept

(B) always increasing

(C) always decreasing

(D) y-intercept 1

(E) asymptote $x = 0$

(F) asymptote $y = 0$

25. What is the y-intercept of the graph of $f(x) = 3 \cdot \left(\frac{1}{2}\right)^x$?

(A) $y = \frac{1}{2}$

(B) $y = 1$

(C) $y = 3$

(D) There is no y-intercept.

26. Match the function g on the left to the description of the transformations applied to the graph of f to obtain the graph of g.

A. $g(x) = 2f(x) + 3$

B. $g(x) = -f(x) - 3$

C. $g(x) = 3f(x) + 2$

D. $g(x) = 2f(x) - 2$

1. reflected across the x-axis and moved down 3 units

2. vertically stretched by a factor of 3 and moved up 2 units

3. vertically stretched by a factor of 2 and moved down 2 units

4. vertically stretched by a factor of 2 and moved up 3 units

I'm in a Learning Mindset!

Is my understanding of exponential models progressing as I anticipated? What, if any, adjustments do I need to make to enhance my learning?

Exponential Growth

A bacteria population starts with only 10 cells, but the number of cells increases by 30% per hour. The population can be modeled by an exponential growth function of the form $P(t) = a(1 + r)^t$ where a is the initial number of bacteria, r is the growth rate expressed as a decimal, and t is the time in hours. The population function, the estimated bacteria population after 5 hours, and the graph of the function are shown below.

Population function:

$$\begin{aligned} P(t) &= a(1 + r)^t \\ &= 10(1 + 0.3)^t \\ &= 10(1.3)^t \end{aligned}$$

Population after 5 hours:

$$\begin{aligned} P(5) &= 10(1.3)^5 \\ &\approx 37 \end{aligned}$$

Graph:

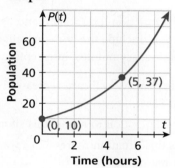

You can rewrite the population function to give the bacteria population for time t in days.

$$P(t) = 10(1.3)^{24t} = 10\left[(1.3)^{24}\right]^t \approx 10(543)^t$$

Exponential Decay

Paul buys a motorcycle for $5000. The motorcycle's value decreases by 15% per year. The value can be modeled by an exponential decay function of the form $v(t) = a(1 - r)^t$ where a is the motorcycle's initial value, r is the decay rate expressed as a decimal, and t is the time in years. The value function, the motorcycle's estimated value after 3 years, and the graph of the function are shown below.

Value function:

$$\begin{aligned} v(t) &= a(1 + r)^t \\ &= 5000(1 - 0.15)^t \\ &= 5000(0.85)^t \end{aligned}$$

Value after 3 years:

$$\begin{aligned} v(3) &= 5000(0.85)^3 \\ &\approx \$3071 \end{aligned}$$

Graph:

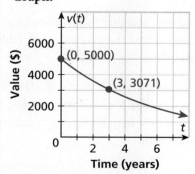

You can rewrite the value function to give the motorcycle's value for time t in months.

$$v(t) = 5000(0.85)^{\frac{t}{12}} = 5000\left[(0.85)^{\frac{1}{12}}\right]^t \approx 5000(0.987)^t$$

Vocabulary

Choose the correct term from the box to complete each sentence.

1. A function of the form $f(x) = ab^x$, where a and b are real numbers with $a > 0$ and $b > 1$, is called an ___?___ function.

2. A function of the form $f(x) = ab^x$, where a and b are real numbers with $a > 0$ and $0 < b < 1$, is called an ___?___ function.

3. An ___?___ is a function of the form $f(x) = ab^x$, where a and b are real numbers with $a \neq 0$, $b > 0$, and $b \neq 1$.

Concepts and Skills

4. Graph the function $f(x) = 4(2)^x$ and use the graph to identify key characteristics of the function. Include the domain, range, intervals where the function is increasing or decreasing, asymptotes, intercepts, and end behavior.

5. The value of a baseball card increases by 8% every year. The card is currently valued at $250.

    A. Write a function to model this situation.

    B. Does this situation represent exponential growth or exponential decay? Explain your reasoning.

    C. What will be the value of the card in 5 years?

    D. Assuming the same rate of growth in the past, what was the value of the card 5 years ago?

6. **(MP) Use Tools** The value of an electronic music device decreases by 11% each year. The device was purchased for $125. What will its value be after 8 years? State what strategy and tool you will use to answer the question, explain your choice, and then find the answer.

7. Compare and contrast exponential growth functions and exponential decay functions. Discuss domain, range, intervals where the functions are increasing or decreasing, asymptotes, intercepts, and end behavior.

8. A friend tells you that the graphs of $f(x) = 2^x$ and $g(x) = \left(\frac{1}{2}\right)^x$ are reflections of each other across the y-axis. Is your friend's statement true? Justify your answer algebraically and graphically.

9. The functions $m_A(t) = 4^t$ and $m_B(t) = 8^t$ represent the masses in grams of bacteria colonies A and B, respectively, t days after the colonies are first observed. Determine how long it takes each colony to double in mass, and compare the doubling times.

10. The population of a city is currently 50,000. The population is projected to increase by 4% per year.

    A. Write a function $f(t)$ giving the city's projected population at time t in years.

    B. Write a function $g(t)$ giving the city's projected population at time t in decades.

    C. Write a function $h(t)$ giving the city's projected population at time t in months.

12

Relationships Among Exponential Functions

Module Performance Task: *Spies and Analysts*™

Social
Media
Half-Life

How can you tell when a post will no longer be seen?

Are You Ready?

Complete these problems to review prior concepts and skills you will need for this module.

Multiply Multi-Digit Decimals

Use the standard algorithm to evaluate each product.

1. -2.124×3.45

2.
$$\begin{array}{r} 6.17 \\ \times\ 3.22 \\ \hline \end{array}$$

3. A sale of 45% off is applied to an item that originally sells for $20.95. Use 0.45×20.95 to determine how much will be taken off the price of this item at the cash register.

4. A collectible coin increased in value by 12% this year. It was purchased for $22.50 at the start of the year. Use 1.12×22.5 to find what the coin was worth at the end of the year.

Transform Linear Functions

Write a rule for the function g that corresponds to each transformation of the graph of $f(x) = x$.

5. a reflection across the x-axis

6. a translation 3 units to the left

7. a vertical stretch by a factor of 3

8. a translation 1 unit up

Compare Linear Functions

For each pair of linear functions, determine which one has the graph with the steeper slope.

9. $y = 3x - 4$ or

x	y
0	−6
1	−4
2	−2
3	0
4	2
5	4

10. $6x + 3y = 12$ or

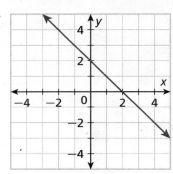

Connecting Past and Present Learning

Previously, you learned:

• to model situations with exponential functions,

• to transform graphs of linear and absolute value functions, and

• to compare properties of linear functions represented in different forms.

In this module, you will learn:

• to transform graphs of exponential functions,

• to interpret characteristics of exponential functions in context, and

• to compare properties of exponential functions represented in different forms.

Transform Exponential Functions

(I Can) graph and identify transformations of exponential functions.

Spark Your Learning

Cars depreciate in value over time as they age. Although the average life span of a car is about 8 years, a manufacturer advertises that a car model will have significant value even after 10 years of depreciation.

The car's value decreases by 16% each year.

Complete Part A as a whole class. Then complete Parts B–D in small groups.

  A. What is a mathematical question you can ask about this situation? What information would you need to know to answer your question?

  B. What variable(s) are needed in this situation? What must be true of the values for these variables in this question?

  C. To answer your question, what strategy and tool would you use along with all the information you have? What answer do you get?

  D. Do you think the manufacturer's advertisement was correct? Explain.

 Turn and Talk How might the model change for different vehicles?

Build Understanding

Exponential Parent Functions

The function $f(x) = b^x$ with base $b > 1$ or $0 < b < 1$ is a parent exponential function. There is no single parent exponential function because each value of b defines a different parent function. Two reference points on the graph of a parent exponential function are $(0, 1)$ and $(1, b)$.

1 ▸ The graphs of two parent exponential functions are shown.

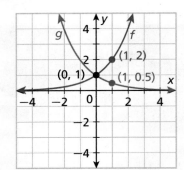

    A. Which reference points allow you to determine the base of each function? Write an equation for each function whose graph is shown.

    B. What reference point is shared by all parent exponential functions? Explain.

    C. Which function is an exponential growth function? Which function is an exponential decay function? Explain how the value of the base determines this characteristic.

Transformations of Exponential Functions

The graph of the function $g(x) = b^x + k$, where k is a real number, is a translation of the graph of the parent exponential function $f(x) = b^x$.

2 ▸ The graph of the parent exponential function $f(x) = 2^x$ is shown, along with the graphs of two other exponential functions g and h.

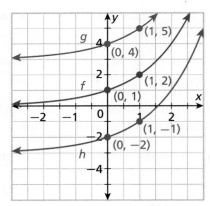

    A. Describe how the graphs of g and h are transformed from the graph of their parent exponential function f.

    B. Identify the values of k for the functions g and h. How can you determine k from the reference points?

    C. Write an equation for each function whose graph is shown.

    D. Identify the domain, range, and end behavior of each function. Explain how the value of k affects these characteristics.

 Turn and Talk Let the reference points for $f(x) = b^x$ be $(0, 1)$ and $(1, b)$. What are the corresponding reference points for the graph of $g(x) = b^x + k$?

The graph of $g(x) = a \cdot b^x$, where a is a nonzero real number, is a vertical stretch or a vertical compression of the graph of the parent exponential function $f(x) = b^x$.

 3 The graph of the parent exponential function $f(x) = 2^x$ is shown, along with the graphs of two other exponential functions g and h.

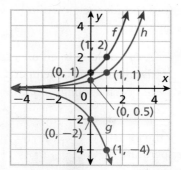

A. Describe how the graphs of g and h are transformed from the graph of their parent exponential function f.

B. Identify the values of a for the functions g and h. How can you determine a from the reference points?

C. Write an equation for each function whose graph is shown.

D. Identify the domain, range, and end behavior of each function. Explain how the value of a affects these characteristics.

E. How do the values of a and b determine whether a function is increasing or decreasing? Explain.

 Turn and Talk Let the reference points for $f(x) = b^x$ be $(0, 1)$ and $(1, b)$. What are the corresponding reference points for the graph of $g(x) = a \cdot b^x$?

When the graph of a parent exponential function $f(x) = b^x$ is transformed to form the graph of $g(x) = a \cdot b^x + k$, the reference points $(0, 1)$ and $(1, b)$ are mapped to the points $(0, a + k)$ and $(1, ab + k)$, respectively.

 4 The graph of a parent exponential function f is transformed into the graph of the exponential function g. Use the reference points to describe how the graph of f is transformed.

	f	g
(0, a + k)	$(0, 1)$	$(0, 7)$
(1, ab + k)	$\left(1, \frac{1}{2}\right)$	$(1, 5)$

A. What is the base of the parent exponential function f? Write an equation for f.

B. How can you use the corresponding reference points of g to form a system of linear equations?

C. Identify the transformations that map the graph of f onto the graph of g. Write a rule for g.

D. The graph of a function h is formed by reflecting the graph of g over the x-axis. Identify the corresponding reference points of h.

E. Identify the transformations that map the graph of f onto the graph of h. Write a rule for h.

F. Graph each function, labeling the y-intercept and asymptote of each graph. Explain how the values of a and k affect the domain, range, and end behavior.

 Turn and Talk How is transforming exponential functions similar to and different from transforming other functions?

Step It Out

Model with Transformations of Exponential Functions

Many situations can be modeled with exponential functions. Examples of these situations include the growth of some animal populations and the depreciation of the value of a car.

5 A cup of soup is left on a countertop to cool. The rate of cooling (that is, the decay rate for the temperature) is r, and t is the time in minutes that the soup has been cooling.

T_0 is the initial temperature of the soup.

The room temperature is T_R.

The temperature can be modeled by an exponential decay function.

Match the description on the left with the corresponding expression on the right.

Description	Expression
A. The base of the function when the rate of cooling is r	1. T_R
B. The difference between the soup's temperature and room temperature	2. $T_0(1-r)^t$
C. The temperature that the soup will approach	3. $T_0(1-r)^t + T_R$
D. The soup's initial temperature	4. $(1-r)$
E. The temperature of the soup at time t	5. T_0

 Turn and Talk According to the model, will the soup ever reach room temperature? Does this aspect of the model accurately reflect reality? Explain.

Check Understanding

1. For $g(x) = \frac{1}{2} \cdot 2^x$, identify the values of a, b, and k.

Shown at the right are the graphs of $f(x) = 3^x$ and a function g whose graph is a transformation of the graph of f. Use the graphs for Problems 2–4.

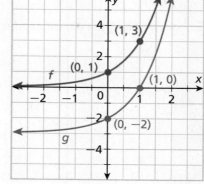

2. What are the reference points for the graph of f and the graph of g? How can you use the reference points to determine a and k?

3. Describe how the graph of f can be transformed into the graph of g. Write a rule for $g(x)$.

4. Let the graph of h be a reflection of the graph of g over the x-axis followed by a translation of 2 units down. Write a rule for $h(x)$.

5. The resale value of a bike decreases by 14% per year. A new bike is valued at $350. Approximate the resale value after 4 years to the nearest dollar.

On Your Own

6. Describe the possible effects of k on the parent function $f(x) = 7^x$ when it is transformed to $g(x) = f(x) + k$.

7. Shown below are the graphs of a parent exponential function f and a function $g(x) = a \cdot f(x)$. What must be true of the sign of a?

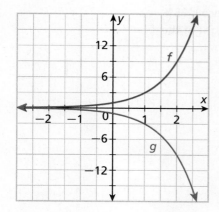

8. (MP) **Reason** How are reference points helpful when graphing transformations of the graph of $f(x) = b^x$ and when writing equations for transformed graphs?

9. Explain why one reference point is not enough to determine a rule for a transformed exponential function. Support your reasoning by providing an example in which one reference point on the graph of f is mapped to the same point on the graphs of two distinct functions g and h.

Tell whether the graph of each function is a vertical stretch or a vertical compression of the graph of the parent function. Also tell whether the graph of the function involves a reflection over the x-axis.

10. $g(x) = 0.7(0.9)^x$

11. $g(x) = -1.1(1.5)^x$

Each graph g is a transformation of the parent exponential function f. Write a rule for f and g.

12.

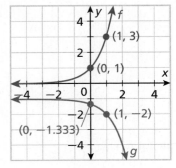

13.

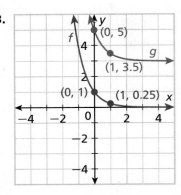

The function f has reference points $(0, 1)$ and $(1, 2)$. What do the reference points become for each transformation given by g?

14. $g(x) = 3 \cdot f(x) - 2$

15. $g(x) = 2 \cdot f(x) + 2$

16. $g(x) = -3 \cdot f(x) + 1$

17. $g(x) = 4 \cdot f(x) - 5$

For Problems 18 and 19, graph the parent function $f(x) = 3^x$ along with the transformation given by g.

18. $g(x) = \frac{1}{3} \cdot f(x) - 1$

19. $g(x) = -1 \cdot f(x) + 6$

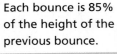

Each bounce is 85% of the height of the previous bounce.

20. A ball is dropped from a height of 12 feet and bounces as shown.

A. Write a function for the ball's height $f(n)$ above the floor on its nth bounce. What is the domain of f?

B. Write a new function $g(n)$ if the ball is dropped from 5 feet instead of 12 feet.

C. What type of transformation could you apply to the graph of f to produce the graph of h?

D. Write a function $h(n)$ for the height of the ball above the floor on its nth bounce if the ball is dropped from 12 feet above a table that is 4 feet tall.

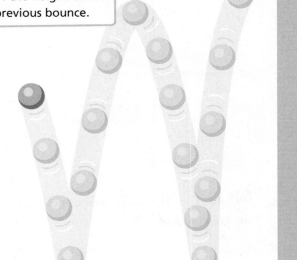

The graph of each function *g* is a transformation of the graph of a parent exponential function *f*. What is the asymptote of the graph of *g*?

21. $g(x) = -2 \cdot f(x) - 2$

22. $g(x) = 4 \cdot f(x) - 5$

23. $g(x) = \frac{1}{2} \cdot f(x) - 1$

24. $g(x) = -f(x) + 8$

25. STEM Maximal oxygen consumption is the maximum rate, in liters per minute, at which the body uses oxygen during exercise. Maximal oxygen consumption varies from person to person, but it decreases with age by about the same percent each year.

Two 25-year-old female athletes have maximal oxygen consumption rates of 4 liters per minute and 3.5 liters per minute.

A. Let the variable *t* represent the time in years after age 25. Write rules for $V_1(t)$ and $V_2(t)$ that model the maximal oxygen consumption for each athlete as a function of *t*.

B. Is this phenomenon modeled by exponential growth or decay? Explain.

C. What do the values $V_1(0)$ and $V_2(0)$ represent in this context?

D. What is the maximal oxygen consumption of each athlete at age 30?

Maximal oxygen consumption decreases with age by about 0.5% per year after age 25 for active adults.

26. (MP) **Reason** Is the domain the same for every exponential function? Is the range the same for every exponential function? Explain.

27. Let *f* be an exponential function with a range of $y > 0$.

A. How does the range of $g(x) = a \cdot f(x)$ relate to the range of *f*?

B. How does the range of $g(x) = f(x) + k$ relate to the range of *f*?

C. Explain how you could determine the range of $g(x) = a \cdot f(x) + k$ using the values of *a* and *k*.

The graph of each function *g* is a transformation of the graph of the corresponding parent exponential function *f*. Given each pair of corresponding reference points, write rules for *f*(*x*) and *g*(*x*).

28.

f	g
(0, 1)	(0, 5)
$\left(1, \frac{1}{2}\right)$	(1, 4)

29.

f	g
(0, 1)	(0, −4)
(1, 3)	(1, −10)

The graph of a parent exponential function *f* is shown. Graph the function *g*, and label the *y*-intercept and asymptote.

30. $g(x) = 3 \cdot f(x) - 2$

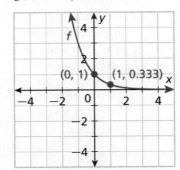

31. $g(x) = -2 \cdot f(x) + 4$

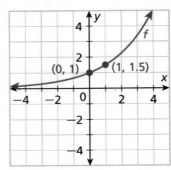

32. (Open Middle™) Using the digits 1 through 9 at most two times each, fill in the boxes to create an exponential function and identify the *y*-intercept and asymptote of the function's graph. Use the greatest possible *y*-intercept.

$$y = \boxed{} \cdot \boxed{}^{\left(x + \boxed{}\right)} + \boxed{}$$

y-intercept: $\boxed{}$ asymptote: $y = \boxed{}$

Spiral Review • Assessment Readiness

33. For $f(x) = b^x$, which statement best describes how $f(x)$ is transformed to $g(x) = 2 \cdot b^x$?

Ⓐ horizontal stretch   Ⓒ horizontal compression

Ⓑ vertical stretch   Ⓓ vertical compression

34. The model $P(t) = 100 \cdot (4)^t$ represents the population $P(t)$ of a bacteria over *t* years. How long does it take for the population of the bacteria to double?

Ⓐ 2 years   Ⓒ 6 months

Ⓑ 1 year   Ⓓ 4 months

35. Which type of function is expressed by $f(x) = b^x, 0 < b < 1$?

Ⓐ exponential decay   Ⓒ linear

Ⓑ exponential growth   Ⓓ quadratic

36. Which function has the greatest growth rate?

Ⓐ $g(x) = 2 \cdot (1.05)^x$ Ⓓ $g(x) = \frac{1}{2} \cdot (2.5)^x$

Ⓑ $g(x) = 3^x$ Ⓔ $g(x) = \frac{1}{4}(3.2)^x$

Ⓒ $g(x) = 2^x$ Ⓕ $g(x) = 3 \cdot (1.5)^x$

I'm in a Learning Mindset!

Is my understanding of transformations of exponential functions progressing as I anticipated? What adjustments can I make to enhance my learning?

Compare Exponential Functions

(I Can) compare exponential functions given in different forms.

Spark Your Learning

A young investor is comparing different investment options. At the end of each year, each investment option earns a fixed percent of the account's balance as interest that gets added to the balance.

Should I invest for 10 years with a 4.0% annual interest rate?

Should I invest for 20 years with a 3.5% annual interest rate?

Complete Part A as a whole class. Then complete Parts B–D in small groups.

A. What is a mathematical question you can ask about this situation? What information would you need to know to answer your question?

B. Describe the variables in this situation. What must be true of the values for these variables in this question?

C. To answer your question, what strategy and tool would you use along with all the information you have? What answer do you get?

D. Does your answer make sense in the context of the situation? How do you know?

Turn and Talk What combination of initial investment ($3000 or $5000), length of investment (10 years or 20 years), and interest rate (3.5% or 4.0%) is guaranteed to produce the greatest amount of total interest? Explain your reasoning.

Build Understanding

Representations of Exponential Functions

Exponential functions can be expressed with a verbal description, an equation, a table, or a graph. The use of each representation has advantages and disadvantages.

1 ▶ Humans start as a single cell that divides into two new cells. Each of these cells divides into two new cells, and the cell division continues in this way, following an exponential pattern. The time it takes for cell division to occur depends on many factors, including what kind of cells they are.

> It takes 1 day for this cell to divide.

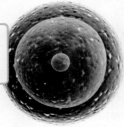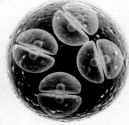

Let t represent time in days and P represent the population, or total number, of cells. The exponential relationship can be represented in different ways, as shown below.

$P(t) = 2^t$

t	P(t)
0	1
1	2
2	4
3	8
4	16
5	32
6	64
7	128
8	256

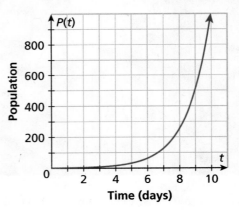

A. What is the initial value of the cell population? Explain how to identify the initial value from the equation, table, and graph.

B. Assuming that the cell division never ends, what is the domain and range of P? How does this appear in the equation, table, and graph?

C. Is P an increasing or decreasing function? Explain how this property appears in the equation, table, and graph.

D. What is the growth factor of the cell population? Explain how to identify the growth rate from the equation, table, and graph.

 Turn and Talk Explain which representation would be most useful to identify each of the following:
- The growth rate
- Any input-output pair
- The end behavior

Step It Out

Compare Growth/Decay Rates

2 Some people collect baseball cards to remember their favorite players. Other people trade and collect baseball cards as investments based on the value of the cards.

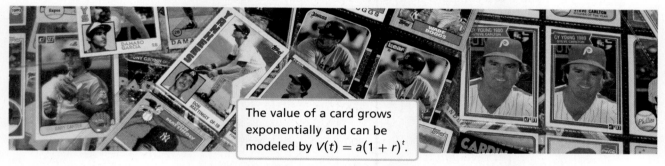

The value of a card grows exponentially and can be modeled by $V(t) = a(1 + r)^t$.

A baseball card is taken to two different appraisers. They both project that the value will grow exponentially. One projection is given in a table while the second projection is given in a graph. Which projection has the higher growth rate?

Projection I

Time (years)	Value ($)
0	300.00
1	390.00
2	507.00
3	659.10
4	856.83
⋮	⋮

Projection II

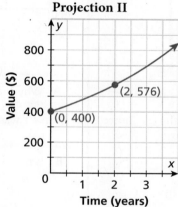

Projection I:

The initial value of the baseball card is $300.

$V_1(t) = 300(1 + r)^t$

$V_1(1) = 300(1 + r)^1 = 390$

$1 + r = 1.3$

$r = 0.3$ or 30%

Projection II:

The initial value of the baseball card is $400.

$V_2(t) = 400(1 + r)^t$

$V_2(2) = 400(1 + r)^2 = 576$

$(1 + r)^2 = 1.44$

$1 + r = 1.2$

$r = 0.2$ or 20%

The first projection has a higher growth rate.

A. Why is $a = 300$?

B. What input-output pair is substituted into the equation?

C. How can you identify the initial value from the graph?

D. Why is only the positive square root considered?

E. How does the growth rate affect the value of the baseball card?

> **Turn and Talk** When will the value of the card from Projection I be the same as the value of the card from Projection II? Use a graph to explain.

Compare Initial Values

The initial value of any exponential function in the form $f(x) = ab^x$ is a because $f(0) = ab^0 = a \cdot 1 = a$. This can often be determined by looking at the table of values or reading the value from the graph. However, this is not always possible.

3 The value V of a computer depreciates exponentially over time t in months. Three brands sell comparable computer models as shown in the equation, table, and graph. Determine the initial value of the computer from each brand and order them from least to greatest.

Brand 1:

$V_1(t) = 485(0.9)^t$

Brand 2	
Time (months)	Value ($)
2	414.00
3	401.58

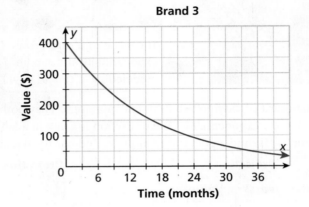

Brand 3

Brand 1 computer:

$V_1(0) = 485(0.9)^0 = 485$

> **A.** Why is a the initial value in $V_1(t) = ab^t$?

The initial value of the computer from Brand 1 was $485.

Brand 2 computer:

$V_2(t) = ab^t$

> **B.** Is $b > 1$ or $0 < b < 1$? Explain

$V_2(3) = ab^3 = 401.58$

$V_2(2) = ab^2 = 414.00$

$b = \dfrac{ab^3}{ab^2} = \dfrac{401.58}{414.00} = 0.97$

> **C.** Why is $b = \dfrac{ab^3}{ab^2}$?

$a(0.97)^2 = 414.00$

> **D.** What do the values 0.97, 2, and 414.00 represent?

$a = \dfrac{414.00}{0.9409} = 440.00$

The initial value of the computer from Brand 2 was $440.

Brand 3 computer:

The initial value of the computer from Brand 3 was $400.

> **E.** How does the initial value appear on the graph?

The initial value of the computer from Brand 3 was the least, Brand 2 was the second greatest, and Brand 1 was the greatest.

 Turn and Talk When is the value of the computer from Brand 1 equal to the value of the computer from Brand 3? Use a graph to explain.

Compare Function Values

When exponential functions are modeling comparable scenarios, you can compare function values for any value of the independent variable, even when they are represented in different ways.

4 ▶ Cyanobacteria, otherwise known as blue-green algae, has the potential to form harmful algal blooms under the right conditions. With sunlight, slow-moving water, nutrients, and the right temperature, populations bloom exponentially.

Under ideal conditions, with a temperature of approximately 27 °C, the population P_1 of a blue-green algal colony reproduces with a growth rate of 92% per day.

An experiment holds the temperature at 20 °C and records the population of algal cells each day in a table.

If both populations start with an initial value of 200, what is the difference between the two populations after 2 weeks?

The algal cells bloom exponentially and can be modeled by $P(t) = a(1 + r)^t$.

Time (days)	0	1	2	3	...
Population	200	284	403	573	...

Ideal Temperature:

$P_1(t) = 200(1.92)^t$

$P_1(14) = 200(1.92)^{14} = 1{,}850{,}321$

> **A.** Why is the function evaluated at $t = 14$?

The algal population with an ideal temperature of 27 °C will be 1,850,321 after 2 weeks.

Controlled Temperature:

$P_2(t) = 200(1 + r)^t$

$P_2(1) = 200(1 + r)^1 = 284$

$1 + r = 1.42$

> **B.** What input-output pair is substituted into the equation?

> **C.** What is the growth rate r?

$P_2(t) = 200(1.42)^t$

$P_2(14) = 200(1.42)^{14} = 27{,}106$

The algal population held at a temperature of 20 °C will be 1,850,321 after 2 weeks.

> **D.** How does the difference compare to $P_1(14)$?

$P_1(14) - P_2(14) = 1{,}850{,}321 - 27{,}106 = 1{,}823{,}215$

After 2 weeks, the algal population with an ideal temperature of 27 °C will have 1,823,215 more cells than the population held at a temperature of 20 °C.

 Turn and Talk How long would it take each algal population to reach 1,000,000,000 cells? Use a graph to explain.

Check Understanding

1. The exponential function f includes the ordered pairs $(0, 6)$ and $(1, 12)$, and $g(x) = 2(3)^x$. Which function has a graph with the greater y-intercept?

2. Which function below has the greater growth rate? Explain.

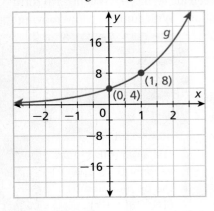

x	f(x)
0	4
1	16
3	64
4	256

3. The exponential function f has a decay rate of 20%, its graph has a y-intercept of 100, and $g(x) = 150(0.9)^x$. Which function has the greater decay rate?

4. $P_1(t) = 200 \cdot 3^t$ and P_2, which includes the ordered pairs $(0, 500)$ and $(1, 1000)$, represent the number of cells in two separate bacteria cultures over time. Which has the greater population when $t = 2$? When $t = 4$? Explain.

On Your Own

5. **(MP) Model with Mathematics**
   When cooking, the term *reduction* refers to a technique that thickens sauce, with volume V in quarts, as it simmers over time t (in hours). Suppose a restaurant uses reduction to thicken two types of sauce, tomato sauce and cream sauce, as shown.

   Tomato sauce:
   $V_c(t) = 20(0.90)^t$

   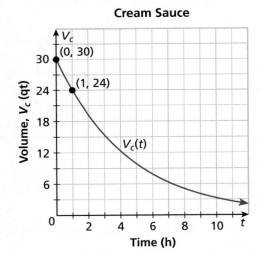
   Cream Sauce

   A. Which sauce has the greater initial volume?

   B. Which sauce reduces at a slower rate? Explain.

   C. Which sauce has the greater volume after 3 hours?

   D. Will the cream sauce always have a greater volume than the tomato sauce? Explain.

6. Justine considers three options for a video game console. The value V, in dollars, depreciates exponentially with time t in years. The value of the first console is given by $V_1(t) = 450(0.9)^t$.

Console 2, $V_2(t)$

- Initial Value: $500
- Value after a year: $400

Console 3, $V_3(t)$

Time (years)	Value ($)
0	$550.00
1	$522.50
2	$496.38
3	$471.56

A. Which console has the greatest initial value?

B. Which console has the lowest decay rate?

C. Which console will have the greatest value after 5 years?

7. Determine which exponential function has the greater growth rate.

x	$f(x)$
−1	$\frac{1}{3}$
0	1
1	3
2	9

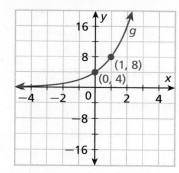

8. Consider the exponential function g, shown in the table, and $f(x) = 12 \cdot 3^x$. Determine which has the greater initial value.

x	1	2	3	4	5	6
$g(x)$	16	32	64	128	256	512

For each pair of exponential functions, determine which has the greater value at the indicated value of x. Show your work.

9. $x = 3$: $f(x) = 2 \cdot 3^x$, and $g(x)$ includes the ordered pairs $(1, 4)$ and $(2, 16)$.

10. $x = 4$: $f(x) = 2 \cdot 4^x$, and $g(x)$ includes the ordered pairs $(1, 6)$ and $(2, 12)$.

11. (MP) **Use Structure** Compare and contrast $f(x) = \frac{1}{3} \cdot 3^x$ and $g(x) = 3 \cdot \left(\frac{1}{3}\right)^x$ in terms of initial values and rates of growth/decay. At what x-value is $f(x) = g(x)$? Use a graph to explain.

Module 12 • Lesson 12.2

12. Exponential decay models for two radioactive samples are shown.

Sample 1

- Initial sample: 800 mg

- After 1 month: 400 mg

Sample 2

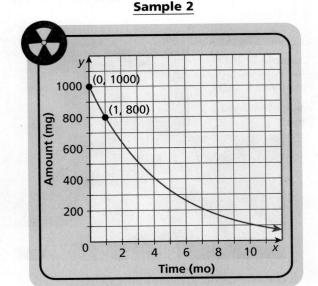

A. Which sample has the greater initial value?

B. Which sample decreases more rapidly (has the higher decay rate)?

C. After 3 months, which sample will have the greater amount of radioactive material? Explain.

13. Financial Literacy The value of a skateboard depreciates exponentially. One year after being purchased, the skateboard was valued at $450.00. One year later, the skateboard was valued at $337.50. The value V of a bike is modeled by the function $V(t) = 400(0.8)^t$ where t is time in years.

A. Which item had the greater initial value? Explain.

B. Which item has the lower decay rate? What does this mean in terms of the item's value?

C. When will the items have the same value? Use a graph to explain.

Spiral Review • Assessment Readiness

14. Which function is equivalent to $f(x) = 2 \cdot 8^x$?

Ⓐ $f(x) = 4 \cdot 2^x$ Ⓒ $f(x) = 2 \cdot 2^{3x}$

Ⓑ $f(x) = 8 \cdot 2^x$ Ⓓ $f(x) = 2 \cdot 3^{2x}$

15. The signed vertical distance between a data point and a line of fit is a ___?___.

Ⓐ residual   Ⓒ regression

Ⓑ scatter plot   Ⓓ correlation

16. The graph of function g is a transformation of the graph of $f(x) = 2^x$. Match each transformation with the corresponding function g.

Transformation

A. Translation

B. Vertical compression

C. Vertical stretch

Function

1. $g(x) = 2^x - 2$

2. $g(x) = 2(2)^x$

3. $g(x) = \frac{1}{2}(2)^x$

 I'm in a Learning Mindset!

Does my work with exponential functions meet expectations? What evidence supports that claim?

Review

Parent Exponential Functions

The function $f(x) = b^x$ with base $b > 1$ or $0 < b < 1$ is a parent exponential function.

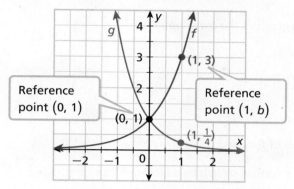

Reference point $(0, 1)$

Reference point $(1, b)$

$f(x) = 3^x$ and $g(x) = \left(\frac{1}{4}\right)^x$ are both parent exponential functions.

Transformations

The graph of the function $g(x) = ab^x + k$ is a transformation of the graph of its corresponding parent exponential function $f(x) = b^x$.

$$g(x) = 2\left(\frac{1}{2}\right)^x + 1$$

- Vertical stretch by a factor of 2

- Vertical translation up 1 unit

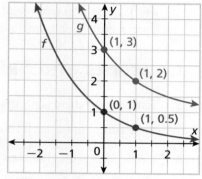

The corresponding reference points are $(0, a + k)$ and $(1, ab + k)$.

Growth Rate and Decay Rate

Daniel is considering purchasing a new car with an initial value $V_1(0) = \$12{,}000$ that depreciates with a decay rate of 15% each year. He is also considering purchasing a used car whose value is shown in the table.

Age (years)	Value ($)	
2	8100	$V_2(2) = a(1 - r)^2$
3	7290	$V_2(3) = a(1 - r)^3$

$$1 - r = \frac{a(1 - r)^3}{a(1 - r)^2} = \frac{V_2(3)}{V_2(2)} = \frac{7290}{8100} = 0.9$$

$$r = 0.1 \text{ or } 10\%$$

The second car has a lower decay rate so it will retain its value longer.

Initial Value

Daniel knows that the initial price of the new car is $V_1(0) = \$12{,}000$ but does not know how much the used car initially cost.

$$V_2(2) = 8100 = a(0.9)^2 = 0.81a$$

$$a = 10{,}000$$

The initial value of the used car was less than the new car.

Car Comparison

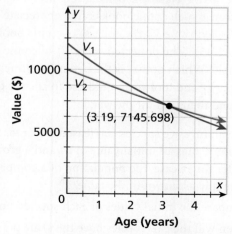

Each car would have the same value $7145.70 when each car is 3.19 years old.

Vocabulary

Choose the correct term from the box to complete each sentence.

1. If the value V of a car is a function of time t, then $V(0)$ represents the ___?___ of the car.

2. For a function $f(x) = a(1 + r)^x$ where a is a nonzero real number and $r > 0$, r is known as the ___?___.

3. For a function $f(x) = a(1 - r)^x$ where a is a nonzero real number and $r > 0$, r is known as the ___?___.

4. For $a > 1$, the graph of $g(x) = ab^x$ is a ___?___ of the graph of the corresponding parent exponential function.

Concepts and Skills

5. Explain why there is no single parent exponential function.

Write the function for each transformation of the graph of $f(x) = 3^x$.

6. a reflection across the x-axis

7. a vertical stretch by a factor of 2 and translated up 3 units

Describe how the graph of the parent exponential function f is transformed to produce the graph of g. Then write an equation for $f(x)$ and $g(x)$.

8.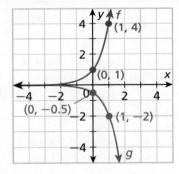

9.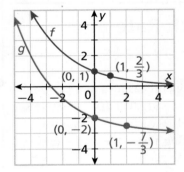

10. **(MP) Use Tools** Natalie is considering investing in a collectible comic book because such comic books often appreciate exponentially over time. The projected value V_A (in dollars) of comic book A in t years is given by $V_A = 60(1.05)^t$. The projected value V_B of comic book B in t years is shown in the table. Which option is the better investment after 10 years? State what strategy and tool you would use to answer the question, explain your choice, and then find the answer.

Time (years), t	Value ($), V_B
0	40.00
1	44.00
2	48.40
3	53.24

11. Suppose an invasive species is released into a foreign ecosystem. Its population P_I has an initial value of 24 and a growth rate of 300% each year. After the release, the population of a competing native species decays exponentially as shown in the table.

Time (years)	Native species population P_N
0	2000
1	1500
2	1125

   A. Compare the initial values of each species' population.

   B. When will the two species have the same population? Use a graph to explain.

Build Exponential Functions and Models

Aeronautical Engineer

STEM
POWERING INGENUITY

Aeronautical engineers are responsible for the mechanics of flight. They undertake theoretical and practical research to accurately predict, measure, and improve an aircraft's safety and performance. To model an aircraft's flight, an aeronautical engineer must balance the forces exerted upon the aircraft.

STEM Task

For an airplane to fly, it must have the right amount of *lift*.

Lift	Weight
Air density: $\rho = 1.2$ kg/m^3	Mass: $m = 362{,}870$ kg
Takeoff velocity: $v = 290$ km/h	Gravity: $g = 9.8$ m/s^2
Wing area: $S = 510$ m^2	

Determine the minimum lift coefficient, C_L, that allows the airplane to take off.

$$L = \frac{1}{2}\rho v^2 S C_L$$

Lift

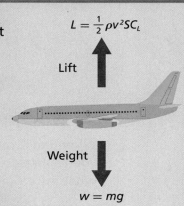

Weight

$$w = mg$$

Learning Mindset
Strategic Help-Seeking Asks Questions

©MIT/NASA

How do you know the right type of questions to ask when you need clarification? Whenever you are working on a learning goal, it is important that you know when and how to ask targeted questions. You want to make sure that your questions are phrased so that the response will get right to the information that will help you most. You may have to rephrase your questions for clarity if the responses you receive are not what you had hoped for. Here are some questions you can ask yourself to make sure you are seeking the right help:

- What information am I looking to gain about the concept of lift? What questions can I ask my teacher to help me better understand the concept of lift?

- How can I encourage my peers to share with me what they know about lift and how to solve the posed task?

- How would I expect an answer to my question to look? Does my question make the expected form of an answer clear? How can I modify my question so that I get the type of answer I expect?

Reflect

Q When have you received an answer that was unhelpful or irrelevant? How could you rephrase your question so that the person has a better understanding of what information you are looking to gain?

Q If you were an aeronautical engineer, what other information might you need to know to ensure a safe flight? What questions could you ask to obtain this information?

Fit Exponential Functions to Data

Harvesting Logistics

Tracking crop growth is important for plant health and predicting the harvest. The table shows data for the height of a sunflower as it grows.

Day	7	14	21	28	35	42	49	56	63	70	77	84
Height (cm)	17.9	36.4	67.8	98.1	131.0	169.5	205.5	228.3	247.1	250.5	253.8	254.5

A. Plot the data and sketch a curve through the points. What does the curve's shape tell you about the sunflower's growth?

B. Is an exponential function a reasonable model for all of the data? Just some of the data? Explain. Use a graphing calculator to create an exponential model with an appropriate domain.

C. Logistic growth can be modeled by the equation $y = \frac{c}{1 + ab^x}$ where a, b, and c are constants. Use a graphing calculator to perform logistic regression. Compare the goodness of fit of your logistic model with your exponential model.

D. Based on the graph alone, when would be an ideal time to harvest? What other factors would you need to consider when choosing an ideal harvest time?

Are You Ready?

Complete these problems to review prior concepts and skills you will need for this module.

Write Equations from Tables and Graphs

Write an equation that represents the table or graph.

1.

x	y
0	0
1	5
2	10
3	15
4	20

2.

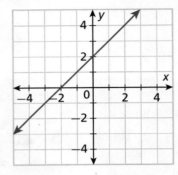

Point-Slope Form

Write the equation of a line in point-slope form using the given information.

3. slope of 4 and passes through the point $(2, 6)$

4. passes through the points $(-2, 8)$ and $(2, 6)$

Scatter Plots and Lines of Fit

Use the table in Problems 5 and 6.

Number of oranges purchased, n	10	15	20	30	40
Price of each orange ($), p	0.75	0.69	0.65	0.54	0.46

5. Create a scatter plot. Then approximate a line of fit.

6. Predict the price per orange when 25 oranges are sold.

Connecting Past and Present Learning

Previously, you learned:

- to fit lines to scatter plots,
- to analyze lines of fit using residuals, and
- to model with exponential functions.

In this module, you will learn:

- to fit exponential functions to data,
- to assess the fit of a model by analyzing residuals, and
- to tell whether a linear or exponential model better fits a set of bivariate data.

Scatter Plots and Fitted Exponential Curves

(I Can) **fit exponential functions to data and make predictions about real-world situations.**

Spark Your Learning

A stamp collector purchases a vintage stamp collection for $100 and plans to sell the collection for a large profit.

The value of the stamps is expected to increase over time.

Complete Part A as a whole class. Then complete Parts B–D in small groups.

A. What is a mathematical question you can ask about this situation? What information would you need to know to answer your question?

B. Does the pattern of data resemble an exponential or linear function? Explain.

C. To answer your question, what strategy and tool would you use along with all the information you have? What answer do you get?

D. Does your answer make sense in the context of the situation? How do you know?

Turn and Talk If the value of the stamp collection was $220 after 10 years and $340 after 20 years, what type of model would you use to represent the data? Explain your reasoning.

Build Understanding

Model Exponential Data and Analyze Residuals

Bivariate data that show a relationship resembling exponential growth or decay can be modeled by an exponential function $f(x) = ab^x$. Recall that a represents the initial value and b represents the growth factor.

1 ▶ The numbers of visitors to an aquarium over time are shown in the table below.

Aquarium Visitors	
Time (years since 2010), t	Visitors (thousands), v
0	250
1	305
2	350
3	420
4	515

A. Make a scatter plot of the data. Do the data appear to show exponential growth or decay? Explain.

B. Using a spreadsheet, create a table like the one shown. Fill down the spreadsheet for cells C3 to C7. What do you notice about the relationship between successive v-values?

C3 ▲▼ ✕ ✓ fx	= B3/B2	
	A	**B**	**C**
1	t	v	ratio of successive v-values
2	0	250	–
3	1	305	1.22
4	2	350	
5	3	420	
6	4	515	
7	5	610	

> Use column C to compute the growth or decay factors between successive v-values.

C. How do your findings in Part B relate to your graph in Part A? Explain.

D. What value would you use for b in an exponential model $v(t) = ab^t$ for the data?

E. What is the value of a? Using the value of b you found in Part D, what is a function you can use to model the data?

 Turn and Talk Do you think your model is a good fit for the data? Explain.

Recall that you compared the goodness of fit of linear models by finding the sum of squared residuals for each model. The model with the least sum of squared residuals is the one that best fits the data. You can use the same method to compare the goodness of fit of exponential models.

2 Using the table of visitors at the aquarium from Task 1, Megan and Austin each found a different function to model the data.

Megan's model:
$$v(t) = 250(1.22)^t$$
based on the ratio of the v-values of the first two data points $(0, 250)$ and $(1, 305)$
$$b = \frac{305}{250} = 1.22$$

Austin's model:
$$v(t) = 250(1.20)^t$$
based on the average of all ratios of v-values of consecutive data points
$$b = \frac{5.98}{5} \approx 1.20$$

A. To analyze Megan's model, use a spreadsheet to create a table like the one shown. Notice the formula you can use to evaluate the number of predicted visitors for year t. Fill down the formula from cell C2 to cell C7.

C2 ▲▼	✕ ✓	fx = 250*(1.22)A2		
	A	**B**	**C**	**D**	**E**
1	t	v (Actual)	v (Predicted)	Residual	Square of residual
2	0	250	250		
3	1	305			
4	2	350			
5	3	420			
6	4	515			
7	5	610			
8			Sum of squared residuals		

The formula calculates $v(t)$ using Megan's model.

B. Recall that a residual is the predicted value subtracted from the actual value. What formula can you use to find the residual in cell D2? Fill down the formula from cell D2 to cell D7.

C. In Part A, you learned that you can use the "^" to indicate an exponent. What formula can you use in cell E2 to represent the squared residual? Fill down the formula from cell E2 to cell E7.

D. Find the sum of squared residuals in cell E8 by adding all of the squared residuals in cells E2 through E7.

E. Create a new spreadsheet for Austin's model by following the steps in Parts A–D. After finding the sum of squared residuals for Austin's model, determine which model better fits the data.

 Turn and Talk Is the sum of residuals or the sum of the squared residuals a better measure of goodness of fit? Explain.

Step It Out

Model Exponential Data Using Technology

Exponential regression is a statistical method used to fit an exponential model to a set of bivariate data. You can use a graphing calculator to find an exponential growth or decay model for the data.

3 ▶ Use the exponential regression feature on a graphing calculator to find and interpret an exponential function that models the aquarium visitor data from Task 1, shown in the table.

Aquarium Visitors	
Time (years since 2010), t	Visitors (thousands), $v(t)$
0	250
1	305
2	350
3	420
4	515
5	610

Enter the data points from the table to create a scatter plot.

A. How can you determine what scale allows you to see the relationship clearly?

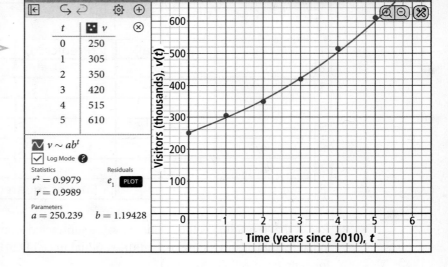

If your graphing calculator offers you the option of Log Mode, select it. There are different ways to perform exponential regression, and choosing Log Mode will perform regression in a way that gives you a correlation coefficient r that helps you assess the goodness of fit, just as with linear regression.

An equation for the exponential model is $v(t) = 250.239(1.19428)^t$.

B. What do the initial value a and the base b of the function represent in this context?

The correlation coefficient is $r = 0.9989$, which indicates an excellent fit of the model to the data. The model itself indicates that attendance at the aquarium is increasing at an annual rate of about 19.4%.

C. Where does the rate 19.4% come from?

> **Turn and Talk** How does the exponential model found in Task 3 compare to the exponential model you wrote in Task 1?

Model Exponential Data Using Piecewise-Defined Functions

A piecewise-defined function can be used to describe data that have different growth rates for different time periods.

4 ▶ In the tables of data shown in the graphing calculator screen below, the *t*-values represent time, measured in decades since 1890, and the *P*-values represent the population, in thousands, of Phoenix, Arizona. Create a model for the data.

The scatter plot shown in the graphing calculator screen indicates that the data from $t = 0$ to $t = 5$ appear to lie along an exponential curve (shown in red), and the data from $t = 6$ to $t = 11$ appear to lie along a different exponential curve (shown in purple).

The population of Phoenix doubled from 5500 in 1890 to 11,100 in 1900.

An exponential model for $t = 0$ to $t = 5$ is $P(t) = 6.6(1.80)^t$.

A. What is the growth rate for this model?

An exponential model for $t = 6$ to $t = 11$ is $P(t) = 104.6(1.28)^t$.

B. What is the growth rate for this model?

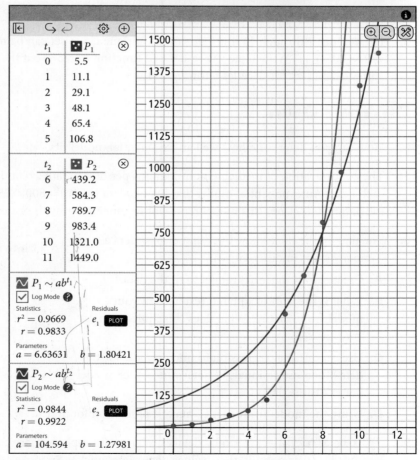

t_1	P_1
0	5.5
1	11.1
2	29.1
3	48.1
4	65.4
5	106.8

t_2	P_2
6	439.2
7	584.3
8	789.7
9	983.4
10	1321.0
11	1449.0

$P_1 \sim ab^{t_1}$
☑ Log Mode ❓
Statistics   Residuals
$r^2 = 0.9669$ e_1 PLOT
$r = 0.9833$

Parameters
$a = 6.63631$ $b = 1.80421$

$P_2 \sim ab^{t_2}$
☑ Log Mode ❓
Statistics   Residuals
$r^2 = 0.9844$ e_2 PLOT
$r = 0.9922$

Parameters
$a = 104.594$ $b = 1.27981$

You can combine the models using a piecewise-defined function:

$$P(t) = \begin{cases} 6.6(1.80)^t, 0 \le t \le 5 \\ 104.6(1.28)^t, 6 \le t \le 11 \end{cases}$$

C. How could you estimate the population 5.5 decades after 1890?

Check Understanding

For Problems 1–5, use the data in the table which gives the estimated value of an antique china set over time.

1. Without using residuals, how can you tell that the data in the table follows an exponential pattern? Do the data show exponential growth or decay?

2. One appraiser uses the growth factor between $(0, 100)$ and $(1, 115)$ to get $v(t) = 100(1.15)^t$ as a model of the data. Another appraiser uses the growth factor between $(3, 179)$ and $(4, 226)$ to get $v(t) = 100(1.26)^t$ as a model. Determine which function best fits the data by comparing the sums of squared residuals.

Antique China Set	
Time (decades since purchase) t	Estimated value ($), $v(t)$
0	100
1	115
2	138
3	179
4	226

3. Use a graphing calculator to find an exponential function that models the data. Compare this model with the models from Problem 2. Which model best fits the data?

4. Use the model you found in Problem 3 to predict the value of the china set 6 decades since it was purchased.

5. For decades 7 through 11, the value of the antique china set can be modeled by $v(t) = 206(1.1)^t$. Write a piecewise-defined function to represent the value of the antique china set for decades 0 through 11.

On Your Own

6. How can you determine how well an exponential model fits data?

7. The concentration of medicine in milligrams per liter in Jade's blood was recorded each hour. An exponential model that fits the data is $C(t) = 800(0.75)^t$. Interpret the parameters. Does this model represent exponential growth or decay? Explain.

8. The data in the table show the number of orders a company ships in different years.

   A. Create an exponential model to fit the data.

   B. What is the sum of squared residuals of your model from Part A? What does this indicate about your model?

   C. Use exponential regression to find a model for the data. Then use residuals to determine which model better fits the data.

   D. Using the model from Part C, make a prediction for $S(10)$.

Time (years since 2014), t	Orders shipped (thousands), $S(t)$
0	100
1	127
2	165
3	179
4	212
5	210

9. (MP) **Use Structure** Electronic devices, such as smartphones, are constantly being improved, and as a result, their values depreciate quickly. Suppose a device costs $1000 new. The phone has a value of $470 one year after purchase and a value of $221 two years after purchase. Model this situation with an exponential function. Interpret the initial value a and base b of the function you wrote. About how many years from the purchase will the smartphone become worth less than $50?

10. **STEM** Santiago measures the temperature of hot water over time and records his data as the difference in the measured temperature and the room temperature as shown. After 5 minutes, he puts an ice cube in the water and then continues measuring the temperatures.

Time (min), t	Temperature difference (°F), T
0	145
1	137
2	132
3	126
4	112
5	102
6	70
7	61
8	51
9	36
10	27

A. Make a scatter plot of the data.

B. Use your scatter plot from Part A to explain why this situation should be modeled using a piecewise-defined function.

C. Use regression to determine the functions that make up the piecewise-defined function.

D. Use the model from Part C to predict the temperature difference after 20 minutes. Is your answer reasonable?

11. A manufacturing company tracks the depreciation of a machine since its purchase as shown in the table.

Time (years since purchased), t	Value ($), $v(t)$
0	35,000
1	26,226
2	22,455
3	18,882
4	15,347
5	12,938

A. Use the first two data points to write an exponential function that models the data.

B. Use a graphing calculator to perform exponential regression on the data. What is the function? Round numbers to 3 significant digits.

C. Find the sum of squared residuals for each model found in Parts A and B. Which model fits the data better?

D. Use the model from Part B to predict the value of the machine after 7 years.

12. The table shows the number of U.S. cell phone subscribers, in millions, since 1985.

Time (years since 1985)	0	5	10	15	20	25
Subscribers (millions)	0.34	5.28	33.76	109.48	207.90	300.52

A. Perform exponential regression on the entire set of data. What do you observe?

B. Look closely at the last three columns of the table. What do you notice about the change in the number of subscribers?

C. What piecewise-defined function best models the data?

1985 cell phone

13. **(MP) Model with Mathematics** A student with an interest-bearing savings account observes the balance in her account at the end of each year.

Time (yr), t	1	2	3	4	5	6
Balance ($), $B(t)$	4,614.32	4,728.92	4,844.69	4,970.12	5,094.75	5,223.79

A. Use exponential regression to write a function that models the data.

B. Use the function from Part A to estimate the amount of money the student deposited in the account initially and the yearly interest rate.

14. The table shows the number of Internet users in the world during a recent 20-year period.

Time (yr), t	1	2	3	4	5	6	7	8	9	10
Users (millions), $U(t)$	16	36	70	147	248	361	719	817	1018	1093

Time (yr), t	11	12	13	14	15	16	17	18	19	20
Users (millions), $U(t)$	1319	1574	1802	2267	2497	2802	3079	3366	3696	4156

A. Why is it a good idea to model the data using a piecewise-defined function?

B. What is the exponential regression model of the data for years 1–10? years 11–20?

C. What is the piecewise-defined function?

D. Predict how many users there will be in year 25.

Spiral Review • Assessment Readiness

15. Which transformation results from adding a constant to an exponential function?

   (A) vertical shift

   (B) vertical compression

   (C) horizontal shift

   (D) horizontal compression

16. Students find the following sums of squared residuals for four linear models. Which squared residual sum comes from the linear model with the best fit?

   (A) 704   (C) 872

   (B) 792   (D) 1064

17. What are the characteristics of the graphs of exponential functions? Select all that apply.

   (A) has a horizontal asymptote

   (B) always has an x-intercept

   (C) always has a y-intercept

   (D) has a vertical asymptote

18. For an investment earning 12.5% simple interest on an initial deposit with no additional deposits, how many years will it take for the investment to double?

   (A) 5   (C) 7

   (B) 6   (D) 8

 I'm in a Learning Mindset!

What resources are available to help me understand how to write functions to model exponential data?

Choose Between Linear and Exponential Models

(I Can) choose between linear and exponential models for given data sets.

Spark Your Learning

Cooper and Logan are training for a marathon. To train, they increase the distance they run each week. Each runner has a different training schedule.

Cooper increases the distance she runs by a constant number of miles.

Logan increases the distance he runs by a constant percent increase.

Complete Part A as a whole class. Then complete Parts B–D in small groups.

  A. What is a mathematical question you can ask about this situation? What information would you need to know to answer your question?

  B. What variables are involved in the situation? What unit of measurement would you use for each variable?

  C. To answer your question, what strategy and tool would you use along with all the information you have? What answer do you get?

  D. Is it possible that Logan can ever surpass the number of miles Cooper runs per week? If so, could Cooper ever catch up to Logan? If not, explain why not.

 Turn and Talk Which runner's training method results in more miles run per week in the short term? In the long term? Explain.

Build Understanding

Compare Linear and Exponential Relationships

1 Two venues are possible meeting places for a yearly convention. Each venue projects a different pattern for the expected attendance at the yearly convention for an eight-year period as shown below.

Venue 1	
Time (yr), _t_	**Attendance, _A(t)_**
0	2500
1	2650
2	2800
3	2950
4	3100
5	3250
6	3400
7	3550

Venue 2	
Time (yr), _t_	**Attendance, _A(t)_**
0	1100
1	1250
2	1420
3	1614
4	1834
5	2084
6	2369
7	2692

A. Which venue projects a common difference of attendees from year to year? How does this relate to the concept of rate of change you studied previously?

B. Which venue projects a fixed percent change of attendees from year to year?

C. Graph each set of data. What type of function does each graph represent? How is the shape of a graph related to whether there is a fixed percent increase or common difference between _A_-values?

D. What happens to the increase in attendance for each yearly interval at the venue that projects a fixed percent change of attendees? Explain why.

 Turn and Talk If the patterns continue, will the projected attendance at Venue 2 ever exceed the projected attendance at Venue 1 for the same year? Explain your reasoning.

Step It Out

Growth of Linear and Exponential Functions

Over equal intervals, linear functions change by equal differences, while exponential functions change by equal factors.

2 Complete the proof that linear functions change by equal differences over equal intervals.

Given: $x_2 - x_1 = x_4 - x_3$
f is a linear function of the form $f(x) = mx + b$.

Prove: $f(x_2) - f(x_1) = f(x_4) - f(x_3)$

Proof: 1. $x_2 - x_1 = x_4 - x_3$ Given

    2. $m(x_2 - x_1) = m(x_4 - x_3)$ _____?_____

> **A.** What property justifies Step 2?

    3. $mx_2 - mx_1 = mx_4 - mx_3$ _____?_____

> **B.** What property justifies Step 3?

    4. $mx_2 + b - mx_1 - b = mx_4 + b - mx_3 - b$ Addition and Subtraction Properties of Equality

    5. $mx_2 + b - (mx_1 + b) = mx_4 + b - (mx_3 + b)$ _____?_____

> **C.** What property justifies Step 5?

    6. $f(x_2) - f(x_1) = f(x_4) - f(x_3)$ Definition of $f(x)$

3 Complete the proof that exponential functions change by equal factors over equal intervals.

Given: $x_2 - x_1 = x_4 - x_3$
g is an exponential function of the form $g(x) = ab^x$.

Prove: $\dfrac{g(x_2)}{g(x_1)} = \dfrac{g(x_4)}{g(x_3)}$

Proof: 1. $x_2 - x_1 = x_4 - x_3$ Given

    2. $b^{(x_2 - x_1)} = b^{(x_4 - x_3)}$ If $x = y$, then $b^x = b^y$.

    3. $\dfrac{b^{x_2}}{b^{x_1}} = \dfrac{b^{x_4}}{b^{x_3}}$ _____?_____

> **A.** What property justifies Step 3?

    4. $\dfrac{ab^{x_2}}{ab^{x_1}} = \dfrac{ab^{x_4}}{ab^{x_3}}$ _____?_____

> **B.** What property justifies Step 4?

    5. $\dfrac{g(x_2)}{g(x_1)} = \dfrac{g(x_4)}{g(x_3)}$ Definition of $g(x)$

Turn and Talk Explain how you can apply what you proved in Tasks 2 and 3 to find $f(x + 1)$ for a linear function and $g(x + 1)$ for an exponential function if you know the values of $f(x)$, $f(x - 1)$, $g(x)$, and $g(x - 1)$.

Compare Linear and Exponential Functions

In real-world situations, when a quantity increases or decreases by a fixed amount, a linear function is the best model. When a quantity increases or decreases by a fixed percent, an exponential function is the best model.

4 ▶ Brooke and Phoebe have both made an investment of $1000. Brooke invested in a bond, while Phoebe invested in a certificate of deposit (CD). The tables show their values of their investments each year. Write functions that model the values of each investment. Graph the models.

Brooke's Investment Value			
Time (yr), t	Value ($), v	Difference $v_2 - v_1$	Ratio $\dfrac{v_2}{v_1}$
0	1000	–	–
1	1040	40	1.04
2	1080	40	1.0384
3	1120	40	1.0370
4	1160	40	1.0357
5	1200	40	1.0345

Phoebe's Investment Value			
Time (yr), t	Value ($), v	Difference $v_2 - v_1$	Ratio $\dfrac{v_2}{v_1}$
0	1000	–	–
1	1037.50	37.50	1.0375
2	1076.41	38.91	1.0375
3	1116.77	40.36	1.0375
4	1158.65	41.88	1.0375
5	1202.10	43.45	1.0375

Determine whether differences or ratios are constant.

For Brooke's investment, the differences are always 40. A linear function is the best type of model for the value of her investment over time.

For Phoebe's investment, the ratios are always 1.0375. An exponential function is the best type of model for value of her investment over time.

Write a model for the value of each investment.

Brooke's investment:
$v = mt + b$
$v = 40t + 1000$

> **A.** What is the real-world meaning of the values of m and b?

Phoebe's investment:
$v = ab^t$
$v = 1000(1.0375)^t$

> **B.** What is the real-world meaning of the values of a and b?

Graph the models.

> **C.** How do the graphs of the models compare?

Graph: Value ($), v versus Time (yr), t. Curves labeled $v = 1000(1.0375)^t$ and $v = 40t + 1000$.

Turn and Talk If interest payments were to continue indefinitely, would the value of Brooke's investment ever exceed the value of Phoebe's investment after year 5? Explain.

Choose Between Linear and Exponential Models

Linear and exponential functions and their graphs can model real-world situations. Often, models do not fit the data exactly, so differences or ratios between successive intervals may not all be equal.

5 A sea turtle population is studied in a coastal area. The data show sea turtle population estimates during a five-year period. Find a model for the data and analyze its fit using a residual plot.

Population over Time		Change per Interval	
Time (yr), t	Population (estimated), $P(t)$	Difference $P(t_n) - P(t_{n-1})$	Ratio $\dfrac{P(t_n)}{P(t_{n-1})}$
0	19,000	–	–
1	17,400	−1600	≈0.92
2	15,400	−2000	≈0.89
3	14,040	−1360	≈0.91
4	13,200	−840	≈0.94
5	12,500	−700	≈0.95

A. Why does an exponential model fit the data?

Use a graphing calculator to find an exponential model that fits the data.

A model that fits the data is $P(t) = 18,700(0.917)^t$.

B. What is the decay factor? How does this compare to the ratios found in the table?

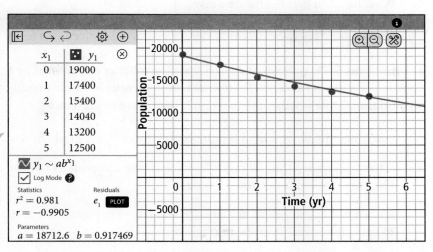

Create a residual plot.

The distribution of residuals is relatively tight, considering the scale of the data. Although the residuals show a pattern that indicates some other curve besides an exponential curve might be a better fit to the data, the exponential model still fits the data well.

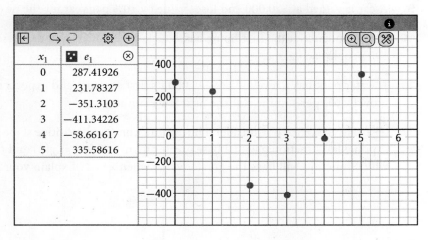

©Rich Carey/Shutterstock

Check Understanding

1. How can you identify whether bivariate data are better represented by a linear function or an exponential function from a data table? from a graph?

2. In the proofs from Tasks 2 and 3, what do $x_2 - x_1$ and $x_4 - x_3$ represent?

3. Copy and complete the table showing a person's salary for several years.

Time (yr), t	Salary ($), S	Difference $S_2 - S_1$	Ratio $\dfrac{S_2}{S_1}$
0	50,000	–	–
1	52,000	?	?
2	54,080	?	?
3	56,243	?	?
4	58,493	?	?

4. What type of function best represents the data given in Problem 3? Support your answer using the values in the table.

5. What function best fits the data given in Problem 3?

On Your Own

For Problems 6–11, state whether each situation is better represented by an exponential function or a linear function. Then write an exponential or linear function to model the situation, and state whether the function is increasing or decreasing.

6. Enrollment in an art school is initially 105 students and grows by 4% per year.

7. A business earns $180,150 in profits its first year and projects to earn another $25,200 per year for the next few years.

8. A town has 35,000 people and predicts a decrease in population of about 200 people per year over the next few years.

9. A car is valued at $20,000 and loses value by 10% per year for the next few years.

10. The attendance at the first home baseball game is 44,330 and decreases by about 105 people each game.

11. A water park has a revenue of $245,000 its first summer and expects revenues to grow by 6% per summer for the next few summers.

12. (MP) **Use Structure** Consider a linear function f with positive slope and an exponential function g with a base greater than 1. If $f(0) = g(0)$ and $f(1) = g(1)$, which function will have the greater value when $x = 2$? Explain your reasoning.

13. Task 2 proved that whenever the differences between any two pairs of x-values are equal, the ___?___ in the corresponding pairs of $f(x)$-values for a linear function f are equal.

14. Task 3 proved that whenever the differences between any two pairs of x-values are equal, the ___?___ in the corresponding pairs of $f(x)$-values for an exponential function f are equal.

15. (MP) **Use Tools** The data show global unit sales of current generation video game consoles (millions of units) during a five-year period.

A. Use a graphing calculator to find a linear model and an exponential model for the data. Interpret the parameters of each model.

B. Analyze the residuals of each model. Which model better fits the data?

C. Use the model you chose in Problem 14 to predict the console sales for year 6.

Video Game Consoles Sold	
Time (yr), t	Consoles (millions), $C(t)$
0	48.62
1	44.73
2	41.95
3	37.46
4	46.78

16. The table below shows the enrollment at a school for several years.

Time (yr), t	0	1	2	3	4	5	6
Students, $S(t)$	1550	1600	1650	1700	1750	1800	1850

A. Does the number of students appear to increase linearly or exponentially? Explain.

B. What is a function that models this situation? Interpret the parameters of the function.

17. **Personal Finance** A worker has a starting salary of $30,000 per year and is offered a choice of an annual $1000 raise or an annual 2% raise. The worker selects the percent raise. Do you agree with the worker's choice? Explain why or why not.

18. The table below shows the total number of comic books sold for several years.

A. Copy and complete the table.

B. Are the data better represented by a linear model or by an exponential model? Explain.

C. How can you use information in the table to create a model of the data? What is the model?

Comic Book Sales			
Time (yr), t	Comic books, $C(t)$	Difference	Ratio
0	110,000	–	–
1	113,300	?	?
2	116,699	?	?
3	120,199	?	?
4	123,806	?	?
5	127,520	?	?

19. Company I and Company II each have 200 employees. Company I increases its workforce by 5% each month. Company II increases its workforce by 21 employees each month. Use a spreadsheet to find after about how many months Company I will have the same number of employees as Company II.

20. (MP) **Use Tools** The data in the tables shows how two factories increase production.

Factory A					Factory B			
Time (month), t	Units produced, U	Change $U_2 - U_1$	Ratio $\dfrac{U_2}{U_1}$		Time (month), t	Units produced, U	Change $U_2 - U_1$	Ratio $\dfrac{U_2}{U_1}$
0	400	–	–		0	800	–	–
1	420	20	1.05		1	900	100	1.13
2	441	21	1.05		2	1000	100	1.11
3	463	22	1.05		3	1100	100	1.1
4	486	23	1.05		4	1200	100	1.09

A. Which type of function should you use to represent the number of units produced by each factory? How do you know?

B. For each factory, write a function that models the number of units it produces.

C. Use a graphing calculator to predict the month when Factory A will produce more units than Factory B.

Spiral Review • Assessment Readiness

21. The function $R(t) = 10(0.97)^t$ models the dollars (in millions) a movie makes in week t after its release. About how much will the movie make 12 weeks after its release?

(A) $6.94 million   (C) $7.73 million

(B) $7.15 million   (D) $69.40 million

22. Which function has the same initial value as the exponential function represented by the table?

x	1	2	3	4
$f(x)$	2200	2420	2662	2928.2

(A) $g(x) = 2200(1.05)^x$ (C) $g(x) = 1450(1.08)^x$

(B) $g(x) = 1500(1.1)^x$ (D) $g(x) = 2000(1.03)^x$

23. What is the common difference of the sequence 25, 32, 39, 46 …?

(A) 1   (C) 5

(B) 4   (D) 7

24. The graph of which function g is the reflection of $f(x) = 2^x$ across the y-axis?

(A) $g(x) = 2^x + 2$ (C) $g(x) = 2^{-x}$

(B) $g(x) = 2^x - 2$ (D) $g(x) = -2^x$

I'm in a Learning Mindset!

Was collaboration an effective tool for understanding how to find if a situation is better modeled by a linear or exponential function? Explain.

Review

Exponential Regression

A coffee shop recorded its sales for 5 months.

Time (months), t	Sales (dollars), S
0	10,400
1	13,900
2	17,900
3	23,800
4	30,700

The exponential regression model is $S(t) = 10,485(1.31)^t$.

Analyzing Fit

When you perform exponential regression on a graphing calculator, the calculator reports a correlation coefficient. As with linear regression, the closer the value of the correlation coefficient is to 1 or -1, the better the fit of the model to the data.

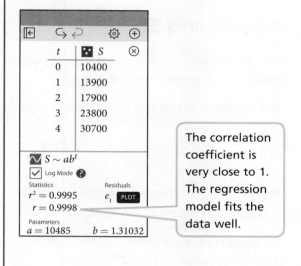

t	S
0	10400
1	13900
2	17900
3	23800
4	30700

$S \sim ab^t$

☑ Log Mode ❓

Statistics   Residuals
$r^2 = 0.9995$ e_1 PLOT
$r = 0.9998$

Parameters
$a = 10485$ $b = 1.31032$

The correlation coefficient is very close to 1. The regression model fits the data well.

Exponential and Linear Models

You can determine whether to use a linear or an exponential function to model the sales at the coffee shop by looking at the differences and ratios of successive S-values.

Coffee Shop Sales			
Time (month), t	Sales (dollars), S	Difference of successive S-values	Ratio of successive S-values
0	10,400	—	—
1	13,900	3500	1.3365
2	17,900	4000	1.2877
3	23,800	5900	1.3296
4	30,700	6900	1.2899

The differences between successive S-values are increasing.

The ratios between successive S-values are approximately equal.

Since linear functions change by equal differences over equal intervals and exponential functions change by equal factors over equal intervals, an exponential model is a good choice to model the sales at the coffee shop.

Vocabulary

Choose the correct term from the box to complete each sentence.

1. A(n) ___?___ is the difference between an actual y-value and a predicted y-value.

2. The values of a(n) ___?___ change by equal differences over equal intervals.

3. The values of a(n) ___?___ change by equal factors over equal intervals.

4. ___?___ is a statistical method used to fit an exponential function to a set of bivariate data.

Concepts and Skills

5. How do exponential functions change over equal intervals? How do linear functions change over equal intervals?

6. The number of tickets sold for a concert decreases each week after the tickets go on sale.

   A. Create a scatter plot of the data. Why is a piecewise-defined function a good model for the data?

   B. What is a piecewise-defined function that models the data?

   C. How many tickets do you think will be sold in week 12?

Time (weeks), t	Tickets sold (1000s), T
0	10.1
1	9.55
2	9.03
3	8.57
4	8.14
5	7.74
6	4.60
7	3.93
8	3.33
9	2.83
10	2.40
11	2.05

7. The number of visitors to two different online stores over five years are shown in the table.

Time (yr), t	0	1	2	3	4
Store 1 visitors (thousands), v_1	8.7	14.5	27.3	46.7	70.2
Store 2 visitors (thousands), v_2	150.2	153.1	155.9	157.2	160.3

   A. For each store, would you use a linear or an exponential function to model the number of visitors? Explain.

   B. For each store, write a function that models the number of visitors. Use residuals to determine the goodness of fit of each model.

   C. Do you think Store 1 will ever have the same number of visitors as Store 2? Explain your reasoning.

8. (MP) **Use Tools** The number of customers who made purchases at a new bookstore for the first five weeks are 150, 176, 208, 240, and 285, respectively. Would you use a linear function or an exponential function as a model for the data? What is an equation for the model? State what strategy and tool you will use to answer the questions, explain your choice, and then find the answers.

Module Performance Task: *Spies and Analysts*™

Computer Contamination

How virulent is a computer virus?

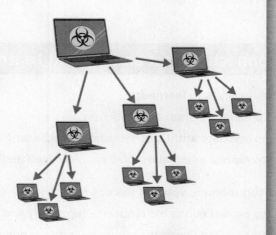

Are You Ready?

Complete these problems to review prior concepts and skills you will need for this module.

Multiply and Divide Rational Numbers

Simplify each expression.

1. $\frac{1}{4} \cdot -\frac{2}{8}$

2. -3.41×0.03

3. $\sqrt{10{,}000} \div 2$

4. $\frac{3}{5} \div \frac{7}{8}$

5. $8.68 \div -6.2$

6. $\sqrt{49} \times \sqrt{81}$

Evaluate Expressions with Exponents

7. Evaluate $5 + x^3$ when $x = 5$.

8. Evaluate $9 - x^2$ when $x = -2$.

9. Evaluate $2x^{-2}$ when $x = 3$.

10. Evaluate $4x^0 + 5$ when $x = 2$.

11. Evaluate $4 + 3x^2$ when $x = -1$.

12. Evaluate $-4x^{-2}$ when $x = -2$.

Arithmetic Sequences

Write an explicit rule and a recursive rule for each sequence.

13. 10, 12, 14, 16, . . .

14. 1, 1.5, 2, 2.5, . . .

15. 100, 80, 60, 40, 20, . . .

16. $\frac{1}{2}, \frac{3}{4}, 1, \frac{5}{4}, \ldots$

17. 3.1, 3.3, 3.5, 3.7, . . .

18. $-2, -11, -20, -29, \ldots$

19. 1.001, 1.005, 1.009, 1.013, . . .

20. $-13, -11.5, -10, -8.5, \ldots$

Connecting Past and Present Learning

Previously, you learned:

- to identify patterns in sequences,
- to associate arithmetic sequences with linear functions, and
- to express arithmetic sequences recursively and explicitly.

In this module, you will learn:

- to express geometric sequences recursively and explicitly,
- to associate geometric sequences with exponential functions, and
- to model with geometric sequences.

Geometric Sequences Defined Recursively

(I Can) write recursive formulas for geometric sequences.

Spark Your Learning

To improve her fitness, Karen swims at the community center pool. Her goal is to increase the time she swims each week for 12 weeks.

Karen swims 90 minutes during the first week.

Complete Part A as a whole class. Then complete Parts B and C in small groups.

A. What is a mathematical question you can ask about this situation? What information would you need to know to answer your question?

B. To answer your question, what strategy and tool would you use along with all the information you have? What answer do you get?

C. Is Karen's goal sustainable over time? Explain.

Turn and Talk For how much time will Karen swim during the 12th week if she swims for 120 minutes during the 1st week and decreases her swimming time by 10% each week? Explain.

Build Understanding

Understand Geometric Sequences

Recall that a sequence is a list of numbers in a specific order. In an arithmetic sequence, consecutive terms differ by the same number d, called the common difference.

$$4, \quad 7, \quad 10, \quad 13, \quad 16, \ldots$$
$$+3 + 3 + 3 + 3 \qquad d = 3$$

A **geometric sequence** is a sequence in which the ratio of successive terms is a constant r, called the **common ratio**, where $r \neq 0$. The geometric sequence shown has a common ratio of 2.

$$1, \quad 2, \quad 4, \quad 8, \quad 16, \ldots$$
$$\cdot 2 \quad \cdot 2 \quad \cdot 2 \quad \cdot 2 \qquad r = 2$$

1 ▸ A bungee jumper jumps from a bridge. The table displays part of a sequence that models the bungee jumper's maximum height $f(n)$ in feet above the water during each rebound n.

n	f(n)
1	200
2	80
3	32

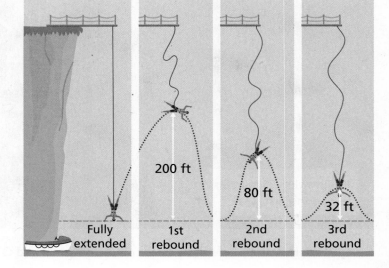

200 ft

80 ft

32 ft

Fully extended | 1st rebound | 2nd rebound | 3rd rebound

A. Is the sequence arithmetic? Explain.

B. Find the ratios of successive terms as shown below. Write the ratios as decimals.

$$\frac{\text{2nd term}}{\text{1st term}} = \frac{80}{200} = \underline{\quad ? \quad}$$

$$\frac{\text{3rd term}}{\text{2nd term}} = \frac{32}{80} = \underline{\quad ? \quad}$$

C. Is the sequence defined by $f(n)$ geometric? If so, what is the common ratio?

D. What are the 4th and 5th terms of the sequence?

 Turn and Talk Can a sequence be both arithmetic and geometric? Explain.

Express Geometric Sequences Recursively

By associating position numbers with the terms of a geometric sequence, you can create a function where the domain of the function is generally the set of natural numbers or whole numbers and the range of the function is the set of the terms of the sequence.

Consider the sequence 50, 100, 200, 400, 800.

Position number, n	1	2	3	4	5
Term of the sequence, $f(n)$	50	100	200	400	800

The domain of the function is {1, 2, 3, 4, 5}.

The range of the function is {50, 100, 200, 400, 800}.

Recall that a recursive rule for a sequence gives the beginning term or terms and a recursive equation that defines the nth term of the sequence by relating it to one or more of the previous terms in the sequence. You can write a recursive rule for a geometric sequence.

General Recursive Rule for a Geometric Sequence

A recursive rule for a geometric sequence with common ratio r is given by:
$f(1)$ = value of 1st term, $f(n) = r \cdot f(n-1)$ for $n \geq 2$

---

2 Consider the sequence 1000, 500, 250, 125, ...

A. Calculate the ratios of consecutive terms. Write the ratios as decimals.

$$\frac{500}{1000} = \underline{\quad?\quad} \qquad \frac{250}{500} = \underline{\quad?\quad} \qquad \frac{125}{250} = \underline{\quad?\quad}$$

B. Is the sequence a geometric sequence? If so, what is the common ratio r?

C. Let $f(n)$ = the value of the nth term of the sequence. What is $f(1)$?

D. What is a recursive rule for the sequence?

E. Copy and complete the table to find the next 4 terms of the sequence.

n	$f(n) = \underline{\quad?\quad} \cdot f(n-1)$
5	$f(5) = \underline{\quad?\quad}$
6	$f(6) = \underline{\quad?\quad}$
7	$f(7) = \underline{\quad?\quad}$
8	$f(8) = \underline{\quad?\quad}$

 Turn and Talk Explain how you would find the tenth term of a geometric sequence given the recursive rule for it. What information do you need to solve the problem?

Step It Out

Graph Geometric Sequences

You can use the position numbers and terms of a sequence to graph the sequence by plotting the ordered pairs $(n, f(n))$. The function is a discrete function, so its graph is made up of unconnected points.

3 Graph the sequence $f(1) = 2, 4 \cdot f(n - 1)$ for $2 \leq n \leq 5$

Use the recursive rule to make a table of values. Then plot the points.

Position number, n	1	2	3	4	5
Term of the sequence, $f(n)$	2	8	32	128	512

> **A.** How does the common ratio r help you find the next term of the sequence? Explain.

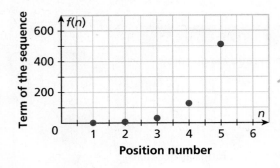

> **B.** Why are the points on the graph not connected?

4 Part of a geometric sequence is shown on the graph. Write a recursive rule for the sequence.

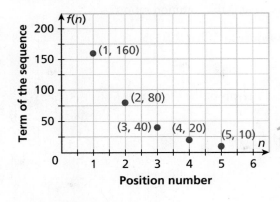

> **A.** How can you find $f(1)$ from the graph?

Find the common ratio, r.

$$\frac{80}{160} = \frac{40}{80} = \frac{20}{40} = \frac{10}{20} = 0.5$$

The recursive rule is $f(1) = 160, f(n) = 0.5 \cdot f(n - 1)$ for $n \geq 2$.

> **B.** Is it possible for $f(n)$ to be a negative number? Explain.

Turn and Talk How are the shapes of the graphs above like the shapes of the graphs of exponential functions?

Apply Geometric Sequences

5 ▶ Micah read that a high school student was able to fold a long piece of tissue paper in half 12 times. Micah folds a piece of notebook paper in half as many times as possible. The table shows Micah's results where $f(n)$ = the number of layers of paper after n folds. Graph Micah's results and write a recursive rule for the sequence. How many layers would there be after 12 folds?

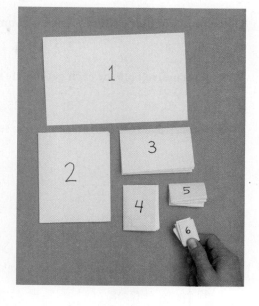

Number of folds, n	1	2	3	4	5	6
Number of layers, $f(n)$	2	4	8	16	32	64

Plot the points $(n, f(n))$ to make a graph of the sequence.

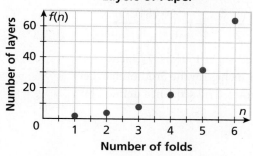

A. Why does the sequence for the number of layers for a folded piece of notebook paper stop at $n = 6$?

The sequence is geometric because consecutive terms have a common ratio.

A recursive rule for the sequence is $f(1) = 2$, $f(n) = 2 \cdot f(n - 1)$ for $n \geq 2$.

B. Why is the common ratio equal to 2?

Find the number of layers after 12 folds.

Number of folds, n	7	8	9	10	11	12
Number of layers, $f(n)$	128	256	512	1024	2048	4096

C. Why do you have to find $f(7)$, $f(8)$, $f(9)$, $f(10)$, and $f(11)$ before finding $f(12)$?

There would be 4096 layers if the paper was folded 12 times.

Turn and Talk Given a recursive rule for a geometric sequence, what tool would you use to find the 20th term of the sequence? Explain.

©Houghton Mifflin Harcourt

Check Understanding

Determine whether each sequence is geometric. If it is geometric, find the common ratio r.

1. 3, 9, 27, 81, …

2. 8, 4, 2, 1, …

3. 6, 9, 12, 15, …

Write a recursive rule for each geometric sequence. Then find the next three terms.

4. 10, 20, 40, 80, …

5. 1, 5, 25, 125, …

6. 5000, 1000, 200, 40, 8, …

Write a recursive rule for the geometric sequence shown on the graph.

7.

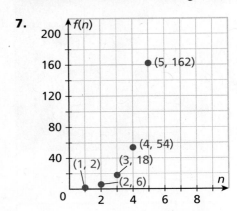

8.

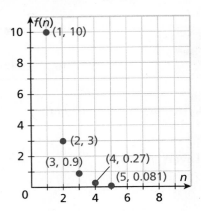

9. The heights to which a ball bounces after it is dropped are as follows: 72 inches on the 1st bounce, 36 inches on the 2nd bounce, and 18 inches on the 3rd bounce. Let $f(n)$ = the height of the ball in inches on the nth bounce. The sequence defined by $f(n)$ is geometric.

   A. Graph the sequence.

   B. Write a recursive rule for the sequence.

   C. What is the height of the ball on the 6th bounce to the nearest tenth of an inch?

On Your Own

Determine whether each sequence is arithmetic or geometric.

10. 200, 195, 190, 185, …

11. 2, 6, 18, 54, …

12. $9, -3, 1, -\frac{1}{3}, \ldots$

Find the common ratio r for each geometric sequence. Then use r to find the next three terms.

13. 5, 15, 45, 135, …

14. 243, 162, 108, 72, …

15. $-2, 6, -18, 54, \ldots$

16. (MP) **Attend to Precision** The hours Myron practices piano each week after he starts taking lessons are given by the sequence 2, 3, 4.5, 6.75, …

   A. Is this a geometric sequence? Explain.

   B. What is the next term in the sequence?

17. (MP) **Reason** Suppose you are given a geometric sequence where all the terms are positive and $0 < r < 1$. Will the sequence be increasing or decreasing? Explain.

18. (MP) **Reason** Suppose you are given a geometric sequence with $r < 0$. What will be true about the signs of the terms of the sequence? Explain.

19. **(MP) Model with Mathematics** Let $f(n) =$ the annual number of sea turtle eggs that hatch on a beach n years from now. Suppose the number of eggs that hatch each year is three times the number of eggs that hatched the previous year.

   A. Write a recursive rule for this sequence.

   B. How many eggs will hatch 4 years from now?

Suppose 50 sea turtle eggs hatch 1 year from now.

Write a recursive rule for each geometric sequence.

20. 4, 20, 100, 500, …

21. 72, 36, 18, 9, …

22. 200, −80, 32, −12.8, …

Find the indicated term of each geometric sequence.

23. 1, 8, 64, … ; 5th term

24. 5, 3, 1.8, … ; 6th term

25. 3, −12, 48; … ; 7th term

26. Part of a geometric sequence is given in the table. Write a recursive rule for the sequence. Then find the 7th term.

Position number, n	1	2	3	4	5
Term of the sequence, $f(n)$	1200	600	300	150	75

27. **(MP) Reason** A geometric sequence has a common ratio of 4. The 5th term is 20. What is the 4th term? What is the 6th term?

Write a recursive rule for the geometric sequence shown on the graph.

28.
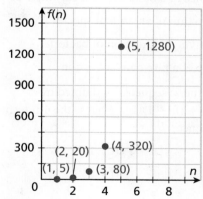

29.
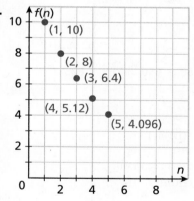

Graph the sequence.

30.
n	1	2	3	4	5
$f(n)$	1	2	4	8	16

31. $f(1) = 200, f(n) = 0.6 \cdot f(n - 1)$ for $2 \le n \le 6$

32. **(MP) Attend to Precision** Ima makes piles of rice. She starts with 1 grain of rice in the first pile and 2 grains of rice in the second pile. Each pile she makes has twice the number of grains of rice as the previous pile. Write a recursive rule for the number of grains of rice $f(n)$ in the nth pile. Then graph the sequence.

33. A population of rabbits has been monitored for many years. The following populations are recorded at the end of each year: 800 rabbits after the 1st year, 1200 rabbits after the 2nd year, 1800 rabbits after the 3rd year, 2700 rabbits after the 4th year.

  A. Write a recursive rule for the sequence that gives the population of rabbits $f(n)$ after n years.

  B. What is the rabbit population after the 6th year?

34. Health and Fitness To increase his fitness, Reggie keeps track of the number of steps he walks each day. He sets a daily step goal for each week. During the 1st week, his daily step goal is 5000 steps. He plans to increase his daily step goal by 10% each week.

  A. Graph the sequence that shows Reggie's daily step goal $f(n)$ during week n.

  B. Write a recursive rule for the sequence.

  C. During which week will Reggie first have a daily step goal of at least 10,000 steps?

35. (**Open Middle**™) Using the digits 1 to 9, at most one time each, fill in the boxes to create two increasing geometric sequences.

Spiral Review • Assessment Readiness

36. Mark saves money every month. What is the b-value for the regression function that best models the data, rounded to three significant digits?

Month	0	1	2	3	4
Savings (dollars)	500	580	650	750	825

  (A) 0.87   (C) 1.12
  (B) 1.03   (D) 1.13

37. Which function is an example of an exponential decay function?

  (A) $f(x) = 5(1.2)^x$ (C) $f(x) = 5(0.2)^x$
  (B) $f(x) = x + 3$ (D) $f(x) = -x + 3$

38. Which scenario could be a real-world example of exponential decay?

  (A) balance of a bank account earning interest
  (B) extinction of an animal species
  (C) a thriving population of bacteria
  (D) value of a rare coin collection

39. An arithmetic sequence is defined by $f(n) = 5 + (n-1)(2)$. What is the 6th term of the sequence?

  (A) 19   (C) 15
  (B) 17   (D) 13

 I'm in a Learning Mindset!

What questions can I ask my teacher to help me understand how to write recursive rules for geometric sequences?

Geometric Sequences Defined Explicitly

(I Can) write explicit rules for geometric sequences.

Spark Your Learning

When Carly was born, a relative purchased a certificate of deposit (CD) in her name. A CD is a savings account that has a fixed interest rate and a fixed redemption date.

The CD is purchased for $1000.

EDUCATION FUND

Complete Part A as a whole class. Then complete Parts B–D in small groups.

A. What is a mathematical question you can ask about this situation? What information would you need to know to answer your question?

B. How can you model this situation using a geometric sequence?

C. To answer your question, what strategy and tool would you use along with all the information you have? What answer do you get?

D. Is the answer reasonable for the situation? Explain.

Turn and Talk What are some limitations of using a recursive rule to find the value of a CD purchased for Carly at birth if the CD is redeemed when she is 20 years old? Explain.

Build Understanding

Express Geometric Sequences Explicitly

Recall that an explicit rule for a sequence defines the *n*th term of the sequence as a function of *n*. You can write explicit rules for geometric sequences.

1 ▶ Karen shares a funny video on social media, and the video is viewed 10 times that day. Each day during the rest of the week, the video gets 3 times the number of views as it did the day before.

Karen's video is viewed 10 times on the first day.

A. Let $v(n)$ = the number of views on the *n*th day. What are the first three terms of the geometric sequence defined by $v(n)$? What is the common ratio?

B. The table shows $v(n)$ expressed as the number of views on the first day multiplied by the common ratio a number of times. Copy and complete the table for the number of views on the 4th, 5th, 6th, and 7th days.

n	$v(n)$
1	$10 \cdot 3^0 = 10$
2	$10 \cdot 3^1 = 30$
3	$10 \cdot 3^2 = 90$

C. Generalize the results from the table by writing an expression for the number of views on the *n*th day.

General Explicit Rule for a Geometric Sequence

An explicit rule for a geometric sequence with common ratio *r* is given by:
$$f(n) = f(1) \cdot r^{n-1}$$

---

2 ▶ Consider the geometric sequence 125, 50, 20, ...

A. Write an explicit rule for the sequence.

B. What is the domain of the function?

C. A geometric sequence is equivalent to an exponential function with a restricted domain. Show that the explicit rule for the sequence can be written as an exponential function of the form $f(n) = ab^n$.

Turn and Talk What is true about the terms of a geometric sequence defined by $f(n) = f(1) \cdot r^{n-1}$ when $r > 1$? when $0 < r < 1$?

Step It Out

Graph Geometric Sequences

You can graph a geometric sequence given the explicit rule for the sequence.

3 Graph the sequence $f(n) = 20(1.5)^{n-1}$ for $1 \le n \le 5$.

Use the explicit rule to make a table of values. Then plot the points.

Position number, n	1	2	3	4	5
Term of the sequence, $f(n)$	20	30	45	67.5	101.25

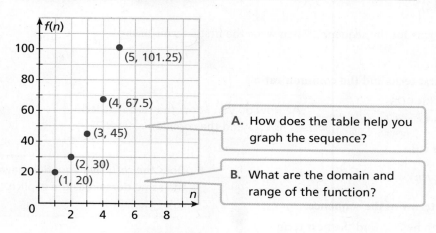

A. How does the table help you graph the sequence?

B. What are the domain and range of the function?

You can also write the explicit rule for a geometric sequence given its graph.

4 Part of a geometric sequence is shown on the graph. Write an explicit rule for the sequence.

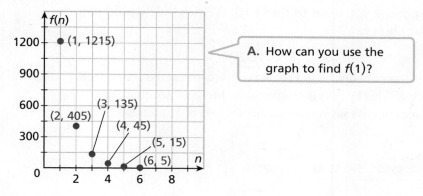

A. How can you use the graph to find $f(1)$?

Find the common ratio, r.

$$\frac{405}{1215} = \frac{135}{405} = \frac{45}{135} = \frac{15}{45} = \frac{5}{15} = \frac{1}{3}$$

An explicit rule is $f(n) = 1215\left(\frac{1}{3}\right)^{n-1}$

B. Why does it make sense that $0 < r < 1$?

Turn and Talk Explain why the graphs above show discrete functions.

Convert Between Forms of Geometric Sequences

Every geometric sequence can be written both recursively and explicitly.

General recursive rule with common ratio r:

$f(1)$ = value of first term, $f(n) = r \cdot f(n-1)$ for $n \geq 2$.

General explicit rule with common ratio r:

$f(n) = f(1) \cdot r^{n-1}$

5 ▷ Consider the geometric sequence defined by the explicit rule shown.

$$f(n) = 0.25(2)^{n-1}$$

Write a recursive rule for the sequence. Then write the first 5 terms of the sequence.

Determine the first term and the common ratio.

The first term $f(1)$ is 0.25.
The common ratio r is 2.

> **A.** How do you know that the first term is 0.25 and the common ratio is 2?

Write a recursive rule.

$$f(1) = 0.25, f(n) = 2 \cdot f(n-1) \text{ for } n \geq 2$$

> **B.** Does the recursive equation have the same domain as the explicit rule? Explain.

Write the first 5 terms of the sequence.

Multiply each term by 2 to find the next term.

0.25, 0.5, 1, 2, 4

•2   •2   •2   •2

> **Turn and Talk** Suppose you want to find $f(10)$. Which rule would you use? Explain your choice.

6 ▷ The table shows the balance in dollars of Leo's savings account at the end of each month. The sequence defined by $b(n)$ is geometric. If this sequence continues, what will be the balance of Leo's savings account at the end of 12 months?

Month, n	1	2	3
Balance, $b(n)$	1500	1530	1560.60

Write a rule for the sequence.

The first term of the sequence is $b(1) = 1500$.

The common ratio r is $\dfrac{1530}{1500} = 1.02$.

> **A.** Why can you use just one ratio to find r?

An explicit rule for the sequence is $b(n) = 1500(1.02)^{n-1}$.

Find $b(12)$.

$b(12) = 1500(1.02)^{12-1} = 1500(1.02)^{11} \approx 1865.06$

The balance at the end of 12 months is $1865.06.

> **B.** Why is an explicit rule written instead of a recursive rule?

Apply Geometric Sequences

7 A biologist estimates the population of ants in a colony at the end of each year for 4 years. The populations are given in the photo.

Year 1: 1000 ants
Year 2: 2400 ants
Year 3: 5760 ants
Year 4: 13,824 ants

Make a graph that shows the population at the end of each year. What will the ant population be at the end of 10 years if the population continues to grow at the same rate?

Graph the data.

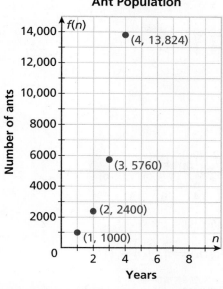

Ant Population

(graph plotting points: (1, 1000), (2, 2400), (3, 5760), (4, 13,824); x-axis labeled "Years" with n, y-axis labeled "Number of ants" with f(n))

A. What general shape do the plotted points appear to have?

Investigate the data.

The sequence 1000, 2400, 5760, 13,824 models the annual ant population. Determine whether the sequence is geometric.

$$\frac{2400}{1000} = \frac{5760}{2400} = \frac{13,824}{5760} = 2.4$$

The sequence is geometric.

B. How do you know that the terms form a geometric sequence?

Write an explicit rule.

Use the first term 1000 and the common ratio 2.4 to write an explicit rule.

$$f(n) = 1000(2.4)^{n-1}$$

Find the population at the end of 10 years.

$$f(10) = 1000(2.4)^{10-1} = 1000(2.4)^9 = 2,641,807.54$$

The ant population after 10 years will be about 2,642,000 ants.

 Turn and Talk Which strategy do you think is most efficient to find the *n*th term of a geometric sequence? Explain.

Check Understanding

Write an explicit rule for the geometric sequence. Then find the indicated term of the sequence.

1. 4, 20, 100, 500, … ; 8th term

2. 6561, 2187, 729, 243, …; 10th term

Graph the sequence.

3. $f(n) = 2 \cdot 3^{n-1}$ for $1 \leq n \leq 6$

4. $f(n) = 1280(0.25)^{n-1}$ for $1 \leq n \leq 5$

Part of a geometric sequence is shown on each graph. Write an explicit rule for the sequence.

5.

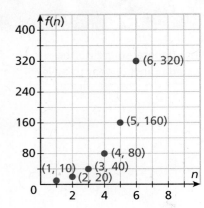

6.

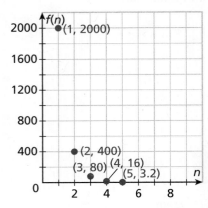

7. Write a recursive rule for the geometric sequence $f(n) = 10(0.3)^{n-1}$.

8. Write an explicit rule for the geometric sequence $f(1) = 9, f(n) = \frac{2}{3} \cdot f(n-1)$ for $n \geq 2$.

9. The heights to which a ball bounces after it is dropped are shown in the table. The heights form a geometric sequence. How high does the ball bounce on the 7th bounce? Round your answer to the nearest centimeter.

Bounce	Height (cm)
1	800
2	560
3	392

On Your Own

10. A geometric sequence is shown in the table.

A. What is the first term of the sequence?

B. What is the common ratio r?

C. What is an explicit rule for the sequence?

D. What is $f(7)$?

n	f(n)
1	400
2	600
3	900
4	1350

Write an explicit rule for the geometric sequence. Then find the indicated term of the sequence.

11. 4, 24, 144, 864, …; 11th term

12. 6, −12, 24, −48, …; 12th term

13. STEM A chemist records the temperature of a solution every 5 minutes as it cools. The recorded temperatures form the geometric sequence 75 °C, 60 °C, 48 °C, 38.4 °C, … . Write an explicit rule for the sequence.

Graph the sequence. Then state the domain and range.

14.

n	1	2	3	4	5
$f(n)$	10	5	2.5	1.25	0.625

15. $f(n) = 300(1.5)^{n-1}$ for $1 \le n \le 5$ **16.** $f(n) = 4(-3)^{n-1}$ for $1 \le n \le 5$

Part of a geometric sequence is shown on each graph. Write an explicit rule for the sequence.

17.

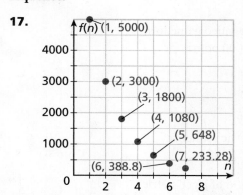

18.

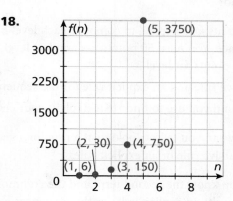

Write a recursive rule for the sequence.

19. $f(n) = 5 \cdot 3^{n-1}$ **20.** $f(n) = 75(0.8)^{n-1}$

Write an explicit rule for the sequence.

21. $f(1) = 10, f(n) = 0.25 \cdot f(n-1)$ for $n \ge 2$

22. $f(1) = 5, f(n) = 2 \cdot f(n-1)$ for $n \ge 2$

23. A wildlife biologist estimates the population of raccoons in an area annually for 4 years.

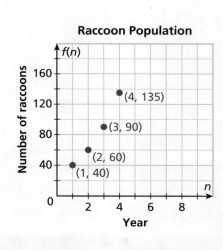

There are about 40 raccoons in the area for the 1st year.

A. Do the estimated populations form a geometric sequence? Explain.

B. What is the projected raccoon population for the 7th year?

C. Explain the method you used to answer the question in Part B.

Module 14 • Lesson 14.2

©sonsedskaya/Adobe Stock

24. The shutter speed settings on a camera form a geometric sequence where $f(n)$ is the shutter speed in seconds and n is the setting number. The shutter speeds for the first three settings are $\frac{1}{960}$, $\frac{1}{480}$, and $\frac{1}{240}$. What is the shutter speed for the 7th setting?

25. The numbers of players remaining in each round of a single-elimination tennis tournament represent a geometric sequence where $f(n)$ is the number of players competing in the nth round. There are 256 players competing in the first round, 128 players in the second round, and 64 players in the third round. How many players are in the 6th round?

26. The numbers of points $f(n)$ needed to complete each level n of a video game form a geometric sequence. You need 50 points to complete level 1, 1000 points for level 2, and 20,000 points for level 3.

   A. Write a recursive rule and an explicit rule for the sequence.

   B. Which rule would you use to find $f(8)$? Explain your choice.

27. (MP) **Reason** How can you tell by looking at a rule for a geometric sequence whether it is a recursive rule or an explicit rule?

28. (MP) **Reason** If you know the second term and the common ratio of a geometric sequence, can you write an explicit rule for the sequence? Explain.

29. (MP) **Reason** Suppose you are given the terms $f(3) = 17$ and $f(5) = 153$ of a geometric sequence. How can you find the common ratio r?

Spiral Review • Assessment Readiness

30. Enrollment in a computer gaming club is 40 people and grows by 5% each year. Which function gives the enrollment after x years?

   (A) $f(x) = 0.05x + 40$

   (B) $f(x) = 5x + 40$

   (C) $f(x) = 40(1.05)^x$

   (D) $f(x) = 40 \cdot 5^x$

31. Which expression is equivalent to $6x^2 + 3x$?

   (A) $6x\left(x + \frac{1}{2}\right)$

   (B) $6\left(-x + \frac{1}{2}x\right)$

   (C) $3\left(2x + \frac{1}{2}\right)$

   (D) $2x\left(3x + \frac{1}{2}x\right)$

32. Match the rule with its description.

   A. $f(1) = 9, f(n) = 4 \cdot f(n - 1)$ for $n \geq 2$

   B. $f(1) = 9, f(n) = f(n - 1) + 4$ for $n \geq 2$

   C. $f(n) = 9 \cdot 4^{n-1}$

   D. $f(n) = 9 + (n - 1)(4)$

   1. Recursive rule for an arithmetic sequence

   2. Explicit rule for an arithmetic sequence

   3. Recursive rule for a geometric sequence

   4. Explicit rule for a geometric sequence

 I'm in a Learning Mindset!

Who can support me in my learning about how to write and graph recursive rules for geometric sequences?

Review

Recursive Rules for Geometric Sequences

Nesting dolls, also known as *matryoshka* dolls, are a popular collector's item. The largest doll separates to fit a smaller doll inside, which has a smaller doll inside of it, and so on. Gabriel measures the heights in centimeters of the first 4 dolls in a set of nesting dolls.

Doll, n	1	2	3	4
Height, $f(n)$	25	20	16	12.8

> The heights of the dolls form a sequence.

> The first term of the sequence is 25.

The sequence is geometric because consecutive terms have a common ratio.

$$\frac{20}{25} = \frac{16}{20} = \frac{12.8}{16} = 0.8$$

You can write a recursive rule for the geometric sequence.

$$f(1) = 25, f(n) = 0.8 \cdot f(n-1) \text{ for } n \geq 2$$

You can use the recursive rule to find the height of the 5th doll in the sequence.

$$f(5) = 0.8 \cdot f(5-1)$$
$$= 0.8 \cdot f(4)$$
$$= 0.8 \cdot 12.8$$

> The value of $f(4)$ is given in the table.

$$= 10.24$$

The height of the 5th doll is 10.24 centimeters.

Explicit Rules for Geometric Sequences

Suppose the set of nesting dolls has 10 dolls. The heights of the dolls, $f(n)$, form a geometric sequence.

The first term, 25, and the common ratio, $\frac{25}{20} = 0.8$, can be used to write an explicit rule for the sequence.

$$f(n) = f(1) \cdot r^{n-1}$$
$$f(n) = 25(0.8)^{n-1}$$

Use the explicit rule to find the height of the 10th doll of the set.

$$f(n) = 25(0.8)^{n-1}$$
$$f(n) = 25(0.8)^{10-1}$$
$$= 25(0.8)^9$$
$$\approx 3.4$$

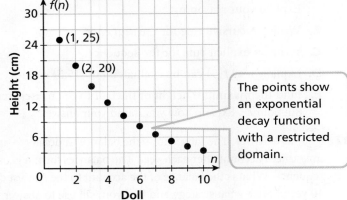

> The points show an exponential decay function with a restricted domain.

The height of the 10th doll is about 3.4 centimeters.

Vocabulary

Choose the correct term from the box to complete each sentence.

1. A sequence in which the ratio of successive terms is a nonzero constant is a(n) ___?___.

2. The ___?___ of the sequence 4, 8, 16, 32, . . . is 2.

3. A sequence with successive numbers having the same difference is a(n) ___?___.

4. A(n) ___?___ defines the *n*th term of a sequence by relating it to previous terms.

5. A(n) ___?___ defines the *n*th term of a sequence as a function of *n*.

Concepts and Skills

6. Suppose all the terms of a geometric sequence are positive and the common ratio is between 0 and 1. Is the sequence increasing or decreasing? Explain.

Write a recursive rule for the geometric sequence. Then find the next three terms.

7. 1, 5, 25, . . .   **8.** 2000, 200, 20, . . .   **9.** 32, 64, 128, . . .

Write an explicit rule for the geometric sequence. Then find the indicated term of the sequence.

10. 2, 18, 162, . . .; 8th term   **11.** 25, 15, 9, . . .; 7th term

Write an explicit rule for the geometric sequence.

12. $f(1) = 7, f(n) = 3 \cdot f(n - 1)$ for $n \geq 2$ **13.** $f(1) = 4, f(n) = 0.8 \cdot f(n - 1)$ for $n \geq 2$

Write a recursive rule for the geometric sequence.

14. $5 \cdot 3^{n-1}$ **15.** $10(0.25)^{n-1}$

16. Leela throws a ball in the air and lets it bounce freely. The maximum height in centimeters of each bounce is shown in the table.

    A. Is the sequence defined by $f(n)$ arithmetic or geometric? Explain your reasoning.

    B. Write a recursive rule for the sequence.

    C. Write an explicit rule for the sequence.

    D. Explain why $f(5)$ can be evaluated but $f(5.5)$ cannot.

    E. Find the maximum height of the ball to the nearest tenth of a centimeter on the 8th bounce. Explain how you found your answer.

Bounce, *n*	Height, *f(n)*
1	800
2	560
3	392

17. (MP) **Use Tools** The table shows the balance in dollars of an investment account after each year. The balances form a geometric sequence. What is the balance of the account to the nearest cent after 10 years? State what strategy and tool you will use to answer the question, explain your choice, and then find the answer.

Year, *n*	Balance, *f(n)*
1	1700
2	2040
3	2448

Polynomial Operations and Models

Computer Scientist

⚡ STEM POWERING INGENUITY

©Pressmaster/Shutterstock

Computer scientists focus on technology and the advancement of computing capabilities through the application of logical mathematical practices. To improve the performance of existing technology and meet the rapidly evolving demands of modern society, they must assess client needs and then develop logical procedures that address them effectively and efficiently.

STEM Task

The language of computers is based on a numeral system that uses 0s and 1s to represent information.

To convert the binary number 10001_2 to its decimal equivalent, multiply each digit by its corresponding power of 2.

$$10001_2 = 1(2^4) + 0(2^3) + 0(2^2) + 0(2^1) + 1(2^0)$$
$$= 16 + 0 + 0 + 0 + 1$$
$$= 17$$

Develop a process for converting a decimal number to its binary equivalent.

Learning Mindset

Resilience Manages the Learning Process

©ImageFlow/Shutterstock

How do you know that you are properly managing your learning? Everyone has a unique learning process, and it is up to you to direct your own learning. As you reflect upon your process, keep in mind the difference between learning and performance. Performance is directly tied to the result, whereas learning is the path you took to get to the result. Identifying your desired learning outcome allows you to break down the process into manageable checkpoints that form your learning path. Here are some questions you can ask yourself to help you manage your learning process:

- What steps am I taking to direct my own learning with mathematical modeling?

- What steps are on my learning path? How will these steps help me achieve my learning outcome?

- How do I know if I am properly managing my learning resources?

- How can I change my learning process and performance by modifying my mindset?

Reflect

Q What is the difference between learning and performance? Is your goal in a task to develop conceptual understanding or procedural fluency? How do you know?

Q How would you as a computer scientist manage your learning process and resources to deliver the best product? Explain.

Module Performance Task: Focus on STEM

Packaging Science

A team of designers wants to produce a package that can hold the largest possible volume while keeping the cost of production low. As illustrated below, the team can program a machine to cut out a square from each corner of a large sheet of construction material to form the framework of the package.

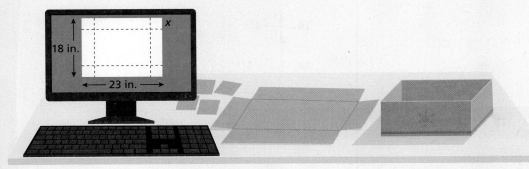

The team needs to choose the size of the square to be cut out from each corner.

A. Write a formula for both the surface area and the volume of the constructed package.

B. Use a graphing calculator or a table to identify the value of x that produces the maximum possible volume for the constructed package.

C. Use a graphing calculator or a table to identify the value of x that produces the maximum possible ratio of volume to surface area for the constructed package.

D. Compare the length of the cut that maximizes the volume with the length of the cut that maximizes the ratio of volume to surface area. Which cut should the team choose for its program? Explain your reasoning.

Are You Ready?

Complete these problems to review prior concepts and skills you will need for this module.

Multiply and Divide Rational Numbers

Simplify each expression.

1. $1\frac{1}{4} \cdot 2\frac{1}{8}$

2. $-3.01(-2.3)$

3. $4^2 \div 2$

4. $1\frac{2}{5} \div \frac{3}{8}$

5. $0.22 \cdot 6$

6. $\frac{5}{4} \div \frac{1}{2}$

The Distributive Property

Simplify each expression.

7. $5(2 + 3) - 6$

8. $2 + 3(6 - 8)$

9. $4(x + y)$

10. $2(x + 4) - 2$

11. $-2(3 - 2x) + 6$

12. $-5(3x + 1) + 8x$

Properties of Exponents

Simplify each expression.

13. $3^2 \cdot 3^3$

14. $2^2 \cdot 3^{-2}$

15. $\frac{4^4}{4^2} \cdot 1^7$

16. $\frac{4^5}{4^2} \cdot 4^4$

17. $3\left(\frac{2}{3}\right)^3$

18. $-3(-3)^{-3}$

Connecting Past and Present Learning

Previously, you learned:

- to use the Distributive Property to combine like terms,
- to use properties of operations to write equivalent expressions, and
- to apply properties of exponents to write equivalent numerical expressions.

In this module, you will learn:

- to apply properties of exponents to find products of monomials,
- to multiply polynomials,
- to understand that the set of polynomials is closed under multiplication, and
- to find special products of binomials.

Multiply Monomials

(I Can) multiply monomials and raise monomials to powers to solve real-world problems.

Spark Your Learning

An artist wants to reproduce a painting using the same ratio of the width to the height, but in a larger size.

The artist has several choices for the scale factor *x*.

Complete Part A as a whole class. Then complete Parts B–D in small groups.

 A. What is a mathematical question you can ask about this situation? What information would you need to know to answer your question?

 B. What expressions can you write to model the length and width of the new painting?

 C. To answer your question, what strategy and tool would you use along with all the information you have? What answer do you get?

 D. What is the unit of measurement for the answer? How do you know?

 Turn and Talk How many times greater is the area of the new painting than the area of the original painting? How is the scale factor related to this number?

Build Understanding

Identify Monomials

A **monomial** is a number, a variable, or a product of numbers and variables with whole-number exponents. A monomial is always an expression with a single term. The general form of a monomial is ax^n, where a is a real number, x is a variable, and n is a whole number.

Monomial

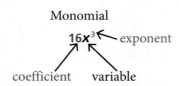

When a monomial consists of only a number, the number is called a constant. When a monomial consists of a constant and at least one variable, the number in the monomial is called a coefficient. A monomial can have multiple variables as long as the exponent of each variable is a whole number. The **degree of a monomial** is the sum of the exponents of the variables in the monomial. The degree of a nonzero constant is 0, and the constant 0 does not have a degree. The first table shows some examples of monomials and identifies the coefficient and the degree of each monomial.

Monomial	Coefficient	Degree
$\sqrt{3}x$	$\sqrt{3}$	1
xy^3	1	4
$-2z^3$	-2	3
$16x^4yz^2$	16	7

A monomial cannot have multiple terms, variables in the denominator, or negative or fractional exponents. Examples of expressions that are not monomials and the reasons why they are not monomials are shown in the second table.

Non-example of a monomial	Reason
$x - 2$	more than one term
$\dfrac{4}{y}$	variable in denominator
x^{-3}	negative exponent
$y^{\frac{1}{3}}$	fractional exponent

1 **A.** What is an example of a monomial that consists of only a number? What is an example of a monomial that consists of only a variable?

B. What is an example of a monomial that consists of a number and a variable? What name do you call the number in this type of monomial?

C. If two monomials have the same coefficient and the same variable, do you know that the two monomials have the same degree? Explain why or why not.

D. When a is constant, what is the value of the expression ax^0? How does this relate to the degree of a nonzero constant monomial?

E. Explain why each of the expressions $-4xy^{-3}$, $0.5 + \sqrt{2}x$, and $\dfrac{3}{x^2}$ is not a monomial.

 Turn and Talk How can you summarize the process for determining if an expression is a monomial?

Multiply Monomials in One Variable

You can use algebra tiles to model multiplying some simple monomials in one variable. To find more complicated products of monomials, algebraic properties can be used.

 The algebra tile diagram shown below on the left represents the product of two monomials. A key for interpreting the tiles is shown below on the right.

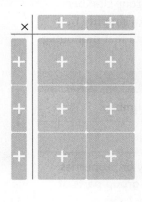

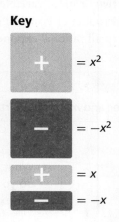

Key

$$+ \quad = x^2$$

$$- \quad = -x^2$$

$$+ \quad = x$$

$$- \quad = -x$$

A. What are the two monomials whose product is modeled by the algebra tile diagram? Explain how you identified each monomial.

B. How does the algebra tile diagram show the product of the two monomials? What is the simplified product?

C. What are the two monomials whose product is modeled by the algebra tile diagram below? What is the simplified product?

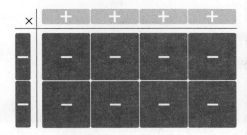

D. Show how you can use properties of exponents to find the products modeled by the two algebra tile diagrams. Give a justification for each of your steps.

E. Can you use algebra tiles to find the product $(3x)(4x^2)$? Why or why not?

F. Find the product $(3x)(4x^2)$ using properties of exponents. Give a justification for each step.

G. You can represent two general monomials in one variable as ax^m and bx^n. What is the product of these monomials? Use properties of exponents to justify your answer.

 Turn and Talk Do you think the set of monomials in a single variable is closed under multiplication? Explain why or why not.

Step It Out

Multiply Monomials in Two or More Variables

When you multiply two monomials, the product is always another monomial.

When multiplying monomials that have two or more variables, first group numbers and like variables. Then you can use the Product of Powers Property to simplify the monomial. Though the property applies to all rational exponents, recall that monomials have only integer exponents.

Product of Powers Property
$a^m \cdot a^n = a^{m+n}$, where a is a real number and m and n are rational numbers

3 ▶ Multiply the monomials

$-2a^2b^2$ and $-5a^7b$.

> **A.** What property or properties do you use to group parts of the expressions?

$(-2a^2b^2)(-5a^7b)$

$= (-2 \cdot (-5))(a^2 \cdot a^7)(b^2 \cdot b)$

$= (-2 \cdot (-5))(a^{2+7})(b^{2+1})$

> **B.** What property justifies this step?

$= 10a^9b^3$

 Turn and Talk Erica says that the product of $2x^3y^2$ and $4x^2y^5$ is $8x^6y^{10}$. Is Erica correct? Explain why or why not.

Find Monomials Raised to Powers

You will use the Power of a Product Property and the Power of a Power Property to raise a monomial to a power.

Power of a Product Property
$(ab)^m = a^m b^m$, where a and b are real numbers and m is a rational number

Power of a Power Property
$(a^m)^n = a^{mn}$, where a is a real number and m and n are rational numbers

4 ▶ Find $(2x^4y^3)^2$.

$(2x^4y^3)^2$

> **A.** What property justifies this step?

$= 2^2(x^4)^2(y^3)^2$

> **B.** What property justifies this step?

$= 4x^{4 \cdot 2}y^{3 \cdot 2}$

$= 4x^8y^6$

 Turn and Talk How is raising monomials to powers similar to raising numbers to powers or products of numbers to powers?

Find Volume

You can use products of monomials to model the volume of three-dimensional figures.

 Home aquariums can be cylinders or rectangular prisms, as well as other shapes. Aquarium A and Aquarium B are shown. What is the volume of each aquarium? How do the volumes of the two aquariums compare? Will one aquarium always have a greater volume given these dimensions? Explain.

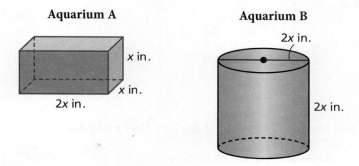

Aquarium A

x in.

x in.

$2x$ in.

Aquarium B

$2x$ in.

$2x$ in.

Find the volume of each aquarium.

For Aquarium A, use the formula for the volume of a rectangular prism: $V = lwh$.

$$V = lwh$$
$$= (2x)(x)(x)$$
$$= 2(x \cdot x \cdot x)$$
$$= 2x^3$$

A. What does each part of this expression represent?

The volume of Aquarium A is $2x^3$ in.^{3}

B. How do you know what units to use for the volumes of the aquariums?

For Aquarium B, use the formula for the volume of a cylinder: $V = \pi r^2 h$.

$$V = \pi r^2 h$$
$$= \pi(x)^2(2x)$$
$$= (\pi \cdot 2)(x^2 \cdot x)$$
$$= 2\pi x^3$$

C. What does each part of this expression represent?

D. What property justifies this step?

The volume of Aquarium B is $2\pi x^3$ in.^{3}

Compare the volumes.

The volumes of both aquariums are monomials in terms of x^3. The coefficient of the monomial that represents the volume of Aquarium B is 2, and the coefficient of the monomial that represents the volume of Aquarium A is 2π. So, the volume of Aquarium B is π times greater than the volume of Aquarium A for any value of x. Aquarium B will always have a greater volume.

 Turn and Talk How do the areas of the base of each aquarium compare?

Check Understanding

1. How many terms does a monomial have?

2. Which expressions are monomials?

   9 $2x$ $\dfrac{2}{x^2}$ $4x^2$ x^{-4} $2 + x$ $5xy^2$

Find each product or power of a monomial.

3. $(6x)(2x)$

4. $(4x)(-3x)$

5. $(3xy)(6x^2y)$

6. $(2xy)(4x^3)$

7. $(-3xy)^2$

8. $(4x^2y)^3$

9. Can you use algebra tiles to find the product $(2x)(6x^2)$? Explain why or why not.

10. A storage crate that is a cube has sides that are $4x$ centimeters long. What is the volume of the crate?

On Your Own

11. What is a monomial? Explain how to identify a monomial.

12. Which of the expressions are monomials?

    2.5 $8x + 2$ $-4x$ $8x^2y$ $x^{\frac{1}{6}}$ $2 - x$ $8xy^2 + 6$

13. Copy and complete the table to list the coefficient and degree of each monomial.

Monomial	Coefficient	Degree
$8x$	?	?
$-3x^2y^2$	?	?
y^5	?	?

14. **(MP) Critique Reasoning** A student says $\dfrac{5}{x}$ is a monomial because it could be rewritten as a multiplication expression. Explain why the student is incorrect.

Explain why each expression is not a monomial.

15. $3x^{-2}$

16. 25^x

17. $-2x^{1.2}$

18. $1 + x^2$

19. $7 - 4x$

20. $\dfrac{6}{x}$

21. Use the algebra tiles diagram.
    A. What are the factors?
    B. What is the product?
    C. Show how you can use the properties of exponents to find the product shown by the algebra tiles.

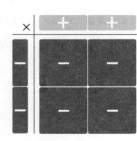

22. The algebra tile diagram shown is incomplete.

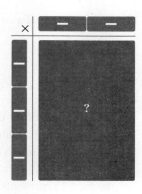

    A. Copy and complete the algebra tile diagram.

    B. What product of monomials does the diagram represent?

    C. Write the simplified product.

    D. Describe a different way you could find the same product.

Find each product.

23. $(5x)(2x)$

24. $(4x)(-6x)$

25. $(3x)(4x^2)$

26. $(2x)(2x^3)$

27. $(5x)(x)(6x)$

28. $(4x^2)(x^3)(7x)$

29. $(4a^2b^2)(2ab)$

30. $(3a^2b^2)(-3a^2b)$

31. $(-5a^3b^2)(2ab)$

32. $(6a^2b^2)(-2ab^3)$

33. (MP) **Reason** The product of two monomials is a monomial with degree 0. What do you know about the two monomial factors? Explain why.

Find the area or volume of each figure.

34.

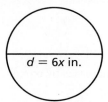

$d = 6x$ in.

35.

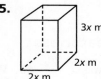

$3x$ m

$2x$ m

$2x$ m

36. The aspect ratio of a screen is the ratio of the screen's width to its height. Two possible aspect ratios of cell phone screens are shown. You can write the width and height of a cell phone screen using the aspect ratio and a scale factor x.

    A. Write a product representing the area of a cell phone screen that has an aspect ratio of 16 : 9. Interpret each factor of the product.

    B. Write a product representing the area of a cell phone screen that has an aspect ratio of 18 : 9. Interpret each factor of the product.

    C. Find the areas of the screens from Parts A and B. How do the areas of the screens compare if you use the same scale factor?

Screens on cell phones can have aspect ratios of 16 : 9 or 18 : 9.

Find each power of a monomial.

37. $(2a^2)^4$

38. $(3a^2b^2)^3$

39. $(5a^4)^2$

40. $(-4a^2b^2)^4$

41. The glass panels on the front of the entrance to an office building are rectangles whose length is 1.5 times the width. There are four rows of glass panels, with the top three rows having 17 panels and the bottom row having only 11 panels to accommodate openings for revolving doors. A model for the total area of the glass in the four rows is $62(1.5x^2)$. In this expression, what does the factor $1.5x^2$ represent? What does the factor 62 represent?

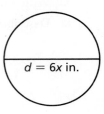

$d = 6x$ in.

42. The dimensions of a terrarium are shown.

A. What is the volume of the terrarium?

B. The surface area of the terrarium is $2(x^2) + 2(36x) + 36x$ in.^{2} Can you write the surface area as a monomial? What does this tell you about the closure of the set of monomials under addition?

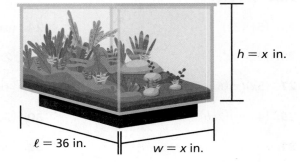

$h = x$ in.

$\ell = 36$ in.

$w = x$ in.

43. ⟨**Open Middle**™⟩ Using the digits 1 to 9, at most one time each, fill in the boxes to make a true statement.

$$\left(\boxed{}x^{\boxed{}}y^{\boxed{}}\right)\left(\boxed{}x^{\boxed{}}y^{\boxed{}}\right) = \boxed{}x^{\boxed{}}y^{\boxed{}}$$

Spiral Review • Assessment Readiness

44. The number of miles Karen walks each week forms a sequence: 10, 12, 14.4, 17.28, . . . What is the common ratio of this sequence?

Ⓐ 0.83

Ⓒ 4

Ⓑ 1.2

Ⓓ 8

45. What is the first term of the sequence with the explicit rule $f(n) = 60(1.2)^{n-1}$?

Ⓐ 50

Ⓒ 72

Ⓑ 60

Ⓓ 86

46. Which type of function increases by equal factors over equal intervals?

Ⓐ decreasing linear

Ⓑ increasing linear

Ⓒ exponential growth

Ⓓ exponential decay

47. What is the solution of the system?
$$\begin{cases} 2x + y = 3 \\ 2x - y = 4 \end{cases}$$

Ⓐ $(1.75, -0.5)$

Ⓒ $(0.5, 1.75)$

Ⓑ $(1.75, 0.5)$

Ⓓ $(-1.75, -0.5)$

 I'm in a Learning Mindset!

What did I learn from the mistakes I made when finding the products of monomials or powers of monomials?

Multiply Monomials, Binomials, and Trinomials

(I Can) write monomials, binomials, and trinomials in standard form and multiply them.

Spark Your Learning

Jumbo TV screens used for outdoor presentations are much larger than home TV screens and require a large area to be displayed.

The dimensions of the *jumbotron* are based on the dimensions of a home TV screen.

Complete Part A as a whole class. Then complete Parts B and C in small groups.

A. What is a mathematical question you can ask about this situation? What information would you need to know to answer your question?

B. To answer your question, what strategy and tool would you use along with all the information you have? What answer do you get?

C. What is the unit of measurement for each answer? How do you know?

Turn and Talk Suppose the home TV screen has a width of 3 feet. What is the area of the jumbotron?

©Marc Dozier/Getty Images

Build Understanding

Classify Polynomials

A **polynomial** is a monomial or a sum of monomials. You can classify a polynomial by the number of its terms. A monomial has one term, a **binomial** has two terms, and a **trinomial** has three terms. An example of a binomial is $2x + 4$, and an example of a trinomial is $4x^2 + 3x + 2$.

Connect to Vocabulary

You can use the prefixes *bi-* and *tri-* to help you remember the number of terms in binomials and trinomials. The prefix *bi-* means two, as in *bicycle*, and the prefix *tri-* means three, as in *tricycle*.

You can also classify a polynomial by its degree. The **degree of a polynomial** is the degree of the term of the polynomial with the greatest degree. To find the degree of a term, calculate the sum of the exponents of the variables in the term.

Polynomial	Term with greatest degree	Degree of the polynomial
$4 - 2x^2$	$-2x^2$	2
$x^2y^4 + 8y^5 + 1$	x^2y^4	6
$2x^3y^4 - 18x^7y$	$-18x^7y$	8

A polynomial in one variable is written in **standard form** when the terms are in order from greatest degree to least degree. The coefficient of the first term of a polynomial written in standard form is the **leading coefficient**.

Polynomial	Standard form	Leading coefficient
$4x + 2x^3 - 8 - x^2$	$2x^3 - x^2 + 4x - 8$	2
$3 - 5x - 7x^6 - 4x^3$	$-7x^6 - 4x^3 - 5x + 3$	-7

1 ▶ **A.** Give an example of an expression that is a polynomial and an example of an expression that is not a polynomial. Explain why the expression is not a polynomial.

B. Identify the degree of each term in the polynomial $-4x^3 + 5x + x^6 - 20$. Which term has the greatest degree?

C. Do you think the polynomial $6x^4 + 2x^2y^3 + y^6$ is written in standard form? How would you define what standard form means for a polynomial with more than one variable?

D. What do you notice about the coefficient of the term with the greatest degree and the leading coefficient of the polynomial $x^2 + 5x^7 - 2x^3 + 19 - x$? Is this relationship true for any polynomial in one variable? Explain.

E. Give an example of a polynomial that has 3 terms, a leading coefficient of 7, and a degree of 5.

 Turn and Talk Can you think of some area or volume formulas that involve binomial or trinomial expressions? Explain.

Analyze Visual Models for Polynomial Multiplication

You have used algebra tiles to find a product of monomials. You can also use algebra tiles to find a product of polynomials.

2 ▶ The algebra tile diagram shows the product of a monomial and a binomial.

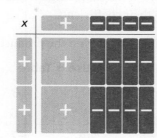

A. What product is shown by the algebra tile diagram? Explain how you identified each factor.

B. How can you use the algebra tiles to represent the product as a polynomial? What is the polynomial?

C. Show how you can use algebraic properties to find the product shown by the algebra tile diagram. Justify each step.

3 ▶ You can use an area model to represent the product of two binomials.

The first diagram below represents the product $(x + 5)(x + 3)$ as the area of a rectangle with dimensions $x + 5$ and $x + 3$. The second diagram shows this rectangle divided into smaller rectangles.

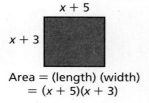

Area = (length) (width)
    = $(x + 5)(x + 3)$

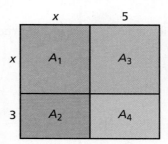

A. Find the area of each colored rectangle in the second diagram.

B. How can you represent the area of the original rectangle in the first diagram, $(x + 5)(x + 3)$, as a polynomial? Use your results from Part A to justify your answer.

C. Write the polynomial for the area of the original rectangle in standard form. What is the degree of the polynomial? What is the leading coefficient?

D. The product $(x + 5)(x + 3)$ is rewritten below using the Distributive Property. Which area(s) given in the second diagram represent the product $x(x + 3)$? Which area(s) represent the product $5(x + 3)$?

$$(x + 5)(x + 3) = x(x + 3) + 5(x + 3)$$

E. If you continue to simplify $x(x + 3) + 5(x + 3)$ and combine like terms, what will the answer be? Explain.

Turn and Talk Suppose the length of the rectangle is $x + 4$ instead of $x + 5$. Will the degree of the polynomial for the area of the original rectangle change? Explain.

Step It Out

Multiply Polynomials

When finding a product of polynomials, you may need to combine like terms. Recall that like terms are terms with the same variables raised to the same exponents. You can combine like terms by adding their coefficients.

Consider the following ways to find the product $(x - 8)(5x + 3)$.

Use a Table

	$5x$	3
x	$5x^2$	$3x$
-8	$-40x$	-24

$$(x - 8)(5x + 3) = 5x^2 + 3x - 40x - 24$$
$$= 5x^2 - 37x - 24$$

Use the Distributive Property

$$(x - 8)(5x + 3) = x(5x + 3) - 8(5x + 3)$$
$$= 5x^2 + 3x - 40x - 24$$
$$= 5x^2 - 37x - 24$$

The methods used to find the product of two binomials can be extended to find products involving trinomials.

4 Two methods are shown for finding the product $(x + 7)(2x^2 - x + 4)$.

Use a table.

First, write subtraction as addition in each polynomial.

$$(x + 7)(2x^2 - x + 4) = (x + 7)\left[2x^2 + (-x) + 4\right]$$

Make a table and find the partial products.

	$2x^2$	$-x$	4
x	$2x^3$	$-x^2$	$4x$
7	$14x^2$	$-7x$	28

The product is $2x^3 - x^2 + 4x + 14x^2 - 7x + 28$, or $2x^3 + 13x^2 - 3x + 28$.

Use the Distributive Property.

$$(x + 7)(2x^2 - x + 4) = x(2x^2 - x + 4) + 7(2x^2 - x + 4)$$
$$= 2x^3 - x^2 + 4x + 14x^2 - 7x + 28$$
$$= 2x^3 + 13x^2 - 3x + 28$$

A. How are the two methods similar?

B. Which method do you prefer? Why?

C. Notice that the product of polynomials is a polynomial. In general, are polynomials closed under multiplication? Explain.

 Turn and Talk In the table used to find the product, what do you notice about diagonal cells in the table? How can this observation help you when simplifying the polynomial?

5 ▶ A stone border is being built around a rectangular rose bed as shown. The width of the border is the same on all sides of the rose bed. Write a polynomial for the combined area of the rose bed and the stone border. What is the combined area when the stone border has a width of 1.5 feet?

Write a polynomial for the combined area.

> **A.** What does $5 + 2x$ represent?

> **B.** What does $4 + 2x$ represent?

Total area $= (5 + 2x)(4 + 2x)$

$\quad = 5(4 + 2x) + 2x(4 + 2x)$

$\quad = 20 + 10x + 8x + 4x^2$

$\quad = 20 + 18x + 4x^2$

Find the combined area when $x = 1.5$.
Total area $= 20 + 18(1.5) + 4(1.5)^2 = 56$

> **C.** Explain why the answer is given in square feet.

The combined area of the rose bed and the stone border is 56 square feet.

6 ▶ A cube has an edge length of x feet. The edge lengths are increased to create the rectangular prism shown. What is the volume of the prism? What polynomial represents the increase in volume?

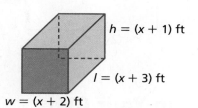

$h = (x + 1)$ ft
$l = (x + 3)$ ft
$w = (x + 2)$ ft

Find the volume.
Area of base $= (x + 2)(x + 3)$

> **A.** What do each of the factors in this product represent?

$= x(x + 3) + 2(x + 3)$

$= x^2 + 3x + 2x + 6$

$= x^2 + 5x + 6$

Volume $= (x^2 + 5x + 6)(x + 1)$

> **B.** What do each of the factors in this product represent?

$= x(x^2 + 5x + 6) + 1(x^2 + 5x + 6)$

$= x^3 + 5x^2 + 6x + x^2 + 5x + 6$

$= x^3 + 6x^2 + 11x + 6$

Find the increase in volume.
The original volume is x^3 cubic feet.
The polynomial that represents the

> **C.** Explain why x^3 cubic feet is the original volume.

increase in volume is the polynomial for the volume of the prism without the x^3 term.

The increase in volume is $(6x^2 + 11x + 6)$ cubic feet.

Turn and Talk The dimensions of the figures are polynomials. Are the expressions you found representing area and volume polynomials as well? Explain.

Check Understanding

Write each polynomial in standard form and identify the leading coefficient.

1. $3x^2 + 1 - x^4$

2. $4x + 3x^2 + 6x^3 + 1$

Identify the type of polynomial and the degree of the polynomial.

3. $2xy + 3x + 2$

4. $xy^4 + 3x^2$

5. How many terms does a binomial have?

6. Can you use algebra tiles to find the product $(x^2)(3x + 8)$? Explain why or why not.

Find each product. Describe the method you used.

7. $(4x)(x - 9)$

8. $(x - 1)(x + 3)$

9. $(2x^2 + 3)(5x + 4)$

10. $(x - 5)(7x^2 + x + 8)$

11. What is the area of the rectangle?

12. What is the volume of the box?

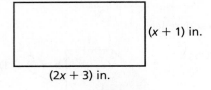
(2x + 3) in.
(x + 1) in.

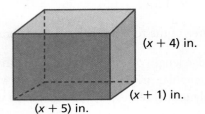
(x + 4) in.
(x + 1) in.
(x + 5) in.

On Your Own

13. Which expressions are binomials?

$9x$ $\qquad$ $2x + 2$ $\qquad$ $4xy$ $\qquad$ $4x^2 - 5$ $\qquad$ $2x^{-4} + 3$ $\qquad$ $2 + x$ $\qquad$ $5xy^2$

14. What is a trinomial? Explain how to identify a trinomial.

Write each polynomial in standard form and identify the leading coefficient.

15. $3 - 6x^4 + x$

16. $x^2 - 7x^3 + 4 - 2x^5$

Identify the type of polynomial and the degree of the polynomial.

17. $3x^2y + 4x + 2y$

18. $2xy + 3$

Determine the factors of the product shown in each table. Then copy and complete the table. What is the product?

19.

	x^2	$12x$	-9
$8x$	?	?	?

20.

	$11x^3$	$-4x^2$	$10x$
$5x$	?	?	?

21. Use the algebra tile diagram.

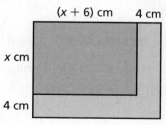

   A. What are the factors of the product shown in the diagram?

   B. Write the product as a polynomial.

   C. Describe a different way you could find the same product.

22. (MP) **Critique Reasoning** Noah found the product $(x - 5)(x^2 + 9x - 2)$ using the method shown. Is Noah's answer correct? Explain why or why not.

	x^2	$9x$	-2
x	x^3	$9x^2$	$-2x$
5	$5x^2$	$45x$	-10

$(x - 5)(x^2 + 9x - 2) = x^3 + 14x^2 + 43x - 10$

Find each product.

23. $x(2x + 4)$

24. $(3xy)(3x + 2y)$

25. $(2x)(6x^2 + 5)$

26. $(4x - 3)(x - 7)$

27. $(9x + 5)(11x - 3)$

28. $(10x)(5x^2 - x + 12)$

29. $(x + 1)(7x^2 + 2x - 15)$

30. $(2x - 4)(9x^2 + 6x + 8)$

31. (MP) **Reason** The factors of an expression are $(8x + 2)$ and $(x + 2)$. Will the product be a polynomial? Explain.

32. When you simplify a polynomial expression, how do you know which monomials to combine?

33. A rectangle is 6 centimeters longer than it is wide. Its length and width are both increased by 4 centimeters.

   A. What do each of the factors in the product $(x + 10)(x + 4)$ represent?

   B. Write a polynomial that represents the area of the larger rectangle.

   C. What is the area of the larger rectangle if $x = 8$?

34. Marco makes the rectangular sign shown to advertise the grand opening of his pizza restaurant. The sign is surrounded by a wood frame that is x inches wide.

   A. What does $(20 + 2x)(30 + 2x)$ represent?

   B. Write a polynomial for the total area of the sign and the frame.

   C. What is the total area of the sign and the frame if the width of the frame is 2 inches?

35. (MP) **Use Structure** The dimensions of a cereal box shaped like a rectangular prism are shown.

A. Write a polynomial that represents the volume of the box.

B. What is the volume of the box if $x = 5$?

$h = (x + 6)$ in.

$w = x$ in. $\ell = (x + 2)$ in.

36. Last year, a cheerleading squad sold tins of popcorn to raise money. They sold 250 tins for $10 each. They are selling tins of popcorn again this year, and they want to raise the price. They estimate that they will lose 15 sales for each $1 increase in the price per tin. The product $(10 + x)(250 - 15x)$ gives the amount of money (in dollars) raised where x is the number of $1 increases.

A. What does $10 + x$ represent? What does $250 - 5x$ represent?

B. Write a polynomial that represents the amount of money raised.

C. Evaluate the polynomial for $x = 1, 2, 3, 4, 5$. Use your results to suggest a price for each tin of popcorn. Explain your reasoning.

37. (Open Middle™) Using the digits 1 to 9, at most one time each, fill in the boxes so that the coefficient of the product's x^2 term is 0.

$$\left(\boxed{} x - \boxed{} \right) \left(\boxed{} x^2 + \boxed{} x + \boxed{} \right)$$

Spiral Review • Assessment Readiness

38. Which expression can be used to represent x if solving this system by substitution?
$$\begin{cases} x + y = 3 \\ 5x - y = 4 \end{cases}$$

(A) $-y + 3$

(B) $\dfrac{y + 4}{5}$

(C) $y + 3$

(D) $y + 4$

39. What is the third term in the sequence given by $f(n) = 5 \cdot 2^{n-1}$?

(A) 5

(B) 10

(C) 20

(D) 25

40. Match the geometric sequence with its common ratio.

A. 50, 55, 60.5, 66.55 . . .

B. 2, 4, 8, 16 . . .

C. 1, 0.5, 0.25, 0.125 . . .

1. 2

2. $\dfrac{1}{2}$

3. 1.1

 I'm in a Learning Mindset!

How can I increase my performance by modifying my mindset?

Special Products of Binomials

(I Can) find special products of binomials.

Spark Your Learning

Mrs. Smith wants to install a hot tub on her deck. The area of the deck that the hot tub covers will need to have more support added to it.

The square hot tub will be installed on a square deck.

Complete Part A as a whole class. Then complete Parts B–D in small groups.

   A. What is a mathematical question you can ask about this situation? What information would you need to know to answer your question?

   B. What expression can you write to model the side length of the hot tub? What unit of measure would you use?

   C. To answer your question, what strategy and tool would you use along with all the information you have? What answer do you get?

   D. What unit of measure is used for the answer? How do you know?

Turn and Talk Predict how your answer would change for each of the following changes in the situation:
   • The minimum side length of the hot tub is doubled.
   • The increase to the side length is doubled.

Build Understanding

Analyze Special Products

Special products of binomials have predictable patterns that can be applied when multiplying the binomials. Algebra tiles and area models can be used to represent special products of binomials.

1 ▶ The algebra tile diagrams show products with binomial factors.

Diagram 1	Diagram 2	Diagram 3

A. Copy and complete the table to represent each diagram as a product with binomial factors and as a polynomial in standard form.

	Diagram 1	Diagram 2	Diagram 3
Product	$(x + 1)(x - 1)$	?	?
Polynomial	?	?	?

B. In the table, how do the terms of each polynomial relate to the terms of the corresponding factors?

C. Use the algebra tile diagrams to explain why there are no x-terms in the polynomials.

D. Generalize the results from the table to write a rule for finding the product $(a + b)(a - b)$.

 Turn and Talk Give an example of two binomials whose product can be written as a difference of two squares.

2 ▶ Consider the square with sides of length $a + b$.

A. The square is divided into smaller squares and rectangles. What is the area of each of the smaller squares and rectangles?

B. How can you represent the area of the square with sides of length $a + b$ as a polynomial in standard form? Use your results from Part A to justify your answer.

C. What is a rule for finding the product $(a + b)^2$?

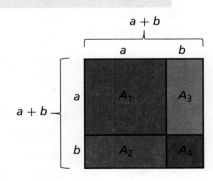

 Turn and Talk Show how you can use algebraic properties to find the product $(a + b)^2$. Justify each step.

400

Step It Out

Find the Product of a Sum and Difference

In Task 1 you discovered the following rule for multiplying $(a + b)(a - b)$. The result $a^2 - b^2$ is called a difference of two squares.

Sum and Difference Pattern
$(a + b)(a - b) = a^2 - b^2$

A mathematical justification of the sum and difference pattern is shown below.

$$(a + b)(a - b) = a(a - b) + b(a - b)$$
$$= a^2 - ab + ab - b^2$$
$$= a^2 + (-1 + 1)ab - b^2$$
$$= a^2 + 0ab - b^2$$
$$= a^2 - b^2$$

3 ▶ **Multiply $(x + 4)(x - 4)$.**

$$(a + b)(a - b) = a^2 - b^2$$
$$(x + 4)(x - 4) = x^2 - 4^2$$
$$= x^2 - 16$$

A. Why can the sum and difference pattern be used to find this product?

Multiply $(-4x + 3)(-4x - 3)$.

$$(a + b)(a - b) = a^2 - b^2$$
$$(-4x + 3)(-4x - 3) = (-4x)^2 - 3^2$$
$$= 16x^2 - 9$$

B. Why is the coefficient of the x^2-term positive?

Multiply $(x^2 + 5)(x^2 - 5)$.

$$(a + b)(a - b) = a^2 - b^2$$
$$(x^2 + 5)(x^2 - 5) = (x^2)^2 - 5^2$$
$$= x^4 - 25$$

C. What expressions replace a and b in the general rule?

 Turn and Talk Will a product of the form $(a + b)(a - b)$ always have a degree of 2? Explain.

Find the Square of a Sum

> **Square of a Sum Pattern**
>
> $(a + b)^2 = a^2 + 2ab + b^2$

A **perfect-square trinomial** is a trinomial that is the result of squaring a binomial. The trinomial $a^2 + 2ab + b^2$ is one form of a perfect-square trinomial.

4 **Multiply $(x + 6)^2$.**

$$(a + b)^2 = a^2 + 2ab + b^2$$

$$(x + 6)^2 = x^2 + 2(x)(6) + 6^2$$

$$= x^2 + 12x + 36$$

A. How can you check the answer?

Multiply $(2x + 2y)^2$.

$$(a + b)^2 = a^2 + 2ab + b^2$$

$$(2x + 2y)^2 = (2x)^2 + 2(2x)(2y) + (2y)^2$$

$$= 4x^2 + 8xy + 4y^2$$

B. Explain why $(2y)^2$ equals $4y^2$ instead of $2y^2$.

Find the Square of a Difference

> **Square of a Difference Pattern**
>
> $(a - b)^2 = a^2 - 2ab + b^2$

The trinomial $a^2 - 2ab + b^2$ is the other form of a perfect-square trinomial.

5 **Multiply $(x - 8)^2$.**

$$(a - b)^2 = a^2 - 2ab + b^2$$

$$(x - 8)^2 = x^2 - 2(x)(8) + 8^2$$

$$= x^2 - 16x + 64$$

A. How do you know that the product will have three terms?

Multiply $(4 - x^2)^2$.

$$(a - b)^2 = a^2 - 2ab + b^2$$

$$(4 - x^2)^2 = 4^2 - 2(4)(x^2) + (x^2)^2$$

$$= 16 - 8x^2 + x^4$$

B. What expressions replace a and b in the general rule?

 Turn and Talk Compare and contrast the patterns for multiplying for $(a + b)^2$ and $(a - b)^2$.

Apply Special Products

6 In a center-pivot irrigation system, the irrigation system is stationary at one end, where the water source is located, and the rest of the system rotates around the fixed end to cover a circular region. The radius of the circular region is equal to the length of the irrigation system.

A farmer will have a center-pivot irrigation system installed in a crop field. The length of each section (*x* feet in the photo) varies depending on the model, but the 8-foot extension on the far end remains constant. The farmer plans to have four sections of length *x* feet installed, as shown.

Write the area of the circular region covered by the irrigation system as a polynomial in standard form.

Write an expression for the radius of the circular region.
The length of four sections of length *x* feet is 4*x* feet. An 8-foot extension is attached to the end of the system. Therefore, the total radius is $(4x + 8)$ feet.

Determine the area of the circular region.
The area A of a circle with radius r is $A = \pi r^2$. Since the radius of the circular region is $(4x + 8)$ feet, the area of the circular region is $A = \pi(4x + 8)^2$ ft^2.

$$A = \pi(4x + 8)^2$$

$$= \pi\left((4x)^2 + 2(4x)(8) + (8)^2\right)$$

$$= \pi(16x^2 + 64x + 64)$$

$$= 16\pi x^2 + 64\pi x + 64\pi$$

A. What rule is used to multiply $(4x + 8)^2$?

B. What is another way you could obtain the product $(4x + 8)^2$?

The area of the circular region is $16\pi x^2 + 64\pi x + 64\pi$ square feet, where *x* is the length of each section of the irrigation system.

C. In this polynomial, what does the term $16\pi x^2$ represent? What does the sum $64\pi x + 64\pi$ represent?

Turn and Talk Suppose that the section of the irrigation system connected to the water source at the center of the circular region is 14 feet shorter than the rest of the sections. How would the solution steps change?

Check Understanding

Write the expression shown by each algebra tile diagram as a product of binomials and as a polynomial in standard form.

1.

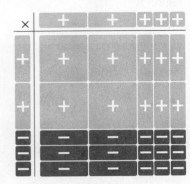

2.

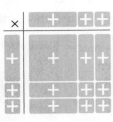

Find each product or power.

3. $(x + 5)^2$

4. $(x + 6)^2$

5. $(x - 4)^2$

6. $(5x - y)^2$

7. $(2x + 6)(2x - 6)$

8. $(x + 10)(x - 10)$

9. The length and width of a rectangle are $(x + 6)$ inches and $(x - 6)$ inches. What is the area of the rectangle?

On Your Own

Write the expression shown by each algebra tile diagram as a product of binomials and as a polynomial in standard form.

10.

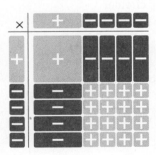

11.

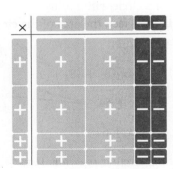

12. The algebra tile diagram shown is incomplete.

   A. Copy and complete the algebra tile diagram.

   B. Write the product shown as a square of a binomial.

   B. Write the product as a polynomial in standard form.

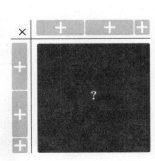

13. (MP) **Construct Arguments** Use algebraic properties to write a justification for $(a - b)^2 = a^2 - 2ab + b^2$.

Find each product or power.

14. $(x + 9)(x - 9)$

15. $(x + 1)(x - 1)$

16. $(6x + y)(6x - y)$

17. $(x^2 + 20)(x^2 - 20)$

18. $(x + 12)(x - 12)$

19. $(2x + 4)(2x - 4)$

20. $(5x + 2)^2$

21. $(4x + 4)^2$

22. $(1 + x^2)^2$

23. $(2x + y^2)^2$

24. $(2x + y)^2$

25. $(4x^2 + 1)^2$

26. $(6x - 3)^2$

27. $(4 - 2x)^2$

28. $(1 - x^2)^2$

29. $(xy - y^2)^2$

30. $(2x - yz)^2$

31. $(3x^2 + 1)^2$

Find each product. Describe the method you used to find the product.

32. $(5x + 1)(1 - 5x)$

33. $(x^2 + y)(x^2 + y)$

34. $(2x^2 + z)(2x^2 - z)$

35. $(4x - 8)(x - 2)$

36. $(10x^2 + 3x)(10x - 3)$

37. $(x^4 + z)(z + x^4)$

38. (MP) **Critique Reasoning** Mike found the power $(2x - 2)^2$ as shown. Explain and correct his error.

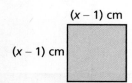

$(2x - 2)^2 = 4x^2 + 4$

39. Special products of binomials can help you find products of certain numbers.

A. The product $21 \cdot 19$ can be written as $(20 + 1)(20 - 1)$. Use mental math to find the product.

B. Rewrite the product $43 \cdot 37$ as a product of two binomials. Then use mental math to find the product.

C. Explain how to find 32^2 using a special product of binomials.

40. Consider the rectangle and square shown.

A. What are the possible values of x? Explain.

B. Does the square or the rectangle have the greater area? Explain.

C. What is the difference in the areas?

x cm

$(x - 2)$ cm

$(x - 1)$ cm

$(x - 1)$ cm

41. A box is shaped like a cylinder, and its radius is 3 centimeters less than its height.

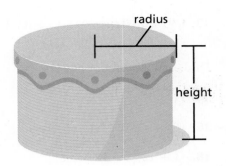

A. The volume V of the cylinder in cubic centimeters is $V = \pi(x - 3)^2(x)$. What does $x - 3$ represent? What does x represent?

B. Write the volume as a polynomial in standard form.

C. Suppose the box has a height of 20 centimeters. What is the volume of the box to the nearest cubic centimeter?

42. The flooring in a room at a library is being replaced. There will be a square rug in the middle of the square floor. The rug will be surrounded by a 6-foot border of wood flooring as shown.

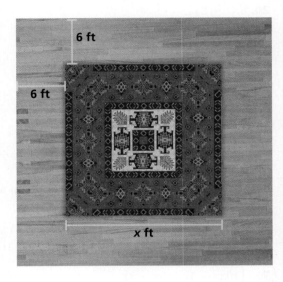

A. Write an expression for the total area of the rug and the exposed wood flooring as a power with a binomial base. What does the binomial represent?

B. Write the total area of the rug and the exposed wood flooring as a polynomial in standard form.

C. What polynomial represents the area of only the exposed wood flooring?

D. Suppose the exposed wood flooring covers an area of 576 square feet. What is the side length of the square rug?

Spiral Review • Assessment Readiness

43. Which expressions are monomials? Select all that apply.

(A) 4

(B) $x^2 + 5x$

(C) $x^{\frac{1}{2}}$

(D) $9xy$

(E) $-7y$

(F) $6x + 1$

44. What is the 5th term of the sequence defined by $f(n) = 5 \cdot 2^{n-1}$?

(A) 20

(B) 40

(C) 80

(D) 160

45. Which pairs of terms are like terms? Select all that apply.

(A) $2x^2, 5x^2$

(B) $3y^2, 3y$

(C) $2xy, 2x$

(D) $8xy, -4xy$

(E) $6x^3, x^6$

(F) $xy^2, 5y^2$

46. What is the degree of the polynomial $9 + 5x^3 - x^2 + 18x$?

(A) 18

(B) 9

(C) 4

(D) 3

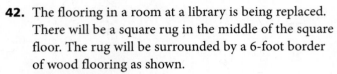

I'm in a Learning Mindset!

Did the mistakes I made stem from the level of challenge of the task or from my level of preparedness? What can I do differently next time?

Multiply Monomials

Joni is designing posters that all have the same ratio of length to width. In the poster below, x represents the scale factor. She wants to find the area of a poster.

$A = lw$
$= (3x)(2x)$
$= (3 \cdot 2)(x \cdot x)$
$= 6x^2$

3x in.

2x in.

> Group the numbers and the variables. Use the properties of exponents to simplify.

The area of the poster is $6x^2$ in.^{2}

Multiply Polynomials

Joni is also working on a group of posters with borders. Each border has a width of x feet. She wants to find the combined area of a poster and its border.

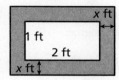

x ft

1 ft

2 ft

x ft

$A = lw$
$= (1 + 2x)(2 + 2x)$
$= 1(2 + 2x) + 2x(2 + 2x)$
$= 2 + 2x + 4x + 4x^2$
$= 2 + 6x + 4x^2$
$= 4x^2 + 6x + 2$

> Use the Distributive Property to find the product.

> The degree of the polynomial is 2.

The combined area of the poster and border is $4x^2 + 6x + 2$ ft^2.

Special Products of Binomials

Some binomial products have patterns that you can use when multiplying.

Square of a sum	Square of a difference	Product of a sum and a difference
$(a + b)^2 = a^2 + 2ab + b^2$	$(a - b)^2 = a^2 - 2ab + b^2$	$(a + b)(a - b) = a^2 - b^2$

The pattern is the square of the first term plus twice the product of the first and second terms plus the square of the second term.

The pattern is the square of the first term minus twice the product of the first and second terms plus the square of the second term.

The pattern is the square of the first term minus the square of the second term. The middle terms sum to 0 because they have opposite signs.

Vocabulary

Choose the correct term from the box to complete each sentence.

1. A __?__ consists of only one term.

2. A __?__ consists of a monomial or the sum of monomials.

3. A __?__ has two terms, and a __?__ has three terms.

4. The __?__ of a polynomial is the coefficient of the term with the greatest __?__.

5. A polynomial is in __?__ when the terms are in order from greatest degree to least degree.

6. A trinomial that is the result of squaring a binomial is called a(n) __?__.

Concepts and Skills

Categorize each expression as a monomial, binomial, or trinomial. Justify your answer.

7. 12

8. $3x$

9. $y - 3$

10. $2 - 3x + x^5$

11. $3 - x^3$

12. 0

Identify the degree and leading coefficient of each product.

13. $(6x)(12x)$

14. $(4x)(-3x + 1)$

15. $(-6x)(6x^2 + 1)$

16. $(2xy)(x^3y)$

17. $(-3xy)^3$

18. $(4xy)(x^2 + x + 1)$

Find each product or power.

19. $(2x^2y^3)(-5xy^4)$

20. $(a^4b^2)(3a^5b^2)$

21. $(3a^2b)^3$

22. $(-2x^2y^3)^2$

23. $(x + 3)(x + 2)$

24. $(x - 4)(x + 6)$

25. $(x + 5)^2$

26. $(x - 8)(x + 8)$

27. $(x - 4)^2$

28. $(x^2 + y)^2$

29. $(3 - x)(2 - x)$

30. $(5 + x)(x - 4)$

31. $(3 - x)^2$

32. $(4 + x)(6 + x)$

33. $(1 - x)(1 + x)$

34. $(7 - x)(x - 8)$

35. (MP) **Use Tools** A city park is adding a garden border that has a uniform width of x feet around a circular fountain. The fountain has a radius of 5 feet. What is the combined area of the fountain and garden border? State what strategy and tool you will use to answer the question, explain your choice, and then find the answer.

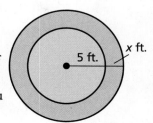

408

Polynomial Addition and Subtraction

Module Performance Task: Focus on STEM

Building Concrete Columns

A team of construction engineers is designing a parking garage. The floors of the garage will be held up by columns formed by encasing steel I-beams in concrete. All of the columns have the same proportions but vary in size. After they are placed, each I-beam is encased in concrete so there is 1 foot of concrete around all sides of the I-beam. The engineers need to calculate how much concrete is needed for each column.

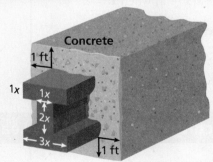

A. Write a polynomial formula that represents the cross-sectional area of the entire column, A_c, and one that represents the cross-sectional area of the I-beam, A_i.

B. Write a polynomial formula that represents the cross-sectional area of the concrete, $A_c - A_i$. Why would an engineer prefer to have a formula instead of a simple number? Explain your reasoning.

C. What is the volume of concrete needed for 50 beams with a length of 20 feet, where 40 beams require x to be 3 inches and 10 beams require x to be 5 inches?

D. What other information would you need to determine the weight the concrete adds to the column?

Are You Ready?

Complete these problems to review prior concepts and skills you will need for this module.

Add and Subtract Rational Numbers

Simplify each expression.

1. $2\frac{1}{4} + 2\frac{3}{8}$

2. $-13.2 + 2.9$

3. $3^2 - 25$

4. $1\frac{3}{5} - \frac{7}{8}$

5. $0.204 + 9.817$

6. $(2.5)^2 - (-5.16)$

Simplify Algebraic Expressions

Simplify each expression.

7. $-12x - 7x + x$

8. $-3x + 6 - (-2x)$

9. $\frac{5}{4}x + x + \frac{11}{4}x$

10. $-0.75x + 1.5x + 0.25 + 5$

11. $10.4x - 3.2 - 5.6x$

12. $6.2 - 4.08x - 21.13 + 3.991x$

Evaluate Expressions with Exponents

Evaluate each expression.

13. Evaluate $x(x + 5)$ when $x = 2$.

14. Evaluate $x + x^3$ when $x = 3$.

15. Evaluate $4x^{-2}$ when $x = -5$.

16. Evaluate $3x^0 + x$ when $x = 2$.

17. Evaluate $2(x^2 - x^{-1})$ when $x = -1$.

18. Evaluate $-2x^{-3} + x^2$ when $x = -2$.

Connecting Past and Present Learning

Previously, you learned:

- to identify monomials, binomials, and trinomials,
- to rewrite and solve variable equations, and
- to understand that the set of polynomials is closed under the operation of multiplication.

In this module, you will learn:

- to understand that the set of polynomials in one variable is closed under the operations of addition and subtraction,
- to interpret the parts of polynomial expressions as single entities, and
- to model real-world scenarios with polynomials.

16.1

Add and Subtract Polynomials

(I Can) add and subtract polynomials.

Spark Your Learning

Pisciculture (fish farming) is the controlled breeding and rearing of fish. Fish can be grown in ponds, tanks, or net pens of various volumes.

Net pen 2

Net pen 1

The depths of net pen 2 and net pen 1 are the same.

Complete Part A as a whole class. Then complete Parts B–D in small groups.

A. What is a mathematical question you can ask about this situation? What information would you need to know to answer your question?

B. How can you determine the expression for volume for each tank? What are the volume expressions?

C. To answer your question, what strategy and tool would you use along with all the information you have? What answer do you get?

D. Is your answer reasonable for all values of *r*? Explain.

Turn and Talk How do you know which net pen has the greater volume? What is the difference of the volumes in the two net pens?

Build Understanding

Simplify Polynomials: Add and Subtract Monomials

To simplify polynomial expressions, combine monomials that are like terms. Remember that like terms have the same variables raised to the same exponents, regardless of their coefficients.

Like terms			Unlike terms		
$2x, 3x$	$3x^2y, 6x^2y$	$a^2b^2, 4b^2a^2$	$2x, 3z$	$3xy, 6x^2y$	$x^2y^2, 4z^2x^2$

To add or subtract monomials in a polynomial, identify like terms. Then add or subtract the coefficients.

Examples of combining like terms	
$2x + 3x + y = (2 + 3)x + y$ $= 5x + y$	$3x^2y - 6x^2y + 4xy^2 = 3x^2y + (-6)x^2y + 4xy^2$ $= \left[3 + (-6)\right]x^2y + 4xy^2$ $= -3x^2y + 4xy^2$

1 Notice in the first example above that even if the polynomial had been written as $3x + 2x + y$, it would still be simplified as $5x + y$ because addition is commutative.

   A. Can you simplify $2x^2y^2 + 3y^2x^2$? Explain.

   B. What is a pair of unlike terms in the monomials below? Which monomial is unlike the other monomials and cannot be added to any other term?

$$\boxed{-4x} \quad \boxed{x^2} \quad \boxed{5x} \quad \boxed{10x^2} \quad \boxed{3xyz^2} \quad \boxed{7xyz^2} \quad \boxed{4z}$$

   C. From Part B, write and simplify the sum of each pair of like terms.

2 Notice in the second example above that if the polynomial had been written as $6x^2y - 3x^2y + 4xy^2$, its simplified form would be $3x^2y + 4xy^2$ because subtraction is not commutative.

   A. Can the order of the terms be changed if you change subtraction to adding the opposite, as in $3x^2y - 6x^2y + 4xy^2 = 3x^2y + \left(-6x^2y\right) + 4xy^2$? Explain.

   B. Look at the monomial terms below. Write two differences for each pair of like terms. Since the order of subtraction matters, you need to write two differences for each pair of like terms.

$$\boxed{7y} \quad \boxed{-5x^2y} \quad \boxed{72xy^3} \quad \boxed{2y} \quad \boxed{3x^2y} \quad \boxed{72y^3x}$$

   C. Simplify each difference you wrote for Part B. Were there any pairs of like terms for which the result was the same for both differences? Explain.

 Turn and Talk How can you simplify $13xyz + 8xyz - 5xyz$? Explain.

Step It Out

Add and Subtract Polynomials

You have added and subtracted pairs of monomials in order to simplify polynomials. Adding and subtracting polynomials is similar, since polynomials have monomials as terms. The steps for adding and subtracting polynomials involve combining like terms.

You can use a vertical format or a horizontal format when adding polynomials.

3 Find the sum $(3x^2 - 7x + 2) + (4x + 5 - x^2)$.

Vertical format:

$$\begin{array}{r} 3x^2 - 7x + 2 \\ +(-x^2 + 4x + 5) \\ \hline 2x^2 - 3x + 7 \end{array}$$

> **A.** Why have the terms of the second polynomial been written in a different order here?

> **B.** What property justifies the grouping of like terms in the sum?

Horizontal format:

$$
\begin{aligned}
(3x^2 - 7x + 2) + (4x + 5 - x^2) &= 3x^2 - 7x + 2 + 4x + 5 + (-x^2) \\
&= (3x^2 + (-x^2)) + (-7x + 4x) + (2 + 5) \\
&= 2x^2 + (-3x) + 7 \\
&= 2x^2 - 3x + 7
\end{aligned}
$$

> **Turn and Talk** How do you know that the sum found in Task 3 is a polynomial? Do you think that the sum of any two polynomials is always another polynomial?

You can also use either format when subtracting polynomials.

4 Find the difference $(5x^2 + 6y - 4) - (-2x^2 + 7x - 3y + 1)$.

Vertical format:

$$\begin{array}{r} 5x^2 \qquad + 6y - 4 \\ -(-2x^2 + 7x - 3y + 1) \\ \hline 7x^2 - 7x + 9y - 5 \end{array}$$

> **A.** Why is there no term above $7x$?

Horizontal format:

$$
\begin{aligned}
(5x^2 + 6y - 4) &- (-2x^2 + 7x - 3y + 1) \\
&= (5x^2 + 6y - 4) + (-1)(-2x^2 + 7x - 3y + 1) \\
&= (5x^2 + 6y - 4) + (2x^2 - 7x + 3y - 1) \\
&= (5x^2 + 2x^2) + (-7x) + (6y + 3y) + (-4 + (-1)) \\
&= 7x^2 + (-7x) + 9y + (-5) \\
&= 7x^2 - 7x + 9y - 5
\end{aligned}
$$

> **B.** What property is used to rewrite the addition in this step?

> **Turn and Talk** How do you know that the difference found in Task 4 is a polynomial? Do you think that the difference of any two polynomials is always another polynomial?

Model with Polynomials

You can use the sums and differences of polynomials to solve real-world problems.

5 Propane delivery trucks come in a variety of sizes, but nearly all of them have tanks that are cylindrical with hemispherical ends. What polynomial expression models the volume of the tank on the propane delivery truck shown at the right?

To find an expression for the volume of the tank, you first need to find expressions for the volume of the cylindrical portion and for the volumes of the two hemispheres on the ends of the tank.

Write a polynomial that represents the volume of the cylindrical portion of the tank.

$$V_1 = \pi r^2 h$$
$$= \pi r^2 (3r + 4)$$
$$= 3\pi r^3 + 4\pi r^2$$

Together, the two hemispherical ends of the tank form a complete sphere. Write a polynomial that represents the volume of this sphere.

$$V_2 = \frac{4}{3}\pi r^3$$

> **A.** How do you know the hemispheres have the same radius, so that a sphere is formed?

Now, write a polynomial that represents the volume of the entire propane tank.

$$V_1 + V_2 = \left(3\pi r^3 + 4\pi r^2\right) + \frac{4}{3}\pi r^3$$
$$= \left(3\pi r^3 + \frac{4}{3}\pi r^3\right) + 4\pi r^2$$
$$= \frac{13}{3}\pi r^3 + 4\pi r^2$$

> **B.** Why is it not possible to combine these two terms?

The volume of the tank on the propane delivery truck is repesented by the polynomial $\frac{13}{3}\pi r^3 + 4\pi r^2$.

Turn and Talk How would the work change if the propane tank only had one hemispherical end and the other end was flat? What polynomial would represent the volume of this propane tank?

Check Understanding

1. Identify the monomials that are like terms with $-3x^2$.

$6x^2$ $2x$ $3x^3$ $4x^2$ $\frac{1}{2}x^2$ x^2y xy^2

Simplify each expression.

2. $9x^2y + 2x^2y + 5$

3. $x^2 + xy + 2xy$

4. $(2xy + 9) - (x^2 - xy - 3)$

5. $(x^2y + 2xy) + (3x^2 - xy + 3)$

6. Copy and complete the difference using the vertical format.

$(3x^2 + 2x + 9) - (x^2 + 2x + 5) = (3x^2 + 2x + 9) + (-x^2 - 2x - 5)$

$$\begin{aligned} 3x^2 + 2x + 9 \\ + (-x^2 - 2x - 5) \\ \hline \underline{\quad?\quad}\ x^2 + \underline{\quad?\quad} \end{aligned}$$

7. The figure at the right represents a mailbox, where x represents the radius of the half-cylinder and all other measurements are in terms of x. What polynomial models the volume of the composite figure?

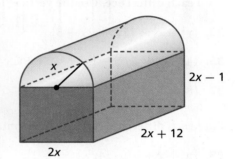

On Your Own

8. Identify the monomials that are like terms with x^2y^2.

$7x^2$ $2x^3$ $3x^2y^2$ $2x^2$ $\frac{1}{4}x^2y^2$ $x^2y\pi$ $6x^2y^2$

Simplify each expression.

9. $2x^2y - 3x^2y$

10. $2x^3 + 5z^3 + 2x^3$

11. $-2xy + 7xy + 3x^2y$

12. $z^2 - 2z^2 + 5z^2$

13. $12r^2 - 8r + r^2$

14. $3a^3 - 5a + 4a^3 + 4a$

15. $-6x^3y - 8x^3y + 10xy^3$

16. $2ab + 4ab + 6ab^2$

17. $2x^2y^2 + 3xy + 9xy$

18. $4x^2 - 3y^2 - 8x^2 + 3y^2$

Create a polynomial to model the area of each composite figure.

19. backyard deck and fish pond

20. countertop

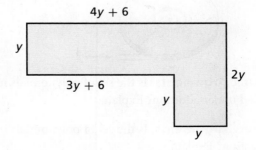

Find each sum. Use the vertical format.

21. $\left(x^2 + xy + 3\right) + \left(x^2 + xy + 2\right)$

22. $\left(2x^2 + 2x + 4\right) + \left(x^2 + x + 5\right)$

23. $\left(3x^2 + 3x + 3\right) + \left(-x^2 - x + 4\right)$

24. $\left(8x^2 + 8xy + 3\right) + \left(x^2 + 4xy + 12\right)$

25. $\left(y^3 + x^2 + x\right) + \left(x^2 + x + 5\right)$

26. $\left(2x^2 + x + 3\right) + \left(x^3 + x + 2\right)$

Find each sum. Use the horizontal format.

27. $\left(2x^2 + x + 5\right) + \left(x^2 + x + 3\right)$

28. $\left(2x^2 + 8x + 3\right) + \left(x^2 + 3x + 5\right)$

29. $\left(2a^2 + 2b + 7\right) + \left(-a^2 - b + 4\right)$

30. $\left(6x^2 + 5z + 2\right) + \left(x^2 + 3z + 4\right)$

31. $\left(2x^3 + x^2 + x\right) + \left(x^2 + 3x + 10\right)$

32. $\left(2x^2 + x + 3\right) + \left(2x^3 + 3x + 5\right)$

Find each difference. Use the vertical format.

33. $\left(y^2 + x\right) - \left(2y^2 + 2x + 5\right)$

34. $\left(-3x^2 + x\right) - \left(x^2 + 2x + 6\right)$

35. $\left(4x^2 + 4x + 3\right) - \left(x^2 + 4x + 5\right)$

36. $\left(2x^3 + x^2 + x\right) - \left(x^2 + 2x + 7\right)$

37. $\left(8x^2 + 2z + 4\right) - \left(7x^2 + 2z + 5\right)$

38. $\left(12m^2 + 5n + 3\right) - \left(14m^2 - 3n + 2\right)$

Find each difference. Use the horizontal format.

39. $\left(y^2 + x + 3\right) - \left(4y^2 + 5x + 2\right)$

40. $\left(4x^2 + x + 2\right) - \left(3x^2 + 2x + 5\right)$

41. $\left(x^2 + 2x + 3\right) - \left(x^2 - 2x - 3\right)$

42. $\left(2x^2 - 4x - 3\right) - \left(x^2 + 8x + 1\right)$

43. $\left(a^2 - 2b + 3\right) - \left(a^2 + 2b\right)$

44. $\left(2x^3 + x^2 + 3\right) - \left(x^2 - 2x - 5\right)$

Create a polynomial to model the area of each composite figure.

45. side of house

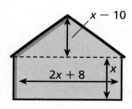

$x - 10$

$2x + 8$

x

46. palladium window

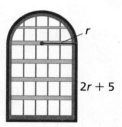

r

$2r + 5$

Create a polynomial to model the volume of each composite figure.

47. fender washer

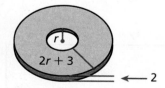

r

$2r + 3$

2

48. trashcan

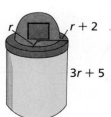

r

$r + 2$

$3r + 5$

49. (MP) **Construct Arguments** Is the set of polynomials in one variable closed under addition? Explain.

50. (MP) **Construct Arguments** Is the set of polynomials in one variable closed under subtraction? Explain.

51. An archery target has a circular "bull's-eye" at its center surrounded by a series of rings of equal width. The target shown at the right has rings that are each 3 inches wide.

   A. Create a polynomial that models the area of the outer white ring.

   B. Create a polynomial that models the area of the black ring.

   C. What polynomial expression represents the difference between the area of the white ring and the area of the black ring?

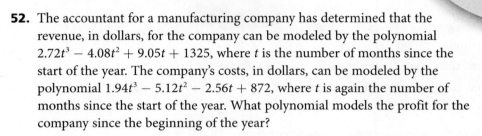

52. The accountant for a manufacturing company has determined that the revenue, in dollars, for the company can be modeled by the polynomial $2.72t^3 - 4.08t^2 + 9.05t + 1325$, where t is the number of months since the start of the year. The company's costs, in dollars, can be modeled by the polynomial $1.94t^3 - 5.12t^2 - 2.56t + 872$, where t is again the number of months since the start of the year. What polynomial models the profit for the company since the beginning of the year?

53. An artist uses painted ceramic blocks to decorate a wall. Each block is a cube with a cylindrical hole passing through it. The sketch below shows the relative dimensions of each block in inches. What polynomial models the volume of ceramic material needed for a block?

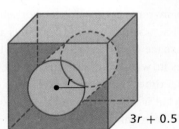

$3r + 0.5$

54. Two businesswomen opened a second coffee shop in their town at the beginning of the year. The profits, in dollars, from their first coffee shop can be modeled by the polynomial $12.4t^2 + 4.9t + 210$, where t is the number of weeks since the beginning of the year. The profits, in dollars, from the new coffee shop can be modeled by the polynomial $1.8t^2 + 6.6t + 105$, where t is again the number of weeks since the beginning of the year. What polynomial models the total profits for the two shops since the beginning of the year?

55. (MP) **Critique Reasoning** When solving a polynomial subtraction problem using the vertical format, Marsha made an error. What was her mistake? What is the correct answer?

$$(4x^2 + 2x + 9) - (x^2 - 2x + 3)$$

$$\begin{array}{r} 4x^2 + 2x + 9 \\ + (-x^2 - 2x + 3) \\ \hline 3x^2 + 12 \end{array} \quad \times$$

56. Alexa makes her own custom jewelry using beads she purchases at an arts and crafts store. She just purchased a large variety of wooden beads like the one shown at the right. There are several sizes, but the hole is the same diameter in all of them.

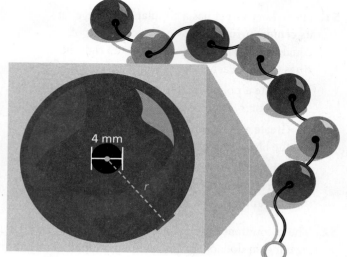

4 mm

A. Since the beads vary in size, let r represent the radius, in millimeters, of a bead. Use the volume formula for a cylinder to approximate the volume of wood that is removed from a bead when the hole is drilled. Leave your answer in terms of π.

B. Explain why your answer to Part A is only an approximation.

C. Create a polynomial that approximates the volume of wood in a bead.

D. What is the volume, to the nearest cubic millimeter, of the wood in a bead if its radius is 15 millimeters?

57. (**Open Middle™**) Using the integers −9 to 9, at most one time each, fill in the boxes to make a true statement.

$$\boxed{}\,x^3 + \boxed{}\,x + \boxed{} \quad \text{plus} \quad \boxed{}\,x^3 + \boxed{}\,x^2 + \boxed{}\,x - \boxed{}$$

$$\text{equals} \quad \boxed{}\,x^3 - \boxed{}\,x^2 + \boxed{}\,x + \boxed{}\,.$$

Spiral Review • Assessment Readiness

58. Which of these is equivalent to $(2y - 1)(3y + 5)$?

  Ⓐ $6y^2 - y - 5$ Ⓒ $5y^2 + 7y + 5$

  Ⓑ $6y^2 + 7y - 5$ Ⓓ $6y^2 + 2y - 5$

59. Match every polynomial with its degree.

  A. $2x^2y + 8$ **1.** 2

  B. $3x^3y^3 + x + 10$ **2.** 3

  C. $4x^2y^2$ **3.** 4

  D. $5xy + x + 6$ **4.** 6

60. A company rents cargo vans for household moves. The company's largest van has an interior space with height, in feet, that is 1.5 times its width and a length, in feet, that is 3.5 times the width. If the width is w feet, what is the volume of the interior of the truck in cubic feet?

  Ⓐ $6w$ Ⓒ $5.25w$

  Ⓑ $5.25w^3$ Ⓓ $6w^3$

⬡ **I'm in a Learning Mindset!**

How can I increase my performance at adding and subtracting polynomials by modifying my mindset?

Model with Polynomials

(I Can) model mathematical and real-world problems with polynomials.

Spark Your Learning

The chess club and the science club at a school have different numbers of members. The clubs have separate meetings.

Both club meetings begin with every club member shaking hands with each of the other club members.

Complete Part A as a whole class. Then complete Parts B–D in small groups.

- **A.** What is a mathematical question you can ask about this situation? What information would you need to know to answer your question?

- **B.** Can you use a visual model of the problem? Do you notice any patterns?

- **C.** To answer your question, what strategy and tool would you use along with all the information you have? What answer do you get?

- **D.** Does your answer make sense? How do you know?

  Turn and Talk What are the advantages of using a formula to find the total number of handshakes rather than counting?

©PeopleImages/E+/Getty Images

Build Understanding

Model Figurate Numbers

Figurate numbers, also known as polygonal numbers, are numbers that can be represented by evenly-spaced dots arranged in a geometric shape. Figurate numbers are commonly modeled with figures that have equal side lengths, such as equilateral triangles, squares, regular pentagons, and regular hexagons. Some figurate numbers can be generalized by a polynomial.

Triangular and square numbers can be represented by an arrangement of points in the shape of an equilateral triangle or square, respectively. The sequence of triangular and square numbers, as well as the polynomial expressions used to calculate the nth number in each sequence, are shown below.

Triangular numbers:

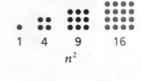

$$\frac{n(n+1)}{2}, \text{ or } \frac{1}{2}n^2 + \frac{1}{2}n$$

Square numbers:

n^2

1 The figures at the right combine the arrangements for triangular numbers and square numbers. The first four figurate numbers for this pattern are 1, 5, 12, and 22. The first arrangement (the single dot) is the first square number.

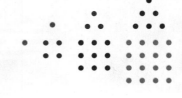

A. How are the second, third, and fourth arrangements formed using the triangular numbers and square numbers?

B. How can you use the polynomials that represent triangular and square numbers to create a polynomial expression that represents the pattern above? What is the expression?

C. Determine the fifth number in the pattern of figurate numbers above by creating a sketch and by using the polynomial expression you wrote in Part B.

 Turn and Talk What is a polynomial expression that represents the cube numbers, 1, 8, 27, 64, ...?

Step It Out

Model with Polynomials

The profit for any business is the difference between its revenue and its costs. If the revenue and the costs for a business are each represented by a polynomial, then the profit for the business is the difference of the two polynomials.

Profit ($)	=	Revenue ($)	−	Cost ($)

2 ▶ Millions of screen protectors for handheld electronic devices are produced and sold each year. A company that produces screen protectors has a revenue (in dollars) given by the polynomial $15x - 0.00001x^2$, where x is the number of screen protectors produced and sold. The cost (in dollars) of producing x screen protectors is $300,000 + 2x + 0.0000097x^2$. Determine the polynomial representing the profit from producing and selling x screen protectors. Then use the polynomial to calculate the profit from producing and selling 400,000 screen protectors.

Profit P	=	Revenue $15x - 0.00001x^2$	−	Cost $300,000 + 2x + 0.0000097x^2$

$P = (15x - 0.00001x^2) - (300,000 + 2x + 0.0000097x^2)$

$= 15x - 0.00001x^2 - 300,000 - 2x - 0.0000097x^2$

A. What property was used to remove the parentheses?

$= -0.00001x^2 - 0.0000097x^2 + 15x - 2x - 300,000$

$= (-0.00001 - 0.0000097)x^2 + (15 - 2)x - 300,000$

B. Why is it useful to write the terms in this order?

$= -0.0000197x^2 + 13x - 300,000$

The profit, in dollars, from producing and selling x screen protectors is represented by this polynomial:

$-0.0000197x^2 + 13x - 300,000$

To find the profit from producing and selling 400,000 screen protectors, evaluate the polynomial when $x = 400,000$:

$-0.0000197(400,000)^2 + 13(400,000) - 300,000 = \$1,748,000$

C. How could you calculate the profit from selling 400,000 screen protectors another way?

 Turn and Talk What is the profit when 0 screen protectors are sold? How can you interpret this?

Check Understanding

1. Write the polynomial expression that gives the number of dots in the nth figure in the sequence of figures shown below. Explain your answer.

2. The number of people in a shopping mall is determined by the rate that people are entering the mall, $p^2 - 2p + 30$, and the rate that people are leaving the mall, $p^2 + 2p + 3$, where p represents the number of people entering or leaving the mall per hour. Write an expression for the net change in the number of people in the mall per hour. What is the change in the number of people when the rate, p, is 3 people per hour?

On Your Own

3. (MP) **Critique Reasoning** John determined that the expression $n^2 + 2n + 1$ represents the sequence of figurate numbers 4, 9, 16, 25, ... Did John solve the problem correctly? Explain why or why not.

4. **STEM** A physicist measures the distance that a rock dropped from a tall bridge falls after $t = 0$ seconds, 1 second, 2 seconds, 3 seconds, and 4 seconds. The list of distances is shown below. Write a polynomial in t that models these distances.

   0, 16, 64, 144, 256

In graph theory, a graph is formed by dots (called vertices) and line segments connecting them (called edges). Use this information for Problems 5 and 6.

5. (MP) **Construct Arguments** In the sequence of graphs below, the vertices are arranged in the shape of a regular polygon, and an edge connects each pair of non-adjacent vertices. Create a polynomial that represents the number of edges in a graph with n vertices. Explain your reasoning.

6. In a complete graph, every pair of vertices is connected by an edge. How many edges are there in a complete graph with n vertices? Explain your reasoning.

7. In a baseball league, the players shake hands with the players of their own team and with the players of the opposing team after a game has ended. If one team has n players and the other team has m players, how many total handshakes are exchanged among the players after the game has ended?

8. The first terms of a sequence of figurate numbers are calculated as shown below.

$$3 = \frac{3(2)}{2} \qquad 3 + 6 = \frac{6(3)}{2} \qquad 3 + 6 + 9 = \frac{9(4)}{2} \qquad 3 + 6 + 9 + 12 = \frac{12(5)}{2}$$

What polynomial can model the nth term of this sequence?

9. The expressions for the cost and revenue from producing and selling x umbrellas are shown in the photo. What is the polynomial that models the profit from producing and selling x umbrellas?

10. STEM Selection sort is a method of sorting an array of numbers by repeatedly finding the minimum value of a list of numbers. Once the minimum value is found, it is removed and placed aside; then the minimum of the remaining numbers is found, and so on. The number of comparisons to sort n numbers in an array is $\frac{1}{2}n^2 - \frac{1}{2}n$, and the number of moves is $3n - 3$. What is the total number of operations (comparisons and moves) required to sort an array of n numbers?

Cost (\$): $100{,}000 + 3x$
Revenue (\$): $15x + 0.00002x^2$

11. Financial Literacy Suppose you invest \$1000 and at the end of the first year the investment has increased $r\%$ in value. Then during the second year, the investment decreases in value by $r\%$. Write a polynomial that represents the value of the investment after 2 years. Use your polynomial to explain why the value of the investment at the end of the second year is less than \$1000.

12. A company opened three new stores at the beginning of last year. Polynomials modeling the total revenue and total costs for each store are shown in the table below, where t is the time in months since the beginning of last year. Which company has the greatest profit?

Store	Revenue	Costs
A	$15t^3 + 7t^2 + 900$	$14t^3 + 5t^2 + 800$
B	$9t^3 + 11t^2 + 1100$	$3t^3 + 2t^2 - 800$
C	$24t^3 + 6t^2 - 700$	$22t^3 + 6t^2 + 800$

13. Open Ended Draw a series of four figures composed of dots, using a pattern. Determine the figurate numbers corresponding to your figures. Then write a polynomial that represents the nth figurate number.

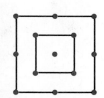

14. The first four figures representing numbers in the sequence of centered square numbers are shown at the right.

A. What are the first four centered square numbers?

B. The centered square numbers are the sums of consecutive square numbers. Recall that n^2 is used to calculate the nth square number. What polynomial represents the $(n + 1)$th square number?

C. Use the expression n^2 and your answer to Part B to write a polynomial that represents the nth centered square number. What is the 15th centered square number?

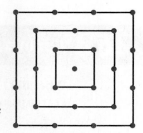

15. Create a polynomial that gives the number of dots in the *n*th figure of the sequence of figures below.

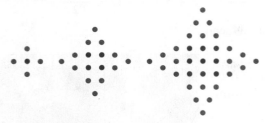

16. A sequence of pentagonal dot arrangements is shown below.

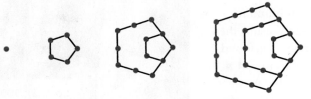

    A. Use the figures to write the first four pentagonal numbers.

    B. The *n*th pentagonal number is given by a polynomial of the form $an^2 + bn$. Write and solve a system of equations to find the values of *a* and *b*.

    C. What is a polynomial for the *n*th pentagonal number?

    D. What is the 20th pentagonal number?

Spiral Review • Assessment Readiness

17. What is the product of $3x^2$ and $2 - x$?

    Ⓐ $6x^2 - 3x$ Ⓒ $-3x^3 + 6x^2$

    Ⓑ $3x^3$ Ⓓ $3x$

18. Which expression gives the area of a room with a width of $(x - 3)$ feet and a length of $(x + 3)$ feet?

    Ⓐ $(x^2 - 3)$ ft^2 Ⓒ $(x^2 + 3)$ ft^2

    Ⓑ $(x^2 - 9)$ ft^2 Ⓓ $(x^2 + 9)$ ft^2

19. Which sums are equal to $-2n^2 + 3$? Select all that apply.

    Ⓐ $(4n - 2) + (-2n - 1)$

    Ⓑ $(-8n^2 + 6) + (6n^2 - 3)$

    Ⓒ $(3n^3 - n^2 + 1) + (-3n^3 - n^2 + 2)$

    Ⓓ $(9n^2 + n - 4) + (-11n^2 - n + 7)$

20. What is the end behavior of the linear function $f(x) = -x + 4$ as $x \to +\infty$?

    Ⓐ $f(x) \to +\infty$ Ⓒ $f(x) \to 0$

    Ⓑ $f(x) \to 4$ Ⓓ $f(x) \to -\infty$

I'm in a Learning Mindset!

What did I learn about modeling real-world situations using polynomials that I can use in my future learning?

Module 16 Review

Add and Subtract Polynomials

Adding and subtracting polynomials requires identifying *like terms*. Like terms have the same variable(s) raised to the same exponent(s).

When adding like terms, use the Distributive Property:

$$
\begin{aligned}
&-3x^4y^2 + 9x^4y^2 \\
&\quad = (-3 + 9)x^4y^2 \\
&\quad = 6x^4y^2
\end{aligned}
$$

Add the coefficients.

Subtracting polynomials involves changing to addition and using the opposites of the coefficients of the polynomial being subtracted.

$$
\begin{aligned}
&(9x^3 + 5x^2 - 6x - 1) - (-3x^3 + x^2 - 4) \\
&\quad = (9x^3 + 5x^2 - 6x - 1) + (+3x^3 - x^2 + 4) \\
&\quad = (9x^3 + 3x^3) + \left(5x^2 + (-x^2)\right) - 6x + (-1 + 4) \\
&\quad = (9 + 3)x^3 + (5 - 1)x^2 - 6x + (-1 + 4) \\
&\quad = 12x^3 + 4x^2 - 6x + 3
\end{aligned}
$$

Closure Under Addition and Subtraction

The set of polynomials is closed under addition and subtraction, which means that sums and difference of polynomials are still polynomials. Subsets of the set of polynomials may or may not be closed under addition and subtraction, as shown in the following examples.

$$(3x^2 + 2) - (x^2 + 2x + 1) = 2x^2 - 2x + 1$$

The result is a polynomial.

The set of monomials in one variable that have the same degree is closed under addition and subtraction.

$$3x^2 + 6x^2 = 9x^2$$

The result is a monomial.

The set of binomials in one variable is not closed under addition and subtraction.

$$(4x + 1) + (2x - 1) = 6x$$

The result may not be a binomial.

Figurate Numbers

A figurate number is a number that can be represented by equally spaced dots in a geometric arrangement. The first four figurate numbers in a sequence are shown below.

Because each figurate number is composed of a square number given by the polynomial n^2 for $n \geq 1$ and two triangular numbers given by the polynomial $\frac{1}{2}n^2 + \frac{1}{2}n$ for $n \geq 1$, the polynomial that gives the nth number in the sequence 3, 10, 21, 36, . . . is

$$n^2 + 2\left(\tfrac{1}{2}n^2 + \tfrac{1}{2}n\right) = 2n^2 + n \text{ for } n \geq 1.$$

So, the fifth number in the sequence is $2(5)^2 + 5 = 50 + 5 = 55$.

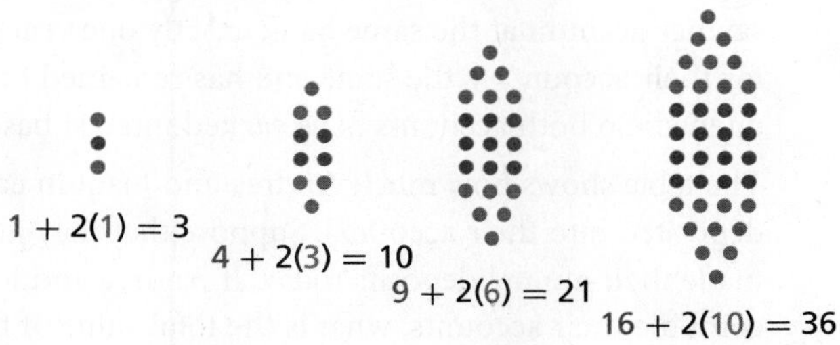

1 + 2(1) = 3
4 + 2(3) = 10
9 + 2(6) = 21
16 + 2(10) = 36

Vocabulary

Choose the correct term from the box to complete each sentence.

1. An expression with three terms is called a ___?___.

2. $3x^2$ and $-4x^2$ are ___?___.

3. A ___?___ is an expression that has a single term.

4. The expression $5w^3 + 4w$ is a ___?___ that has a ___?___ of 5 and a ___?___ of 3.

Concepts and Skills

Simplify each expression.

5. $-4x^2 + 3x^2$

6. $2x^3yz + 4x^3yz$

7. $\left(4xy^2 - 3xy + 2x^2\right) + \left(2xy^2 + 5xy - 2x^2\right)$

8. $\left(3x^2 - 4x - 5\right) + \left(2x^2 + 2x - 2\right)$

9. $\left(5x^2y + 2xy - 5\right) - \left(2x^2y + 2xy + 12\right)$

10. $\left(2z^3 + 3z - 1\right) - \left(6z^2 + z + 4\right)$

11. Collin is building a storage shed for his backyard. He found plans for a shed that allow him to decide on a size that fits his needs. A diagram of the shed shown in the plans is at the right. Write a polynomial that represents the volume of the shed.

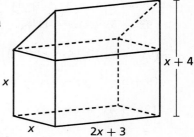

12. Show that when you add $4x^2 + 2x - 6$ and $-3x^2 + 6x + 10$ the sum is still a polynomial.

13. The first three figurate numbers in a sequence are represented by the geometric dot arrangements at the right. The arrangements are formed using the first three triangular numbers and the first three square numbers.

    A. What are the three figurate numbers represented here?

    B. Write a polynomial that represents the total number of dots needed for the *n*th figurate number in the sequence.

    C. What is the 12th number in the sequence.

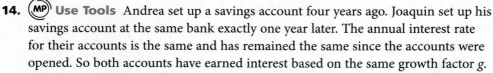

14. (MP) **Use Tools** Andrea set up a savings account four years ago. Joaquin set up his savings account at the same bank exactly one year later. The annual interest rate for their accounts is the same and has remained the same since the accounts were opened. So both accounts have earned interest based on the same growth factor *g*.

    The table shows how much Andrea and Joaquin each deposited into their accounts. Suppose that they just made their annual deposits today. If Andrea and Joaquin combine their accounts, what is the total value of the combined account in terms of *g*? What is the value of the account in dollars if $g = 1.03$? State what strategy and tool you will use to answer the question, explain your choice, and then find the answer.

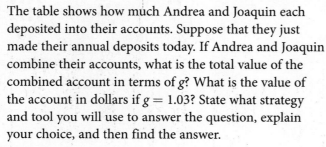

	Initial deposit	Amount of annual deposit
Andrea	$1000	$1000
Joaquin	$750	$750

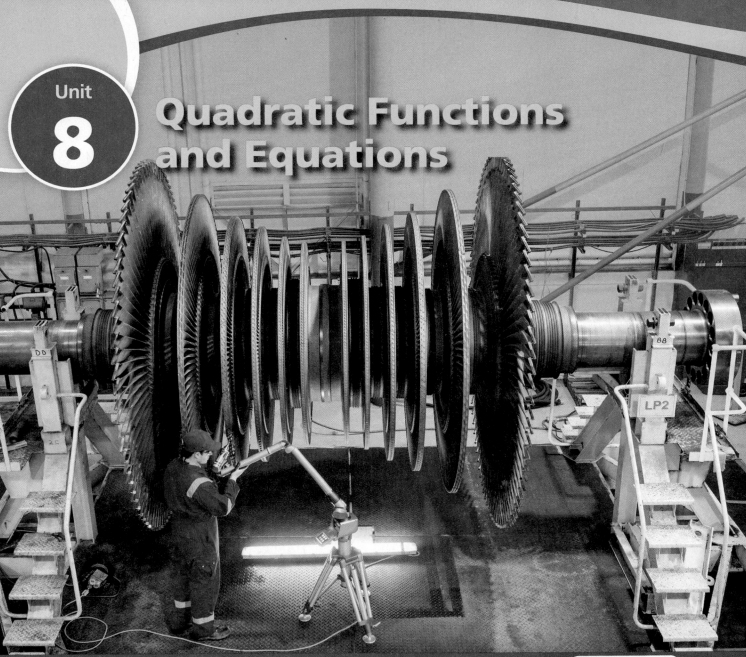

Quadratic Functions and Equations

Mechanical Engineer

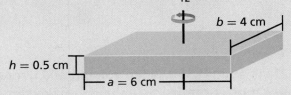

Mechanical engineers are involved in the development of a wide range of products and require a broad knowledge base. They must research and assess project requirements during the development phase and then design, prototype, and test their product. In order to ensure that the final product is durable, mechanical engineers must analyze how it reacts to different stresses.

STEM Task

The moment of inertia of an object describes its resistance to changes in its rotational motion. For a thin rectangular prism with mass M in grams, $I = \frac{1}{12}M(a^2 + b^2)$.

The rectangular prism above has a density of 42 g/cm³ and is to be rotated about an axis through its center. Calculate its moment of inertia.

©adventtr/E+/Getty Image

How do you know that your plan is going to help you meet your learning goals? As you approach a new topic, developing a clear plan will aid you in your path to success. Planning ahead requires an understanding of the learning outcomes, deliverable products, and the overall time allotment for the task. Breaking the task into smaller parts and setting a timeline for each part will make your plan more manageable. Writing down your plan and sharing it with others is a great way to keep yourself accountable. Here are some questions you can ask yourself to help you plan to meet your learning goals:

- What are my current learning goals? Are my goals attainable? If not, how can I refine them?

- What action steps do I need to complete in order to master quadratic functions?

- What factors can I use to establish timelines for my goals?

- What social factors impact my goals?

- How will I know when my goal is met successfully?

Reflect

Q Think about times when you did and did not plan ahead. How can you use those experiences to help you develop plans for your current goals?

Q What does a mechanical engineer need to incorporate into his or her planning process to ensure that the final product is successful?

Use Graphing and Factoring to Solve Quadratic Equations

Module Performance Task: *Spies and Analysts*™

Air Melon

Where would the watermelon land?

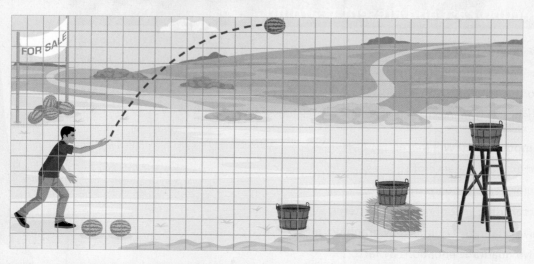

Are You Ready?

Complete these problems to review prior concepts and skills you will need for this module.

Factor Linear Expressions

Factor out the greatest common factor from each expression.

1. $2x - 8$

2. $9x - 81$

3. $25x - 5$

4. $14x + 35$

5. $24x + 36$

6. $12x + 20$

Solve Two-Step Equations

Solve each equation.

7. $3x - 1 = 8$

8. $6(x + 4) = 18$

9. $5(x - 3) = 30$

10. $4x + 5 = 21$

11. $3(x + 2) = -3$

12. $8x - 34 = 6$

Multiply Binomials

Determine each binomial product.

13. $(3x + 2)(x - 4)$

14. $(x - 4)(3x - 1)$

15. $(2x - 5)^2$

16. $(5x + 1)^2$

17. $(6x - 1)(6x + 1)$

18. $(-2x + 3)(-2x - 3)$

Connecting Past and Present Learning

Previously, you learned:

- to develop polynomials to model figurate numbers,
- to model with polynomials, and
- to algebraically manipulate polynomial expressions.

In this module, you will learn:

- to factor the difference of squares,
- to factor perfect square trinomials,
- to factor using special factoring patterns,
- to solve quadratic equations by graphing, and
- to solve quadratic equations by factoring.

Solve Quadratic Equations by Graphing Quadratic Functions

(I Can) understand the key features of the graph of a quadratic function and solve quadratic equations approximately by graphing.

Spark Your Learning

A rectangular area of a lawn needs to be covered with sod.

There are 4 skids. There is enough sod on each skid to cover about 400 square feet.

Complete Part A as a whole class. Then complete Parts B–D in small groups.

A. What is a mathematical question you can ask about this situation? What information would you need to know to answer your question?

B. What variable(s) are needed in this situation? What must be true of the values for the variable(s) in this question?

C. To answer your question, what strategy and tool would you use along with all the information you have? What answer do you get?

D. Does your answer make sense in the context of the situation? How do you know?

Turn and Talk Predict how your answer would change for each of the following changes in the situation:
- Another skid of sod is used.
- The width and length are equal.
- The length is 20 feet longer than the width.

Build Understanding

Graph Quadratic Functions of the Form $f(x) = ax^2 + bx$

A **quadratic function** is a function that can be written in the form $f(x) = ax^2 + bx + c$, where a, b, and c are real numbers and $a \neq 0$. The graph of a quadratic function is called a **parabola**. The **vertex of a parabola**, or turning point, is the highest or lowest point on the parabola. Recall that an x-intercept is the x-coordinate of a point where a graph intersects the x-axis. Also recall that an axis of symmetry, or *line of symmetry*, is a line that divides a plane figure or a graph into two congruent reflected halves.

1 ▶ The graph of the quadratic function $f(x) = 2x^2 - 4x$ is shown.

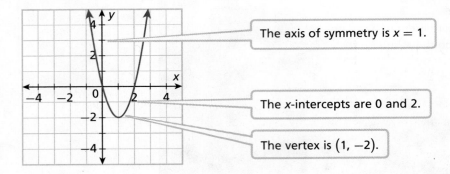

The axis of symmetry is $x = 1$.

The x-intercepts are 0 and 2.

The vertex is $(1, -2)$.

A. Explain why f satisfies the definition of a quadratic function.

Using the key features of the graph of f, you will draw and analyze the graph of another quadratic function, $g(x) = 3x^2 - 12x$.

B. Use a table of x-values from -2 to 8 and the corresponding $g(x)$-values to plot points on the graph of g in a coordinate plane. Then connect the points with a smooth curve to obtain a parabola. Describe the shape of the parabola. Which direction does it open?

C. Identify the x-intercepts of the graph of g.

D. Determine the coordinates of the vertex of the graph of g. For this parabola, is the vertex the highest or lowest point?

E. Draw the axis of symmetry on the graph and indicate its equation. How is this line related to the vertex?

F. Notice that the rule for g, $3x^2 - 12x$, has two terms with a common factor of $3x$. You can use the Distributive Property to rewrite $3x^2 - 12x$ as $3x(x - 4)$. Because it gives the function's rule as a product of factors, $g(x) = 3x(x - 4)$ is called the *factored form* of g. How does the factored form make identifying the x-intercepts easier?

G. How could you use the x-intercepts to find the axis of symmetry?

 Turn and Talk What are the domain and range of the function f whose graph is shown above?

Graph Quadratic Functions of the Form $f(x) = ax^2 + bx + c$

 2 The function $g(x) = 2x^2 - 4x - 2$, whose graph is shown below in red, is related to the function $f(x) = 2x^2 - 4x$ from Task 1, whose graph is shown below in blue.

A. Was the graph of f translated up or down to create the graph of g?

B. Write $g(x)$ in terms of $f(x)$. How does this confirm what you observed about the graphs in Part A?

C. What are the approximate x-intercepts of the graph of g? Are these the same as the x-intercepts of the graph of f? When you translate a quadratic function vertically, are the x-intercepts affected?

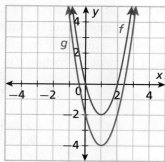

D. What is the axis of symmetry of the graph of g? Compare this to the axis of symmetry of the graph of f. When you translate a quadratic function vertically, is the axis of symmetry affected?

E. What is the vertex of the graph of g? Compare this to the vertex of the graph of f. When you translate a quadratic function vertically, how is the vertex affected?

 Turn and Talk How are the domain and range of a quadratic function affected by a vertical translation?

Graph Quadratic Functions of the Form $f(x) = -\left(ax^2 + bx + c\right)$

 3 Suppose you multiply $g(x) = 2x^2 - 4x - 2$ by -1 to get $h(x) = -\left(2x^2 - 4x - 2\right)$. The graph of g is shown below in red and the graph of h is shown below in green.

A. How are the graphs of g and h related?

B. Identify which of the key features of a parabola listed below are affected when $g(x)$ is multiplied by -1 to get $h(x) = -g(x)$. Explain.

- x-intercepts
- axis of symmetry
- vertex
- direction parabola opens

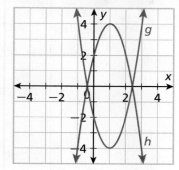

 Turn and Talk How are the domain and range of a quadratic function affected by multiplying the function by -1?

Step It Out

Solve Quadratic Equations Graphically

A **zero** of a function f is any number x such that $f(x) = 0$. The zeros of a function are the x-intercepts of the graph of the function. For the quadratic function $f(x) = ax^2 + bx + c$, any zero of the function satisfies the equation $ax^2 + bx + c = 0$. Therefore, to solve the quadratic equation $ax^2 + bx + c = 0$, identify any x-intercepts on the graph of the related function $f(x) = ax^2 + bx + c$.

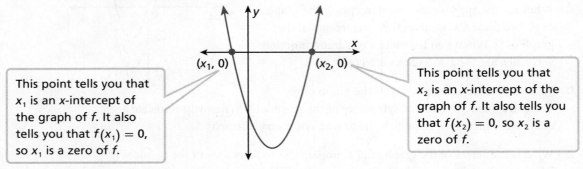

This point tells you that x_1 is an x-intercept of the graph of f. It also tells you that $f(x_1) = 0$, so x_1 is a zero of f.

This point tells you that x_2 is an x-intercept of the graph of f. It also tells you that $f(x_2) = 0$, so x_2 is a zero of f.

It is important to understand that any solution acquired from a graph must be considered an approximate solution unless it is verified by substitution to be an exact solution.

4 Solve $3x^2 - 18x + 15 = 0$ graphically.

The solutions of the equation are the zeros of the function $f(x) = 3x^2 - 18x + 15$, which are graphically represented by the x-intercepts.

Graph $f(x) = 3x^2 - 18x + 15$ using a graphing calculator. Based on the graph, the x-intercepts appear to be 1 and 5.

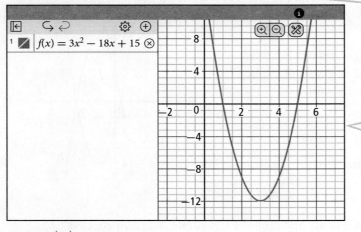

A. How do you know that these are the only x-intercepts?

B. How do you determine an appropriate viewing window when graphing the function?

$f(1) = 3(1^2) - 18(1) + 15 = 3 - 18 + 15 = 0$

$f(5) = 3(5^2) - 18(5) + 15 = 75 - 90 + 15 = 0$

The solutions are 1 and 5.

 Turn and Talk Is it possible for a quadratic equation to have no solution or only one solution? If so, describe the graph of the related quadratic function.

Solve Real-World Quadratic Equations Graphically

The distance that a falling object travels over time due to gravity can be modeled by the quadratic function $d(t) = 16t^2$, where d is the distance in feet and t is the time in seconds since the object begins falling.

5 A professional cliff-diving competition uses a platform that can be set to a range of heights. Use the function $d(t) = 16t^2$ to determine the time it would take for a diver to reach the water from the platform height shown.

Since the total distance the diver must fall to the water is 65 feet, solve the equation $65 = 16t^2$.

Write the quadratic equation as $65 - 16t^2 = 0$, and graph the related function $f(t) = 65 - 16t^2$.

A. Knowing that 65 is the diver's initial height and $16t^2$ is the distance that the diver has fallen at time t, what does $65 - 16t^2$ represent?

The platform height is set at 65 ft.

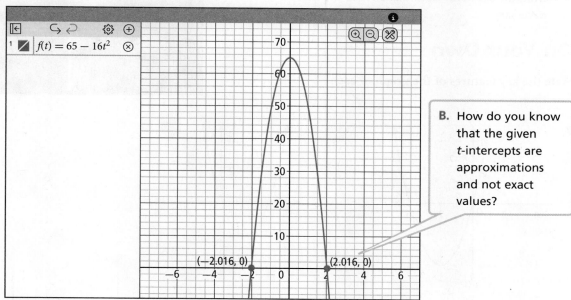

B. How do you know that the given t-intercepts are approximations and not exact values?

Based on the graph, the t-intercepts are about -2 and 2.

The solutions of the equation $65 = 16t^2$ are $t \approx -2$ and $t \approx 2$.

The solution $t \approx -2$ is not valid in this situation.

C. Why is the solution $t \approx -2$ not valid?

Therefore, it takes about 2 seconds for the diver to reach the water.

Turn and Talk How long would it take for a diver to reach the water if the platform was at 85 feet? Round to the nearest tenth if necessary.

Check Understanding

1. A quadratic function of the form $f(x) = ax^2 + bx$ has an x-intercept at $x = -6$. What could be the equation of this function? Is there more than one function that could be used to answer this question? Explain.

2. What are the similarities and differences between the graphs of $f(x) = 5x^2 + 3x$ and $g(x) = 5x^2 + 3x + 4$?

3. How are the graphs of $f(x) = 2x^2 - 5x + 2$ and $g(x) = -2x^2 + 5x - 2$ related?

4. Find the x-intercepts of the graph of $f(x) = 2x^2 + 6x - 36$.

5. How long does it take for an object dropped from 144 feet to reach the ground?

6. The Grand Canyon Skywalk is a cantilevered bridge with a glass walkway. It was opened to the general public in March of 2007. How long would it take an object to hit the canyon floor if it were to be accidentally dropped from the skywalk? Round answer to the nearest tenth if necessary.

720 feet

On Your Own

State the key features of the graph of each function.

7.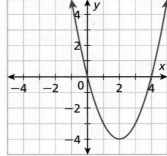

8.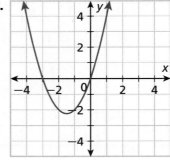

Graph each function to determine its zeros.

9. $f(x) = x^2 + 3x + 2$

10. $f(x) = x^2 - 9$

11. $f(x) = x^2 + 5x$

12. $f(x) = x^2 + 8x + 16$

13. $f(x) = x^2 - x - 12$

14. $f(x) = -x^2 + 5x - 6$

15. $f(x) = 2x^2 - 10x - 28$

16. $f(x) = 3x^2 + 18x - 81$

17. $f(x) = 4x^2 - 12x$

18. $f(x) = -x^2 - 8x - 7$

19. $f(x) = -3x^2 - 6x + 144$

20. $f(x) = -2x^2 - 2x + 60$

21. The graph of $f(x) = x^2 + 2x$ is shown.

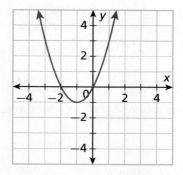

A. Copy the graph on a blank coordinate plane and draw the graph of $g(x) = f(x) - 3$. What are the key features of the graph of g?

B. On the same coordinate plane from Part A, draw the graph of $h(x) = -g(x)$. What are the key features of the graph of h?

22. (MP) **Critical Thinking** A quadratic function has a minimum value when the function's graph opens upward and a maximum value when the graph opens downward. What can you say about a when $f(x) = ax^2$ has a minimum value? a maximum value?

23. (MP) **Use Repeated Reasoning** Jackson wants to determine the x-values for which the two functions $f(x) = x^2 - 4x + 11$ and $g(x) = 3x - 1$ are equal.

A. Write an equation that he can use to solve the problem. Explain your answer.

B. Write the equation from Part A in the form $ax^2 + bx + c = 0$.

C. Use a graphing calculator with the equation you wrote in Part B to solve the problem.

24. (MP) **Construct Arguments** Cynthia was asked to solve the equation $x^2 + 2x + 2 = 0$ but is unsure what to do next, as she cannot find a viewing window where the graph of $f(x) = x^2 + 2x + 2$ crosses the x-axis. What does this mean in terms of the question she has been asked to solve? Explain.

25. A snowboarder sitting in a lift chair dropped her glove.

A. What equation can you use to determine how long it takes for the glove to reach the ground?

B. Use a graph to find all solutions of the equation. Round to the nearest tenth if necessary.

C. How long does it take for the glove to reach the ground? Is the solution exact or an approximation? Explain your answer.

D. How could you improve the precision of the solution?

40 ft

26. An apple is hanging from a tree 25 feet above the ground.

A. What equation can you use to determine how long it takes for the apple to reach the ground when it falls?

B. Find all solutions to the equation.

C. How long does it take for the apple to reach the ground when it falls?

27. A rectangular garden has an area of 400 square feet. The garden is 10 feet longer than it is wide.

A. What equation can you write to model this situation? Define any variables that you use.

B. Rewrite your equation from Part A in the form $ax^2 + bx + c = 0$.

C. Use a graph to find all solutions to the equation. Round to the nearest tenth if necessary.

D. What are the approximate dimensions of the garden?

E. Are there solutions to the equation that are not solutions to the problem? Explain.

28. Open Ended Use a graphing calculator to help you write three quadratic equations: one with no solutions, one with exactly one solution, and one with two solutions.

29. (**Open Middle**™) Using the integers -9 to 9, at most one time each, fill in the boxes to create a quadratic function and identify the x-intercepts and the vertex of the function's graph.

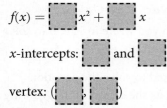

$$f(x) = \boxed{}\, x^2 + \boxed{}\, x$$

x-intercepts: $\boxed{}$ and $\boxed{}$

vertex: $(\,\boxed{}\,,\,\boxed{}\,)$

Spiral Review • Assessment Readiness

30. The cost for a school fundraiser is defined by the polynomial $x^2 + 3x + 2$ and the revenue is defined by the polynomial $2x^2 + x$. Which polynomial represents the profit?

Ⓐ $-x^2 + 2x + 2$　　Ⓒ $3x^2 + 4x + 2$

Ⓑ $x^2 - 2x - 2$　　Ⓓ $-3x^2 - 4x - 2$

31. Which expressions simplify to $16x^2y + 4xy$? Select all that apply.

Ⓐ $4x(xy + y)$　　Ⓓ $4(4x^2y + xy)$

Ⓑ $16(x^2y + xy)$　　Ⓔ $2x^2y(8x + 2y)$

Ⓒ $4xy(4x + 1)$　　Ⓕ $2y(8x^2 + 2x)$

32. Match the expressions with their correct simplified expressions.

A. $x^2 - 4 + (2x^2 + 3)$　　　　**1.** $-2xy - 8y$

B. $3x^2 + xy - 6y - (3x^2 + 3xy + 2y)$　　**2.** $3x^2 + x - 1$

C. $2x^2 + 6x + 7 + (x^2 - 5x - 8)$　　**3.** $3x^2 - 1$

D. $3x^2y - 9y - (5x^2y - y)$　　　**4.** $-2x^2y - 8y$

I'm in a Learning Mindset!

What are my action steps to solve quadratic equations using their graphs?

Solve Quadratic Equations by Factoring $x^2 + bx + c$

(I Can) use the Zero Product Property to solve quadratic equations in standard form with a leading coefficient of 1.

Spark Your Learning

A contractor needs to determine the length, in yards, of a rectangular foundation to cover with gravel.

The area of the rectangular foundation can be represented by $x^2 + 30x$ where x is the width in yards.

Complete Part A as a whole class. Then complete Parts B–D in small groups.

A. What is a mathematical question you can ask about this situation? What information would you need to know to answer your question?

B. How can you represent the information you know with an equation?

C. To answer your question, what strategy and tool would you use along with all the information you have? What answer do you get?

D. Does your answer make sense in the context of the situation? How do you know?

 Turn and Talk Predict how your answer would change for each of the following changes in the situation:

- The length needs to be 50 yards longer than the width.
- The length and the width need to be equal.
- The area of the foundation needs to be 100 square yards greater.

Build Understanding

Factor Quadratic Expressions of the Form $x^2 + bx$

The greatest common factor (GCF) of an expression is the product of the greatest integer and the greatest power of each variable that divide evenly into each monomial of the expression.

An expression such as $x^2 + 3x$ can be factored using a common factor. Each term in the expression has a common factor of x because each term is divisible by x.

$$x^2 + 3x = x \cdot x + 3 \cdot x$$
$$= x(x + 3)$$

Factoring enables you to rewrite an expression in an equivalent form that can reveal properties of the quantity the expression represents.

1 ▷ A developer wants to construct buildings on different-sized square lots in a city. The city has a setback rule that requires buildings to be a minimum distance from the street. The development company plans to use the entire area that it is allowed to build on.

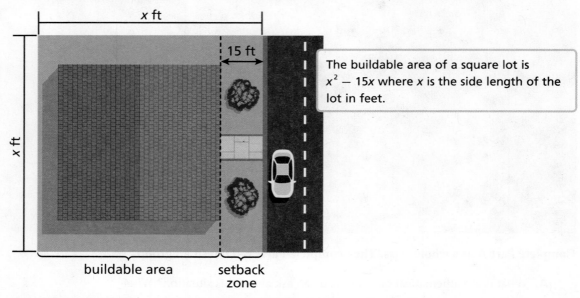

The buildable area of a square lot is $x^2 - 15x$ where x is the side length of the lot in feet.

buildable area   setback zone

A. What do the expressions x^2 and $15x$ represent in this context?

B. What is the greatest common factor of x^2 and $15x$?

C. Write the factored form for the buildable area on a square lot in the city. What does each factor of the expression represent in this context?

D. What is the minimum number of feet that the building must be set back from the street? What restriction does this place on the side length of a lot that can be built on?

E. If the developer chooses to construct a building on a square lot with a side length of 60 feet, what is the maximum area of one floor of the building?

 Turn and Talk What is the factored form of $x^2 + bx$?

Factor Quadratic Expressions of the Form $x^2 + bx + c$

The Distributive Property can be used to expand the product $(x + p)(x + q)$. The result is a quadratic expression of the form $x^2 + bx + c$, where b is the sum of the constants p and q and c is the product of p and q.

$$\overset{x^2 \qquad pq}{(x + p)(x + q)} = x^2 + (p + q)x + pq$$
$$\underset{qx}{px}$$
$$x^2 + bx + c$$

The goal of factoring is to reverse this process by starting with the quadratic expression $x^2 + bx + c$ and finding integer values of p and q so that $x^2 + bx + c = (x + p)(x + q)$.

2 Suppose you want to write $x^2 + 8x + 12$ in the factored form $(x + p)(x + q)$.

A. Identify the value of c. Since c is the product of p and q, find all the factor pairs of c.

B. Identify the value of b. Since b is the sum of p and q, find the pair of factors p and q that have a sum of b.

C. Write $x^2 + 8x + 12$ in factored form. Multiply the factors to check your answer.

D. How can you use the factor pairs you found in Part A to factor $x^2 - 8x + 12$? What is the factored form of this expression?

E. Suppose you want to factor an expression $x^2 + bx + c$ where $c < 0$, such as $x^2 + x - 12$. What must be true about the signs of p and q in this case? What is the factored form of $x^2 + x - 12$?

F. Consider the expression $x^2 - 5x - 12$. Can you write this expression in factored form $(x + p)(x + q)$ where p and q are integers? Explain.

 Turn and Talk Describe how the process for factoring an expression $x^2 + bx + c$ depends on the signs of b and c. Consider each of the following cases.

- $b > 0$ and $c > 0$
- $b < 0$ and $c > 0$
- $b > 0$ and $c < 0$
- $b < 0$ and $c < 0$

Step It Out

Solve Quadratic Equations Using the Zero Product Property

A quadratic equation $ax^2 + bx + c = 0$ is said to be written in **standard form**. In this lesson, all equations have the form $x^2 + bx + c = 0$ (that is, the value of a is 1). You can use factoring to solve such an equation by writing it as $(x + p)(x + q) = 0$ and then applying the Zero Product Property.

> ### Zero Product Property
>
> Let A and B be real numbers or algebraic expressions. If $AB = 0$, then $A = 0$ or $B = 0$.

3 Solve the equation $x^2 + 5x = 6$ algebraically, and check the solution.

Write the equation in standard form.

$x^2 + 5x - 6 = 0$

> **A.** Why is solving the equation $x^2 + 5x - 6 = 0$ equivalent to solving $x^2 + 5x = 6$?

Factor the quadratic expression.

$(x + 6)(x - 1) = 0$

> **B.** How does factoring the expression $x^2 + 5x - 6$ help you solve the equation?

Apply the Zero Product Property.

$x + 6 = 0$	or	$x - 1 = 0$
$x = -6$	or	$x = 1$

Check each solution.

Check $x = -6$:

$$x^2 + 5x = 6$$
$$(-6)^2 + 5(-6) \overset{?}{=} 6$$
$$36 - 30 \overset{?}{=} 6$$
$$6 = 6 \checkmark$$

Check $x = 1$:

$$x^2 + 5x = 6$$
$$(1)^2 + 5(1) \overset{?}{=} 6$$
$$1 + 5 \overset{?}{=} 6$$
$$6 = 6 \checkmark$$

> **C.** How do the solutions appear when $f(x) = x^2 + 5x$ and $g(x) = 6$ are graphed together?

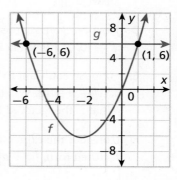

State the solution.

The solutions of the equation $x^2 + 5x = 6$ are $x = -6$ and $x = 1$.

> **D.** How would the solutions appear in the graph of $h(x) = x^2 + 5x - 6$?

 Turn and Talk Does a quadratic equation always have two solutions? Explain.

Solve Real-World Quadratic Equations

4 Tia is contracted to expand a rectangular deck that currently measures 10 feet by 6 feet. Two sides of the deck are up against the house. Tia plans to increase the length and width of the deck by the same amount so that the deck's new area is 165 square feet. By how much does she need to increase the length and width of the deck?

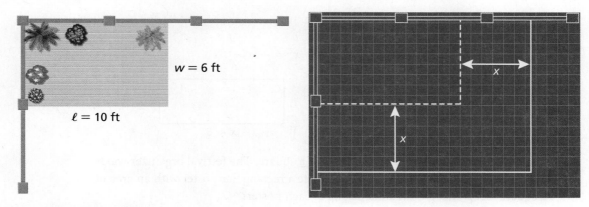

$w = 6$ ft

$\ell = 10$ ft

Use a verbal model.

New deck length (ft)			New deck width (ft)		New deck area (ft²)
Increase in length (ft)	Current deck length (ft)		Increase in width (ft)	Current deck width (ft)	New deck area (ft²)
x	10		x	6	165

The verbal model reads: (Increase in length + Current deck length) · (Increase in width + Current deck width) = New deck area

Write an equation.

$(x + 10)(x + 6) = 165$

Solve the equation.

$x^2 + 16x + 60 = 165$

$x^2 + 16x - 105 = 0$

$(x + 21)(x - 5) = 0$

$x + 21 = 0$ or $x - 5 = 0$

$x = -21$ or $x = 5$

> **A.** Why is it important to place grouping boxes around the new length and new width?

> **B.** Why can't the Zero Product Property be applied here even though the left side is factored?

> **C.** What strategies could you use to factor $x^2 + 16x - 105$?

> **D.** Why doesn't the negative solution make sense in this context?

Answer the question.

Tia should increase the length and width of the deck by 5 feet so that the new dimensions are 15 feet by 11 feet.

 Turn and Talk Create a function that would allow you to solve the problem by finding the x-intercepts of its graph. Draw the graph and label the x-intercepts.

Check Understanding

1. Identify the greatest common factor of the expressions x^2 and $5x$.

Factor each expression.

2. $x^2 - 2x$ **3.** $x^2 + 7x + 10$ **4.** $x^2 + 3x - 4$

Solve each equation algebraically.

5. $x^2 + 6x + 8 = 0$ **6.** $x^2 = -8x - 16$

7. The rectangle shown has an area of 84 square inches. Find the dimensions of the rectangle.

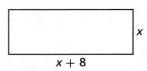

x

$x + 8$

8. A poster for a film festival is in the shape of a square. The festival organizer wants to increase the dimensions as shown to create a rectangular poster with an area of 72 square feet. What are the dimensions of each poster?

Before:

x ft

x ft

After:

$(x + 3)$ ft

$(x + 4)$ ft

On Your Own

One dimension of each rectangle is x in. Factor the expression for the rectangle's area to find the other dimension.

9.

$A = x^2 + 8x$ in.^{2}

10.

$A = x^2 - 6x$ in.^{2}

11. In the rectangles above, what would be the restriction on the variable?

Factor each quadratic expression.

12. $x^2 - 7x + 6$ **13.** $x^2 + 7x + 12$

14. $x^2 + 5x + 6$ **15.** $x^2 - 14x + 48$

16. $x^2 + 8x + 15$ **17.** $x^2 + 10x + 16$

Solve each equation.

18. $x^2 + 8x + 15 = 0$

19. $x^2 + 4x - 12 = 0$

20. $x^2 = 3x + 10$

21. $x^2 + x = 12$

22. $x^2 + 9x + 4 = -10$

23. $x^2 - 5x = 24$

24. (MP) **Critique Reasoning** Wendy attempted to solve for the x-intercepts of the graph of $f(x) = x^2 + 8x + 10$, but she could not factor the expression $x^2 + 8x + 10$ using integers. She concluded that this means the graph of the function does not cross the x-axis. Is her conclusion correct? Explain.

25. A hammock holder can be modeled by the quadratic function shown, where $h(x)$ represents the height in inches off of the ground and x represents the horizontal distance in feet from the left supporting leg of the holder.

A. What does the value $h(0)$ represent in this context?

B. What is the height of the right supporting leg? Write an equation that you can use to find the location on the x-axis of the right supporting leg.

C. How far apart are the supporting legs of the hammock holder?

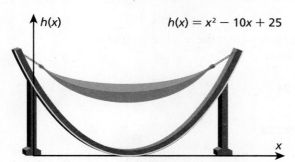

$h(x) = x^2 - 10x + 25$

26. **Open Ended** Give an example of a quadratic expression that can be factored using integers and an example of a quadratic expression that cannot be factored using integers. Explain.

27. (MP) **Model with Mathematics** A roped-off swimming area on a beach is shaped like a rectangle with the shore as one side. The owners of a beachfront resort want to increase the size of the swimming area by adding x yards to the width and $2x$ yards to the length.

The width of the swimming area is 20 yards and the length is 30 yards.

A. Write expressions for the length and width of the swimming area after the increase.

B. What value of x will result in an area of 1000 square yards for the new swimming area? What will be the new dimensions of the swimming area?

©krolya25/Shutterstock

28. Trevor has a square piece of wood that measures x inches on each side. To make a piece with the dimensions he needs, he plans on cutting 3 inches off of one side to form a rectangle.

  A. Draw and label a diagram of the rectangular piece of wood. In terms of x, what are the dimensions of the rectangular piece of wood Trevor has made?

  B. Write an expression representing the area of the piece of wood.

  C. Write an equation you can use to find the dimensions of the rectangular piece of wood, given that the area is 54 square inches.

  D. What are the dimensions of the rectangular piece of wood?

29. (MP) **Use Tools** The area of the shaded region is 16 square meters. What is the value of x in meters? State what strategy and tool you will use to answer the question, explain your choice, and then find the answer.

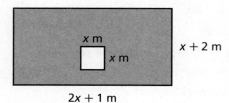

30. (**Open Middle™**) Using any integer, fill in the box so that the quadratic expression is factorable using integers. Find all possible values.

$$x^2 + \boxed{}\,x - 24$$

Spiral Review • Assessment Readiness

31. Which of the expressions simplify to $3x + 4$? Select all that apply.

  (A) $2x + 1 + x + 3$ (D) $x - 3 + 2x + 7$

  (B) $5x + 1 - (2x - 3)$ (E) $2x - 1 + x + 4$

  (C) $x + 2 - (2x + 2)$ (F) $8x + 1 - (5x + 5)$

32. The figures in a sequence are each composed of dots. The number of dots in the nth figure is given by the polynomial $\frac{n(n-1)}{2}$. Which could be the number of dots in one of the figures?

  (A) $\frac{3}{2}$ (C) 8

  (B) 7   (D) 15

33. How is the graph of $f(x) = x^2 + 3x$ translated to produce the graph of $g(x) = x^2 + 3x - 25$?

  (A) 25 units down   (C) 25 units up

  (B) 3 units left   (D) 3 units right

34. Simplify $(10x)(-4x + 4)$.

  (A) $6x^2 + 4$ (C) $-40x^2 + 4$

  (B) $-6x^2 + 10x + 40$ (D) $-40x^2 + 40x$

I'm in a Learning Mindset!

What factors should I consider when establishing a timeline for my learning goal?

Solve Quadratic Equations by Factoring $ax^2 + bx + c$

(I Can) use the Zero Product Property to solve quadratic equations in standard form when the leading coefficient is not 1.

Spark Your Learning

The car is at rest when the light turns green. A bus moving at a constant speed passes the car without needing to slow down for the light.

The bus approaches the light as it turns green, and it does not need to stop.

Complete Part A as a whole class. Then complete Parts B–D in small groups.

A. What is a mathematical question you can ask about this situation? What information would you need to know to answer your question?

B. What variables are needed in this situation? What must be true of the values for these variables?

C. To answer your question, what strategy and tool would you use along with all the information you have? What answer do you get?

D. Does your answer make sense in the context of the situation? How do you know?

 Turn and Talk Predict how your answer would change for each of the following changes in the situation:
- The bus is traveling faster.
- The car has a greater acceleration.
- The bus is initially closer to the car.

Build Understanding

Factor Quadratic Expressions of the Form $ax^2 + bx$

In the last lesson, you factored expressions of the form $x^2 + bx$ by factoring out the greatest common factor. You can use the same process to factor an expression of the form $ax^2 + bx$ when the leading coefficient a is not 1. For example, consider the expression $3x^2 + 9x$.

$3x^2 + 9x$
$= 3x \cdot x + 3x \cdot 3$
$= 3x(x + 3)$

> Here, the greatest common factor of 3x is shown in blue.

1 An expression for the area of a flag is given, where x represents the width of the flag.

> The area is $A = 5x^2 - 10x$.

A. What is the greatest common factor of the terms of $5x^2 - 10x$?

B. Write the factored form of the area.

C. What is an expression for the length of the flag in terms of the width x?

D. What restriction is placed on the possible values of the area? What restriction does this place on the possible values of x?

Factor $ax^2 + bx + c$ when $c > 0$

Given an expression of the form $ax^2 + bx + c$ with integer coefficients, you may be able to factor the expression as $(mx + p)(nx + q)$ for integers m, n, p, and q. By expanding $(mx + p)(nx + q)$, you can see how the constants in the factored and unfactored forms are related. Notice that m and n are a factor pair for a and p and q are a factor pair for c.

$$(mx + p)(nx + q) = mnx^2 + mqx + npx + pq$$
$$= \underset{a}{mnx^2} + \underset{b}{(mq + np)x} + \underset{c}{pq}$$

2 Factor $6x^2 + 13x + 5$.

A. What are the values of a, b, and c?

B. Suppose you want to factor $6x^2 + 13x + 5$ as $(mx + p)(nx + q)$ where m and n are both positive. Explain why p and q must both be positive as well. Also explain why $mn = 6$, $pq = 5$, and $mq + np = 13$.

C. Make a spreadsheet like the one shown. Based on the spreadsheet, what is the factored form of $6x^2 + 13x + 5$? Explain.

	A	B	C	D	E
1	Factors of 6 (m and n)		Factors of 5 (p and q)		$mq + np$
2	6	1	5	1	11
3	6	1	1	5	31
4	3	2	5	1	13
5	3	2	1	5	17

D. Leah thinks the spreadsheet in Part C doesn't account for all possibilities. She adds four more rows by swapping the values in columns A and B as shown. Explain why adding these rows is not necessary.

	A	B	C	D	E
1	Factors of 6 (m and n)		Factors of 5 (p and q)		$mq + np$
6	1	6	5	1	31
7	1	6	1	5	11
8	2	3	5	1	17
9	2	3	1	5	13

E. Consider the expression $2x^2 - 9x + 10$. If you want to factor the expression as $(mx + p)(nx + q)$ where m and n are positive, what must be true about the signs of p and q? What is the factored form of the expression?

F. Sometimes the terms of an expression $ax^2 + bx + c$ have a common factor that you should factor out first before completing the factorization. Use this process to factor $18x^2 + 39x + 6$.

 Turn and Talk Which expression is more difficult to factor, $12x^2 + 67x + 16$ or $13x^2 + 30x + 17$? Explain.

Factor $ax^2 + bx + c$ when $c < 0$

3 ▶ To factor an expression such as $2x^2 - 7x - 15$ where $c < 0$, you can make a table that is similar to the spreadsheet you created in Task 2.

Factors of a	Factors of c	Outer product + Inner product
1 and 2	1 and -15	$(1)(-15) + (2)(1) = -13$
1 and 2	3 and -5	$(1)(-5) + (2)(3) = 1$
1 and 2	5 and -3	$(1)(-3) + (2)(5) = 7$
1 and 2	15 and -1	$(1)(-1) + (2)(15) = 29$
1 and 2	-1 and 15	$(1)(15) + (2)(-1) = 13$
1 and 2	-3 and 5	$(1)(5) + (2)(-3) = -1$
1 and 2	-5 and 3	$(1)(3) + (2)(-5) = -7$
1 and 2	-15 and 1	$(1)(1) + (2)(-15) = -29$

A. Explain why the factors of c must have different signs.

B. Why are the factors of a in the table the same while the factors of c are different?

C. What is the factored form of $2x^2 - 7x - 15$?

 Turn and Talk In the expression given in Task 3, suppose the value of b changes from -7 to 7. How does the factored form of the expression change?

Step It Out

Solve Quadratic Equations by Factoring

You can solve some equations of the form $ax^2 + bx + c = 0$ by factoring and then applying the Zero Product Property.

4 ▶ The cross section of a portable speaker is designed to have a parabolic shape defined by the equation $y = -2x^2 + 7x$, where x is the horizontal distance (in inches) along the front of the speaker and y is the vertical distance (in inches) of the parabolic casing from the front of the speaker. The designer needs to attach bolts to the casing where the casing is 6 inches from the front of the speaker.

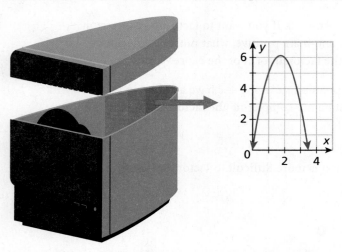

Determine the distances x at which the casing is 6 inches from the front of the speaker.

$-2x^2 + 7x = 6$	Given
$-2x^2 + 7x - 6 = 0$	Subtraction Property of Equality
$2x^2 - 7x + 6 = 0$	Multiply both sides by -1.
$(2x - 3)(x - 2) = 0$	?
$2x - 3 = 0$ or $x - 2 = 0$	?
$x = \dfrac{3}{2}$ or $x = 2$	Solve each equation for x.

A. For what reason is 6 subtracted from both sides of the equation?

B. What is done to rewrite the equation as a product?

C. What property justifies writing $(2x - 3)(x - 2) = 0$ as two separate equations?

D. How can you be sure the quadratic expression is factored correctly?

The casing reaches a distance of 6 inches from the front of the speaker when $x = 1.5$ inches and when $x = 2$ inches.

 Turn and Talk Compare and contrast solving a quadratic equation graphically and by factoring. Be sure to attend to the precision of each method.

5 ▶ An inground pool is being installed with a concrete path of uniform width on all four sides. The pool along with the concrete path will have a total area of 96 square meters. What is the width x of the path?

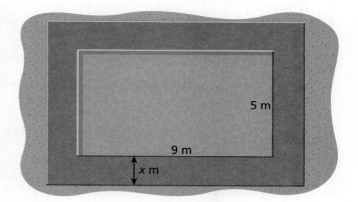
5 m
9 m
x m

The area of the pool along with the concrete path can be modeled by multiplying the total length by the total width.

Use a verbal model.

Total length (m)

Twice width of path (m) **2x**	+	Pool length (m) **9**

$\cdot$

Total width (m)

Twice width of path (m) **2x**	+	Pool width (m) **5**

$=$

Total area (m²) **96**

Write an equation.

$(2x + 9)(2x + 5) = 96$

Solve the equation.

$(2x + 9)(2x + 5) = 96$

> **A.** The left side of the equation is written as a product. Why can't the Zero Product Property be applied yet?

$4x^2 + 28x + 45 = 96$

$4x^2 + 28x - 51 = 0$

> **B.** What strategy and tool can you use to factor the quadratic expression?

$(2x - 3)(2x + 17) = 0$

$2x - 3 = 0 \text{ or } 2x + 17 = 0$

$x = \dfrac{3}{2} \text{ or } \qquad x = -\dfrac{17}{2}$

> **C.** Why isn't $-\dfrac{17}{2}$ a valid solution?

Answer the question.

The width of the concrete path is $\dfrac{3}{2}$, or 1.5 meters.

> **D.** What is the area of the concrete path?

 Turn and Talk Create a function that gives the volume V of concrete required if the width of the path is x meters and the thickness of the path is h meters.

Check Understanding

1. What is the factored form of the expression $3x^2 - 15x$?

2. Outline the steps you will need to follow and identify the tools you will use in order to factor the expression $2x^2 + 13x + 15$.

3. What is the factored form of the expression $3x^2 + 11x - 4$?

4. Solve the equation $3x^2 - 3x - 36 = 0$ by factoring.

5. The area of the parallelogram shown is $2x^2 - 17x - 9$ square inches. Find an expression for the height of the parallelogram.

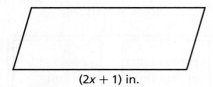

(2x + 1) in.

On Your Own

Write an equation that will allow you to solve for x. Then find the solution.

6.
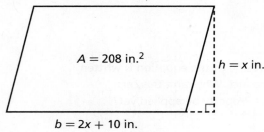

$A = 208$ in.^{2}
$h = x$ in.
$b = 2x + 10$ in.

7.
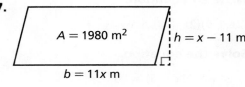

$A = 1980$ m^2
$h = x - 11$ m
$b = 11x$ m

Factor each expression.

8. $6x^2 + 11x + 4$

9. $2x^2 + 9x + 9$

10. $6x^2 + 13x + 6$

11. $4x^2 + 17x + 15$

12. $2x^2 + x - 10$

13. $3x^2 + 17x - 6$

14. $6x^2 + x - 15$

15. $5x^2 - 13x - 6$

16. $2x^2 - 7x - 9$

17. $16x^2 + 2x - 3$

18. $3x^2 - 5x - 28$

19. $6x^2 - 17x - 45$

20. $2x^2 + 7x - 15$

21. $8x^2 + 34x + 21$

22. **Open Ended** Write a quadratic expression in the form $ax^2 + bx + c$ that cannot be factored using integers. Explain.

23. If a quadratic expression can be factored using integers, are the zeros of the corresponding function necessarily integers? Explain.

24. How do the zeros of the function $f(x) = 2x^2 - x - 3$ relate to the zeros of the function $g(x) = -2x^2 + x + 3$? Support your answer algebraically and graphically.

25. **(MP) Critique Reasoning** Maureen solved the equation $3x^2 + x = 9$ as shown.

$$3x^2 + x = 9$$
$$x(3x + 1) = 3 \cdot 3$$
$$x = 3 \text{ or } 3x + 1 = 3$$
$$x = 3 \text{ or } \qquad x = \frac{2}{3}$$

Is her solution correct? Explain.

26. **STEM** A particle is moving along a path given by $y = 2x^2 + 5x - 4$ while a sheet of thin gold foil is placed at $y = 38$. Solve the equation $2x^2 + 5x - 4 = 38$ to find the positive x-coordinate of the point at which the particle will collide with the foil.

Write and solve an equation to find the point(s) where the graphs of f and g intersect. Then graph both functions and label the point(s) of intersection.

27. $f(x) = 4x^2 + x - 2$ and $g(x) = x^2 - 4x$

28. $f(x) = 4x^2 + 2x - 3$ and $g(x) = -6x + 2$

29. $f(x) = 5x^2 - 9x - 7$ and $g(x) = 2x + 5$

30. $f(x) = 7x^2 - 9x - 9$ and $g(x) = x^2 + 2x + 1$

31. $f(x) = 10x^2 + 29x + 9$ and $g(x) = 2x + 4$

32. $f(x) = 2x^2 + 13x - 5$ and $g(x) = -10x^2 + 2x$

33. $f(x) = 9x^2 - 2x - 13$ and $g(x) = 2x^2 - 8$

34. $f(x) = -17x + 13$ and $g(x) = -12x^2 + 4$

Graph each function. Label the x-intercepts, the axis of symmetry, and the vertex.

35. $f(x) = 3x^2 + x - 2$

36. $f(x) = 6x^2 + 9x + 3$

37. $f(x) = 4x^2 - 2x - 2$

38. $f(x) = -3x^2 - 18x - 15$

39. $f(x) = 2x^2 + 8x + 6$

40. $f(x) = -2x^2 + 2x + 4$

41. $f(x) = -4x^2 + 8x + 5$

42. $f(x) = 3x^2 + 5x - 2$

43. The white frame of the window shown forms a rectangle with a vertical strip down the middle that divides the window into two sections. The width of each part of the frame is x inches.

A. Write an expression for the total area of the glass in the window.

B. Write an equation that will allow you to determine the width x of the window frame if the total area of the glass is 186 square inches.

C. Solve your equation from Part B. Are both solutions viable? Explain.

D. What is the width of the frame?

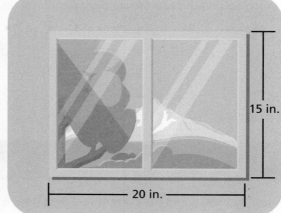

15 in.

20 in.

44. For what value of x does the area of the shaded region equal 478 square feet?

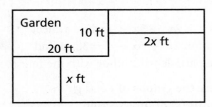

3x + 4 ft

x ft

x ft

2x − 3 ft

45. The dimensions of a rectangular garden are to be increased as shown.

Garden

10 ft

20 ft

2x ft

x ft

For what value of x is the garden's new area equal to 800 square feet?

46. (Open Middle™) Fill in the box with an integer so that the resulting quadratic expression can be factored using integers.

$$3x^2 + 4x + \boxed{}$$

Spiral Review • Assessment Readiness

47. Which properties are true for $f(x) = x^2 - 4x$? Select all that apply.

Ⓐ The y-intercept is at $y = 0$.

Ⓑ The zeros are at $x = 0$ and $x = -4$.

Ⓒ The vertex is $(-2, 12)$.

Ⓓ The line of symmetry is $x = 2$.

Ⓔ The vertex is $(2, -4)$.

Ⓕ The graph opens downwards.

48. Which is an equivalent form of the expression $(2x - 5)(2x + 5)$?

Ⓐ $4x^2 - 20x - 25$

Ⓑ $4x^2 + 20x - 25$

Ⓒ $4x^2 - 25$

Ⓓ $2x^2 - 25$

49. Match each expression on the left with an equivalent form on the right.

A. $x^2 + 4x - 21$

B. $x^2 + 6x + 5$

C. $x^2 + 4x - 5$

D. $x^2 - 4x - 21$

1. $(x + 3)(x - 7)$

2. $(x + 5)(x + 1)$

3. $(x - 3)(x + 7)$

4. $(x + 5)(x - 1)$

⬡ I'm in a Learning Mindset!

How will I know when my current learning goal is met successfully? What are my next steps?

Use Special Factoring Patterns to Solve Quadratic Equations

(I Can) use special factoring patterns to solve quadratic equations.

Spark Your Learning

A rider on this amusement park ride accidentally drops a wallet.

The riders are lifted high into the air before the ride starts to spin.

Complete Part A as a whole class. Then complete Parts B–C in small groups.

A. What mathematical question can you ask about this situation? What information would you need to know to answer your question?

B. To answer your question, what strategy and tool would you use along with all the information you have? What answer do you get?

C. Does your answer make sense in the context of the situation? How do you know?

> **Turn and Talk** Predict how your answer would change for each of the following changes in the situation:
> - The wallet fell a distance of 250 feet.
> - The wallet was thrown towards the ground, not dropped.

Build Understanding

Factor the Difference of Squares

Recall that the product of a sum and a difference in the form $(a + b)(a - b)$ generates the expression $a^2 - b^2$ when expanded. For example, $(x + 2)(x - 2)$ can be found using the table to the right.

	x	−2
−x	x^2	−2x
2	2x	−4

The resulting expression of $x^2 - 4$ is called a difference of squares.

You can factor expressions that are differences of squares by using the factoring pattern shown below.

Difference of Squares	
Factoring pattern	**Examples**
$a^2 - b^2 = (a + b)(a - b)$	$x^2 - 9 = x^2 - 3^2$ $\quad = (x + 3)(x - 3)$ $9x^2 - 1 = (3x)^2 - 1^2$ $\quad = (3x + 1)(3x - 1)$

To completely factor an expression, factor out its greatest common factor. This greatest common factor may include variables.

1 Consider the polynomial $4x^2 - 64$.

A. What properties of this expression suggest that it is a difference of squares?

B. Use the Distributive Property to expand $(2x + 8)(2x - 8)$ and confirm that it is equivalent to $4x^2 - 64$. Why is $(2x + 8)(2x - 8)$ an incomplete factored form of $4x^2 - 64$?

C. The leading coefficient and last term of $4x^2 - 64$ have two common factors: 2 and 4. Rewrite $4x^2 - 64$ by factoring out 2, and then rewrite $4x^2 - 64$ by factoring out 4.

D. Choose the expression from Part C from which you factored out the greatest common factor. Use the pattern of differences of squares to completely factor $4x^2 - 64$.

E. How do you know that your answer to Part D is the completely factored form of $4x^2 - 64$?

 Turn and Talk Describe the steps you would need to factor $81x^4 - 1$ completely. Show the factored form as you describe the steps.

Step It Out

Factor Perfect-Square Trinomials

Previously, you have learned how the square of a binomial sum is given by $(a + b)^2 = a^2 + 2ab + b^2$ and how the square of a binomial difference is given by $(a - b)^2 = a^2 - 2ab + b^2$. For example, $(x + 2)(x + 2)$ can be found using the table to the right.

	x	2
$-x$	x^2	$2x$
2	$2x$	4

The resulting expression of $x^2 + 4x + 4$ is called a perfect-square trinomial.

You can factor expressions that are perfect-square trinomials by using the factoring patterns shown below.

Perfect-Square Trinomials	
Factoring pattern	**Examples**
$a^2 + 2ab + b^2 = (a + b)(a + b)$ $\qquad\qquad\quad = (a + b)^2$	$x^2 + 6x + 9 = (x + 3)(x + 3)$ $\qquad\qquad\quad = (x + 3)^2$
$a^2 - 2ab + b^2 = (a - b)(a - b)$ $\qquad\qquad\quad = (a - b)^2$	$x^2 - 10x + 25 = (x - 5)(x - 5)$ $\qquad\qquad\qquad = (x - 5)^2$

2 ▶ Factor $5x^2 + 30x + 45$.

First, recognize that the terms have a greatest common factor. After factoring out the GCF, check to see if the trinomial fits a factoring pattern.

$$5x^2 + 30x + 45 = 5(x^2 + 6x + 9) \qquad \text{Factor out the GCF, 5.}$$
$$= 5(x^2 + 2(x \cdot 3) + 3^2) \qquad \text{Recognize the form } a^2 + 2ab + b^2.$$
$$= 5(x + 3)(x + 3) \qquad \text{Factor the trinomial.}$$
$$= 5(x + 3)^2 \qquad \text{Write as the square of a binomial.}$$

A. What are the values of a and b in this case?

Turn and Talk Suppose that the polynomial in Task 2 is $5x^2 + 30xy + 45y^2$. How would the factored form of the polynomial change?

3 ▶ Factor $12x^3 - 84x^2 + 147x$.

Again, look for a GCF and factor it out before looking for a factoring pattern.

A. Why is x included in the GCF?

$$12x^3 - 84x^2 + 147x = 3x(4x^2 - 28x + 49) \qquad \text{Factor out the GCF, } 3x.$$
$$= 3x[(2x)^2 - 2(2x \cdot 7) + 7^2] \qquad \text{Recognize the form } a^2 - 2ab + b^2.$$
$$= 3x(2x - 7)(2x - 7) \qquad \text{Factor the trinomial.}$$
$$= 3x(2x - 7)^2 \qquad \text{Write as the square of a binomial.}$$

Turn and Talk Suppose that the polynomial in Task 3 is $12x^4 - 84x^3 + 147x^2$. How would the factored form of the polynomial change?

Solve Quadratic Equations Using Special Factoring Patterns

If $ax^2 + bx + c$ is a difference of squares or is a perfect-square trinomial, then equations in the form $ax^2 + bx + c = 0$ can be solved using the Zero Product Property.

4 The volume of the fish tank pictured is 9 cubic feet. What are its dimensions?

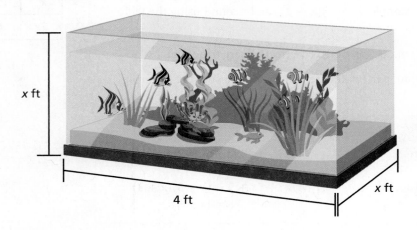

x ft

4 ft

x ft

You can use a factoring pattern and the Zero Product Property to find the dimensions.

Write a quadratic equation for the volume.

$4 \cdot x \cdot x = 9$

$4x^2 = 9$

> **A.** Explain what each of the four quantities represents.

Solve the equation for x.

$4x^2 = 9$

$4x^2 - 9 = 0$

$(2x + 3)(2x - 3) = 0$

> **B.** Write a step after this one that could help you recognize $4x^2 - 9$ as a difference of squares.

> **C.** What solutions satisfy the Zero Product Property here?

Answer the question.

The dimensions of the tank are 4 feet by 1.5 feet by 1.5 feet.

 Turn and Talk The factored form suggested two different possible values for x. Why aren't both valid solutions in this situation?

Solve Real-World Quadratic Equations

Projectile motion describes the height of a dropped or launched object as it freefalls due to gravity.

Quantity	Description	Units
t	time since the object was dropped or launched	seconds
v_0	initial vertical velocity (positive if upward; negative if downward)	feet per second
h_0	initial height of the object when it was dropped or launched	feet
$h(t)$	height of the object from the ground t seconds after being dropped or launched	feet

The height of the object above the ground is modeled by $h(t) = -16t^2 + v_0 t + h_0$, where $h = 0$ represents ground level.

When the object is dropped, the model simplifies to $h(t) = -16t^2 + h_0$ because $v_0 = 0$.

5 While standing at a lookout, Antonio sent a couple of pebbles to the canyon floor below. The illustrations show the two methods he used.

How long after Antonio released them did each pebble fall before reaching the canyon floor?

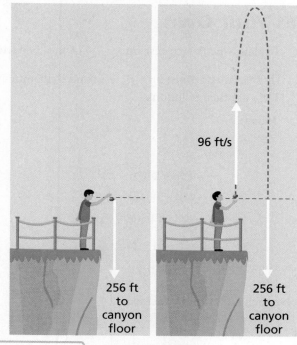

96 ft/s

256 ft to canyon floor

256 ft to canyon floor

Dropped pebble

$h_D(t) = -16t^2 + 256$

$0 = -16t^2 + 256$

$0 = -16(t^2 - 16)$

$0 = -16(t - 4)(t + 4)$

$t = 4$ or $t = -4$

A. Explain the reasoning for these models.

B. Why are the strategies for factoring these expressions different?

C. Why aren't the solutions $t = -4$ and $t = -2$ valid?

Thrown pebble

$h_T(t) = -16t^2 + 96t + 256$

$0 = -16t^2 + 96t + 256$

$0 = -16(t^2 - 6t - 16)$

$0 = -16(t - 8)(t + 2)$

$t = 8$ or $t = -2$

The dropped pebble reaches the canyon floor after 4 seconds, and the thrown pebble reaches the canyon floor after 8 seconds.

 Turn and Talk Explain how the solution for the thrown pebble would have changed if Antonio had thrown the pebble down with an initial velocity of 96 ft/s.

Check Understanding

Factor each expression.

1. $x^2 - 64$

2. $25x^2 - 4$

3. Explain how you would factor $2x^2 - 18$.

Solve each equation by factoring.

4. $x^2 + 12x + 36 = 0$

5. $4x^2 - 28x + 49 = 0$

6. Write and solve a quadratic equation that models how long it takes an ear of corn to freefall 16 feet to the bottom of a corn crib.

On Your Own

7. Explain why the expression $x^2 + 4$ cannot be factored over the real numbers.

8. (MP) **Critique Reasoning** Jesse and Benjamin are asked to factor $100x^2 - 100$. Here are their solutions.

Jesse:

$$100x^2 - 100 = (10x)^2 - 10^2$$
$$= (10x - 10)(10x + 10)$$
$$= 10(x - 1)(10)(x + 1)$$
$$= 100(x - 1)(x + 1)$$

Benjamin:

$$100x^2 - 100 = 100(x^2 - 1)$$
$$= 100(x - 1)(x + 1)$$

Who is correct? Explain.

Solve each equation by factoring.

9. $x^2 - 4 = 0$

10. $9x^2 - 1 = 0$

11. $4x^2 + 16x + 16 = 0$

12. $x^2 + 10x + 25 = 0$

13. $9x^2 + 12x + 4 = 0$

14. $4x^2 + 28x + 49 = 0$

15. $x^2 - 16x + 64 = 0$

16. $9x^2 - 12x + 4 = 0$

17. $16x^2 - 8x + 11 = 10$

18. $25x^2 - 20x - 5 = -9$

19. $9x^2 - 24x + 7 = -9$

20. $4x^2 = 1$

21. $8x^2 - 40x + 50 = 0$

22. $3x^2 - \dfrac{4}{3} = 0$

23. $36x^2 - 12x + 2 = 1$

24. $98x^2 + 5 = 7$

25. Arturo is building a storage chest in the shape of a rectangular prism with dimensions x feet by x feet by 6 feet. He wants the chest to have a volume of 96 cubic feet. What are the unknown dimensions of the chest?

26. A seagull drops a clam from a height of 36 feet in order to break open the clam's shell on the rocks below. For what amount of time does the clam fall?

27. (MP) **Critique Reasoning** Juan and Julio were asked to factor $x^2 - 10x + 25$. Juan's strategy was to look for the factors of 25 and then determined the sum of these factors to find the combination that generated the value -10. Julio's strategy was to look at the pattern of $x^2 - 2bx + b^2$. Who is correct? Explain.

For each function, determine the x-intercepts of the function's graph by factoring.

28. $f(x) = 2x^2 - 72$

29. $g(x) = 9x^2 + 30x + 25$

30. A rock falls from where the dashed line meets the cliff.

    A. Write the projectile motion model for this situation.

    B. Find the time it takes for the rock to hit the water.

    C. Does doubling the height from which the rock falls double the time it takes to fall? If so, use the falling rock to demonstrate why. If not, determine the height from which the rock must fall for the time to double.

100 feet

Factor each polynomial.

31. $27x^4 - 3x^2$

32. $32x^5 - 18x^3$

33. $100x^3 - 36x$

34. $80x^5 - 5x^3$

35. $4x^4 - x^2$

36. $36x^4 - 16x^2$

37. $-18x^6 - 24x^5 - 8x^4$

38. $75x^5 + 30x^4 + 3x^3$

39. $-16x^3 + 8x^2 - x$

40. $6x^3 - 216x$

41. $-12x^3 + 147x$

42. $8x^4 + 40x^3 + 50x^2$

43. Trina creates a sequence of triangles with equal base and height. Each triangle is created from the previous one by a rule. Let x represent the base of the first triangle.

    A. The area of the second triangle is $2x^2 + 4x + 2$. What are its dimensions?

    B. The area of the third triangle is $8x^2 + 24x + 18$. What are its dimensions?

    C. Use the dimensions of the first, second, and third triangles to describe how each triangle is related to the previous triangle.

44. If you kick a ball on the ground upward with an initial vertical velocity of 64 feet per second, does the ball reach a height of 64 feet? If so, how long does it take the ball to reach that height?

45. (MP) **Model with Mathematics** Three students are participating in their school's egg drop competition. Each has a unique way to keep a raw egg from breaking and a different way to release the protected egg.

For each method, determine how long it takes the protected egg to hit the ground from the flat roof of their school building, 32 feet above the ground.

    A. The first student throws the protected egg upward with an initial vertical velocity of 16 feet per second.

    B. The second student throws the protected egg downward with an initial vertical velocity of 16 feet per second.

    C. The third student simply drops the protected egg. If you cannot factor the quadratic that models this case over the set of rational numbers, try factoring it over the set of irrational numbers.

Spiral Review • Assessment Readiness

46. Which is the correct factored form of $2x^2 - x - 6$?

    Ⓐ $(x + 3)(2x - 2)$

    Ⓑ $(2x + 3)(x - 2)$

    Ⓒ $(2x - 3)(x + 2)$

    Ⓓ $(x - 3)(2x + 2)$

47. What are the x-intercepts of the graph of the function $f(x) = -2x^2 + 12x - 16$?

    Ⓐ $x = 2, x = 4$

    Ⓑ $x = -2, x = 4$

    Ⓒ $x = 2, x = -4$

    Ⓓ $x = -2, x = -4$

48. Match the factored forms with their corresponding trinomials.

    A. $(x - 2)(x + 3)$ **1.** $x^2 + 5x - 6$

    B. $(x + 2)(x - 3)$ **2.** $x^2 + x - 6$

    C. $(x - 6)(x + 1)$ **3.** $x^2 - x - 6$

    D. $(x + 6)(x - 1)$ **4.** $x^2 - 5x - 6$

 I'm in a Learning Mindset!

What social factors impact my goals? What are the positive impacts?

Solve by Graphing

A gardener wants to enlarge a rectangular garden that is 5 feet by 8 feet. The gardener will increase both the width and length by x feet.

The area of the garden is this polynomial:

$$(5 + x)(8 + x) = x^2 + 13x + 40$$

If the gardener wants the enlarged garden to have an area of 70 square feet, then solve this equation:

$$x^2 + 13x + 40 = 70, \quad \text{or} \quad x^2 + 13x - 30 = 0$$

One way to solve the equation is by graphing the left side as a function and using the graph to determine the zeros of the function.

> The only positive x-intercept is 2, so add 2 feet to the width and length.

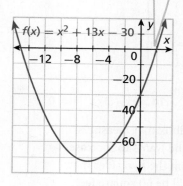

Solve by Factoring $x^2 + bx + c$

Another way to solve the equation

$$x^2 + 13x - 30 = 0$$

is by factoring the left side. You can use a table to list the factors of the constant term, -30, and then see which pair of factors has a sum equal to the x-term's coefficient, 13.

Factors of -30	Sum of factors
1 and -30	-29
-1 and 30	29
2 and -15	-13
-2 and 15	13
3 and -10	-7
-3 and 10	7
5 and -6	-1
-5 and 6	1

From the table, you see that the factors -2 and 15 have a sum of 13. This means that you can write $x^2 + 13x + 30$ in factored form as $(x - 2)(x + 15)$. Now solve:

$$(x - 2)(x + 15) = 0$$

$$x - 2 = 0 \quad \text{or} \quad x + 15 = 0$$

$$x = 2 \quad \text{or} \quad x = -15$$

> Use the Zero Product Property.

The only positive solution is 2, so add 2 feet to the width and length.

Solve by Factoring $ax^2 + bx + c$

Suppose the gardener wants to add x feet to all four sides of the garden to create an enlarged area of 88 square feet. The new equation and solution are:

$$(5 + 2x)(8 + 2x) = 88$$

$$40 + 26x + 4x^2 = 88$$

$$4x^2 + 26x - 48 = 0$$

$$2(2x^2 + 13x - 24) = 0$$

$$2(2x - 3)(x + 8) = 0$$

> Use the Zero Product Property.

$$2x - 3 = 0 \quad \text{or } x + 8 = 0$$

> The only positive solution is $\frac{3}{2}$, or 1.5, so add 1.5 feet to the width and length.

$$x = \frac{3}{2} \quad \text{or} \quad x = -8$$

Vocabulary

Choose the correct term from the box to complete each sentence.

1. A function of the form $f(x) = ax^2 + bx + c$, where a, b, and c are real numbers and $a \neq 0$, is called a(n) ___?___.

2. The graph of a quadratic function is called a(n) ___?___.

3. A(n) ___?___ is any number that makes the function equal 0.

4. The ___?___ states that if A and B are real numbers or algebraic expressions and $AB = 0$, then $A = 0$ or $B = 0$.

5. A line that divides a graph into two congruent reflected halves is a(n) ___?___.

6. The ___?___ of a parabola is the highest or lowest point on the parabola.

Concepts and Skills

Graph each function and find its x-intercepts. Round to the nearest tenth if necessary.

7. $f(x) = 3x^2 - 6x$

8. $f(x) = -x^2 + 7x$

9. $f(x) = 2x^2 + 5x - 4$

10. $f(x) = -x^2 - 2x + 10$

11. How is the graph of $f(x) = -x^2 - 2x + 5$ related to the graph of $g(x) = x^2 + 2x - 5$?

Solve each equation using the Zero Product Property.

12. $x^2 - 8x = 0$

13. $x^2 + 6x + 8 = 0$

14. $x^2 - 3x - 4 = 0$

15. **(MP)** **Use Tools** Melissa wants to expand her rectangular sandbox that measures 4 feet by 8 feet. Two sides of the sandbox are against a fence. She wants to increase the length and the width of the sandbox by the same amount on the two sides that are not against the fence. The total area of the new sandbox will be 60 square feet. What is the amount of increase? State what strategy and tool you will use to answer the question, explain your choice, and then find the answer.

Factor each expression.

16. $6x^2 + 15x$

17. $12x^2 - 7x + 1$

18. $15x^2 - 11x - 12$

19. A rectangular prism has a height of x feet and a base area of $2x^2 + 3x - 14$ square feet. If the width of the base is $x - 2$ feet, find the length of the base.

Solve each equation by factoring.

20. $x^2 - 121 = 0$

21. $9x^2 - 24x + 16 = 0$

22. $4x^2 + 12x = -9$

23. Ed is outside on his balcony when he accidentally knocks his sunglasses off the railing. The height h, in feet, of his sunglasses above the ground at time t, in seconds, is given by the function $h(t) = -16t^2 + h_0$. How long will it take his sunglasses to hit the ground if the railing is 25 feet above the ground?

Use Square Roots to Solve Quadratic Equations

Automotive Racing

Two race cars are competing in a 50 km race.

Car 1	Car 2
Car 1 reaches the 35 km marker traveling $v = 180$ km/h.	Car 2 reaches the 40 km marker traveling $v = 150$ km/h.

A. If each car continues traveling at its respective velocity, which car would win the race?

B. The function for the position s of an object at time t is $s(t) = \frac{1}{2}at^2 + vt + s_0$, where a represents acceleration with units of km/h². Create a verbal model for the position function. Use the units of each component to explain why the function makes sense.

C. If Car 1 accelerates at a constant rate of 750 km/h² until it reaches the finish line, which car would win the race? Explain your reasoning.

D. What is the minimum acceleration needed for Car 1 to win the race if Car 2 does not accelerate? What is the minimum acceleration needed for Car 1 to win the race if Car 2 does accelerate? State your answer in terms of Car 2's acceleration.

Are You Ready?

Complete these problems to review prior concepts and skills you will need for this module.

Evaluate Algebraic Expressions

Evaluate each expression for the given value(s).

1. $4x^2 - 3x + 5;$
$x = -3$

2. $-x^2 - 4x + 3y^2;$
$x = -3, y = -2$

3. $-2x^2 + 5y + 3;$
$x = 2, y = -1$

4. $3xy^2 - 2y;$
$x = 4, y = 2$

5. $x^2y + 2x + y;$
$x = -2, y = 5$

6. $2x^2y^2 + 4xy + 8;$
$x = -1, y = -4$

Square Roots and Cube Roots

Simplify each expression.

7. $\sqrt{16}$

8. $\sqrt{49}$

9. $\sqrt[3]{8}$

10. $\sqrt[3]{27}$

11. $\sqrt[3]{-125}$

12. $\sqrt[3]{-64}$

Solve Literal Equations

Solve each equation for the indicated variable.

13. $y = mx + b$ for b

14. $C = 2\pi r$ for r

15. $A = \frac{1}{2}bh$ for h

16. $4x - 3y = -2$ for x

Connecting Past and Present Learning

Previously, you learned:
- to simplify expressions using properties of exponents,
- to solve quadratic equations by graphing, and
- to choose between different models when fitting functions to data.

In this module, you will learn:
- to develop and use the Quadratic Formula,
- to model real-world problems with quadratic equations, and
- to choose an appropriate method to solve quadratic equations.

Solve Simple Quadratic Equations

(I Can) solve quadratic equations of the form $ax^2 = c$ by using square roots and determine whether there are one, two, or no real solutions.

Spark Your Learning

Eda is designing a pendulum with a length of 5 feet.

The time it takes a pendulum to swing back and forth one time, called the period, depends on the length of the pendulum.

Complete Part A as a whole class. Then complete Parts B–D in small groups.

A. What is a mathematical question you can ask about this situation? What information would you need to know to answer your question?

B. What variable(s) are involved in this situation? What unit of measurement would you use for each variable?

C. To answer your question, what strategy and tool would you use along with all the information you have? What answer do you get?

D. Speculate how you could determine different periods given different pendulum lengths.

Turn and Talk Discuss each of the following questions:
- Eda halves the length of her pendulum. What would its period be?
- Eda wants her pendulum to swing back and forth 10 times per minute. How should she change its length?

Build Understanding

Solve $x^2 = c$

Previously, you learned to solve the quadratic equation $x^2 - 4 = 0$ by factoring the difference of squares on the left side. You can also solve the equation by rewriting it as $x^2 = 4$ and using square roots.

Square Roots and Quadratic Equations	
Definition of square root	**What it means for quadratic equations**
A number b is a square root of a nonnegative number a when $b^2 = a$. **Examples:** 2 is a square root of 4 because $2^2 = 4$. -2 is a square root of 4 because $(-2)^2 = 4$. In general, every positive number has two square roots, which are opposites. The symbols $\sqrt{}$ and $-\sqrt{}$ are used to indicate a positive square root and its opposite. **Examples:** $\sqrt{4} = 2$ and $-\sqrt{4} = -2$ 0 has only one square root: $\sqrt{0} = -\sqrt{0} = 0$. Square roots of negative numbers do not exist in the real number system.	The quadratic equation $x^2 = 4$ is equivalent to the question, "What numbers when squared are equal to 4?" The answer to this question is, of course, 2 and -2, which are the square roots of 4. The definition of square root allows you to rewrite the equation $x^2 = 4$ as $x = \pm\sqrt{4}$. Recall that the symbol $\pm$ is read "plus or minus." In general, given an equation of the form $x^2 = a$ where a is a nonnegative number, you can write: $x^2 = a$ Given equation $x = \pm\sqrt{a}$ Definition of square root

Square roots have two properties that are useful when solving quadratic equations. Each property is a direct consequence of a property of rational exponents.

Square Roots and Quadratic Equations	
Multiplication property of square roots	For $a \geq 0$ and $b \geq 0$, $\sqrt{ab} = \sqrt{a} \cdot \sqrt{b}$.
Quotient property of square roots	For $a \geq 0$ and $b > 0$, $\sqrt{\dfrac{a}{b}} = \dfrac{\sqrt{a}}{\sqrt{b}}$.

1   **A.** The steps for solving the equations $x^2 = 12$ and $x^2 = \frac{16}{9}$ are shown. State a reason for each step.

     B. When $\sqrt{12}$ is written as $2\sqrt{3}$, it is said to be in *simplest form* because the radicand no longer contains any perfect-square factors (other than 1). What is the simplest form of $\sqrt{18}$?

     C. Show how to solve the equation $x^2 = \frac{27}{25}$.

$$x^2 = 12$$
$$x = \pm\sqrt{12}$$
$$= \pm\sqrt{4 \cdot 3}$$
$$= \pm\sqrt{4} \cdot \sqrt{3}$$
$$= \pm 2\sqrt{3}$$

$$x^2 = \frac{16}{9}$$
$$x = \pm\sqrt{\frac{16}{9}}$$
$$= \pm\frac{\sqrt{16}}{\sqrt{9}}$$
$$= \pm\frac{4}{3}$$

 Turn and Talk What properties of rational exponents can you use to justify the two properties of square roots knowing that $\sqrt{ab} = (ab)^{\frac{1}{2}}$ and $\sqrt{\frac{a}{b}} = \left(\frac{a}{b}\right)^{\frac{1}{2}}$?

Solve $ax^2 = c$

You learned in the previous task that you can use square roots to solve quadratic equations of the form $x^2 = c$ where c is a perfect square. You can also use square roots to solve quadratic equations of the forms $ax^2 - c = 0$ and $ax^2 = c$, where a and c are real numbers and $a \neq 0$.

2 ▶ Suppose a gully has left and right walls as shown. The gully is roughly shaped as a parabola, where x represents the horizontal position, in feet, and $h(x)$ represents the vertical displacement, in feet, with respect to the top of the gully. The corners are located at the x-intercepts of $h(x)$ as shown. How wide is the gully?

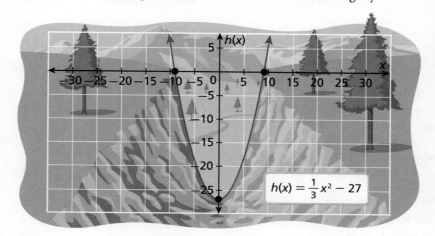

$$h(x) = \frac{1}{3}x^2 - 27$$

A. What is the first step in solving the problem?

B. Show how to write the equation in the form $x^2 = c$.

C. Find the solutions of the equation and determine the width of the gully.

3 ▶ Given that $c \geq 0$, you can solve the equation $x^2 = c$ by using square roots to get $x = -\sqrt{c}$ or $x = \sqrt{c}$.

A. If c is a positive real number, but NOT a perfect square, does the equation $x^2 = c$ still have solutions? If so, tell what type of numbers the solutions are. If not, explain why not.

B. How can you express the solutions to $x^2 = 5$ exactly and approximately?

C. Solve the literal equation $ax^2 = c$.

D. Use the general solution you wrote in Part C to solve $3x^2 = 6$ and $-4x^2 = -5$. What are the exact solutions in radical form? What are the approximate solutions written as decimals rounded to the nearest tenth?

E. Solving the equation $2x^2 = 1$ gives $x = \pm\sqrt{\frac{1}{2}} = \pm\frac{1}{\sqrt{2}}$. To avoid having a square root in the denominator, you can multiply both the numerator and denominator by $\sqrt{2}$. What result do you get? Why do you think this step is called *rationalizing the denominator*?

 Turn and Talk When does the quadratic equation $ax^2 = c$ have two real solutions? When does it have no real solution?

Solve $a(x + b)^2 = c$

 The equation $a(x + b)^2 = c$ can be solved using a strategy similar to the one used to solve the equation $ax^2 = c$. See the general solution method below.

A. Copy the solution, and supply the reason for each step.

$$a(x + b)^2 = c$$

$$(x + b)^2 = \frac{c}{a} \qquad \underline{\quad ? \quad}$$

$$x + b = \pm\sqrt{\frac{c}{a}} \qquad \underline{\quad ? \quad}$$

$$x = -b \pm\sqrt{\frac{c}{a}} \qquad \underline{\quad ? \quad}$$

B. State any restrictions on a, b, and c.

C. For what values of a and c will the equation $a(x + b)^2 = c$ have two solutions? For what values will the equation have no solution? Explain your reasoning.

D. Does the value of b have any impact on the number of solutions of $a(x + b)^2 = c$? Explain your reasoning.

E. The steps for solving the equation $3(x + 1)^2 = 150$ are shown on the left below and the justifications of those steps on the right. The steps and justifications are scrambled.

Write the solution steps in the correct order.	Write the justifications in the correct order.
$x = -1 \pm \sqrt{25} \cdot \sqrt{2}$	Definition of square root
$(x + 1)^2 = 50$	Product Property of Square Roots
$x + 1 = \pm\sqrt{50}$	Given equation
$3(x + 1)^2 = 150$	Write $\sqrt{25}$ as 5.
$x = -1 \pm 5\sqrt{2}$	Write 50 as $25 \cdot 2$.
$x = -1 \pm \sqrt{25 \cdot 2}$	Subtraction Property of Equality
$x = -1 \pm \sqrt{50}$	Division Property of Equality

 Turn and Talk How many solutions, if any, does the equation $-3(x - 4)^2 = 39$ have? How do you know?

Step It Out

Solve Real-World Quadratic Equations by Using Square Roots

When modeling a real-world situation, you may use a formula that contains a squared variable. You can solve for that variable by using square roots.

5 A cylindrical water tank for a fish farm is shown. The volume of the tank can be modeled by the formula $V = \pi r^2 h$, where V is the capacity, r is the radius, and h is the height. What is the radius of this tank to the nearest tenth of a foot?

radius r

Volume V: 370 ft³
Height h: 4.5 ft

$$V = \pi r^2 h \quad \text{Original formula}$$

$$370 = \pi r^2(4.5) \quad \text{Substitute.}$$

A. What property justifies this step?

$$\frac{370}{4.5\pi} = \frac{4.5\pi r^2}{4.5\pi} \quad \underline{?}$$

$$\frac{370}{4.5\pi} = r^2 \quad \text{Simplify.}$$

$$\pm\sqrt{\frac{370}{4.5\pi}} = r \quad \text{Definition of square root}$$

$$\pm 5.1 \approx r \quad \text{Use a calculator to approximate the square roots.}$$

C. Why is this expression considered the exact solution?

B. Which value of r is not reasonable in this situation? Explain.

The radius is $\sqrt{\dfrac{370}{4.5\pi}}$ feet, or approximately 5.1 feet.

> **Turn and Talk** Predict how the radius would change for each of the following changes in the situation:
> - The height is doubled.
> - The volume is doubled.
> - The volume is halved.

Check Understanding

1. Show how to solve $x^2 = 121$ two ways: by factoring and by using square roots.

Solve each equation.

2. $m^2 = 81$

3. $a^2 = 32$

4. $2x^2 - 18 = 0$

5. $3a^2 = 147$

6. $4(x + 1)^2 = 100$

7. $-11(y - 2)^2 = -99$

8. A ball is dropped from the top of a building. The function $h(t) = -16t^2 + 160$ models the ball's height h, in feet, at time t, in seconds. How long will it take the ball to hit the ground? Round to the nearest tenth of a second.

On Your Own

Solve each equation by using square roots. If the equation has no real-number solution, write *no real solution*.

9. $n^2 = 144$

10. $a^2 = 25$

11. $x^2 - 49 = 0$

12. $v^2 = \dfrac{25}{81}$

13. $3x^2 = 0$

14. $-5x^2 = -500$

15. $4z^2 - 64 = 0$

16. $6a^2 + 24 = 0$

17. $\dfrac{1}{4}t^2 - 4 = 0$

18. $(x + 2)^2 = 169$

19. $(a + 10)^2 = 121$

20. $(r - 16)^2 = 484$

21. $(x + 1)^2 - 3 = 13$

22. $(t - 4)^2 - 64 = 0$

23. $(2y - 2)^2 + 5 = 41$

24. $(x - 4)^2 - 4 = -5$

25. $(y + 3)^2 + 2 = 3$

26. $(2z + 1)^2 - 40 = 81$

27. $2(x - 8)^2 - 3 = 5$

28. $(m + 1)^2 + 5 = 2$

29. $3(a + 4)^2 + 4 = 31$

Solve each equation. Give the solutions in radical form. Then use a calculator to approximate the solutions to two decimal places, if necessary.

30. $c^2 = 216$

31. $t^2 - 135 = 0$

32. $f^2 - 14 = 65$

33. $w^2 - 5 = 73$

34. $5b^2 + 6 = 306$

35. $5z^2 - 65 = 0$

36. $(b + 3)^2 = 28$

37. $(d + 4)^2 = 48$

38. $(x + 6)^2 - 18 = 0$

39. $(k + 4)^2 - 16 = 16$

40. $12(c + 7)^2 = 2160$

41. $7(x - 2)^2 - 9 = 432$

42. $2(y + 2)^2 + 12 = 26$

43. $(a - 3)^2 + 4 = 6$

44. $-2(z - 10)^2 = -26$

45. $-(x + 11)^2 + 11 = 8$

46. $3(x + 1)^2 = 15$

47. $4(m + 6)^2 + 6 = 14$

48. **STEM** A ball is released from the top of a ramp. As it rolls down, it accelerates (that is, its velocity increases). The ball's acceleration is $a = 4$ ft/s². The formula $d = \frac{1}{2}at^2$ gives the distance d, in feet, that the ball travels in time t, in seconds. If the length of the ramp is 24 feet, after how much time does the ball reach the bottom of the ramp? Give the answer as a simplified radical and as a decimal rounded to the nearest tenth.

49. In a movie, a spyglass falls from the crow's nest of a ship. The distance, in feet, that it falls can be modeled by the function $d(t) = 16t^2$, where t is time, in seconds. If the spyglass has fallen 112 feet, for how many seconds has it fallen? Give the answer as a simplified radical and as a decimal rounded to the nearest tenth.

For Problems 50–52, write a quadratic equation to model each situation. Then solve the equation. When necessary, give the answer in simplest radical form, and as a decimal approximation rounded to the nearest tenth.

50. Find the side length of a square if the area is 289 square meters.

51. Find the radius of a circle if the area is 400π square inches.

52. Find the length of a side s of an isosceles right triangle whose area A is 24 square feet given that $A = \frac{1}{2}s^2$.

53. (MP) **Critique Reasoning** Two students try to solve $n^2 + 256 = 0$ as shown. Which student made an error? Describe and correct the error made.

Jacob

$n^2 + 256 = 0$
$n^2 = 256$
$n = \pm\sqrt{256}$
$n = \pm 16$

Anakin

$n^2 + 256 = 0$
$n^2 = -256$
no real solution

54. The rug shown is in the shape of a semicircle with the given area. What is the rug's diameter? Write an equation to model the situation, and then solve it using square roots, rounding the diameter to the nearest tenth of a foot.

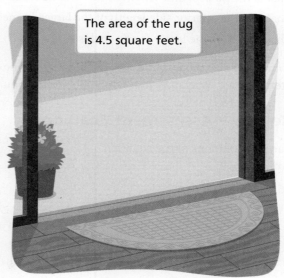

The area of the rug is 4.5 square feet.

55. The population of a town was 52,000 in 2000. The model $P(t) = 8t^2 + 52{,}000$ gives the projected population P at time t in years since 2000. In about how many years is the population expected to be twice the population in 2000?

56. Explain why the quadratic equation $x^2 + b = 0$ where $b > 0$ has no real solution, but the quadratic equation $x^2 - b = 0$ where $b > 0$ has two real solutions.

57. Part of a beach is being enclosed to restore sand dunes. The area is an isosceles right triangle with an area of 9000 square feet. There is already a fence along the hypotenuse. How many feet of fencing is needed for the other two sides? Define a variable and use it to write an equation to model the situation. Then solve the equation using square roots, rounding the length of fencing to the nearest foot.

58. Soybeans fall from a conveyor and settle into a pile shaped like a cone. The volume of this cone-shaped pile of soybeans can be modeled by the formula $V = \frac{1}{3}\pi r^2 h$, where r is the radius, in feet, of the base of the cone and h is the height, in feet, of the cone. To the nearest tenth of a foot, what is the radius of a cone-shaped pile of soybeans that has a volume of 1250 cubic feet and a height of 6 feet?

59. Write an equation to represent the distance d above the water after t seconds of the highest possible dive in a professional diving competition. Assume the diver does not leap upward from the platform. If the platform is the highest allowed, how long will it take the diver to reach the water? Round to the nearest tenth of a second.

Competitive professional divers can dive from heights up to 85 feet.

60. Construction workers are dropping debris down a vertical chute that terminates in a trash bin. The function $h(t) = -16t^2 + h$ gives the height, in feet, of a piece of debris at time t, in seconds, dropped from a height of h, in feet. How much time does it take a piece of debris to fall from a height of 900 feet?

61. Two different sizes of square picture frames are offered from an online art supply store. The smaller frame has an interior side length that is 2 inches less than the larger frame and encloses an area of 200 square inches. For Parts A–C, express answers in radical form.

  A. What is the interior side length of the smaller frame?

  B. What was the interior side length of the larger frame?

  C. What area does the larger frame enclose?

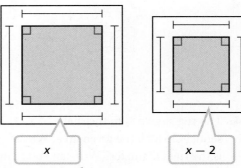

x

$x - 2$

62. **(MP) Reason** Solve the formula $d = 16t^2$ for t. Describe how you can use this rewritten formula. Why does it use only the positive square root?

Spiral Review • Assessment Readiness

63. What are the solutions of the equation $x^2 + 8x + 12 = 0$?

Ⓐ $-6, -2$ Ⓒ $2, 6$

Ⓑ $6, -2$ Ⓓ $2, -6$

64. What are the solutions to the equation $4a^2 - 30a + 36 = 0$?

Ⓐ $-6, -\dfrac{3}{2}$ Ⓒ $-\dfrac{3}{2}, 6$

Ⓑ $-6, \dfrac{3}{2}$ Ⓓ $\dfrac{3}{2}, 6$

65. Match the equation on the left with its solution(s) on the right.

  A. $x^2 - 49 = 0$ **1.** $x = -7$

  B. $x^2 + 14x + 49 = 0$ **2.** $x = -7, 7$

  C. $4x^2 - 16x + 16 = 0$ **3.** $x = \dfrac{1}{2}$

  D. $16x^2 - 16x + 4 = 0$ **4.** $x = 2$

 I'm in a Learning Mindset!

What have I learned to help me reach my goal of using square roots to solve quadratic equations?

Solve Quadratic Equations by Completing the Square

(I Can) solve quadratic equations of the form $ax^2 + bx + c = 0$ by completing the square.

Spark Your Learning

Suppose you are planning to build a rectangular boat dock.

The design requires 400 square feet of wood for the dock's platform.

Complete Part A as a whole class. Then complete Parts B–D in small groups.

A. What is a mathematical question you can ask about this situation? What information would you need to know to answer your question?

B. What variable(s) are involved in this situation?

C. To answer your question, what strategy and tool would you use along with all the information you have? What answer do you get?

D. Does your answer make sense in the context of the situation? How do you know?

 Turn and Talk Predict how your answer would change for each of the following changes in the situation:
- The area is doubled.
- The area is the same, but the width is 12 feet less than the length.

Build Understanding

Complete the Square for $x^2 + bx + c$

Recall that a perfect-square trinomial is a trinomial whose factored form is the square of a binomial.

$$a^2 - 2ab + b^2 = (a - b)^2$$
$$a^2 + 2ab + b^2 = (a + b)^2$$

Completing the square is a process used to form a perfect-square trinomial.

1 You can visualize completing the square using algebra tiles.

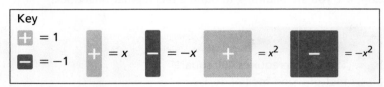

A. Use algebra tiles to model the expression $x^2 - 4x$. Arrange the tiles as shown.

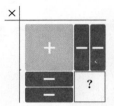

To form a perfect-square trinomial, add positive unit tiles to create a square shape. How many do you need to add?

Write the perfect-square trinomial that the algebra tiles model after you add unit tiles.

B. Copy and complete the table. Use algebra tiles or draw a diagram.

Original expression	Number of unit tiles to form a perfect-square trinomial	Perfect-square trinomial formed
$x^2 + 6x$	?	?
$x^2 + 8x$	?	?
$x^2 + 10x$	?	?

C. How is the number of unit tiles that you add related to the coefficient of x?

D. Use your answer to Part C to make a conjecture about how the value of c is related to the value of b in a perfect-square trinomial of the form $x^2 + bx + c$.

E. Use your answer to Part D to rewrite a perfect-square trinomial of the form $x^2 + bx + c$ in terms of only x and b. Then show an equivalent squared binomial in terms of only x and b.

F. Consider the expression $x^2 - 12x + c$, where the value of b in $x^2 + bx + c$ is negative. Find the value of c that will make $x^2 - 12x + c$ a perfect-square trinomial. Then write the expression as the square of a binomial.

Turn and Talk Will the value of c always be positive if $x^2 + bx + c$ is a perfect-square trinomial? Why or why not?

Complete the Square for $ax^2 + bx + c$
When a Is a Perfect Square

In Task 1 you formed perfect-square trinomials from quadratic expressions of the form $x^2 + bx$. In this task you will learn to form perfect-square trinomials from quadratic expressions of the form $ax^2 + bx$, where a is a perfect square and $a \neq 1$.

2 **A.** Use algebra tiles to model the expression $4x^2 + 8x$. Arrange the tiles as shown.

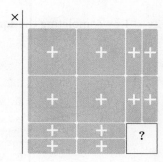

To form a perfect-square trinomial, add positive unit tiles to create a square shape. How many do you need to add?

Write the perfect-square trinomial that the algebra tiles model after you add unit tiles.

B. Write the perfect-square trinomial you formed in Part A as the square of a binomial.

C. Copy and complete the table. Use algebra tiles or draw a diagram.

Original expression	Perfect-square trinomial formed	Binomial squared
$4x^2 + 12x$	$4x^2 + 12x + \underline{\ ?\ }$	$\left(2x + \underline{\ ?\ }\right)^2$
$9x^2 + 6x$	$9x^2 + 6x + \underline{\ ?\ }$	$\left(3x + \underline{\ ?\ }\right)^2$
$9x^2 + 12x$	$9x^2 + 12x + \underline{\ ?\ }$	$\left(\underline{\ ?\ }x + \underline{\ ?\ }\right)^2$

D. The quadratic trinomial $ax^2 + bx + c$ is a perfect-square trinomial if $c = \dfrac{b^2}{4a}$. Show that this is true for each perfect-square trinomial formed in Part C.

E. Consider the expression $4x^2 - 12x + c$, where the value of b in $ax^2 + bx + c$ is negative. Find the value of c that will make $4x^2 - 12x + c$ a perfect-square trinomial. Then write the expression as the square of a binomial.

Turn and Talk Explain how $c = \dfrac{b^2}{4a}$ is obtained as follows:
- When you complete the square on $ax^2 + bx$, what expression involving a gives the number of rows and the number of columns of x^2-tiles?
- The b x-tiles are divided into two groups, with each group arranged alongside either the rows or the columns of x^2-tiles. What expression involving a and b gives the number of rows and the number of columns of x-tiles?
- This creates an empty square to be filled by unit tiles. What expression involving a and b gives the number of unit tiles you need to add?

Step It Out

Solve Equations by Completing the Square

You can solve equations of the form $ax^2 + bx = c$ by completing the square. When doing so, you must be careful to keep the resulting equation equivalent to the original equation.

3 Solve $3x^2 + 2x = 1$ by completing the square.

Method 1:

$$3x^2 + 2x = 1$$

$$3(3x^2 + 2x) = 3(1)$$

> **A.** What procedure is used to get a perfect-square coefficient of x^2?

$$9x^2 + 6x = 3$$

$$9x^2 + 6x + 1 = 3 + 1$$

> **B.** Why is 1 added to both sides?

$$9x^2 + 6x + 1 = 4$$

$$(3x + 1)^2 = 4$$

$$3x + 1 = \pm\sqrt{4}$$

> **C.** How is the definition of square root used?

$$3x = -1 \pm 2$$

$$3x = 1 \ \text{ or } \ 3x = -3$$

$$x = \frac{1}{3} \ \text{ or } \ x = -1$$

> **D.** Why are there two possible answers?

Method 2:

$$3x^2 + 2x = 1$$

$$\frac{1}{3}(3x^2 + 2x) = \frac{1}{3} \cdot 1$$

> **E.** What procedure is used to get a coefficient of 1 for the x^2-term?

$$x^2 + \frac{2}{3}x = \frac{1}{3}$$

$$x^2 + \frac{2}{3}x + \left(\frac{1}{3}\right)^2 = \frac{1}{3} + \left(\frac{1}{3}\right)^2$$

> **F.** How do you find the value $\left(\frac{1}{3}\right)^2$ used to complete the square?

$$\left(x + \frac{1}{3}\right)^2 = \frac{4}{9}$$

$$x + \frac{1}{3} = \pm\frac{2}{3}$$

$$x = -\frac{1}{3} \pm \frac{2}{3}$$

$$x = \frac{1}{3} \ \text{ or } \ x = -1$$

Check by substitution in $3x^2 + 2x = 1$.

Check $x = \frac{1}{3}$: $3\left(\frac{1}{3}\right)^2 + 2\left(\frac{1}{3}\right) = 1$ ✔   Check $x = -1$: $3(-1)^2 + 2(-1) = 1$ ✔

 Turn and Talk Which method do you prefer: Method 1 or Method 2? Explain.

Solve Real-World Equations by Completing the Square

You can use completing the square to solve real-world problems.

4 A company builds tables with decorative legs as shown, where the arch of the leg is a parabola modeled by the equation $y = -\frac{1}{32}x^2 + \frac{3}{2}x - 2$ and x and y are in inches. What is the exact width of the arch at its base? What is the approximate width to the nearest tenth?

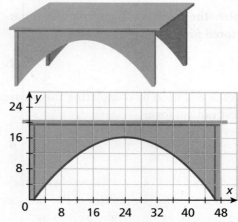

Complete the square to find the x-intercepts.

$$-\frac{1}{32}x^2 + \frac{3}{2}x - 2 = 0$$

A. Why does multiplying each term of the equation by -32 make solving easier?

$$-32\left(-\frac{1}{32}x^2 + \frac{3}{2}x - 2\right) = -32(0)$$

$$x^2 - 48x + 64 = 0$$

B. Why was the equation written in this form?

$$x^2 - 48x = -64$$

$$x^2 - 48x + 576 = -64 + 576$$

C. Explain why 576 has to be added to both sides of the equation.

$$(x - 24)^2 = 512$$

$$x - 24 = \pm\sqrt{512}$$

D. Show that $\sqrt{512}$ is equivalent to $16\sqrt{2}$.

$$x = 24 \pm 16\sqrt{2}$$

$$x = 24 + 16\sqrt{2} \text{ or } x = 24 - 16\sqrt{2}$$

Find the width by subtracting the x-intercepts.

$$w = \left(24 + 16\sqrt{2}\right) - \left(24 - 16\sqrt{2}\right)$$

E. How do you know which way to subtract?

$$= 24 + 16\sqrt{2} - 24 + 16\sqrt{2}$$

$$= 32\sqrt{2}$$

The width of the arch at its base is exactly $32\sqrt{2}$ inches or approximately 45.3 inches.

F. How do you know if this answer is reasonable?

 Turn and Talk Could you have solved the equation by multiplying through by 32 instead of -32? Why or why not?

Check Understanding

Complete the square to form a perfect-square trinomial. Then write each trinomial in factored form.

1. $x^2 + 6x$

2. $9x^2 - 4x$

Solve each equation by completing the square. When necessary, give answers in simplest radical form.

3. $x^2 + 8x - 9 = 0$

4. $4x^2 - 6x = -1$

5. A cross section of a crystal vase with thick sides is shown. The interior of the vase can be modeled by the parabola given by $y = 3x^2 - 12x + 6$, where x and y are inches. What is the width of the interior of the vase at its opening? Round your answer to the nearest tenth.

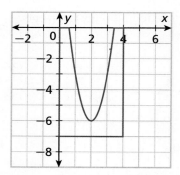

On Your Own

Complete the square to form a perfect-square trinomial. Then write each trinomial in factored form.

6. $x^2 - 12x$

7. $4x^2 + 20x$

8. $x^2 + 10x$

9. $25x^2 + 10x$

10. $x^2 - x$

11. $9x^2 - 8x$

12. **(MP) Critique Reasoning** Jun was instructed to complete the square on $16x^2 + 40x$ to form a perfect-square trinomial and then to rewrite the trinomial in factored form. His solution is shown. Explain his error. What is the correct solution?

$16x^2 + 40x$
$16x^2 + 40x + 400$
$(4x + 20)^2$ ✗

Solve each equation by completing the square. When necessary, give answers in simplest radical form.

13. $x^2 + 4x = 5$

14. $x^2 - 6x = 2$

15. $x^2 - 2x = 0$

16. $x^2 + 8x - 5 = 0$

17. $x^2 + 4x - 15 = 0$

18. $x^2 + 10x - 12 = 0$

19. $x^2 + 4x = 2$

20. $x^2 + 6x - 4 = 0$

21. $x^2 - 2x = 1$

22. $x^2 + 12x - 4 = 0$

23. $x^2 - 5x - 1 = 0$

24. $x^2 + 2x - 3 = 0$

25. $x^2 + 4x + 8 = 5$

26. $x^2 + 6x = 3$

The height h, in feet, of a projectile can be modeled by the equation $h(t) = -16t^2 + v_0 t + h_0$ where t is the time in seconds, h_0 is the projectile's initial height in feet, and v_0 is the projectile's initial vertical velocity in feet per second. Solve each projectile motion problem by completing the square. Round to the nearest tenth of a second.

27. A lacrosse player throws a ball into the air from a height of 8 feet with an initial vertical velocity of 30 feet per second. When will the ball hit the ground? Round to the nearest tenth of a second.

28. A soccer player kicks a soccer ball from the ground with an initial vertical velocity of 14 feet per second. When will the ball land back on the ground?

29. (MP) **Model with Mathematics**
The window of the museum shown can be modeled by the quadratic function

$$y = -\frac{9}{50}(x^2 - 18x + 31)$$

where x and y are in meters.

A. What are the exact values of the x-intercepts of the graph of the function written in radical form?

B. What is the approximate width of the window at its base to the nearest tenth of a meter?

Solve each equation by completing the square. When necessary, give answers in simplest radical form.

30. $6x - 4 = -5x^2$

31. $2x^2 - 18x = 6 + 6x$

32. $-4x = -x^2$

33. $-18x + 8 = -x^2$

34. $2x^2 = -3x + 8$

35. $8x^2 - 3 = -6x$

36. $8x^2 + 6x = 16$

37. $25x^2 = 6x + 8$

38. $-4x^2 + 8x = -21$

39. $16x^2 = 16x + 5$

40. $-2x^2 + 6x + 5 = 0$

41. $6x = 32 - 6x^2$

42. An architect is designing the rectangular lobby of a new office building as shown in the sketch. He knows that the length will be 8 yards greater than the width.

$x + 8$

x | The area is 8000 yd².

A. What are the exact dimensions of the lobby in radical form?

B. What are the approximate dimensions rounded to the nearest tenth of a yard?

43. A water arc from a fountain like the one shown can be modeled by the quadratic function

$$y = -\frac{2}{3}(x^2 - 4x + 1)$$

where x and y are in feet. The graph shows a side view of the fountain.

A. Describe how you could use the quadratic function to find the horizontal distance covered by the water arc.

B. What is the horizontal distance that the water arc covers? Round to the nearest tenth.

44. (MP) **Use Structure** Compare how to solve $5x^2 - 10x - 12 = 0$ by completing the square in two different ways.

A. First use division to get the coefficient of x^2 to be 1. Then find the exact solutions of the equation.

B. First use multiplication to get the coefficient of x^2 to be a perfect square other than 1. Then find the exact solutions of the equation.

C. For this problem, was it easier to first use multiplication or division? Explain.

45. (Open Middle™) Fill in the spaces below using the digits 0 to 9, at most once each, to make a true statement.

$$\boxed{}x^2 + \boxed{}x + \boxed{} = \left(x + \boxed{}\right)^2 - \boxed{}$$

Spiral Review • Assessment Readiness

46. What are the factors of $x^2 - 36$? Select all that apply.

Ⓐ $x - 36$ Ⓓ $x + 6$

Ⓑ $x + 36$ Ⓔ $x - 18$

Ⓒ $x - 6$ Ⓕ $x + 18$

47. Simplify $\sqrt{4^2 + 4}$.

Ⓐ $\sqrt{10}$ Ⓒ 10

Ⓑ $2\sqrt{5}$ Ⓓ $4\sqrt{10}$

48. A rectangular fenced-in playground has an area of 48 square meters. The width w is given by $3w^2 = 48$. What is w?

Ⓐ $2\sqrt{3}$ m   Ⓒ $4\sqrt{3}$ m

Ⓑ 4 m   Ⓓ $2\sqrt{15}$ m

49. What are the solution(s) of $2x^2 + 2x = 12$? Select all that apply.

Ⓐ -4 Ⓓ 2

Ⓑ -3 Ⓔ 3

Ⓒ -2 Ⓕ 4

 I'm in a Learning Mindset!

What are my action steps to solving quadratic equations by completing the square?

Use the Quadratic Formula to Solve Equations

(I Can) use the method of completing the square to derive the Quadratic Formula, and solve equations by using the Quadratic Formula.

Spark Your Learning

For a contest, a member of the science club is testing a slingshot she has built.

The projectile motion model $h(t) = -16t^2 + v_0 t + h_0$ can be used to model the height of a projectile, such as a pumpkin, during its flight.

Complete Part A as a whole class. Then complete Parts B–D in small groups.

A. What is a mathematical question you can ask about this situation? What information would you need to know to answer your question?

B. What variable(s) are involved in this situation? What unit of measurement would you use for each variable?

C. To answer your question, what strategy and tool would you use along with all the information you have? What answer do you get?

D. How can you determine what initial velocities are unreasonable in this situation given the initial height?

 Turn and Talk Predict how your answer would change for each of the following changes in the situation:

- The initial vertical velocity is 30 feet per second.
- The initial vertical velocity is 15 feet per second and the initial height is 2 feet.

Build Understanding

Derive the Quadratic Formula

Previously, you learned how you can solve a literal equation for a specified variable. You can use completing the square to solve the general quadratic equation $ax^2 + bx + c = 0$ for x. The resulting formula, called the **Quadratic Formula**, can be used to find the solutions of any quadratic equation.

Quadratic Formula

For any quadratic equation of the form $ax^2 + bx + c = 0$ and $a \neq 0$:

$$x = \frac{-b \pm \sqrt{b^2 - 4ac}}{2a}$$

---

1 To derive the Quadratic Formula, solve the general quadratic equation for x by completing the square.

Step 1: Write the general quadratic equation where $a \neq 0$.

$$ax^2 + bx + c = 0$$

Step 2: Subtract the constant from both sides of the equation.

$$ax^2 + bx = -c$$

Step 3: Multiply both sides of the equation by $4a$.

$$4a^2x^2 + 4abx = -4ac$$

Step 4: Add b^2 to both sides of the equation.

$$4a^2x^2 + 4abx + b^2 = b^2 - 4ac$$

Step 5: Write the left side of the equation as a square of a binomial.

$$\left(2ax + b\right)^2 = b^2 - 4ac$$

Step 6: Use the definition of square root to rewrite the equation.

$$2ax + b = \pm\sqrt{b^2 - 4ac}$$

Step 7: Subtract b from both sides of the equation.

$$2ax = -b \pm \sqrt{b^2 - 4ac}$$

Step 8: Divide both sides of the equation by $2a$.

$$x = \frac{-b \pm \sqrt{b^2 - 4ac}}{2a}$$

A. Why is the second step to rewrite $ax^2 + bx + c = 0$ as $ax^2 + bx = -c$?

B. Why do you multiply all terms by $4a$ in Step 3?

C. Why do you add b^2 to both sides in Step 4?

D. What property of equality justifies Step 2? Step 3? Step 4? Step 7? Step 8?

Turn and Talk Look back at Step 6. What can you conclude about the solutions of the quadratic equation when $b^2 - 4ac$ is positive? When $b^2 - 4ac$ is zero? When $b^2 - 4ac$ is negative?

Use the Discriminant

In the Quadratic Formula, the expression $b^2 - 4ac$ under the radical sign is called the **discriminant**. It determines the number of real solutions of a quadratic equation of the form $ax^2 + bx + c = 0$. All quadratic equations have either two real solutions, one real solution, or no real solution.

2 The chart shows possible values of the discriminant, the number of solutions of the associated quadratic equation, and a sample graph of $f(x) = ax^2 + bx + c$.

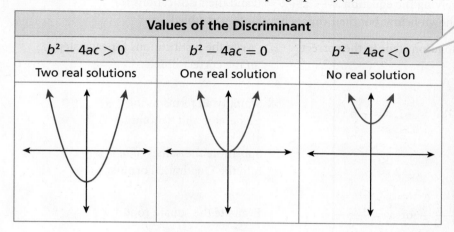

Values of the Discriminant		
$b^2 - 4ac > 0$	$b^2 - 4ac = 0$	$b^2 - 4ac < 0$
Two real solutions	One real solution	No real solution

When $b^2 - 4ac < 0$, there are two non-real solutions that are called *complex numbers*. You will study complex numbers in Algebra 2. In this book, it is sufficient to say that the answer is *no real solution*.

A. How does the graph of $f(x) = ax^2 + bx + c$ tell you how many real solutions the equation $ax^2 + bx + c = 0$ has?

B. For $x^2 - 2x - 15 = 0$, what are the values of a, b, and c? Why is the value of the discriminant 64? What does the value 64 tell you about the equation?

C. In the spreadsheet below, the formula in cell D2 evaluates the discriminant for $4x^2 + 13x + 9 = 0$. What does the value in cell D2 tell you?

D2 ⬍ ✕ ✓ *fx* = B2^2–4*A2*C2				
A	**B**	**C**	**D**	**E**
a	*b*	*c*	**Discriminant**	
4	13	9	25	
−4	13	9		
4	−13	9		
4	12	9		
4	13	12		

D. What quadratic equations are represented in rows 3–6 in the spreadsheet? Give your answers in the form $ax^2 + bx + c = 0$.

E. Fill down the formula from cell D2 through cell D5. What do you observe? What can you say about the solutions for the equations you found in Part D?

Turn and Talk How can the discriminant tell you whether you will have rational or irrational solutions when $b^2 - 4ac \geq 0$?

Step It Out

Solve Quadratic Equations Using the Quadratic Formula

The Quadratic Formula can be used to solve any quadratic equation in standard form. If the equation is not in standard form, you will first need to rewrite it. Then determine the values for a, b, and c and substitute them into the formula.

3 The steps for solving the equation $x^2 - x - 6 = 0$ and the justifications for each step are shown below, but their orders have been scrambled.

A. Write the solution steps in the correct order.

$$a = 1, b = -1, c = -6$$

$$x = \frac{1 \pm 5}{2}$$

$$x = \frac{1 + 5}{2} \text{ or } x = \frac{1 - 5}{2}$$

$$x = \frac{-(-1) \pm \sqrt{(-1)^2 - 4(1)(-6)}}{2(1)}$$

$$x = \frac{1 \pm \sqrt{25}}{2}$$

$$x = 3 \text{ or } x = -2$$

B. Write the justifications for each step in the correct order.

Simplify all terms in the numerator and denominator.

Substitute the values of a, b, and c into the Quadratic Formula.

Evaluate the square root.

Write the equation with $\pm$ in it as two separate equations.

Simplify both equations.

Identify a, b, and c.

C. The solutions are 3 and -2. To verify the solutions, use a graphing calculator. Graph $y = x^2 - x - 6$. How does the graph verify the solutions?

D. How would a graphing calculator help you verify real solutions that are not integers?

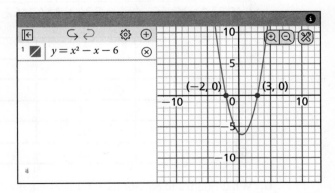

 Turn and Talk Suppose that for the equation $ax^2 + bx + c = 0$, the values of a, b, and c are rational numbers.

- Under what circumstances does the Quadratic Formula produce solutions that are rational numbers?
- Under what circumstances does the Quadratic Formula produce solutions that are irrational numbers?

Solve Real-World Quadratic Equations Using the Quadratic Formula

Given a real-world situation that is modeled by a quadratic equation, you can determine the number of real solutions using the discriminant and then solve using the Quadratic Formula. In the metric system, the height $h(t)$ of a projectile is $h(t) = -4.9t^2 + v_0t + h_0$ where $h(t)$ and h_0 are in meters, v_0 is in meters per second, and t is in seconds.

4 ▶ A volleyball player serves a ball overhand to start a play. How long is the ball at least 5 meters above the ground? Round to the nearest hundredth of a second.

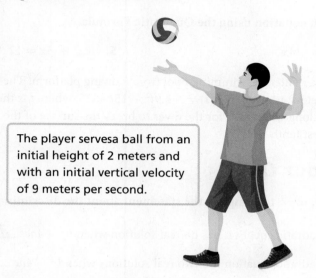

The player serves a ball from an initial height of 2 meters and with an initial vertical velocity of 9 meters per second.

$h(t) = -4.9t^2 + v_0t + h_0$	Projectile motion model
$5 = -4.9t^2 + 9t + 2$	Substitute.
$-4.9t^2 + 9t - 3 = 0$	Write in standard form.
$a = -4.9, b = 9, c = -3$	Identify a, b, and c.
$t = \dfrac{-9 \pm \sqrt{9^2 - 4(-4.9)(-3)}}{2(-4.9)}$	Quadratic Formula.
$t = \dfrac{-9 \pm \sqrt{22.2}}{-9.8}$	Simplify.
$t = \dfrac{-9 + \sqrt{22.2}}{-9.8}$ or $t = \dfrac{-9 - \sqrt{22.2}}{-9.8}$	Write as two equations.
$t \approx 0.438$ or $t \approx 1.399$	Simplify.
$1.399 - 0.438 = 0.961$	Subtract.

A. How is this equation obtained?

B. What does the discriminant $9^2 - 4(-4.9)(-3) = 22.2$ tell you about the solutions?

C. What do these times represent?

D. Why do you subtract the two values for t?

E. Why is only the final solution rounded to the nearest hundredth?

The ball is at least 5 meters above the ground for about 0.96 second.

 Turn and Talk What is the exact solution of the problem in radical form?

Check Understanding

1. When you derive the Quadratic Formula, what is the restriction on a?

Use the discriminant to determine the number of real solutions of the equation.

2. $3x^2 - 4x + 7 = 0$
3. $x^2 = -6x - 9$

Solve each equation using the Quadratic Formula.

4. $3x^2 = -4x + 15$
5. $2x^2 + 5x = 12$

6. A diver enters a swimming pool from a diving platform. The diver's height h, in meters, is given by $h(t) = -4.9t^2 + 15t + 25$, where t is the time in seconds. How long will it take for the diver to break the surface of the water? Round to the nearest tenth.

On Your Own

Use $>$, $<$, or $=$ to complete the statement about the discriminant.

7. A quadratic equation has no real solution when $b^2 - 4ac$ ___?___ 0.

8. A quadratic equation has two real solutions when $b^2 - 4ac$ ___?___ 0.

9. A quadratic equation has one real solution when $b^2 - 4ac$ ___?___ 0.

Use the discriminant to determine the number of real solutions of each equation.

10. $6x^2 + 12x + 6 = 0$
11. $2x^2 + 5x = 10$

12. $3x^2 - x - 7 = 0$
13. $5x^2 + 2x + 6 = 0$

14. $2x^2 = -3x - 2$
15. $12x + 1 = -2x^2$

16. When deriving the Quadratic Formula in Task 1, you could have divided by a in Step 2. Using this method, what would have been the resulting equation in Step 4? Does one derivation method appear to be simpler than the other? Explain.

Solve using the Quadratic Formula. When necessary, give answers in simplest radical form.

17. $x^2 + x - 6 = 0$
18. $2x^2 + 7x - 2 = 0$

19. $2x^2 + 6x + 2 = 0$
20. $4x^2 = 12x - 9$

21. $2x^2 + x - 6 = 0$
22. $2x^2 - 7x - 2 = 0$

23. $4x^2 = 16x - 14$
24. $5x^2 = 14x - 2$

25. $2x^2 - 10x = 12$
26. $3x^2 - 3 = 0$

27. $5x^2 - 25x + 20 = 0$
28. $4x^2 = 36$

29. $3x^2 + 4x + 1 = 5$
30. $6x^2 - x = 2x + 10$

Use the Quadratic Formula to solve each equation. Write your answers in decimal form rounded to the nearest hundredth. When necessary, write *no real solution*.

31. $x^2 - 3x - 1 = 0$

32. $-2x^2 = -5x - 8$

33. $x^2 + 3x + 1 = 0$

34. $-3x^2 - 5x = -8$

35. $5x^2 + 2x - 1 = 0$

36. $x^2 = 4x - 6$

37. $-x^2 = -6x - 8$

38. $3x^2 = 6x - 10$

39. A chicken coop shaped like a rectangular prism has a height of x meters and a base area of $x^2 + 8x + 5$ square meters.

    A. If the base area is 20 square meters, what equation can you solve to find x?

    B. What is the height to the nearest tenth of a meter?

    C. Are all solutions of the equation from Part A reasonable? Explain.

40. (MP) **Critique Reasoning** Chloe solves the equation $-4.9x^2 + 6x + 12 = 0$ as shown. Is she correct? If yes, explain. If not, correct her error.

Use $h(t) = -4.9t^2 + v_0 t + h_0$ for Problems 41–43. Round answers to the nearest tenth.

$$a = -4.9, b = 6, c = 12$$

$$x = \frac{-(6) \pm \sqrt{(6)^2 - 4(-4.9)(12)}}{2(-4.9)}$$

$$x = \frac{-6 \pm \sqrt{36 - 235.2}}{-9.8}$$

$$x = \frac{-6 \pm \sqrt{-199.2}}{-9.8}$$

Since the discriminant is -199.2, the equation has no solution.

41. An earthquake causes a rock to fall, with no initial vertical velocity, from the side of a cliff 8 meters above a river. How long will it take for the rock to land in the river?

42. A circus performer gets launched from a large cannon. The mouth of the cannon sits 6 meters off the ground, and the performer is launched with an initial vertical velocity of 15 meters per second. How long will it take for the performer to land on the safety net that is 5 meters off the ground?

43. You are standing on the ground when a friend standing on a balcony asks you to toss him his keys. He can catch the keys as long as they are at least 4 meters above the ground. If you toss the keys from an initial height of 2 meters with an initial vertical velocity of 14 meters per second, how long does your friend have to catch his keys?

44. **(MP)** **Model with Mathematics** Adede and Celia are cyclists that leave school at the same time. Celia travels south and Adede travels east. After Celia cycles 6 miles, the distance between them is 3 miles less than twice the distance cycled by Adede.

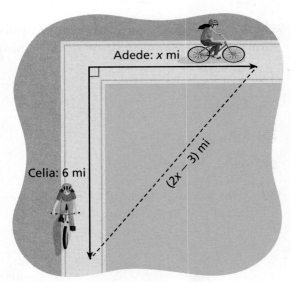

Adede: x mi

Celia: 6 mi

$(2x - 3)$ mi

   A. Use the Pythagorean Theorem to write an equation to find how far Adede has cycled.

   B. Use the Quadratic Formula to solve your equation from Part A. Round to the nearest tenth. Are both answers for x valid? Explain.

   C. To the nearest tenth, what is the approximate distance between the cyclists?

45. **STEM** The concentration of medicine m, in milligrams per liter, that exists in the bloodstream of a patient with an initial injection and then an IV drip is given by the function $m(t) = -0.25t^2 + 3t + 4$ where t is the time in hours. How many hours does it take for the medication to completely leave the bloodstream? Round to the nearest tenth.

46. **(Open Middle™)** Using the digits 1 to 9, at most one time each, create three quadratic equations in standard form such that one has no real solution, one has one real solution, and one has two real solutions.

$$\boxed{}x^2 + \boxed{}x + \boxed{} = 0 \qquad \boxed{}x^2 + \boxed{}x + \boxed{} = 0 \qquad \boxed{}x^2 + \boxed{}x + \boxed{} = 0$$

   no real solutions   1 real solution   2 real solutions

Spiral Review • Assessment Readiness

47. Solve $(x + 3)^2 = 10$.

   (A) $x = -8, x = 2$ (C) $x = -3 \pm \sqrt{10}$

   (B) $x = 2$ (D) $x = 3 \pm \sqrt{10}$

49. Which expression is a perfect-square trinomial? Select all that apply.

   (A) $4x^2 + 20x + 25$ (D) $6w^2 - 24w + 24$

   (B) $4x^2 + 20x - 25$ (E) $9y^2 + 18y + 36$

   (C) $16w^2 - 24w + 9$ (F) $9y^2 + 36y + 36$

48. A car bumper sticker is in the shape of a parallelogram. The base of the parallelogram is given by $10x - 5$ where x is the height in centimeters. If the area of the sticker is 15 square centimeters, what is the value of x?

   (A) 10 centimeters   (C) 2 centimeters

   (B) 3 centimeters   (D) 1.5 centimeters

50. Solve $x^2 - 24x + 14 = 0$ by completing the square.

   (A) $x = 12 \pm \sqrt{130}$ (C) $x = -12 \pm \sqrt{130}$

   (B) $x = 12 \pm \sqrt{158}$ (D) $x = -12 \pm \sqrt{158}$

 I'm in a Learning Mindset!

How will I know when my goal of solving quadratic equations using the Quadratic Formula is met successfully?

Choose a Method for Solving Quadratic Equations

(I Can) solve quadratic equations using a variety of methods and choose an appropriate method based on the initial form of the equation.

Spark Your Learning

Students are organizing a car wash to raise funds for a field trip. They need to raise $470.

If they charge customers too little, they may not raise enough money. If they charge customers too much, they may not attract enough customers to raise enough money.

Complete Part A as a whole class. Then complete Parts B–D in small groups.

A. What is a mathematical question you can ask about this situation? What information would you need to know to answer your question?

B. What variable(s) are involved in this situation? What unit of measurement would you use for each variable?

C. To answer your question, what strategy and tool would you use along with all the information you have? What answer do you get?

D. Does your answer make sense in the context of the situation? How do you know?

 Turn and Talk How could you find the least amount the students could charge per car wash if they needed to raise $380 for the field trip?

Build Understanding

Compare Methods for Solving Quadratic Equations

Previously, you have learned different methods for solving quadratic equations: graphing, factoring, using square roots, completing the square, and using the Quadratic Formula. Some of these methods will work for all quadratic equations, whereas others can be used only for specific types of quadratic equations. For all equations in the table, $a \neq 0$.

Method	Equation form	Example	Note
Graphing	$ax^2 + bx + c = 0$	$3x^2 + 4x - 4 = 0$	Apparent exact solutions must be checked by substituting them into the equation.
Factoring	$ax^2 + bx + c = 0$	$x^2 - 11x + 24 = 0$ $2x^2 - x - 15 = 0$	The factors are two binomials.
Using square roots	$ax^2 + c = 0$ or $a(x + b)^2 = c$	$4x^2 - 17 = 0$ $9(x + 2)^2 = 13$	This method can be used when there is no x-term.
Completing the square	$ax^2 + bx + c = 0$	$x^2 + 2x - 1 = 0$ $16x^2 + 2x - 1 = 0$	Best to use this method when a is a perfect square, but will work for any quadratic equation.
Quadratic Formula	$ax^2 + bx + c = 0$	$x^2 - 3x - 5 = 0$	If $b^2 - 4ac$ is a perfect square, the factoring method can also be used.

1 ▶ **A.** What are all the methods you can use to solve $4x^2 - 29 = 0$? Which method would you choose? Explain your reasoning.

B. What are all the methods you can use to solve $x^2 - 5x - 6 = 0$? Which method would you choose? Explain your reasoning.

C. Which two methods could you use to solve $3x^2 + 5x + 1 = 0$? Explain your reasoning.

D. Is the Quadratic Formula the most efficient method for solving $x^2 - x - 42 = 0$? What other method could you use? Explain your reasoning.

E. Consider the equation $3x^2 - 5x = 2$. What is this equation written in standard form?

F. Which methods could you use to solve the equation from part E? Which method would you choose. Explain your reasoning.

 Turn and Talk For each of the four non-graphing methods listed above, summarize the characteristics of quadratic equations that are best solved by each method.

Step It Out

Choose Methods to Solve Quadratic Equations

Before choosing which non-graphing method to use when solving a quadratic equation, consider the characteristics of the given quadratic equation.

2 ▶ Which non-graphing method is the most appropriate for solving $3x^2 - 4x - 8 = 0$? Give a reason why you chose this method. Then solve the equation.

Evaluate solution methods.

Method	Evaluation of method
Factoring	The equation is not factorable, so this is not an appropriate method.
Using square roots	The equation is not in the correct form, so this is not an appropriate method.
Completing the square	This method can be used on any quadratic equation. However, in this equation, a is not a perfect square, which means this method may be time consuming.
Using the Quadratic Formula	This method can be used on any quadratic equation. Because a is not a perfect square, this method may be faster than completing the square.

A. How can you verify that the equation is not factorable?

B. How do you know the equation is not in the correct form?

Solve the equation.

Solve by completing the square.

$$3x^2 - 4x - 8 = 0$$

$$3(3x^2 - 4x - 8) = 3(0)$$

$$9x^2 - 12x - 24 = 0$$

$$9x^2 - 12x = 24$$

$$9x^2 - 12x + 4 = 24 + 4$$

$$(3x - 2)^2 = 28$$

$$3x - 2 = \pm\sqrt{28}$$

$$x = \frac{2 \pm 2\sqrt{7}}{3}$$

$$x = \frac{2 + 2\sqrt{7}}{3} \text{ or } x = \frac{2 - 2\sqrt{7}}{3}$$

Use the Quadratic Formula to solve.

$$3x^2 - 4x - 8 = 0$$

C. What must be true of the equation before you identify a, b, and c?

$$a = 3, b = -4, c = -8$$

$$x = \frac{-(-4) \pm \sqrt{(-4)^2 - 4(3)(-8)}}{2(3)} = \frac{4 \pm \sqrt{112}}{6}$$

$$x = \frac{4 \pm 4\sqrt{7}}{6} = \frac{2(2 \pm 2\sqrt{7})}{6} = \frac{2 \pm 2\sqrt{7}}{3}$$

$$x = \frac{2 + 2\sqrt{7}}{3} \text{ or } x = \frac{2 - 2\sqrt{7}}{3}$$

Both methods give the same solution, $x = \dfrac{2 + 2\sqrt{7}}{3}$ or $x = \dfrac{2 - 2\sqrt{7}}{3}$.

 Turn and Talk How is the first step in solving by completing the square different from solving by using the Quadratic Formula?

Solve Real-World Quadratic Equations Using Any Method

3 A video game development company plans to release a new video game. The company uses a quadratic model to predict the future revenue R, in millions of dollars, based on the number v, in tens of thousands, of video games sold. The total cost C for developing the game is in millions of dollars. The profit P is the difference of the revenue and the cost. How many video games does the company need to sell in order to break even (that is, make a profit of $0)?

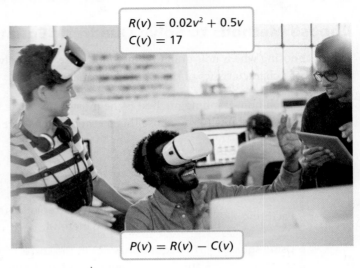

$R(v) = 0.02v^2 + 0.5v$

$C(v) = 17$

$P(v) = R(v) - C(v)$

Write equation.

Use the given model to write an equation for the situation.

$$R(v) - C(v) = P(v)$$

$$0.02v^2 + 0.5x - 17 = 0$$

> **A.** What does the number 17 represent in this equation?

Solve the equation.

$a = 0.02, b = 0.5, c = -17$

$$v = \frac{-0.5 \pm \sqrt{(0.5)^2 - 4(0.02)(-17)}}{2(0.02)}$$

> **B.** Why is using the Quadratic Formula a good method for solving this equation?

$$v = \frac{-0.5 \pm \sqrt{1.61}}{0.04}$$

$$v \approx 19.22 \text{ or } v \approx -44.22$$

Interpret any solutions. Then check by graphing.

The negative solution does not make sense in this context because the company cannot sell a negative number of video games. The model predicts that the company will break even if approximately 192,200 video games are sold. The graph supports this result.

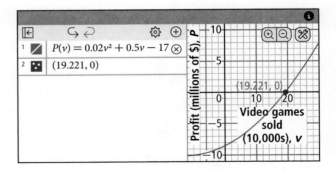

Turn and Talk How would the equation that models how many games the company needs to sell to break even change if the cost to develop the game was $18 million?

Check Understanding

State the method of solving that requires the fewest steps for each quadratic equation: graphing, factoring, using square roots, completing the square, or using the Quadratic Formula.

1. $x^2 - 3x - 10 = 0$

2. $-5x^2 = -30$

3. $2x^2 - 3x - 7 = 0$

4. $4x^2 + 16x = 3$

5. Consider the quadratic equation $0 = -2x^2 + 110x - 900$.

   A. Speculate which solution method is the most appropriate to solve the equation. Give a reason why you chose the method.

   B. What is the solution?

6. The height h, in feet, of a ball thrown into the air is modeled by $h(t) = -16t^2 + 32t + 4$, where t is the time in seconds after the ball is thrown. You want to determine when the ball will reach the ground.

   A. Which method is the most appropriate for solving $0 = -16t^2 + 32t + 4$?

   B. After how many seconds will the ball reach the ground? If necessary, round your answer to the nearest hundredth of a second.

On Your Own

7. **(MP) Critique Reasoning** Greta uses the graph shown to solve the quadratic equation $-2x^2 + 6 = 0$. She says the exact solution is $x = -1.8$ or $x = 1.8$. Is Greta's solution correct? Explain why or why not. If not, find the correct solution.

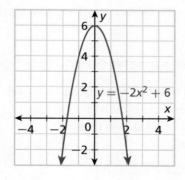

Speculate which solution method is the most appropriate for solving each equation. Explain your reasoning and solve. If necessary, leave answers in radical form.

8. $4x^2 + 12x = 3$

9. $3x^2 + x - 1 = 0$

10. $2x^2 - 3x - 5 = 0$

11. $2x^2 - 8 = 0$

12. $x^2 - x - 12 = 0$

13. $-4x^2 = -20$

14. $2x^2 + x - 10 = 0$

15. $-4x^2 + 4x + 8 = 0$

16. $-2x^2 + 5x = -3$

17. $3x^2 = -x + 7$

18. **Open Ended** Write three different equations—each as an example that is best solved using square roots, completing the square, or using the Quadratic Formula. Explain your reasoning.

19. (MP) **Use Structure** What do you look for in a given quadratic equation to determine if completing the square is the best solution method to use?

20. (MP) **Model with Mathematics** A bait shop is building a rectangular container with a total volume of 50 ft³ to hold a worm farm. The dimensions are shown.

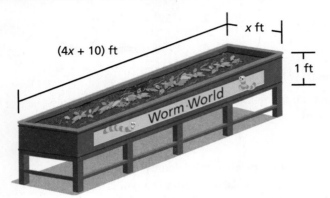

A. Write a quadratic equation to represent the volume of the container.

B. Which solution method is the most appropriate for finding the measurements of the length and width of the container? Find the length and width.

21. (MP) **Reason** Suppose you attempt to factor the equation $ax^2 + bx + c = 0$ where a, b, and c are integers but cannot find any factors of the form $mx + p$ and $nx + q$ where m, n, p, and q are integers. Does that mean that the equation has no real solutions? Explain.

Spiral Review • Assessment Readiness

22. When solving $4x^2 + 8x = -2$ by completing the square, what number would you add to both sides in order for the left side to be a perfect-square trinomial?

  Ⓐ 1   Ⓒ 4

  Ⓑ 2   Ⓓ 8

23. Solve $-x^2 + 2x + 2 = 0$ using the Quadratic Formula.

  Ⓐ $-2 \pm \sqrt{3}$ Ⓒ $1 \pm \sqrt{3}$

  Ⓑ $1 \pm 2\sqrt{3}$ Ⓓ $2 \pm \sqrt{3}$

24. Match each function with its zeros.

  A. $f(x) = 3x^2 - 6x$ **1.** $x = -1, 3$

  B. $f(x) = 3x^2 - 6x - 9$ **2.** $x = 0, 2$

  C. $f(x) = -(3x^2 + 9x)$ **3.** $x = -2, 0$

  D. $f(x) = -(3x^2 + 6x)$ **4.** $x = -3, 0$

I'm in a Learning Mindset!

What factors did I use to establish timelines for my goal of being able to choose the best methods for solving quadratic equations?

Solve by Using Square Roots

The floor area of a square room is 132 square feet. What are the dimensions of the room to the nearest tenth of a foot?

Let x represent the length, in feet, of one side of the square room. The area of the room can be modeled by the expression $x \cdot x = x^2$.

$x^2 = 132$

> Definition of square root

$x = \pm\sqrt{132}$

$x \approx \pm 11.5$

> Use a calculator to approximate the square root.

The dimensions of the square room are approximately 11.5 feet by 11.5 feet.

> Determine which value for x is reasonable in this context and answer the question.

Solve by Completing the Square

The height, in feet, of a ball thrown upwards can be modeled by $h(t) = -16t^2 + 128t + 6$, where t is time, in seconds. Find when the ball falls to the ground, rounded to the nearest tenth of a second.

$-16t^2 + 128t + 6 = 0$

$-\dfrac{1}{16}(-16t^2 + 128t + 6) = -\dfrac{1}{16}(0)$

$t^2 - 8t - \dfrac{6}{16} = 0$

$t^2 - 8t = \dfrac{6}{16}$

$t^2 - 8t + 16 = \dfrac{6}{16} + 16$

$(t - 4)^2 = \dfrac{262}{16}$

> Adding 16 to both sides makes the left side a perfect-square trinomial and keeps the equation balanced.

$t - 4 = \pm\sqrt{\dfrac{262}{16}}$

$t = 4 \pm \dfrac{\sqrt{262}}{4}$

> Definition of square root

The ball falls to the ground after $t = 4 \pm \dfrac{\sqrt{262}}{4}$ seconds, or approximately 8.0 seconds.

Solve by Using the Quadratic Formula

Use the Quadratic Formula to solve any quadratic equation of the form $ax^2 + bx + c = 0$, where a, b, and c are real numbers and $a \neq 0$.

$-16t^2 + 128t + 6 = 0$

> $a = -16$, $b = 128$, $c = 6$

$t = \dfrac{-b \pm \sqrt{b^2 - 4ac}}{2a}$

$= \dfrac{-128 \pm \sqrt{(128)^2 - 4(-16)(6)}}{2(-16)}$

> Substitute.

$= \dfrac{-128 \pm \sqrt{16768}}{-32}$

> Evaluate the discriminant.

$= 4 \pm \dfrac{\sqrt{262}}{4}$

> Simplify.

Using the Quadratic Formula results in the same solutions given by completing the square.

Choose the Best Method

The best method for solving a quadratic equation depends upon the numbers in the equation. For a quadratic equation in standard form, $ax^2 + bx + c = 0$ where a, b, and c are real numbers and $a \neq 0$, consider the following cases.

Case	Method
There is no bx term (that is, $b = 0$).	Solve for x^2 and use the definition of square roots.
$a = 1$, and b is even. Or, more generally, a is a perfect square and $2\sqrt{a}$ is a factor of b.	Complete the square.
Any case other than the two above.	Use the Quadratic Formula.

Vocabulary

Choose the correct term from the box to complete each sentence.

> **Vocabulary**
>
> completing the square
> discriminant
> perfect-square trinomial
> Quadratic Formula
> square root

1. All quadratic equations of the form $ax^2 + bx + c = 0$, where a, b, and c are real numbers and $a \neq 0$, can be solved by ___?___ or using the ___?___.

2. To solve $x^2 = 16$ for x, use the definition of the ___?___.

3. The ___?___ is the expression $b^2 - 4ac$ that appears in the Quadratic Formula.

4. $4x^2 + 12x + 9$ is an example of a ___?___.

Concepts and Skills

5. Explain the relationship between completing the square and the Quadratic Formula.

6. Explain why a quadratic equation with a positive discriminant has two real solutions, a quadratic equation with a negative discriminant has no real solution, and a quadratic equation with a discriminant of zero has one real solution.

Use the discriminant to determine the number of solutions.

7. $3x^2 + 5x - 1 = 0$

8. $x^2 + 4x + 8 = 0$

9. $-2x^2 - 4x = -32$

10. $4x^2 = 24x - 36$

Solve each equation. When necessary, give answers in simplest radical form.

11. $2x^2 = 32$

12. $(x + 4)^2 = 36$

13. $2x^2 - 4x - 3 = 0$

14. $x^2 - x - 6 = 0$

15. $2x^2 + 4x + 2 = 0$

16. $3x^2 + 2x = 2$

17. (MP) **Use Tools** A stone falls from a train trestle. The stone's height, in meters, above the ground is modeled by the function $h(t) = -4.9t^2 + 155$, where t is time in seconds. To the nearest tenth of a second, how long does it take the stone to hit the ground? State what strategy and tool you will use to answer the question, explain your choice, and then find the answer.

18. The height, in feet, of a launched water balloon is modeled by the function $h(t) = -16t^2 + 20t + 15$, where t is time, in seconds.

   A. At what time does the projectile have a height of 10 feet?

   B. How long is the projectile in the air?

   C. What are a reasonable domain and range for the function? Explain your reasoning.

Functions and Models

Demographer

STEM
POWERING INGENUITY

A demographer studies populations to identify trends and predict regional needs. Analyzing data collected from various communities aids in planning for and making decisions about utilities and services such as housing, hospitals, schools, water, and transportation infrastructure.

©electravk/Getty Images

STEM Task

Determine if recent population data demonstrates linear, quadratic, or exponential growth. Justify your reasoning.

World Population Statistics for 1960–2015			
Year	Population (billions)	Year	Population (billions)
1960	2.88	1990	5.31
1965	3.29	1995	5.72
1970	3.69	2000	6.12
1975	4.10	2005	6.53
1980	4.50	2010	6.93
1985	4.91	2015	7.34

Learning Mindset

Perseverance Collects and Tries Multiple Strategies

How can you choose the strategy that will work best for the given task? When problem-solving, there are often multiple ways to start moving towards the solution. Gathering and organizing your resources and strategies at the onset of the task gives you flexibility on your learning path. Sometimes you will have to choose a different path if the first strategy is not working out. Here are some questions you can ask yourself when selecting a strategy.

- What organizational tools and strategies are available for this task?

- What is important to consider when analyzing population growth? Which strategies can offer you insight into this data?

- What is my strategy for analyzing population growth? Can it be improved? How?

- What other strategies can I try if the first strategy I try does not work?

- How much time do I have to finish this task? What will I do if it is taking me too much time trying to select an effective strategy?

Reflect

Q When have you had to stop and approach a problem with a different strategy? What did you do when you realized that the original strategy did not work?

Q What would you need to do as a demographer if your first strategy for collecting data is not working? What should you do if you think your initial analysis needs to be revised? Explain your reasoning.

Build Quadratic Functions and Models

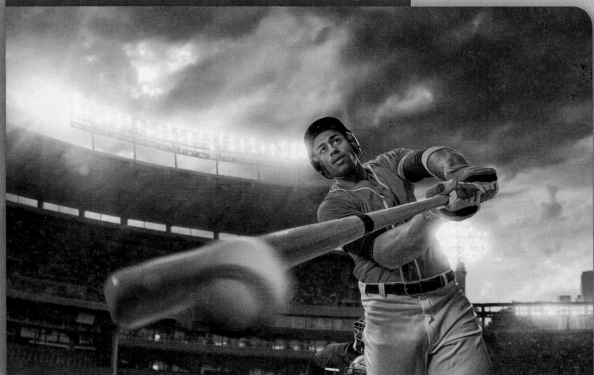

Home Run Derby

How can you measure the distance of a home run?

Are You Ready?

Complete these problems to review prior concepts and skills you will need for this module.

Compare Linear Functions

Compare the functions *f* and *g*.

$$f(x) = 2x + 3$$

x	0	1	2	3
g(x)	4	$4\frac{1}{3}$	$4\frac{2}{3}$	5

1. The graph of which function has the greater slope?

2. The graph of which function has the greater *y*-intercept?

3. Which function has the greater value when $x = 1$?

Transform Linear Functions

Create a graph to show the transformation of the parent linear function $f(x) = x$.

4. a translation down 3 units

5. a vertical stretch by a factor of 4

6. $g(x) = x + 2$

7. $g(x) = -2x$

Scatter Plots and Lines of Fit

The temperature, in °F, can be approximated by counting the number of cricket chirps in 15 seconds. Use the graph to solve each problem.

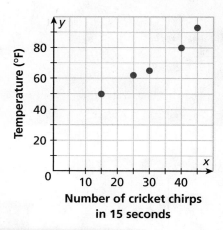

8. Draw a line of fit for the function.

9. If 20 cricket chirps are heard in 15 seconds, approximately what is the temperature?

10. Approximately how many cricket chirps would be heard in 15 seconds if the temperature is 70 °F?

Connecting Past and Present Learning

Previously, you learned:

- to rewrite linear and exponential functions to identify key characteristics,
- to solve quadratic equations by factoring,
- to compare linear and exponential functions in different forms, and
- to use linear and exponential regression to model a data set.

In this module, you will learn:

- to write quadratic functions in vertex, standard, and intercept form,
- to compare quadratic functions and models using key characteristics, and
- to fit quadratic functions to a data set using quadratic regression.

Quadratic Functions in Vertex Form

(I Can) write and graph quadratic functions in vertex form.

Spark Your Learning

The height of a free throw shot in basketball can be modeled by a quadratic function.

The ball is released at a different height for the two shots, but both shots reach the same maximum height.

Complete Part A as a whole class. Then complete Parts B–D in small groups.

    A. What is a mathematical question you can ask about this situation? What information would you need to know to answer your question?

    B. What variable(s) are involved in this situation? What unit of measurement would you use for each variable?

    C. To answer your question, what strategy and tool would you use along with all the information you have? What answer do you get?

    D. Does your answer make sense in the context of the situation?

 Turn and Talk What are the similarities and differences between the models for the two free throw shots?

Build Understanding

Identify Characteristics of the Parent Quadratic Function $f(x) = x^2$

A function that can be written in the form $f(x) = ax^2 + bx + c$ is called a quadratic function. The most basic quadratic function is the parent function $f(x) = x^2$.

1 A. Copy and complete the table for $f(x) = x^2$. Use the points from the table to graph $f(x) = x^2$. Draw a smooth curve through the plotted points.

x	$f(x) = x^2$
−4	?
−3	9
?	4
−1	?
?	0
1	?
2	?
?	9
4	?

Recall that the graph of a quadratic function is called a parabola. The highest or lowest point on a parabola is the vertex.

B. What is the shape of the graph of $f(x) = x^2$? Which point on the graph is the vertex?

C. In Lesson 8.2, an axis of symmetry was defined as a line that divides a graph into two symmetrical halves. Notice that for every point (x, y) on the graph of $f(x) = x^2$, the point $(-x, y)$ is also on the graph. What is the axis of symmetry for $f(x) = x^2$?

D. What is the x-intercept of the graph of f? What is the y-intercept?

E. For what values of x in the domain of $f(x)$ is the graph of f decreasing? For what values of x is the graph of f increasing?

F. The value of the function $f(x) = x^2$ is positive for all x-values other than $x = 0$. Why is the value of the function never negative?

G. What are the domain and range of $f(x) = x^2$? What happens to the graph of f as the value of x approaches negative infinity? As the value of x approaches positive infinity?

H. Does $f(x)$ increase fastest for $0 < x < 2$, for $2 < x < 4$, or for $4 < x < 6$? Explain.

 Turn and Talk Where is the vertex of a parabola in relationship to its axis of symmetry? Is the y-coordinate of the vertex a maximum or a minimum value for $f(x) = x^2$?

Identify Transformations of the Graph of $f(x) = x^2$

Previously, you learned how to stretch or compress, translate, and reflect the graph of a linear function. You can also perform similar transformations of the graph of the parent quadratic function $f(x) = x^2$.

2 ▶ **Stretch, Compression, or Reflection**

You can vertically stretch or compress the graph of the parent function by multiplying the range values by a nonzero number a. You can reflect the graph of the parent function across the x-axis by multiplying the range values by -1.

$f(x) = x^2$ $g(x) = -x^2$

$p(x) = 2x^2$ $q(x) = \frac{1}{2}x^2$

$r(x) = -2x^2$ $s(x) = -\frac{1}{2}x^2$

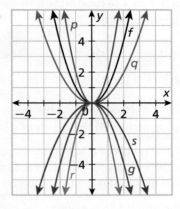

A. Which graph represents a stretch of the graph of f? A compression? A reflection? A stretch and a reflection? A compression and a reflection?

Horizontal Translation

You can translate the graph of the parent function horizontally by adding a nonzero number h to the domain values of the function.

$f(x) = x^2$

$m(x) = (x + 2)^2$

$n(x) = (x - 2)^2$

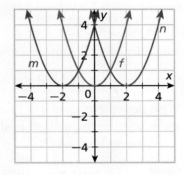

B. Which graph represents a translation of the graph of f to the right? A translation to the left?

Vertical Translation

You can translate the graph of the parent function vertically by adding a nonzero number k to the range values of the function.

$f(x) = x^2$

$v(x) = x^2 + 2$

$w(x) = x^2 - 2$

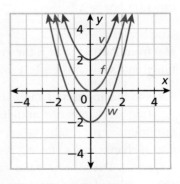

C. Which graph represents a translation of the graph of f up? A translation down?

 Turn and Talk How is the vertex of the graph of $g(x) = -x^2$ related to the vertex of the graph of $f(x) = x^2$? Describe how the vertex of each of the other transformed graphs in Task 2 is related to the vertex of the graph of f.

Graph Quadratic Functions in Vertex Form

Previously, you studied the standard form of a quadratic function. Now you will study the **vertex form of a quadratic function** which is $f(x) = a(x - h)^2 + k$, where a, h, and k are constants. You can graph quadratic functions written in vertex form by using the constants a, h, and k to determine how the graph is a transformation of the graph of the parent function $f(x) = x^2$.

Transformations of the Graph of the Parent Function $f(x) = x^2$
The graph of the function $g(x) = a(x - h)^2 + k$ is a transformation of the graph of $f(x) = x^2$. The vertex of the graph of g is the point (h, k). The axis of symmetry of the graph of g is the line $x = h$.
If $\lvert a \rvert > 1$, the graph of g is a vertical stretch of the graph of f. If $\lvert a \rvert < 1$, the graph of g is a vertical compression of the graph of f. If $a < 0$, the graph of g is a reflection across the x-axis of the graph of f.
If $h > 0$, the graph of g is a horizontal translation h units to the right of the graph of f. If $h < 0$, the graph of g is a horizontal translation $\lvert h \rvert$ units to the left of the graph of f.
If $k > 0$, the graph of g is a vertical translation k units up of the graph of f. If $k < 0$, the graph of g is a vertical translation $\lvert k \rvert$ units down of the graph of f.

Use a graphing calculator to complete Parts A–C.

3 **A.** Graph both $f(x) = x^2$ and $g(x) = -3x^2$.

What does the value of a in function g tell you about how the graph of g is related to the graph of the parent function f?

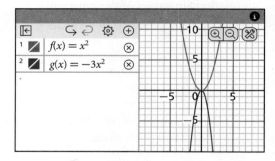

B. Graph $p(x) = -3(x - 2)^2$. How is the graph of p related to the graph of g from Part A? How is the graph of p related to the graph of the parent function $f(x) = x^2$?

C. Graph $q(x) = -3(x - 2)^2 + 5$. How is the graph of q related to the graph of p from Part B? How is the graph of q related to the graph of the parent function $f(x) = x^2$?

D. Refer to the graphs of f and q. Compare ranges, end behavior, where the functions are increasing and decreasing, whether the functions have a minimum or maximum value, and what that value is. Compare the average rate of change in $f(x)$ for $0 \le x \le 1$ to the average rate of change in $q(x)$ for $2 \le x \le 3$. Describe how the values of a, h, and k impact the key characteristics of $q(x)$ as compared to $f(x)$.

 Turn and Talk If a quadratic function has a graph that is symmetric across the line $x = -1$, has a minimum value of 2, and has an average rate of change of 3 for $-1 \le x \le 0$, what could be the vertex form of the function?

Step It Out

Write Quadratic Functions in Vertex Form

You can use the graph of a parabola to write the corresponding equation for a quadratic function in vertex form.

4 A coffee cup manufacturer is developing a new paraboloid-shaped cup design, where the interior surface of the cup forms a parabola for any cross section through the central axis of the cup (excluding the handle).

The shape of a coffee cup has an impact on heat retention and the comfort of drinking from it.

A cross section of the new coffee cup is shown in the graph. The cross section is placed on the coordinate grid so that the base and leftmost edge are on the x- and y-axes, respectively. Units are measured in centimeters. What is the distance between the two inside edges at the top of the cup?

Identify the vertex of the parabola.
The vertex is at $(3.5, 1)$.

> **A.** Why is another point needed to write the function?

Identify another point on the graph.
One other point on the graph is $(2.5, 2)$.

Write the vertex form of the function.
The vertex form of a quadratic function for the inside edge of the cup is $f(x) = a(x - 3.5)^2 + 1$.

Find the value of a.
Use the equation $2 = a(2.5 - 3.5)^2 + 1$ to find that $a = 1$.

Write the function.
The inside edge of the cup is modeled by $f(x) = (x - 3.5)^2 + 1$.

> **B.** What information was used to write this equation?

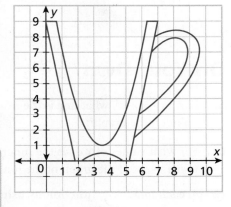

Answer the question.
Solve the equation $9 = (x - 3.5)^2 + 1$ to find the horizontal locations of the inside edges of the top of the cup, $x = 3.5 \pm 2\sqrt{2}$.

> **C.** How was this equation formed?

The distance between the inside edges is $(3.5 + 2\sqrt{2}) - (3.5 - 2\sqrt{2}) \approx 5.66$ centimeters.

Turn and Talk Does a coffee cup with an inside edge modeled by $g(x) = (x - 3.4)^2 + 0.8$ have the same parabolic shape as the cup modeled by $f(x) = (x - 3.5)^2 + 1$? Why or why not?

Check Understanding

1. Given the function $g(x) = 2x^2$, for what values of x is $g(x) \geq 0$? For what values of x is the function decreasing? For what values of x is the function increasing? What line is the axis of symmetry?

2. Identify the transformations of the graph of $f(x) = x^2$ that result in the graph of g. What rule, in vertex form, can you write for $g(x)$?

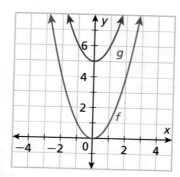

3. Graph the function $g(x) = 2(x + 1)^2 - 3$. What line is the axis of symmetry, and what point is the vertex of the graph?

4. Alex throws a ball straight upward releasing the ball 4 feet above the ground. At 1.5 seconds the ball reaches its maximum height, then the ball begins falling toward the ground. The graph represents the height of the ball over time. Use the graph to write the function in the form $h(t) = a(t - h)^2 + k$, where h is the height of the ball (in feet) and t is time (in seconds). Alex catches the ball 3 feet above the ground. How long is the ball in the air before it is caught?

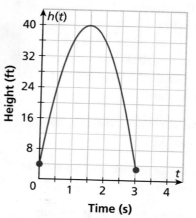

On Your Own

5. For $f(x) = -x^2$, what line is the axis of symmetry? Why is the vertex the highest point on the graph?

6. For what values of x does the function $f(x) = \frac{1}{2}x^2$ increase? What are the x- and y-intercepts of the graph of the function?

Graph each quadratic function by using a table of values. Identify how the graph is related to the graph of the parent quadratic function. Identify the axis of symmetry and the vertex.

7. $g(x) = (x + 3)^2 + 2$

8. $g(x) = 2(x)^2 + 4$

9. $g(x) = -(x + 1)^2 - 5$

State the values for a, h, and k and how they affect the graph of the parent function $f(x) = x^2$.

10. $g(x) = -4(x - 1)^2 + 2$

11. $g(x) = -\frac{1}{3}(x + 2)^2 - 3$

12. $g(x) = \frac{1}{4}(x - 3)^2 + 4$

13. $g(x) = \frac{3}{2}(x + 1)^2 - 2$

For each graph, identify the transformation (stretch, compression, reflection, translation) of the graph of the parent function $f(x) = x^2$ that results in the graph of the function g.

14. $g(x) = (x + 5)^2$

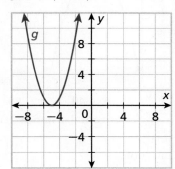

15. $g(x) = 3x^2$

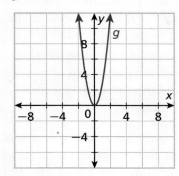

16. $g(x) = -\dfrac{1}{2}x^2$

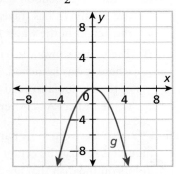

17. $g(x) = (x - 2)^2$

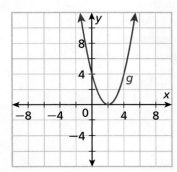

18. $g(x) = x^2 + 4$

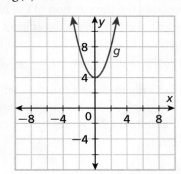

19. $g(x) = -(x + 2)^2 + 6$

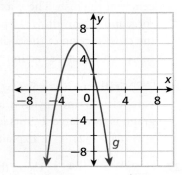

Write the vertex form of a quadratic function for each graph.

20.

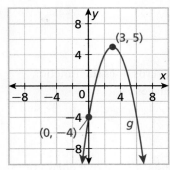

(3, 5)

(0, −4)

g

21.

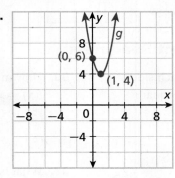

(0, 6)

g

(1, 4)

22.

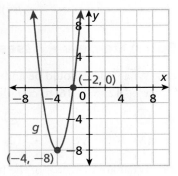

(−2, 0)

g

(−4, −8)

23. Use a graphing calculator to graph both $f(x) = x^2$ and $g(x) = -2(x - 3)^2 + 4$.

   A. Identify the values of a, h, and k in the function g.

   B. What effect does the value of a have on the graph of g when compared to the graph of f?

   C. What effect do the values of h and k have on the graph of g when compared to the graph of f?

   D. Describe the overall effects of the constants a, h, and k on the graph of $g(x) = a(x - h)^2 + k$ when compared to the graph of the parent function $f(x) = x^2$.

24. (MP) **Attend to Precision** Marcus builds a water balloon launcher. He launches the balloon from the ground.

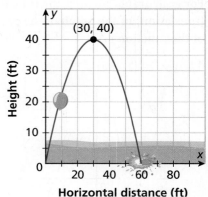

A. Write a quadratic function in vertex form to model the location of the water balloon if x represents the horizontal distance the water balloon has traveled from where it was launched, and y is the height of the water balloon above the ground.

B. The figure shows the balloon landing at about 60 feet from where it was launched. How can you use the axis of symmetry of the parabola to verify this distance? Does the function you wrote in Part A also verify this distance?

25. (MP) **Use Structure** A parabolic satellite dish has a diameter of 3 feet. It is mounted so that the center is 2 feet above and 6 feet from the edge of a flat roof. Points on the dish that are 1 foot from the center are 2.5 feet above the roof. Suppose a coordinate plane is perpendicular to the roof and passes through the center of the dish. The x-axis represents the intersection of the plane and the roof, and the origin is the point where the line meets the edge of the roof. Sketch the cross section of the dish and write a function with an appropriate domain to represent the cross section. What is the depth of the dish at its center? Explain.

26. (MP) **Critique Reasoning** Juan is trying to write a function whose graph is a parabola obtained by translating the graph of the parent quadratic function. The graph is translated 2 units left and 2 units up. He writes the function $g(x) = (x - 2)^2 + 2$. Explain the error.

27. (Open Middle™) Using the digits 1 to 9, at most one time each, complete the equation to create a quadratic function in vertex form with the least minimum value.

$$f(x) = \boxed{}\left(x - \boxed{}\right)^2 + \boxed{}$$

Spiral Review • Assessment Readiness

28. What value should be added to each side of $x^2 + 12x = -16$, to complete the square?

　(A) 12　　　　　　　(C) 144

　(B) 36　　　　　　　(D) 256

29. What are the zeros of the function $f(x) = x^2 - 7x - 8$?

　(A) $x = 1, x = 8$　　　(C) $x = -1, x = -8$

　(B) $x = -1, x = 8$　　(D) $x = 1, x = -8$

30. How many real zeros does the function $f(x) = x^2 + 36$ have?

　(A) 0　　　　　　　(C) 2

　(B) 1　　　　　　　(D) 3

31. What is the standard form of a quadratic function?

　(A) $y = mx + b$　　　(C) $y = ax^2 + bx + c$

　(B) $Ax + By = C$　　(D) $y = a(x - h) + k$

 I'm in a Learning Mindset!

Did I manage my time effectively while I was learning about quadratic functions in vertex form? What steps did I take to manage my time?

Quadratic Functions in Standard Form

(I Can) graph quadratic functions in standard form and convert between standard and vertex forms of quadratic functions.

Spark Your Learning

Although the shape of the Gateway Arch in St. Louis is a flattened catenary curve, it can be approximated by a parabola.

The width of the Gateway Arch is approximately 630 feet.

Complete Part A as a whole class. Then complete Parts B–D in small groups.

A. What is a mathematical question you can ask about this situation? What information would you need to know to answer your question?

B. What variable(s) are involved in this situation?

C. To answer your question, what strategy and tool would you use along with all the information you have? What answer do you get?

D. Does your answer make sense in the context of the situation? How do you know?

 Turn and Talk Suppose an arch similar to the Gateway Arch is being designed. Predict how the height of the structure would change for each of the following.

- The quadratic model of the Gateway Arch is multiplied by a number greater than 1.
- The quadratic model is multiplied by a number between 0 and 1.

Build Understanding

Convert from Vertex Form to Standard Form

You can convert a quadratic function written in vertex form, $f(x) = a(x - h)^2 + k$, to standard form, $f(x) = ax^2 + bx + c$, by expanding $(x - h)^2$.

$$f(x) = a(x - h)^2 + k \qquad \text{Vertex form}$$

$$= a(x^2 - 2hx + h^2) + k \qquad \text{Square the binomial.}$$

$$= ax^2 - 2ahx + ah^2 + k \qquad \text{Distribute } a \text{ to the terms of the trinomial.}$$

$$= ax^2 + (-2ah)x + (ah^2 + k) \qquad \text{Write as a sum of an } x^2\text{-term, an } x\text{-term, and a constant.}$$

$$= ax^2 + bx + c, \qquad \text{Relate to standard form.}$$

where $b = -2ah$ and $c = ah^2 + k$

1 **A.** When a quadratic function is written in vertex form, the axis of symmetry is the line $x = h$. Solve $b = -2ah$ for h. What is the equation of the axis of symmetry, in terms of a and b, for the graph of a quadratic function written in standard form?

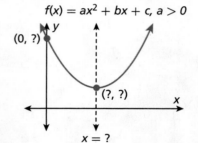

B. When a quadratic function is written in vertex form, the maximum or minimum value of the function is $f(x) = k$. Solve $c = ah^2 + k$ for k. Then substitute the expression for h in terms of a and b found in Part A. What is the maximum or minimum value, in terms of a, b, and c, for a quadratic function written in standard form?

C. In Parts A and B you found expressions for h and k in terms of a, b, and c. Write the ordered pair, in terms of a, b, and c, for the vertex of the graph of a quadratic function written in standard form.

D. Recall that the y-intercept of the graph of a function occurs when $x = 0$. What is the y-intercept, in terms of a, b, and c, for the graph of a quadratic function written in standard form?

E. Recall that the x-intercepts of the graph of a function occur when $f(x) = 0$. What expression can you use to find the x-intercepts for the graph of a quadratic function written in standard form?

F. The equation for a function is $f(x) = x^2 - 6x + 11$. Identify the axis of symmetry, maximum or minimum value, vertex, y-intercept, and any x-intercepts.

Turn and Talk How can you use the value $x = -\frac{b}{2a}$ and the function $f(x) = ax^2 + bx + c$ to find the maximum or minimum value of the function? Explain.

Convert from Standard Form to Vertex Form

You can use the technique of completing the square to convert the standard form of a quadratic equation, $f(x) = ax^2 + bx + c$, to the vertex form, $f(x) = a(x - h)^2 + k$.

$f(x) = ax^2 + bx + c$ Standard form

$= a\left(x^2 + \dfrac{b}{a}x\right) + c$ Factor a from the variable terms.

$= a\left(x^2 + \dfrac{b}{a}x + \left(\dfrac{b}{2a}\right)^2 - \left(\dfrac{b}{2a}\right)^2\right) + c$ Add and subtract $\left(\dfrac{b}{2a}\right)^2$ to complete the square.

$= a\left(x^2 + \dfrac{b}{a}x + \left(\dfrac{b}{2a}\right)^2\right) + c - a\left(\dfrac{b}{2a}\right)^2$ Distribute a to $-\left(\dfrac{b}{2a}\right)^2$.

$= a\left(x + \dfrac{b}{2a}\right)^2 + c - \dfrac{b^2}{4a}$ Factor the trinomial; simplify the constant.

$= a\left(x + \dfrac{b}{2a}\right)^2 + \dfrac{4ac - b^2}{4a}$ Vertex form

2 ▶ A. For the form $f(x) = a(x - h)^2 + k$, the vertex is the point (h, k). Use the vertex form of $f(x) = ax^2 + bx + c$ shown above to write (h, k) in terms of a, b, and c.

B. Use the vertex form of $f(x) = ax^2 + bx + c$ shown above to determine the equation of the axis of symmetry. How is this equation related to the ordered pair you wrote in Task 1?

C. Evaluate the vertex form of $f(x) = ax^2 + bx + c$ at $x = -\dfrac{b}{2a} - d$ and $x = -\dfrac{b}{2a} + d$, where d is an arbitrary number. What do you notice about $f\left(-\dfrac{b}{2a} - d\right)$ and $f\left(-\dfrac{b}{2a} + d\right)$? What is the relationship between the points $\left(-\dfrac{b}{2a} - d, f\left(-\dfrac{b}{2a} - d\right)\right)$ and $\left(-\dfrac{b}{2a} + d, f\left(-\dfrac{b}{2a} + d\right)\right)$

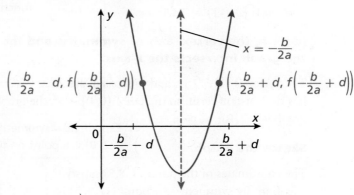

and the axis of symmetry of the graph? What does this relationship confirm about the parabola shown?

D. Use the vertex form of $f(x) = ax^2 + bx + c$ shown above to find the zeros of the function. What do you notice about the expressions for the zeros?

E. Follow the process for completing the square to rewrite $f(x) = 2x^2 + 6x + 5$ in vertex form. What are the coordinates of the vertex?

Turn and Talk Explain why you do not need to memorize that the vertex of a quadratic function in standard form is $\left(-\dfrac{b}{2a}, \dfrac{4ac - b^2}{4a}\right)$.

Step It Out

Graph Quadratic Functions Given in Standard Form

To graph a quadratic function given in standard form, it is helpful to rewrite the function in vertex form.

 3   Arches have been used in the construction of buildings and bridges for centuries. Suppose the larger arch of the structure shown is approximated by the function $y = -0.1x^2 + 2.2x$, where x is the distance, in feet, along the ground from the left end of the arch to the right and y is the height in feet. Draw the parabola that models the shape of the arch by graphing the function.

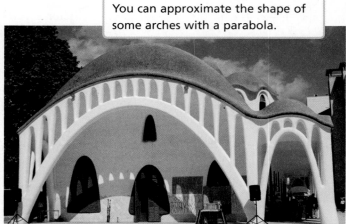

> You can approximate the shape of some arches with a parabola.

Rewrite the equation in vertex form by completing the square.

$$y = -0.1x^2 + 2.2x$$
$$= -0.1(x^2 + 22x)$$
$$= -0.1(x^2 - 22x + 121) + 0.1(121)$$
$$= -0.1(x - 11)^2 + 12.1$$

> **A.** Why is it helpful to write the function in vertex form?

Identify the vertex, axis of symmetry, and the two points where the graph intersects the x-axis.

The vertex is $(11, 12.1)$, and the axis of symmetry is $x = 11$. The given equation has no constant term, so the point $(0, 0)$ is on the graph. Another point on the graph is $(22, 0)$.

> **B.** Explain how symmetry was used to determine $(22, 0)$ is a point on the graph.

Sketch the graph.

The coordinates of the point $(5, 8.5)$ satisfy the equation. By symmetry, the point $(17, 8.5)$ is also on the graph. Plot points at $(0, 0)$, $(5, 8.5)$, $(11, 12.1)$, $(17, 8.5)$, and $(22, 0)$. Use these points and symmetry to sketch a parabola that models the shape of the arch.

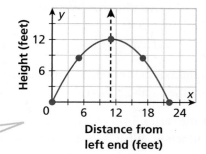

Distance from left end (feet)

> **C.** Why is the axis of symmetry helpful when sketching the graph?

 Turn and Talk How could you improve the accuracy of the graph?

Analyze Real-World Quadratic Functions in Standard Form

Recall that the projectile motion model describes the height of a projectile over time. The projectile's height is determined by this function:

$$h(t) = -16t^2 + v_0 t + h_0$$

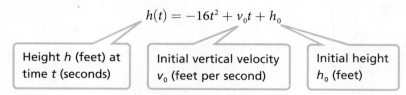

Height h (feet) at time t (seconds)

Initial vertical velocity v_0 (feet per second)

Initial height h_0 (feet)

The projectile motion model is an example of a quadratic function in standard form.

4 ▶ Olivia is practicing catching a baseball by throwing it straight up into the air. She throws the baseball at a speed of 32 feet per second. What is the maximum height that the baseball reaches and the time at which that height is reached?

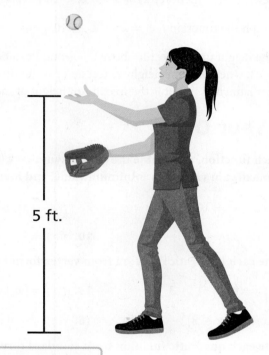

Since the initial velocity v_0 is 32 feet per second and the initial height h_0 is 5 feet, the height of the baseball above the ground can be modeled by $h(t) = -16t^2 + 32t + 5$, where t is the time in seconds since Olivia released the baseball.

5 ft.

The vertex of the graph of a quadratic function with a negative leading coefficient gives the function's maximum value, so the vertex of the graph of h gives the maximum height reached by the ball. Rewrite the function h in vertex form.

$h(t) = -16t^2 + 32t + 5$

$= -16(t^2 - 2t) + 5$

$= -16(t^2 - 2t + 1) + 5 + 16(1)$

$= -16(t - 1)^2 + 21$

A. Why is the first step to factor out -16?

B. Why is 16(1) added to the expression at this step?

This form of the function reveals the vertex to be the point $(1, 21)$.

C. What is the baseball's maximum height?

D. How many seconds after Olivia releases the baseball does it reach its maximum height?

Turn and Talk If Olivia were able to throw the baseball up in the air at double the initial vertical velocity (64 feet per second instead of 32 feet per second), does the maximum height of the baseball also double? If so, explain why. If not, how does the new maximum height relate to the maximum height when the baseball was thrown at 32 feet per second?

Check Understanding

1. The function $f(x) = x^2 - 4x + 3$ is in standard form.

   A. What is the axis of symmetry?

   B. What is the vertex?

   C. Does the function have a maximum value or a minimum value?

   D. Identify any x- and y-intercepts.

2. Rewrite the function $f(x) = (x - 2)^2 + 3$ in standard form.

3. Rewrite the function $f(x) = x^2 + 8x + 20$ in vertex form.

4. Graph the function $f(x) = x^2 + 4x + 10$.

5. The height of a projectile above the ground can be modeled by $h(t) = -16t^2 + 32t + 64$, where h is the height in feet and t is the time in seconds since the projectile was launched. What is the maximum height of the projectile?

On Your Own

For each function, determine the axis of symmetry, the vertex, whether the function has a maximum value or a minimum value, and identify any x- and y-intercepts.

6. $f(x) = x^2 + 10x + 25$

7. $f(x) = x^2 + 14x + 33$

8. $f(x) = -2x^2 - 12x + 14$

9. $f(x) = 3x^2 - 12x + 36$

10. $f(x) = -x^2 - 20x + 156$

11. $f(x) = -3x^2 + 18x - 24$

Rewrite each quadratic function from vertex form to standard form.

12. $f(x) = (x - 5)^2 + 3$

13. $f(x) = (x + 4)^2 + 6$

14. $f(x) = 2(x - 3)^2 + 8$

15. $f(x) = -(x + 8)^2 - 12$

16. $f(x) = -3(x - 4)^2 + 25$

17. $f(x) = 3(x + 2)^2 + 4$

Rewrite each quadratic function from standard form to vertex form.

18. $f(x) = x^2 + 12x + 20$

19. $f(x) = x^2 - 8x + 15$

20. $f(x) = 2x^2 + 12x + 2$

21. $f(x) = 4x^2 + 24x + 40$

22. $f(x) = -2x^2 - 20x - 12$

23. $f(x) = -4x^2 + 16x + 6$

24. You can approximate the shape of a banana using a parabola. Positioning the y-axis at the left end of the banana and the x-axis on the tabletop underneath the banana, you get the equation shown, where x and y are measured in centimeters. Rewrite the equation in vertex form and use the result to estimate the length of the banana, the thickness of the banana halfway along its length, and the height of the left end of the banana above the tabletop. Explain your reasoning.

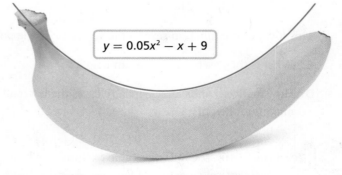

$y = 0.05x^2 - x + 9$

25. (MP) Attend to Precision The arc of water from a water fountain has the shape of a parabola. Positioning the y-axis where the water emerges from the fountain and the x-axis on the surface of the water in the fountain, you get the equation shown, where x and y are measured in feet. Rewrite the equation in vertex form and use the result to estimate how high the water arc goes and how wide the water arc is at its base. Explain your reasoning.

$y = -x^2 + 5x$

26. (MP) Reason Suppose $f(x) = (x - h)^2 + k$. Write the function f in standard form.

27. (MP) Reason Can every quadratic function in standard form be rewritten in vertex form? Explain.

28. (MP) Use Repeated Reasoning Consider a quadratic function given in standard form, $f(x) = ax^2 + bx + c$.

  A. How do you identify the vertex of the graph of the function?

  B. How do you know whether the graph has a minimum or maximum?

  C. How can you identify the y-intercept of the graph?

Graph each quadratic function.

29. $f(x) = x^2 + 4x + 8$

30. $f(x) = x^2 + 2x - 6$

31. $f(x) = 2x^2 + 8x + 1$

32. $f(x) = 3x^2 + 3x + 6$

33. $f(x) = -x^2 - 5x + 2$

34. $f(x) = -5x^2 - 10x + 25$

35. (MP) Use Structure How does the symmetry of a parabola help you graph a quadratic function? Explain.

36. Open Ended When do you think the vertex form of a quadratic function is most useful? the standard form?

37. During an eruption, a volcano that is 10,000 feet tall shoots a rock into the air with an initial vertical velocity of 220 feet per second. What is the maximum height of the rock?

38. A compressed air rocket is shot from the ground with an initial vertical velocity of 30 feet per second. After how many seconds does the rocket reach its maximum height?

39. Molly is practicing kicking a soccer ball. She kicks the ball with an initial vertical velocity of 40 feet per second.

  A. What quadratic function, in standard form, models the height of the soccer ball?

  B. What is the maximum height of the soccer ball?

  C. After how many seconds does the soccer ball reach its maximum height?

2.5 ft

40. Robert is at tennis practice. His coach asks all of the players to warm up by bouncing a tennis ball on their racket while keeping the racket at the same height above the court. Robert bounces his tennis ball with an upward velocity of 8 feet per second.

> Robert's tennis racket is 4 feet above the ground.

A. What quadratic function, in standard form, models the height of the tennis ball above the court?

B. What is the y-intercept of the graph of the function you wrote? What does it represent?

C. What is the maximum height of the tennis ball?

D. How long after Robert hits the tennis ball the first time does the ball reach its maximum height?

E. How long after he hits the ball the first time will the ball return to its starting height?

F. Use a graph of the function you wrote to approximate how long it would take for the ball to hit the court if Robert misses it with his racket.

41. **(MP) Critique Reasoning** Marvin wrote $f(x) = -6(x + 3)^2 - 18$ in standard form as $f(x) = -6x^2 + 6x - 9$. What is his error? Explain his mistake and write the standard form of the function correctly.

42. **(Open Middle™)** Using the digits 1 to 9, at most one time each, copy the equation and fill in the boxes to create a quadratic equation in standard form with the least minimum value.

$$y = \boxed{}\, x^2 + \boxed{}\, x + \boxed{}$$

Spiral Review • Assessment Readiness

43. Use the Quadratic Formula to identify the zeros of $f(x) = x^2 + 0.75x + 0.125$.

Ⓐ $x = -0.25, -0.5$ Ⓒ $x = 0.25, 0.5$

Ⓑ $x = -0.25, 0.5$ Ⓓ $x = 0.25, -0.5$

44. The graph of which quadratic function has its vertex at $(4, 5)$ and passes through the point $(5, 6)$?

Ⓐ $f(x) = (x + 4)^2 + 5$

Ⓑ $f(x) = (x - 4)^2 + 5$

Ⓒ $f(x) = (x - 4)^2 - 5$

Ⓓ $f(x) = (x + 4)^2 - 5$

45. Which method would you use to find the zeros of $f(x) = x^2 - 22x + 121$?

Ⓐ Factor.

Ⓑ Complete the square.

Ⓒ Use square roots.

Ⓓ Use the Quadratic Formula.

46. How many x-intercepts does the graph of $f(x) = -x^2 + 10x - 1$ have?

Ⓐ 0   Ⓒ 2

Ⓑ 1   Ⓓ 3

 I'm in a Learning Mindset!

How effective was completing the square for identifying the vertex of quadratic functions written in standard form?

Quadratic Functions in Intercept Form

(I Can) write and graph quadratic functions in intercept form.

Spark Your Learning

The arch supporting the bridge can be modeled by the graph of a quadratic function. Three points on the graph are shown.

Complete Part A as a whole class. Then complete Parts B–D in small groups.

A. What is a mathematical question you can ask about this situation? What information would you need to know to answer your question?

B. What is the significance of points *A*, *B*, and *C*?

C. To answer your question, what strategy and tool would you use along with all the information you have? What answer do you get?

D. Does your answer make sense in the context of the situation? How do you know?

Turn and Talk How could you find the length of the road supported by the parabolic arch between points *A* and *B*?

Build Understanding

Investigate Different Forms of Quadratic Functions

When a quadratic function is written in vertex form, you can identify certain key characteristics of the graph of the function. In the following task, you will investigate another form of a quadratic function that reveals other key characteristics of the graph of the function.

1 The graphs of four quadratic functions are shown below.

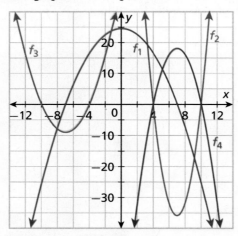

A. The four functions shown above are written in vertex form in the table below. Copy and complete the table to determine whether the graph of each function opens up or down, the graph's axis of symmetry, and which labeled graph above corresponds to the function.

Function	Does graph open up or down?	Axis of symmetry	Graph
$g(x) = (x - 7)^2 - 9$	?	$x =$?	?
$h(x) = -2(x + 7)^2 + 18$	?	$x =$?	?
$j(x) = -\frac{1}{2}x^2 + \frac{49}{2}$	?	$x =$?	?
$k(x) = 4(x - 7)^2 - 36$	?	$x =$?	?

B. Rewrite each function in standard form. Then use what you have learned about factoring quadratic expressions to write each function in the form $f(x) = a(x - x_1)(x - x_2)$. How are the values of x_1 and x_2 for each function related to the graph of the function?

C. For a function written in the form $f(x) = a(x - x_1)(x - x_2)$, how can you determine if its graph opens up or down? How can you determine the axis of symmetry of its graph?

D. Describe the steps you would take to graph a function written in the form $f(x) = a(x - x_1)(x - x_2)$.

 Turn and Talk Give an example of a function written in the form $f(x) = a(x - x_1)$ $(x - x_2)$ that has a graph that opens down and x-intercepts at $(2, 0)$ and $(6, 0)$.

Write Quadratic Functions in Intercept Form

The **intercept form of a quadratic function** is $f(x) = a(x - x_1)(x - x_2)$ where x_1 and x_2 are the x-intercepts of the graph of the function. You have learned that the x-intercepts of the graph of a function are the zeros of the function. So, x_1 and x_2 are the zeros of the function $f(x) = a(x - x_1)(x - x_2)$.

When given a quadratic function in standard form, you can use what you have learned about factoring quadratic expressions to rewrite the function in intercept form.

2▸ Consider the three quadratic functions shown below. You are given the standard form of the function, the intercept form of the function, and the graph of the function.

$f(x) = x^2 + 3x - 4$ $g(x) = -4x^2 - 8x - 4$ $h(x) = x^2 + 2x + 5$

$f(x) = (x + 4)(x - 1)$ $g(x) = -4(x + 1)^2$ No intercept form

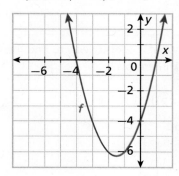   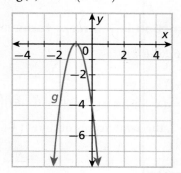 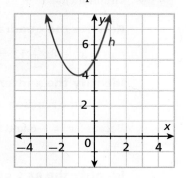

A. What do you observe about the relationship between the intercept form of each function and its corresponding graph?

B. Copy and complete the table using the given information.

Function description	Number of x-intercepts of graph
$f(x) = a(x - x_1)(x - x_2)$ where $x_1 \neq x_2$	?
$f(x) = a(x - x_1)(x - x_2)$ where $x_1 = x_2$	?
The function cannot be written in intercept form.	?

C. For the function $g(x) = -4(x + 1)^2$, why is it incorrect to say that the x-intercept of the graph of g is 1? How could you write the rule for $g(x)$ to make the x-intercept more apparent?

D. Explain why every quadratic function cannot be written in intercept form.

 Turn and Talk Give an example of a quadratic function written in intercept form where the vertex of the graph of the function is also the only x-intercept of the graph of the function.

Step It Out

Graph Quadratic Functions in Intercept Form

You can identify key characteristics of the graph of a quadratic function when it is written in intercept form $f(x) = a(x - x_1)(x - x_2)$. The values of x_1 and x_2 are the x-intercepts of the graph of the function. The axis of symmetry is halfway between $(x_1, 0)$ and $(x_2, 0)$, so the axis of symmetry is $x = \frac{x_1 + x_2}{2}$.

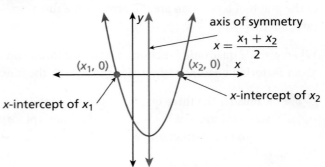

axis of symmetry

$x = \frac{x_1 + x_2}{2}$

$(x_1, 0)$ $(x_2, 0)$ x

x-intercept of x_1

x-intercept of x_2

3 ▶ Graph $f(x) = x^2 + 8x + 12$.

Rewrite the quadratic function in intercept form.

$f(x) = x^2 + 8x + 12 = (x + 6)(x + 2)$

> **A.** What is another way to find the x-intercepts?

Identify the x-intercepts.

Rewrite the function as $f(x) = (x + 6)(x + 2) = \left(x - (-6)\right)\left(x - (-2)\right)$.

Because $x_1 = -6$ and $x_2 = -2$, the x-intercepts occur at $(-6, 0)$ and $(-2, 0)$.

Identify the axis of symmetry.

$x = \dfrac{x_1 + x_2}{2} = \dfrac{-6 + (-2)}{2} = -4$

Identify the vertex.

The x-coordinate of the vertex is -4.

> **B.** Why is the x-coordinate of the vertex -4?

The y-coordinate of the vertex is as follows:

$f(-4) = (-4)^2 + 8(-4) + 12 = -4$.

The vertex is $(-4, -4)$.

> **C.** How is the y-coordinate of the vertex found?

Graph the function.

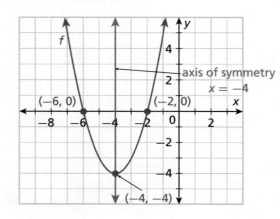

axis of symmetry
$x = -4$

$(-6, 0)$ $(-2, 0)$

$(-4, -4)$

> **D.** How are the key characteristics of the graph used to draw the graph?

Choose an Appropriate Form of a Quadratic Function

4 ▶ Ahiyana dives from a diving board into a pool. Her height h, in feet, above the surface of the water is a function of the time t, in seconds, after she starts her dive. Three different forms of this function are given below.

- How long is Ahiyana above the surface of the water during the dive?
- What is Ahiyana's maximum height during her dive?

The standard form is
$h(t) = -16t^2 + 16t + 32$.

The intercept form is
$h(t) = -16(t + 1)(t - 2)$.

The vertex form is
$h(t) = -16(t - 0.5)^2 + 36$.

Determine how long Ahiyana is above the water.

Ahiyana enters the water at a height of 0 feet. To find the time when $h(t) = 0$, find the zeros of $h(t) = -16t^2 + 16t + 32$.

To find the zeros of a function, use the function written in intercept form.

$h(t) = -16(t + 1)(t - 2)$

> **A.** What does $t = 2$ represent in this situation?

The zeros of the function are -1 and 2.

Ahiyana is above the surface of the water for 2 seconds.

> **B.** Why is $t = -1$ ignored?

Determine the maximum height.

Ahiyana's maximum height during her dive is at the vertex of the graph of the function. To find the vertex of the graph, use the function written in vertex form.

> **C.** What does the vertex of the graph represent in this situation?

$h(t) = -16(t - 0.5)^2 + 36$

The vertex of the graph is $(0.5, 36)$.

Ahiyana's maximum height during the dive is 36 feet.

Check your answers by graphing the function.

Note that the parts of the function's graph outside Quadrant I aren't relevant to this situation.

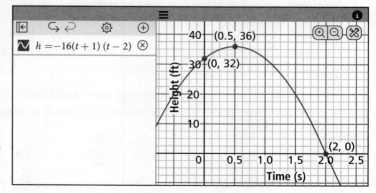

Turn and Talk What does the y-intercept of the graph represent in this situation?

Check Understanding

1. What are the x-intercepts of the graph of $f(x) = -2(x - 2)(x - 4)$?

Write each quadratic function in intercept form. Then determine the x-intercepts of the graph of each function.

2. $f(x) = x^2 - 31x + 220$

3. $f(x) = 3x^2 - 6x - 105$

4. How are the vertex and the x-intercepts of the graph of $f(x) = 4(x - 9)^2$ related?

5. How can you use the x-intercepts of the graph of $f(x) = -(x - 12)(x - 14)$ to find the axis of symmetry of the graph?

6. The height, in feet, of an object at time t, in seconds, after it is launched into the air can be represented by the functions below.

$$h(t) = -16(t + 2)(t - 3)$$

$$h(t) = -16(t - 0.5)^2 + 100$$

$$h(t) = -16t^2 + 16t + 96$$

   A. Which function would you use to find the maximum height reached by the object? What is the maximum height?

   B. Which function would you use to find the time the object is in the air? How long is the object in the air?

On Your Own

For Problems 7–9, use parabolas A, B, and C graphed at the right.

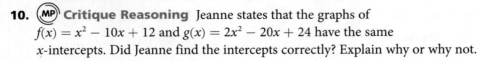

7. Which parabola represents $f(x) = (x + 1)(x - 4)$? $g(x) = -(x + 5)(x - 1)$? $h(x) = -\frac{1}{3}(x + 5)(x - 6)$?

8. Which two functions have graphs with a common x-intercept? Explain how you know by observing the functions and their graphs.

9. **Open Ended** Write a new function j in intercept form with a graph that has the same x-intercepts as parabola B.

10. (MP) **Critique Reasoning** Jeanne states that the graphs of $f(x) = x^2 - 10x + 12$ and $g(x) = 2x^2 - 20x + 24$ have the same x-intercepts. Did Jeanne find the intercepts correctly? Explain why or why not.

If possible, write each function in intercept form and identify the x-intercepts of the graph of the function. If the function cannot be written in intercept form, write *not factorable*.

11. $f(x) = -3x^2 + 9x - 6$

12. $f(x) = -x^2 + 5x - 9$

13. $f(x) = 3x^2 - 12x - 135$

14. $f(x) = x^2 - 3x - 154$

15. $f(x) = x^2 - 15x + 44$

16. $f(x) = x^2 - x - 132$

17. $f(x) = x^2 - 17x + 72$

18. $f(x) = 2x^2 - 22x - 24$

19. $f(x) = 2x^2 + 5x - 3$

20. **Use Repeated Reasoning** Identify any pairs of functions whose graphs have the same x-intercepts.

$f_1(x) = x^2 - 20x - 69$ $\qquad$ $f_2(x) = x^2 - 20x + 69$ $\qquad$ $f_3(x) = x^2 + 20x + 69$

$f_4(x) = -x^2 + 20x - 69$ $\qquad$ $f_5(x) = x^2 + 20x - 69$ $\qquad$ $f_6(x) = -x^2 + 20x + 69$

Write each function in intercept form. Identify the x-intercepts, the axis of symmetry, and the vertex of the graph of the function. Then graph the function.

21. $f(x) = x^2 + 10x + 24$ $\qquad\qquad$ **22.** $f(x) = x^2 + 4x - 32$

23. $f(x) = -x^2 - 12x - 27$ $\qquad\qquad$ **24.** $f(x) = -2x^2 + 20x - 32$

25. $f(x) = 2x^2 - 8x - 64$ $\qquad\qquad$ **26.** $f(x) = -x^2 - 6x + 72$

27. A cross-section of a satellite dish is given by graph of $f(x) = -\frac{1}{30}x^2 + \frac{4}{5}x$, where x is the horizontal distance, in inches, from the left edge and $f(x)$ is the depth, in inches, of the satellite dish x inches from the left edge.

 A. Rewrite the given function in intercept form. Then identify and interpret the x-intercepts of the graph of the function in this situation.

 B. Rewrite the function in vertex form. Then identify and interpret the vertex of the graph of the function in this situation.

 C. Use a graphing calculator to verify your solutions.

28. The monthly profit P, in dollars, of a party-planning business after time t, in months, is given by $P(t) = -30t^2 + 1260t - 2400$.

 A. Write the function in intercept form. What are the x-intercepts of the graph of the function? What do they mean in this situation?

 B. What is the y-intercept of the graph of the function? How would you interpret the y-intercept in this situation?

 C. Write the function in vertex form. What is the vertex of the graph of the function? How would you interpret the vertex in this situation?

29. A storage container with a rectangular base is being designed. The perimeter of the base is fixed at 44 feet. So, $2l + 2w = 44$ and $l = 22 - w$. Write a function for the area of the base, in square feet, in terms of the width w. What is the maximum area of the base for the given perimeter?

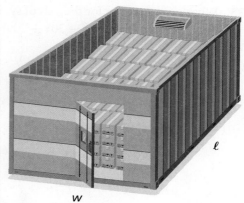

ℓ

w

30. The graph of a quadratic function has a vertex at $(1, 6)$ and x-intercepts at $(-3, 0)$ and $(5, 0)$.

 A. Use the given information to find the value of a in the intercept form of the function $f(x) = a(x - x_1)(x - x_2)$. The write the function in intercept form.

 B. Use the function rule to identify a fourth point on the graph. Repeat Part A using the new point and the x-intercepts. Is the value of a the same?

31. Henry is building a model train tunnel using a parabola for the shape of the tunnel opening. The shape of the tunnel opening is given by $f(x) = -\frac{1}{5}(x^2 - 13x + 12)$, where $f(x)$ is the height, in inches, of a point on the parabola x inches from the left of the tunnel's base. How wide is the opening of the tunnel at its base?

32. Ravi is tossing a lacrosse ball with a lacrosse stick. The height, in feet, of the ball at time t (in seconds) during Ravi's overhand toss is given by $h_1(t) = -16(t + 0.25)(t - 1.5)$. The height, in feet, of the ball at time t, in seconds, during Ravi's underhand toss is given by $h_2(t) = -16(t - 0.75)^2 + 10$. During which toss did the ball go higher? How much higher?

33. The shape of the hill of a roller coaster can be modeled by the function $h(x) = -\frac{1}{5}x^2 + 4x + 300$, where $f(x)$ is the height, in feet, of a point on the shape of the hill x inches from the left of a support beam.

A. Write h in intercept form.

B. What are the x-intercepts, y-intercept, and vertex of the graph of the function?

C. What is a reasonable domain for h based on your answer in Part A? What does this domain represent?

D. Sketch a graph of h over the reasonable domain you specified. Label the points from Part B on your graph.

Spiral Review • Assessment Readiness

34. What is the solution to the equation $x^2 + 2x - 14 = 1$?

Ⓐ $x = 5, x = -3$

Ⓑ $x = -5, x = -3$

Ⓒ $x = -5, x = 3$

Ⓓ $x = 5, x = 3$

35. What is an equation for the axis of symmetry of the graph of $f(x) = x^2 - 30x + 209$?

Ⓐ $x = -15$

Ⓑ $x = 15$

Ⓒ $x = -5$

Ⓓ $x = 5$

36. Which of the following functions represents a vertical compression and a vertical shift up of the graph of $f(x) = 10(x - 3)^2 + 5$?

Ⓐ $f(x) = 10(x - 3)^2 + 4$

Ⓑ $f(x) = 5(x - 3)^2 + 10$

Ⓒ $f(x) = 4(x - 3)^2 - 5$

Ⓓ $f(x) = 10(x - 5)^2 + 5$

37. Which of the following functions have graphs that represent a vertical stretch of the graph of the parent function $f(x) = x^2$? Select all that apply.

Ⓐ $f(x) = -\frac{3}{4}(x - 3)^2 - 5$

Ⓑ $f(x) = -3x^2 + 2x + 1$

Ⓒ $f(x) = 2.5(x - 4)(x + 5)$

Ⓓ $f(x) = -2.5(x - 4)(x + 5)$

 I'm in a Learning Mindset!

What did I learn about quadratic functions in intercept form that I can use in my future learning?

Compare Quadratic Functions

(I Can) compare quadratic functions represented in different forms.

Spark Your Learning

The owners of a dance studio consider two ways to lower the studio rental fee to maximize their monthly revenue.

The dance studio rental fee is $100 per hour. The studio is rented 40 hours per month.

Complete Part A as a whole class. Then complete Parts B–D in small groups.

A. What is a mathematical question you can ask about this situation? What information would you need to know to answer your question?

B. What variable(s) are involved in this situation?

C. To answer your question, what strategy and tool would you use along with all the information you have? What answer do you get?

D. Does your answer make sense in the context of the situation? How do you know?

 Turn and Talk How did you manipulate the revenue functions in order to analyze the difference in maximum monthly revenues?

Build Understanding

Analyze Different Forms of Quadratic Functions

You have learned how to write quadratic functions in standard form, vertex form, and intercept form. Each form gives you direct information about some key characteristics of the function's graph.

1 The quadratic function represented by the graph is written in three forms.

Standard form
$$f(x) = \frac{1}{10}x^2 - \frac{12}{5}x + 8$$

Vertex form
$$f(x) = \frac{1}{10}(x - 12)^2 - \frac{32}{5}$$

Intercept form
$$f(x) = \frac{1}{10}(x - 4)(x - 20)$$

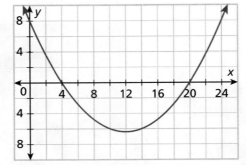

A. Which form would you use to determine the x-intercepts of the graph of the function? Explain your reasoning.

B. Which form would you use to determine the minimum value of the function? Explain your reasoning.

C. Which form would you use to determine the y-intercept of the graph of the function? Explain your reasoning.

D. Copy and complete the table, replacing the three functions with "Standard," "Vertex," and "Intercept," respectively. Then put an "X" in each cell for which the key characteristic of the graph can be determined only by looking at the corresponding form of the quadratic function.

Function	Parabola opens up or down	Axis of symmetry	Vertex	x-intercepts	y-intercept
$f(x) = \frac{1}{10}x^2 - \frac{12}{5}x + 8$	?	?	?	?	?
$f(x) = \frac{1}{10}(x - 12)^2 - \frac{32}{5}$	?	?	?	?	?
$f(x) = \frac{1}{10}(x - 4)(x - 20)$	?	?	?	?	?

E. Do the function rules for each form have any single quantity in common? If so, what does this quantity tell you about the graph of the function?

> **Turn and Talk** What is the value of the function when $x = 8$? Which form of the function did you use to find the answer? Explain your choice.

Step It Out

Compare Quadratic Functions with Different Representations

2 The graphs of quadratic functions f and g are parabolas that open up. Which function has the lesser minimum value?

$f(x) = 3(x - 5)^2 - 6$

x	−2	−1	3	4
g(x)	10	0	0	10

> **A.** How can the vertex of the graph of a function be used to find the minimum value of the function?

Start by finding the vertex of the graph of each function.

Find the vertex of the graph of f.

The function $f(x) = 3(x - 5)^2 - 6$ is written in vertex form.

So, the vertex is $(5, -6)$.

> **B.** How is the vertex found?

Find the vertex of the graph of g.

Points $(-1, 0)$ and $(3, 0)$ in the table show that the graph of the function has x-intercepts of -1 and 3. Use these values to write the function in intercept form.

$$g(x) = a(x + 1)(x - 3)$$

Use the coordinates of another point on the graph to find the value of a.

$$g(x) = a(x + 1)(x - 3)$$
$$10 = a(4 + 1)(4 - 3)$$
$$10 = 5a$$
$$2 = a$$

> **C.** What point on the graph of the function is used to find the value of a?

So, $g(x) = 2(x + 1)(x - 3)$.

Use the intercept form of the function to find the axis of symmetry of its graph.

$$\text{axis of symmetry} = \frac{-1 + 3}{2} = 1$$

> **D.** How is the y-coordinate of the vertex found?

The x-coordinate of the vertex is 1.

The y-coordinate of the vertex is $y = 2(1 + 1)(1 - 3) = -8$.

The vertex of the graph of g is $(1, -8)$.

Compare the vertices.

The minimum value of function f is -6, and the minimum value of function g is -8. Function g has the lesser minimum value.

The graphs of the functions show that g has a lesser minimum value since the vertex of its graph is lower.

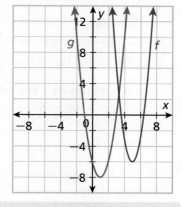

 Turn and Talk Which function has the greater y-intercept?

Compare Real-World Quadratic Functions

3 A marching band drum major practices throwing her baton into the air. During two practice throws, she does not catch the baton, and it lands on the ground.

The height, in feet, of her baton after t seconds during her first throw is modeled by the graph of the quadratic function h_1. The height of the baton during the second throw is modeled by the quadratic function h_2 in the photo.

Which throw has a greater initial vertical velocity? After how many seconds is the baton at the same height at the same time during the two missed throws?

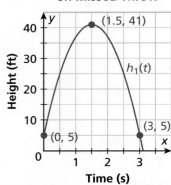

Height of Baton on Missed Throw

The height, in feet, of the baton after t seconds during the second missed throw is given by $h_2(t) = -16t^2 + 32t + 6$.

Find the initial vertical velocity of each missed throw.

The graph for the first missed throw shows an initial height of 5 feet. Use this information to write a projectile motion model for the first throw.

$$h_1(t) = -16t^2 + v_0t + h_0 = -16t^2 + v_0t + 5$$

A. How do you know the initial height is 5 feet?

Use the point $(3, 5)$ on the graph to find the value of v_0.

$$5 = -16(3)^2 + v_0(3) + 5$$
$$144 = 3(v_0)$$
$$48 = v_0$$

B. Why can't the point $(0, 5)$ be used to find the value of v_0?

So, $h_1(t) = -16t^2 + 48t + 5$, and the initial vertical velocity of the first missed throw is 48 feet per second.

The function $h_2(t) = -16t^2 + 32t + 6$ is already written as a projectile motion model. The initial vertical velocity of the second throw is 32 feet per second.

The first missed throw has a greater initial vertical velocity.

Find the value of t for which $h_1(t) = h_2(t)$.

$$-16t^2 + 48t + 5 = -16t^2 + 32t + 6$$
$$16t = 1$$
$$t = 0.0625$$

C. Suppose h_1 and h_2 are graphed on the same coordinate plane. What should happen where $t = 0.0625$?

The baton is at the same height at the same time exactly 0.0625 second into the two missed throws.

 Turn and Talk Which throw reaches a greater maximum height?

Check Understanding

For Problems 1 and 2, use the graph of the quadratic function g.

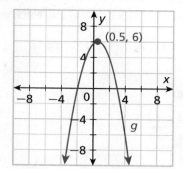

1. Suppose you want to find the y-intercept of the graph. Would you prefer to use the standard form, vertex form, or intercept form of the quadratic function? Explain your reasoning.

2. Consider the quadratic function $f(x) = -x^2 + 4x + 5$. Does the graph of f or g have the greater maximum? Explain.

3. Two objects are projected into the air at the same time. The height, in feet, of Object A after t seconds is modeled by the graph of h_A. The height, in feet, of Object B after t seconds is modeled by $h_B(t) = -16t^2 + 64t + 80$.

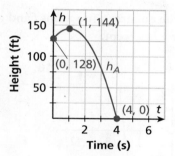

   A. Which object was projected from a greater initial height?

   B. At what point does the graph of h_A intersect the graph of h_B? What does this point represent in the context of the situation?

On Your Own

4. Three equivalent forms of the quadratic function f are shown. Decide which form(s) can be used to determine each key characteristic of the graph of f by just looking at the form.

Standard form	Vertex form	Intercept form
$f(x) = -x^2 + 8x + 9$	$f(x) = -(x-4)^2 + 25$	$f(x) = -(x+1)(x-9)$

   A. The y-intercept

   B. The x-intercepts

   C. Whether the graph opens up or down

5. (MP) **Critique Reasoning** Justin states that the y-intercept of the graph of a quadratic function can be directly determined by looking at the intercept form of the function. Is Justin correct? Explain why or why not.

Consider the quadratic functions $f(x) = -2x^2 - 8x - 4$ and $g(x) = \frac{1}{2}(x+3)^2 - 4$.

6. What is the axis of symmetry of the graph of each function?

7. Does the graph of each function open up or down?

8. What is the vertex of the graph of each function?

9. What is the minimum or maximum value of each function?

10. What is the y-intercept of the graph of each function?

11. At which point(s) do the graphs of the functions intersect? Use a graphing calculator to estimate the coordinates of the point(s).

Consider the quadratic functions *f* and *g*. If the graphs of *f* and *g* open up, determine which function has a lesser minimum value. When the graphs of *f* and *g* open down, determine which function has a greater maximum value.

12. $f(x) = -3(x + 4)(x + 12)$

x	g(x)
0	−16
−2	−6
−4	0
−8	0
−10	−6

13. $f(x) = \frac{1}{4}(x + 1)^2 - 3$

x	g(x)
−2	0
−1	−3
1	−3
2	0
3	5

14. $f(x) = 2x^2 - 8x - 12$

x	g(x)
−3	0
−2	−12
0	−12
1	0
2	20

Consider the quadratic functions *f* and *g*. Determine whether the graph of *f* or *g* has the greater *y*-intercept.

15. $f(x) = x^2 - x - 8$

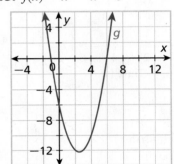

16. $f(x) = -(x + 1)^2 + 1$

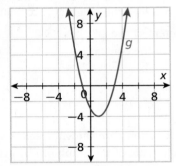

17. $f(x) = -(x - 9)(x - 3)$

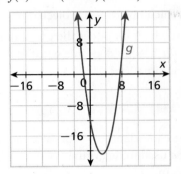

(MP) **Use Tools** Functions *f* and *g* are quadratic functions. Use a graphing calculator to estimate the value(s) of *x* for which $f(x) = g(x)$.

18. $f(x) = 2(x - 1)^2 + 3$

$g(x) = -x^2 + 4x + 5$

19. $f(x) = 0.7x^2 + 6x - 1.9$

$g(x) = -(x - 5.2)(x + 4.1)$

20. $f(x) = 0.25(x + 8)(x - 6)$

The graph of *g* has a vertex at $(7, 20)$ and passes through $(1, -16)$.

21. $f(x) = -(x - 2)^2 + 15$

The graph of *g* has *x*-intercepts of −4 and 6 and passes through $(5, -9)$.

For each pair of quadratic functions, determine whether it is more efficient to use the function rule for *f* or *g* to find the *x*-intercepts of the graphs of the functions. Then determine which function's graph has the greater positive *x*-intercept.

22. $f(x) = x^2 - x - 6$

$g(x) = (x + 1)(x - 6)$

23. $f(x) = -x^2 + x + 6$

$g(x) = (x + 2)(x - 1)$

24. $f(x) = x^2 - 4x - 5$

$g(x) = -(x - 2)(x + 4)$

25. $f(x) = 2(x + 4)(x - 8)$

$g(x) = x^2 - 2x - 24$

26. $f(x) = -5(x + 5)(x - 1)$

$g(x) = (x - 3)^2 - 12$

27. $f(x) = (x - 1)^2 - 6$

$g(x) = x^2 + 7x - 18$

Functions *g* and *h* are quadratic functions. For each pair of functions, determine which function's graph has a greater magnitude of vertical stretch or compression compared to the graph of the parent function $f(x) = x^2$.

28. $g(x) = -\frac{1}{2}x^2 + 6x - 2$

The graph of *h* is shown below.

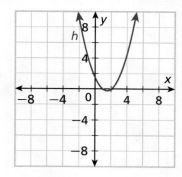

29. $g(x) = 1.5(x + 1)^2 + 6$

The graph of *h* is shown below.

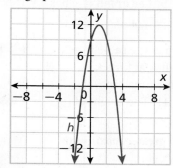

30. $g(x) = 2x^2 + 2x - 5$

The graph of *h* is shown below.

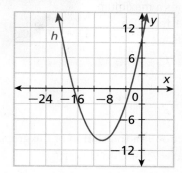

31. $g(x) = -(x - 2)(x - 2)$

The graph of *h* is shown below.

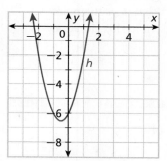

32. Two discus throwers are analyzing their techniques. The height, in feet, of the discus at time *t*, in seconds, after Jennyfer throws it can be modeled by $h_J(t) = -16t^2 + 30t + 5$. Aiden's throw is described in the photo.

A. Who threw the discus higher? Explain.

B. Who threw from a higher initial height? Explain.

C. Who threw with the greater initial vertical velocity? Explain.

D. Whose throw resulted in a shorter flight time? Explain.

Aiden releases the discus at a height of 6 feet with an initial vertical velocity of 24 feet per second.

©Shahjehan/Shutterstock

For each pair of quadratic functions, identify which function has a graph with a vertex having a greater y-coordinate, a graph with a greater y-intercept, and a graph with a greater vertical stretch compared to the graph of the parent function $f(x) = x^2$.

33. Let $f(x) = (x + 1)^2 + 4$. The graph of g has x-intercepts of -1 and -5 and passes through $(0, 10)$.

34. Let $f(x) = 3x^2 + 12x - 15$. The graph of g has a vertex of $(1, 1)$ and passes through $(3, 3)$.

35. Two baseballs are thrown at the same time. The height, in feet, of Ball A at time t, in seconds, is modeled by the function $A(t) = -16(t - 1.5)^2 + 41$. The height of Ball B is described in the photo.

A. Which ball reaches a greater maximum height?

B. Which ball has a greater initial vertical velocity?

C. Suppose the two functions are graphed. At what point do the graphs of the two functions intersect? What does the point of intersection represent in this situation?

Ball B reaches a maximum height of 31 feet after 1.25 seconds.

Spiral Review • Assessment Readiness

36. What is the vertex form of $f(x) = 3x^2 - 12x + 19$?

Ⓐ $f(x) = 3(x + 19)(x + 1)$

Ⓑ $f(x) = 2(x - 3)^2 + 6$

Ⓒ $f(x) = 3(x - 2)^2 + 7$

Ⓓ $f(x) = 3(x - 2)(x + 2) + 7$

37. What is the standard form of $f(x) = -4(x + 1)(x - 2)$?

Ⓐ $f(x) = 4x^2 + 4x + 8$

Ⓑ $f(x) = -4x^2 - 4x + 8$

Ⓒ $f(x) = 8x^2 + 4x - 2$

Ⓓ $f(x) = -4x^2 + 4x + 8$

38. Which function is a translation of the graph of $f(x) = -2(x - 7)^2 + 2$ to the left?

Ⓐ $g(x) = -2(x - 9)^2 + 4$

Ⓑ $g(x) = -4(x - 7)^2 + 2$

Ⓒ $g(x) = -2(x - 5)^2 + 2$

Ⓓ $g(x) = -(x - 7)^2 + 4$

39. Solve the system of equations by substitution.

$$\begin{cases} 3x + y = 11 \\ x + y = 3 \end{cases}$$

Ⓐ $(4, -1)$ Ⓒ $(-2, 5)$

Ⓑ $(2, 5)$ Ⓓ $(7, -10)$

 I'm in a Learning Mindset!

What did I learn when comparing the special features of quadratic functions in different forms?

Scatter Plots and Fitted Quadratic Curves

(I Can) fit quadratic functions to data by hand and by quadratic regression.

Spark Your Learning

Erika is a champion motocross rider. The time-lapse photo shows the parabolic path of one of her jumps.

Complete Part A as a whole class. Then complete Parts B–D in small groups.

A. What is a mathematical question you can ask about this situation? What information would you need to know to answer your question?

B. What form of a quadratic function would you use to model the path? Explain.

C. To answer your question, what strategy and tool would you use along with all the information you have? What answer do you get?

D. Does your answer make sense in the context of the situation? How do you know?

Turn and Talk Assuming the ground is level, what is the horizontal distance covered by Erika's jump, measured from the end of the jump ramp?

Build Understanding

Use Second Differences to Identify Quadratic Data

Given a set of data pairs (x, y) with evenly spaced x-values, you know that the data can be modeled by a linear function if the first differences in the y-values are constant. If the first differences are not constant but the second differences in the y-values are constant and nonzero, then the data can be modeled by a quadratic function.

Connect to Vocabulary

First differences are differences between the y-values of a function for evenly spaced x-values. The differences between the first differences are called the **second differences**.

1 ▶ **A.** Copy and complete the table.

x	$y = f(x)$	First difference	Second difference
1	1	–	–
2	4	$4 - 1 = 3$	–
3	9	$9 - 4 = 5$	$5 - 3 = 2$
4	16	?	?
5	25	?	?

B. Are the x-values evenly spaced? Explain.

C. Are the first differences constant? What does this mean?

D. Are the second differences constant? What does this mean?

E. Create a table to find the second differences for the data shown in the graph below.

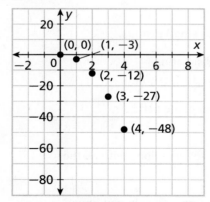

F. What is true about the second differences from Part E? What is true about the data?

 Turn and Talk Are there any limitations to identifying data that can be modeled by a quadratic function using the method of second differences? Explain.

Step It Out

Fit a Quadratic Function to Data by Hand

When the points on a scatter plot appear to represent a quadratic relationship, you can determine a function that models the data. You can do so by estimating the vertex and a second point that is visibly close to the pattern of the data. Those two points can be used to write a quadratic function in vertex form.

2 The scatter plot shows data points that roughly follow a parabola. Find a quadratic function that models the data.

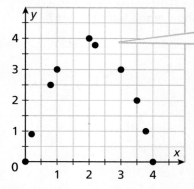

A. What point appears to be the vertex?

Substitute the coordinates of the vertex into the vertex form of a quadratic function.

$$f(x) = a(x - h)^2 + k$$

$$f(x) = a(x - 2)^2 + 4$$

B. What is another point that could have been chosen to represent the data?

Use a second point that is representative of the data, such as $(1, 3)$, to solve for a.

$f(x) = a(x - 2)^2 + 4$	Original function
$3 = a(1 - 2)^2 + 4$	Substitute $x = 1$ and $f(x) = 3$.
$3 = a + 4$	Simplify.
$-1 = a$	Subtract 4 from each side.

C. Does it make sense that a is negative? Explain.

The data can be modeled by the function $f(x) = -(x - 2)^2 + 4$.

 Turn and Talk How could a graph of the function be used to determine if the function is a good model for the data?

Fit a Quadratic Function to Real-World Data

For the projectile motion function $h(t) = -16t^2 + v_0t + h_0$, sometimes values of v_0 and h_0 are not known. In such cases, you may need to solve a system of equations to determine a function that models the data.

3 A coin is tossed off of a bridge into a river. The height h (in feet) of the coin above the river at time t (in seconds) is shown in the table. Find a quadratic model for the data.

t	h
1	414
2	373
3	300
4	195
5	58

A. Do the data show a quadratic pattern? Explain.

The values of v_0 and h_0 are unknown, so substitute two data pairs into the projectile motion function to create a system of equations. For example, you can use (1, 414) and (3, 300).

$$\begin{cases} 414 = -16(1)^2 + v_0(1) + h_0 \\ 300 = -16(3)^2 + v_0(3) + h_0 \end{cases} \rightarrow \begin{cases} 414 = -16 + v_0 + h_0 \\ 300 = -144 + 3v_0 + h_0 \end{cases} \rightarrow \begin{cases} 430 = v_0 + h_0 \\ 444 = 3v_0 + h_0 \end{cases}$$

Solve the system of equations.

$$v_0 + h_0 = 430$$
$$-\left(3v_0 + h_0 = 444\right)$$
$$\overline{-2v_0 = -14}$$
$$v_0 = 7$$

B. Does it matter which two data pairs are chosen? Explain.

C. What does $v_0 = 7$ mean in the context of the situation?

Substitute $v_0 = 7$ into one of the original equations and solve for h_0.

$$v_0 + h_0 = 430$$
$$7 + h_0 = 430$$
$$h_0 = 423$$

D. What does $h_0 = 423$ mean in the context of the situation?

So, a quadratic model for the given situation is $h(t) = -16t^2 + 7t + 423$.

 Turn and Talk How would the general form of the equation have been different if the coin was dropped straight down from the bridge?

Use Quadratic Regression to Find a Model

A scatter plot of real-world data may have a shape that is only approximately parabolic. You can perform **quadratic regression** on a graphing calculator to find the quadratic function that best fits the data. The calculator may also give a statistic called the **coefficient of determination**, which is a value from 0 to 1 that is denoted by R^2 and that tells you how well the function fits the data. The closer R^2 is to 1, the better the fit.

4 The table shows the speed of a car over time. Use regression to find a function that fits the data. Then predict the speed of the car after 11 seconds.

> The speed of a car is measured every 2 seconds as it accelerates from rest on a test track.

Time (seconds)	Speed (mi/h)
2	31
4	49
6	61
8	72
10	79

> **A.** How can you quickly tell that the data are not linear?

Enter the data pairs from the table into a graphing calculator to find the quadratic regression function.

> **B.** Does the coefficient of determination indicate that the function fits the data well? Explain.

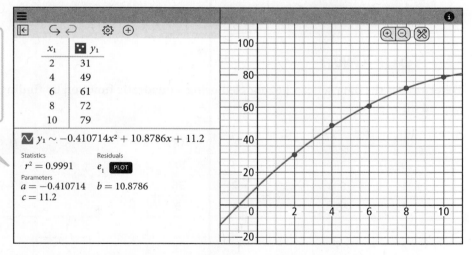

The quadratic function that best models the data is $f(x) = -0.411x^2 + 10.9x + 11.2$.

To predict the speed of the car after 11 seconds, substitute $x = 11$ into the function.

$$f(11) = -0.411(11)^2 + 10.9(11) + 11.2 \approx 81$$

The speed of the car after 11 seconds is about 81 miles per hour.

> **Turn and Talk** Will the quadratic function found by regression model the car's speed accurately as time continues to increase beyond 11 seconds? Explain.

Check Understanding

1. Determine if the data are quadratic by finding the second differences.

x	1	2	3	4	5	6
y	−2	−1	4	13	26	43

2. Plot the points $(0, 0)$, $(1, -3)$, $(-1, -4)$, $(2, -10)$, $(-2, -11)$, $(3, -25)$, and $(-3, -27)$. Then fit a quadratic function, in vertex form, to the data.

3. The table shows the height of a soccer ball in feet for every half-second after a goalie dropkicks the ball. Find a quadratic model for the given situation using the projectile motion function.

Time	0.5	1.0	1.5	2.0	2.5	3.0	3.5
Height	31	54	69	76	75	66	49

4. A company that makes flying discs to use as promotional materials will produce flying discs in a variety of diameters. The table shows the price of 100 flying discs for four diameters. Use a graphing calculator to find the quadratic regression function that fits the data, and then use the function to predict the price of 100 discs that are 8 inches in diameter.

Diameter (inches)	4	5	6	7
Price (dollars)	35	55	80	108

On Your Own

Determine if the data set can be modeled using a quadratic function by finding the second differences.

5.

x	f(x)
0	2
1	9
2	26
3	53
4	90

6.

x	f(x)
−3	103
−2	36
−1	9
0	4
1	3

7.

x	f(x)
−2	−19
−1	−9
0	−3
1	−1
2	−3

8. Create a table to find the second differences for the data shown in the graph. Are the data quadratic?

9. If a table of values has a constant difference in x-values and a constant difference in y-values, what type of function does this indicate?

10. If a table of values has a constant difference in x-values and the second differences of the y-values are constant, what type of function does this indicate?

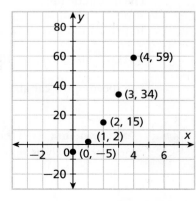

540

Fit a quadratic function, in vertex form, to the data pairs plotted in each graph.

11.

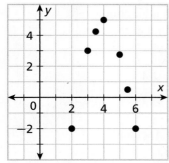

12.

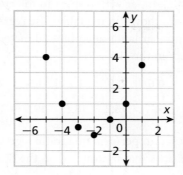

13. Throwing the javelin is one of the field events at some track meets. Data about the flight of the javelin thrown by a competitor at a meet are shown in the table at the right.

   A. Use two data points and the projectile motion function to create a model for the data.

   B. Use your model to find the maximum altitude reached by the javelin.

   C. How long does it take the javelin to reach its maximum altitude?

Time since release (sec)	Altitude (ft)
0.5	25.5
1.0	36.0
1.5	38.5
2.0	33.0
2.5	19.5

(MP) **Model with Mathematics** Use the projectile motion function to create a model for the data given in each table.

14.

t	h
0	20
1	72
2	92
3	80
4	36

15.

t	h
1	84
2	111
3	106
4	69
5	0

16.

t	h
0.5	31
1	44
1.5	49
2	46
2.5	35

17. An archery student shoots arrows toward a target downrange. The table shows the height, in feet, of an arrow t seconds after being released. Use the projectile motion function to create a model for the data given in the table.

Time (seconds)	0	1	2	3	4
Height (feet)	5	64	91	86	49

18. Several data points for the height of a projectile over time are known. However, the data point corresponding to its greatest height is not one of these points. Is it still possible to determine the quadratic function that models the data? Explain.

19. (MP) **Use Tools** The images from a high definition camera were used to measure the height, in meters, of a ski jumper with respect to the end of the takeoff ramp every 0.3 second. The data are shown in the table. Use regression to find a function that fits the data. If the ski jumper lands at a point 30 meters below the end of the ramp, how long was the skier in the air?

Time (seconds)	0.3	0.6	0.9	1.2	1.5	1.8	2.1	2.4
Height (meters)	11.2	14.1	16.3	18.5	19.5	20.5	21.0	21.0

20. A graphing calculator was used to perform quadratic regression on a data set and found that $R^2 = 0.51$. What does that indicate about the fit of the curve?

21. (Open Middle™) Using the integers -9 to 9, at most one time each, copy the following and fill in the boxes twice to create two quadratic functions with corresponding x- and y-coordinates, one with a maximum value and one with a minimum value.

x	y
⬚	⬚
⬚	⬚
⬚	⬚

$$y = \boxed{}\, x^2 + \boxed{}$$

Spiral Review • Assessment Readiness

22. A function is given in the form $f(x) = a(x - m)(x - n)$. Suppose $f(x) = 0$. Which of the following terms can be applied to the solutions? Select all that apply.

(A) zeros

(B) vertex

(C) x-intercepts

(D) y-intercept

(E) vertical asymptotes

(F) horizontal asymptote

23. The heights over time of two falling objects are modeled by the functions $h(t) = -16t^2 + 4$ and $g(t) = -16t^2 + 4t + 10$, where h and g are in feet and t is in seconds. Which statement is correct?

(A) The initial speed of $h(t)$ is 4 ft/s.

(B) The initial height of $g(t)$ is 10 ft.

(C) The maximum speed of both is -16 ft/s.

(D) The initial height of both is -16 ft.

24. Match the type of function to a characteristic that indicates that type.

A. linear

B. exponential

C. quadratic

D. constant

1. The ratio of consecutive y-values is constant.

2. The graph is U-shaped.

3. There is no variable quantity in the function rule.

4. The first difference is constant.

I'm in a Learning Mindset!

Did I manage my time effectively while I was studying quadratic regression? What steps did I take to manage my time?

Vertex Form of a Quadratic Function

A quadratic function can be written in vertex form by identifying key points on its graph.

The *y*-intercept occurs at (0, 16).

The vertex is $(h, k) = (3, -2)$.

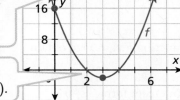

The vertex form of the quadratic function *f* is

$f(x) = a(x - h)^2 + k$

$= a(x - 3)^2 - 2$

Substitute 3 for *h* and −2 for *k*.

Use the fact that $f(0) = 16$ to solve for *a*.

$f(0) = 16 = a(0 - 3)^2 - 2$

$16 = 9a - 2$

$18 = 9a$

$a = 2$

$f(x) = 2(x - 3)^2 - 2$

Standard Form of a Quadratic Function

The vertex form of a quadratic function can be expanded to obtain the standard form of a quadratic function, $f(x) = ax^2 + bx + c$.

The terms are placed in order from greatest degree to least degree.

$f(x) = 2(x - 3)^2 - 2$ Expand $(x - 3)(x - 3)$.

$= 2(x^2 - 6x + 9) - 2$

Distribute.

$= 2x^2 - 12x + 18 - 2$

$= 2x^2 - 12x + 16$ Collect like terms.

The *y*-intercept is given by $(0, c) = (0, 16)$.

The axis of symmetry is given by $x = -\frac{b}{2a} = 3$.

The vertex is given by $\left(-\frac{b}{2a}, \frac{4ac - b^2}{4a}\right) = (3, -2)$.

Intercept Form of a Quadratic Function

The zeros of a quadratic function appear as the *x*-intercepts of its graph.

$f(x) = 2(x - 3)^2 - 2$

$= 2x^2 - 12x + 16$ Factor out the GCF.

$= 2(x^2 - 6x + 8)$

$= 2(x - 4)(x - 2)$

$-4 + (-2) = -6$ and $(-4)(-2) = 8$.

Set the function equal to 0, then use the Zero Product Property to determine the zeros.

$0 = x - 4$ or $0 = x - 2$

$x = 4$ or $x = 2$

The zeros of the function *f* occur when $x = 4$ and $x = 2$.

Quadratic Regression

Just like linear and exponential regression, quadratic regression fits a quadratic function to data while minimizing the sum of the squared residuals.

x	1	2	3	4	5
y	9.8	4	1.9	4.3	9.7

A graphing calculator gives the regression equation $y = 1.92x^2 - 11.52x + 19.36$.

The coefficient of determination is $R^2 = 0.9976$.

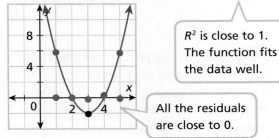

R^2 is close to 1. The function fits the data well.

All the residuals are close to 0.

Vocabulary

Choose the correct term from the box to complete each sentence.

1. The ___?___ of a quadratic function is $f(x) = a(x - h)^2 + k$.

2. The factored form of a quadratic function, $f(x) = a(x - x_1)(x - x_2)$, is called ___?___.

3. The ___?___ of a quadratic function is $f(x) = ax^2 + bx + c$.

4. You can use ___?___ to fit a quadratic function to a data set.

Concepts and Skills

5. Describe the transformations of the graph of the parent function $f(x) = x^2$ to obtain the graph of the function $g(x) = a(x - h)^2 + k$.

6. Rewrite the function $f(x) = 2x^2 - 4x - 16$ in vertex and intercept form.

Graph each function and identify the vertex, the axis of symmetry, and the *x*- and *y*-intercepts of the graph.

7. $f(x) = x^2 - 5x - 6$ **8.** $f(x) = -2(x - 3)(x + 5)$ **9.** $f(x) = 4(x - 2)^2 + 5$

10. The fuel efficiency of a vehicle, measured in miles per gallon (mi/gal), is dependent on the speed, measured in miles per hour (mi/h).

A. Create a scatter plot of the data. Why would a quadratic model be a good fit for the data?

Speed (mi/h)	5	15	25	45	55	65
Fuel efficiency (mi/gal)	10	21	27	31	30	27

B. Use quadratic regression to obtain a quadratic function that models the relationship between speed and fuel efficiency. How do you know that the function is a good fit for the data?

C. Use the quadratic function to predict the fuel efficiency at a speed at 30 mi/h.

11. Determine which function has the greatest maximum value.

$f(x) = -2x^2 - 20x - 47$

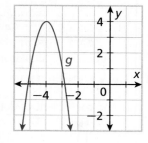

x	h(x)
−8	−44
−6	−12
−4	4
−2	4
0	−12

12. (MP) **Use Tools** The prom committee created a parabolic arch made of balloons to serve as the background for photos taken of couples attending the prom. The arch is given by the equation $y = 5x - x^2$ where x and y are measured in feet. How tall is the arch and how wide is it at its base? State what strategy and tool you will use to answer the question, explain your choice, and then find the answer.

Motel Madness

How has Fantastic 5 Motel changed its prices compared to inflation?

Are You Ready?

Complete these problems to review prior concepts and skills you will need for this module.

Simplify Algebraic Expressions

Simplify each expression.

1. $5(x + 3) - 2$

2. $-x^2 + 3(x - 5) + 6$

3. $-(x + 4) + 3(x - 8)$

4. $-\frac{1}{2}x + 3(x - 3) + 9$

Solve Systems of Linear Equations by Substitution

Solve each system of equations using the substitution method.

5. $\begin{cases} y = 2x - 4 \\ 3x + 2y = 13 \end{cases}$

6. $\begin{cases} y - 4 = 3x \\ -4x - 3y = 1 \end{cases}$

7. $\begin{cases} 5x - 2y = 29 \\ -3x + 3y = -21 \end{cases}$

8. $\begin{cases} y - x = -10 \\ 3x - 2y = 24 \end{cases}$

Fit Exponential Functions to Data

Model each data set with an exponential function.

9.

x	y
0	2
1	8
2	32
3	128
4	512

10.

x	y
0	16
1	8
2	4
3	2
4	1

Connecting Past and Present Learning

Previously, you learned:

- to write and solve linear, quadratic, and exponential equations,
- to write and solve systems of linear equations, and
- to model real-world situations with expressions, equations, and inequalities.

In this module, you will learn:

- to write and solve nonlinear systems of equations,
- to compose functions when constructing models, and
- to choose between linear, exponential, and quadratic functions when modeling real-world situations.

Choose Among Linear, Exponential, and Quadratic Models

(**I Can**) determine whether a given data set is best modeled by a linear, exponential, or quadratic function.

Spark Your Learning

Gael buys a new boat to use for fishing and recreation. He plans to sell the boat in 10 years.

Gael paid $20,000 for the boat.

Complete Part A as a whole class. Then complete Parts B–D in small groups.

A. What is a mathematical question you can ask about this situation? What information would you need to know to answer your question?

B. What variable(s) are involved in this situation? What unit of measurement would you use for each variable?

C. To answer your question, what strategy and tool would you use along with all the information you have? What answer do you get?

D. Does your answer make sense in the context of the situation? How do you know?

Turn and Talk How did you decide which type of function to use to model the boat's value over time?

©Robert Daly/Caiaimage/Getty Images

Build Understanding

Evaluate Models for a Data Set

Given a table of data pairs (x, y), you can use several tools to determine which type of function best models the data. You can graph a proposed model on a scatter plot of the data and visually assess how well the model fits the data. You can also plot the residuals for the model. If the points on the residual plot are close to the x-axis and appear randomly distributed above and below the x-axis, then the model fits the data well.

1 The table shows the data from the previous page that give a boat's value y (in dollars) at time x (in years after the boat was purchased).

x	0	1	2	3	4	5	6	7	8
y	20,000	16,100	12,700	10,300	8100	6600	5200	4200	3300

Below are the linear, exponential, and quadratic functions obtained by performing regression on the data. Following each function is the graph of the function on a scatter plot of the data and then a residual plot for the function.

Linear function:	Exponential function:	Quadratic function:
$y = -2020x + 17{,}700$	$y = 20{,}100(0.799)^x$	$y = 219x^2 - 3770x + 19{,}700$

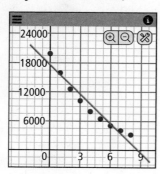 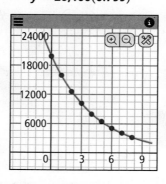 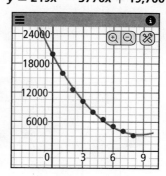

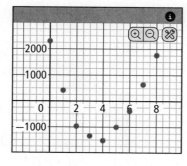 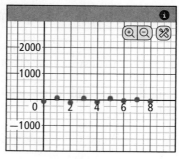 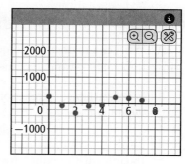

A. How do the linear function's graph and residual plot suggest that the function is not a good model for the data?

B. The graphs of the exponential and quadratic functions both are close to all the data points. Which function do you think is the better model? Why?

 Turn and Talk Which of the three functions do you think would most accurately predict the boat's value after 10 years? Explain.

Step It Out

Choose a Quadratic Model

Previously you saw that when regression is used to fit a quadratic function to a data set, the coefficient of determination R^2 indicates how well the function fits the data. A coefficient of determination can also be generated when you use regression to fit linear and exponential functions to data. For linear and exponential functions, the coefficient of determination equals the square of the correlation coefficient r; that is, $R^2 = r^2$.

If a linear, exponential, and quadratic function are each fit to the same data set, you can compare the values of R^2 for the functions to help you decide which function models the data best. In general, the closer R^2 is to 1, the better the function fits the data.

2 ▶ A study found that the average fuel economy for a sample of cars varied by driving speed as shown in the table. Find a function that models the data well. Then use the function to predict the average fuel economy for a driving speed of 60 mi/h.

Speed (mi/h), x	15	25	35	45	55	65	75
Fuel economy (mi/gal), y	24.4	30.5	31.2	31.6	32.4	29.2	24.8

Make a scatter plot of the data, and use regression to find a good model.
Enter the data pairs into a graphing calculator and make a scatter plot. The data points rise and then fall, which suggests a quadratic model. The coefficient of determination for a quadratic model, $R^2 \approx 0.9419$, is also reasonably close to 1. A good model for the data is $y = -0.00848x^2 + 0.762x + 15.4$.

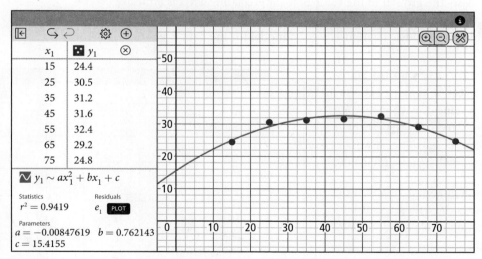

Predict the average fuel economy for a driving speed of 60 mi/h.
Find the value of y when $x = 60$: $y = -0.00848(60)^2 + 0.762(60) + 15.4 \approx 30.6$. The average fuel economy for a speed of 60 mi/h is about 30.6 mi/gal.

A. Use regression on a graphing calculator to find a linear function and an exponential function that model the data. What is the coefficient of determination R^2 for each function? Do the values of R^2 support the conclusion that a quadratic model is best?

B. Use the quadratic model. What driving speed maximizes fuel economy?

Choose an Exponential Model

3 ▶ Unlike new cars, which usually decrease in value in the years after they are purchased, a classic car can increase in value.

The table below shows how the value of one classic car has increased since it was purchased by a car museum. Find a function that models the data well. Then use the function to predict the car's value 50 years after it was purchased.

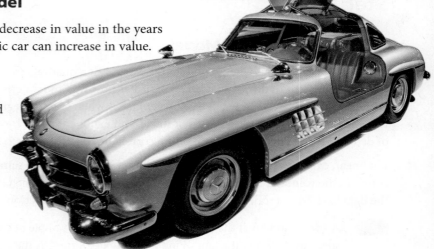

Time (years), x	0	5	10	15	20	25	30	35	40
Value (thousands of $), y	5.0	6.2	8.1	10.6	13.1	17.1	21.4	27.8	35.0

Make a scatter plot of the data, and use regression to find a good model.
Enter the data pairs into a graphing calculator and make a scatter plot. The data points clearly follow a curve rather than a line, so a linear function can be eliminated as a possible model. The coefficient of determination for an exponential model, $R^2 \approx 0.9996$, is slightly closer to 1 than that for a quadratic model. Also, the growth in the value of an appreciating asset is typically expressed as a percent increase per year, which supports using an exponential model. Therefore, a good model for the data is $y = 4.96(1.05)^x$.

Predict the car's value 50 years after it was purchased.
Find the value of y when $x = 50$:
$y = 4.96(1.05)^{50} \approx 56.9$. The value of the car 50 years after it was purchased will be about $56,900.

A. Find a quadratic function that models the data set. Is this function also a good model? Explain.

B. Compare the values of the classic car predicted by the exponential and quadratic models as the time since the car was purchased increases.

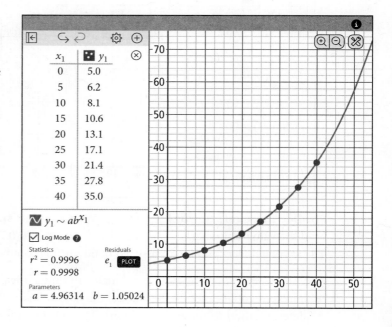

©Mikhail Kolesnikov/Shutterstock

Choose a Linear Model

4 The Johnson family is taking a vacation to Niagara Falls by car. The table shows how the odometer reading on their car changes over time as they travel.

Time (hours), x	Odometer (miles), y
0	25,500
1	25,563
2	25,614
3	25,674
4	25,720
5	25,774
6	25,839

Find a function that models the data well. Then use the function to predict the odometer reading after 8 hours of travel.

Make a scatter plot of the data, and use regression to find a good model.

Enter the data into a graphing calculator and make a scatter plot. The data points lie close to a line, which suggests a linear model. The coefficient of determination for a linear model, $R^2 = r^2 \approx 0.9986$, is also very close to 1. A good model is $y = 55.179x + 25{,}504$.

Predict the odometer reading after 8 hours of travel.

Find the value of y when $x = 8$: $y = 55.179(8) + 25{,}504 \approx 25{,}945$. After 8 hours of travel, the odometer will read about 25,945 miles.

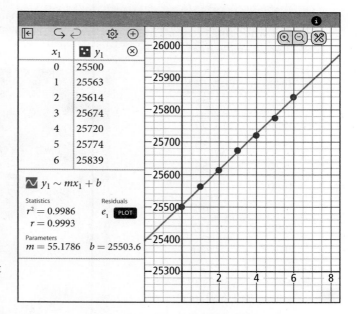

A. Use regression to find a quadratic model for the data. Which model— the linear model or the quadratic model—more clearly indicates the approximate average rate of change in the odometer reading with respect to time for $0 \le x \le 6$? Explain.

B. Consider what happens to the linear and quadratic models as the time x increases beyond the values shown in the table. Which model do you think more accurately represents the situation for increasingly greater values of x? Explain.

Turn and Talk Why might you prefer the linear model to the quadratic model even though the value of R^2 for the quadratic model is closer to 1?

Check Understanding

1. When choosing among a linear, exponential, and quadratic function to model bivariate data, how can you use residual plots to help make your selection?

2. When choosing among a linear, exponential, and quadratic function to model bivariate data, how can you use coefficients of determination to help make your selection?

3. The table shows the percent of people living in central cities of the United States over time.

   A. Let t = the time in years since 1910, and let p = the percent of people living in central cities of the United States. Use regression to find a model that fits the data well.

   B. Explain why you chose your model over other possible models.

   C. According to the model you selected, what percent of people were living in central cities in the United States in 2000?

Year	Percent of people
1910	21.2
1920	24.2
1930	30.8
1940	32.5
1950	32.8
1960	32.3
1970	31.4
1980	30.0

On Your Own

4. The table shows the population of the world's last remaining natural migratory flock of whooping cranes. The flock spends winters in Texas but migrates to northern Canada in early spring.

Year	Population
1940	22
1950	34
1960	33
1970	56
1980	76
1990	146
2000	177
2010	281

Whooping cranes are an endangered species and are protected in both the United States and Canada.

   A. Let t = the time in years since 1940, and let P = the whooping crane population. Find a model that fits the data well. Explain why you chose your model over other possible models.

   B. Use your model to predict the whooping crane population in 2020.

   C. Use your model to predict the year when the whooping crane population will reach 700.

   D. How could you use your model to estimate the whooping crane population in 1930? What population does your model give for 1930?

Use regression to find a linear, exponential, and quadratic function that model the data. Which type of function best models the data? Support your answer using the shape of the scatter plot and the coefficient of determination.

5.

Time (weeks), t	0	1	2	3	4	5	6
Sales (thousands of $), s	75	35	15	10	7	4	1

6.

Time (weeks), t	0	1	2	3	4	5	6
Sales (thousands of $), s	75	35	15	5	3	1	4

7. The table shows the total sales, in millions of dollars, at a car dealership for several years since 2013.

Years since 2013, t	Car sales (millions of dollars), s
0	49.3
1	52.9
2	56.7
3	59.6
4	59.7
5	61.2

A. Use regression to find a linear function, an exponential function, and a quadratic function that model the data.

B. Which function do you think best models the data? Support your answer using residuals and the coefficient of determination.

C. Use the model you selected in Part B to predict the dealership's total sales in the year 2023.

8. The data in the table give the speed s, in meters per second, of a space program's rocket t seconds after launch.

Time since launch (s), t	0	1	2	3	4	5	6	7	8
Speed (m/s), s	0	3	4	7	10	12	15	16	20

A. Use regression to find a linear function, an exponential function, and a quadratic function that model the data.

B. Which function would you use to model the data? Explain your choice.

9. (MP) **Reason** Use regression on a graphing calculator to fit a quadratic function $y = ax^2 + bx + c$ to the data in the table below. What do you notice about the function the calculator gives you? Explain why this makes sense.

x	0	1	2	3	4	5
y	5	8	11	14	17	20

10. (Open Middle™) Using the integers −9 to 9 at most one time each, fill in the boxes twice to create two functions (one linear and one quadratic) such that each function has the input-output pairs given in the table.

x	y
▨	▨
▨	▨
▨	▨

$$y = \boxed{} x^{\boxed{}} + \boxed{}$$

Spiral Review • Assessment Readiness

11. Which function best fits the data shown in the table?

x	0	1	2	3	4
y	1	3.5	5	4	0

(A) $y = -(x - 2)^2 + 5$ (C) $y = -(x - 2)^2 + 4$

(B) $y = -2(x - 2)^2 + 5$ (D) $y = -2(x - 2)^2 + 4$

12. Let $a = 4x - 4$ and $b = 2x^2 - 6x - 8$. Which expression is equivalent to $a - b$?

(A) $-2x^2 + 10x - 4$ (C) $2x^2 - 10x - 4$

(B) $-2x^2 + 10x + 4$ (D) $2x^2 - 10x + 4$

13. The quadratic function $g(x)$ is represented by the table and $f(x) = 2x^2 - 6x - 20$. Identify the function that has each characteristic.

x	1	2	3	4
g(x)	−15	−16	−15	−12

Characteristic	f(x)	g(x)
A. greater positive *x*-intercept	?	?
B. lesser minimum value	?	?
C. greater *y*-intercept	?	?

I'm in a Learning Mindset!

How did I proactively seek to fill any gaps in my understanding of modeling data with linear, exponential, and quadratic functions?

Perform Operations with Functions

(I Can) **perform operations with functions in mathematical and real-world contexts.**

Spark Your Learning

The head swim coach at a college is ordering spirit gear for the swim team and coaches to wear to swim meets. Each person will receive one shirt and one jacket/pants combo.

Swim Team Online Shop

Your Logo Here

$15 per shirt

$65 per combo

SHOP NOW

Complete Part A as a whole class. Then complete Parts B–D in small groups.

A. What is a mathematical question you can ask about this situation? What information would you need to know to answer your question?

B. What function models the cost $S(x)$ of the shirts for x swim team members and coaches? What function models the cost $J(x)$ of the jacket/pants combos?

C. To answer your question, what strategy and tool would you use along with all the information you have? What answer do you get?

D. Does your answer make sense in the context of the situation? How do you know?

 Turn and Talk What single function $T(x)$ could you write to model the total cost of all clothing items for x swim team members and coaches? Explain.

Build Understanding

Investigate Operations with Functions

You have already performed arithmetic operations with algebraic expressions to create new expressions. In a similar way, you can perform operations with functions to create new functions.

Operations with Functions		
Operation	**Definition**	**Example for $f(x) = x^2 - 9$, $g(x) = x + 3$**
Addition	$(f + g)(x) = f(x) + g(x)$	$\begin{aligned}(f + g)(x) &= f(x) + g(x)\\ &= (x^2 - 9) + (x + 3)\\ &= x^2 + x - 6\end{aligned}$
Subtraction	$(f - g)(x) = f(x) - g(x)$	$\begin{aligned}(f - g)(x) &= f(x) - g(x)\\ &= (x^2 - 9) - (x + 3)\\ &= x^2 - x - 12\end{aligned}$
Multiplication	$(f \cdot g)(x) = f(x) \cdot g(x)$	$\begin{aligned}(f \cdot g)(x) &= f(x) \cdot g(x)\\ &= (x^2 - 9)(x + 3)\\ &= x^3 + 3x^2 - 9x - 27\end{aligned}$
Division	$\left(\dfrac{f}{g}\right)(x) = \dfrac{f(x)}{g(x)}, \ g(x) \neq 0$	$\begin{aligned}\left(\dfrac{f}{g}\right)(x) &= \dfrac{f(x)}{g(x)}\\[4pt] &= \dfrac{x^2 - 9}{x + 3}\\[4pt] &= \dfrac{(x + 3)(x - 3)}{x + 3}\\[4pt] &= x - 3, \text{ where } x \neq -3\end{aligned}$

1 Use the functions $f(x) = x^2 - 9$ and $g(x) = x + 3$ from the last column of the table above.

A. Find $(g + f)(x)$ and compare the result with $(f + g)(x)$. In general, is it true that $(f + g)(x) = (g + f)(x)$? Explain.

B. Find $(g - f)(x)$ and compare the result with $(f - g)(x)$. In general, is it true that $(f - g)(x) = (g - f)(x)$? Explain.

C. Find $(g \cdot f)(x)$ and compare the result with $(f \cdot g)(x)$. In general, is it true that $(f \cdot g)(x) = (g \cdot f)(x)$? Explain.

D. Find $\left(\dfrac{g}{f}\right)(x)$ and compare the result with $\left(\dfrac{f}{g}\right)(x)$. In general, is it true that $\left(\dfrac{f}{g}\right)(x) = \left(\dfrac{g}{f}\right)(x)$? Explain.

 Turn and Talk Are there unique functions f and g such that $(f + g)(x) = 5x + 8$? Explain.

Step It Out

Add Two Models

Sometimes solving a real-world problem requires combining functions that represent different quantities by performing an operation on the functions. Adding two functions is often useful when the problem involves finding a total.

 A rental car agency charges $45 per day to rent a midsize car. Optional rental insurance costs $22 per day. Write equations for the following quantities as functions of the rental time: the cost to rent a midsize car without insurance, the cost of insurance, and the total cost of the rental if insurance is purchased. Then find the total cost of renting a midsize car with insurance for 5 days.

Write a function for the rental cost (without insurance).

Rental cost ($) $R(t)$	=	Rental rate ($/day) 45	·	Time (days) t

$R(t) = 45t$

Write a function for the cost of insurance.

Insurance cost ($) $I(t)$	=	Insurance rate ($/day) 22	·	Time (days) t

$I(t) = 22t$

Write a function for the total cost if insurance is purchased.

Total cost ($) $T(t)$	=	Rental cost ($) $R(t)$	+	Insurance cost ($) $I(t)$

$T(t) = R(t) + I(t)$

$T(t) = 45t + 22t$

$T(t) = 67t$

Find the total cost of renting a midsize car with insurance for 5 days.

$T(5) = 67(5) = 335$

The total cost is $335.

A. What type of functions are $R(t)$, $I(t)$, and $T(t)$?

B. In general, what can you say about the sum of two linear functions?

 Turn and Talk Suppose that the rental car agency raises the cost of renting a midsize car by 10% and the cost of insurance by 15%. How does the function $T(t)$ for the total cost of the rental with insurance change?

Subtracting functions can help you compare two quantities by telling you when one of the quantities is greater than or less than the other quantity and by how much.

3 A laboratory has cultures of two types of bacteria, Type A and Type B. Information about the Type A bacteria is shown in the photo. The initial population of Type B bacteria is 1500, and the population decreases by 75 bacteria per day.

Write equations that give the following quantities as functions of time: the population of Type A bacteria, the population of Type B bacteria, and the difference between the Type B and Type A populations. Then evaluate the difference function at times of 4 days and 11 days, and interpret the results.

> The initial population of Type A bacteria is 100. The population grows by 25% per day.

Write an equation for the Type A bacteria population as a function of time.

Let $P_A(t)$ = the population of Type A bacteria at time t (in days). Because the population increases by a fixed percent per day, it can be modeled by an exponential growth function. The initial population is 100 and the growth rate (as a decimal) is 0.25.

$$P_A(t) = 100(1 + 0.25)^t$$

$$P_A(t) = 100(1.25)^t$$

Write an equation for the Type B bacteria population as a function of time.

Let $P_B(t)$ = the population of Type B bacteria at time t (in days). Because the population decreases by a fixed number of bacteria per day, it can be modeled by a linear function. The initial population is 1500 and the rate of decrease is 75 bacteria per day.

$$P_B(t) = 1500 - 75t$$

Write an equation for the difference between the Type B and Type A populations.

Let $D(t)$ = the difference between the Type B and Type A bacteria populations at time t (in days).

$$D(t) = P_B(t) - P_A(t)$$

$$D(t) = 1500 - 75t - 100(1.25)^t$$

> **A.** Can the equation for $D(t)$ be simplified further? Explain.

Evaluate $D(t)$ when $t = 4$ and $t = 11$, and interpret the results.

$$D(4) = 1500 - 75(4) - 100(1.25)^4 \approx 956$$

$$D(11) = 1500 - 75(11) - 100(1.25)^{11} \approx -489$$

> **B.** What does a negative value of $D(t)$ mean in this situation?

After 4 days, there are about 956 *more* Type B bacteria than Type A bacteria.
After 11 days, there are about 489 *fewer* Type B bacteria than Type A bacteria.

Turn and Talk How can you use a graphing calculator and the function $D(t)$ to find the time when the two bacteria populations are equal? When are the populations equal?

Multiply Two Models

4 ▸ Use the information in the photo to write equations that give the following quantities as functions of the number of $0.50 price increases: the magazine's price, the number of subscribers, and the monthly revenue from magazine sales. Then find the sales price that maximizes monthly revenue and the maximum revenue.

The price of a monthly magazine is $4 per issue.

The magazine has 8000 subscribers. For each $0.50 increase in price, the magazine will lose 500 subscribers.

Let $x =$ the number of $0.50 price increases. Let $P(x)$, $S(x)$, and $R(x)$ be the magazine's price, the number of subscribers, and the monthly revenue from magazine sales, respectively.

$P(x) = 4 + 0.5x$

$S(x) = 8000 - 500x$

> **A.** In the equation for $S(x)$, what do the terms 8000 and $-500x$ represent?

$R(x) = P(x) \cdot S(x)$

> **B.** Why does $R(x)$ equal the product of $P(x)$ and $S(x)$?

$\quad = (4 + 0.5x)(8000 - 500x)$

$\quad = 32{,}000 - 2000x + 4000x - 250x^2$

$\quad = -250x^2 + 2000x + 32{,}000$

$R(x)$ is a quadratic function that has a maximum value when $x = -\frac{b}{2a} = -\frac{2000}{2(-250)} = 4$. So the magazine price that maximizes revenue is $P(4) = 4 + 0.5(4) = \$6$. The maximum monthly revenue is $R(4) = -250(4)^2 + 2000(4) + 32{,}000 = \$36{,}000$.

Divide Two Models

5 ▸ A shipping company organizes boxes by width, x (in centimeters). The volume of a box is given by $V(x) = x^3 + 8x^2 + 15x$, and the area of the box's base is $B(x) = x(x + 5)$. What function represents the box's height?

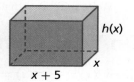

Use the fact that the volume of a rectangular prism is the product of the prism's base area and its height.

$V(x) = B(x) \cdot h(x)$

$x^3 + 8x^2 + 15x = x(x + 5) \cdot h(x)$

$\dfrac{x^3 + 8x^2 + 15x}{x(x + 5)} = h(x)$

> **A.** What property justifies dividing each side by $x(x + 5)$?

$\dfrac{x(x + 3)(x + 5)}{x(x + 5)} = h(x)$

> **B.** Show that $x^3 + 8x^2 + 15x = x(x + 3)(x + 5)$.

$x + 3 = h(x)$

> **C.** How was the equation for $h(x)$ simplified?

The function $h(x) = x + 3$ represents the box's height.

>
>
> **Turn and Talk** The company in Task 5 wants to ship an item with a height of 21 cm. Will the item fit in a box that has a width of 15 cm? Explain.

Check Understanding

Given $f(x) = x - 4$, $g(x) = x^2 - 16$, and $h(x) = x$, find the indicated function. State any restrictions on x.

1. $(f + g)(x)$

2. $(f - h)(x)$

3. $(g \cdot h)(x)$

4. $\left(\dfrac{g}{f}\right)(x)$

5. The price of gasoline at a certain gas station is $2.75 per gallon before tax, and there is a state tax of $0.24 per gallon. Write equations that give the following quantities as functions of the amount g of gas purchased (in gallons): the before-tax cost $B(g)$, the amount of tax $T(g)$, and the total cost $C(g)$.

6. Each year a wildlife biologist estimates the squirrel population in two forests, Forest A and Forest B. The estimated populations in Forest A and Forest B are given by the functions $A(t) = -10t + 500$ and $B(t) = 100(1.2)^t$, respectively, where t is the time in years since 2010.

   A. Write a function $D(t)$ that represents the difference between the squirrel populations in Forest A and Forest B.

   B. Find $D(5)$ and interpret the result.

7. The owner of a movie theater is considering raising the price of tickets to matinees. The theater currently charges $6 for a matinee ticket and sells an average of 200 matinee tickets per day. The owner estimates that each $1 increase in the ticket price will reduce the number of tickets sold per day by 20. What ticket price will maximize the theater's daily revenue? What is the maximum daily revenue?

8. The base of a rectangular prism has a width of x inches and a length of $(x + 3)$ inches. The volume of the prism is given by the function $V(x) = 3x^3 + 13x^2 + 12x$. Write functions that give the prism's base area $B(x)$ and height $h(x)$.

On Your Own

Given $f(x) = 2x$, $g(x) = 4x^2 - 25$, $h(x) = 2x + 5$, and $a(x) = 4(1.5)^x$, find the indicated function. State any restrictions on x.

9. $(f + g)(x)$

10. $(f + a)(x)$

11. $(h - f)(x)$

12. $(f \cdot h)(x)$

13. $\left(\dfrac{g}{f}\right)(x)$

14. $\left(\dfrac{g}{h}\right)(x)$

15. $(g \cdot h)(x)$

16. $(g - h)(x)$

17. $\left(\dfrac{a}{f}\right)(x)$

18. $(a - g)(x)$

19. $(a \cdot h)(x)$

20. $(g \cdot a)(x)$

21. $(f + h)(x)$

22. $(h + a)(x)$

23. $(h - a)(x)$

24. $(f \cdot g)(x)$

25.  **Model with Mathematics** Your neighbor is building a rectangular chicken coop. Copy and complete the table to find four sets of possible dimensions and areas for the coop. Then write functions giving the chicken coop's width $w(x)$ and area $A(x)$ if x is the length of the coop.

The width of the chicken coop must be 8 feet less than the length.

Length (ft)	Width (ft)	Area (ft²)
11	?	33
?	4	?
13	?	?
?	?	84

26. The width of a rectangle is given by the function $w(x) = x + 4$, and the length is given by $\ell(x) = 3x + 2$, both in feet. Write a function $P(x)$ that represents the perimeter of the rectangle.

27. A state's Department of Fish and Wildlife is tracking the populations of smallmouth bass and walleye in a lake. The initial populations of smallmouth bass and walleye were estimated to be 1600 and 400, respectively. Each population has been growing by 5% per year.

   A. What functions $B(t)$ and $W(t)$ give the smallmouth bass and walleye populations, respectively, at time t (in years)?

   B. What function $T(t)$ gives the total population of both species of fish?

   C. What function $D(t)$ gives the difference between the smallmouth bass and walleye populations?

   D. What function $R(t)$ gives the ratio of the smallmouth bass population to the walleye population? What do you notice about the ratio?

28. For a high school volleyball team with x members, the cost of jerseys is given by $J(x) = 25x$ and the cost of shorts is given by $S(x) = 15x$. Both costs are in dollars.

   A. What function $T(x)$ gives the total cost of uniforms for the volleyball team, where a uniform consists of a jersey and a pair of shorts?

   B. If a volleyball team has 12 members, what is the cost of uniforms for the team?

29. Open Ended Write a function $h(x)$ and show that it is a product of two other functions, $f(x)$ and $g(x)$.

30. A terrarium in the shape of a rectangular prism has a width of x inches and a length of $(2x + 5)$ inches. The volume of the terrarium is given by $V(x) = 2x^3 + 17x^2 + 30x$.

   A. Write a function that gives the terrarium's base area $B(x)$.

   B. Write a function that gives the terrarium's height $h(x)$.

   C. If the terrarium's width is 11 inches, what are its length, height, base area, and volume?

31. **(MP)** **Model with Mathematics** A company offers customers unlimited online storage of photos, videos, and other files for $10 per month. The company currently has 52,000 subscribers to this service and estimates that the number of subscribers would decrease by 2000 for each $1 increase in the monthly price.

   A. What is the company's current monthly revenue?

   B. Write an equation that gives the monthly revenue $R(x)$, in thousands of dollars, as a function of the number x of $1 increases in the monthly price of the service.

   C. What two prices could the company charge to increase monthly revenue to $550,000? Explain.

   D. What price maximizes monthly revenue? What is the maximum revenue?

32. The graphs of a linear function f and a quadratic function $g(x) = x^2 - x - 2$ are shown.

   A. Write an equation for the function $h(x) = (f - g)(x)$.

   B. How are the values of x for which $h(x) = 0$ related to the graphs of f and g?

   C. For what values of x is $h(x) > 0$? What is true about the graphs of f and g for these x-values?

   D. For what values of x is $h(x) < 0$? What is true about the graphs of f and g for these x-values?

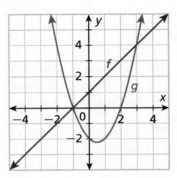

Spiral Review • Assessment Readiness

33. The graph of a quadratic function f has x-intercepts at 1 and 5 and a y-intercept at -10. The quadratic function g is given by the equation $g(x) = -x^2 + 2x + 14$. Which function has the greater maximum value?

   Ⓐ the function f

   Ⓑ the function g

   Ⓒ The maximum values are equal.

   Ⓓ cannot be determined

34. What type of function would best fit a data set whose x-values are evenly spaced and whose y-values have constant, nonzero second differences?

   Ⓐ linear

   Ⓑ quadratic

   Ⓒ absolute value

   Ⓓ exponential

35. A scatter plot of a data set has a parabolic shape. The vertex of the parabola is at $(5, 30)$, and another point on the parabola is $(2, 3)$. What quadratic function models the data?

   Ⓐ $f(x) = (x - 5)^2 + 30$

   Ⓑ $f(x) = (x + 5)^2 + 30$

   Ⓒ $f(x) = -3(x - 5)^2 + 30$

   Ⓓ $f(x) = -\dfrac{27}{49}(x + 5)^2 + 30$

36. What is the solution of the system?
$$\begin{cases} 2x + 3y = 5 \\ x - 2y = 6 \end{cases}$$

   Ⓐ $(4, -1)$ Ⓒ $(-4, 1)$

   Ⓑ $(4, 1)$ Ⓓ $(-4, -1)$

 I'm in a Learning Mindset!

Did I manage my time effectively while learning about operations with functions? What steps did I take to manage my time?

Solve Nonlinear Systems

(I Can) use graphs, tables, and successive approximations to solve nonlinear systems involving linear, quadratic, and exponential equations.

Spark Your Learning

Consumer demand for electric vehicles has been projected to grow over the next few years.

93.56 million gas vehicles were sold in 2018.

1.23 million battery electric vehicles (BEV) were sold in 2018.

Complete Part A as a whole class. Then complete Parts B–D in small groups.

A. What is a mathematical question you can ask about this situation? What information would you need to know to answer your question?

B. What variable(s) are involved in this situation? What unit of measurement would you use for each variable?

C. To answer your question, what strategy and tool would you use along with all the information you have? What answer do you get?

D. Does your answer make sense in the context of the situation? How do you know?

 Turn and Talk Determine the average rate of change for the projected sales of each vehicle. How do these rates imply that they will eventually have the same amount of sales?

Build Understanding

Determine the Number of Solutions of Nonlinear Systems

A nonlinear system of equations has at least one equation that is nonlinear, such as a quadratic or exponential equation. You can determine the solutions of a nonlinear system by graphing each function and identifying any points of intersection.

1 The possible number of solutions for some nonlinear systems are shown.

	3 solutions	2 solutions	1 solution	No solutions
Linear-quadratic	Not possible			
Linear-exponential	Not possible			
Quadratic-exponential				

A. Explain why the x-coordinates of the points where the graphs of the equations $y = f(x)$ and $y = g(x)$ intersect are the solutions of the equation $f(x) = g(x)$.

B. Use a graphing calculator to graph $f(x) = x^2$ and $g(x) = 2x$. Translate either function vertically to find linear-quadratic systems with 2, 1, and 0 solutions. Explain why it is not possible for a linear-quadratic system to have more than two solutions.

C. Use a graphing calculator to graph $f(x) = x^2$ and $g(x) = 2^x$. Translate and/or reflect either function vertically to find quadratic-exponential systems with 3, 2, 1, and 0 solutions.

 Turn and Talk How many solutions are possible for a system of two quadratic functions? Explain.

Step It Out

Solve Nonlinear Systems Graphically

2 ▶ A baseball player hits a ball over the left field wall into the stands for a home run. The height of the ball h_b, in feet, is modeled by the equation $h_b(x) = -\frac{1}{1000}x^2 + \frac{1}{2}x + 3$ where x is the horizontal distance from home plate, in feet.

The stands rise at a rate of 7 feet for every 20 feet of run with the farthest row being 455 feet from home plate. Determine where in the stands the ball lands to the nearest foot.

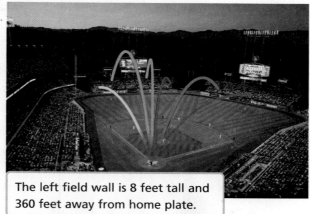

The left field wall is 8 feet tall and 360 feet away from home plate.

The height of the stands can be modeled by the function $h_s(x) = \frac{7}{20}(x - 360) + 8$ for $360 \le x \le 455$.

Solve the following system by setting the two height functions equal.

$$\begin{cases} h_b(x) = -\dfrac{1}{1000}x^2 + \dfrac{1}{2}x + 3 \\ h_s(x) = \dfrac{7}{20}(x - 360) + 8 \end{cases}$$

A. What does the point (360, 8) represent in this situation?

B. For what values of x would a solution be possible?

The x-coordinate of the point where the graphs of $y = h_b(x)$ and $y = h_s(x)$ intersect is the solution of $h_b(x) = h_s(x)$, so graph both functions on the same coordinate plane.

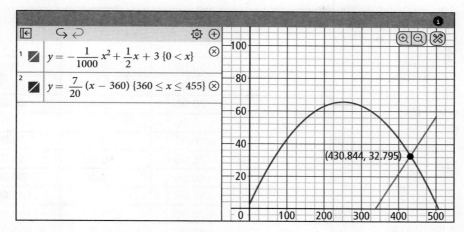

The ball will land in the stands with a horizontal distance of 431 feet from home plate and 33 feet off the ground.

C. How many solutions can a linear-quadratic system have? Why is there only one solution in this situation?

Turn and Talk How could you find the answer if you used a table instead of a graph?

Solve Nonlinear Systems Using Successive Approximations

Methods of successive approximations begin by approximating a solution and then refining the approximation until a desired level of precision is reached.

Given the system of equations $y = f(x)$ and $y = g(x)$, a solution can be approximated by analyzing the function $h(x) = f(x) - g(x)$. Begin with a reasonable interval of values that contains the solution. Then divide the interval into subdivisions of equal length and look for a sign change in $h(x)$. When $h(x)$ changes from positive to negative or from negative to positive, the subdivision where the sign change occurs becomes a more precise interval that contains the solution.

  In an action movie, the hero is on an enclosed ramp, at a distance of 50 feet (as measured along the ramp) from the exit at the bottom of the ramp. The villain releases a large boulder at a distance of 60 feet from the bottom of the ramp.

The hero runs away from the boulder at a constant speed of 15 feet per second. The rolling boulder, however, is accelerating at a rate of 10 feet per second every second. The distance the boulder travels in time t, in seconds, is given by the formula $d = \frac{1}{2} at^2$ where $a = 10$ ft/s^2 in this case. Does the hero make it to the end of the ramp and get out of the way of the boulder?

The distances of the hero and the boulder from the end of the ramp are modeled by the following system of equations:

$$\begin{cases} d_h(t) = 50 - 15t \\ d_b(t) = 60 - \frac{1}{2}(10)t^2 = 60 - 5t^2 \end{cases}$$

A. Are these functions increasing or decreasing? How do you know that the system has a solution?

For the villain's plan to work, then $d_h(t)$ must equal $d_b(t)$ before the hero makes it to the end of the ramp.

Create a spreadsheet to analyze the sign of $d_h(t) - d_b(t)$.

The sign of $d_h(t) - d_b(t)$ changes from negative to positive between $t = 3$ and $t = 4$. The hero and the boulder have the same position sometime between 3 and 4 seconds.

B. Why must the solution to $d_h(t) = d_b(t)$ occur between these two times?

	A	B	C	D
1	t	$d_h(t)$	$d_b(t)$	$d_h(t) - d_b(t)$
2	0	50.00	60.00	−10.00
3	1	35.00	55.00	−20.00
4	2	20.00	40.00	−20.00
5	3	5.00	15.00	−10.00
6	4	−10.00	−20.00	10.00
7	5	−25.00	−65.00	40.00
8	6	−40.00	−120.00	80.00
9	7	−55.00	−185.00	130.00
10	8	−70.00	−260.00	190.00
11	9	−85.00	−345.00	260.00
12	10	−100.00	−440.00	340.00

Refine the interval to $3 < t < 4$.

	A	B	C	D
1	t	$d_h(t)$	$d_b(t)$	$d_h(t) - d_b(t)$
2	3	5.00	15.00	−10.00
3	3.1	3.50	11.95	−8.45
4	3.2	2.00	8.80	−6.80
5	3.3	0.50	5.55	−5.05
6	3.4	−1.00	2.20	−3.20
7	3.5	−2.50	−1.25	−1.25
8	3.6	−4.00	−4.80	0.80
9	3.7	−5.50	−8.45	2.95
10	3.8	−7.00	−12.20	5.20
11	3.9	−8.50	−16.05	7.55
12	4	−10.00	−20.00	10.00

C. What is an approximate solution at this step? What is the level of precision?

The sign of $d_h(t) - d_b(t)$ changes from negative to positive between $t = 3.5$ and $t = 3.6$. The hero and the boulder have the same position at sometime between 3.5 and 3.6 seconds.

Refine the interval to $3.5 < t < 3.6$.

	A	B	C	D
1	t	$d_h(t)$	$d_b(t)$	$d_h(t) - d_b(t)$
2	3.50	−2.50	−1.25	−1.25
3	3.51	−2.65	−1.60	−1.05
4	3.52	−2.80	−1.95	−0.85
5	3.53	−2.95	−2.30	−0.65
6	3.54	−3.10	−2.66	−0.44
7	3.55	−3.25	−3.01	−0.24
8	3.56	−3.40	−3.37	−0.03
9	3.57	−3.55	−3.72	0.17
10	3.58	−3.70	−4.08	0.38
11	3.59	−3.85	−4.44	0.59
12	3.60	−4.00	−4.80	0.80

D. Why is a spreadsheet a useful tool for this process?

The sign of $d_h(t) - d_b(t)$ changes from negative to positive between $t = 3.56$ and $t = 3.57$. The hero and the boulder have the same position at sometime between 3.56 and 3.57 seconds.

The hero will reach the end of the ramp when $d_h(t) = 0$.

$$0 = 50 - 15t$$
$$15t = 50$$
$$t = \frac{50}{15} \approx 3.33 \text{ seconds}$$

E. How much time did the hero escape with?

The hero reaches the end of the ramp after approximately 3.33 seconds, narrowly escaping the boulder.

 Turn and Talk What is another way to solve the problem?

Check Understanding

Determine the number of solutions for each system.

1.

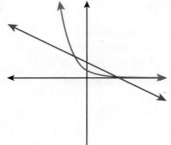

2.

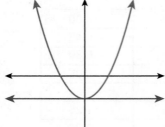

3.

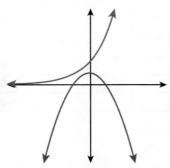

4. (MP) **Attend to Precision** Two populations are modeled by the functions $P_1(t) = 100(2)^t$ and $P_2(t) = 25t^2 + 200$ where t is time, in days. Approximate when they have the same population size. Explain how precise your approximation is.

	A	B	C	D
1	t	$P_1(t)$	$P_2(t)$	$P_2(t) - P_2(t)$
2	0.00	100.00	200.00	−100.00
3	0.25	118.92	201.56	−82.64
4	0.50	141.42	206.25	−64.83
5	0.75	168.18	214.06	−45.88
6	1.00	200.00	225.00	−25.00
7	1.25	237.84	239.06	−1.22
8	1.50	282.84	256.25	26.59
9	1.75	336.36	276.56	59.80
10	2.00	400.00	300.00	100.00

5. A system is composed of the equations $y = x - 3$ and $y = -x^2 - \frac{1}{2}x$. Use a graphing calculator to find the solutions to the system. Round to the nearest hundredth.

On Your Own

Determine the number of solutions for each system.

6.

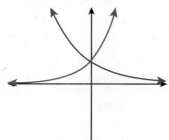

7.

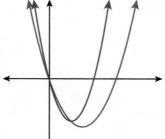

8.

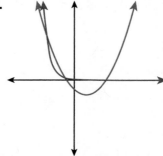

Determine the number of solutions for each system.

9. $y = 2^x$
$y = 5x - 4$

10. $y = 3^x$
$y = 2x^2$

11. $y = -4^x$
$y = x^2 - 3$

12. $y = x^2$
$y = x - 1$

13. $y = 1.2^x + 2$
$y = 2x^2 + 1$

14. $y = -x^2 + 3$
$y = (x - 2)^2 + 1$

15. A rock climber is scaling a cliff that is 200 feet tall at a rate of 15 feet per minute. The height of the climber, in feet, after t seconds is given by $h_p(t) = 0.25t$. Their climbing partner drops a coil of rope from directly above them. The height of the coil, in feet, after t seconds is given by $h_r(t) = -16t^2 + 200$. At what time does the coil of rope reach the climber?

16. **(MP) Use Tools** The height h_s, in feet, of the stands in a hockey arena is represented by $h_s(x) = \frac{1}{2}(x - 10)$ for $x \geq 10$ where x is the horizontal distance, in feet, from a T-shirt cannon. The function representing the height of a T-shirt shot by the cannon is shown.

   A. State what strategy and tool you will use to solve $h_s(x) = h_t(x)$. Explain your choice.

   B. For what value of x is $h_s(x)$ are $h_t(x)$ equal? What does this represent in this situation?

   C. At what height will the T-shirt land in the stands? Explain.

$h_t(x) = -\dfrac{1}{32}x^2 + x + 10$

17. **(MP) Reason** A ball is kicked into the air and lands on the roof of a house. The height h_b, in feet, of the ball is given by $h_b(x) = -\frac{1}{8}x^2 + 3x$ where x is its horizontal position, in feet. The height h_r, in feet, of the roof is given by $h_r(x) = \frac{1}{2}(x + 3)$ where x is its horizontal position in feet over the interval $15 \leq x \leq 25$. Use successive approximations to approximate where the ball hits the roof to the nearest hundredth of a foot.

Given the two functions, use successive approximations to find any solutions to the system. Round to the nearest hundredth.

18. $y = -x + 1$ and $y = -x^2 + 4x - 3$

19. $y = 3x - 1$ and $y = x^2 - 4x + 3$

20. $y = 2^x$ and $y = -2x + 5$

21. $y = -3x^2 + 1$ and $y = x^2 - 4x$

22. $y = x + 4$ and $y = x^2 - 4x + 5$

23. $y = -x^2 + 8$ and $y = -2^x + 2$

24. **(MP) Use Tools** During a beanbag-toss game, players attempt to toss a beanbag into a hole on a slanted wooden board. The height h_b, in feet, of one beanbag tossed during the game is given by $h_b(x) = -\frac{1}{4}x^2 + x + \frac{9}{2}$ where x is the horizontal distance, in feet. The height h_w of the wooden board is given by $h_w(x) = \frac{1}{2}(x - 6)$ for $6 \le x \le 8$. Will the beanbag land in the hole? State what strategy and tool you will use to answer the question, explain your choice, and then find the answer.

4.5 ft

0.8 ft

25. **Health and Fitness** During its practice, a volleyball team does serving drills. The height $h_1(t)$, in feet, of a volleyball being served for one player is $h_1(t) = -16t^2 + 29t + 5.6$. The height of another ball being hit simultaneously is $h_2(t) = -16t^2 + 27x + 5.8$. For each, t is the time, in seconds. At what time will the volleyballs be at the same height?

26. **Open Ended** Write a system of nonlinear functions that has three solutions and state the solutions. The functions must be either linear, quadratic, or exponential.

Spiral Review • Assessment Readiness

27. Given $f(x) = 6x^2 - 17x - 14$ and $g(x) = x^2 - 2x$, what is $f(x) - g(x)$?

Ⓐ $5x^2 - 15x - 14$ Ⓒ $5x^2 + 15x + 14$

Ⓑ $5x^2 + 15x - 14$ Ⓓ $7x^2 - 19x - 14$

28. Given $f(x) = x^2 - x - 6$ and $g(x) = x - 3$, what is $\frac{f(x)}{g(x)}$?

Ⓐ $x - 3$ Ⓒ $x^3 - 4x^2 - 3x + 18$

Ⓑ $x + 2$ Ⓓ $\frac{1}{x + 2}$

29. A car is purchased for $25,425 and depreciates at an annual rate of 9%. Which function represents the value of the car at time t, in years.

Ⓐ $25,425(1.09)^t$ Ⓒ $25,425 + 9t$

Ⓑ $25,425(0.91)^t$ Ⓓ $25,425 - 9t$

30. Which functions are exponential? Select all that apply.

Ⓐ $y = 3^x$ Ⓓ $y = x^2 + 12$

Ⓑ $y = 3x$ Ⓔ $y = \frac{1}{3}x - 1$

Ⓒ $y = 14\left(\frac{1}{5}\right)^x$ Ⓕ $y = 8(0.2)^x$

 I'm in a Learning Mindset!

How did I learn from my mistakes while working with nonlinear systems?

Cubic Functions

(I Can) analyze cubic functions and their behaviors.

Spark Your Learning

An architect is designing a series of rectangular prism-shaped buildings that will meet the different space requirements of her clients.

The length and height of each building is dependent on the width of the building.

Complete Part A as a whole class. Then complete Parts B–C in small groups.

A. What is a mathematical question you can ask about this situation? What information would you need to know to answer your question?

B. What variable(s) are involved in this situation? What unit of measurement would you use for each variable?

C. To answer your question, what strategy and tool would you use along with all the information you have? What answer do you get?

Turn and Talk Predict how your answer would change for the following changes in the situation:

- The length of the base is equal to the width.
- The height is 50 meters greater than the width.

Build Understanding

Characteristics of Cubic Functions

A function defined by a third-degree polynomial expression is called a **cubic function**. The **standard form of a cubic function** is $f(x) = ax^3 + bx^2 + cx + d$, where a, b, c, and d are real numbers and $a \neq 0$. The parent cubic function is $f(x) = x^3$.

Just like quadratic functions, you may be able to rewrite cubic functions in intercept form, $f(x) = a(x - x_1)(x - x_2)(x - x_3)$, where x_1, x_2, and x_3 are the function's zeros as well as the x-intercepts of the function's graph.

1 ▶ Consider the following cubic functions written in intercept form.

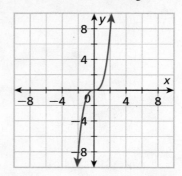

$$f(x) = x^3$$

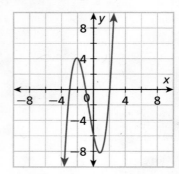

$$f(x) = (x + 3)(x + 1)(x - 2)$$

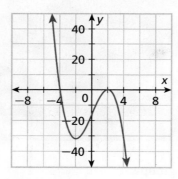

$$f(x) = -(x + 4)(x - 2)^2$$

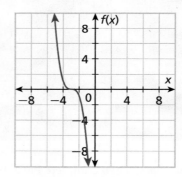

$$f(x) = -(x + 3)^3$$

A. Describe the end behavior of each function. How does the sign of the leading coefficient a affect the end behavior?

B. How many turning points can the graph of a cubic function have? Does the graph of a cubic function always have a turning point? Explain.

C. How many distinct x-intercepts can the graph of a cubic function have? Explain.

D. Does the graph of a cubic function always cross the x-axis at an x-intercept? Explain how this observation relates to the number of times a factor is repeated when written in intercept form.

 Turn and Talk Does a cubic function always attain positive and negative values? Explain.

Step It Out

Write Cubic Functions in Intercept Form

Factoring a cubic function will help you identify the zeros of a cubic function. You learned that quadratic functions can have 0, 1, or 2 zeros; cubic functions can have 1, 2 or 3 zeros.

Cubic function	Intercept form	Zeros and x-intercepts
$f(x) = x^3 + 2x^2 - 15x$	$f(x) = x(x - 3)(x + 5)$	0, 3, and −5
$g(x) = 2x^3 + 4x^2 + 2x$	$g(x) = 2x(x + 1)^2$	0 and −1
$h(x) = x^3$	$h(x) = x^3$	0

 2 Identify the zeros of the cubic functions $f(x) = -2x^3 - 4x^2 + 48x$ and $g(x) = (x + 1)(3x^2 - 9x - 12)$.

> **A.** Why is the first step to write the functions in intercept form?

Write the functions in intercept form.

$f(x) = -2x^3 - 4x^2 + 48x$

$\quad = -2x(x^2 + 2x - 24)$

$\quad = -2x(x + 6)(x - 4)$

> **B.** Compare the strategies for factoring $f(x)$ and $g(x)$.

$g(x) = (x + 1)(3x^2 - 9x - 12)$

$\quad = (x + 1)(3(x^2 - 3x - 4))$

$\quad = 3(x + 1)(x - 4)(x + 1)$

$\quad = 3(x + 1)^2(x - 4)$

Identify the zeros.

> **C.** What property allows you to conclude that x_1 is a zero given that $x - x_1$ is a factor?

The function f can be written in the form $f(x) = -2(x - 0)(x + 6)(x - 4)$. The factors $x - 0$, $x + 6$, and $x - 4$ indicate that 0, −6, and 4 are zeros of f.

The factors $x + 1$ and $x - 4$ indicate that −1 and 4 are zeros of g.

> **D.** Why does the factor $x - 4$ in the rule for $f(x)$ produce 4 as a zero? Why does the factor $x + 1$ in the rule for $g(x)$ produce −1 as a zero?

 Turn and Talk How can the zeros of a function help you sketch its graph?

Graph Cubic Functions

By identifying the zeros and end behavior of a cubic function, you can create a rough sketch of the function's graph.

3 Create a rough sketch of the graph of $f(x) = -x^3 + 12x^2 - 36x$.

Determine the end behavior.

There are two possible end behaviors for a cubic function, depending on the sign of the leading coefficient. Since the sign of the x^3 term is negative in $f(x)$, the end behavior is the opposite of the end behavior of the parent cubic function.

As $x \to -\infty$, $f(x) \to +\infty$, and as $x \to +\infty$, $f(x) \to -\infty$.

> **A.** Why does the end behavior only depend on the sign of the x^3 term?

Identify the *x*-intercepts.

Factor the cubic expression to write the function in intercept form.

$$f(x) = -x^3 + 12x^2 - 36x$$
$$= -x(x^2 - 12x + 36)$$
$$= -x(x - 6)^2$$

> **B.** Explain the steps used to factor the cubic expression.

The factors of x and $x - 6$ indicate that 0 and 6 are x-intercepts of the functions graph.

Sketch the graph.

Based on the end behavior, the left end of the graph should go up and the right end of the graph should go down.

The graph must cross the x-axis at 0. The graph touches the x-axis when $x = 6$ but does not cross it.

> **C.** How do you know that the graph crosses the x-axis at 0? How do you know that the graph does not cross the x-axis at 6?

The graph has positive values when $x < 0$. The graph has negative values when $0 < x < 6$ and $x > 6$.

The graph starts at the upper left, crosses the x-axis when $x = 0$, turns between 0 and 6 to come back up and touch the x-axis when $x = 6$, and then turns and continues to the lower right.

> **D.** Why is it better not to label the y-axis scale for this graph?

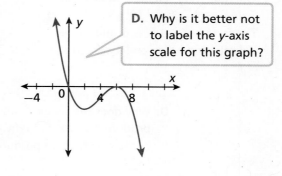

 Turn and Talk How could you improve the accuracy of your sketch of the graph?

Analyze Real-World Cubic Functions

Since the volume of an object is a measurement of three-dimensional space, the volume may be modeled with a cubic function if each dimension of the object has a linear relationship with the same variable.

 4 Hector is designing a scooper in the shape of a right triangular prism. He will start with a 10-inch by 15-inch sheet of plastic and cut out two squares from the corners on one side and two triangles from the corners on the other side as shown. Then he will fold the sides up, glue the edges that meet, and attach a handle to create the scooper. What size squares should Hector cut out to obtain the scooper with the maximum volume?

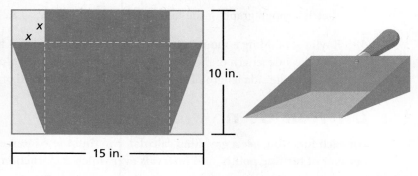

Use a verbal model.

Volume (in³) V	$= \frac{1}{2}$	Length (in.) $15 - 2x$	$\cdot$	Width (in.) $10 - x$	$\cdot$	Height (in.) x

Define the domain.

If Hector does not cut any squares, then $x = 0$. The largest squares he can cut have a side length of 7.5 inches since the long side of the sheet of plastic is 15 inches long. The domain is $0 \le x \le 7.5$.

A. Explain why each dimension is dependent on x.

B. What is the volume when $x = 7.5$? Why?

Find the maximum.

Use a graphing calculator to graph the function $V(x) = \frac{1}{2}(15 - 2x)(10 - x)x$ on the domain.

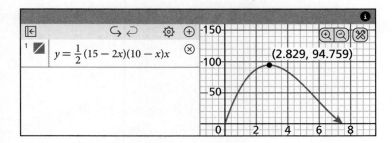

Answer the question.

The maximum volume of the scooper is approximately 94.8 in³. To create a scooper with this volume, Hector should cut squares with a side length of approximately 2.8 inches.

C. What are the dimensions of the scooper when $x = 2.8$?

 Turn and Talk What is the maximum volume of the scooper if Hector cuts squares from the 10-inch side instead of the 15-inch side?

Check Understanding

1. Use a graphing calculator to identify the end behavior, x-intercepts, approximate turning points, and intervals where the function $f(x) = -2x^3 + 62x + 60$ is positive and negative.

2. Write the function $f(x) = 4x^3 - 100x$ in intercept form.

3. Sketch a rough graph of the function $f(x) = (x + 4)(x^2 - 8x + 12)$.

4. Kaylin is building a model pyramid with a square base. The height is 2 inches less than the side length of the base. Write a function for the volume of the pyramid based on the side length of the base x. Specify the domain of the function.

On Your Own

For each function, use a graphing calculator to find the x-intercepts, end behavior, number of turning points, and intervals over which the function is positive and negative.

5. $f(x) = x^3 - 3x^2$

6. $f(x) = -x^3 + 2x^2 + 8x$

7. $f(x) = -2x^3 + 6x^2 + 18x + 10$

8. $f(x) = x^3 - x$

9. $f(x) = x^3 - 6x^2 + 12x - 8$

10. $f(x) = -x^3 + 13x + 12$

Write each function in intercept form.

11. $f(x) = 3x^3 + 21x^2 - 24x$

12. $f(x) = -4x^3 + 16x$

13. $f(x) = (x + 3)(x^2 + 2x - 35)$

14. $f(x) = (2 - x)(x^2 + 4x + 3)$

15. $f(x) = (x - 4)(-2x^2 - 2x + 40)$

16. $f(x) = -x^3 - 2x^2 - x$

17. $f(x) = -2x^3 + 18x$

18. $f(x) = (x + 2)(3x^2 - 18x + 24)$

Sketch a rough graph of each function.

19. $f(x) = x^3 + x^2 - 12x$

20. $f(x) = -(x + 3)(x^2 - 6x + 5)$

21. Consider the graph of the cubic function f shown.
    A. What are the zeros of f?
    B. Describe the end behavior of f.
    C. For which values of x is $f(x)$ negative? For which values is $f(x)$ positive?
    D. Write a possible rule for the function that is graphed.

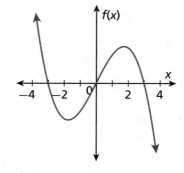

22. The intercept form of the cubic function $f(x)$ includes the factor $x^2 + 4$. If the standard form of the function is $f(x) = 2x^3 + x^2 + 8x + 4$, what is the intercept form? Multiply your answer to confirm.

23. (MP) **Use Structure** Graph the function $f(x) = x^3 + 6x^2 + 11x + 6$ to identify the x-intercepts. Use the x-intercepts to write the intercept form of the function. Multiply your answer to confirm.

24. (MP) **Reason** One of the graphs at the right represents the cubic function $f(x) = x^3 + 3x^2 - 2x - 12$.

A. Identify the graph representing the given function.

B. How are the graphs of the two functions related?

C. Find the function that corresponds to the other graph, using the relationship between the given graphs.

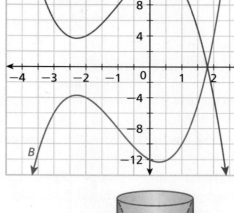

25. The figure shows a cylinder with a cone removed. The base radius of the cylinder and cone is x, and the height of both is $x + 5$. Write a function that gives the volume of the cylinder with the cone removed.

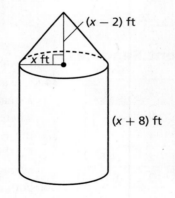

26. (MP) **Model with Mathematics**
An architect is assigned to develop a formula to find the volumes of silos with varying dimensions as shown in the sketch. Develop a mathematical model that gives the volume of the silo.

$(x - 2)$ ft

x ft

$(x + 8)$ ft

27. Consider the four graphs of cubic functions shown.

A. Which functions in the graph have repeated zeros?

B. Do any of the functions have a negative leading coefficient? Explain.

C. Identify the widest interval over which all the functions are positive.

28. The product of three consecutive odd numbers is a function of positive integers. Develop a cubic function that represents the product of the numbers given the value of the first of the three numbers.

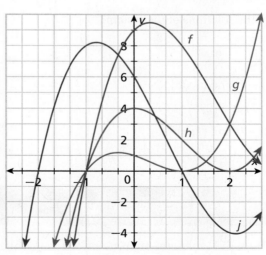

29. Four squares, each with a side length of x inches, are cut out from the corners of a 20 in. by 30 in. piece of sheet metal. Then all four sides are folded as shown to create a box. What is the maximum volume of the box?

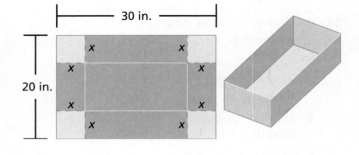

30 in.

20 in.

30. For stability, the height of a rectangular pyramid is designed to be 5 feet less than the width of the base. The perimeter of the base must be 70 feet.

A. Write a cubic function that gives the volume of the pyramid for any given width.

B. What is the maximum volume of the pyramid? What are the dimensions of the pyramid that produce the maximum volume?

31. (**Open Middle**™) Using the integers -9 to 9, at most two times each, fill in the boxes to create a polynomial function with distinct zeros that are as close as possible to each other.

$$y = \boxed{}x^3 + \boxed{}x^2 + \boxed{}x + \boxed{} \qquad x = \boxed{}, \boxed{}, \boxed{}$$

Spiral Review • Assessment Readiness

32. Which type of function best models the data in the table?

Ⓐ constant

Ⓑ linear

Ⓒ quadratic

Ⓓ exponential

x	y
0	2
1	3
2	4.5
3	6.75

33. What are the solutions of the system?
$$\begin{cases} 6x - y = -5 \\ x^2 + 3x - y = 5 \end{cases}$$

Ⓐ $(-2, -7)$ and $(5, 35)$

Ⓑ $(1, -7)$ and $(2, 5)$

Ⓒ $(-2, -7)$ and $(2, 5)$

Ⓓ $(1, -7)$ and $(5, 35)$

34. The average cost of driving and maintaining a small sedan is given by $C_s(t) = 529.5t$, where time t is measured in months. Similarly, the average cost for a pickup truck is $C_p(t) = 837.83t$. Which function gives the average total cost of driving and maintaining both a small sedan and a pickup truck?

Ⓐ $C_T(t) = 308.33t$ Ⓒ $C_T(t) = 1146.16t$

Ⓑ $C_T(t) = 683.67t$ Ⓓ $C_T(t) = 1367.33t$

35. On a football team, 14 out of 40 players weigh more than 250 pounds. What percent of the players weigh more than 250 pounds?

Ⓐ 35%   Ⓒ 14%

Ⓑ 28%   Ⓓ 5.6%

 I'm in a Learning Mindset!

How did I manage my time effectively while I was learning about characteristics of cubic functions? What steps did I take to manage my time?

Review

Choose a Model

Amara owns a collector car. She tracks the value V of the car over time t in years since it was produced.

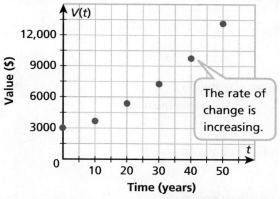

Amara uses a graphing calculator and regression to model the data with an exponential function.

$$V(t) = 3000(1.03)^t; R^2 = 0.9995$$

The rate of change is increasing.

The coefficient of determination is very close to 1.

Function Operations

Amara must pay expenses E on the collector car, such as insurance and maintenance. She pays $250 per year on expenses.

$$E(t) = -250t$$

The net worth N of the classic car is found by adding the expenses to the car's value.

$$N(t) = V(t) + E(t) = 3000(1.03)^t - 250t$$

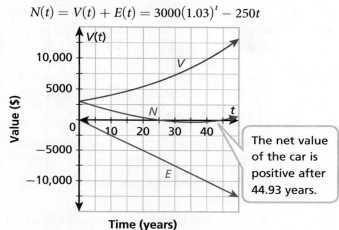

The net value of the car is positive after 44.93 years.

Nonlinear Systems

After 20 years, when the car is worth $5400, Amara considers selling the car and buying another classic car that costs $4500 and appreciates at a growth rate of 4%. How many years from now will the second car have the same value as the first car?

$$V_1(t) = 5400(1.03)^t \qquad V_2(t) = 4500(1.04)^t$$

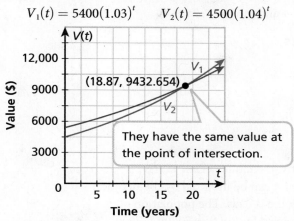

They have the same value at the point of intersection.

The second car would have the same value 18.89 years in the future.

Cubic Functions

To draw a rough graph, write the function in intercept form.

$$f(x) = x^3 - 25x$$
$$= x(x^2 - 25)$$
$$= x(x + 5)(x - 5)$$

Factor out the GCF.

Factor a difference of squares.

Plot the x-intercepts.

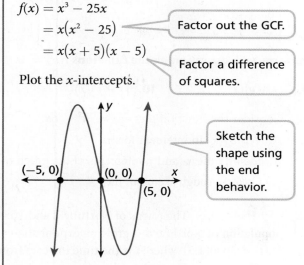

Sketch the shape using the end behavior.

Vocabulary

Choose the correct term from the box to complete each sentence.

1. A ___?___ is a third-degree polynomial function.

2. A(n) ___?___ has a rate of change that is constant,
   a(n) ___?___ has a second difference that is constant, and
   a(n) ___?___ has a common ratio that is constant.

3. A(n) ___?___ contains two or more equations, where at least one of the equations is not linear.

Concepts and Skills

4. How can you use residual values to determine if an equation is a good fit for a set of data? How can you use the coefficient of determination to determine if an equation is a good fit for a set of data?

5. How can you tell if a data set can be modeled with a linear, quadratic or exponential function? Explain your reasoning.

6. Elizabeth and Hannah keep track of the number of books they have read.

   A. What type of function would best fit each student's reading habits? Explain your reasoning.

   B. Use regression to create a model for each student's reading habits.

   C. If this trend continues, how long will it take each student to read 50 books?

   D. Is it likely that these trends will continue? Explain your reasoning.

Year	Elizabeth's books	Hannah's books
1	4	1
2	9	2
3	13	5
4	17	9
5	20	15

Solve each nonlinear system of equations.

7. $\begin{cases} 8x + 2y = -10 \\ x^2 - 1 = y \end{cases}$

8. $\begin{cases} x^2 + y = 11 \\ 2^x - 7 = y \end{cases}$

Perform each operation on the functions $f(x) = 3x + 4$ and $g(x) = -2x - 9$.

9. $(f + g)(x)$

10. $(f - g)(x)$

11. $(f \cdot g)(x)$

12. Consider the function $f(x) = x^3 + x^2 - 6x$.

   A. Write $f(x)$ in intercept form.

   B. Identify the x- and y-intercepts of the graph of $f(x)$.

   C. Create a rough sketch of $f(x)$.

13. **(MP) Use Tools** The towns of Northfield and Westfield conduct a census. The population of Northfield is growing exponentially and can be modeled by the function $P_N(t) = 3000(1.5)^t$ where t is the time in years from the census. The population of Westfield is growing at a steady rate and can be modeled by $P_W(t) = 5000t + 7000$. When will the towns have the same population? State what strategy and tool you will use to answer the question, explain your choice, and then find the answer.

Data Analysis

Ecologist

The relationship between living things and their environment is complex. An ecologist studies these relationships by gathering, analyzing, and modeling data such as population counts of species. The science done by ecologists can provide insights into the world we live in and the environmental issues that impact it.

STEM Task

After the reintroduction of wolves to Yellowstone, ecologists observed shifts in the populations of the elk in the park.

Write an equation that models the relationship between the wolf and elk populations in Yellowstone. Explain why you chose the model you did.

Yellowstone Wolf and Elk Population		
Year	Wolf	Elk
2000	177	13400
2002	271	9215
2004	324	8335
2006	390	6588
2008	449	6279
2010	501	4635

Learning Mindset
Resilience Notices Others

When solving a problem, you may be inclined to handle a task alone. You can accelerate your learning by tapping into the understanding and insights that others have. Take notice of what others around you are doing during a learning task. Navigating your way through a task can become easier as others can help fill in gaps in your understanding. By working together, you may even come up with a completely new way forward, something that none of you would have thought about on your own. Here are some questions you can ask yourself to enhance how you notice others while engaging in the learning process:

■ How does my perspective on the wolf and elk populations compare to my peers' perspectives? How can observing or consulting with my peers during this task open my mind to different modes of reasoning?

■ While listening to the thoughts of others, how can I determine if what they are saying is fact or opinion? How can I convey disagreement while keeping the conversation focused on the topic?

■ Am I empathetic to my peers when they express opinions that differ from my own? How? Why is it important to empathize with others?

■ How can I best take notice of a peer who needs help? What strategy can I use to support the learning of my peers?

Reflect

Q What caused you to take notice of your peers as you modeled the data about wolf and elk populations in Yellowstone? If you and your peers thought about the data differently, how did you address your differences?

Q If you were an ecologist, what would you need to do to make sure that your analysis was conducted in an unbiased and transparent manner? How would you respond to feedback critical of your work?

21 Categorical Data

Music to My Ears

Is there an association between mathematical and musical proficiencies?

Are You Ready?

Complete these problems to review prior concepts and skills you will need for this module.

Write Decimals and Fractions as Percents

Express each number as a percent, rounded to the nearest tenth.

1. 0.012

2. 2.65

3. $\frac{2}{3}$

4. $\frac{15}{16}$

Scatter Plots and Association

Marcie records the high temperature on the days that her business sells lemonade.

Temperature (°F)	65	66	72	78	80	80	83	86	90
Lemonade sales (cups)	200	210	240	275	268	280	300	320	300

5. Construct a scatter plot to represent the data.

6. Is there an association between the temperature and lemonade sales? Explain.

Two-Way Frequency Tables

Randomly selected students were surveyed about how they get to school. Of students in Grade 9, 35 take public transportation and 25 walk. Of students in Grade 10, 35 take public transportation and 5 walk.

7. Construct a two-way frequency table to model the data.

8. How many are in the Grade 9 category?

9. What percent of students surveyed walk to school?

Connecting Past and Present Learning

Previously, you learned:

- to construct and interpret two-way frequency tables and relative frequency tables,
- to construct and interpret scatter plots for bivariate data to investigate association, and
- to use random sampling to produce representative samples and support inferences.

In this module, you will learn:

- to summarize categorical data for two categories in two-way frequency tables,
- to interpret relative frequencies in the context of data, and
- to recognize possible associations between categorical variables.

Two-Way Frequency and Relative Frequency Tables

(I Can) read, create, and interpret two-way frequency tables and relative frequency tables.

Spark Your Learning

A survey of randomly selected high school students from all four grades is conducted about whether they play a musical instrument in school.

> The percent of students who are seniors and play a musical instrument in school is lower than other grades.

Complete Part A as a whole class. Then complete Parts B–D in small groups.

 A. What is a mathematical question you can ask about this situation? What information would you need to know to answer your question?

 B. What variable(s) are involved in this situation? How can you assess or compare the variable(s)?

 C. To answer your question, what strategy and tool would you use along with all the information you have? What answer do you get?

 D. Does your answer make sense in the context of this situation? How do you know?

  Turn and Talk Predict how your answer may change for each of the following changes in the situation:
 • All students surveyed are members of the school's concert band or marching band.
 • The number of students surveyed is considerably larger.

Build Understanding

Understand Types of Data

1 Quantitative data are numerical data. **Categorical data** are qualitative in nature, such as "blue" and "red," or "slow" and "fast."

Quantitative	Categorical
age 15, age 19	under age 18, over age 18

A. Why do you think "Under age 18" and "Over age 18" are categorical instead of quantitative?

B. What is an example of quantitative data that describe temperature?

C. What is an example of categorical data that describe temperature?

 Turn and Talk Although numbers used for counts and measurements are quantitative data, sometime numbers are used as categorical data. Give an example of using numbers as categorical data.

Read and Interpret Two-Way Frequency Tables

A **two-way frequency table** shows frequency data for two categorical variables. Each **frequency** indicates the number of items in a data set that belong to both a specific category for one of the categorical variables and another specific category for the other categorical variable.

2 The two-way frequency table shows the results of a survey of 200 randomly selected movie lovers about how they prefer to watch movies.

		Preferred Method of Watching Movies			
		Theater	Handheld device	Television	Total
Age	15–49	28	?	44	160
	50+	20	6	14	?
	Total	?	94	58	200

A. Copy and complete the two-way frequency table. Explain how you found the missing values.

B. You can see that 28 people of age 15–49 preferred theater and only 20 people aged 50 and older preferred theater. Is it valid to conclude that theater is more popular for people of age 15–49? Explain.

 Turn and Talk How many ways can you determine the total number of people surveyed who are 50 and older? Describe them.

Read and Interpret Two-Way Relative Frequency Tables

A **two-way relative frequency table** is a two-way frequency table that displays relative frequencies. Recall that a **relative frequency** is the quotient of any frequency in a two-way frequency table and the total number of data values.

$$\text{relative frequency} = \frac{\text{frequency in a two-way frequency table}}{\text{total number of data values}}$$

3 ▶ A two-way relative frequency table for the data from Task 2 is shown.

		Preferred Method of Watching Movies			
		Theater	Handheld device	Television	Total
Age	15–49	0.14	0.44	0.22	0.80
	50+	0.10	0.03	0.07	0.20
	Total	0.24	0.47	0.29	1.00

A. Using the definition of *relative frequency*, explain how the entry for movie watchers of ages 15–49 who prefer watching movies on a handheld device was calculated. What does this entry mean?

B. What does the entry 1.00 in the "Total" row and "Total" column represent?

Two-way tables display two types of relative frequencies.

A **joint relative frequency** is a relative frequency representing a combination of one category of the categorical variables and another category from the other categorical variable.

A **marginal relative frequency** is the sum of the joint relative frequencies in a row or column of a two-way table.

Joint relative frequencies

		Preferred Method of Watching Movies			
		Theater	Handheld device	Television	Total
Age	15–49	0.14	0.44	0.22	0.80
	50+	0.10	0.03	0.07	0.20
	Total	0.24	0.47	0.29	1.00

Marginal relative frequencies

C. What percent of those surveyed are ages 50+ who prefer watching on a handheld device? What type of relative frequency is this?

D. Where do you see 47% in the two-way table? What type of relative frequency is this, and what does it mean in the context of the survey?

 Turn and Talk Is a marginal relative frequency always greater than a joint relative frequency? Explain.

Step It Out

Create Two-Way Tables

4 A survey of 200 randomly selected drivers was conducted asking whether they knew about the law that prohibits texting while driving. What percent of the surveyed drivers responded no?

| Under age 25 | Yes: 40 / No: 40 / Unsure: 20 |
| Ages 23+ | Yes: 20 / No: 77 / Unsure: 3 |

Create a two-way frequency table.

		Awareness of the Law			
		Yes	**No**	**Unsure**	**Total**
Age	**Under 25**	40	40	20	100
	25+	20	77	3	100
	Total	60	117	23	200

A. How can you find the marginal frequencies highlighted in the table?

Convert the two-way frequency table to a two-way relative frequency table.

B. Why is every entry divided by 200?

		Awareness of the Law			
		Yes	**No**	**Unsure**	**Total**
Age	**Under 25**	$\frac{40}{200} = 0.200$	$\frac{40}{200} = 0.200$	$\frac{20}{200} = 0.100$	$\frac{100}{200} = 0.500$
	25+	$\frac{20}{200} = 0.100$	$\frac{77}{200} = 0.385$	$\frac{3}{200} = 0.015$	$\frac{100}{200} = 0.500$
	Total	$\frac{60}{200} = 0.300$	$\frac{117}{200} = 0.585$	$\frac{23}{200} = 0.115$	$\frac{200}{200} = 1.000$

The percent of the surveyed drivers who responded that they did not know that it is illegal to text while driving is 58.5%.

C. What joint relative frequencies contribute to this value? What do they represent?

Turn and Talk Would a two-way frequency table or a two-way relative frequency table be more useful if the marginal frequencies for the categories are equal? If they are different?

Analyze Data Using Two-Way Relative Frequency Tables

5 The results of a random survey about whether triathletes prefer cycling, running, or swimming are shown in the two-way relative frequency table. A vendor is selling sports equipment at this triathlon. Based on the results of the survey, for which sport should the vendor promote its products for the most? For what age group should the vendor target its promotion of that sport?

		Preferred Sport			
		Cycling	Running	Swimming	Total
Age	Under 50	0.10	0.35	0.12	0.57
	50 to under 65	0.10	0.10	0.20	0.40
	65 and older	0.01	0.00	0.02	0.03
	Total	0.21	0.45	0.34	1.00

A. Does this relative frequency tell you how many triathletes were surveyed? Explain.

Compare the marginal relative frequencies.
21% < 34% < 45%

Running is the preferred sport with the greatest marginal relative frequency. The vendor should promote its running products the most.

B. Interpret each percent in this situation.

C. Why is the greatest marginal relative frequency important to the vendor?

Compare the joint relative frequencies.
0% < 10% < 35%

The joint relative frequency representing triathletes under 50 who chose running as their preferred sport is the greatest. The vendor should target the promotion of its running products to triathletes under the age of 50 the most.

D. Why are only these three joint relative frequencies considered?

E. Why is the greatest joint relative frequency important to the vendor?

Turn and Talk If the triathlon limits the number of participants to 7500 triathletes, how many potential clients will the vendor reach with its promotion?

©Chris Cheadle/Alamy

Check Understanding

1. Compare and contrast quantitative and categorical data.

2. Randomly selected language students were surveyed about what language they study and for how long they have been studying. Use the data in the two-way frequency table to answer the questions.

<table>
<tr><td rowspan="2"></td><td rowspan="2"></td><td colspan="4">Language</td></tr>
<tr><td>Spanish</td><td>French</td><td>Other</td><td>Total</td></tr>
<tr><td rowspan="4">Length of study</td><td>Less than 1 year</td><td>15</td><td>22</td><td>3</td><td>40</td></tr>
<tr><td>More than 1 year</td><td>22</td><td>17</td><td>1</td><td>40</td></tr>
<tr><td>Total</td><td>37</td><td>39</td><td>4</td><td>80</td></tr>
</table>

A. How many language students surveyed have been studying Spanish for more than one year?

B. What is the expression to calculate the relative frequency of language students surveyed that have been studying Spanish for more than one year? What type of frequency is this?

C. Create a two-way relative frequency table. Where do you see 5% in the two-way table? What does it mean in the context of the survey?

D. What percent of language students surveyed study French? What type of frequency is this?

On Your Own

3. What question can you ask yourself to determine if data are quantitative or categorical?

4. Randomly selected students were surveyed about their preferred school subject. The data is summarized in the two-way frequency table shown.

<table>
<tr><td rowspan="2"></td><td rowspan="2"></td><td colspan="4">Preferred Subject</td></tr>
<tr><td>Math</td><td>Science</td><td>Art</td><td>Total</td></tr>
<tr><td rowspan="3">Grade</td><td>K–5</td><td>42</td><td>37</td><td>46</td><td>125</td></tr>
<tr><td>6–9</td><td>36</td><td>18</td><td>21</td><td>75</td></tr>
<tr><td>Total</td><td>78</td><td>55</td><td>67</td><td>200</td></tr>
</table>

A. Create a two-way relative frequency table.

B. What percent of students surveyed are in Grades 6–9 and say they prefer science?

C. What percent of all students surveyed say they prefer art?

D. In which grade range (K–5 or 6–9) do a greater number of students surveyed prefer math? In which grade range do a greater percent of students surveyed prefer math? Explain.

5. **(MP)** **Attend to Precision**

The cafeteria director surveyed randomly selected high school students about their preferred fruit.

A. Create a two-way relative frequency table. Round to the nearest hundredth.

B. What does the relative frequency 23% mean in the context of the survey?

C. How many pears should the cafeteria provide if 500 students are eating lunch? Explain.

	Preferred Fruit			
	Apple	**Orange**	**Pear**	**Total**
9	25	22	12	59
10	28	17	5	50
Total	53	39	17	109

Grade (row label on left)

6. **(MP)** **Use Structure** Use the two-way frequency table to answer the questions.

	Vegetable Preference		
	Broccoli	**Asparagus**	**Total**
Yes	5	13	18
No	22	10	32
Total	27	23	50

Vegan? (row label on left)

A. Create a two-way relative frequency table to display the results.

B. What does the relative frequency 36% mean in the context of the survey?

C. What percent of respondents say they are vegan and prefer asparagus?

7. **STEM** Engineering is a diverse field with a wide variety of specializations. Engineering students at two universities were randomly surveyed about which program they were enrolled in.

	Engineering Specialty			
	Electrical Engineering	**Mechanical Engineering**	**Other**	**Total**
1	173	122	43	338
2	152	113	67	332
Total	325	235	110	670

University (row label on left)

A. Create a two-way relative frequency table. Round to the nearest hundredth.

B. What is the relative frequency of a student from University 1 studying electrical engineering? What type of frequency is this?

C. What does the relative frequency 35% mean in the context of the survey?

D. If 50 new students were to enroll in engineering programs at these universities, how many would be expected to enroll in an electrical engineering program?

Module 21 • Lesson 21.1

591

8. A survey of 72 people was conducted about their favorite places to spend leisure time. Children responded: 20 park, 10 shopping center, and 5 home. Adults responded: 2 shopping center, 20 home, and 15 park.

   A. Create a two-way relative frequency table to display the data.

   B. When reading the two-way table, what is the difference between finding the percent of adults who prefer spending leisure time in a park and finding the percent of people who prefer spending leisure time in a park?

   C. What is the difference between finding the percent of people who prefer spending leisure time in a park and the percent of people who do not prefer spending leisure time in a park?

9. **Open Ended** A town committee is deciding what project they should complete with the remaining funds in the budget. They randomly surveyed the citizens of the town about which project they thought was most important.

		Project			
		Repave Main Street	Construct a Park	Open a Senior Center	Total
Age	**18–29**	91	93	16	200
	30–49	82	48	70	200
	50+	24	68	108	200
	Total	197	209	194	600

   Which project should the town committee choose? Explain.

Spiral Review • Assessment Readiness

10. At a zoo, 60% of all animals are mammals. Zebras represent 3% of all animals at the zoo. What percent of mammals are zebras?

    (A) 20%   (C) 180%

    (B) 57%   (D) 5%

11. What are the zeros of the function $f(x) = x^3 + 6x^2 + 9x$?

    (A) $-3, 0, 3$ (C) $-3, 0$

    (B) $0, 3$ (D) $-1, -3, 0$

12. Match each function f with the type of function it represents.

    A. linear   **1.** $f(x) = 2(0.97)^x$

    B. exponential   **2.** $f(x) = 2x + 3$

    C. quadratic   **3.** $f(x) = x^2 + 6x + 9$

 I'm in a Learning Mindset!

How can observing or consulting with my peers help me resist negative influences and fixed-mindset thoughts?

Recognize Possible Associations Between Categorical Variables

(I Can) calculate conditional relative frequencies and use them to identify possible associations between categorical variables.

Spark Your Learning

Automobile insurance costs most for teen drivers.

Statistics show that those of ages 16 to 24 are most likely to have traffic accidents.

Complete Part A as a whole class. Then complete Parts B–D in small groups.

A. What is a mathematical question you can ask about this situation? What information would you need to know to answer your question?

B. What are the categorical variables in this situation? What categories are associated with each variable? What do the numbers in the table represent?

C. To answer your question, what strategy and tool would you use along with all the information you have? What answer do you get?

D. Does your answer make sense in the context of this situation? How do you know?

 Turn and Talk How would the data have to change to indicate that drivers of ages 40 to 49 are most likely to have traffic accidents?

Build Understanding

Calculate and Interpret Conditional Relative Frequencies

A **conditional relative frequency** is the ratio of a joint relative frequency to a related marginal relative frequency in a two-way table.

$$\text{conditional relative frequency} = \frac{\text{joint relative frequency}}{\text{marginal relative frequency}}$$

You can determine whether there is an association between categories in a two-way relative frequency table by comparing a conditional relative frequency to a corresponding marginal relative frequency.

		Preferred Pet		
		Dog	**Cat**	**Total**
Age	**6–17**	0.20	0.24	0.44
	18–49	0.11	0.45	0.56
	Total	0.31	0.69	1.00

1 ▶ A group of people of age 6–49 are asked whether they prefer dogs or cats as pets. The results of the survey are shown in the two-way relative frequency table.

A. What is the percent of all those surveyed who are age 6–17?

B. What is the percent of all those surveyed who are age 6–17 and prefer dogs?

C. Of the people age 6–17 surveyed, what percent prefer dogs? To answer this question, you need to find a conditional relative frequency.

$$\boxed{\begin{array}{c}\text{Percent of age 6–17 surveyed} \\ \text{who prefer dogs}\end{array}} = \frac{\boxed{\begin{array}{c}\text{Percent of all surveyed who are} \\ \text{age 6–17 and prefer dogs}\end{array}}}{\boxed{\begin{array}{c}\text{Percent of all surveyed} \\ \text{who are age 6–17}\end{array}}}$$

D. What percent of those surveyed prefer dogs? Where in the table do you get this information?

E. If age doesn't matter as far as dog preference is concerned, you could expect the percent of dog-preferring people who are age 6–17 to be the same as the percent of dog-preferring people of all ages surveyed. Is this the case? Explain.

F. Would you say there *is* an association or there is *no* association between being age 6–17 and preferring dogs? Explain your reasoning.

G. Think of the categories of being age 6–17 and preferring dogs the other way: Of those people who prefer dogs, what percent are age 6–17? If dog preference doesn't matter as far as age is concerned, the percent of people age 6–17 who prefer dogs would be about the same as the percent of all people age 6–17 surveyed. Do the two percents that you found agree? (If so, you can conclude that there is no association between being age 6–17 and preferring dogs. If not, you can conclude there is an association.)

 Turn and Talk Suppose the table showed the counts from surveying 100 people instead of the relative frequencies. How would you change the calculation to decide whether there is an association between being age 6–17 and preferring dogs?

Step It Out

Identify Possible Associations

2 ▶ The results of a survey of 200 high school students about their method of transportation to school are shown.

- Find the conditional relative frequency of those who arrive at school by car, given that they are in 10th grade.
- Determine whether there is an association between being in 10th grade and arriving at school by car.

		Method of Transportation			
		Car	**Bus**	**Other**	**Total**
Grade	**9**	0.05	0.15	0.02	0.22
	10	0.04	0.14	0.12	0.30
	11	0.12	0.06	0.07	0.25
	12	0.14	0.05	0.04	0.23
	Total	0.35	0.40	0.25	1.00

Find the conditional relative frequency.

$$\text{Conditional relative frequency that a student arrives at school by car, given that the student is in 10th grade} = \frac{\text{Joint relative frequency that a student arrives at school by car and is in 10th grade}}{\text{Marginal relative frequency that student is in 10th grade}}$$

$$= \frac{0.04}{0.30}$$

$$\approx 0.13$$

$$= 13\%$$

The percent of 10th grade students surveyed who arrive at school by car is 13%.

A. Explain how this percent is different than the percent of all students surveyed who are in 10th grade and arrive at school by car.

Determine if there is an association.

If there is no association, then the percent of 10th grade students surveyed who arrive at school by car should be 35%.

B. Why should the percent of 10th grade students surveyed who arrive at school by car be 35% if there is no association?

However, the percent of 10th grade students surveyed who arrive at school by car is 13%.

This means that there is an association between being in 10th grade and arriving at school by car.

 Turn and Talk What is another way to show that there is an association between being in 10th grade and arriving at school by car?

Recognize Trends in Data

3 Each table shows the results of a survey about preferred electronic communication. One survey was conducted in 2009, and the other was conducted in 2019.

Determine whether there is an association between being under 25 and preferring text messages. Then determine if the data show a trend.

2009 Preferred Communication

Age		Email	Text message	Total
	Under 25	0.18	0.24	0.42
	25+	0.47	0.11	0.58
	Total	0.65	0.35	1.00

2019 Preferred Communication

Age		Email	Text message	Total
	Under 25	0.25	0.38	0.63
	25+	0.19	0.18	0.37
	Total	0.44	0.56	1.00

Determine whether there is an association.

For both 2009 and 2019, find the conditional relative frequency of people surveyed who prefer text messages, given that they are under 25. Then compare the conditional relative frequency to an appropriate marginal frequency for each survey.

> **A.** What will be true about the frequencies if there is no association?

Description of group	2009 survey	2019 survey
People surveyed who prefer text messages, given that they are under 25	$\frac{0.24}{0.42} \approx 57\%$	$\frac{0.38}{0.63} \approx 60\%$
All people surveyed who prefer text messages	$0.35 = 35\%$	$0.56 = 56\%$

There is an association between being under 25 and preferring text messages

Determine if there is a trend.

In both surveys, the percent of people under 25 surveyed who prefer text messages is greater than the percent of all people surveyed who prefer text messages. So, people who are under 25 are more likely to prefer text messages.

> **B.** What evidence supports this conclusion?

However, the two frequencies for 2019 are much closer than those for 2009. The association between being under 25 and preferring text messages has almost disappeared.

Turn and Talk For both 2009 and 2019, determine whether there is an association between being 25 and over and preferring email. Then determine if the data show a trend.

Check Understanding

Visitors at a science museum are asked how many times they visit the museum during a year and whether or not they have a membership with museum. The results are shown in the realtive freqeuncy table.

		Visits per year			
		1 or 2	3 or 4	5 or more	Total
Membership	Member	0.15	0.29	0.06	0.50
	Non member	0.32	0.17	0.01	0.50
	Total	0.47	0.46	0.07	1.00

1. Consider the relative frequency 0.32 in the table. Is 0.32 a joint relative frequency or a marginal relative frequency? Explain.

2. Find the conditional relative frequency for visiting the museum 1 or 2 times in a year, given that the visitor is not a member. Is there an association between visiting the museum 1 or 2 times in a year and not being a member? Explain.

3. The same survey was given 5 years ago. In that survey, the conditional relative frequency that a person who visits the museum 1 or 2 times in a year, given that the visitor is not a member, was 51%. What does this tell you about any trend between visiting the museum 1 or 2 times a year and not being a member?

On Your Own

4. The two-way frequency table shows the results of a survey about preferred frozen yogurt flavor.

		Preferred Frozen Yogurt Flavor			
		Chocolate	Strawberry	Vanilla	Total
Age	Under 25	0.20	0.10	0.17	0.47
	25+	0.24	0.10	0.18	0.53
	Total	0.44	0.21	0.35	1.00

A. Consider the conditional relative frequency of those who prefer cholcolate frozen yogurt, given that they are under 25. Describe the joint relative frequency and the marginal relative frequency used to find this conditional relative frequency.

B. What is the conditional relative frequency of those who prefer cholcolate frozen yogurt, given that they are under 25? Write your answer as a percent.

C. How can you use the conditional relative frequency from Part B to determine whether there is an association between being under 25 and preferring chocolate frozen yogurt? Is there an association? Explain why or why not.

5. (MP) **Reason** When finding a conditional relative frequency, can the joint relative frequency used be greater than the marginal frequency used? Explain.

6. At a high school dance, three students competed for the most creative duct tape formal wear. The two-way relative frequency table shows the results of the vote for most creative design.

		Contestant			
		1	**2**	**3**	**Total**
Voters	**Junior**	0.40	0.13	0.06	0.59
	Senior	0.17	0.22	0.02	0.41
	Total	0.57	0.35	0.08	1.00

A. What is the conditional realative frequency of those who voted for contestant 1, given they are a junior? Write your answer as a percent.

B. Is there an association between voting for contestant 1 and being a junior? Explain.

C. (MP) **Critique Reasoning** Henry states that a voter likely chose contestant 1, given that the voter is a senior. Is Henry correct? Explain why or why not.

In Problems 7–11, the results of a customer survey give levels of customer satifaction for different age groups. Classify each statement about the survey as describing a *joint, marginal,* **or** *conditional* **relative frequency.**

7. In the survey, 16% of the participants rate the service as good, given that they are under age 25.

8. In the survey, 9% of the participants are ages 25–50 and rate the service as bad.

9. In the survey, 30% of the participants are under age 25.

10. In the survey, 11% of the participants rate the service as average and are over age 50.

11. In the survey, 8% of the participants are under ages 25–50, given that they rate the service as excellent.

12. The results of a survey about preferred movie genres are shown in the relative frequency table below. Is there is an association between preferring a horror movie and being age 30–49? Explain your reasoning.

		Movie Genre Preferred			
		Comedy	**Drama**	**Horror**	**Total**
Age	**10–17**	0.23	0.11	0.04	0.38
	18–29	0.13	0.15	0.02	0.30
	30–49	0.14	0.14	0.04	0.32
	Total	0.50	0.40	0.10	1.00

13. Jaywalking occurs when a pedestrian crosses a street without regard for traffic, and it is a violation of a pedestrian law. Participants of a survey are asked whether they are aware of the pedestrian law for crossing a street and whether they obey the law. The results are shown in the relative freqeuncy table.

There were 500 participants in each survey.

		Knows the Law		
		Yes	No	Total
Obeys the Law	Yes	0.45	0.30	0.75
	No	0.12	0.13	0.25
	Total	0.57	0.43	1.00

A. What is the conditional relative frequency that survey participants obey the law, given that they know the law? Write your answer as a percent.

B. Is there an association between obeying the law for crossing the street and knowing the law? Explain.

C. Do the survey results support the argument that more resources should be utilized to educate people about pedestrian laws? Explain.

14. The owner of a comic book store sells comic books at her store and online. The tables show the relative frequencies of comic book sales for 2008 and 2018.

	2008 Comic Book Sales		
	Online	In Store	Total
18–29	0.26	0.31	0.57
Age **30 and up**	0.09	0.34	0.43
Total	0.35	0.65	1.00

	2018 Comic Book Sales		
	Online	In Store	Total
18–29	0.29	0.10	0.39
Age **30 and up**	0.43	0.18	0.61
Total	0.72	0.28	1.00

A. For both 2008 and 2018, find the conditional relative frequency of a comic book sold online, given that it was purchased by someone of age 18–29. Write each answer as a percent.

B. For both 2008 and 2018, determine if there an association between purchasing a comic book online and being age 18–29. Explain your reasoning.

C. Use the answer to Part B to determine whether there are any trends in the data. Explain your reasoning.

15. **(MP)** **Critique Reasoning** Sanjay collected data from a survey on vegetables. To find the conditional relative frequency of those who like broccoli, given they also like asparagus, he divided 0.32 by 0.42. Will this result in the correct conditional relative frequency? Explain.

		Likes Asparagus		
		Yes	No	Total
Likes Broccoli	Yes	0.32	0.10	0.42
	No	0.46	0.12	0.58
	Total	0.78	0.22	1.00

16. **(MP)** **Critique Reasoning** The results of a survey of preferred fruit among students in Grades 6 and 7 are shown in the two-way relative frequency table. Using these results, Karen claims that there is an association between preferring oranges and being in 6th grade. Do you agree? Explain why or why not.

		Preferred Fruit			
		Apple	Orange	Pear	Total
Grade	6	0.23	0.20	0.11	0.54
	7	0.26	0.16	0.04	0.46
	Total	0.49	0.36	0.15	1.00

Spiral Review • Assessment Readiness

17. What are the zeros of the function
$f(x) = x^3 - 5x^2 + 6x$?

Ⓐ 0, 2, 3
Ⓒ 1, 2, 3
Ⓑ 0, 1, 6
Ⓓ −3, −2, 1

18. Which is a linear system of equations?

Ⓐ $\begin{cases} x^2 + y^2 = 6 \\ 2x + 2y = 2 \end{cases}$
Ⓒ $\begin{cases} x + y = 12 \\ x + 2y = -2 \end{cases}$

Ⓑ $\begin{cases} x + y = 8 \\ 2xy = 2 \end{cases}$
Ⓓ $\begin{cases} y^2 = 14 \\ x + 2y = 16 \end{cases}$

19. What data are quantitative? Select all that apply.

Ⓐ hair colors
Ⓓ movie genres
Ⓑ building heights
Ⓔ school subjects
Ⓒ floor areas
Ⓕ state populations

20. Ava's test scores are 50, 95, 90, 85, 88. What is the mean of the test scores?

Ⓐ 72.5
Ⓒ 88
Ⓑ 81.6
Ⓓ 89.5

 I'm in a Learning Mindset!

How do I differentiate between statements of fact and opinion?

Two-Way Frequency and Relative Frequency Tables

A survey of 50 randomly selected people asked about their use of social media.

		Use of Social Media			
		Often	Sometimes	Never	Total
Age	15–29	15	3	2	20
	30–49	8	9	3	20
	50+	1	3	6	10
	Total	24	15	11	50

The frequencies shown in the two-way table above can be converted to the relative frequencies show in the two-way table below by dividing every number by 50.

		Use of Social Media			
		Often	Sometimes	Never	Total
Age	15–29	0.30	0.06	0.04	0.40
	30–49	0.16	0.18	0.06	0.40
	50+	0.02	0.06	0.12	0.20
	Total	0.48	0.30	0.22	1.00

Special Relative Frequencies

In a two-way relative frequency table, a joint relative frequency occurs at the intersection of two categories, one from each categorical variable. Example: 30% of those surveyed are people of age 15–29 who use social media often.

In a two-way relative frequency table, a marginal relative frequency is a row total or column total for a particular category. Examples: 40% of those surveyed are people of age 15–29, and 48% of those surveyed use social media often.

In a two-way relative frequency table, a conditional relative frequency is the ratio of a joint relative frequency and a corresponding marginal relative frequency. Example: Of the people surveyed who are age 15–29, the relative frequency of those who use social media often is $\frac{0.30}{0.40} = 0.75$, or 75%.

Association Between Categories

To determine whether there is an association between being age 15–29 and using social media often, compare the conditional relative frequency with the marginal relative frequency.

$$75\% \neq 48\%$$

75% of the people surveyed who are age 15–29 use social media often.

48% of all people surveyed use social media often.

If there were no association, you could expect that 48% of the people surveyed who are age 15–29 would use social media often. Since the conditional relative frequency is significantly different from 48%, there is an association between being age 15–29 and using social media often.

Vocabulary

Choose the correct term from the box to complete each sentence.

1. A __?__ occurs at the intersection of two categories, one from each categorical variable.

2. In a two-way frequency table, a __?__ is a row total or column total for a particular category.

3. In a two-way frequency table, a __?__ is the ratio of a joint relative frequency and a corresponding marginal relative frequency.

4. __?__ are numerical, while __?__ are qualitative.

Concepts and Skills

5. Compare and contrast joint relative frequency, marginal relative frequency, and conditional relative frequency.

6. Explain why a comparison between conditional relative frequency and marginal relative frequency can be used to determine if there is an association between variables.

7. **(MP) Use Tools** A survey of randomly selected people were asked about their preference for unflavored or flavored water. Suppose you work for an advertising agency and one of your accounts is a manufacturer of flavored water. What age group would you target in your ad campaign for the flavored water?

	Water Preference		
Age	Unflavored	Flavored	Total
15–29	18	20	?
30–50	16	22	?
50+	28	10	?
Total	62	52	?

State what strategy and tool you will use to answer the question, explain your choice, and then find the answer.

8. A survey of randomly selected adults were asked if they had children and if they had pets.

   A. Create a two-way relative frequency table to represent the data.

   B. Calculate the conditional relative frequency for an adult who has a pet given that they have children.

   C. Is there an association between adults having children and pets? Explain.

	Children		
Adults	Yes	No	Total
Yes	18	28	46
No	30	12	42
Total	48	40	88

22 Numerical Data

Module Performance Task: *Spies and Analysts*™

Ace in the Hole

Which player is more consistent?

Volleyball STATS

	Game	1	2	3	4	5	6	TOTAL
Player	**#1**	10	10	10	10	10	10	60
	#2	5	15	5	15	5	15	60

SERVICE ACES (SA)

©Augustas Cetkauskas/Adobe Stock

Are You Ready?

Complete these problems to review prior concepts and skills you will need for this module.

Dot Plots

Create a dot plot for each data set.

1. 6, 6, 7, 8, 9, 10, 12, 12, 12

2. 85, 85, 75, 60, 75, 70, 75, 75, 80, 90, 80, 85, 85, 90, 105

Measures of Center

Find the mean, median, and mode for each data set. Round to the nearest hundredth.

3. 6, 6, 6, 3, 3, 9, 4, 5

4. 0.25, 0.14, 0.23, 0.55, 0.06, 0.7, 0.14

5. 200, 300, 400, 400, 250, 700, 825, 900

6. 95, 100, 105, 88, 62, 64, 72

7. 0.5, 0.9, 0.1, 0.3, 0.5, 0.8

8. 8, 2, 12, 9, 13, 8, 2, 2, 12, 9, 10

Measures of Variability

Find the range and interquartile range of each data set.

9. 21, 20, 12, 12, 14, 14, 15

10. 2, 17, 18, 18, 17, 20, 24, 20

11. 5, 7, 3, 4

12. 0.5, 1.2, 0.9, 0.8, 1.0, 0.6, 0.6, 0.7

Connecting Past and Present Learning

Previously, you learned:

- to represent and display statistics in a variety of ways,
- to relate the choice of measure of center to the context of a data set, and
- to relate the variability with the data distribution.

In this module, you will learn:

- to interpret differences in shape, center, and spread in context,
- to choose appropriate statistics to characterize a set of data,
- to identify the effect of removing an outlier from a set of data, and
- to use box plots and histograms to compare two or more data sets.

Data Distributions and Appropriate Statistics

(**I Can**) identify distribution shapes and outliers and use them to choose appropriate measures of center and spread.

Spark Your Learning

Of the people in a small town's community choir, 20 members are either bass or soprano singers.

> The ages of the bass and soprano singers range from 24 to 63.

Complete Part A as a whole class. Then complete Parts B and C in small groups.

A. What is a mathematical question you can ask about this situation? What information would you need to know to answer your question?

B. To answer your question, what strategy and tool would you use along with all the information you have? What answer do you get?

C. Does your answer make sense in the context of this situation? How do you know?

Turn and Talk If you were to guess the age of a randomly selected bass singer or soprano singer without seeing the singer, how likely do you think it would be to guess within 3 years of the correct age? Explain your reasoning.

©Igor Bulgarin/Shutterstock

Build Understanding

Identify Distribution Shapes

A **dot plot** is a statistical graph using dots or other marks to show the frequency of distinct data values. A data distribution can be described by its shape when the data are displayed in a dot plot or other statistical graph.

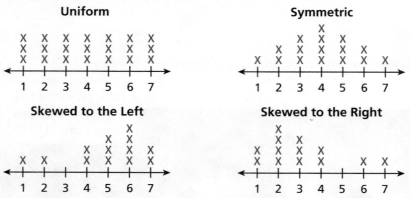

Uniform

Symmetric

Skewed to the Left

Skewed to the Right

1 The frequency table shows how often two different soccer teams scored the given total number of goals per game during one season.

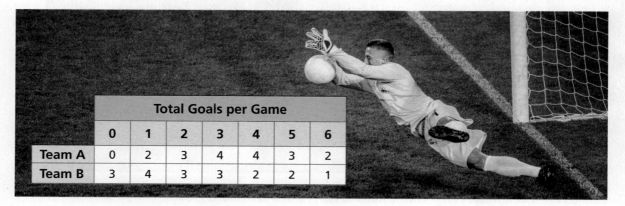

Total Goals per Game							
	0	**1**	**2**	**3**	**4**	**5**	**6**
Team A	0	2	3	4	4	3	2
Team B	3	4	3	3	2	2	1

A. Create and label a dot plot to display the frequencies for each team.

B. When you drew the number lines for your dot plots, why didn't you use a scale of 0.5 (to show the numbers 0, 0.5, 1, 1.5, . . .) or a scale of 2 to show the numbers (0, 2, 4, and 6)?

C. How are the data distributions alike? How are the data distributions different?

D. What is the shape of the data distribution shown in each dot plot?

E. Find the mean for each data set. Then find the percent of data less than each mean. What do you observe? How can you explain what you observe in terms of the shape of each data distribution?

> **Turn and Talk** Which of these two teams do you think is more likely to win in a game against each other? Explain your reasoning.

Identify Measures of Center and Spread

A **statistic** is a number that characterizes a data set. The *mean* and *median* are two statistics that measure the central tendency, or center, of a data set.

Measures of Center
Mean: Denoted by μ, the sum of all the values in a data set divided by the number of data values. Also called the *average*.
Median: For an ordered data set with an odd number of values, the median is the middle value. For an ordered data set with an even number of values, the median is the average of the two middle values. The median is sometimes denoted by Q_2.

The *interquartile range* and *standard deviation* are two statistics that measure the dispersion, or spread, of a data set.

Measures of Spread
Interquartile range (IQR): The difference of the third quartile, denoted Q_3, and the first quartile, denoted Q_1. Q_1 is also called the lower quartile, as it is the median of the lower half of the data. Q_3 is also called the upper quartile, as it is the median of the upper half of the data.
Standard deviation: Denoted by lowercase Greek letter *sigma*, σ, the square root of the variance, which is calculated as shown for the data set $\{x_1, x_2,..., x_n\}$ with n elements and mean μ: $$\sigma = \sqrt{\frac{(x_1 - \mu)^2 + (x_2 - \mu)^2 + \cdots + (x_n - \mu)^2}{n}}$$

Statisticians distinguish between statistics for sample data and statistics for population data. In this book, only statistics for population data are used.

2 ▶ The amount of money Sanjay earned from selling T-shirts at seven basketball games is listed below.

Game	1	2	3	4	5	6	7
Amount ($)	54	46	68	62	63	65	104

A. What are the mean and the median of the given data set? Why are these statistics considered measures of center? Use the given data to support your answer.

B. For the given data set, the IQR is 14 and the standard deviation is about 16.98. Why are these statistics considered measures of spread?

C. If one data set has a greater IQR than another data set, what conclusions can you draw about the values in the two data sets?

D. Which measure of spread tells you how the values in a data set vary from the mean? Explain.

Step It Out

Find Measures of Spread and Identify Outliers

An **outlier** is a data value that is far removed from the rest of the data. A data value x is considered to be an outlier in either of the following cases:

- x is less than the first quartile Q_1, and its distance from Q_1, given by $Q_1 - x$, is more than 1.5 times the IQR. In other words, $Q_1 - x > 1.5(IQR)$, or $x < Q_1 - 1.5(IQR)$.

- x is greater than the third quartile Q_3, and its distance from Q_3, given by $x - Q_3$, is more than 1.5 times the IQR. In other words, $x - Q_3 > 1.5(IQR)$, or $x > Q_3 + 1.5(IQR)$.

3 ▶ The attendance secretary at Seminole High School made a list of the number of student absences each day for seven days. What are the IQR and the standard deviation of this data set? Does the data set have any outliers?

Absences

Day 1: 15
Day 2: 12
Day 3: 8
Day 4: 10
Day 5: 11
Day 6: 26
Day 7: 9

Find the IQR.

Order the data set. Find the median, Q_2.
8, 9, 10, 11, 12, 15, 26

Find Q_1 by finding the median of {8, 9, 10}.
8, 9, 10, 11, 12, 15, 26

Find Q_3 by finding the median of {12, 15, 26}.
8, 9, 10, 11, 12, 15, 26

The IQR is the difference between Q_3 and Q_1:
$15 - 9 = 6$

Find the standard deviation.

The mean of the data set is 13.

> **A.** How do you find the mean?

$$\sigma = \sqrt{\frac{(15-13)^2 + (12-13)^2 + (8-13)^2 + (10-13)^2 + (11-13)^2 + (26-13)^2 + (9-13)^2}{7}}$$

> **B.** What does the 7 represent?

$$= \sqrt{\frac{(2)^2 + (-1)^2 + (-5)^2 + (-3)^2 + (-2)^2 + (13)^2 + (-4)^2}{7}}$$

$$= \sqrt{\frac{4 + 1 + 25 + 9 + 4 + 169 + 16}{7}} = \sqrt{\frac{228}{7}} \approx 5.7$$

The standard deviation is about 5.7.

Identify any outliers.

$Q_1 - 1.5(IQR) = 9 - 1.5(6) = 9 - 9 = 0$

$Q_3 + 1.5(IQR) = 15 + 1.5(6) = 15 + 9 = 24$

> **C.** How do these values help you determine whether or not there are any outliers?

So, 26 is an outlier in this data set.

Turn and Talk What happens to the mean, median, standard deviation, and IQR if the outlier is removed?

Choose Appropriate Statistics

Although the mean and standard deviation are commonly used statistics, they can be greatly influenced by outliers. Therefore, the mean and standard deviation are best used when describing a data set with no outliers. The median and IQR are best used when a data set has one or more outliers.

 4 The school's basketball coach records the number of assists for three players on the team. What are the appropriate statistics to use when describing each player's number of assists?

Tanya	6	6	7	8	9	6	20	10
Celia	7	6	7	8	9	6	9	8
Betina	6	6	7	8	9	6	10	7

Find measures of center and spread for each data set.

Tanya	Celia	Betina
Mean = 9	Mean = 7.5	Mean = 7.375
$\sigma \approx 4.40$	$\sigma \approx 1.12$	$\sigma \approx 1.41$
Median = 7.5	Median = 7.5	Median = 7
$Q_1 = 6$	$Q_1 = 6.5$	$Q_1 = 6$
$Q_3 = 9.5$	$Q_3 = 8.5$	$Q_3 = 8.5$
IQR = 9.5 − 6 = 3.5	IQR = 8.5 − 6.5 = 2	IQR = 8.5 − 6 = 2.5

A. For which data set(s) are the mean and median similar values?

Identify any data set that has an outlier.

Find $Q_1 - 1.5(\text{IQR})$ and $Q_3 + 1.5(\text{IQR})$ for each data set to determine outliers.

- Tanya: $6 - 1.5(3.5) = 0.75$ and $9.5 + 1.5(3.5) = 14.75$

  So, the value 20 is an outlier because it is greater than 14.75.

- Celia: $6.5 - 1.5(2) = 3.5$ and $8.5 + 1.5(2) = 11.5$

  This data set does not have an outlier.

- Betina: $6 - 1.5(2.5) = 2.25$ and $8.5 + 1.5(2.5) = 12.25$

  This data set does not have an outlier.

B. Why can Celia's and Betina's assists be described by the mean and standard deviation?

Choose appropriate statistics for each data set.

To describe Tanya's assists per game, use the median and IQR. Both Celia's and Betina's assists per game can be described by either the mean and standard deviation or the median and IQR.

 Turn and Talk What statistics should you use to compare all three data sets? Explain your reasoning.

Check Understanding

Identify the shape of each data distribution.

1.

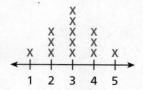

```
            X
            X
      X  X  X
      X  X  X
X  X  X  X  X
+--+--+--+--+--+->
1  2  3  4  5
```

2.

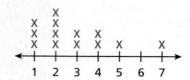

```
      X
   X  X
   X  X  X  X
X  X  X  X  X      X
+--+--+--+--+--+--+--+->
1  2  3  4  5  6  7
```

3. The table shows the wingspans, in inches, of six Australian parrots.

Wingspans (in.)	12.5	19.5	14.5	13	19.5	11

   A. Create a dot plot of the data set and identify the shape of its distribution.

   B. What are the mean and median of the data set?

   C. What are the IQR and standard deviation of the data set?

   D. Explain what the values of these statistics tell you about the data set.

4. To determine your final grade, why might you prefer your teacher use the mean of your test scores to determine your final grade instead of the median?

5. The frequency table gives the prices of books in a clearance bin at two different bookstores.

Store A	7	6	5	4	5	5	6	3
Store B	15	4	7	5	8	6	4	7

   A. Does either data set have an outlier? Explain.

   B. Which measures of center and spread are better for describing the data for Store A? What are the values of those statistics?

   C. Which measures of center and spread are better for describing the data for Store B? What are the values of those statistics?

On Your Own

6. If the spread of data on one side of the median of a data set is much greater than the spread of data on the other side, then what shape does the data distribution have? Explain.

Create a dot plot for each data set and identify the shape of the distribution.

7. Ticket prices, in dollars, for nine shows:
   {20, 30, 40, 20, 30, 70, 30, 30, 20}

8. Shoe sizes of ten people:
   {5, 8, 9, 7, 8, 11, 10, 10, 13, 9}

9. **Open Ended** Write a data set with 10 values that would produce a symmetric dot plot. Explain how you chose the data.

Calculate the mean and standard deviation for each data set. Round to the nearest hundredth.

10. Lengths, in inches, of fish caught:
   {5, 3, 6, 7, 7, 9, 15, 17, 18}

11. Weights, in ounces, of nine books:
   {29, 28, 21, 18, 17, 15, 19, 17, 17}

Calculate the median and IQR for each data set.

12. Heights, in centimeters, of seven people:
{162, 173, 165, 183, 175, 158, 177}

13. Days per month with precipitation:
{13, 11, 13, 12, 13, 12, 11, 10, 10, 10, 11, 11}

For each data set, determine if an outlier exists.

14. Cash, in dollars, in five wallets:
{2, 3, 20, 25, 30}

15. Wait time, in minutes, at nine restaurants:
{0, 0, 10, 12, 14, 16, 12, 12, 32}

16. The top scores for a video game achieved by two different players are shown.

Player A	3393	2442	1945	1593	1355	1254	1144	1088	1042
Player B	2629	2065	1740	1690	1264	1184	1139	1102	1024

A. What are the mean and median for each data set?

B. What are the IQR and standard deviation for each data set?

C. What do the statistics tell you about these data sets?

17. STEM At a robotics competition, robots pick up and then throw a ball. The distances, in meters, that eight robots can throw a ball are recorded. Identify the outlier in the data set. Explain how you know it is an outlier.

Distance thrown (m)	10.1	10.1	10.2	10.2	10.3	10.1	10.2	9.8

18. The average bowling scores of seven bowlers are 175, 210, 230, 220, 230, 225, and 240.

A. What are the appropriate statistics for this data set? Explain.

B. Calculate the appropriate statistics for this data set.

19. **(MP) Attend to Precision** Marnie and Beth both swim the 200 meter butterfly. The coach tracks their times in seconds.

Marnie's times (s)	228	242	222	219	229	237	239	203
Beth's times (s)	216	221	208	226	211	200	226	231

A. Which data set has a greater mean? greater median?

B. Which data set has a greater standard deviation? greater IQR?

C. Does either data set have an outlier? Explain.

D. Who do you think is the better swimmer? On which statistics do you base your answer? Justify your decision.

20. (MP) **Reason** The dot plot shows the number of people renting bicycles over a 9-day period.

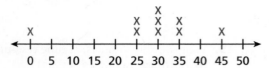

A. If the greatest value in the data set is increased by 10, is the median affected? Is the mean affected?

B. If the least value in the data set is removed, is the standard deviation affected? Is the IQR affected?

C. Summarize the effects of removing the greatest or least value on the statistics.

21. (Open Middle™) Using the digits 1 to 9, at most one time each, fill in the boxes to make a data set with the following constraints.

- a range of 5
- least possible interquartile range
- skewed left
- least possible median

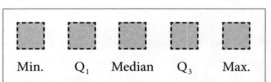

Spiral Review • Assessment Readiness

22. In a survey, 70 people were asked about their preference for a pet. Twenty responded cats, 30 dogs, and 20 none. What is the relative frequency of those who prefer dogs?

(A) 30%   (C) 70%

(B) 43%   (D) 100%

23. A joint relative frequency of 0.12 and a marginal relative frequency of 0.4 in a two-way table are used to calculate a conditional relative frequency. What is the conditional relative frequency?

(A) 0.08   (C) 0.3

(B) 0.16   (D) 0.48

24. Identify what statistic each value represents for the data set $\{-1, -4, 10, 15, 7, 8, 22\}$.

Value	Mean	Median	IQR	Standard deviation
A. 8	?	?	?	?
B. ≈ 8.14	?	?	?	?
C. ≈ 8.24	?	?	?	?
D. 16	?	?	?	?

I'm in a Learning Mindset!

How can observing or consulting with my peers help me resist negative influences and fixed-mindset thoughts?

Compare Data Distributions

(I Can) compare data distributions using box plots and histograms.

Spark Your Learning

The Blue Socks and the Bluebirds are in the same softball league.

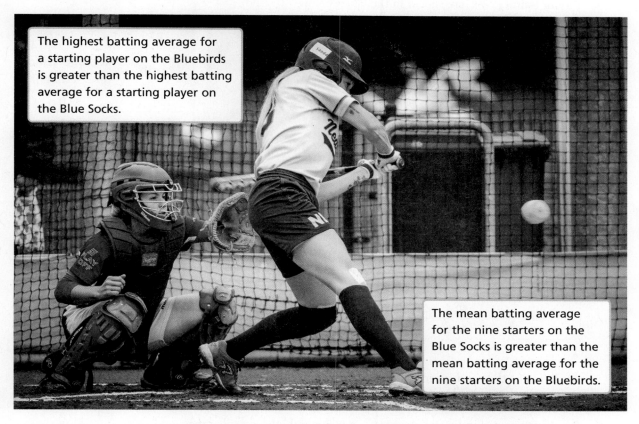

The highest batting average for a starting player on the Bluebirds is greater than the highest batting average for a starting player on the Blue Socks.

The mean batting average for the nine starters on the Blue Socks is greater than the mean batting average for the nine starters on the Bluebirds.

Complete Part A as a whole class. Then complete Parts B–C in small groups.

A. What is a mathematical question you can ask about this situation? What information would you need to know to answer your question?

B. To answer your question, what strategy and tool would you use along with all the information you have? What answer do you get?

C. Does your answer make sense in the context of this situation? How do you know?

Turn and Talk Predict how your answer would change for each of the following changes in the situation.

- The highest batting average is omitted from both data sets.
- The lowest batting average is omitted from both data sets.

Build Understanding

Compare Two Data Sets

Statistical measures offer a way to compare sets of data to one another. You have studied the various statistical measures for single-variable data sets.

1 ▶ The monthly average wind speed data for Mount Washington, NH, and Mount Rainier, WA, are shown in the tables below.

Mount Washington, NH	
Month	Average wind speed (mi/h)
Jan.	46.0
Feb.	44.1
Mar.	40.3
Apr.	34.7
May	29.1
Jun.	27.6
Jul.	25.7
Aug.	24.0
Sep.	28.6
Oct.	34.7
Nov.	40.4
Dec.	44.9

A wind gust of 231 miles per hour occurred on Mount Washington, NH, in 1934.

Mount Rainier, WA	
Month	Average wind speed (mi/h)
Jan.	39.0
Feb.	38.1
Mar.	44.1
Apr.	36.5
May	30.8
Jun.	29.7
Jul.	30.3
Aug.	32.8
Sep.	23.7
Oct.	31.0
Nov.	49.8
Dec.	49.8

©Robert F. Bukaty/AP Images

A. Examine the wind speeds shown in the two tables. Does either data set appear to have any outliers? If so, identify the outlier(s).

B. Which pair of statistical measures—median and interquartile range, or mean and standard deviation—do you think is more appropriate for comparing the two sets of data? Justify your answer.

C. Determine the median and interquartile range of the wind speeds on each mountain. Which mountain has the greater median? Which has the greater interquartile range?

D. Use a graphing calculator to compute the mean and standard deviation of the wind speeds on each mountain. Compare these measures for the two mountains.

 Turn and Talk Mount Washington is frequently cited as the windiest mountain on Earth due to the record wind gust in 1934. Based on your comparison of the wind speed data for Mount Washington and Mount Rainier, would you agree or disagree that Mount Washington is the windiest mountain? Explain your answer.

Step It Out

Create Histograms

A **histogram** is a statistical graph used to display data grouped into intervals of equal width. Histograms are useful for displaying the shape of a distribution of data.

To create a histogram, first group the data values into intervals of equal width. Use a frequency table to help you organize the data into these intervals before constructing the histogram. Then display the intervals on the *x*-axis and show the frequency on the *y*-axis. Bars are used to show the number of data values that fall into each of the intervals.

2▶ Crazy Claw Cactus Shop sells a variety of domestic indoor cacti.

Heights (in.) of 50 Cacti				
2	13	8	16	4
31	26	18	20	19
1	2	22	6	35
18	22	14	24	2
19	4	13	25	32
11	14	24	5	23
3	8	19	4	7
25	22	32	26	29
7	39	2	3	16
4	20	17	10	5

A. Why do you need to create a frequency table first?

Create a frequency table. The data values range from 1 to 39, so use an interval width of 5 or 10.

Height (in.)	Frequency
0–4	11
5–9	7
10–14	6
15–19	8
20–24	8
25–29	5
30–34	3
35–39	2

B. Why should the sum of frequencies be 50?

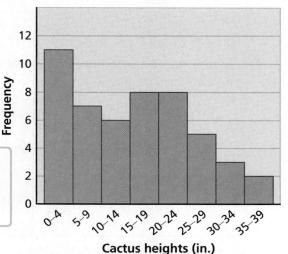

Make sure that the sum of the frequencies is 50.

Turn and Talk Would the shape of the distribution in the histogram appear differently if a different interval width were used?

Use Box Plots to Describe Data

A **box plot** is another statistical graph that shows how values in a data set are distributed. Five key values that summarize a data set are displayed in a box plot.

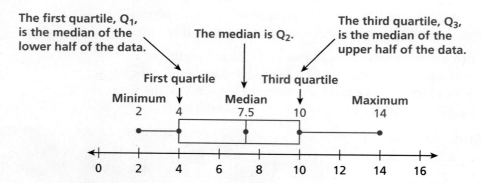

The first quartile, Q_1, is the median of the lower half of the data.

The median is Q_2.

The third quartile, Q_3, is the median of the upper half of the data.

First quartile   Third quartile

Minimum   Median   Maximum
2   4   7.5   10   14

0   2   4   6   8   10   12   14   16

3 The calendar shows the daily high temperature, in °F, on each of the first 21 days in January at a weather station. Create a box plot that models these data.

January

Sun	Mon	Tue	Wed	Thu	Fri	Sat
	15 ¹	16 ²	20 ³	22 ⁴	22 ⁵	17 ⁶
30 ⁷	31 ⁸	32 ⁹	23 ¹⁰	24 ¹¹	17 ¹²	17 ¹³
40 ¹⁴	45 ¹⁵	32 ¹⁶	32 ¹⁷	45 ¹⁸	45 ¹⁹	53 ²⁰
54 ²¹	22	23	24	25	26	27
28	29	30	31			

Determine the five key values for the data.

Arrange the data from least to greatest.

15, 16, 17, 17, 17, 20, 22, 22, 23, 24, 30, 31, 32, 32, 32, 40, 45, 45, 45, 53, 54

Identify the minimum and maximum values directly from the list.
minimum: 15   maximum: 54

There are 21 data values, so the median (Q_2) is the 11th number in the list.
median: 30

> **A.** Is 30 part of the upper or lower half of the data? Explain.

So there are 10 data values on either side of the median, 30. Identify the values of the first quartile (Q_1) and the third quartile (Q_3).

first quartile: $Q_1 = \dfrac{17 + 20}{2} = 18.5$

> **B.** Why is Q_1 the mean of 17 and 20?

third quartile: $Q_3 = \dfrac{40 + 45}{2} = 42.5$

> **C.** Why is Q_3 the mean of 40 and 45?

Draw the box plot.

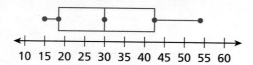

10 15 20 25 30 35 40 45 50 55 60

Turn and Talk How would the addition of a much greater value affect the box plot?

Compare Two Data Distributions

4 Angela and Kaitlin compete for different local high school teams in the long jump event at track meets. The measures of their best jump in each of the last 10 track meets are shown in the table.

The histograms and box plots below display the data for the two girls.

Jump Distances (m)	
Angela	**Kaitlin**
4.24	4.70
4.67	5.03
4.88	5.08
5.03	4.82
4.33	5.23
4.95	5.18
4.80	5.36
4.90	5.46
4.63	4.98
5.56	5.21

A. How are the two distributions alike and how are they different?

B. Why would you not use the mean and standard deviation to compare the data sets?

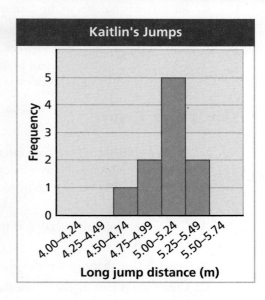

C. What do the box plots show about the consistency of the girls' jumps?

D. Why does the box plot for Angela show a dot that is separated from the rest of the plot?

E. Which of the girls is more likely to jump farther in tomorrow's track meet, where both teams are competing? Explain your reasoning.

Turn and Talk For this situation, which statistical graph do you think is better to compare the data sets? Explain.

©Roberto Peri/Cultura/Getty Images

Check Understanding

1. A histogram is created from a data set.

   A. How many data values are in the data set?

   B. What does the general shape of the histogram tell you about the data set?

   C. What is the width of each interval?

   D. Is it possible to redraw the histogram using an interval width of 4? Explain.

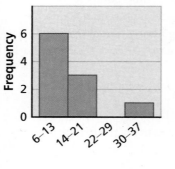

2. The data set shows the number of hours Rebecca babysat each week for 10 weeks.

   $$\{0, 10, 11, 12, 9, 6, 16, 14, 12, 30\}.$$

   A. Create a histogram with 0–8 as the first interval.

   B. Create a box plot.

   C. Identify any outliers in the data set.

   D. Lyndon also babysits. This data set represents the number of hours Lyndon babysat during the same 10-week period as Rebecca: {18, 10, 11, 18, 18, 12, 16, 14, 14, 17}. Create a box plot to display the data set. Compare the box plots to determine whether Rebecca or Lyndon babysat more hours. Justify your answer.

On Your Own

3. Scientists recorded the breathing intervals, in minutes, for a group of gray whales in the Pacific Ocean. The times are shown in the table.

   A. Create a histogram, with 0–4 as the first interval.

   B. Describe the shape of this distribution.

   C. Create a box plot to display the data.

   D. Describe how the box plot reflects the shape of the distribution as indicated by the histogram.

Breathing Intervals (min)				
8	5	13	7	16
9	15	11	8	6
10	9	9	11	14
12	13	15	16	11
14	9	15	6	14

4. Listed are the ages of the first 45 U.S. Presidents on the date of their first inauguration:

   57, 61, 57, 57, 58, 57, 61, 54, 68, 51, 49, 64, 50, 48, 65, 52, 56, 46, 54, 49, 51, 47, 55, 55, 54, 42, 51, 56, 55, 51, 54, 51, 60, 62, 43, 55, 56, 61, 52, 69, 64, 46, 54, 47, 70

   A. Create a histogram, with 40–44 as the first interval.

   B. Describe the shape of this distribution.

   C. Create a box plot to display the data.

   D. Describe how the box plot reflects the shape of the distribution as indicated by the histogram.

5. Listed are the circumferences, in inches, for prize-winning pumpkins in 2 locations over the past 10 years.

Location 1   Circumferences (in.)
122, 100, 115, 120, 140, 100, 125, 128, 140, 144

Location 2   Circumferences (in.)
104, 151, 112, 126, 137, 144, 142, 118, 107, 139

A. Create histograms for the winning pumpkin circumferences in both locations.

B. How are the distributions alike and how are they different?

C. Which location has a greater mean circumference?

D. Create box plots to compare the data sets.

E. Which location has a greater median circumference?

F. Which location has circumferences that are less spread out?

Create a histogram for each data set.

6. Car sales by salespersons this month:
{1, 5, 6, 2, 2, 7, 3, 4, 8, 5}

7. Fish caught by scouts on fishing trip:
{3, 4, 8, 12, 7, 5, 4, 12, 3, 9}

8. Low temperature, in °F, for 10 days:
{50, 62, 34, 37, 44, 44, 36, 37, 42, 36}

9. Days of sunshine for 10 months:
{15, 24, 17, 21, 20, 12, 17, 21, 25, 21}

Create a box plot for each data set.

10. Time, in hours, worked each week:
{48, 44, 42, 37, 47, 40, 38, 54, 43, 34}

11. Rainfall, in inches, each month:
{8, 6, 10, 12, 6, 3, 3, 5, 6}

12. Daily class absences for 10 days:
{2, 10, 10, 11, 14, 16, 12, 13, 17, 25}

13. Heights, in inches, of karate students:
{42, 40, 51, 48, 45, 50, 49, 45, 45, 40}

14. A movie theater manager has gathered data on popcorn and frozen yogurt sales for the past 9 weeks.

	Week								
	1	**2**	**3**	**4**	**5**	**6**	**7**	**8**	**9**
Popcorn	10	12	11	10	9	12	13	9	10
Frozen yogurt	11	11	11	10	5	6	7	8	10

A. Create histograms for the sales of popcorn and frozen yogurt.

B. How are the distributions alike and how are they different?

C. Which item has a greater mean number of sales?

D. Create box plots to compare the data sets.

E. Which item has a greater median number of sales?

F. Which item has more consistent sales?

15. (MP) **Use Structure** John and Pablo compare how many points they score playing a game.

Games										
	1	**2**	**3**	**4**	**5**	**6**	**7**	**8**	**9**	**10**
John	45	50	25	35	40	80	25	30	35	40
Pablo	25	25	25	40	40	100	40	30	30	35

    A. Who had the highest individual score?

    B. Which data set has the greater median?

    C. Based on the data values, who do you think is the better player? Explain.

16. (MP) **Reason** How can you estimate the IQR of a data set from a histogram?

17. (MP) **Use Structure** If the maximum value of a data set and the third quartile value are the same, describe the appearance of a box plot of the data.

Spiral Review • Assessment Readiness

18. A survey of 100 children, adults, and elder adults asks about their preference for a pet. Which expression is a conditional relative frequency?

    (A) $\dfrac{\text{children who prefer cats}}{\text{total people surveyed}}$ (C) $\dfrac{\text{children who prefer cats}}{\text{total cat-preferring people}}$

    (B) $\dfrac{\text{children who prefer dogs}}{\text{total adults surveyed}}$ (D) $\dfrac{\text{people who prefer cats}}{\text{total people surveyed}}$

19. Roger's test scores in percentages are 94, 93, 92, 95, 88, 66, 100. What is the standard deviation of the data set, to the nearest whole number?

    (A) 105   (B) 11   (C) 10   (D) 733

20. Which measure of center should be used for each data set?

Data set	Mean	Median	Either
A. 15, 18, 19, 22, 2, 18, 17, 19	?	?	?
B. 3, 3, 3, 3, 3, 3, 3	?	?	?
C. 2, 3, 4, 5, 6, 6, 7, 8, 9	?	?	?
D. 2, 3, 3, 6, 7, 10, 12, 40, 3	?	?	?

 I'm in a Learning Mindset!

What strategies do I use to support others in their pursuit of learning goals?

Review

Analyze a Data Distribution

Roscoe surveyed 10 of his classmates about the time, to the nearest 5 minutes, that they spend commuting to school. He displayed the data in the dot plot below.

The data distribution is skewed left because the dots are more spread out on the left side.

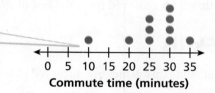

Commute time (minutes)

He then calculated measures of center and spread.

Measures of center	Measures of spread
Mean: $$\frac{10 + 20 + 3(25) + 4(30) + 35}{10}$$ $$= 26$$ Median: $\frac{25 + 30}{2} = 27.5$	Standard deviation: $$\sqrt{\frac{(10-25)^2 + (20-25)^2 + 3(25-25)^2 + 4(30-25)^2 + (35-25)^2}{10}}$$ $$\approx 6.6$$ IQR: $Q_3 - Q_1 = 30 - 25 = 5$

The mean is less than the median because the mean is pulled in the direction of skew.

The standard deviation uses all the data, whereas the IQR uses only the upper and lower quartiles.

Compare Data Distributions

Roscoe surveyed 10 students at another school to see how their commute times compared with students at his school. The histogram shows the other school's data distribution.

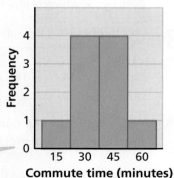

Commute time (minutes)

This distribution appears to be symmetric.

He created box plots to compare the commute times for the two schools.

The two schools have the same median, but the second school's data are more spread out.

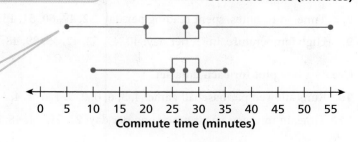

Commute time (minutes)

Vocabulary

Choose the correct term from the box to complete each sentence.

1. A graph that uses a number line with marks to show frequency is a(n) ____?____.

2. A(n) ____?____ is a number that characterizes a data set.

3. The ____?____ measures the dispersion of a data set.

4. A(n) ____?____ is a value that is far removed from the rest of the set.

Concepts and Skills

5. The scores from a basketball team's games are displayed in the dot plot.

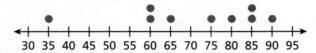

30 35 40 45 50 55 60 65 70 75 80 85 90 95

  A. Describe the shape of the distribution. Explain your reasoning.

  B. Identify the mean and median, rounding to the nearest tenth.

  C. Identify the standard deviation and the IQR, rounding to the nearest tenth.

  D. Does an outlier exist? Explain your reasoning.

  E. Explain which is more appropriate, the mean or the median.

6. Avery's finishing times for an obstacle course, in seconds, were 84, 90, 86, 110, 82, 89, 83, 125, 84, 93, 83, and 85.

  A. Describe the shape of the distribution. Explain your reasoning.

  B. Find the mean and standard deviation of the data, rounding to the nearest tenth.

  C. Find the median and IQR of the data, rounding to the nearest tenth.

  D. Are there any outliers? If so, identify them. If not, explain.

  E. Explain which is more appropriate, the mean or the median.

7. **(MP) Use Tools** The table shows bowling scores over 11 games.

Game	1	2	3	4	5	6	7	8	9	10	11
James	114	110	120	125	130	112	112	95	128	132	70
Raoul	140	100	114	105	120	110	125	135	130	100	105

Which bowler do you think is better? State what strategy and tool you will use to answer the question, explain your choice, and then find the answer.

Create a histogram for each data set.

8. Time, in minutes, spent reading per day: 52, 47, 60, 51, 15, 45, 63, 44, 52, 42

9. High temperature, in °F, per day: 40, 47, 52, 42, 35, 39, 48, 55, 60, 71, 58, 45

Create a box plot for each data set.

10. Runs allowed per baseball game: 4, 3, 6, 0, 2, 3, 1, 6, 1, 4, 12, 6, 1, 3, 3, 5, 2

11. Time, in minutes, spent practicing per day: 22, 29, 31, 48, 27, 33, 0, 20, 34, 33, 45

UNIT 1

MODULE 1, LESSON 1.1
On Your Own

7. irrational; The sum is 8.14159…

9. rational; The product is a whole number.

11. rational; The product is a whole number.

13. rational; The decimal form is a repeating number.

15. rational; The root is a whole number.

17. rational; 2 is a whole number.

19. rational; 3 is a whole number.

21. irrational; The area is the product of a positive integer and π.

23. Let $\frac{a}{b}$ and $\frac{c}{d}$ be two rational numbers. Then $\frac{a}{b} \cdot \frac{c}{d} = \frac{ac}{bd}$. By the definition of rational number, a, b, c, and d are integers. Because integers are closed under multiplication, ac and bd are integers. Therefore, by definition of rational number, $\frac{ac}{bd}$ is a rational number.

Spiral Review • Assessment Readiness

27. C

MODULE 1, LESSON 1.2
On Your Own

5. false; $\sqrt[3]{-27} = \sqrt[3]{(-3)^3} = -3$

7. false; $(-2)^3 = -8$. If n is even, then it is true.

9. 4

11. $\frac{1}{3}$

13. 9

15. 49

17. 1000

19. 32

21. 97

23. $\frac{1}{2}$

25. $1000x^3y^6$

27. $27x^3y^{12}$

29. $2x\sqrt[3]{x^2y}$

31. $2x^3y\sqrt{3x}$

33. When Alicia uses this, she will be left to evaluate $(27)^{\frac{1}{3}}$, which is 3.

35.A. 36 m: about 26 m/s; 72 m: about 37 m/s; 144 m: about 53 m/s

B. When initial height is multiplied by 4, the result is double.
$$4.41\sqrt{4h} = 4.41\sqrt{2^2 \cdot h} = 4.41 \cdot 2\sqrt{h}$$

C. 9 m: about 13 m/s; 144 m: about 53 m/s; When initial height is multiplied by 16, the result is quadrupled.
$$4.41\sqrt{16h} = 4.41\sqrt{4^2 \cdot h} = 4.41 \cdot 4\sqrt{h}$$

D. If the increase in initial height is x, then the velocity is increased by a factor of $\sqrt{x}$.

37. Adrian is incorrect. The correct simplified expression is $2x^2y^2 \cdot \sqrt[3]{x^2y^2}$.

Spiral Review • Assessment Readiness

41. A, C, D

43. A, D, F

MODULE 1, LESSON 1.3
On Your Own

7.A. Answers may vary. Possible answer: the measurement of a spark plug for a car; The fit must be tight so that compression in the cylinder can occur.

B. Answers may vary. Possible answer: measuring the distance between two major cities on a map in California; The distance can be off by an amount that makes it insignificant to the measurement.

9. 9.15 cm to 9.25 cm

11. 3

13. 2

15. 1

17. 3

19. 1

21. 8 ft²

23. 6.5 m/s

25. 1.2 cm/h

27.A. 94.48 g

B. 12.0 mL

C. 7.87 g/mL

29. Possible answer: The caricatures will have accentuated features, so the accuracy is low, but "from the same artist" implies that precision will be high because the caricatures will all be very much alike.

31. Since all values cannot be accurate until the expense is incurred, the budget can have a low level of estimation to give the family an idea of what they are spending or can spend on items each month.

MODULE 2, LESSON 2.1

On Your Own

7.A. no; Possible answer: The time for an episode of Heather's show is given in minutes. Hours are used for the units in the advertisement.

B. Possible answer: One episode is $\frac{48}{60} = \frac{4}{5}$ hour long.

C. $2.50 + 0.50\left(\frac{4}{5}s - 10\right)$

9.A. $48t + 18\left(\frac{5}{6} - t\right)$

B. $48t$ is the distance the skater travels while sprinting; $18\left(\frac{5}{6} - t\right)$ is the distance the skater travels while recovering.

C. $30t + 15$

D. 35 km

11. $17x + 4$

13. $14x + 4$

15. $8x + 23$

17. $14 - 10x$

19. $-1.42x + 2.8$

21.A. $34b$; $b + 2$; $72(b + 2)$; Possible answers: To find the number of beads used in a specific number of bracelets, multiply the number of bracelets by 34. To find the number of necklaces he makes, add 2 to the number of bracelets he makes. To find the number of beads used for a specific number of necklaces, add 2 to the number of bracelets and then multiply that number by 72.

B. $34b + 72(b + 2)$

C. $106b + 144$; The coefficient 106 represents the number of beads used in one bracelet and one necklace, the constant 144 represents the number of beads used in the necklaces made in excess of the number of bracelets made, and the variable b still represents the number of bracelets.

D. yes; $34b + 72(b + 2) = 34b + 72b + 144$ by the Distributive Property; $34b + 72b + 144 = 106b + 144$ by combining like terms.

23. Possible answer: $2(x + 3) - 3(x - 2)$; $-x + 12$; When I substitute any value of x into both expressions, they have the same value.

Spiral Review • Assessment Readiness

25. B

27.A. 3 significant digits

B. 1 significant digit

C. 2 significant digits

MODULE 2, LESSON 2.2

On Your Own

5. no; Mark multiplied 9 by $\frac{2}{3}$ instead of dividing 9 by $\frac{2}{3}$.

7. $x = 4$

9. $x = -\dfrac{3}{4}$

11. $x = -1$

13. $x = -3$

15. $x = -1$

17. $x = -0.8$

19. 28 weeks

21. Possible answer:
Using Subtraction and Division: $3x + 4 = 13$; $3x + 4 - 4 = 13 - 4$; $3x = 9$; $\frac{3x}{3} = \frac{9}{3}$; $x = 3$
Using Addition and Multiplication: $3x + 4 = 13$; $3x + 4 + (-4) = 13 + (-4)$; $3x = 9$; $\frac{1}{3}(3x) = \frac{1}{3}(9)$; $x = 3$

23. 12 oz, or 0.75 lb, of peanuts

Spiral Review • Assessment Readiness

27. A

29. C, E

MODULE 2, LESSON 2.3

On Your Own

5.A. time; $r_b(t_1 + t) = r_y t$; $t = \dfrac{r_b t_1}{r_y - r_b}$

B. The numerator is the initial distance between the yellow car and the blue car. The denominator is the rate at which the yellow car closes the initial distance; It makes sense to divide the numerator by the denominator because the time to close the initial distance equals the initial distance divided by the rate.

7. $h = \dfrac{2A}{b}$

9. $h = \dfrac{S - 2\pi r^2}{2\pi r}$

11.A. $v = \dfrac{m}{D}$

B. about 8.85 cm^3

C. about 2.07 cm

13. $x = \dfrac{b}{a}$; $a \neq 0$

15. $x = \dfrac{c}{a} - b$; $a \neq 0$

17. $x = \dfrac{d - b}{a - c}$; $a \neq c$

19.A. Let g = the number of guests and C = the estimated total cost of the food; $C = 15.9g$

B. $g = \dfrac{C}{15.9}$

C. 157 guests

21. Jen is not correct; She must first multiply each side of the formula by 2 to get $x_1 + x_2 = 2x$. Then, she must subtract x_2 from each side to get $x_1 = 2x - x_2$.

23. Solving $d = 2r$ for r gives $r = \frac{d}{2}$, so
$A = \pi r^2 = \pi\left(\frac{d}{2}\right)^2 = \frac{\pi d^2}{4}$; Solving $C = 2\pi r$
for r gives $r = \frac{C}{2\pi}$, so $A = \pi r^2 = \pi\left(\frac{C}{2\pi}\right)^2 = \frac{\pi C^2}{4\pi^2} = \frac{C^2}{4\pi}$.

Spiral Review • Assessment Readiness

25. D

MODULE 2, LESSON 2.4

On Your Own

7.A.

Total Cost for Orange Taxi   Total Cost for Blue Taxi

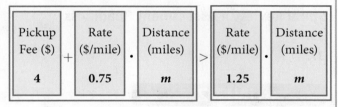

B. $4 + 0.75m > 1.25m$; $8 > m$

C. When the ride is less than 8 miles, Blue Taxi is the better deal.

9.A. *See below.*

B. $15c + 140$; $30c + 50$

C. $c < 6$; Possible answer: The new pricing is better when it is less than the old pricing. Therefore, when the number of classes is less than 6, the new pricing is better.

D. Possible answer: For the manager, the new pricing is better when it brings in more money than the old pricing. So the manager might use the inequality $30c + 50 > 15c + 140$, whose solution is $c > 6$.

11. $n \geq -5$

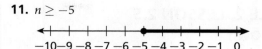

13. $r < \dfrac{1}{2}$

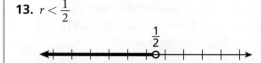

15. $x < 2$

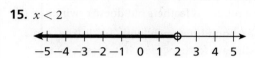

17. $n \leq -2$

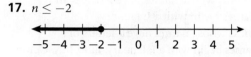

19. $n \geq -7$

21. $x \geq -5.6$

23.A. $50 + 24t \leq 250$; $t \leq 8\frac{1}{3}$

B. $80 + 18t \leq 250$; $t \leq 9\frac{4}{9}$

C. Possible answer: The band should rent Room B because they can have it for longer.

25.A. $x > \dfrac{-b(d + c)}{a}$

B. $x \geq \dfrac{b}{a} + c$

C. $x < \dfrac{d + b}{a - c}$

D. $x \leq \dfrac{d - ac}{a + b}$

27. Possible answer: $\frac{x}{5} + 9 \geq 15$; You can also add -9 to each side and then divide each side by $\frac{1}{5}$.

Spiral Review • Assessment Readiness

31. B   **33.** B

9.A.

Number of classes	Cost under old model ($)	Cost under new model ($)
2	2(15) + 140 = 170	2(30) + 50 = 110
4	4(15) + 140 = 200	4(30) + 50 = 170
5	5(15) + 140 = 215	5(30) + 50 = 200
6	6(15) + 140 = 230	6(30) + 50 = 230
7	7(15) + 140 = 245	7(30) + 50 = 260

MODULE 2, LESSON 2.5

On Your Own

5.A. The statement, *All birds have feathers.*, is true. Birds are the only mammals that have feathers. The statement, *All birds swim.*, is false. A puffin does swim, but other birds do not.

B. The compound statement with "and" is not true. Puffins, for example, have feathers and do swim, while a robin has feathers but doesn't swim.

C. The compound statement with "or" is true. Any bird will have feathers, even if it doesn't swim.

7. AND: months whose names have 7 letters and whose names begin with a J; January
OR: months whose names have 7 letters or whose names begin with a J; January, June, July, October

9. AND: prime numbers less than 30 and perfect cubes less than 30; No numbers exist in this set.
OR: prime numbers less than 30 or perfect cubes less than 30; 1, 3, 5, 7, 8, 11, 13, 17, 19, 23, 27, 29

11. AND: states that border on bodies of salt water and states whose names begin with an "M"; Mississippi, Maryland, Massachusetts, Maine
OR: states that border on bodies of salt water or states whose names begin with an "M"; Hawaii, Alaska, Washington, Oregon, California, Texas, Louisiana, Mississippi, Alabama, Florida, Georgia, South Carolina, North Carolina, Virginia, Delaware, New Jersey, New York, Connecticut, Rhode Island, New Hampshire, Massachusetts, Maine, Maryland, Michigan, Minnesota, Missouri, Montana

13. $a \geq 14$ OR $a \leq 4$

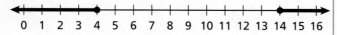

15. $x \geq -7$ or $x < -8$

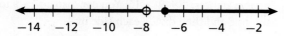

17. $p > -3$ OR $p < 5$; all real numbers

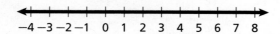

19. $8 < x \leq 10$

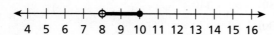

21. $-6 < n \leq -3$

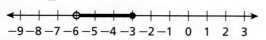

23. AND; $-6 < x < 3$

25. OR; $x < 3$ or $x \geq 6$

27. $15 \leq \frac{9}{5}(t - 32) \leq 25$; $40.3 \leq t \leq 45.9$; The temperature of the pond should be between 40 °F and 46 °F, inclusive.

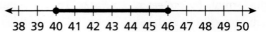

29. $90 \leq 2.5q \leq 100$; $36 \leq q \leq 40$; Mario must get between 36 and 40 questions correct, inclusive.

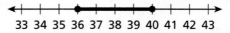

31. The amount that the athlete is supposed to squat is between 70% and 80% of his or her bodyweight; $84 \leq p \leq 96$; The athlete should be able to squat between 84 and 96 pounds, inclusive.

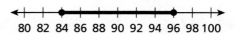

Spiral Review • Assessment Readiness

35. C

37. D, F

UNIT 2

MODULE 3, LESSON 3.1

On Your Own

5. Possible answers: Linear equations:
$2x - 3y = 9$, $4x - 5y = 20$
Nonlinear equations:
$y = x^2 + 3$, $x^2 + y^2 = 9$

7. no

9. yes

11. yes

13. no

15. yes

17. $x = 2, y = -4$

19. $x = 8, y = 2$

21. $x = 16, y = -12$

23. $x = 2, y = 4$

25. no x-intercept, $y = 2$

27.A. $(32, 0), \left(0, -\frac{160}{9}\right)$

© Houghton Mifflin Harcourt Publishing Company

B.

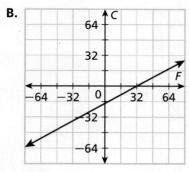

29. Infinitely many solutions exist.
Possible answers: $x = 3, x = -1, x = 5$

31.A. $2l + 1.75m = 18$, where $l =$ number of large eggs and $m =$ number of medium eggs

    B. $(9, 0), (2, 8)$

33.A. $(10, 0), (8, 3), (6, 6), (4, 9), (2, 12)$, and $(0, 15)$, where the x-coordinates represent the number of candle packs sold and the y-coordinates represent the number of soap sets sold

    B. All of the ordered pairs listed in Part A are on the graph of $30x + 20y = 300$ and are solutions of the equation.

    C. Possible answer: $(-2, 18)$ is a solution of $30x + 20y = 300$, but $(-2, 18)$ is not a reasonable answer because Dennis cannot sell -2 candle sets. Likewise, rational number solutions of $30x + 20y = 300$ are not reasonable answers either.

35.A. $x + 6y = 50$

    B. 20 lb of seeds

    C. $3\frac{1}{3}$ lb of cranberries

Spiral Review • Assessment Readiness

37. A, C

39. B

MODULE 3, LESSON 3.2

On Your Own

5. Possible answer: Martha; She is correct because the positive and negative values of the slopes indicate whether the line moves up or down as they move to the right. Both lines would make the same angle to the horizontal axis.

7. She is incorrect. The correct slope is $-\frac{3}{1}$. It would appear that Julia used $\frac{\text{run}}{\text{rise}}$, not $\frac{\text{rise}}{\text{run}}$.

9. $m = -\frac{1}{3}$

11. $m = -2$

13. $m = \frac{3}{2}$

15. $m = \frac{4}{5}$

17. $m = -1$

19. Possible answer: $(2, 3)$

21. Possible answer: $(9, 9)$

23. 500 ft/min; $\frac{400}{3} \approx 133.33$ ft/min; 280 ft/min

25.A. Many points exist. Possible answer: Coupled with $(-2, -5)$, $(0, 0)$ would result in a positive slope.

    B. Many points exist. Possible answer: Coupled with $(-2, -5)$, $(1, -10)$ would result in a negative slope.

27. 35 in./day; It is the average vertical growth rate of the plant.

29.A. 2.5 inches

    B. 1.5 hours

    C. about 1.7 in./h

Spiral Review • Assessment Readiness

31. A, C, F

33.A. 4

    B. 1

    C. 2

    D. 3

MODULE 4, LESSON 4.1

On Your Own

5. For the relation to be a function, any vertical line drawn should only pass through the graph once. If any vertical line passes through the graph of a relation more than once, the relation is not a function.

7. yes

9. $f(-1) = -7, f(1) = -1, f(3) = 5$

11.A. $C(0)$ represents the cost of a large cheese pizza with no toppings. $C(2)$ represents the cost of a large cheese pizza with 2 toppings.

    B. $C(0) = 10.95, C(2) = 12.95$

    C.

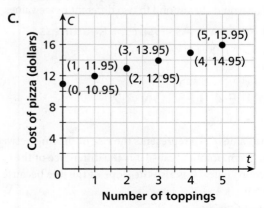

no; The domain is only nonnegative integers because you cannot have partial or negative toppings.

13.

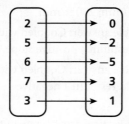

Domain   Range

15. The relation in Problem 13 is a function since all elements of the domain have a unique element in the range; The relation in Problem 14 is not a function since some elements in the domain correspond to more than one element in the range.

17. no

19. no

21. 0

23. 0

25.A. yes; Every day will have only one number of people who see the movie.

  B. 12,000 people saw the movie on opening day.

  C. Fewer people saw the movie 10 days after it was released than saw the movie 5 days after it was released.

  D. The combined number of people who saw the movie on the 3rd and 4th days after its release was 19,000.

  E. For that value of t, no one saw the movie.

27. no

29. Possible answer: The relation is likely to not be a function. Since there are 100 individuals, it is likely that at least one pair of individuals will have the same age but different heart rates. This would mean that one domain value would correspond to two different range values.

Spiral Review • Assessment Readiness

31. A

33. C

MODULE 4, LESSON 4.2

On Your Own

5. The value $q - p$ represents the rise of the line between the given points because it is the difference of the y-coordinates. It is also the slope of the line because the run is $4 - 3 = 1$.

7.

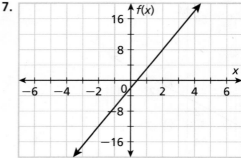

9.

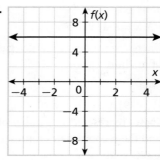

11.

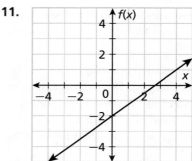

13.A. $W(t) = 8 + 1.5t$

  W is weight in pounds.

  t is time in weeks.

  B. $0 \leq t \leq 30$

15. The domain is all real numbers from -3 to 4. The range is all real numbers from 1 to 8.

17. The domain is all real numbers from 0 to 4. The range is all real numbers from 0 to 4.

19. $m = -3; f(x) = -3x + 5$

21. $m = 0; f(x) = 9$

23. $m = \frac{1}{2}; f(x) = \frac{1}{2}x - 3$

25. Wendy is incorrect; Since the variable x is in the denominator, this is not a linear function.

27. Both are correct; You can start at any point on the line and locate a second point by moving according to the slope.

29. Answers will vary. Possible answer: Monica walked home from a position that was 400 yards away at a rate of 10 yards per second.

31.A. 12 feet represents the y-intercept, and $\frac{1}{24}$ foot per hour represents the slope, or 144 inches represents the y-intercept, and 1 inch per 2 hours represents the slope.

B. $h(t) = 12 - \frac{1}{24}t$, where t is the time in hours and h is the height of the water in feet above the base of the dam, or $h(t) = 144 - 0.5t$, where t is the time in hours and h is the height of the water in inches above the base of the dam

C. t is all real numbers greater than or equal to 0 and less than or equal to 24.

D. If the units are in feet, $w(0) = 12$ and $w(24) = 11$, so the range is $11 \leq w \leq 12$. If the units are in inches, $w(0) = 144$ and $w(24) = 132$, so the range is $132 \leq w \leq 144$.

33.A. 200 ft

B. $\frac{250}{3}$ ft/h

C. $f(t) = \frac{250}{3}t + 200$

Spiral Review • Assessment Readiness

35. B, C, D, E

37.A. 2

B. 3

C. 1

D. 4

MODULE 4, LESSON 4.3

On Your Own

7. $g(x) \rightarrow +\infty$ as $x \rightarrow +\infty$; $g(x) \rightarrow -\infty$ as $x \rightarrow -\infty$

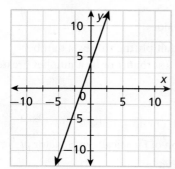

9. The function is increasing.

11. $y = -x + 5$

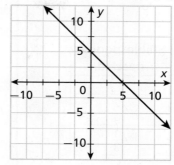

13. $y = x - 1$

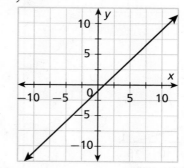

15. min: -12, max: 13

17. There is no minimum or maximum.

19. min: $-\frac{22}{3}$, max: -4

21. min: 0, min: 5

23. $\frac{1}{5}$

25. 2

27. The initial value would be the starting deposit, and the investment will grow from there, so the minimum value will be your initial investment. As long as the investment is left in the bank, it will continue to become a larger and larger value, so there is no maximum value.

29. zero: $\frac{3}{4}$, y-intercept: -3, maximum: 9, minimum: -7

31. The y-intercept is 1 cm. It represents the car's initial starting point.

33. The maximum is 16 and the minimum is 1. These represent the starting and ending points of the car.

Spiral Review • Assessment Readiness

37. A, C, D, F

MODULE 4, LESSON 4.4

On Your Own

3.A.

Teaspoons used	Tablespoons needed
0	5
1	$4\frac{2}{3}$
2	$4\frac{1}{3}$
3	4
⋮	⋮

B.

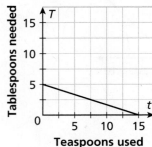

C. The T-intercept is 5, and it represents the total number of tablespoons needed for the recipe. The t-intercept is 15, and it represents the number of teaspoons required to equal 5 tablespoons.

D. The function is decreasing because you will need less tablespoons as you add more teaspoons.

E. $T(t) = 5 - \frac{1}{3}t$. $T(10)$ represents the number of tablespoons still needed after measuring out 10 teaspoons.

5.A. $C(\ell) = 15\ell$

B. The C-intercept is \$0. There will be no cost of 0 meters of sidewalk.

C. The minimum value is 0, which is the cost of not building a sidewalk. There is no function maximum, as the cost keeps increasing as the length increases, but there is a practical maximum, because sidewalks are built in very limited lengths.

D. C increases without bound as ℓ increases without bound because the cost always increases by \$15/m, but there is a practical limit in this context.

7.A. $A(t) = 35,000 - 500t$

B. decreasing

C. domain: $0 \le t \le 70$, range: $0 \le A \le 35,000$

D. 35,000 ft; the altitude of the airplane when it begins its final approach

E. 500 ft/min; the speed of the airplane as it makes its final approach

F. the altitude of the airplane 30 minutes into its final approach

9. $y - 2 = \frac{1}{3}x$

11. $y - 2 = 2(x + 5)$

13. $y - 6 = 0$

15. $y - 6 = \frac{7}{3}(x - 4)$

17. $y - 2 = 0$

19.A.

Depth (m)	Temperature (°C)
15	13
25	12

B. The slope is -1 °C per 10 meters.

C. $T(d) = -\frac{1}{10}x + 11.5$

D. The value $T(45)$ represents the temperature of the water at a depth of 45 m below the surface.

Spiral Review • Assessment Readiness

23. C

25. A, B

MODULE 5, LESSON 5.1

On Your Own

5. Compress the graph of f vertically by a factor of $\frac{1}{4}$.

7. Translate the graph of f right 5 units.

9. Translate the graph of f up 7 units.

11. Stretch the graph of f vertically by a factor of 5.

13. different range values

15. different domain values

17. Possible answer: Multiply the rule by a number greater than 0 and less than 1 or by a number greater than 1.

19. Multiply the rule by -1.

21. Translate the graph of f up 4 units.

23. Compress the graph of f vertically by a factor of $\frac{1}{4}$ and reflect it across the x-axis.

25. Translate the graph of f right 3 units.

27. Stretch the graph of f vertically by a factor of 3 and reflect it across the x-axis.

29. Translate the graph of f down 5 units.

31. Possible answer: Guy wires 1, 3, and 5 are vertically stretched by some factor greater than 1 to produce guy wires 2, 4, and 6, respectively.

33. no; To make a semicircle, she will have to transform the range by multiplying by -1 to flip the quarter circle over.

35.

$g(x) = -f(x)$		$h(x) = f(-x)$	
x	**y**	**x**	**y**
-2	-4	-2	4
-1	-1	-1	1
0	0	0	0
1	-1	1	1
2	-4	2	4

The graph of g is a reflection of the graph of f across the x-axis. The graph of h is a reflection of the graph of f across the y-axis.

37. $g(x) = f(x) - 2$

39. $g(x) = f(x + 3)$

41. $g(x) = f(x - 2) + 4$

43. $g(x) = 8f(x + 1)$

45.

g	
x	**g(x)**
-2	2
-1	-2
0	1
1	-9

47. Stretch the graph of f vertically by a factor of 2, compress it horizontally by a factor of $\frac{1}{2}$, reflect it across the x-axis, and reflect it across the y-axis.

Spiral Review • Assessment Readiness

49. B

MODULE 5, LESSON 5.2

On Your Own

5. Possible answer: All the graphs pass through the origin.

7.A. h

 B. g

 C. j

9. The parent linear function is translated down 2 units; $g(x) = f(x) - 2$

11. reflected in the y-axis, and then translated 7 units to the right

13. $g(x) = f(x) + 50$

15. $g(x) = -\frac{1}{2}f(x)$

17. Translate the graph of f up 5 units.

19. Vertically stretch the graph of f by a factor of 6.

21. Reflect the graph of f in the y-axis, and then vertically stretch the graph by a factor of 3.

23. Vertically compress the graph of f by a factor of $\frac{1}{2}$.

25. Reflect the graph of f in the y-axis, vertically stretch the graph by a factor of 3, and then vertically translate the graph 5 units up.

27. Translate the graph of f up 9 units.

29.A. $f(t) = 1800 - 120t$

 B. $g(t) = f(t) - 800$; Vertically translate the graph of f down 800 units to obtain the graph of g.

 C. $h(t) = \frac{2}{3}f(t) + 600$; Vertically compress the graph of f by a factor of $\frac{2}{3}$, and then translate the graph 600 units up to obtain the graph of h.

Spiral Review • Assessment Readiness

31. B

33. B

MODULE 5, LESSON 5.3

On Your Own

5. $h(x)$

7. $f(x)$ and $g(x)$

9. They all have the same end behavior.

11. j: -5, g: -3, both f and h: -2

13. For f, substitute in $x = 20$ and simplify. For h, add 1 to the x-value and -2 to the output until $x = 20$. For g, draw the line $x = 20$ and identify the point of intersection. For j, add 2 to the x-value and -5 to the output until $x = 20$.

15.A. The value 0.5 represents Tamara's distance from the start of the trail at noon. The units are in miles.

 B. $f(t) = 4t$

 C. Tamara

17.A Best Online Tutors

 B. Best Online Tutors

 C. Best Online Tutors

Spiral Review • Assessment Readiness

19. A

21. B

MODULE 5, LESSON 5.4

On Your Own

7.

x	y
5	−2
2	−1
−1	0
−4	1
−7	2

The inverse is a function; Every x-value is mapped onto one y-value.

9. $f(g(x)) = f\left(\frac{2}{7}x\right)$

$\quad = \frac{7}{2}\left(\frac{2}{7}x\right)$

$\quad = x$

$g(f(x)) = g\left(\frac{7}{2}x\right)$

$\quad = \frac{2}{7}\left(\frac{7}{2}x\right)$

$\quad = x$

11. $f(g(x)) = f\left(\frac{1}{5}x + 2\right)$

$\quad = 5\left(\frac{1}{5}x + 2\right) - 10$

$\quad = x + 10 - 10$

$\quad = x$

$g(f(x)) = g(5x - 10)$

$\quad = \frac{1}{5}(5x - 10) + 2$

$\quad = x - 2 + 2$

$\quad = x$

13. no; The graph of the inverse is the vertical line $x = c$, which is not a function.

15. yes; The graphs are reflections across the x-axis.

17. $f^{-1}(x) = x + 7$

19. $f^{-1}(x) = \frac{x - 4}{3}$

21. $f^{-1}(x) = -4x - 32$

23.A. $E = 250t + 5500$

B. $t = \frac{E}{250} - 22$

C. 18 years

25. $f^{-1}(x) = \frac{x - b}{a}; f^{-1}(x) = \frac{x + 2}{7}$

27. yes; The graphs of such functions are their own inverses across the x-axis and have the form $f(x) = x$ or $f(x) = -x + b$, for any real number b.

Spiral Review • Assessment Readiness

29. C

31. B

UNIT 3

MODULE 6, LESSON 6.1

On Your Own

5. positive correlation; x-values and y-values increase together.

7. no correlation; As x-values increase, y-values appear to have no pattern

9. close to 1.

11. strong negative correlation; Possible answer: As the amount of water in the container increases, the amount of empty space in the container decreases.

13. weak positive correlation; Possible answer: As the outside temperature increases, it is likely that the number of people at the beach will also increase.

15. As age increases, the number of hours children sleep decreases. Possible answer: Correlation could be due to causation because older children need less sleep.

17. As number of movie tickets sold at one theater increases, it also increases at another theater. Possible answer: This is not due to causation. It could be caused by an external variable, like a popular movie was released recently and is showing in both theaters.

19.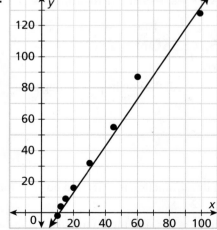

correlation is strong positive; line of fit: $y \approx -1.5x - 17$

21.A. strong positive correlation

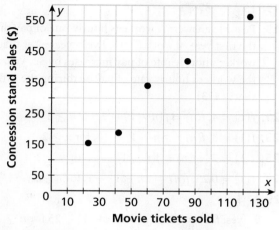

B. Possible answer: yes; More people at the movies probably causes the concession stand to sell more.

C.

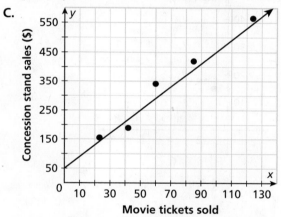

$$y \approx 4x + 50$$

D. Slope represents the increase in concession stand sales in dollars per movie ticket sold; y-intercept represents the concession stand sales when no movie tickets are sold.

E. $y \approx 4(75) + 50 = 350$; Concession stand sales would be predicted to be about $350; interpolation

F. $y \approx 4(200) + 50 = 850$; Concession stand sales would be predicted to be about $850; extrapolation

23.A.

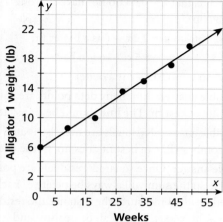

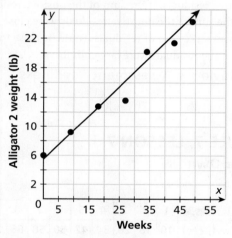

B. Alligator 1: $y \approx \frac{3}{10}x + 5\frac{1}{2}$; Alligator 2: $y \approx \frac{4}{10}x + 5\frac{1}{2}$

Alligator 2 has a slightly faster rate of growth because $\frac{4}{10} > \frac{3}{10}$.

25. Possible answer: Although number of hours to complete the job decreases as number of people working increases, the scatter plot shows the points lie along a curve, not a straight line. Because correlation implies a linear relationship, Stanley is incorrect about a strong negative correlation between the variables.

Spiral Review • Assessment Readiness

27. A

29. A

MODULE 6, LESSON 6.2

On Your Own

3. Possible answer: The line of best fit for a set of bivariate data with a strong correlation is one that has the least sum of squared residuals.

5. This means that the data do not have a strong relationship.

7. $152.4 < 156$, so $y = 2.2x + 6$ is a better fit.

9. $17.5 < 21$, so $y = -3.5x + 16$ is a better fit.

11. $6.5 < 7$, so $y = 4.5x - 2$ is a better fit.

13.A. Possible answer: Too many data points are above the line of best fit. The line should be translated up.

   B. Possible answer: Residuals are not distributed randomly so line of best fit does not fit the data well.

15. Possible answer: Once squared, residuals are positive numbers so the sum will always be positive. Each squared residual measures the distance the residuals are from the x-axis. There can be positive and negative residuals. If the sum of the positive residuals and the sum of the negative residuals were close to opposites, the sum of residuals would be close to 0 even if the residuals were large numbers.

Spiral Review • Assessment Readiness

17. D

19. D

MODULE 7, LESSON 7.1

On Your Own

7.A. 5 tickets cost $42

   B.

Tickets, t	1	2	3	4	5	6	7	8	9	10
Cost, $c(t)$	10	18	26	34	42	50	58	66	74	82

   C. 9 tickets

9. yes; All infinite arithmetic sequences have the same domain because the domain corresponds to the term number. no; Infinite arithmetic sequences can have different ranges because the range corresponds to the terms.

11. no; The differences between consecutive terms are not the same.

13. $g(1) = 8$, $g(n) = g(n - 1) - 10$, for $2 \leq n \leq 6$

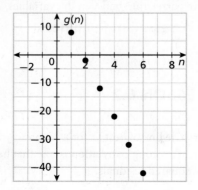

15. 295

17. 15

19. Possible answer: A worker's hourly rate of pay during the first year of work is $15. Every year after that, the worker's hourly rate of pay increases by $2. What will the worker's hourly rate of pay be during the fifth year? ($23)

21. $f(1) = 4$, $f(n) = f(n - 1) - 7$, for $n \geq 2$

23. $f(1) = 3$, $f(n) = f(n - 1) + 14$, for $n \geq 2$

25. $f(1) = 2\frac{1}{3}$, $f(n) = f(n - 1) - \frac{1}{3}$, for $n \geq 2$

27. $f(1) = 0.25$, $f(n) = f(n - 1) - 1$, for $n \geq 2$

29.A. $125

   B. yes; $f(1) = 125$, $f(n) = f(n - 1) + 25$ for $n \geq 2$

   C. $350

31.

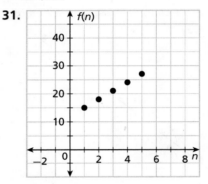

33.

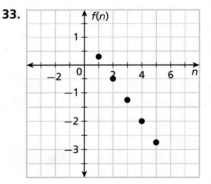

Spiral Review • Assessment Readiness

35. A

37. B

MODULE 7, LESSON 7.2

On Your Own

5.A. yes; 3

   B. 3 times; 4 times

7.A. $f(1) = 12, f(n) = f(n-1) + 9$ for $n \geq 2$;
$f(n) = 3 + 9n$

   B. $39; Possible explanation: I substituted 4 for n in
$f(n) = 3 + 9n$ and simplified.

9. $g(n) = 94 - 6n$ for $n \geq 1$

11.A.

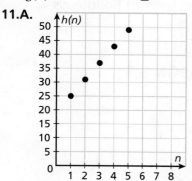

   B. 5

   C. $h(1) = 25, h(n-1) + 6$ for $2 \geq n \geq 5$

13.A. $f(1) = 52, f(n) = f(n-1) - 8$

   B. $f(n) = 60 - 8n$

   C. $4

   D. Week 8

15. $f(n) = 32 + 8n$ for $n \geq 1$

17. $f(n) = 300 + 50n$ for $n \geq 0$

Spiral Review • Assessment Readiness

19. B

MODULE 8, LESSON 8.1

On Your Own

5.A. $C(p) = \begin{cases} 0.15p & \text{if } p \leq 20 \\ 0.12p & \text{if } 20 > p \geq 50 \\ 0.10p & \text{if } p > 50 \end{cases}$

   B. $6.00

   C. $6.50

7. $v(t) = \begin{cases} 4t & \text{if } 0 \leq t < 10 \\ t + 30 & \text{if } 10 \leq t < 20 \\ 50 & \text{if } 20 \leq t < 40 \\ -\dfrac{42}{5}t + 386 & \text{if } 40 \leq t < 45 \\ 8 & \text{if } 45 \leq t < 55 \\ -\dfrac{8}{5}t + 96 & \text{if } 55 \leq t < 60 \end{cases}$

9. $-2; 9; 18; -1$

11. $2; -2; 0; 10; 35$

13.

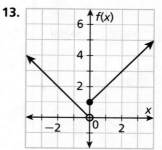

15.

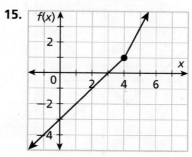

17. $f(x) = \begin{cases} \vdots \\ -2 & \text{if } -3 < x \leq -2 \\ -1 & \text{if } -2 < x \leq -1 \\ 0 & \text{if } -1 < x \leq -0 \\ 1 & 0 < x \leq 1 \\ 2 & 1 < x \leq 2 \\ 3 & 2 < x \leq 3 \\ \vdots \end{cases}$

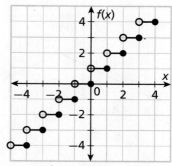

19. $A(t) = \begin{cases} 8000 + 500t & \text{if } 0 \leq t \leq 20 \\ 18{,}000 - 800t & \text{if } 20 < t \leq 42.5 \end{cases}$

21. $f(x) = \begin{cases} x + 1 & \text{if } x < 0 \\ 2 & \text{if } x \geq 0 \end{cases}$

23. $f(x) = \begin{cases} -4 & \text{if } x \leq 1 \\ -3 & \text{if } 1 < x \leq 2 \\ 2x - 4 & \text{if } x \geq 3 \end{cases}$

25.A. Multiply B1 and B2. Divide the product by B3 and round down.

   B. $\text{INT}\left(\dfrac{B1 \ast B2}{B3}\right)$

© Houghton Mifflin Harcourt Publishing Company

Spiral Review • Assessment Readiness

27. A, D

29. D

MODULE 8, LESSON 8.2

On Your Own

7. yes; it is the same as $f(x) = \begin{cases} -x, & x < 0 \\ x, & x \geq 0 \end{cases}$

9.

x	y
−4	−2
3	3
−2	−2
0	0

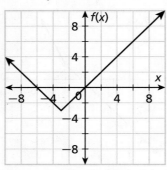

11.

x	y
−3	2
−2	0
−1	−2
0	0

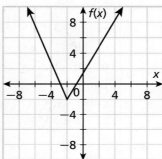

13.

x	y
0	4.5
1	5
3	6
5	5

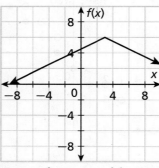

15. $a = -4$; The graph is a transformation of the graph of the parent function. It is reflected across the x-axis and stretched vertically by a factor of 4.

17. $a = -1, h = 1, k = -3$; translate 1 right, reflect across x-axis, translate 3 down

19. $a = \frac{2}{5}, h = 0, k = 6$; compress by a factor of $\frac{2}{5}$, translate 6 up

21. $(-2, 2)$

23. $(9, 0)$

25. $f(x) = |x - 2| - 4$

27. $f(x) = -2|x + 1| + 4$

29.A. 98.6

 B. horizontal translation 98.6 units to the right

 C. The range is from 0 to 1.6 °F.

Spiral Review • Assessment Readiness

31. B

33. C

MODULE 8, LESSON 8.3

On Your Own

7. $x = \frac{2}{3}$

9. $x = 1$ or $x = -3$

11. no solution

13. $x > 10$ or $x < -2$

15. $-2 < x < 2$

17. no solution

19. $-2 \leq x \leq 7$; The solutions are between the x-coordinates of the intersection points and include those x-coordinates.

21. $-2 < x < 7$; The solutions are between the x-coordinates of the intersection points but exclude those x-coordinates.

23.A. 150 ft and 330 ft from left-hand shore

 B. The points of intersection would decrease 2 ft, and the x-coordinates would move closer toward the axis of symmetry.

25. Possible answers: time, distance, height, length, speed

27. $|115.76 - t| \leq 1.72$

29.A. $|x + 3| + 1 = 4$

 B. Possible answer: $|x + 3| + 1 < 4$

 C. no; only one possible equation from graph

 D. yes; many possible inequalities from graph

Spiral Review • Assessment Readiness

31. C

33. C

UNIT 4

MODULE 9, LESSON 9.1

On Your Own

7. infinitely many solutions

9. $(0, 5)$

11. $(1.5, -1.5)$

13.

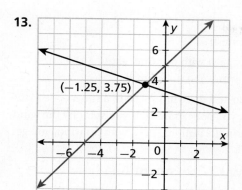

$(-1, 4)$

15.

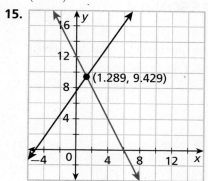

$(1, 9)$

17.

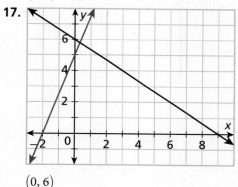

$(0, 6)$

19. six hours; level nine

21. The lines will intersect.

23. The system could have either no solution or infinitely many solutions.

25. The slope and y-intercept are the same, so the lines are the same, and the system has infinite solutions.

27.A. Let x be the number of high school students and y be the number of middle school students.

B. $\begin{cases} 5x + 3y = 41 \\ x + y = 10 \end{cases}$

C.

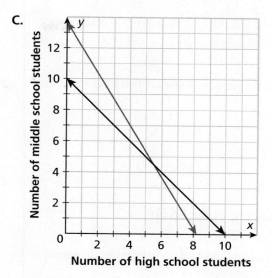

$(5.5, 4.5)$

D. 5.5 high school students and 4.5 middle school students

E. no; You cannot have a fraction of a student.

Spiral Review • Assessment Readiness

31. A

33. A, B, C, D

MODULE 9, LESSON 9.2

On Your Own

7. $(2, 5)$

9. $(6, -1)$

11. $(5, 0)$

13. $(-2, 3)$

15. $(2, -2)$

17. $(-8, -6)$

19. $(1, 3)$

21. $(3.3, -0.6)$

23. infinitely many solutions

25. infinitely many solutions

27. $\left(\dfrac{2}{5}, \dfrac{3}{5}\right)$

29. no solution

31. $\left(\dfrac{1}{4}, \dfrac{3}{10}\right)$

33. $(-0.3, 0.25)$

35. You can substitute the solution into both equations to see if they both make a true statement.

37.A. $\begin{cases} 10x + 12y = 136 \\ 12x + 15y = 168 \end{cases}$

B. Pickles are $4 a jar, and olives are $8 a jar.

C. The graph would have two lines intersecting at $(4, 8)$.

Spiral Review • Assessment Readiness

39. C

41.A. 1

  B. 4

  C. 3

  D. 2

MODULE 9, LESSON 9.3

On Your Own

9. The coefficients of one of the variables must be the same or opposites.

11. $(-3, 1)$

13. $(1, 6)$

15. no solution

17. $a + 6r = 39$ and $a + 9r = 51$; cost of admission: $15; cost of a ride: $4

19.A. San Francisco to Washington, D.C.: 488 mi/h; return trip: about 407 mi/h

  B. $\begin{cases} n + w = 488 \\ n - w = 407 \end{cases}$

$$\begin{aligned} n + w &= 488 \\ +n - w &= 407 \\ \hline 2n &= 895 \\ n &= 447.5 \text{ mi/h} \end{aligned}$$

$$n + w = 488$$

$$447.5 + w = 488$$
$$w = 40.5 \text{ mi/h}$$

airliner's speed with no wind: about 447.5 mi/h; speed of wind: about 40.5 mi/h

  C. yes; If you add the wind speed to airliner speed with no wind, you get 488 mi/h. If you subtract the wind speed from the airliner speed with no wind, you get 407 mi/h.

Spiral Review • Assessment Readiness

21. D

23. C

MODULE 9, LESSON 9.4

On Your Own

7. when like terms do not have the same or opposite coefficient

9. $(0, 5)$

11. $(-2, 3)$

13. $(-1, 1)$

15. $(-3, 4)$

17. $(5, 6)$

19. $(2.5, 6.5)$

21. She must multiply the first equation by 7, but also the second equation by 2.

23. $(4, 1)$

25. $(-1, 2)$

27. $(5, -1)$

29. *See below.*

29.A. The variables are the number of oranges and the number of apples. Use x to represent the total number of oranges and y to represent the total number of apples.

B.

  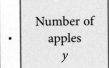 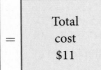

| Cost of an orange $.65 | · | Number of oranges x | + | Cost of an apple $.75 | · | Number of apples y | = | Total cost $11 |

C.

| Number of oranges x | + | Number of apples y | = | Number of pieces of fruit 16 |

D. $\begin{cases} 0.65x + 0.75y = 11 \\ x + y = 16 \end{cases}$

E. 10 oranges and 6 apples

31. In order to eliminate a variable, find the least common multiple of coefficients of the same variable in different equations. Multiply each equation by the number required in order to produce that coefficient. When the least common multiple of coefficients of the same variable in different equations is one of the coefficients, then you need to multiply only one of the equations.

33. $\begin{cases} 3a + 3c = 84 \\ 2a + 4c = 6 \end{cases}$; Adult tickets are \$18, and child tickets are \$10.

35.A. $\begin{cases} 8b + 6s = 27.10 \\ 10b + 7s = 32.75 \end{cases}$

   B. \$1.70

   C. \$2.25

   D. bus; bus costs less than subway

37. They are both correct. Nina's method will result in x being eliminated. Kara's method will result in y being eliminated.

39.A. $\begin{cases} x + 2y = -4 \\ 3x + y = -32 \end{cases}$

$$x = -2y - 4$$
$$3(-2y - 4) + y = -32$$
$$-6y - 12 + y = -32$$
$$-5y - 12 = -32$$
$$-5y = -20$$
$$y = 4$$
$$x + 2(4) = -4$$
$$x + 8 = -4$$
$$x = -12$$
$$(-12, 4)$$

   B. $\begin{cases} x + 2y = -4 \\ 3x + y = -32 \end{cases}$

$$-2(3x + y) = -2(-32)$$
$$-6x - 2y = 64$$
$$x + 2y = -4$$
$$\underline{+ \ -6x - 2y = 64}$$
$$-5x = 60$$
$$x = -12$$
$$3(-12) + y = -32$$
$$-36 + y = -32$$
$$y = 4$$
$$(-12, 4)$$

C. yes; Possible answer: Multiplying the first equation by 3 resulted in a system where subtracting one equation from the other eliminated the variable x and resulted in the same ordered pair solution, $(-12, 4)$, as found using the substitution method.

Spiral Review • Assessment Readiness

43. C

45. C, F

MODULE 10, LESSON 10.1

On Your Own

  5. yes

  7. no

  9. on or below the line

11. no

13. no

15. yes

17. no

19. no

21.

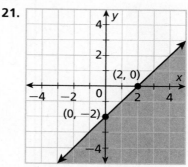

23.

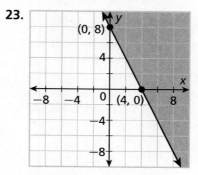

25.

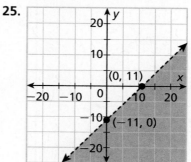

27.

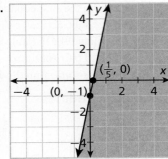

29.

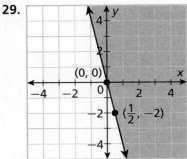

31.

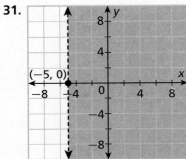

33. $y \leq 3x + 10$

35. Possible answer: First look at the boundary line to determine what equality symbol should be used. Then identify the slope and y-intercept to write the inequality in slope-intercept form.

37. $x + y \leq 860$; Possible answer: One of the solutions is (360, 500), which represents a 360-lb bobsled and 500 lb total weight of athletes.

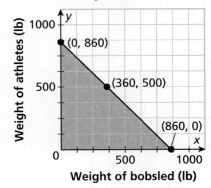

39. $y \leq 0.30x$

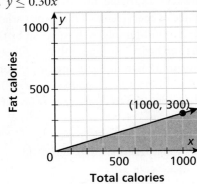

One solution is (1000, 300). This means that according to the study, if you consume 1000 total calories per day, then 300 of those calories can be from fat.

Spiral Review • Assessment Readiness

43. A

45. A, D

MODULE 10, LESSON 10.2
On Your Own

11. no

13. no

15. no; The inequalities have parallel boundary lines, and the half-planes shaded do not overlap.

17. $\begin{cases} y \geq 0 \\ x \geq 0 \end{cases}$

19.

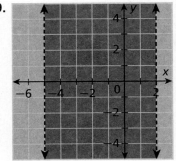

21.

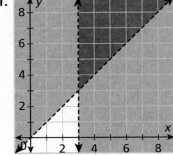

23.

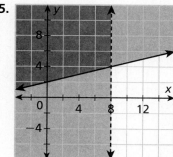

25.

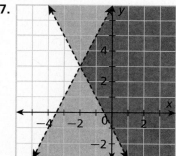

27.

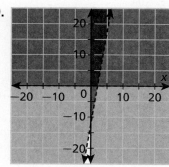

29.

31.A. $\begin{cases} x + y \geq 9 \\ 6x + 5y \leq 50 \end{cases}$

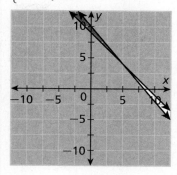

B. yes

C. no

D. The graphs of the individual equalities would no longer overlap. The system of inequalities would no longer have a solution.

33.A. Let x represent the number of pants and y the number of shirts.

$\begin{cases} 30x + 20y \leq 200 \\ x + y \geq 6 \end{cases}$

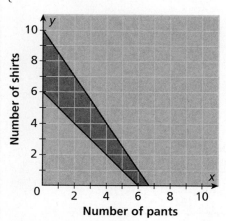

B. yes; yes

C. yes; It is not reasonable given the context of the situation. You cannot have fractional values.

Spiral Review • Assessment Readiness

37. D

39. D

UNIT 5

MODULE 11, LESSON 11.1

On Your Own

7. $a = 3, b = 2$

9.

x	y
−3	$\frac{1}{125}$
−2	$\frac{1}{25}$
−1	$\frac{1}{5}$
0	1
1	5
2	25
3	125

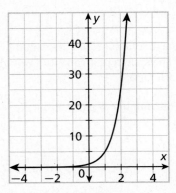

11.

x	y
−3	$\frac{3}{64}$
−2	$\frac{3}{16}$
−1	$\frac{3}{4}$
0	3
1	12
2	48
3	192

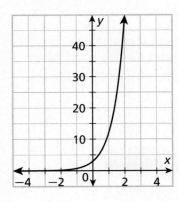

13. The *y*-intercept is at $y = 10$, the domain is all real numbers, and the range is all real numbers greater

than zero. As *x* goes to negative infinity, $f(x)$ goes to 0, and as *x* goes to positive infinity, $f(x)$ goes to positive infinity.

15. Possible answer: They all have a *y*-intercept of 1.

17. *f*

19. $f(x) = 4(2)^x$

21.

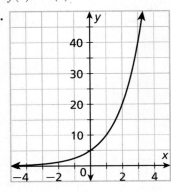

23.

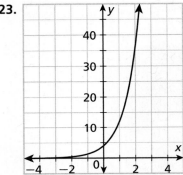

25.A. $r = 0.04$

 B. $1 + r = 1 + 0.04 = 1.04$

 C. $A(t) = 25,000(1.04)^t$, where *A* is the value of the investment and *t* is the time in years

 D. $45,023.59

27. The options are plans 1 and 3, since the investment is under 3 years; Plan 1 is the better plan, as it has the higher interest rate.

29. The only option is plan 3, since the investment is under 3 years and under $40,000.

31. $f(x) = 0.5(4)^x$

33.A. $r = 0.5$

 B. $1 + r = 1 + 0.5 = 1.5$

 C. $A(t) = 200(1.5)^t$, where *A* is the number of bacteria cells and *t* is the time in weeks

 D. The population will be about 25,949 cells.

Spiral Review • Assessment Readiness

35. C

37. A, C

MODULE 11, LESSON 11.2

On Your Own

7. $a = \dfrac{5}{3}, b = \dfrac{1}{4}$

9.

x	y
−3	15.625
−2	6.25
−1	2.45
0	1
1	0.4
2	0.16
3	0.064

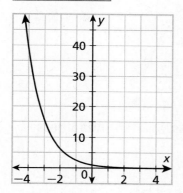

11.

x	y
−3	192
−2	48
−1	12
0	3
1	$\dfrac{3}{4}$
2	$\dfrac{3}{16}$
3	$\dfrac{3}{64}$

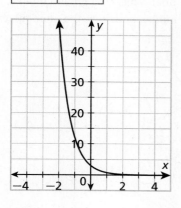

13. as $x \to +\infty, f(x) \to 0$, and as $x \to -\infty, f(x) \to +\infty$

15. The y-intercept is $(0, 15)$, the domain is all real numbers, and the range is all values greater than zero. As x goes to negative infinity, $g(x)$ goes to positive infinity, and as x goes to positive infinity, $g(x)$ goes to 0.

17. the y-intercept; The new y-intercept is a.

19. g

21. $f(x) = 10\left(\dfrac{1}{2}\right)^x$

23.

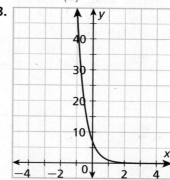

25. The exponential decay function should be $f(x) = 2000(0.7)^x$. The student forgot to subtract the rate of depreciation from 1 before solving.

27. Possible answer: The value of a motorhome depreciates at a rate of 4% per year. With a purchase price of $40,000, its value after t years is modeled by $f(t) = 40,000(0.96)^t$.

29.A. $A = 250(0.79)^t$

   B. about 23.67 mg

31. $v(t) = 1000(0.94)^t$, where v is the value in dollars and t is the time in years; $538.62

33. $v(t) = 1800(0.8)^t$; $590

Spiral Review • Assessment Readiness

35. C, D

37. C

MODULE 11, LESSON 11.3

On Your Own

7. 0.247% monthly

9. $A(t) = 25,000(1.79)^t$

11.A. $P(t) = 1200(0.95)^t$

   B. $P(t) = 1200(0.9957)^t$

   C. about 3.6 years

13.A. $v(t) = 45,000(0.75)^t$

   B. $v(t) = 45,000(0.9763)^t$

15.A. $A(t) = 300(1.03)^t$

B. about $347.78

C. $A(t) = 300(1.0025)^t$

D. about $324.95

17.A. $v(t) = 3,400,000(0.9761)^t$

B. about $2.8 million

C. $v(t) = 3,400,000(0.9980)^t$

D. about $3.1 million

19. If r_a is the annual growth rate and r_m is the monthly growth rate, then in general it is not true that $r_m = \frac{r_a}{12}$. Instead, r_m is the value for which $(1 + r_m)^{12} = 1 + r_a$, so $r_m = (1 + r_a)^{\frac{1}{12}} - 1$. If $r_a = 12\% = 0.12$, then $r_m = (1.12)^{\frac{1}{12}} - 1 \approx 0.0095$, or about 0.95% (not 1%).

21. $\frac{1}{4}$ year, or about 3 months

Spiral Review • Assessment Readiness

25. C

MODULE 12, LESSON 12.1

On Your Own

7. The value of a is negative.

9. Possible answer: There are many different transformations that could map the reference point of f to a given reference point of a transformed function. For example, the reference point $(0, 1)$ of $f(x) = 2^x$ is mapped to $(0, -1)$ of $g(x) = -2^x$ by a reflection over the x-axis and to $(0, -1)$ of $h(x) = 2^x - 2$ by a translation down 2 units. Given only the reference point $(0, -1)$, there is no way of knowing which transformation produced the point.

11. vertical stretch and reflection

13. $f(x) = \left(\frac{1}{4}\right)^x$ and $g(x) = 2\left(\frac{1}{4}\right)^x + 3$

15. $(0, 4), (1, 6)$

17. $(0, -1), (1, 3)$

19.

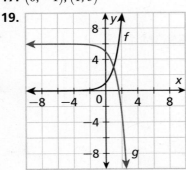

21. $y = -2$

23. $y = -1$

25.A. $V_1(t) = 4(0.995)^t$ and $V_2(t) = 3.5(0.995)^t$

B. exponential decay because the base is less than 1

C. They represent the maximal oxygen consumption rate at age 25 of each athlete.

D. $V_1(30) = 4(0.995)^{30} \approx 3.44$ liters per minute
$V_2(30) = 3.5(0.995)^{30} \approx 3.01$ liters per minute

27.A. If $a > 0$, the range of g is $y > 0$. If $a < 0$, the range of g is $y < 0$.

B. The range of g is $y > k$.

C. If $a > 0$, then the range of g is $y > k$. If $a < 0$, then the range of g is $y < k$.

29. $f(x) = 3^x$ and $g(x) = -3(3)^x - 1$

31.

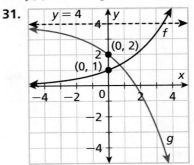

Spiral Review • Assessment Readiness

33. B

35. A

MODULE 12, LESSON 12.2

On Your Own

5.A. cream sauce

B. tomato sauce

C. cream sauce

D. no; The volume of the cream sauce has a greater decay rate and so eventually will reduce to a volume lower than that of the tomato sauce.

7. f

9. g

11. g has the greater initial value; f is a growth model, while g is a decay model. Both have the same values at $x = 1$.

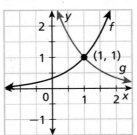

13.A. the skateboard; From the function for the value of the bike, the initial value of the bike is $400. After one year, the skateboard had a value of $450, so it had a greater initial value.

B. the bike; This means that the skateboard will lose value more quickly and eventually be worth less than the bike.

C. The bike and the skateboard will have the same value after 6.283 years. The graphs of each item's value intersect when $t = 6.283$ years , which is when $V_S(t) = V_B(t)$.

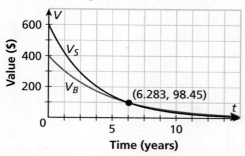

Spiral Review • Assessment Readiness

15. A

11.A. $v(t) = 35{,}000(0.75)^t$

B. $v(t) = 33{,}400(0.824)^t$

C. Residuals for $v(t) = 35{,}000(0.75)^t$:

t	v (Actual)	v (Predicted)	Residual	Square of residual
0	35,000	35,000	0	0
1	26,226	26,250	−24	576
2	22,455	19,688	2767	7,656,289
3	18,882	14,766	4116	16,941,456
4	15,347	11,074	4273	18,258,529
5	12,938	8306	4632	21,455,424
			Sum of squared residuals	64,312,274

Residuals for $v(t) = 33{,}400(0.824)^t$:

t	v (Actual)	v (Predicted)	Residual	Square of residual
0	35,000	33,400	1600	2,560,000
1	26,226	27,522	−1296	1,679,616
2	22,455	22,678	−223	49,729
3	18,882	18,687	195	38,025
4	15,347	15,398	−51	2601
5	12,938	12,688	250	62,500
			Sum of squared residuals	4,392,471

The sum of squared residuals for the first model is about 64 million, and the sum of squared residuals for the regression model is about 4 million. Since 4 million < 64 million, the regression model fits the data better.

D. about $8615

UNIT 6

MODULE 13, LESSON 13.1
On Your Own

7. Possible answer: The initial amount of medicine was approximately 800 units. 75% of the previous hour's amount of medicine remains after each hour; it represents exponential decay because the concentration is decreasing over time.

9. $v(t) = 1000(0.47)^t$; The initial value represents the original cost of the phone, $1000. The base 0.47 represents the value of the phone in terms of the year before. So each year, the phone's value is 47% of the previous year's value; after 4 years the value drops below $50.

11. *See below.*

13.A. $B(t) = 4500.18(1.0252)^t$

B. about $4500, 2.5%

Spiral Review • Assessment Readiness

15. A

17. A, C

MODULE 13, LESSON 13.2

On Your Own

7. linear; $f(x) = 25{,}200x + 180{,}150$; increasing

9. exponential; $v(t) = 20{,}000(0.9)^t$; decreasing

11. exponential; $f(x) = 245{,}000(1.06)^x$; increasing

13. differences

15.A. $f(x) = -1.095x + 47.19$;
$f(x) = 47.2(0.97)^x$

B. Linear: $y = -1.095x + 47.19$

x	y (Actual)	y (Predicted)	Residual	Squared residuals
1	48.62	46.10	2.53	6.38
2	44.73	45.00	−0.27	0.07
3	41.95	43.91	−1.96	3.82
4	37.46	42.81	−5.35	28.62
5	46.78	41.72	5.07	25.65
		Sum of squared residuals		64.55

Exponential: $f(x) = 47.2(0.97)^x$

x	y (Actual)	y (Predicted)	Residual	Squared residuals
1	48.62	45.78	2.84	8.04
2	44.73	44.41	0.32	0.10
3	41.95	43.08	−1.13	1.27
4	37.46	41.79	−4.33	18.71
5	46.78	40.53	6.25	39.03
		Sum of squared residuals		67.16

Although the sum of squared residuals is very close, the linear model has the lowest value, so that is the best-fit model.

C. $-1.095(6) + 47.19 \approx 40.6$ million consoles

17. Possible answer: no; It would take more than 48 years for the salary with the percent increase to equal the salary with the constant increase after the first year.

19. about 28 months

Spiral Review • Assessment Readiness

21. A

23. D

MODULE 14, LESSON 14.1

On Your Own

11. geometric

13. $r = 3$; 405, 1215, 3645

15. $r = -3$; −162, 486, −1458

17. decreasing; Since $0 < r < 1$, the next term in the sequence will be a positive term that is less than the previous term.

19.A. $f(1) = 50, f(n) = 3 \cdot f(n-1)$ for $n \geq 2$

B. 1350 eggs

21. $f(1) = 72, f(n) = 0.5 \cdot f(n-1)$ for $n \geq 2$

23. 4096

25. 12,288

27. 5; 80

29. $f(1) = 10, f(n) = 0.8 \cdot f(n-1)$ for $2 \leq n \leq 5$

31.

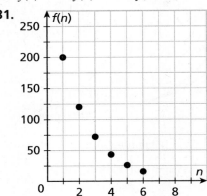

33.A. $f(1) = 800, f(n) = 1.5 \cdot f(n-1)$ for $n \geq 2$

B. 6075 rabbits

Spiral Review • Assessment Readiness

37. C

39. C

MODULE 14, LESSON 14.2

On Your Own

11. $f(n) = 4 \cdot 6^{n-1}$; 241,864,704

13. $f(n) = 75(0.8)^{n-1}$

15.

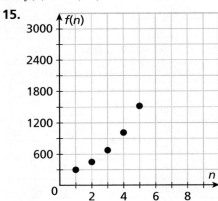

17. $f(n) = 5000(0.6)^{n-1}, 1 \leq n \leq 7$

19. $f(1) = 5, f(n) = 3 \cdot f(n-1)$ for $n \geq 2$

21. $f(n) = 10(0.25)^{n-1}$

23.A. yes; The populations 40, 60, 90, and 135 form a geometric sequence because consecutive terms have a common ratio of 1.5.

B. about 456 raccoons

C. Possible answer: I wrote an explicit rule for the geometric sequence. Then I used the rule to find the 7th term of the sequence.

25. 8 players

27. Possible answer: If it is a recursive rule, $f(1)$ will be given.

29. $153 = 17r^2$
$9 = r^2$
$\pm 3 = r$

Spiral Review • Assessment Readiness

31. A

UNIT 7

MODULE 15, LESSON 15.1
On Your Own

11. Possible answer: A monomial is a number, variable with whole number exponent, or product of those; To identify a monomial, look for expressions that only have one term. The term can be a number, variable, or product of both. The term cannot have variables in the denominator or negative or fractional exponents.

13.

Monomial	Coefficient	Degree
$8x$	8	1
$-3x^2y^2$	-3	4
y^5	1	5

15. negative exponent

17. exponent is not a whole number

19. difference of two monomials

21.A. $-2x, 2x$

B. $-4x^2$

C. $-2x(2x) = (-2 \cdot 2)(x \cdot x)$
$= -4x^2$

23. $10x^2$

25. $12x^3$

27. $30x^3$

29. $8a^3b^3$

31. $-10a^4b^3$

33. Each of the monomial factors must be a constant. Because you add the exponents of any like variables when multiplying and monomials cannot have variables with a negative degree, the degree of each of the original factors must be 0. This means they are constants.

35. $12x^3 \, m^3$

37. $16a^8$

39. $25a^8$

41. The factor $1.5x^2$ represents the area of each panel. The factor 62 represents the total number of glass panels.

Spiral Review • Assessment Readiness

45. B

47. A

MODULE 15, LESSON 15.2
On Your Own

13. $2x + 2, 4x^2 - 5, 2 + x$

15. $-6x^4 + x + 3; -6$

17. trinomial, degree of 3

19. $(8x)(x^2 + 12x - 9); 8x^3 + 12x^2 - 72x$

$\bullet$	x^2	$12x$	-9
$8x$	$8x^3$	$12x^2$	$-72x$

21.A. $-2x$ and $x + 3$

B. $-2x^2 - 6x$

C. Possible answer: I can use the Distributive Property:
$(-2x)(x + 3) = (-2x)(x) + (-2x)(3)$
$= -2x^2 - 6x.$

23. $2x^2 + 4x$

25. $12x^3 + 10x$

27. $99x^2 + 28x - 15$

29. $7x^3 + 9x^2 - 13x - 15$

31. yes; The simplified product is $8x^2 + 18x + 4$, which is three monomials joined by addition, so it is a polynomial.

33.A. The expression $x + 10$ represents the length of the larger rectangle, and $x + 4$ represents the width of the larger rectangle.

  B. $x^2 + 14x + 40$

  C. 216 cm²

35.A. $(x^3 + 8x^2 + 12x)$ in.³

  B. 385 in.³

Spiral Review • Assessment Readiness

39. C

MODULE 15, LESSON 15.3

On Your Own

11. $(2x - 2)(2x + 2)$, $4x^2 - 4$

13. Possible answer:

$(a - b)^2 = (a - b)(a - b)$ — Write power as product.

$\quad = a(a - b) - b(a - b)$ — Distributive Property.

$\quad = a^2 - ab - ab + b^2$ — Multiply.

$\quad = a^2 - 2ab + b^2$ — Simplify.

15. $x^2 - 1$

17. $x^4 - 400$

19. $4x^2 - 16$

21. $16x^2 + 32x + 16$

23. $4x^2 + 4xy^2 + y^4$

25. $16x^4 + 8x^2 + 1$

27. $16 - 16x + 4x^2$

29. $x^2y^2 - 2xy^3 + y^4$

31. $9x^4 + 6x^2 + 1$

33. $x^4 + 2x^2y + y^2$; square of a sum

35. $4x^2 - 16x + 16$; square of a difference

37. $x^8 + 2x^4z + z^2$; square of a sum

39.A. 399

  B. $(40 + 3)(40 - 3)$; 1591

  C. Possible answer: Write 32^2 as $(30 + 2)^2$, and then find the power using the square of a sum pattern. $(30 + 2)^2 = 900 + 120 + 4 = 1024$

41.A. the radius; the height

  B. $\pi x^3 - 6\pi x^2 + 9\pi x$

  C. 18,158 cm³

Spiral Review • Assessment Readiness

43. A, D, E

45. A, D

MODULE 16, LESSON 16.1

On Your Own

9. $-x^2y$

11. $5xy + 3x^2y$

13. $13r^2 - 8r$

15. $-14x^3y + 10xy^3$

17. $2x^2y^2 + 12xy$

19. $\left(\frac{3}{4}\pi + 3\right)r^2 + 29r + 40$

21. $2x^2 + 2xy + 5$

23. $2x^2 + 2x + 7$

25. $y^3 + 2x^2 + 2x + 5$

27. $3x^2 + 2x + 8$

29. $a^2 + b + 11$

31. $2x^3 + 2x^2 + 4x + 10$

33. $-y^2 - x - 5$

35. $3x^2 - 2$

37. $x^2 - 1$

39. $-3y^2 - 4x + 1$

41. $4x + 6$

43. $-4b + 3$

45. $3x^2 + 2x - 40$

47. $16\pi r^2 + 36\pi r + 18\pi$

49. yes; The sum of two polynomials in one variable always results in another polynomial in the same variable since no other variables appear in the terms being added. The number of terms may differ from one or both of the polynomials being added, but the result is a polynomial.

51.A. $6\pi r + 63\pi$

  B. $6\pi r + 45\pi$

  C. 18π

53. $(3r + 0.5)^3 - \pi r^2(3r + 0.5)$, or $(27 - 3\pi)r^3 + (13.5 - 0.5\pi)r^2 + 2.25r + 0.125$

55. She wrote the opposite monomials incorrectly; The answer should be $3x^2 + 4x + 6$.

Spiral Review • Assessment Readiness

59.A. 2

  B. 4

  C. 3

  D. 1

MODULE 16, LESSON 16.2

On Your Own

3. yes; Each number is a perfect square. The first number is 2^2, the second number is 3^2, and so on. This means that the nth number is $(n + 1)^2$, and $(n + 1)^2 = n^2 + 2n + 1$. This matches what John found.

5. $\frac{n(n - 3)}{2}$; Possible answer: Each of the n vertices is connected to $n - 3$ other vertices since there are $n - 1$ other vertices in general and two of those are adjacent to the given vertices. This means there are $n(n - 3)$ edges between the vertices, but this counts each edge twice, one time for the vertex at each end of the edge. Therefore, divide $n(n - 3)$ by 2 to find the total number of edges.

7. $mn + \frac{1}{2}n(n - 1) + \frac{1}{2}m(m - 1)$

9. $0.00002\,x^2 + 12x - 100{,}000$

11. $1000 - \frac{1}{10}r^2$; The value of $\frac{1}{10}r^2$ is positive, so the value of $1000 - \frac{1}{10}r^2$ is less than 1000.

13. Possible answer:

$2, 7, 15, 26$; $\frac{3}{2}n^2 + \frac{1}{2}n$

15. $3n^2 + 2n$

Spiral Review • Assessment Readiness

17. C

19. B, C, D

UNIT 8

MODULE 17, LESSON 17.1

On Your Own

7. The y-intercept is at $y = 0$, the x-intercepts are at 0 and 4. The line of symmetry is at $x = 2$. The domain is all real numbers and the range is all real numbers greater than or equal to -4.

9. $-2, -1$

11. $-5, 0$

13. $-3, 4$

15. $-2, 7$

17. $0, 3$

19. $-8, 6$

21.A.

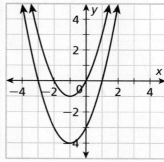

x-intercepts: -3 and 1, vertex: $(-1, -4)$, axis of symmetry: $x = -1$, opens up

B.

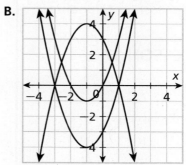

x-intercepts: -3 and 1, vertex: $(-1, 4)$, axis of symmetry: $x = -1$, opens down

23.A. $x^2 - 4x + 11 = 3x - 1$; The functions are equal when $f(x) = g(x)$. Substitute the expressions for the two functions to get $x^2 - 4x + 11 = 3x - 1$.

B. $x^2 - 7x + 12 = 0$

C. The functions are equal when $x = 3$ or $x = 4$.

25.A. $16t^2 = 40$ or $16t^2 - 40 = 0$

B. $t \approx -1.6$ or $t \approx 1.6$

C. It takes about 1.6 seconds for the glove to hit the ground. A negative value of t (time) does not make sense in this context. So, -1.6 seconds is an invalid solution; The solution is an approximation because I had to round it.

D. I could improve the precision of the solution by zooming in farther (if using the trace function) or by including more decimal places (if having the calculator determine the intercept).

27.A. Let w represent the width of the garden; $400 = w(w + 10)$

B. $w^2 + 10w - 400 = 0$

C.

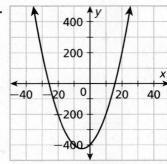

$w \approx -25.6$ or $w \approx 15.6$

D. 25.6 ft by 15.6 ft

E. yes; The dimensions of the garden cannot be negative.

Spiral Review • Assessment Readiness

31. C, D, F

MODULE 17, LESSON 17.2

On Your Own

9. $x + 8$ in.

11. Problem 9: $x > 0$; Problem 10: $x > 6$

13. $(x + 3)(x + 4)$

15. $(x - 6)(x - 8)$

17. $(x + 2)(x + 8)$

19. $x = -6, x = 2$

21. $x = 3, x = -4$

23. $x = -3, x = 8$

25.A. $h(0)$ represents the height of the hammock above the left supporting leg.

B. 25 inches

C. 10 feet

27.A. $30 + 2x, 20 + x$

B. 5 yards; 40 yards by 25 yards

29. 2

Spiral Review • Assessment Readiness

31. A, B, D

33. A

MODULE 17, LESSON 17.3

On Your Own

7. $11x(x - 11) = 1980$; 20 m

9. $(x + 3)(2x + 3)$

11. $(x + 3)(4x + 5)$

13. $(x + 6)(3x - 1)$

15. $(5x + 2)(x - 3)$

17. $(2x + 1)(8x - 3)$

19. $(2x - 9)(3x + 5)$

21. $(4x + 3)(2x + 7)$

23. no; An example would be $(2x + 1)x = 0$, where the zeros are $x = 0$ and $x = -\frac{1}{2}$.

25. The solution is incorrect because Maureen is applying the Zero Product Property when the product is 3, not 0.

27. $x = -2, x = \frac{1}{3}$

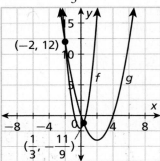

29. $x = -\frac{4}{5}, x = 3$

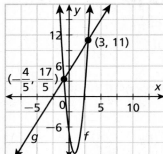

31. $x = -\frac{5}{2}, x = -\frac{1}{5}$

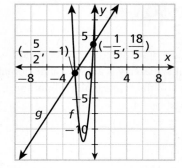

33. $x = -\dfrac{5}{7}, x = 1$

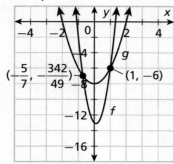

35.

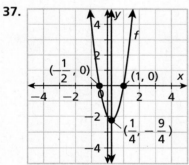

37.

39.

41.

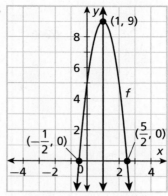

43.A. $(20 - 3x)(15 - 2x)$

B. $(20 - 3x)(15 - 2x) = 186$

C. $x = \dfrac{3}{2}$ inches or $x = \dfrac{38}{3}$ inches; Only $x = \dfrac{3}{2}$ inches is viable as the other solution would be too large for the window.

D. The width of the frame is 1.5 inches.

45. $x = 10$

Spiral Review • Assessment Readiness

47. A, D, E

49.A. 3

B. 2

C. 4

D. 1

MODULE 17, LESSON 17.4

On Your Own

7. This is a sum of squares, not a difference of squares. If someone thinks it can be factored as $(x + 2)^2$, this expands to $x^2 + 4x + 4$, not just $x^2 + 4$.

9. $x = 2, -2$

11. $x = -2$

13. $x = -\dfrac{2}{3}$

15. $x = 8$

17. $x = \dfrac{1}{4}$

19. $x = \dfrac{4}{3}$

21. $x = \dfrac{5}{2}$

23. $x = \dfrac{1}{6}$

25. 4 ft, 4 ft

27. They are both correct; Both methods lead to the same factored form, and so either method is valid in factoring the given trinomial.

29. $x = -\dfrac{5}{3}$

31. $3x^2(3x + 1)(3x - 1)$

33. $4x(5x + 3)(5x - 3)$

35. $x^2(2x + 1)(2x - 1)$

37. $-2x^4(3x + 2)^2$

39. $-x(4x - 1)^2$

41. $-3x(2x + 7)(2x - 7)$

43.A. $2x + 2$ and $2x + 2$

   B. $4x + 6$ and $4x + 6$

   C. The dimensions of each triangle are 2 more than 2 times the dimensions of the previous triangle.

45.A. 2 seconds

   B. 1 second

   C. approximately 1.414 seconds

Spiral Review • Assessment Readiness

47. A

MODULE 18, LESSON 18.1

On Your Own

9. $n = \pm 12$

11. $x = \pm 7$

13. $x = 0$

15. $z = \pm 4$

17. $t = \pm 4$

19. $a = -21, 1$

21. $x = -5, 3$

23. $y = -2, 4$

25. $y = -4, -2$

27. $x = 6, 10$

29. $a = -7, -1$

31. $t = \pm 3\sqrt{15}; t = -11.62, 11.62$

33. $w = \pm\sqrt{78}; w = -8.83, 8.83$

35. $z = \pm\sqrt{13}; z = -3.61, 3.61$

37. $d = -4 \pm 4\sqrt{3}; d = -10.93, 2.93$

39. $k = -4 \pm 4\sqrt{2}; k = -9.66, 1.66$

41. $x = 2 \pm 3\sqrt{7}; x = -5.94, 9.94$

43. $a = 3 \pm\sqrt{2}; a = 1.59, 4.41$

45. $x = -11 \pm\sqrt{3}; x = -12.73, -9.27$

47. $m = -6 \pm\sqrt{2}; m = -7.41, -4, 59$

49. $\sqrt{7}$ s or about 2.6 s

51. $400\pi = \pi r^2; 20$ in.

53. Jacob; Jacob should have subtracted 256 from both sides instead of added. There is no solution because you can't have a square root of a negative number.

55. $t \approx 81$ years

57. x is both the length and width of the isosceles triangle; $\frac{1}{2}x^2 = 9000$; 268 ft

59. $d = -16t^2 + 85$; 2.3 s

61.A. $10\sqrt{2}$ in.

   B. $2 + 10\sqrt{2}$ in.

   C. $204 + 40\sqrt{2}$ in^2

Spiral Review • Assessment Readiness

63. A

65.A. 2

   B. 1

   C. 4

   D. 3

MODULE 18, LESSON 18.2

On Your Own

7. $4x^2 + 20x + 25; (2x + 5)^2$

9. $25x^2 + 10x + 1; (5x + 1)^2$

11. $9x^2 - 8x + \dfrac{16}{9}; \left(3x - \dfrac{4}{3}\right)^2$

13. $x = -5$ or $x = 1$

15. $x = 0$ or $x = 2$

17. $x = -2 \pm \sqrt{19}$

19. $x = -2 \pm \sqrt{6}$

21. $x = 1 \pm\sqrt{2}$

23. $x = \dfrac{5 \pm \sqrt{29}}{2}$

25. $x = -1$ or $x = -3$

27. 2.1 s

29.A. $x = 9 + 5\sqrt{2}, x = 9 - 5\sqrt{2}$

   B. 14.1 ft

31. $x = 6 \pm\sqrt{39}$

33. $x = 9 \pm\sqrt{73}$

35. $x = \dfrac{-3 \pm\sqrt{33}}{8}$

37. $x = \dfrac{3 \pm\sqrt{209}}{25}$

39. $x = -\dfrac{1}{4}, \dfrac{5}{4}$

41. $x = \dfrac{-3 \pm\sqrt{201}}{6}$

43.A. As the ends of the arc are at $y = 1$, you can set the quadratic function equal to 1 to get $-\frac{2}{3}(x^2 - 4x + 1) = 1$. Alternatively, you can first translate the function down 1 unit so that the ends of the arc are on the x-axis and then set the function equal to 0 to get $-\frac{2}{3}(x^2 - 4x + 1) - 1 = 0$.

B. about 2.4 feet

Spiral Review • Assessment Readiness

47. B

49. B, D

MODULE 18, LESSON 18.3

On Your Own

7. <

9. =

11. 105; 2 real solutions

13. -116; no real solution

15. 136; 2 real solutions

17. $x = -3$ or $x = 2$

19. $x = \dfrac{-3 \pm \sqrt{5}}{2}$

21. $x = \dfrac{3}{2}$ or $x = -2$

23. $x = 2 \pm \dfrac{\sqrt{2}}{2}$

25. $x = -1$ or $x = 6$

27. $x = 1$ or $x = 4$

29. $x = -2$ or $x = \dfrac{2}{3}$

31. $x \approx 3.30$ or $x \approx -0.30$

33. $x \approx -0.38$ or $x \approx -2.62$

35. $x \approx 0.29$ or $x \approx -0.69$

37. $x \approx -1.12$ or $x \approx 7.12$

39.A. $x^2 + 8x + 5 = 20$

B. about 1.6 m

C. no; The solution -9.6 is not reasonable because the coop's height cannot be negative.

41. 1.3 s

43. 2.6 s

45. $t \approx 13.2$ hours

Spiral Review • Assessment Readiness

47. C

49. A, C, F

MODULE 18, LESSON 18.4

On Your Own

7. no; The graph provides an approximate solution. The exact solution is $x = \pm\sqrt{3}$.

9. Possible answer: Quadratic Formula; The Quadratic Formula works for all solvable equations and is usually less work than completing the square when a is not a perfect square; $x = \dfrac{-1 \pm \sqrt{13}}{6}$

11. Possible answer: square roots; Taking square roots is the easiest approach and least likely to result in an error due to the minimal number of computations, but it only works for values when $b = 0$ in standard form; $x = \pm 2$.

13. Possible answer: square roots; Taking square roots is the easiest approach and least likely to result in an error due to the minimal number of computations, but it only works for values when $b = 0$ in standard form; $x = \pm\sqrt{5}$.

15. Possible answer: factoring; When the equation is easy to factor, use factoring rather than the other methods; $x = -1, 2$.

17. Possible answer: Quadratic Formula; The Quadratic Formula works for all solvable equations and is usually less work than completing the square when a is not a perfect square; $x = \dfrac{-1 \pm \sqrt{85}}{6}$.

19. if the leading coefficient is a perfect square

21. no; Possible answer: The equation can have irrational solutions. For example, when $x^2 - 3 = 0$, $a = 1$, $b = -0$, and $c = -3$ are integers.

Spiral Review • Assessment Readiness

23. C

UNIT 9

MODULE 19, LESSON 19.1

On Your Own

5. The axis of symmetry is $x = 0$; The vertex of $(0, 0)$ is the highest point since the graph changes from increasing to decreasing in value at $x = 0$.

7.

x	$g(x) = (x + 3)^2 + 2$
−3	2
−2	3
−1	6
0	11
1	18
2	27
3	38

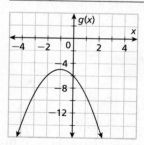

The graph of the parent function is translated left 3 units and up 2 units; axis of symmetry: $x = -3$; vertex: $(-3, 2)$

9.

x	$g(x) = (x + 1)^2 - 5$
−3	−9
−2	−6
−1	−5
0	−6
1	−9
2	−14
3	−21

The graph of the parent function is reflected across the x-axis, translated 1 unit left and 5 units down; axis of symmetry: $x = -1$; vertex: $(-1, -5)$

11. $a = -\frac{1}{3}$ compresses the graph of the parent function by a factor of $\frac{1}{3}$ and reflects it across the x-axis; $h = -2$ translates the graph 2 units to the left; $k = -3$ translates the graph down 3 units

13. $a = \frac{3}{2}$ stretches the graph of the parent function by a factor of $\frac{3}{2}$ or 1.5; $h = -1$ translates the graph 1 unit to the left; $k = -2$ translates the graph down 2 units.

15. The graph is stretched.

17. The graph is translated right.

19. The graph is a reflection across the x-axis followed by a translation to the left and up.

21. $g(x) = 2(x - 1)^2 + 4$

23.A. $a = -2, h = 3, k = 4$

B. The value of a reflects the graph of g across the x-axis and vertically stretches the graph.

C. The value of h translates the graph of g right. The value of k translates the graph of g up.

D. The graph of g is a vertical stretch by a factor of 2, a reflection across the x-axis, a translation 3 units right, and a translation 4 units up of the graph of f.

25.

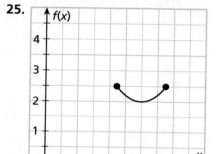

$y = \frac{2}{9}(x - 6)^2 + 2$; domain: $4.5 \le x \le 7.5$; depth at center: 0.5 ft; The points at the ends of the domain are $(4.5, 2.5)$ and $(7.5, 2.5)$, so the depth of the dish is $2.5 - 2 = 0.5$ ft.

Spiral Review • Assessment Readiness

29. B

31. C

MODULE 19, LESSON 19.2

On Your Own

7. $x = -7, (-7, -16)$, minimum, x-intercepts: −3 and −11 and y-intercept: 33

9. $x = 2, (2, 24)$, minimum, x-intercepts: none and y-intercept: 36

11. $x = 3, (3, 3)$, maximum, x-intercepts: 2 and 4 and y-intercept: −24

13. $f(x) = x^2 + 8x + 22$

15. $f(x) = -x^2 - 16x - 76$

17. $f(x) = 3x^2 + 12x + 16$

19. $f(x) = (x - 4)^2 - 1$

21. $f(x) = 4(x + 3)^2 + 4$

23. $f(x) = -4(x - 2)^2 + 22$

25. $y = -(x - 2.5)^2 + 6.25$; height: 6.25 ft, width: 5 ft; The vertex is at $(2.5, 6.25)$ which reveals the maximum height of the arc of water is 6.25 feet. Since $(0, 0)$ is on the graph, by symmetry the point $(5, 0)$ is also on the graph, so the width of the arc of water is 5 feet.

27. yes; Possible answer: There are no restrictions on completing the square for a quadratic function.

29.

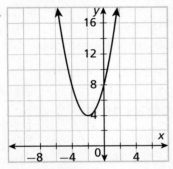

31.

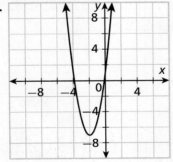

33.

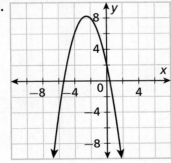

35. Possible answer: For every point plotted to the left of the vertex you can plot the reflection of that point across the line of symmetry to plot every point to the right of the line of symmetry.

37. about 10,756 feet

39.A. $h(t) = -16t^2 + 40t + 2.5$

B. 27.5 ft

C. 1.25 s

41. Marvin distributed -6 to only the first term after expanding $(x + 3)^2$; $f(x) = -6x^2 - 36x - 72$

Spiral Review • Assessment Readiness

43. A

45. C

MODULE 19, LESSON 19.3
On Your Own

7. $f(x)$: C; $g(x)$: A; $h(x)$: B

9. Possible answer: $j(x) = 3(x + 5)(x - 6)$

11. $f(x) = -3(x - 1)(x - 2)$
x-intercepts: 1, 2

13. $f(x) = 3(x + 5)(x - 9)$
x-intercepts: -5, 9

15. $f(x) = (x - 4)(x - 11)$
x-intercepts: 4, 11

17. $f(x) = (x - 9)(x - 8)$
x-intercepts: 8, 9

19. $f(x) = 2\left(x - \dfrac{1}{2}\right)(x + 3)$
$x = -3, x = \dfrac{1}{2}$

21. $f(x) = (x + 6)(x + 4)$; x-intercepts: -6, -4; axis of symmetry: $x = -5$;
vertex: $(-5, -1)$

23. $f(x) = -(x + 3)(x + 9)$; x-intercepts: -3, -9; axis of symmetry: $x = -6$;
vertex: $(-6, 9)$

25. $f(x) = 2(x - 8)(x + 4)$; x-intercepts: 8, -4; axis of symmetry: $x = 2$;
vertex: $(2, -72)$

27.A. $f(x) = -\dfrac{1}{30} x(x - 24)$; The x-intercepts are 0 and 24. The width is 24 inches.

B. $f(x) = -\dfrac{1}{30}(x - 12)^2 + 4.8$; The vertex is $(12, 4.8)$. At the center, 12 inches from the left edge, the maximum depth is 4.8 inches.

Selected Answers

C.

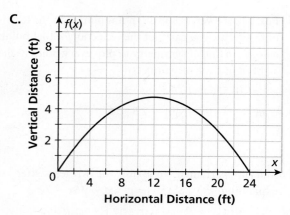

29. $A(w) = -w^2 + 22w$; 121 ft²

31. 11 in.

33.A. $h(x) = -\dfrac{1}{5}(x - 50)(x + 30)$

B. x-intercepts: -30 and 50; y-intercept: (300); vertex: $(10, 320)$

C. $-30 \le x \le 50$; The domain represents the width of the hill of 80 ft.

D.

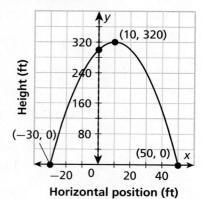

Spiral Review • Assessment Readiness

35. B

37. B, C, D

MODULE 19, LESSON 19.4

On Your Own

5. no; The x-intercepts of the graph of the function can be directly determined by looking at the intercept form of the function, not the y-intercept.

7. f: down, g: up

9. f: maximum of 4; g: minimum of -4

11. $(-3.94, -3.56)$ and $(-0.46, -0.76)$

13. The function f has a lesser minimum value.

15. the graph of g

17. the graph of g

19. $x \approx -5.4, x \approx 2.5$

21. $x \approx -2.9, x \approx 5.9$

23. $g; f$

25. $f; f$

27. $g; f$

29. The graph of h has a greater magnitude of stretch.

31. The graph of h has a greater magnitude of stretch.

33. vertex with greater y-coordinate: graph of f; greater y-intercept: graph of g; greater stretch: graph of g

35.A. Ball A

B. Ball A

C. $(0.125, 10.75)$; Both balls are at the same height, 10.75 feet, after 0.125 seconds.

Spiral Review • Assessment Readiness

37. D

39. A

MODULE 19, LESSON 19.5

On Your Own

5.

x	y = f(x)	First difference	Second difference
0	2	—	—
1	9	7	—
2	26	17	10
3	53	27	10
4	90	37	10

yes

7.

x	y = h(x)	First difference	Second difference
−2	−19	—	—
−1	−9	10	—
0	−3	6	−4
1	−1	2	−4
2	−3	−2	−4

yes

9. linear

11. $f(x) = -2(x - 4)^2 + 5$

13.A. $h(t) = -16t^2 + 45t + 7$

B. about 38.6 ft

C. about 1.4 s

15. $h(t) = -16t^2 + 75t + 25$

17. $h(t) = -16t^2 + 75t + 5$

19. $h(t) \approx -2.64t^2 + 11.76t + 7.95$; about 6.6 s

Spiral Review • Assessment Readiness

23. B

MODULE 20, LESSON 20.1

On Your Own

5. linear: $s = -10.4t + 52.3$; exponential: $s = 70.2(0.525)^t$; quadratic: $s = 3.26t^2 - 30t + 68.6$; The exponential function models the data best. The data decrease quickly at first and then continue to decrease at a slower rate, which suggests exponential decay. Also, the coefficient of determination for the exponential function, 0.965, is closer to 1 than is the coefficient of determination for the linear function, 0.7331, or for the quadratic function, 0.9482.

7.A. linear: $s = 2.37t + 50.7$; exponential: $s = 50.7(1.0436)^t$; quadratic: $s = -0.452t^2 + 4.62t + 49.1$

B. quadratic; The coefficient of determination for the quadratic function is 0.9888, which is closer to 1 than is the coefficient of determination for the linear function, 0.9174, or for the exponential function, 0.906. Also, overall the residuals for the quadratic function are closer to the t-axis than are the residuals for the other two functions.

C. about $50.1 million

9. $y = 0x^2 + 3x + 5$, or $y = 3x + 5$; The function is a linear function. This makes sense because the data points from the table all lie precisely on the same line.

Spiral Review • Assessment Readiness

11. A

13.A. $g(x)$

B. $f(x)$

C. $g(x)$

MODULE 20, LESSON 20.2

On Your Own

9. $(f + g)(x) = 4x^2 + 2x - 25$

11. $(h - f)(x) = 5$

13. $\left(\dfrac{g}{f}\right)(x) = \dfrac{4x^2 - 25}{2x}, x \neq 0$

15. $(g \cdot h)(x) = 8x^3 + 20x^2 - 50x - 125$

17. $\left(\dfrac{a}{f}\right)(x) = \dfrac{2(1.5)^x}{x}, x \neq 0$

19. $(a \cdot h)(x) = 8x(1.5)^x + 20(1.5)^x$

21. $(f + h)(x) = 4x + 5$

23. $(h - a)(x) = 2x + 5 - 4(1.5)^x$

25.

Length (ft)	Width (ft)	Area (ft²)
11	3	33
12	4	48
13	5	65
14	6	84

$w(x) = x - 8$
$A(x) = x^2 - 8x$

27.A. $B(t) = 1600(1.05)^t$; $W(t) = 400(1.05)^t$

B. $T(t) = 2000(1.05)^t$

C. $D(t) = 1200(1.05)^t$

D. $R(t) = 4$; The ratio is constant.

29. Possible answer:

$h(x) = 2x^2 + 5x - 12$
$h(x) = (x + 4)(2x - 3)$
$f(x) = x + 4$
$g(x) = 2x - 3$

31.A. $520,000

B. $R(x) = -2x^2 + 32x + 520$

C. $11 per month or $25 per month; The equation $R(x) = 550$, or $-2x^2 + 32x + 520 = 550$, has two solutions: $x = 1$, corresponding to a monthly price of $10 + $1 = $11, and $x = 15$, corresponding to a monthly price of $10 + $15 = $25.

D. $18 per month; $648,000

Spiral Review • Assessment Readiness

33. B

35. C

MODULE 20, LESSON 20.3

On Your Own

7. two solutions

9. two solutions

11. two solutions

13. two solutions

15. The coil of rope will reach the climber after approximately 3.528 seconds.

17. The ball will hit the roof approximately 19.38 feet horizontally from its initial spot with a height of 11.19 feet.

19. $(0.63, 0.88), (6.37, 18.12)$

21. $(-0.21, 0.87), (1.21, -3.37)$

23. $(-2.49, 1.82)$

25. 0.1 s

Spiral Review • Assessment Readiness

27. A

29. B

MODULE 20, LESSON 20.4

On Your Own

5. x-intercepts: 0 and 3; end behavior: $f(x) \to -\infty$ as $x \to -\infty$ and $f(x) \to +\infty$ as $x \to +\infty$; turning points: 2; positive: $(3, +\infty)$; negative: $(-\infty, 0)$ and $(0, 3)$

7. x-intercepts: -1 and 5; end behavior: $f(x) \to +\infty$ as $x \to -\infty$ and $f(x) \to -\infty$ as $x \to +\infty$; turning points: 2; positive: $(-\infty, -1)$ and $(-1, 5)$; negative: $(5, +\infty)$

9. x-intercepts: 2; end behavior: $f(x) \to -\infty$ as $x \to -\infty$ and $f(x) \to +\infty$ as $x \to +\infty$; turning points: 0; positive: $(2, +\infty)$; negative: $(-\infty, 2)$

11. $f(x) = 3x(x - 1)(x + 8)$

13. $f(x) = (x + 3)(x - 5)(x + 7)$

15. $f(x) = -2(x - 4)^2(x + 5)$

17. $f(x) = -2x(x + 3)(x - 3)$

19.

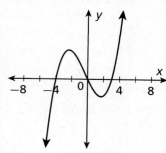

21.A. -3, 0, and 3

B. $f(x) \to +\infty$ as $x \to -\infty$ and $f(x) \to -\infty$ as $x \to +\infty$

C. negative: $(-3, 0)$ and $(3, +\infty)$; positive: $(-\infty, -3)$ and $(1, 5)$

D. Possible answer: $f(x) = -x(x + 3)(x - 3)$

23. $f(x) = (x + 3)(x + 2)(x + 1)$

25. $V(x) = \frac{2}{3}\pi x^2 (x + 5)$

27.A. g, h

B. no; Possible answer: If a function had a negative leading coefficient, then the end behavior would be $f(x) \to +\infty$ as $x \to -\infty$ and $f(x) \to -\infty$ as $x \to +\infty$. None of the graphs have this end behavior.

C. $(-1, 1)$

29. approximately 1056 in^3

Spiral Review • Assessment Readiness

33. A

35. A

UNIT 10

MODULE 21, LESSON 21.1

On Your Own

3. Possible answer: I can ask myself if I can describe the category with a number. If I can, it is quantitative. If I cannot, it is categorical.

5. *See below.*

5.A.

		Preferred Fruit			
		Apple	Orange	Pear	Total
Grade	9	0.23	0.20	0.11	0.54
	10	0.26	0.16	0.05	0.47
	Total	0.49	0.36	0.16	≈1.00

B. The relative frequency of 23% means that 23% of all the high school students surveyed are in grade 9 and prefer apples.

C. 78 pears because when 16% of all high school students surveyed pears is scaled to 500 students, the result is 78 pears.

7. *See below.*

9. Possible answer: The town committee should choose to fund the project to construct a park because it had the highest marginal relative frequency and the most consistent joint relative frequencies among the different age groups.

Spiral Review • Assessment Readiness

11. C

MODULE 21, LESSON 21.2

On Your Own

5. no; The joint relative frequency represents a part of the marginal relative frequency, so the joint relative frequency will always be less than the marginal relative frequency.

7. conditional

9. marginal

11. conditional

13.A. about 79%

　B. no; The conditional relative frequency from Part A is very close to the marginal relative frequency for participants who obey the law, 75%.

　C. no; As described in Part B, there is no association between knowing the law and obeying the law. Educating people about the law will not increase the number of those who obey the law by a significant amount.

15. no; Possible answer: To find the conditional relative frequency of those who like broccoli, given that they like asparagus, divide the joint relative frequency of those who like broccoli and asparagus, 0.32, by the marginal relative frequency of those who like asparagus (for the column), 0.78.

Spiral Review • Assessment Readiness

17. A

19. B, C, F

MODULE 22, LESSON 22.1

On Your Own

7. skewed to the right

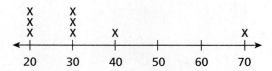

9. Possible Answers: 4, 4, 5, 5, 6, 6, 7, 7, 8, 8; For ten values, I divided 10 by 5 to get 2, then made sure there were 2 entries of each of 4, 5, 6, 7, and 8.

11. 20.11; 4.75

13. 11; 2

15. 32

17. The outlier is 9.8 because it is less than $Q1 - 1.5(IQR) = 10.1 - 1.5(0.15) = 9.875$.

19.A. Marnie's; Marnie's

　B. The data for Marnie has the larger standard deviation and the larger IQR.

　C. Neither data set has an outlier; For each of the data sets all of the data values are between $Q1 + 1.5(IQR)$ and $Q3 - 1.5(IQR)$.

　D. Possible answer: Beth; I think Beth is the better swimmer because her mean time is lower.

Spiral Review • Assessment Readiness

23. C

7.A.

		Engineering Specialty			
		Electrical engineering	**Mechanical engineering**	**Other**	**Total**
University	**1**	.26	.18	.06	.50
	2	.23	.17	.10	50
	Total	.49	.35	.16	1.00

　B. The joint relative frequency is 26%.

　C. The relative frequency 35% means that 35% of all the engineering students surveyed are enrolled in a mechanical engineering program.

　D. 24 students

MODULE 22, LESSON 22.2

On Your Own

3.A.

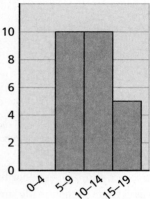

B. Possible answer: At intervals of five, the histogram's shape is relatively symmetric, with a slight skew to the right.

C.

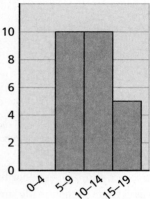

D. Possible answer: The box plot is relatively symmetric, just like the histogram, with its maximum and minimum values nearly the same distance from the median. The location of the box portion of the plot shows that the data is slightly skewed to the right.

5.A. Possible answer, at intervals of 10:

See below.

B. Possible answer: The distributions are alike in ranging from approximately 100 to 150 inches in circumference. Both also have two values in the smallest interval, and never exceed four values for the intervals that I chose. The distributions are different in clustering: the data from Location 2 is much less clustered than is the data from Location 1.

C. Location 2 has a greater mean circumference.

D.

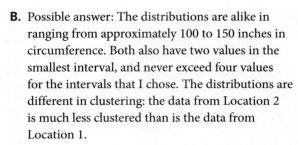

E. Location 2 has a greater median circumference.

F. Location 1 has circumferences that are less spread out.

7. Possible answer using intervals of 3:

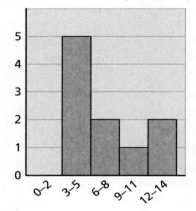

5.A.

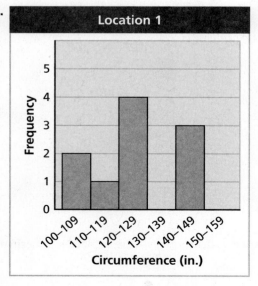

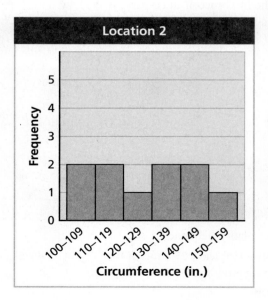

9. Possible answer using intervals of 4:

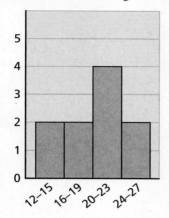

11.

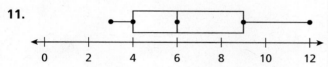

13.

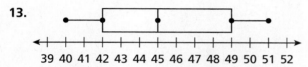

15.A. Pablo

B. John

C. John, because his points scored have the higher median for the data set and the quartiles.

17. If the maximum and the third quartile are the same, the box plot would have no "whisker" on the right side.

Spiral Review • Assessment Readiness

19. C

A

English	Spanish	Examples
absolute value The absolute value of x is the distance from zero to x on a number line, denoted $\lvert x \rvert$. $$\lvert x \rvert = \begin{cases} x & \text{if } x \geq 0 \\ -x & \text{if } x < 0 \end{cases}$$	**valor absoluto** El valor absoluto de x es la distancia de cero a x en una recta numérica, y se expresa $\lvert x \rvert$. $$\lvert x \rvert = \begin{cases} x & \text{si } x \geq 0 \\ -x & \text{si } x < 0 \end{cases}$$	$\lvert 3 \rvert = 3$ $\lvert -3 \rvert = 3$
absolute-value equation An equation that contains algebraic expressions within absolute value bars.	**ecuación de valor absoluto** Ecuación que contiene expresiones algebraicas entre barras de valor absoluto.	$\lvert x + 4 \rvert = 7$
absolute-value function A function whose rule contains algebraic expressions within absolute value bars.	**función de valor absoluto** Función cuya regla contiene expresiones algebraicas entre barras de valor absoluto.	$y = \lvert x + 4 \rvert$
absolute-value inequality An inequality that contains algebraic expressions within absolute value bars.	**desigualdad de valor absoluto** Desigualdad que contiene expresiones algebraicas entre barras de valor absoluto.	$\lvert x + 4 \rvert > 7$
accuracy The closeness of a given measurement or value to the actual measurement or value.	**exactitud** Cercanía de una medida o un valor a la medida o el valor real.	
algebraic expression An expression that contains at least one variable.	**expresión algebraica** Expresión que contiene por lo menos una variable.	
arithmetic sequence A sequence whose successive terms differ by the same number d, called the common difference.	**sucesión aritmética** Sucesión cuyos términos sucesivos difieren en el mismo número d, denominado *diferencia común*.	4, 7, 10, 13, 16, … $+3\ +3\ +3\ +3 \qquad d = 3$
asymptote A line that a graph gets closer to as the value of x increases or decreases without bound.	**asíntota** Recta a la cual se aproxima una gráfica a medida que el valor de x aumenta o disminuye sin límite.	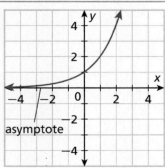

Glossary/Glosario

English	Spanish	Examples
axis of symmetry A line that divides a plane figure or a graph into two congruent reflected halves.	**eje de simetría** Línea que divide una figura plana o una gráfica en dos mitades reflejadas congruentes.	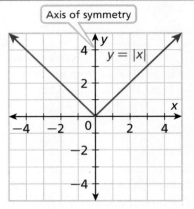

B

English	Spanish	Examples
binomial A polynomial with two terms.	**binomio** Polinomio con dos términos.	$x + y$ $2a^2 + 3$ $4m^3n^2 + 6mn^4$
bivariate data Paired values of two variables, such as a series of measurements of air temperature at different times of day.	**datos bivariados** Valores de dos variables agrupados en pares, como una serie de mediciones de la temperatura del aire en diferentes momentos del día.	Time / Temperature (°F) table below
boundary line A line that divides a coordinate plane into two half-planes.	**línea de límite** Línea que divide un plano cartesiano en dos semiplanos.	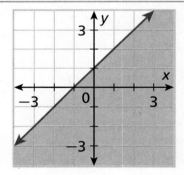

Time	Temperature (°F)
8 A.M.	65
9 A.M.	69
10 A.M.	72

English	Spanish	Examples

box plot A statistical graph, also known as a box-and-whisker plot, that divides a data set into four equal parts using quartiles. A box is drawn from the first (or lower) quartile to the third (or upper) quartile. The box is divided into two parts at the median (the second quartile). Line segments (or "whiskers") are drawn from each end of the box out to the least and greatest data values. If the data set includes outliers, they are sometimes removed from the whiskers and shown as individual points.

gráfica de caja Gráfica estadística, también conocida como gráfica de mediana y rango, que divide un conjunto de datos en cuatro partes iguales usando cuartiles. Se dibuja una caja desde el primer cuartil (o inferior) hasta el tercer cuartil (o superior). Se divide la caja en dos partes en la mediana (el segundo cuartil). Se dibujan segmentos de recta (o "brazos") desde cada extremo de la caja hasta el valor más bajo y el valor más alto. Si el conjunto de datos incluye valores extremos, algunas veces se los remueve de los brazos y se los muestra como puntos individuales.

First quartile · Third quartile
Minimum · Median · Maximum
0 2 4 6 8 10 12 14

C

categorical data Data that are qualitative in nature, such as "liberal," "moderate," and "conservative."

datos categóricos Datos de índole cualitativa, como "liberal", "moderado" y "conservador".

closure A set of numbers is said to be closed, or to have closure, under a given operation if the result of the operation on any two numbers in the set is also in the set.

cerradura Se dice que un conjunto de números es cerrado, o tiene cerradura, respecto de una operación determinada, si el resultado de la operación entre dos números cualesquiera del conjunto también está en el conjunto.

The set of natural numbers is closed under addition because the sum of two natural numbers is always a natural number.

coefficient The numerical factor in a term. If a term has no numerical factor, the coefficient is understood to be 1.

coeficiente Factor numérico de un término. Si un término no tiene factor numérico, se entiende que el coeficiente es 1.

In the expression $2x + 3y$, 2 is the coefficient of x and 3 is the coefficient of y.

common difference In an arithmetic sequence, the constant difference of any term after the first and the previous term.

diferencia común En una sucesión aritmética, diferencia constante entre cualquier término después del primero y el término anterior.

In the arithmetic sequence 3, 5, 7, 9, 11, …, the common difference is 2.

common ratio In a geometric sequence, the constant ratio of any term after the first and the previous term.

razón común En una sucesión geométrica, la razón constante entre cualquier término después del primero y el término anterior.

In the geometric sequence 32, 16, 8, 4, 2, . . ., the common ratio is $\frac{1}{2}$.

English	Spanish	Examples
completing the square A process used to form a perfect-square trinomial. To complete the square for $x^2 + bx$, add $\left(\frac{b}{2}\right)^2$.	**completar el cuadrado** Proceso utilizado para formar un trinomio cuadrado perfecto. Para completar el cuadrado para $x^2 + bx$, hay que sumar $\left(\frac{b}{2}\right)^2$.	$x^2 + 6x + \blacksquare$ Add $\left(\frac{6}{2}\right)^2 = 9.$ $x^2 + 6x + 9$
compound inequality Two inequalities that are combined into one statement by the word *and* or *or*.	**desigualdad compuesta** Dos desigualdades unidas en un enunciado por la palabra *y* u *o*.	$x \geq 2$ AND $x < 7$ (also written $2 \leq x < 7$) 0 2 4 6 8 $x < 2$ OR $x > 6$ 0 2 4 6 8
conditional relative frequency The ratio of a joint relative frequency to a related marginal relative frequency in a two-way table.	**frecuencia relativa condicional** Razón de una frecuencia relativa conjunta a una frecuencia relativa marginal en una tabla de doble entrada.	
consistent system A system of equations or inequalities that has at least one solution.	**sistema consistente** Sistema de ecuaciones o desigualdades que tiene por lo menos una solución.	$\begin{cases} x + y = 6 \\ x - y = 4 \end{cases}$ solution: $(5, 1)$
constant A value that does not change. It may be a number or a letter that stands for a fixed number.	**constante** Valor que no cambia. Puede ser un número o una letra que represente un número fijo.	$3, 0, \pi$
continuous function on an interval A function whose graph on an interval of the x-axis is connected, with no gaps or breaks.	**función continua en un intervalo** Función cuya gráfica en un intervalo del eje x está conectada, sin espacios ni interrupciones.	$f(x) = 2^x$
correlation A measure of the strength and direction of a linear relationship between the two variables in a set of bivariate data.	**correlación** Medida de la fuerza y dirección de una relación lineal entre las dos variables en un conjunto de datos bivariados.	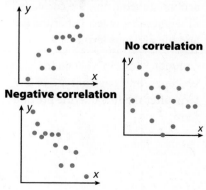

English	Spanish	Examples
correlation coefficient A number r, where $-1 \le r \le 1$, that describes how closely the points in a scatter plot cluster around the least-squares line.	**coeficiente de correlación** Número r, donde $-1 \le r \le 1$, que describe a qué distancia de la recta de mínimos cuadrados se agrupan los puntos de un diagrama de dispersión.	An r-value close to 1 describes a strong positive correlation. An r-value close to 0 describes a weak correlation or no correlation. An r-value close to -1 describes a strong negative correlation.
cubic function A function that can be written in the form $f(x) = ax^3 + bx^2 + cx + d$, where a, b, c, and d are real numbers and $a \neq 0$.	**función cúbica** Función que se puede expresar como $f(x) = ax^3 + bx^2 + cx + d$, donde a, b, c y d son números reales y $a \neq 0$.	$f(x) = x^3 + 2x^2 - 6x + 8$

D

English	Spanish	Examples
decreasing function on an interval A function whose output decreases (or stays the same) as the input increases. For a decreasing function, $f(b) \le f(a)$ for any a and b in the interval such that $b > a$.	**función decreciente en un intervalo** Función cuyo valor de salida disminuye (o permanece igual) a medida que el valor de entrada aumenta. Dada una función decreciente, $f(b) \le f(a)$ para cualquier valor de a y b en el intervalo, tal que $b > a$.	$f(x)$ is decreasing on the interval $x < 0$.
degree of a monomial The sum of the exponents of the variables in the monomial.	**grado de un monomio** Suma de los exponentes de las variables del monomio.	$4x^2y^5z^3$ Degree: $2 + 5 + 3 = 10$ $5 = 5x^0$ Degree: 0
degree of a polynomial The degree of the term of the polynomial with the greatest degree.	**grado de un polinomio** Grado del término del polinomio con el grado máximo.	$3x^2y^2 + 4xy^5 - 12x^3y^2$ Degree 6 Degree 4 Degree 6 Degree 5
dependent system A system of equations that has infinitely many solutions.	**sistema dependiente** Sistema de ecuaciones que tiene soluciones infinitas.	$\begin{cases} x + y = 2 \\ 2x + 2y = 4 \end{cases}$
dependent variable The output of a function; a variable whose value depends on the value of the input, or independent variable.	**variable dependiente** Valor de salida de una función; variable cuyo valor depende del valor de la entrada, o variable independiente.	For $y = 2x + 1$, y is the dependent variable. input: x output: y
difference of two squares A polynomial of the form $a^2 - b^2$, which may be written as the product $(a + b)(a - b)$.	**diferencia de dos cuadrados** Polinomio del tipo $a^2 - b^2$, que se puede expresar como el producto $(a + b)(a - b)$.	$x^2 - 4 = (x + 2)(x - 2)$

Glossary/Glosario

English	Spanish	Examples
discrete function A function whose graph is made up of unconnected points.	**función discreta** Función cuya gráfica está compuesta por puntos no conectados.	
discriminant The discriminant of the quadratic equation $ax^2 + bx + c = 0$ is $b^2 - 4ac$.	**discriminante** El discriminante de la ecuación cuadrática $ax^2 + bx + c = 0$ es $b^2 - 4ac$.	The discriminant of $2x^2 - 5x - 3 = 0$ is $(-5)^2 - 4(2)(-3)$ or 49.
domain The set of all first elements (or x-values) of the ordered pairs that constitute a relation or function.	**dominio** Conjunto de todos los primeros elementos (o valores de x) de los pares ordenados que constituyen una función o relación.	The domain of the function $\{(-5, 3), (-3, -2), (-1, -1), (1, 0)\}$ is $\{-5, -3, -1, 1\}$.
dot plot A statistical graph using dots or other marks to show the frequency of distinct data values.	**diagrama de puntos** Gráfica estadística que usa puntos u otras marcas para mostrar la frecuencia de valores de datos distintos.	

E

English	Spanish	Examples
elimination method A method used to solve a system of equations in which one variable is eliminated by adding or subtracting two equations of the system.	**eliminación** Método utilizado para resolver un sistema de ecuaciones por el cual se elimina una variable sumando o restando dos ecuaciones del sistema.	
end behavior The trends in the y-values of a function as the x-values increase or decrease without bound.	**comportamiento extremo** Tendencia de los valores de y de una función a medida que los valores de x aumentan o disminuyen sin límite.	$f(x) = x^2$ As $x \rightarrow -\infty, f(x) \rightarrow +\infty$. As $x \rightarrow +\infty, f(x) \rightarrow +\infty$.
equation A mathematical statement that two expressions are equal.	**ecuación** Enunciado matemático que indica que dos expresiones son iguales.	$x + 4 = 7$ $2 + 3 = 6 - 1$ $(x - 1)^2 + (y + 2)^2 = 4$
equivalent equations Equations that have the same solution(s).	**ecuaciones equivalentes** Ecuaciones que tienen la misma solución o las mismas soluciones.	$3x + 1 = 10$ and $3x = 9$ are equivalent equations.
explicit rule for nth term of a sequence A rule that defines the nth term of a sequence as a function of n.	**fórmula explícita** Fórmula que define el enésimo término de una sucesión como una función de n.	The explicit rule $f(n) = 3 + 2(n - 1)$ for $n \geq 1$ generates the sequence $3, 5, 7, 9, \ldots$

English	Spanish	Examples
exponential decay function An exponential function of the form $f(x) = ab^x$ in which $a > 0$ and $0 < b < 1$. If r is the rate of decay, then the function can be written $f(t) = a(1 - r)^t$, where a is the initial amount and t is the time.	**función de disminución exponencial** Función exponencial del tipo $f(x) = ab^x$ en la cual $a > 0$ y $0 < b < 1$. Si r es la tasa de disminución, entonces la función se puede expresar como $f(t) = a(1 - r)^t$, donde a es la cantidad inicial y t es el tiempo.	$f(t) = 3(0.5)^t$ 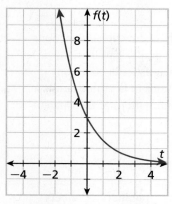
exponential function A function of the form $f(x) = ab^x$, where a and b are real numbers with $a \neq 0$, $b > 0$, and $b \neq 1$. Translating the graph of f vertically by k units produces the function $g(x) = ab^x + k$, which is also an exponential function.	**función exponencial** Función del tipo $f(x) = ab^x$, donde a y b son números reales con $a \neq 0$, $b > 0$ y $b \neq 1$. Al representar la gráfica de f verticalmente en k unidades, se genera la función $g(x) = ab^x + k$, que es también una función exponencial.	$f(x) = 3 \cdot 2^x$ 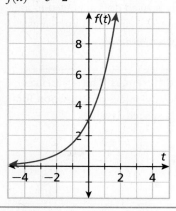
exponential growth function An exponential function of the form $f(x) = ab^x$ in which $a > 0$ and $b > 1$. If r is the rate of growth, then the function can be written $f(t) = a(1 + r)^t$, where a is the initial amount and t is the time.	**función de crecimiento exponencial** Función exponencial del tipo $f(x) = ab^x$ en la que $a > 0$ y $b > 1$. Si r es la tasa de crecimiento, entonces la función se puede expresar como $f(t) = a(1 + r)^t$, donde a es la cantidad inicial y t es el tiempo.	$f(t) = 2(1.5)^t$ 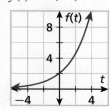
exponential regression A statistical method used to fit an exponential model to a given data set.	**regresión exponencial** Método estadístico utilizado para ajustar un modelo exponencial a un conjunto de datos determinado.	
expression A mathematical phrase that contains numbers and/or variables combined with operations.	**expresión** Frase matemática que contiene números y/o variables combinados con operaciones.	$6x + 1$
extrapolation Making a prediction using a value of the independent variable outside of a model's domain.	**extrapolación** Hacer una predicción con un valor de la variable independiente que esté fuera del dominio de un modelo.	

F

English	Spanish	Examples
family of functions Functions whose graphs have basic characteristics in common. Functions in the same family are transformations of their parent function.	**familia de funciones** Funciones cuyas gráficas tienen características básicas en común. Las funciones de la misma familia son transformaciones de su función madre.	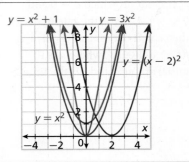
figurate numbers Numbers that can be represented by evenly-spaced dots arranged in a geometric shape. Also known as *polygonal numbers*.	**números figurados** Números que se pueden representar mediante puntos espaciados uniformemente y ordenados en una forma geométrica. También conocidos como *números poligonales*.	
first differences The differences between *y*-values of a function for evenly spaced *x*-values.	**primeras diferencias** Diferencias entre los valores de *y* de una función para valores de *x* espaciados uniformemente.	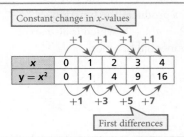
first quartile The median of the lower half of a data set, denoted Q_1. Also called *lower quartile*.	**primer cuartil** Mediana de la mitad inferior de un conjunto de datos, expresada como Q_1. También se llama *cuartil inferior*.	Lower half Upper half 18, ㉓ 28, 29, 36, 42 **First quartile**
frequency table An organized table that lists the number of times, or frequency, that each data value occurs.	**tabla de frecuencia** Tabla organizada que enumera la cantidad de veces que ocurre cada valor de datos, o la frecuencia.	Data set: 1, 1, 2, 2, 3, 4, 5, 5, 5, 6, 6, 6, 6 Frequency table:

Frequency table:

Data	Frequency
1	2
2	2
3	1
4	1
5	3
6	4

English	Spanish	Examples
function A relation in which every domain value is paired with exactly one range value.	**función** Relación en la que a cada valor de dominio corresponde exactamente un valor de rango.	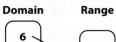 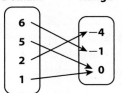

English	Spanish	Examples
function notation If x is the independent variable and y is the dependent variable, then the function notation for y is $f(x)$, read "f of x," where f names the function.	**notación de función** Si x es la variable independiente e y es la variable dependiente, entonces la notación de función para y es $f(x)$, que se lee "f de x," donde f nombra la función.	equation: $y = 2x$ function notation: $f(x) = 2x$
function rule An algebraic expression that defines a function.	**regla de función** Expresión algebraica que define una función.	$f(x) = 2x^2 + 3x - 7$ ↑ **function rule**

G

English	Spanish	Examples
geometric sequence A sequence in which the ratio of successive terms is a constant r, called the common ratio, where $r \neq 0$.	**sucesión geométrica** Sucesión en la que la razón de los términos sucesivos es una constante r, denominada razón común, donde $r \neq 0$.	1, 2, 4, 8, 16, … $\cdot 2$ $\cdot 2$ $\cdot 2$ $\cdot 2$ $r = 2$
graph of a function In the coordinate plane, the set of all points with coordinates (x, y), where x is in the domain of the function f and $y = f(x)$.	**gráfica de una función** En el plano cartesiano, conjunto de todos los puntos con coordenadas (x, y), donde x está en el dominio de la función f e $y = f(x)$.	
graph of a system of inequalities in two variables The region in the coordinate plane consisting of all points whose coordinates (x, y) are solutions of all of the inequalities in the system.	**gráfica de un sistema de desigualdades en dos variables** Región de un plano cartesiano que consta de todos los puntos cuyas coordenadas (x, y) son soluciones de todas las desigualdades del sistema.	(2, 1) is in the overlapping shaded regions, so it is a solution
graph of an inequality in one variable All solutions of the inequality plotted as points on a number line.	**gráfica de una desigualdad en una variable** Todas las soluciones de una desigualdad representadas como puntos en una recta numérica.	$x \geq 2$
graph of an inequality in two variables In the coordinate plane, the set of all points whose coordinates (x, y) are solutions of the inequality.	**gráfica de una desigualdad en dos variables** En el plano cartesiano, conjunto de todos los puntos cuyas coordenadas (x, y) son soluciones de la desigualdad.	$y \leq x + 1$

English	Spanish	Examples
greatest integer function A function denoted by $f(x) = \lfloor x \rfloor$ in which the number x is rounded down to the greatest integer that is less than or equal to x.	**función de entero mayor** Función expresada como $f(x) = \lfloor x \rfloor$ en la cual el número x se redondea hacia abajo hasta el entero mayor que sea menor o igual a x.	

H

English	Spanish	Examples
half-plane The part of the coordinate plane on one side of a line. The half-plane may or may not include the line.	**semiplano** La parte del plano cartesiano de un lado de una recta. El semiplano puede o no incluir la recta.	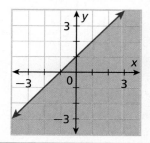
histogram A statistical graph used to display data grouped into intervals of equal width.	**histograma** Gráfica estadística utilizada para mostrar datos agrupados en intervalos de igual ancho.	
horizontal line A line described by the equation $y = b$, where b is the y-intercept.	**línea horizontal** Línea descrita por la ecuación $y = b$, donde b es la intersección con el eje y.	$y = 4$ 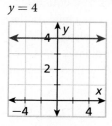
horizontal translation (of a graph) A shift of a graph to the left or right, with no change in the shape of the graph.	**traslación horizontal (de una gráfica)** Desplazamiento de una gráfica hacia la izquierda o hacia la derecha, sin producir cambios en la forma de la gráfica.	

I

English	Spanish	Examples
inconsistent system A system of equations or inequalities that has no solution.	**sistema inconsistente** Sistema de ecuaciones o desigualdades que no tiene solución.	$\begin{cases} x + y = 0 \\ x + y = 1 \end{cases}$

English	Spanish	Examples
increasing function on an interval A function whose output increases (or stays the same) as the input increases. For an increasing function, $f(b) \geq f(a)$ for any a and b in the interval such that $b > a$.	**función creciente en un intervalo** Función cuyo valor de salida aumenta (o permanece igual) a medida que el valor de entrada aumenta. Dada una función creciente, $f(b) \geq f(a)$ para cualquier valor de a y b en el intervalo, tal que $b > a$.	$f(x)$ is increasing on the interval $x > 0$.
independent system A system of equations that has exactly one solution.	**sistema independiente** Sistema de ecuaciones que tiene sólo una solución.	$\begin{cases} x + y = 7 \\ x - y = 1 \end{cases}$ Solution: $(4, 3)$
independent variable The input of a function; a variable whose value determines the value of the output, or dependent variable.	**variable independiente** Entrada de una función; variable cuyo valor determina el valor de la salida, o variable dependiente.	For $y = 2x + 1$, x is the independent variable.
index In the radical $\sqrt[n]{x}$, which represents the nth root of x, n is the index. In the radical $\sqrt{x}$, the index is understood to be 2.	**índice** En el radical $\sqrt[n]{x}$, que representa la enésima raíz de x, n es el índice. En el radical $\sqrt{x}$, se da por sentado que el índice es 2.	The radical $\sqrt[3]{8}$ has an index of 3.
inequality A mathematical statement that compares two expressions by using one of the following signs: $<, >, \leq, \geq,$ or $\neq$.	**desigualdad** Enunciado matemático que compara dos expresiones utilizando uno de los siguientes signos: $<, >, \leq, \geq$ o $\neq$.	$x \geq 2$
intercept See x-intercept and y-intercept.	**intersección** Ver intersección con el eje x e intersección con el eje y.	
intercept form of a quadratic function A quadratic function written in the form $f(x) = a(x - x_1)(x - x_2)$, where x_1 and x_2 are the x-intercepts of the function's graph.	**forma de intercepto de una función cuadrática** Función cuadrática expresada en la forma $f(x) = a(x - x_1)(x - x_2)$, donde x_1 y x_2 son intersecciones de x de la gráfica de la función.	
interpolation Making a prediction using a value of the independent variable from within a model's domain.	**interpolación** Hacer una predicción con un valor de la variable independiente a partir del dominio de un modelo.	
interquartile range (IQR) The difference of the third (upper) and first (lower) quartiles in a data set.	**rango entre cuartiles** Diferencia entre el tercer cuartil (superior) y el primer cuartil (inferior) de un conjunto de datos.	Interquartile range: $36 - 23 = 13$

Glossary/Glosario

English	Spanish	Examples
inverse of a function The relation that results from reversing the input and output values of a function.	**inverso de una función** Relación que se genera al invertir los valores de entrada y de salida de una función.	
irrational number A real number that cannot be expressed as the ratio of two integers. Its decimal form is non-repeating and non-terminating.	**número irracional** Número real que no se puede expresar como una razón de enteros. Su forma decimal es infinita y no se repite.	$\sqrt{2}$, π, e

J

English	Spanish	Examples
joint relative frequency In a two-way frequency table, the ratio of the frequency in a particular category to the total number of data values.	**frecuencia relativa conjunta** En una tabla de frecuencia de doble entrada, la razón entre la frecuencia en una categoría determinada y el número total de valores de datos.	

L

English	Spanish	Examples
leading coefficient The coefficient of the first term of a polynomial in standard form.	**coeficiente principal** Coeficiente del primer término de un polinomio en forma estándar.	$3x^2 + 7x - 2$ Leading coefficient: 3
least-squares line The line of fit for which the sum of the squares of the residuals is as small as possible.	**línea de mínimos cuadrados** Línea de ajuste en que la suma de cuadrados de los residuos es la menor.	
like terms Terms with the same variables raised to the same exponents.	**términos semejantes** Términos con las mismas variables elevadas a los mismos exponentes.	$4xy^2$ and $-5xy^2$ are like terms.
line of best fit The line that comes closest to all of the points in a scatter plot of bivariate data.	**línea de mejor ajuste** Línea que más se acerca a todos los puntos de un diagrama de dispersión de datos bivariados.	
line of fit A line on a scatter plot that helps show the correlation between variables more clearly.	**línea de ajuste** Línea en un diagrama de dispersión que ayuda a mostrar más claramente la correlación entre variables.	**Fundraiser**

English	Spanish	Examples
line of symmetry *See* axis of symmetry.	**línea de simetría** *Ver* eje de simetría.	
linear equation in one variable An equation that can be written in the form $ax = b$ where a and b are real numbers. When $a \neq 0$, the equation has just one solution. When $a = 0$, the equation can have either no solution or all real numbers as solutions depending on the value of b.	**ecuación lineal en una variable** Ecuación que puede expresarse en la forma $ax = b$ donde a y b son números reales. Cuando $a \neq 0$, la ecuación tiene solo una solución. Cuando $a = 0$, la ecuación puede tener ninguna solución o todos los números reales como soluciones, según el valor de b.	$x + 1 = 7$
linear equation in two variables An equation that can be written in the form $Ax + By = C$ where A, B, and C are constants and A and B are not both 0.	**ecuación lineal en dos variables** Ecuación que puede expresarse en la forma $Ax + By = C$ donde A, B y C son constantes y A y B no son ambas 0.	$2x + 3y = 6$
linear function A function that can be written in the form $f(x) = mx + b$, where x is the independent variable and m and b are real numbers. Its graph is a line.	**función lineal** Función que puede expresarse en la forma $f(x) = mx + b$, donde x es la variable independiente y m y b son números reales. Su gráfica es una línea.	$y = x - 1$
linear inequality in one variable An inequality that can be written in one of the following forms: $ax < b$, $ax > b$, $ax \leq b$, $ax \geq b$, or $ax \neq b$, where a and b are constants and $a \neq 0$.	**desigualdad lineal en una variable** Desigualdad que puede expresarse de una de las siguientes formas: $ax < b$, $ax > b$, $ax \leq b$, $ax \geq b$ o $ax \neq b$, donde a y b son constantes y $a \neq 0$.	$3x - 5 \leq 2(x + 4)$
linear inequality in two variables An inequality that can be written in one of the following forms: $Ax + By < C$, $Ax + By > C$, $Ax + By \leq C$, $Ax + By \geq C$, or $Ax + By \neq C$, where A, B, and C are constants and A and B are not both 0.	**desigualdad lineal en dos variables** Desigualdad que puede expresarse de una de las siguientes formas: $Ax + By < C$, $Ax + By > C$, $Ax + By \leq C$, $Ax + By \geq C$ o $Ax + By \neq C$, donde A, B y C son constantes y A y B no son ambas 0.	$2x + 3y > 6$
linear regression A statistical method used to fit a linear model to a given data set.	**regresión lineal** Método estadístico utilizado para ajustar un modelo lineal a un conjunto de datos determinado.	

English	Spanish	Examples
literal equation An equation where letters represent constants.	**ecuación literal** Ecuación donde las letras representan constantes.	$ax + b = c$ where $a \neq 0$
lower quartile *See* first quartile.	**cuartil inferior** *Ver* primer cuartil.	

M

English	Spanish	Examples
mapping diagram A diagram that shows how the elements in the domain are mapped to the elements in the range of a relation or function.	**diagrama de correspondencia** Diagrama que muestra cómo los elementos del dominio se corresponden con los elementos del rango de una relación o función.	**Mapping Diagram**
marginal relative frequency The sum of the joint relative frequencies in a row or column of a two-way table.	**frecuencia relativa marginal** Suma de las frecuencias relativas conjuntas en una fila o columna de una tabla de doble entrada.	
maximum value of a function The y-coordinate of the highest point on the graph of the function.	**máximo de una función** Coordenada de y del punto más alto en la gráfica de la función.	The maximum value of the function is 2.
mean The sum of all the values in a data set divided by the number of data values. Also called the *average*.	**media** Suma de todos los valores de un conjunto de datos dividida entre el número de valores de datos. También llamada *promedio*.	Data set: 4, 6, 7, 8, 10 Mean: $\dfrac{4 + 6 + 7 + 8 + 10}{5}$ $= \dfrac{35}{5} = 7$
measure of center A measure that describes the center of a data set.	**medida central** Medida que describe el centro de un conjunto de datos.	mean, median, or mode
measure of spread A measure that describes how spread out values in a data set are.	**medida de dispersión** Medida que describe cuán dispersos están los valores en un conjunto de datos.	range, interquartile range, or standard deviation
median For an ordered data set with an odd number of values, the median is the middle value. For an ordered data set with an even number of values, the median is the average of the two middle values.	**mediana** Dado un conjunto de datos ordenado con un número impar de valores, la mediana es el valor medio. Dado un conjunto de datos con un número par de valores, la mediana es el promedio de los dos valores medios.	8, 9, 9, 12, 15 Median: 9 4, 6, 7, 10, 10, 12 Median: $\dfrac{7 + 10}{2} = 8.5$

English	Spanish	Examples
minimum value of a function The y-coordinate of the lowest point on the graph of the function.	**mínimo de una función** Coordenada de y del punto más bajo en la gráfica de la función.	 $(0, -2)$ The minimum value of the function is -2.
mode The value or values that occur most frequently in a data set; if all values occur with the same frequency, the data set is said to have no mode.	**moda** Valor o valores que se presentan con mayor frecuencia en un conjunto de datos. Si todos los valores se presentan con la misma frecuencia, se dice que el conjunto de datos no tiene moda.	Data set: 3, 6, 8, 8, 10 Mode: 8 Data set: 2, 5, 5, 7, 7 Modes: 5 and 7 Data set: 2, 3, 6, 9, 11 No mode
monomial A number, a variable, or a product of a number and variables with whole-number exponents; a polynomial with one term.	**monomio** Número, variable o producto de un número y variables con exponentes de números enteros; polinomio con un término.	$3x^2y^4$

N

English	Spanish	Examples
negative correlation In a set of bivariate data, the two variables have a negative correlation if there is a linear relationship such that one variable decreases as the other variable increases.	**correlación negativa** En un conjunto de datos bivariados, las dos variables tienen una correlación negativa si existe una relación lineal tal que una variable disminuye a medida que la otra variable aumenta.	
no correlation In a set of bivariate data, the two variables have no correlation if there is no linear relationship between the variables.	**sin correlación** En un conjunto de datos bivariados, las dos variables no tienen correlación si no existe una relación lineal entre las variables.	
nonlinear system of equations A system of equations in which at least one of the equations is not linear.	**sistema no lineal de ecuaciones** Sistema de ecuaciones en el cual por lo menos una de las ecuaciones no es lineal.	A system that contains one quadratic equation and one linear equation is a nonlinear system.
nth root The nth root of a number a, written as $\sqrt[n]{a}$ or $a^{\frac{1}{n}}$, is a number that is equal to a when it is raised to the nth power.	**enésima raíz** Enésima raíz de un número a, que se escribe $\sqrt[n]{a}$ o $a^{\frac{1}{n}}$, es un número igual a a cuando se eleva a la enésima potencia.	$\sqrt[5]{32} = 2$, because $2^5 = 32$.
numerical expression An expression that contains only numbers and operations.	**expresión numérica** Expresión que contiene únicamente números y operaciones.	$\dfrac{3^2 + 1}{6 - 1}$

Glossary/Glosario

O

English	Spanish	Examples
outlier A data value that is greater than the result of adding 1.5 times the interquartile range to the third (or upper) quartile, or that is less than the result of subtracting 1.5 times the interquartile range from the first (or lower) quartile.	**valor extremo** Valor de datos que es mayor que el resultado de sumar 1.5 veces el rango entre cuartiles al tercer cuartil (o superior), o que es menor que el resultado de restar 1.5 veces el rango entre cuartiles del primer cuartil (o inferior).	For the data values 2, 3, 5, 5, 7, 8, 8, and 20, the value 20 is an outlier.

P

English	Spanish	Examples
parabola The shape of the graph of a quadratic function.	**parábola** Forma de la gráfica de una función cuadrática.	
parent function The simplest function with the defining characteristics of the family. Functions in the same family are transformations of their parent function.	**función madre** Función más básica que tiene las características distintivas de una familia. Las funciones de la misma familia son transformaciones de su función madre.	$f(x) = x^2$ is the parent function for $g(x) = x^2 + 4$ and $h(x) = (5x + 2)^2 - 3$.
perfect-square trinomial A trinomial whose factored form is the square of a binomial. A perfect-square trinomial has the form $a^2 - 2ab + b^2 = (a - b)^2$ or $a^2 + 2ab + b^2 = (a + b)^2$.	**trinomio cuadrado perfecto** Trinomio cuya forma factorizada es el cuadrado de un binomio. Un trinomio cuadrado perfecto tiene la forma $a^2 - 2ab + b^2 = (a - b)^2$ o $a^2 + 2ab + b^2 = (a + b)^2$.	$x^2 + 6x + 9$ is a perfect-square trinomial, because $x^2 + 6x + 9 = (x + 3)^2$.
piecewise-defined function A function that has different rules for different parts of its domain.	**función definida a trozos** Función que tiene reglas diferentes para partes diferentes de su dominio.	$f(x) = \begin{cases} 2 & \text{if } x < 1 \\ 2x & \text{if } x \geq 0 \end{cases}$
point-slope form A linear equation in two variables written in the form $y - y_1 = m(x - x_1)$, where m is the slope and (x_1, y_1) is a point on the line.	**forma de punto y pendiente** Ecuación lineal en dos variables expresada en la forma $y - y_1 = m(x - x_1)$, donde m es la pendiente y (x_1, y_1) es un punto en la línea.	$y - 3 = 2(x - 3)$
polynomial A monomial or a sum of monomials.	**polinomio** Monomio o suma de monomios.	$2x^2 + 3xy - 7y^2$

English	Spanish	Examples
positive correlation In a set of bivariate data, the two variables have a positive correlation if there is a linear relationship such that one variable increases as the other variable increases.	**correlación positiva** En un conjunto de datos bivariados, las dos variables tienen correlación positiva si existe una relación lineal tal que una variable aumenta mientras la otra variable aumenta.	
precision The level of detail of a measurement, determined by the unit of measure.	**precisión** Detalle de una medición, determinado por la unidad de medida.	A ruler marked in millimeters has a greater level of precision than a ruler marked in centimeters.

Q

English	Spanish	Examples
quadrant One of the four regions into which the x- and y-axes divide the coordinate plane.	**cuadrante** Una de las cuatro regiones en las que los ejes x y y dividen el plano cartesiano.	
quadratic equation An equation that can be written in the standard form $ax^2 + bx + c = 0$, where a, b, and c are real numbers and $a \neq 0$.	**ecuación cuadrática** Ecuación que se puede expresar de forma estándar como $ax^2 + bx + c = 0$, donde a, b y c son números reales y $a \neq 0$.	$x^2 + 3x - 4 = 0$ $x^2 - 9 = 0$
Quadratic Formula The formula $x = \dfrac{-b \pm \sqrt{b^2 - 4ac}}{2a}$, which gives solutions of equations in the form $ax^2 + bx + c = 0$, where $a \neq 0$.	**fórmula cuadrática** La fórmula $x = \dfrac{-b \pm \sqrt{b^2 - 4ac}}{2a}$, que da soluciones para las ecuaciones del tipo $ax^2 + bx + c = 0$, donde $a \neq 0$.	The solutions of $2x^2 - 5x - 3 = 0$ are given by $$x = \frac{-(-5) \pm \sqrt{(-5)^2 - 4(2)(-3)}}{2(2)}$$ $$= \frac{5 \pm \sqrt{25 + 24}}{4} = \frac{5 \pm 7}{4}$$ $$x = 3 \text{ or } x = -\frac{1}{2}$$
quadratic function A function that can be written in the form $f(x) = ax^2 + bx + c$, where a, b, and c are real numbers and $a \neq 0$. Its graph is a parabola.	**función cuadrática** Función que se puede expresar como $f(x) = ax^2 + bx + c$, donde a, b y c son números reales y $a \neq 0$. Su gráfica es una parábola.	$f(x) = x^2 - 6x + 8$
quadratic regression A statistical method used to fit a quadratic model to a given data set.	**regresión cuadrática** Método estadístico utilizado para ajustar un modelo cuadrático a un conjunto de datos determinado.	

R

English	Spanish	Examples
radical expression An expression that contains a radical sign.	**expresión radical** Expresión que contiene un signo de radical.	$\sqrt{x+3}+4$
radical sign The symbol $\sqrt{}$ used to denote a root. The symbol is used alone to indicate a square root or with an index, $\sqrt[n]{}$, to indicate an nth root.	**signo de radical** Símbolo $\sqrt{}$ que se utiliza para expresar una raíz. Puede utilizarse solo para indicar una raíz cuadrada, o con un índice, $\sqrt[n]{}$, para indicar una enésima raíz.	$\sqrt{36}=6$ $\sqrt[3]{27}=3$
radicand The expression under a radical sign.	**radicando** Número o expresión debajo del signo de radical.	Expression: $\sqrt{x+3}$ Radicand: $x+3$
range of a data set The difference of the greatest and least values in the data set.	**rango de un conjunto de datos** Diferencia del mayor y menor valor en un conjunto de datos.	The data set $\{3, 3, 5, 7, 8, 10, 11, 11, 12\}$ has a range of $12-3=9$.
range of a function or relation The set of all second elements (or y-values) of the ordered pairs that constitute a function or relation.	**rango de una función o relación** Conjunto de todos los segundos elementos (o valores de y) de los pares ordenados que constituyen una función o relación.	The range of the function $\{(-5, 3), (-3, -2), (-1, -1), (1, 0)\}$ is $\{-2, -1, 0, 3\}$.
rate of change A ratio that compares the amount of change in a dependent variable to the amount of change in an independent variable.	**tasa de cambio** Razón que compara la cantidad de cambio de la variable dependiente con la cantidad de cambio de la variable independiente.	Mark is filling his car's tank with gas. The tank has 7 gallons of gas after 1 minute and 17 gallons of gas after 3 minutes. The rate of change in the tank's volume of gas with respect to time is: $\dfrac{\text{change in volume}}{\text{change in time}}$ $=\dfrac{17-7}{3-1}=\dfrac{10}{2}$ $=5 \text{ gal/min}$
rational exponent An exponent that can be expressed as $\frac{m}{n}$ such that if m and n are integers, then $b^{\frac{m}{n}}=\sqrt[n]{b^m}=\left(\sqrt[n]{b}\right)^m$.	**exponente racional** Exponente que se puede expresar como $\frac{m}{n}$ tal que si m y n son enteros, entonces $b^{\frac{m}{n}}=\sqrt[n]{b^m}=\left(\sqrt[n]{b}\right)^m$.	$64^{\frac{1}{6}}=\sqrt[6]{64}$
rational number A number that can be written in the form $\frac{a}{b}$, where a and b are integers and $b \neq 0$.	**número racional** Número que se puede expresar como $\frac{a}{b}$, donde a y b son enteros y $b \neq 0$.	$3, 1.75, 0.\overline{3}, -\frac{2}{3}, 0$
rationalizing the denominator Rewriting a fraction by multiplying by another fraction that is equivalent to 1 in order to remove radical terms from the denominator.	**racionalizar el denominador** Escribir nuevamente una fracción multiplicándola por otra fracción equivalente a 1 a fin de eliminar los términos radicales del denominador.	$\dfrac{1}{\sqrt{2}} \cdot \dfrac{\sqrt{2}}{\sqrt{2}} = \dfrac{\sqrt{2}}{2}$

English	Spanish	Examples
real number A rational or irrational number. Every point on the number line represents a real number.	**número real** Número racional o irracional. Cada punto de la recta numérica representa un número real.	
recursive rule for nth term of a sequence A rule for a sequence in which one or more previous terms are used to generate the next term.	**fórmula recurrente para hallar el enésimo término de una sucesión** Fórmula para una sucesión en la cual uno o más términos anteriores se usan para generar el término siguiente.	Given that $f(1) = 3$, the recursive rule $f(n) = f(n-1) + 2$ generates the sequence 3, 5, 7, 9, . . .
reflection across the x-axis A transformation that reflects, or "flips," a graph or figure across the x-axis.	**reflexión sobre el eje x** Transformación en la que una gráfica o figura se refleja o se invierte sobre el eje x.	
relation A set of ordered pairs.	**relación** Conjunto de pares ordenados.	$\{(0, 5), (0, 4), (2, 3), (4, 0)\}$
relative frequency The relative frequency of a category is the frequency of the category divided by the total of all frequencies.	**frecuencia relativa** La frecuencia relativa de una categoría es la frecuencia de la categoría dividida por el total de todas las frecuencias.	
residual The signed vertical distance between a data point and a line of fit.	**residuo** La diferencia vertical entre un dato y una línea de ajuste.	
residual plot A scatter plot of points whose x-coordinates are the values of the independent variable and whose y-coordinates are the corresponding residuals.	**diagrama de residuos** Diagrama de dispersión de puntos en el que la coordenada x representa los valores de la variable independiente y la coordenada y representa los residuos correspondientes.	

S

English	Spanish	Examples
scatter plot A graph of the ordered pairs from a set of bivariate data.	**diagrama de dispersión** Gráfica de los pares ordenados de un conjunto de datos bivariados.	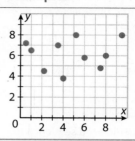
second differences Differences between first differences of a function.	**segundas diferencias** Diferencias entre las primeras diferencias de una función.	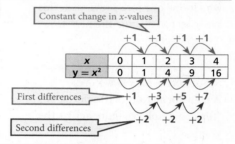
sequence A list of numbers in a specific order.	**sucesión** Lista de números en un orden específico.	$1, 2, 4, 8, 16, \ldots$
significant digits The digits used to express the precision of a measurement.	**dígitos significativos** Dígitos usados para expresar la precisión de una medida.	
skewed distribution A type of distribution in which the data values on one side of the median are more spread out than the data values on the other side. In a distribution skewed to the left, the mean is less than the median. In a distribution skewed to the right, the mean is greater than the median.	**distribución sesgada** Tipo de distribución en la que los valores de los datos de un lado de la mediana están más dispersos que los valores de los datos en el otro lado. En una distribución sesgada a la izquierda, la media es menor que la mediana. En una distribución sesgada a la derecha, la media es mayor que la mediana.	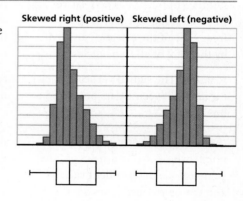
slope A measure of the steepness and direction of a line. If (x_1, y_1) and (x_2, y_2) are any two points on the line, the slope of the line, known as m, is represented by the equation $m = \frac{y_2 - y_1}{x_2 - x_1}$.	**pendiente** Medida de la inclinación y la dirección de una línea. Dados dos puntos (x_1, y_1) y (x_2, y_2) en una línea, la pendiente de la línea, denominada m, se representa con la ecuación $m = \frac{y_2 - y_1}{x_2 - x_1}$.	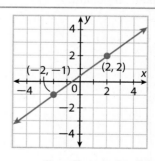

$$m = \frac{y_2 - y_1}{x_2 - x_1} = \frac{-1 - 2}{-2 - 2} = \frac{3}{4}$$

English	Spanish	Examples
slope-intercept form A linear equation in two variables written in the form $y = mx + b$, where m is the slope and b is the y-intercept.	**forma de pendiente-intersección** Ecuación lineal en dos variables expresada en la forma $y = mx + b$, donde m es la pendiente y b es la intersección con el eje y.	$y = -2x + 4$ The slope is -2. The y-intercept is 4.
solution of an equation in one variable Any value of the variable that makes the equation true.	**solución de una ecuación en una variable** Cualquier valor de la variable que hace que la ecuación sea verdadera.	Equation: $x - 3 = 5$ Solution: $x = 8$
solution of an equation in two variables Any ordered pair that makes the equation true.	**solución de una ecuación en dos variables** Cualquier par ordenado que hace que la ecuación sea verdadera.	$(4, 2)$ is a solution of $x + y = 6$.
solution of an inequality in one variable Any value of the variable that makes the inequality true.	**solución de una desigualdad en una variable** Cualquier valor de la variable que hace que la desigualdad sea verdadera.	Inequality: $x + 2 < 6$ Solution: $x < 4$
solution of an inequality in two variables Any ordered pair that makes the inequality true.	**solución de una desigualdad en dos variables** Cualquier par ordenado que hace que la desigualdad sea verdadera.	$(3, 1)$ is a solution of $x + y < 6$.
solution of a system of equations Any ordered pair that satisfies all the equations in a system of equations.	**solución de un sistema de ecuaciones** Cualquier par ordenado que resuelva todas las ecuaciones de un sistema de ecuaciones.	$\begin{cases} x + y = -1 \\ -x + y = -3 \end{cases}$ The solution of the system is the ordered pair $(1, -2)$.
solution of a system of inequalities Any ordered pair that satisfies all the inequalities in a system of inequalities.	**solución de un sistema de desigualdades** Cualquier par ordenado que resuelva todas las desigualdades de un sistema de desigualdades.	$\begin{cases} y \le x + 1 \\ y < -x + 4 \end{cases}$ (2, 1) is in the overlapping shaded regions, so it is a solution
standard form of a linear equation A linear equation in two variables written in the form $Ax + By = C$, where A, B, and C are real numbers and A and B are not both 0.	**forma estándar de una ecuación lineal** Ecuación lineal en dos variables expresada en la forma $Ax + By = C$, donde A, B y C son números reales y A y B no son ambos cero.	$2x + 3y = 6$

English	Spanish	Examples
standard form of a polynomial A polynomial in one variable written with its terms in order from greatest degree to least degree.	**forma estándar de un polinomio** Polinomio de una variable expresado con sus términos ordenados de mayor a menor grado.	$4x^5 - 2x^4 + x^2 - x + 1$
standard form of a quadratic equation A quadratic equation in one variable written in the form $ax^2 + bx + c = 0$, where a, b, and c are real numbers and $a \neq 0$.	**forma estándar de una ecuación cuadrática** Ecuación cuadrática en una variable escrita en la forma $ax^2 + bx + c = 0$, donde a, b y c son números reales y $a \neq 0$.	$2x^2 + 3x - 1 = 0$
standard deviation A measure of dispersion of a data set. The standard deviation σ is the square root of the variance, which is calculated by summing the squared deviations of the data values from the mean and then dividing the sum by the number of data values.	**desviación estándar** Medida de dispersión de un conjunto de datos. La desviación estándar σ es la raíz cuadrada de la varianza, la cual se calcula sumando las desviaciones cuadradas de los valores de los datos de la media y luego dividiendo la suma entre el número de valores de los datos.	Data set: $\{6, 7, 7, 9, 11\}$ Mean: $\dfrac{6 + 7 + 7 + 9 + 11}{5} = 8$ Variance: $\dfrac{1}{5}(4 + 1 + 1 + 1 + 9) = 3.2$ Standard deviation: $\sigma = \sqrt{3.2} \approx 1.8$
statistics Numbers that characterize a set of data.	**estadísticas** Números que caracterizan un conjunto de datos.	
step function A piecewise-defined function that is constant over each interval in its domain.	**función escalón** Función definida a trozos que es constante en cada intervalo en su dominio.	
substitution method A method used to solve a system of equations by solving one of the equations for one of its variables and substituting the resulting expression for that variable into the other equation(s).	**sustitución** Método utilizado para resolver un sistema de ecuaciones resolviendo una de las ecuaciones para una de sus variables y sustituyendo la expresión resultante para esa variable en las demás ecuaciones.	
symmetric distribution A type of distribution in which the right and left sides of its display are mirror images of each other. In a symmetric distribution, the mean and median are equal.	**distribución simétrica** Tipo de distribución en la que los lados derecho e izquierdo son idénticos. En una distribución simétrica, la media y la mediana son iguales.	
system of equations Two or more equations having the same variables.	**sistema de ecuaciones** Dos o más ecuaciones que tienen las mismas variables.	$\begin{cases} 2x + 3y = -1 \\ x - 3y = 4 \end{cases}$
system of inequalities Two or more inequalities having the same variables.	**sistema de desigualdades** Dos o más desigualdades que tienen las mismas variables.	$\begin{cases} 2x + 3y > -1 \\ x - 3y \leq 4 \end{cases}$

T

English	Spanish	Examples
term of a sequence One of the numbers in the sequence. A particular term is identified by its position in the sequence.	**término de una sucesión** Uno de los números de la sucesión. Un término particular se identifica por su posición en la sucesión.	5 is the third term in the sequence 1, 3, 5, 7, …
term of an expression The parts of the expression that are added together.	**término de una expresión** Partes de una expresión que deben sumarse.	$3x^2 - 6x + 8 = 3x^2 + (-6x) + 8$ Term Term Term
third quartile The median of the upper half of a data set. Also called *upper quartile*.	**tercer cuartil** Mediana de la mitad superior de un conjunto de datos. También se llama *cuartil superior*.	Lower half Upper half 18, 23, 28, 29, ⃝36 42 Third quartile
tolerance The amount by which a measurement is permitted to vary from a specified value.	**tolerancia** Cantidad por la que una medida se permite variar de un valor especificado.	
transformation A change in the position, size, or shape of a figure or graph. Introducing a constant k into a function's rule results in a transformation of the function's graph. The graphs of $f(x + k)$ and $f(x) + k$ are both translations (shifts) of the graph of $f(x)$, and the graph of $k \cdot f(x)$ is a vertical stretch or vertical compression of the graph of $f(x)$ along with a reflection (flip) of the graph of $f(x)$ across the x-axis if $k < 0$.	**transformación** Cambio en la posición, tamaño o forma de una figura o gráfica. Introducir una constante k en la regla de una función da como resultado una transformación de la gráfica de la función. Las gráficas de $f(x + k)$ y $f(x) + k$ son traslaciones (desplazamientos) de la gráfica de $f(x)$, y la gráfica de $k \cdot f(x)$ es un estiramiento vertical o una compresión vertical de la gráfica de $f(x)$ junto con una reflexión (inversión) de la gráfica de $f(x)$ sobre el eje x si $k < 0$.	$y = x^2 + 1$ $y = 3x^2$ $y = (x - 2)^2$ $y = x^2$
translation of a graph *See* horizontal translation of a graph *and* vertical translation of a graph.	**traslación de una gráfica** *Ver* traslación horizontal de una gráfica *y* traslación vertical de una gráfica.	
trinomial A polynomial with three terms.	**trinomio** Polinomio con tres términos.	$4x^2 + 3xy - 5y^2$

English | **Spanish** | **Examples**

two-way frequency table A frequency table that displays two-variable categorical data in rows and columns.

tabla de frecuencia de doble entrada Tabla de frecuencia que muestra los datos categóricos de dos variables organizados en filas y columnas.

		Preference		
		Inside	Outside	Total
Pet	Cats	35	15	50
	Dogs	20	30	50
	Total	55	45	100

two-way relative frequency table A relative frequency table that displays two-variable categorical data in rows and columns.

tabla de frecuencia relativa de doble entrada Tabla de frecuencia relativa que muestra los datos categóricos de dos variables en filas y columnas.

		Preference		
		Inside	Outside	Total
Pet	Cats	0.35	0.15	0.50
	Dogs	0.20	0.30	0.50
	Total	0.55	0.45	1.00

U

unlike terms Terms with different variables or the same variables raised to different powers.

términos distintos Términos con variables diferentes o las mismas variables elevadas a potencias diferentes.

$4xy^2$ and $6x^2y$ are unlike terms.

upper quartile *See* third quartile.

cuartil superior *Ver* tercer cuartil.

V

value of a function The result of replacing the independent variable in a function's rule with a number and simplifying.

valor de una función Resultado de reemplazar la variable independiente en la regla de una función por un número y luego simplificar.

The value of the function $f(x) = x + 1$ for $x = 3$ is $f(3) = 4$.

value of an expression The result of replacing the variables in an expression with numbers and simplifying.

valor de una expresión Resultado de reemplazar las variables de una expresión por números y luego simplificar.

The value of the expression $x + 1$ for $x = 3$ is 4.

variable A symbol used to represent a quantity that can change.

variable Símbolo utilizado para representar una cantidad que puede cambiar.

In the expression $2x + 3$, x is the variable.

vertex form of a quadratic function A quadratic function written in the form $f(x) = a(x - h)^2 + k$, where a, h, and k are constants and (h, k) is the vertex of the function's graph.

forma en vértice de una función cuadrática Función cuadrática expresada en la forma $f(x) = a(x - h)^2 + k$, donde a, h y k son constantes y (h, k) es el vértice de la gráfica de la función.

English	Spanish	Examples
vertex of a parabola The highest or lowest point on the parabola.	**vértice de una parábola** Punto más alto o más bajo en la parábola.	The vertex is $(0, -2)$.
vertex of an absolute-value graph The highest or lowest point on the graph of an absolute-value function.	**vértice de una gráfica de valor absoluto** El punto más alto o más bajo en la gráfica de una función de valor absoluto.	The vertex is $(0, 0)$.
vertical compression of a graph A transformation that pushes the points of a graph toward the x-axis. Any point on the x-axis remains unchanged.	**compresión vertical de una gráfica** Transformación que desplaza los puntos de una gráfica hacia el eje x. Todos los puntos del eje x permanecen iguales.	
vertical line A line whose equation is $x = a$, where a is the x-intercept.	**línea vertical** Línea cuya ecuación es $x = a$, donde a es la intersección con el eje x.	
vertical line test A test used to determine whether a relation is a function. If any vertical line crosses the graph of a relation more than once, the relation is not a function.	**prueba de la línea vertical** Prueba utilizada para determinar si una relación es una función. Si una línea vertical corta la gráfica de una relación más de una vez, la relación no es una función.	Function Not a function
vertical stretch of a graph A transformation that pulls the points of a graph away from the x-axis. Any point on the x-axis remains unchanged.	**estiramiento vertical de una gráfica** Transformación que desplaza los puntos de una gráfica en forma vertical alejándolos del eje x. Todos los puntos del eje x permanecen iguales.	
vertical translation (of a graph) A shift of graph up or down, with no change in the shape of the graph.	**traslación vertical (de una gráfica)** Desplazamiento de una gráfica hacia arriba o hacia abajo, sin producir cambios en la forma de la gráfica.	

Glossary/Glosario

English	Spanish	Examples
x-intercept The x-coordinate of a point where a graph intersects the x-axis.	**intersección con el eje x** Coordenada x de un punto donde una gráfica corta el eje x.	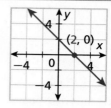 The x-intercept is 2.

English	Spanish	Examples
y-intercept The y-coordinate of a point where a graph intersects the y-axis.	**intersección con el eje y** Coordenada y de un punto donde una gráfica corta el eje y.	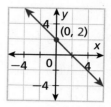 The y-intercept is 2.

English	Spanish	Examples
zero of a function For the function f, any number x such that $f(x) = 0$.	**cero de una función** Dada la función f, todo número x tal que $f(x) = 0$.	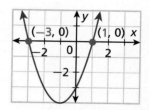 The zeros are −3 and 1.

A

absolute value equations
solving algebraically, 228
solving graphically, 226
absolute value functions
constructing functions for
transformations of, 220–221
graphing, 217–224
parent, 218
absolute value inequalities
solving algebraically, 229
solving graphically, 227
accuracy, 20
in calculations, 19–26
addition
closure properties and, 8
of irrational numbers, 7
models in, 557
of monomials, 412
operations with functions, 556
of polynomials, 411–418, 556
of rational numbers, 7, 186, 410
significant digits and, 22
solving linear systems by, 253–258
Addition Property of Equality,
38, 40, 43
Addition Property of Inequality, 54
algebra
*The development of algebra skills and
concepts is found throughout the
book.*
equations in
simplifying, 30
writing and solving, 37–44
writing two-step, 30
expressions in, 30, 31, 32, 34
constant, 32
defined, 32
equivalent, 33, 38
terms in, 32
variable, 32
writing, interpreting, and
simplifying, 31–36
inequalities in
compound, 61–68
writing two-step, 30
properties of operations
Addition Property of Equality,
38, 40, 43
Addition Property of Inequality, 54
Distributive Property, 31, 33, 36,
39, 441
Division Property of Equality, 38,
43, 471
Division Property of Inequality, 54
Multiplication Property of Equality,
38, 43, 155
Multiplication Property of
Inequality, 54, 57

Subtraction Property of Equality,
38, 43
Subtraction Property of Inequality,
54, 155
variable, linear equations and
inequalities in one, 29–70
rewriting formulas and solving
literal equations, 45–52
writing, interpreting, and
simplifying, 31–36
writing and solving compound
inequalities, 61–68
writing and solving equations,
37–44
writing and solving inequalities,
53–60
algebraic equations, evaluating, 466
algebraic expressions
compound statement involving, 227
evaluating, 4, 164
simplifying, 15, 30, 32, 34, 238,
410, 546
involving rational exponents, 15
writing, 31, 32
AND
compound statements involving,
62, 227
solving compound inequalities
involving, 63
approximations, solving nonlinear
systems by successive, 566–567
area, finding, 395
with products of monomials, 387
Are You Ready?, appears in every
module. 4, 30, 74, 94, 130, 164,
206, 238, 270, 292, 318, 340, 360, 382,
410, 430, 466, 502, 546, 584, 604
arguments, data trends in
supporting, 596
arithmetic sequences, 360, 362
converting between general forms
for, 197
defined recursively, 187–202
explicitly defined, 195–202
explicit rules for, 196
graphing, 190, 198
modeling with, 191, 199
recursive rules for, 188–189
art, 223, 417
assessment
Are You Ready?, appears in every
module. 4, 30, 74, 94, 130, 164,
186, 206, 238, 270, 292, 318, 340,
360, 382, 410, 430, 466, 502, 546,
584, 604
Check Understanding, appears in
every lesson. *See, for example,* 9,
16, 24, 34, 42, 57, 66, 80, 88
Module Review, appears in every
module. 27–28, 69–70, 91–92,
183–184, 203–204, 233–234,

267–268, 287–288, 315–316,
335–336, 357–358, 425–426,
463–464, 497–498, 543–544,
579–580, 601–602, 621–622
associations, 584
between categorical variables,
593–600
identifying possible, 595
asymptote, 295
axis of symmetry, 218

B

base, 12
best-fit lines, residuals and, 175–185
binomials, 392
multiplication of monomials,
trinomials, and, 391–398
special products of, 399–406
bivariate data, 166
boundary line, 273
box plots, in describing data, 616
brackets ([ ]), 33

C

calculations, precision and accuracy
in, 19–26
careers
aeronautical engineer, 337
aerospace engineer, 71
chemist, 1
computer scientist, 379
demographer, 499
ecologist, 581
electrical engineer, 235
geologist, 161
industrial engineer, 289
mechanical engineer, 427
categorical data, 583–622
associations between categorical
variables and, 593–600
two-way frequency and relative
frequency tables, 585–592
categorical variables, recognizing
associations between, 593–600
causation, distinguishing between
correlation and, 168
ceiling functions, 215
center, measures of, 604, 607, 608
Check Understanding, appears in
every lesson. *See, for example,* 9, 16,
24, 34, 42, 57, 66, 80, 88
closure, 6, 7
properties of, 8
proving, 6
coefficient, 32, 384
leading, 392

Index

© Houghton Mifflin Harcourt Publishing Company

Index

LENGTH

1 meter (m) = 1000 millimeters (mm)

1 meter = 100 centimeters (cm)

1 meter ≈ 39.37 inches

1 kilometer (km) = 1000 meters

1 kilometer ≈ 0.62 mile

1 inch = 2.54 centimeters

1 foot (ft) = 12 inches (in.)

1 yard (yd) = 3 feet

1 mile (mi) = 1760 yards

1 mile = 5280 feet

1 mile ≈ 1.609 kilometers

CAPACITY

1 liter (L) = 1000 milliliters (mL)

1 liter = 1000 cubic centimeters

1 liter ≈ 0.264 gallon

1 kiloliter (kL) = 1000 liters

1 cup (c) = 8 fluid ounces (fl oz)

1 pint (pt) = 2 cups

1 quart (qt) = 2 pints

1 gallon (gal) = 4 quarts

1 gallon ≈ 3.785 liters

MASS/WEIGHT

1 gram (g) = 1000 milligrams (mg)

1 kilogram (kg) = 1000 grams

1 kilogram ≈ 2.2 pounds

1 pound (lb) = 16 ounces (oz)

1 pound ≈ 0.454 kilogram

1 ton = 2000 pounds

TIME

1 minute (min) = 60 seconds (s)

1 hour (h) = 60 minutes

1 day = 24 hours

1 week = 7 days

1 year (yr) = about 52 weeks

1 year = 12 months (mo)

1 year = 365 days

1 decade = 10 years

Tables of Measures, Symbols, and Formulas

SYMBOLS

$=$	is equal to	x^2	x squared
$\neq$	is not equal to	x^3	x cubed
$\approx$	is approximately equal to	$\lvert x \rvert$	absolute value of x
$>$	is greater than	$\frac{1}{x}$	reciprocal of x ($x \neq 0$)
$<$	is less than	$\sqrt{x}$	square root of x
$\geq$	is greater than or equal to	$\sqrt[3]{x}$	cube root of x
$\leq$	is less than or equal to	x_n	x sub n ($n = 0, 1, 2, \ldots$)

FORMULAS

Perimeter and Circumference

Polygon	$P = $ sum of the lengths of sides
Rectangle	$P = 2\ell + 2w$
Square	$P = 4s$
Circle	$C = \pi d$ or $C = 2\pi r$

Area

Rectangle	$A = \ell w$
Parallelogram	$A = bh$
Triangle	$A = \frac{1}{2}bh$
Trapezoid	$A = \frac{1}{2}h(b_1 + b_2)$
Square	$A = s^2$
Circle	$A = \pi r^2$

Volume

Right Prism	$V = \ell wh$ or $V = Bh$
Cube	$V = s^3$
Pyramid	$V = \frac{1}{3}Bh$
Cylinder	$V = \pi r^2 h$
Cone	$V = \frac{1}{3}\pi r^2 h$
Sphere	$V = \frac{4}{3}\pi r^3$

Surface Area

Right Prism	$S = Ph + 2B$
Cube	$S = 6s^2$
Square Pyramid	$S = \frac{1}{2}P\ell + B$

Pythagorean Theorem

$$a^2 + b^2 = c^2$$